SECOND YEAR LATIN

JENNEY'S

SECOND YEAR LATIN

CHARLES JENNEY, JR.

ERIC C. BAADE

DAVID D. COFFIN

ROGERS V. SCUDDER

PRENTICE HALL

Needham, Massachusetts   Englewood Cliffs, New Jersey

PROGRAM CONSULTANTS

Bernard Barcio
Carmel High School
Carmel, Indiana

Doris Kays
Foreign Language Consultant
Northeast ISD
San Antonio, Texas

Michael Mitchusson
Sherman High School
Sherman, Texas

Maureen O'Donnell
Formerly of W.T. Woodson High School
Fairfax, Virginia

Grady L. Warren III
Northeast High School
Clarksville, Tennessee

STAFF CREDITS

PROJECT EDITOR:
Rita R. Riley

PRODUCT DEVELOPMENT:
Thomas Maksym

ART DIRECTOR:
L. Christopher Valente

TEXT DESIGNER AND PRODUCTION COORDINATOR:
Carol H. Rose

SENIOR DESIGNER:
Richard E. Dalton

PHOTO RESEARCHERS:
Susan Van Etten
Laurel Anderson/Photosynthesis

PHOTO COORDINATOR:
Katherine S. Diamond

PRODUCTION EDITOR:
Shyamol Bhattacherya

MANUFACTURING:
Roger Powers

COVER DESIGN:
John Martucci and L. Christopher Valente

MAPS
Sanderson Associates

ISBN: 0-13-797390-0

3   6 7 8 9 97 96 95   91 90

A Simon & Schuster Company

(*page i*) Mosaic floor from Tunisia showing
Diana hunting

(*page ii*) Impressionist rural landscape from a
villa at Pompeii

About the Authors . . .

Charles Jenney, Jr., senior author, was graduated from Harvard University and did graduate work there as well as at the University of Toulouse in France and the American Academy at Rome. He taught at Belmont Hill School, Belmont, Massachusetts for fifty-four years serving not only as teacher, but as Head of the Latin Department, Director of Studies, and Assistant Headmaster.

Eric C. Baade received both his B.A. degree and Ph.D. from Yale University and is currently the Chairman of the Department of Classics at Brooks School, North Andover, Massachusetts. He has co-authored many texts on Latin authors and on the teaching of Latin, and has had considerable teaching experience on both the high school and college levels. He has also conducted Archaeology Field Courses in Italy for both high school and college classes. In 1987 he received an award for the Massachusetts Classics Teacher of the year.

David D. Coffin received his B.A. degree in Classics summa cum laude from Yale University and received his M.A. degree there also. He taught in the Department of Classics at Phillips Exeter Academy, Exeter, New Hampshire both as an instructor and as Chairman of the Classics Department. He has edited and co-authored many texts on Latin authors and on the teaching of Latin.

Rogers V. Scudder was graduated magna cum laude from Harvard University and received his M.A. in Classics at the University of Wisconsin, and a Diploma of Classical Archaeology at Oxford University in England. He served as Director of the Library at the American Academy in Rome and is currently teaching at the Groton School, Groton, Massachusetts.

Contributing Author

Thomas K. Burgess was graduated cum laude in Classics from Harvard University and received a Master of Philosophy in Classics at the University of London. He has taught Latin, Greek, Ancient History, and Roman Topography at St. Stephen's School in Rome, Italy and is presently a teacher of Classics at Brooks School, North Andover, Massachusetts.

The authors dedicate this volume to the best of editors, Rita Riley.

CONTENTS

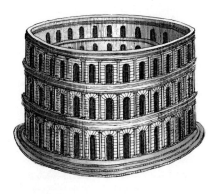

PREFACE

This edition of SECOND YEAR LATIN continues the thorough grammar presentation which formed the basis of FIRST YEAR LATIN and stresses participles, gerunds, and forms and uses of the subjunctive. The format of the first twenty lessons is basically the same as FIRST YEAR LATIN and includes all the features of the first level text including the cultural program "*If You Lived in Ancient Rome . . .,*" *Learning English through Latin, the Philosopher's Handbook,* and the continuation of reading selections based on the history of Rome. By the end of Lesson 20 students are prepared to read the section on Caesar's *Gallic War* which follows this lesson. The second half of the text is a brief anthology of a variety of Latin readings and includes selections on biography, narrative poetry, epigrams, comedy and history. It is not the intention of the authors to have every class read every selection. These readings should be considered as optional, and selections should be chosen according to the needs and capabilities of individual classes. Further readings, *The Twelve Labors of Hercules, The Argonauts, Ulysses,* and *Sabina and Cotta* from Book 5 of the Gallic Wars, are included on blackline masters in the accompanying Teacher's Resource Book.

The core material of the last two units (lessons 33–40) of FIRST YEAR LATIN is also provided on blackline masters in the Teacher's Resource Book, thus providing a bridge program between the two texts. This material can be used as the initial presentation for those classes which were unable to finish the first-year-text or as review material for the beginning weeks of the second year.

The goal of the Jenney Latin Program is to guide students as soon as possible to the reading of Latin authors through the mastery of the language itself, and every effort has been made to provide teachers with the means to accomplish this goal. The ancillary materials enhance the program by offering a variety of options for reinforcing the grammar and capturing the essential highlights of the anthology selections.

Italy and Sicily

Po R.

*ADRIATIC
SEA*

Arretium •

Clusium •

ETRURIA

Tiber R.

Tarquinii •

CORSICA

Veii •

Caere •

Fidenae

Rome •

Ostia •

SAMNIUM

LATIUM

VOLSCI

Capua •

VIA APPIA

CAMPANIA

Cumae •

• Pompeii

Brundisium •

SARDINIA

TYRRHENIAN SEA

Crimisus •

Crotona •

*MEDITERRANEAN
SEA*

Segesta •

SICILY

Acis •

IONIAN SEA

Syracuse •

Carthage •

Malta

AFRICA

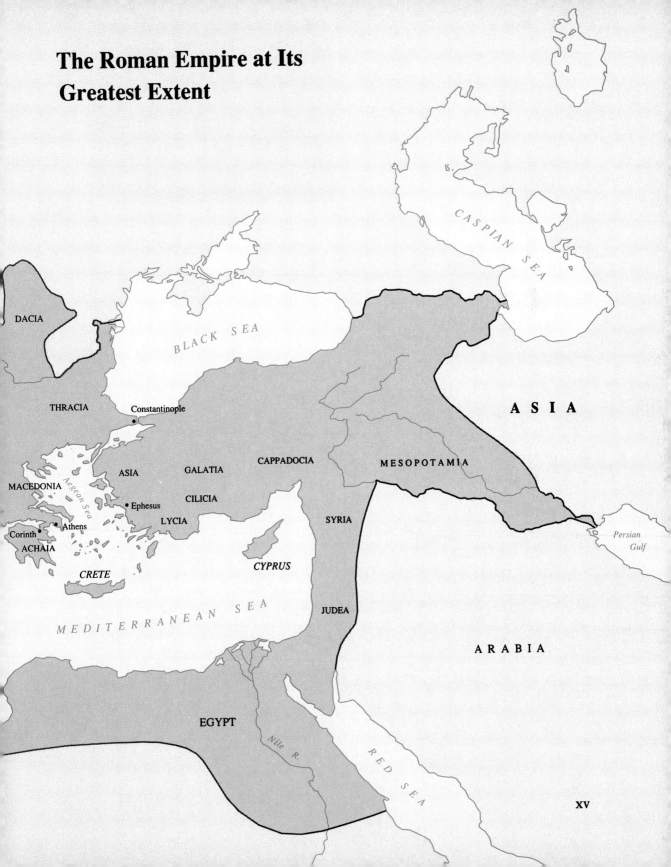

The Roman Empire at Its Greatest Extent

DACIA

BLACK SEA

CASPIAN SEA

THRACIA

Constantinople

ASIA

MESOPOTAMIA

ASIA

CAPPADOCIA

GALATIA

MACEDONIA

Aegean Sea

CILICIA

• Ephesus

LYCIA

SYRIA

Corinth •

• Athens

ACHAIA

CRETE

CYPRUS

Persian Gulf

JUDEA

MEDITERRANEAN SEA

ARABIA

EGYPT

Nile R.

RED SEA

XV

LESSON 1

Participles

An aerial view of the center of ancient Rome. In the very foreground is the east side of the Circus Maximus. Across the modern street are the ruins of the imperial palaces on the Palatine.

THE SITE
OF YOUR CITY

When Romulus and Remus and their men were looking for a site to build their city, the Palatine Hill would have seemed perfect. It was a fairly flat-topped rectangular hill such as the Latins seem to have preferred, and the streams of the Consus and Cloaca provided it with an almost complete magical water boundary. It was steep on three sides and hence easily fortified with a palisade; the saddle dividing its two heights provided an easy ascent and a natural place for a gate on its fourth side. Not far from this gate was the level (if somewhat marshy) ground needed for markets and public assemblies, later to become the Forum. When the Sabines under Titus Tatius joined the Romans as fellow-citizens, their hill, the Esquiline, must have been included in the city, the two settlements being joined by the Velia, just below which lay the common graveyard of the two peoples.

The site was far enough from the sea to offer protection from marauding pirates, yet near enough for access to salt and fish. The sea could be reached easily by rafts or barges on the Tiber, and the breaking down of the river bank caused by the inflowing of the Cloaca and the Consus made a natural landing place. Near this landing was another flat area (later the **Forum Boārium** and the **Forum Holitōrium**) where products brought to Rome via the river could be sold at market. The presence of the Tiber island made crossing the river easier at this spot, as well.

It may well have been the fact that the city controlled this crossing which led the Etruscans to take it under their control in the sixth century B.C., when they were spreading their sphere of influence south to Campania. The building of the great temple on the Capitoline Hill gave the city the conformation which the Etruscans liked, a plateau (the Palatine) guarded by a higher, smaller citadel (the Capitoline). Under the Etruscan kings the city also made use of the plain protected by the loop of the Tiber (the

(Continued)

Campus Martius). This was used for the military musters which formed the basis of government under the constitution of Servius Tullius. It was the Etruscan kings also who drained the Forum, thereby creating the city's first sewer.

Model of the Capitoline Hill (*below right*) and the Palatine Hill and Circus Maximus *(below left)* as they appeared in imperial Rome. The Forum Boarium and the Forum Holitorium occupy the open areas near the river.

ANCIENT ROME LIVES ON . . .

What can modern architects learn from the Romans about choosing sites for their projects?

FORMS

◼ PARTICIPLES

A participle (**participium,** *part-taker*) is so called because it is part verb and part adjective. Its attributes are *tense* (present, perfect, or future), *voice* (active or passive), *gender* (masculine, feminine, or neuter), *number* (singular or plural), and *case* (nominative, vocative, genitive, dative, accusative, or ablative).

A regular Latin verb has four participles: present active, perfect passive, future active, and future passive. There is no present passive or perfect active participle.

Present Active Participle

The present active participle is formed in the first two conjugations by adding **-ns** to the present stem. In the last two conjugations it adds **-ēns** to the present stem.

1ST CONJUGATION:	vocā- + -ns > vocāns, *calling*
2D CONJUGATION:	habē- + -ns > habēns, *having*
3D CONJUGATION:	pōn- + -ēns > pōnēns, *placing*
	capi- + -ēns > capiēns, *taking*
4TH CONJUGATION:	audī- + -ēns > audiēns, *hearing*

The present active participle is declined as a one-termination adjective of the third declension, with **-e** (not **-ī**) in the ablative singular:

DECLENSION OF THE PRESENT ACTIVE PARTICIPLE

	SINGULAR		PLURAL	
	MASC. & FEM.	NEUT.	MASC. & FEM.	NEUT.
NOM.	vocāns	vocāns	vocantēs	vocantia
GEN.	vocantis	vocantis	vocantium	vocantium
DAT.	vocantī	vocantī	vocantibus	vocantibus
ACC.	vocantem	vocāns	vocantīs	vocantia
ABL.	vocante	vocante	vocantibus	vocantibus

Perfect Passive Participle

The perfect passive participle is the fourth principal part, declined as a first- and second-declension adjective.

1ST CONJUGATION:	vocātus, -a, -um, *having been called*
2D CONJUGATION:	habitus, -a, -um, *having been had*
3D CONJUGATION:	positus, -a, -um, *having been placed*
	captus, -a, -um, *having been taken*
4TH CONJUGATION:	audītus, -a, -um, *having been heard*

Future Active Participle

The future active participle is the same as the future active infinitive, declined as a first- and second-declension adjective.

1ST CONJUGATION:	vocātūrus, -a, -um, *about to call*
2D CONJUGATION:	habitūrus, -a, -um, *about to have*
3D CONJUGATION:	positūrus, -a, -um, *about to place*
	captūrus, -a, -um, *about to take*
4TH CONJUGATION:	audītūrus, -a, -um, *about to hear*

Future Passive Participle

The future passive participle is formed in the first two conjugations by adding **-ndus** to the present stem. In the last two conjugations it adds **-endus** to the present stem. It is declined as a first- and second-declension adjective.

1ST CONJUGATION:	vocā- + -ndus > vocandus, -a, -um, *to be called*
2D CONJUGATION:	habē- + -ndus > habendus, -a, -um, *to be had*
3D CONJUGATION:	pōn- + -endus > pōnendus, -a, -um, *to be placed*
	capi- + endus > capiendus, -a, -um, *to be taken*
4TH CONJUGATION:	audī- + -endus > audiendus, -a, -um, *to be heard*

Participles of Deponent Verbs

Deponent verbs have all four participles, including the two active ones.

The meaning of the perfect passive participle of a deponent verb is active. The meaning of the future passive participle of a deponent verb, however, is passive.

verēns, verentis, *fearing*
veritus, -a, -um, *having feared*
veritūrus, -a, -um, *about to fear*
verendus, -a, -um, *to be feared*

SUMMARY OF PARTICIPLES

Each verb has only four participles. How to tell them apart when you meet them in Latin:

The present active will have **-ns** or **-nt-** followed by 3d declension endings.
The perfect passive will have **-s-**, **-t-**, or **-x-**, followed by 1st and 2d declension endings.
The future active will have **-ūr-**, followed by 1st and 2d declension endings.
The future passive will have **-nd-**, followed by 1st and 2d declension endings.

SYNTAX

■ PARTICIPLES: AGREEMENT, TENSES, CONSTRUCTIONS

A participle, like an adjective, modifies a substantive, and agrees with the word it modifies in gender, number, and case.

Like a verb, a participle has tense and voice. Its tense, like that of an infinitive, is relative to the tense of the verb of its clause. The present is used for an action going on at the same time as that of the verb, the perfect for an action preceding that of the verb, and the future for an action coming after that of the verb.

A participle will govern the same constructions as the verb from which it is derived, e.g. a direct object, an indirect object, an ablative of means, or an infinitive construction.

Mīlitēs urbe potītī cīvium bona occupāvērunt.
Having gotten possession of the city, the soldiers seized the citizens' goods.

Linguae oblītus auxilium rogāre nōn potest.
Having forgotten the language, he cannot ask for aid.

Puer rēgem aditūrus cessāvit.
About to approach the king, the boy paused.

Manēre cupiēns dubitābit discēdere.
Wanting to remain, he will hesitate to depart.

Anguem avibus nocentem vīderat.
He had seen the snake harming the birds.

■ TRANSLATION OF PARTICIPLES

The basic translations of the participles are as follows:

PRESENT ACTIVE:	vocāns, *calling, while calling, in the act of calling*
PERFECT PASSIVE:	vocātus, *called, having been called*
FUTURE ACTIVE:	vocātūrus, *about to call, going to call,*
	intending to call, destined to call
FUTURE PASSIVE:	vocandus, *to be called, having to be called*

Participles are often used in Latin where a clause would be used in English. This must be kept in mind when translating either from Latin to English or from English to Latin.

Equum inventum
domum dūcet.

$\left\{\begin{array}{l}\end{array}\right.$ *He will lead his horse, which he has found, home.*
When he has found his horse, he will lead it home.
Since he has found his horse, he will lead it home.
If he finds his horse, he will lead it home.

One of the first public works projects of the Etruscan kings was channeling the Cloaca, the stream running between the Palatine and Capitoline hills, so that they could drain the Forum. The culvert of the Cloaca can still be seen today where it flows into the Tiber River (*right*).

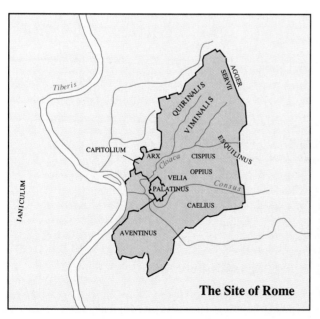

The Site of Rome

VOCABULARY

BASIC WORDS

membrum, -ī, n.   *part ⟨of the body⟩, organ, limb*

minister, ministrī, m.   *waiter, attendant, servant*

prōlēs, prōlis, f.   *offspring*

sermō, sermōnis, m.   *talk, conversation*

voluptās, voluptātis, f.   *pleasure*

agō, -ere, ēgī, actum   *drive, set in motion, do, act*

alō, -ere, aluī, alitum   *feed, nourish, support, rear*

flectō, -ere, flexī, flexum   *bend*

fleō, -ēre, flēvī, flētum (intrans.) *weep,* (trans.) *weep for*

pellō, -ere, pepulī, pulsum   *strike, push; rout*

quaerō, -ere, quaesīvī, quaesītum   *seek, search for, ask for*

reddō, -ere, reddidī, redditum   *give back; render*

Notes: 1. **Agō** is an all-purpose verb which has very many meanings in English. It cannot be translated until the subject and object are known. Here are some examples of its use:

Age dīc mihi.   *Come on, tell me.*

Aetatēm in rē publicā ēgit. $\left\{ \begin{array}{l} \textit{He devoted his life to politics.} \\ \textit{He spent his time on politics.} \end{array} \right.$

Animam ēgit.   *She gave up the ghost.*

Diēs sacrōs agēmus.   *We shall observe the holy days.*

Id agite.   *Pay attention to this.*

In Senātū dē hāc rē agunt.   *They are discussing this matter in the Senate.*

Male tēcum agēbat.   *She was treating you badly.*

Prīmās partēs ēgerat.   *She had played leading roles.*

Sē mēcum saepe agit.   *He often spends his time with me.*

Sēdecimum annum agō.   *I am in my sixteenth year.*

Tibi grātiās agō.   *I thank you.*

Tuam rem age.   *Mind your own business.*

2. **Reddō**, meaning *render*, may take a predicate accusative (objective complement):

Hoc mē reddidit fēlīcissimum.   *This has rendered me very happy.*

Building Vocabulary

Note this derivative of **agō**:

agitō, -āre, -āvī, -ātum   *put in constant motion* (+ all other meanings of **agō** with the additional idea of repetition or continuance)

Note the following compounds of **pellō**:

appellō, -ere, appulī, appulsum   *push to, drive to, direct to*
expellō, -ere, expulī, expulsum   *push out, expel*
impellō, -ere, impulī, impulsum   *push on, strike upon*

◼ LEARNING ENGLISH THROUGH LATIN

alimentary	*nourishing; connected with food or nutrition*
dismember	*mutilate by cutting or tearing the limbs*
flexible	*pliant; adjustable to change*
membrane	*a thin, soft layer of tissue covering an organ in the body*
prolific	*fruitful; fertile; producing ⟨something⟩ in abundance*
quest	*a pursuit, a seeking*
sermonize	*to preach to, exhort; lecture*
voluptuous	*characterized by luxury, elegance, and sensual pleasure*

▰ PRACTICE ▰

A.   Complete the following sentences by using derivatives from this lesson:

1. The ___ canal is a passage in the body through which food passes and is digested.   2. My schedule is very ___, so I will come at your convenience. 3. He is certainly a ___ writer, and has had many of his works published. 4. Diogenes was on a ___ for an honest man.   5. The detective said that the corpse was not only beheaded but was ___ as well.   6. Please don't ___; I already understand what I did wrong.   7. The Sirens were very ___, and lured sailors to their death by their seductive singing.

B.   Three of the verbs in the Vocabulary have a large number of English derivatives. Find and define at least four for each (see clues on p. 10):

1. **flectō** (stems will appear as *-flect* and *-flex*)   2. **quaerō** (*-quīrō* in compounds; stems will be *-quire* and *-quisit-*)   3. **pellō** (stems will be *-pel* and *-puls-*)

C. Name (by tense and voice) and translate the following participles:

1. agitātūrus   2. ārsūrus   3. clausus   4. sciēns   5. versandus
6. negāns   7. monendus   8. dēbitus   9. servītūrus   10. sedēns

D. Give tense, voice, gender(s), number(s), and case(s):

1. agitātīs   2. agenda   3. alentī   4. appulsō   5. expulsūre   6. flectentia
7. flētum   8. flentium   9. flendum   10. flētūrum

E. Give, name, and translate all participles of each verb:

1. agitō   2. agō   3. dō   4. gaudeō   5. impellō   6. inveniō
7. oblīvīscor   8. optō   9. quaerō   10. reddō

F. Pronounce and translate, giving at least two translations for each participle:

1. Optimōs versūs saepissimē legendōs tibi trādam.   2. Ad aedem flūminī proximam pervenientēs deae imāginem aspeximus.   3. Quālem ventum potissimum spērās nāvigātūrus in Hispāniam?   4. Hominī in ultimās terrās discessūrō nihil huius modī ūsuī erit.   5. Post proelium faciem cuiusque cīvis hūmī iacentis vīdimus ad hostium moenia versam.

FROM THE PHILOSOPHER'S HANDBOOK . . .

Quam sē ipse amāns—sine rivāle!
Himself loving himself so much—without a rival!
—CICERO

Would this be an appropriate saying for someone with a large ego? Can you see the relationship between the English *ego* and the Latin **ego**?

READING

Developing Reading Skills

These Latin words which you have already learned will help you in determining the meaning of some of the unfamiliar words in this Reading: cēdō, dō, fleō, lēgātus, mīles, mīlle, minister, mittō, mōveō, nōbilis, prōdō, sentiō, super, and turba.

If you know the meanings of the following English words you can guess intelligently at the meanings of unfamiliar words: *apparent, clemency, conciliate, consent, conspire, create, defend, dental, disturb, divide, exhaust, famine, indignation, intestine, legation, mature, militia, nobility, quiet, secede, sedition, tribute, vein, ventral,* and *vigorous.*

A Fable and a Woman Save Rome

Sextō decimō annō post rēgēs exactōs populus Rōmānus, quod tribūtīs et mīlitiā ā Senātū exhauriēbātur, sēditiōnem fēcit. Magna pars plēbis urbem relīquit et in montem trāns Aniēnem amnem sēcessit. Tum Patrēs turbātī Menēnium Agrippam ad plēbem mīsērunt eam Senātuī conciliātum. Is intrōmissus in plēbis castra nihil aliud atque hoc narrāvisse fertur:

"Tempore quō in homine nōn ut nunc omnia in ūnum cōnsentiēbant, sed singulīs membrīs suum cuique cōnsilium et suus sermō fuit, reliquae partēs indīgnātae ventrī 'Nostrā' inquiunt 'cūrā, nostrō labōre ac ministeriō tibi omnia quaeruntur. Tū intereā in mediō sedēns quiētus nihil aliud ac datīs

5

---

1. post rēgēs exactōs: Latin sometimes uses a concrete noun modified by a participle where English would use an abstract noun with *of.* Examples: **Trīcēsimō septimō annō post urbem conditam obiit Rōmulus.** *Romulus died in the thirty-seventh year after the founding of the city.* **Cāsus urbis nūntiātus omnīs in fugam dedit.** *The news of the fall of the city put everyone to flight.*   **4. conciliātum:** Be careful not to confuse the supine with the perfect passive participle. Here you can see that **conciliātum** must be a supine because it has the direct object **eam,** and a passive could not take a direct object.   **5 and 9. nihil aliud:** object of some infinitive understood, e.g. **agere** or **ēgisse**

10 voluptātibus frueris.' Cōnspīrāvērunt inde iubentēs manūs ad ōs cibum nōn
ferre, nec ōs accipere datum, nec dentīs acceptum cōnficere. Hāc īrā, quā
ventrem fame domātūrōs sē spērāverant, ipsa ūnā membra tōtumque corpus
ad extrēmam tābem vēnērunt. Inde apparuit ministerium ventris quoque
haud segne esse, et reliqua membra sēnsērunt ventrem nōn magis alī quam
15 alere, reddentem in omnīs corporis partīs hunc quō vīvimus vigēmusque,
dīvīsum pariter in vēnās mātūrum cōnfectō cibō sanguinem. Vidētis hinc
intestīnam corporis sēditiōnem similem esse īrae plēbis in Patrēs." Quā
fābulā flēxit mentīs hominum quī igitur in urbem rediērunt. Tum prīmum
Tribūnī Plēbis creātī sunt, quī plēbem adversus nōbilitātis superbiam dēfēn-
20 sūrī erant.

Octāvō decimō annō post exactōs rēgēs C. Mārtius, vocātus Coriolānus
ab urbe Volscōrum Coriolīs quam bellō cēperat, plēbī invīsus factus est.
Quā rē urbe expulsus ad Volscōs, ācerrimōs Rōmānōrum hostīs, contendit,
ā quibus dux exercitūs factus Rōmānōs saepe vīcit. Iam usque ad quīntum
25 mīlliārium urbis accesserat, nec ūllīs cīvium suōrum lēgātiōnibus clēmentiam
prō patriā rogantium flectī poterat. Dēnique cum Volumniā uxōre aliīsque
mātrōnīs Veturia māter ex urbe ad eum vēnit, quae fīliō sē complectī cupientī
"Priusquam" inquit "complexum accipiō dīc mihi: Utrum ad hostem an ad
fīlium vēnī? Captīva an māter in castrīs tuīs sum?" Cuius flētū et prēcibus
30 commōtus exercitum remōvit Coriolānus patriaeque pepercit, quam ob rem
ā Volscīs ut prōditor occīsus esse dīcitur.

READING COMPREHENSION

1. Why did the populace of Rome revolt?   2. What did they do?   3. Who
was sent to reconcile them with the Senate?   4. What did he do?   5. What
did the plebeians gain in the end?   6. When Coriolanus was driven out of
the city, where did he go and what did he do?   7. What is the significance
of the following? "Priusquam complexum accipiō dīc mihi: Utrum ad hostem
an ad fīlium vēnī? Captīva an māter in castrīs tuīs sum?"   8. What
happened to Coriolanus?

---

11. datum, acceptum: treat as conditional   **12. ūnā ⟨viā⟩:** *together, along with*   **15. hunc:**
masculine because it looks forward to **sanguinem**, line 16   **16. mātūrum cōnfectō cibō:** i.e.
prepared by the digestion of the food; Roman physiologists thought that the stomach
converted food to blood

LESSON 2

Participles of Irregular Verbs; Active and Passive Periphrastic; Dative of Agent

The southwest side of the Roman Forum is still graced by the elegant columns of the Temple of Castor and Pollux.

YOUR
CIVIC CENTER

Throughout the Republic the civic center of Rome was not at its geographical center. It was on the edge of town, the whole Campus Martius to the north and west of the Forum and Capitoline, inside the curve of the Tiber, being uninhabited. The buildings of the Forum area grew up in a natural but haphazard way, without any master plan.

Already in the late Monarchy the marshy part of the Forum had been drained by deepening and covering the Cloaca and filling in the gully which ran down from the Velia. The Regia and the Temple of Vesta, just inside the city's sacred boundary, on the edge of the Forum, were also built during the time of the Kings. During the reign of the Etruscans the first Comitium and Curia were placed at the northeast corner of the Forum, and rows of shops were built along the west end of its south side (**Tabernae Veterēs**) and the east end of its north side (**Tabernae Novae**).

The beginning of the Republic saw the building of the Temple of Saturn and the Temple of Castor at the southwest and southeast corners of the Forum; and in 336 B.C. the Temple of Concordia was built at the west end, under the Capitoline. The growth of commerce and banking, now that Rome was ruling all of Latium, led to the building of the shops called the **Argentāriae Novae** between the **Tabernae Novae** and the Curia, at about this same time. Because the Forum was used for gladiatorial shows and other spectacles, the shops of the **Argentāriae Novae** were built with balconies, and balconies were added to the **Tabernae Veterēs,** just across the Forum. This work was sponsored by the Consul Gaius Maenius, and so **maeniānum** became the Latin word for *balcony* (**meniano** still means *balcony* in Italian). Maenius also decorated the speakers' platform of the Comitium with the beaks (**rostra**) of the ships he had captured from the

(Continued)

14

A PHRASE TO USE

Urbem laterīcium invēnit, marmoream relīquit.

He found the city a city of bricks; he left it a city of marble. (The boast of the emperor Augustus)

people of Antium, in the Latin Wars. The platform was thereafter known as the **rostra,** and has given us an English word.

Business, both public and commercial, continued to grow, and the need for a covered space for various legal and business transactions caused M. Porcius Cato to build the first basilica, the Basilica Porcia, to replace the **Argentāriae Novae,** in 184 B.C. This was closely followed by the building of the Basilica Aemilia, behind the **Tabernae Novae,** and the Basilica Sempronia, behind the **Tabernae Veterēs.**

By the middle of the 2d century B.C., when Rome had come to rule all the Mediterranean lands, the city must have presented a strangely primitive appearance to the many ambassadors who came from all over the classical world. Used to the glories of Athens, Syracuse, Alexandria, and other marvels of architecture and city planning, they must have been astounded by this city of mud-brick dwellings and low-eaved temples of soft tufa, with little or no decoration, and by the haphazardness of the city plan and the placement of its important buildings.

(*below*) The small, round Temple of Vesta enshrined the eternal flame of the royal hearth in the time of the early kings.

ANCIENT ROME LIVES ON . . .

State the changes that time has brought to your town or city over the past five years.

FORMS

PARTICIPLES OF IRREGULAR VERBS

Sum and its compounds have only the following participles:

PARTICIPLES OF SUM AND ITS COMPOUNDS

	PRESENT ACTIVE	FUTURE ACTIVE
sum	——	futūrus, *about to be*
absum	absēns, *absent*	āfutūrus, *about to be absent*
adsum	——	adfutūrus, *about to be present*
possum	potēns, *powerful*	——
prōsum	——	prōfutūrus, *about to be profitable*

Eō and its compounds form the present active and future passive participles irregularly.

DECLENSION OF THE PRESENT ACTIVE PARTICIPLE OF EŌ

	SINGULAR		PLURAL	
	MASC. & FEM.	NEUT.	MASC. & FEM.	NEUT.
NOM.	iēns	iēns	euntēs	euntia
GEN.	euntis	euntis	euntium	euntium
DAT.	euntī	euntī	euntibus	euntibus
ACC.	euntem	iēns	euntīs	euntia
ABL.	eunte	eunte	euntibus	euntibus

Future passive participle of **adeō: adeundus, -a, -um,** *to be approached.*
The participles of **ferō** are formed regularly: **ferēns, lātus, lātūrus, ferendus.**

SYNTAX

ACTIVE AND PASSIVE PERIPHRASTIC

The word *periphrastic* (meaning *expressed in a roundabout way*) is a hard-sounding name for two very simple constructions, the use of the future active and future passive participles as predicate adjectives (subjective complements).

Active Periphrastic

The future active participle may be used with the verb **sum** as another way of expressing the future tense. It may also indicate intention or destiny. The use comes quite naturally from the four meanings of the future active participle.

Hoc factūrus est.
$\begin{cases} \textit{He is going to do this.} \\ \textit{He is about to do this.} \\ \textit{He is intending to do this (He intends to do this).} \\ \textit{He is destined to do this.} \end{cases}$

This use is called the active periphrastic (or the first periphrastic).

Passive Periphrastic

The future passive participle may be used with the verb **sum** to express necessity or obligation. This also comes quite naturally from the meaning of the participle.

Hoc faciendum est.
$\begin{cases} \textit{This is to be done.} \\ \textit{This has to be done.} \\ \textit{This must be done.} \\ \textit{This should be done.} \\ \textit{This ought to be done.} \end{cases}$

Hoc faciendum erat.
$\begin{cases} \textit{This was to be done.} \\ \textit{This had to be done.} \\ \textit{This should have been done.} \\ \textit{This ought to have been done.} \end{cases}$

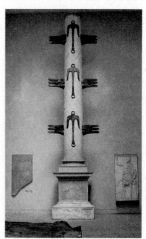

Reconstruction of the **columna rostrāta** of Gaius Duilius, who captured the **rostra** adorning it from enemy ships in 260 B.C.

This use is called the passive periphrastic (or the second periphrastic).

Since intransitive verbs can be used only impersonally in the passive, their passive periphrastic also must be impersonal.

> Ad montēs ante noctem perveniētur.
> *The mountains will be reached before night.*
> Ad montēs ante noctem perveniendum erit.
> *The mountains will have to be reached before night.*

> Diū et ācriter pugnātum est. *The fighting was long and fierce.*
> Diū et ācriter pugnandum erat. *The fighting had to be long and fierce.*

> Captīvīs nōn nocētur. *The captives are not being harmed.*
> Captīvīs nōn nocendum est. *The captives ought not to be harmed.*

▪ DATIVE OF AGENT

With the passive periphrastic, agency is expressed by the dative case rather than by the Ablative of Agent.

Hoc mihi faciendum erat.
> *This was to be done by me.*
> *This had to be done by me.*
> *I had to do this.*
> *This should have been done by me.*
> *I should have done this.*
> *This ought to have been done by me.*
> *I ought to have done this.*

This use of the dative comes from its use as the dative of possession.

> Hoc mihi faciendum erat. *I had this to do > I had to do this.*

If the future passive participle already has a dative, the Ablative of Agent is used.

> Dōnum tibi ā mē dandum est. *I must give you a gift.*
> Patrī ā tē parendum est. *You must obey your father.*
> Eī ā nōbīs credendum erat. *We should have believed her.*

VOCABULARY

BASIC WORDS

cīvitās, cīvitātis, f. *citizenship, citizenry*
clāmor, clāmōris, m. *shout, cry*
fīnis, fīnis, m. or f. (i-stem) *end, boundary*
littera, -ae, f. *letter ⟨of the alphabet⟩; (pl.) document, letter; literature*
officium, -ī, n. *duty*
opēs, opum, f. (pl.) *resources*

humānus, -a, -um *human; humane*

āiō, ___, ___, ___ *say yes; affirm, assert, state*
contemnō, -ere, contēmpsī, contemptum *despise, feel contempt for, belittle*
sequor, -ī, secūtus sum *follow*
trahō, -ere, trāxī, tractum *draw, drag*

ferē (adv.) *almost, nearly; generally, usually; nōn ferē, hardly*

Note: **Āiō** is defective; it has only these forms:

PRESENT:	āiō	—	IMPERFECT:	āiēbam	āiēbāmus
	āis	—		āiēbas	āiēbātis
	āit	āiunt		āiēbat	āiēbant

PRESENT ACTIVE PARTICIPLE: āiēns

FROM THE PHILOSOPHER'S HANDBOOK . . .

Vītanda est imprōba sīrēn dēsidia.
One must steer clear of the wicked temptress, Laziness.
—HORACE

Why do you think Horace considered Laziness a wicked temptress? What harm can you see in being lazy?

■ LEARNING ENGLISH THROUGH LATIN

clamorous	*loud, noisy*
contemptuous	*scornful, disdainful, full of contempt*
copious	*plentiful, abundant*
illiterate	*not knowing how to read or write; showing limited knowledge of a particular field*
infinite	*having no measurable or definable limits; without beginning or end*
obsequious	*overly submissive; much too willing to serve or obey*
officious	*offering unnecessary and unwarranted advice; meddlesome*
opulence	*wealth, riches*

Building Vocabulary

Note the following compounds of **sequor** and **trahō:**

consequor, -ī, consecūtus sum   *follow ⟨as a consequence⟩; catch up with, get, obtain*

persequor, -ī, persecūtus sum   *follow constantly, pursue, persecute*

abstrahō, -ere, abstrāxī, abstractum   *drag away*

dētrahō, -ere, dētrāxī, dētractum   *drag down; remove; humiliate, slander*

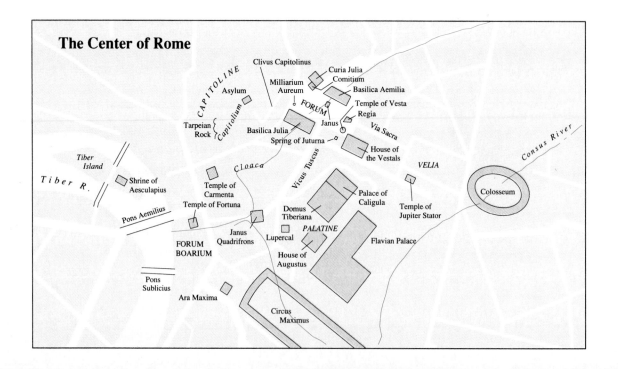

The Center of Rome

PRACTICE

A. Using a derivative from this lesson, restate each sentence to say the same thing.

1. The lecture was so interesting! I took profuse notes for you to review. 2. He is really ignorant when it comes to musical composition. 3. The objections to the proposal were stated in such a scornful manner that I withdrew my support from the whole project. 4. She is a good neighbor, but sometimes I am upset with her meddlesome ways. 5. His attitude reminded me of the fawning courtiers of old. 6. Let us not measure success by affluence. 7. I knew the home team had won when I heard the vociferous cheers. 8. I am weary of his sermonizing and endless repetition.

B. Find and define at least ten derivatives of **trahō** (stem *-tract-*).

C. **Subtrahō** means *remove from below;* **revereor** means about the same as **vereor.** Give the original meanings of:

1. addenda   2. Amanda   3. referendum   4. reverend   5. subtrahend

Translation Help

Beause participles can take all the same constructions as verbs, it becomes important in a Latin sentence to make it clear whether any given construction goes with the participle or with the verb. This is done by means of word order: a construction that goes with a participle should be placed between the participle and the substantive it modifies. If the participle is used as a noun, or if the substantive it modifies is not expressed but understood, the construction which goes with the participle should be put on the other side of the participle from the verb.

Mīlitēs rēgī parentēs ducī pepercērunt. *Obeying the king, the soldiers spared the leader.*

Mīlitēs ducī parentēs rēgī pepercērunt. *Obeying the leader, the soldiers spared the king.*

Crēvit patrem secūta avem. *Having followed a bird, she beheld her father.*

Crēvit avem secūta patrem. *Having followed her father, she beheld a bird.*

D. Give tense, voice, gender(s), number(s), and case(s) of each form:

1. abiēns 2. absēns 3. illātīs 4. illātūrīs 5. īnferendīs 6. īnferentis
7. trānseunda 8. trānseuntia 9. trānsita 10. trānsitūra

E. Give, name, and translate all the participles of the following:

1. obeō 2. possum 3. sequor 4. tollō 5. trahō

F. Identify (by tense and voice) the following participles of verbs you have not seen:

1. fluxūrīs 2. quassōrum 3. linquendum 4. picta 5. scandēns
6. accēnse 7. conandīs 8. nexō

G. Give all possible translations of these examples of the first and second periphrastics:

1. Num nostrae cīvitātī amīcitiae speciē impositūra es? 2. Utrī hostēs, hī an illī, nostrīs persequendī sunt? 3. Vocem deī quōcumque vocābit semper secūtūrus est. 4. Quisquis reī publicae nocuerat abstrahendus et dē arce coniciendus erat. 5. Aiēbant Fāta: "Hic puer aut maximā cum glōriā proeliō mortem obitūrus aut vītam humilem sed longam actūrus est."

H. Translate, using the second periphrastic:

1. You must not harm your parents. 2. They should never have obeyed that evil man. 3. You must remember posterity. 4. We ought to leave the city. 5. We shall have to give the supreme god a golden statue.

I. Pronounce and translate:

1. Sē nūllī invidēre pecūniamque contemnere aiēns maiōrēs opēs tamen cōnsequī quam aliī semper temptābat. 2. Īdem hostibus dextimē imposuit in nōs impetum factūrīs. 3. In silvam procul urbe parvum numerum captīvōrum interficiendōrum haud hūmānē trāxērunt.

Composite columns in the Roman style

(*below*) The north side of the Forum in reconstruction shows the elaborate backdrop of temples and public buildings which impressed visitors to imperial Rome. (*right*) The same view today shows, from right to left: the Arch of Septimius Severus, the arches of the **Tabulārium** as the understructure of the modern-day City Hall, and the columns of the Temple of Saturn.

READING

Developing Reading Skills

Latin words which will help in determining the meaning of new words: **agō, currō, dominus, ex, ferō, iūs, ob, plēbs, prō, properō, rogō, sedeō, servus, stō,** and **ūnus.**

English words which will help: *abdicate, appellation, arable, client, create, domination, effusive, exercise, fossil, implore, injury, intent, mandate, opinion, plebeian, salute, toga, tribunal, triumph,* and *unique.*

Abdication and Abduction

Annō quīnquāgēsimō secundō post rēgēs exactōs placuit Senātuī quoniam exercitus Rōmānus in Algidō monte ab Aequīs obsidēbātur Dictātōrem creāre. Omnēs ferē Patrēs exīstimābant L. Quīnctium Cincinnātum ad eum honōrem dēligendum esse. Operae pretium est audīre quī omnia prae dīvitiīs
5 hūmāna contemnunt neque honōrī magnō locum neque virtūtī putant esse sine effūsīs opibus: spēs ūnica imperī Populī Rōmānī, L. Quīnctius, trāns Tiberim quattuor iūgerum colēbat agrum. Ibi ab lēgātīs, seu fossam fodiēns pālae innixus, seu arāns, operī certē—id quod cōnstat—rūsticō intentus, inventus salūtātusque maximē admīrātus est, rogitānsque "Satīn salvē?"
10 togam properē ē tuguriō sibi ferre uxōrem Racīliam iubet, nam putat mandāta Senātūs sibi audienda esse togātō. Statim Racīlia eī hanc adfert, quā amīctum illī Dictātōrem eum cōnsalūtant. Aequōs superāvit et triumphum magnā cum glōriā ēgit; tum officiō functus sextō decimō diē postquam togam praetextam accēpit Dictātūrā sē abdīcavit contrā opīniōnem omnis

---

4. Operae pretium: *"the price of the effort"* = *"worthwhile"* **quī:** supply as antecedent **eōs** (as subject of **audīre**)   **7. quattuor iūgerum** = *ca. 2⅔ acres*   **9. Sati⟨s⟩n⟨e⟩ salvē?:** *"Safely enough?"* = *"Is everything all right?"*   **11. togātō:** For farming he would have been wearing a girt up tunic or exomis (a tunic opened up to leave one or both shoulders bare). **14. praetextam:** The toga of the Dictator had a purple stripe, to show that he had the powers of a king.

plebis quae tantam potestātem in ūnō virō positam timēbat atque ad agrum 15
et labōrem suum rediit.

Hōc tempore plēbs clamāre coepit lēgēs scrībendās esse, "nam aliter"
inquiunt omnēs "quōmodo iūra nostra aut iniūriās nōbilitātis adversus nōs
cognitūrī sumus?" Annō trēcēsimō ergō et alterō ab urbe conditā Decemvirī
creātī sunt ā quibus cīvitātī lēgēs scrībendae erant. Hī prīmō annō bene 20
ēgērunt; secundō autem dominātiōnem exercēre coepērunt. At dēnique
sublāta est Decemvirīs potestās quibus nōn fīnis sōlum īdem quī rēgibus sed
causa etiam eadem imperī āmissī erat. Ūnum ex eīs Ap. Claudium virginis
cuiusdam plēbēiae cupīdō occupāvit, quī igitur illud cōnsilium cēpit: virginī
venientī in Forum—ibi namque in tabernāculīs litterārum lūdī erant—Appī 25
cliēns quīdam M. Claudius minister Decemvirī cupīdinis manum iniēcit,
servā suā nātam servamque appellāns, sequīque sē iubēbat; cunctantem vī
abstractūrum. Clāmor nūtrīcis fidem Quirītum implōrantis concursum fēcit.
Iam ā vī tūta erat, cum adsertor nihil opus esse multitūdine concitātā ait;
sē iūre grassārī, nōn vī. Vocat puellam in iūs; ad tribūnal Appī perventum 30
est . . .

End of a Roman hoe-mattock

■ READING COMPREHENSION

1. What decision did the Senate make in the 52d year after the expulsion
of the kings?   **2.** Who was their choice?   **3.** What was he doing when the
envoys arrived?   **4.** What did he ask his wife to do and why?   **5.** How
did he ease the anxiety of the plebs, who feared the settling of so much
power on one man?   **6.** What was the purpose of appointing the Decemvirs?
7. Why was their power taken from them?   **8.** What was the plan of Appius
Claudius?   **9.** What brought the mob running?   **10.** What was the assertion
of the claimant?

---

22. sōlum as an internal accusative = *only*   **27. servā:** When the perfect passive participle
of **nāscor** is used as a noun (*son* or *daughter*), the ablative without a preposition is used
instead of the genitive of possession; this use is called the Ablative of Source.   **27. cunctantem
vī abstractūrum:** Indirect statements often omit the verb of saying and pronoun subjects and
objects. The full form would be **Dīxit sē eam cunctantem vī abstractūrum.** Translate
cunctantem as a conditional clause.

LESSON 3

Other Uses of Participles; Ablative Absolute

The arch of Septimius Severus was originally built as a monumental pedestal for a bronze triumphal chariot that contained a statue of the Emperor.

THE MONUMENTAL FORUM

The Romans' growing familiarity with other capital cities led to the first embellishments of the Forum. In 121 B.C. the Temple of Concord was rebuilt to a grander design and a basilica was built alongside it, thus giving a colonnaded border to the east end of the Forum. In the same year the first triumphal arch was built. These strange constructions were not designed, as is sometimes thought, for the triumphal procession to pass through on its way to the Capitolium, but rather as enormous pedestals for the statue of the triumphator in his four-horse chariot. The Roman invention of vaulting made it unnecessary for these pedestals to be solid, and their designers soon saw the decorative possibilities of these huge vaults.

The Dictator Sulla was the first to apply an overall plan to the Forum. In 78 B.C. he had the record office (**Tabulārium**) built on the saddle joining the two peaks of the Capitoline; its rear facade, standing on a huge substructure, provided a decorative backdrop to the west end of the Forum. He also relocated the Temple of Castor, lining it up with the Basilica Sempronia, rebuilt the Basilica Aemilia, and had most of the Forum paved. Most of the Forum, however, was still edged with shops, and its central area was crowded with various monuments placed more or less at random.

It was left to Julius Caesar to make a really radical rearrangement of the Forum. He replaced the Basilica Sempronia with a new Basilica Julia, with no shops, but with a colonnade edging the Forum on its south side. He also built a new Basilica Aemilia, screening the shops in front of it with a colonnade, and a new Curia in line with it, so that the north and south sides of the Forum, like the west end, now had a more or less continuous row of columns. The Comitium was dismantled and only part of it, the Rostra, rebuilt, but in a new location at the west end, facing down the length of the Forum. He ruthlessly removed the monuments from the central area, sparing only those (e.g. the little shrine of Cloacina) of which religion

(Continued)

27

forbade displacement; some of these monuments he buried under his new pavement.

After Caesar's assassination, the mob cremated his body at the east end of the Forum, and there Augustus built the Temple of the Deified Julius, fronting it with another Rostra, which faced the original one at the west end. Augustus also added the **Milliārium Aureum.** Later emperors, except for Septimius Severus, whose great triumphal arch was built near the west end, respected the Caesarian design.

(*below*) The ruins of the Basilica Julia. Julius Caesar undertook the first wholesale urban renewal of the Roman city center.

OTHER USES OF PARTICIPLES

Participles are often used as mere adjectives, and as such may be compared.

> Nōs parātiōrēs eīs fore spērāmus.
> *We hope that we shall be more prepared than they.*
> Amantissimus omnium hominum est.
> *He is the most loving person in the world.*

Participles are frequently used as nouns, especially the following:

> amāns, amantis, m.   *a lover*
> audientēs, audientium, m.   *the audience*
> doctī, doctōrum, m.   *the learned*
> nāta, -ae, f.   *a daughter*
> nātus, -ī, m.   *a son*
> victī, victōrum, m.   *the conquered*

ABLATIVE ABSOLUTE

The circumstances under which an action occurs are often expressed by a substantive in the ablative modified by a participle. This construction is called the Ablative Absolute. The basic translation uses *with;* but the construction, like other participial uses, is often best translated by a clause in English.

> Hostibus nōs persequentibus cessāre nōn possumus.
> *With the enemy pursuing us, we cannot pause.*
> *Since the enemy are pursuing us, we cannot pause.*
> *When the enemy are pursuing us, we cannot pause.*
> *If the enemy are pursuing us, we cannot pause.*

> Auxiliō nōbīs allātō servābimur.
> *With help having been brought to us, we shall be saved.*
> *Since help has been brought to us, we shall be saved.*
> *When help is brought to us, we shall be saved.*
> *If help is brought to us, we shall be saved.*

Since **sum** has no present participle, an ablative absolute sometimes consists of two nouns or a noun and an adjective.

> Caesare duce, hostīs vincēmus.
> *With Caesar as our leader, we shall conquer the enemy.*

Since Caesar is our leader, we shall conquer the enemy.
When Caesar is our leader, we shall conquer the enemy.
If Caesar is our leader, we shall conquer the enemy.

Etrūscīs inimīcīs ad montīs nōn preveniētur.
With the Etruscans being unfriendly, the mountains will not be reached.
Since the Etruscans are unfriendly, the mountains will not be reached.
When the Etruscans are unfriendly, the mountains will not be reached.
If the Etruscans are unfriendly, the mountains will not be reached.

The ablative absolute is not used when the substantive to be modified by the participle has some other syntactical role to play in the sentence.

Hostīs nōs persequentēs fugere nōn possumus.
We cannot escape the enemy pursuing us.
We cannot escape the enemy who are pursuing us.
With the enemy pursuing us, we cannot escape.
Since the enemy are pursuing us, we cannot escape.
When the enemy are pursuing us, we cannot escape.
If the enemy are pursuing us, we cannot escape.

Auxilium nōbīs allātum nōs servābit.
The help brought to us will save us.
The help which has been brought to us will save us.
Since help has been brought to us, it will save us.
When help is brought to us, it will save us.
If help is brought to us, it will save us.

Latin does not have a perfect active participle (although the perfect passive participles of deponent verbs have an active meaning) but English does. Therefore it is often less clumsy to translate a Latin perfect passive participle by an English perfect active participle. Analyse the following sentences:

Hostibus superātīs oppidum cēpērunt.
Having defeated the enemy, they took the town.
Hostīs secūtī oppidum cēpērunt.
Having followed the enemy, they took the town.
Oppidō captō rēgem occupāvērunt.
Having taken the town, they seized the king.
Oppidō potītī rēgem occupāvērunt.
Having gotten possession of the town, they seized the king.
Rēgem occupātum interfēcērunt.   *Having seized the king, they killed him.*
Rēgī occupātō perpercērunt.   *Having seized the king, they spared him.*
Rēge occupātō Rōmam rediērunt.
Having seized the king, they returned to Rome.

VOCABULARY

BASIC WORDS

comes, comitis, m. or f. *companion*

mora, -ae, f. *delay*

pudor, pudōris, m. *shame, modesty, decency;* ⟨*a woman's*⟩ *honor*

improbus, -a, -um *bad, depraved, shameless*

mortuus, -a, -um *dead*

cadō, -ere, cecidī, cāsum *fall*

caedō, -ere, cecīdī, caesum *fell, cut down*

canō, -ere, cecinī, cantum (trans. and intrans.) *sing, play* ⟨*on a musical instrument*⟩

loquor, -ī, locūtus sum *speak*

morior, -ī, moritūrus *die*

rapiō, -ere, rapuī, raptum *snatch*

sūmō, -ere, sūmpsī, sūmptum *take; put on* ⟨*clothing*⟩

Notes: 1. **Comes** is from **cum** + **eō**, a *"goer-with"*.
  2. **Morior** has no perfect passive participle (**moritūrus** is future active). The missing form is replaced by the adjective **mortuus:**

Mortua est.   *She is dead = She has died = She died.*

A composite capital

LEARNING ENGLISH THROUGH LATIN

improbity	*dishonesty*
incantation	*the chanting of words or formulas to cast a spell*
loquacity	*excessive talkativeness*
moribund	*dying*
rapacious	*plundering, grasping, voracious*
rapture	*the state of being carried away with joy, love, etc.; ecstasy*
sumptuous	*lavish, magnificent, splendid*

Building Vocabulary

1. **Cadō** in compounds becomes **-cidō, -cidere, -cidī, -cāsum.**
   EXAMPLE: occidō, -ere, occidī, occāsum *fall down, sink*

2. **Caedō** in compounds becomes **-cīdō, -cīdere, -cīdī, -cīsum.**
   EXAMPLE: occīdō, -ere, occīdī, occīsum *cut down, kill*

3. **Rapiō** in compounds becomes **-ripiō, -ripere, -ripuī, -reptum.**
   EXAMPLE: ēripiō, -ere, ēripuī, ēreptum *snatch out, rescue*

■ PRACTICE ■

A. Using a word from the derivative list in this lesson, restate each of the following sentences to say the opposite.

1. The hostess served a very meager meal to the visiting dignitaries. 2. The defendant's reticence disturbed everyone in the courtroom. 3. The chairman's integrity amazed all the members of the board. 4. The explorer did not expect to be in such a state of dejection after his adventure. 5. The artifacts we excavated seemed to indicate a nascent civilization.

B. Give and define at least five examples each of derivatives of **cadō** (stems in *-cid-* and *-cas-*) and **caedō** (stems in *-cide* and *-cis-*).

EXAMPLES: **cadō,** *occident;* **caedō,** *suicide.*

C. Give and define at least five examples each of derivatives of **loquor** (stems in *-loqu-* and *-locut-*) and **sūmō** (stems in *-sume* and *-sumpt-*). Use the list of prefixes in the Appendix.

D. Give tense, voice, gender(s), number(s), case(s), and degree of each participle:

1. loquentiōribus   2. cāsūrissima   3. raptiōrēs   4. agitātissimīs
5. flectentiōra

E. Rewrite each sentence, replacing the subordinate clause with an ablative absolute; then pronounce and translate:

1. Cor fēminae ubi omnem pudōrem āmīsit est parātum ad omnia genera rērum improbārum.   2. Sī Caesaris prōlēs dux erit nōbīs nōn timēmus. 3. Quoniam sacra virgō bonam fortūnam canit nōs hostīs victūrōs scīmus. 4. Postquam sōl super montem aspiciētur spēs nova animīs aderit.   5. Simul ac sōl super montem sē ōstendet spēs nova animīs aderit.

F. Pronounce and translate, using the English perfect active participle in each sentence:

1. Nātō numquam repertō quōmodo domum redīre audēbit?   2. Mīlitēs fīne bellī factō Rōmam sine mōrā rediērunt.   3. Quandō rēgīna amante amissō dolēre dēsinet?   4. Circā duās hōrās audientibus locūta sibi nōn diūtius loquendum esse sēnsit.   5. Dea nātam apud īnfimum Dītem inventam ad sedīs priōrēs dūxit.

G. Which of the Latin sentences are correct? What is wrong with the others?

1. Having killed his shameless companion, he returned home.
   a. Improbum comitem occīsus domum redīvit.
   b. Improbum comitem occīsum domum redīvit.
   c. Improbō comite occīsō domum redīvit.
   d. Improbum comitem occīsō domum redīvit.

2. Having followed the sun, he arrived in Outer Spain.
   a. Sōlem sequēns in Hispāniam Ulteriōrem pervēnit.
   b. Sōle secūtō in Hispāniam Ulteriōrem pervēnit.
   c. Sōlem secūtum in Hispāniam Ulteriōrem pervēnit.
   d. Sōlem secūtus in Hispāniam Ulteriōrem pervēnit.

3. Having written a letter in a foreign language, he brought it to Caesar.
   a. Litterīs linguā aliēnā scriptīs eās ad Caesarem tulit.
   b. Litterās linguā aliēnā scriptās ad Caesarem tulit.
   c. Litterās linguā aliēnā scriptus eās ad Caesarem tulit.
   d. Litterās linguā aliēnā scrībēns eās ad Caesarem tulit.

H. Pronounce and translate:

1. Ā dextrā fēminārum clāmōrēs quōs ut solēbant diūtissimē eiciēbant, simul ā sinistrā cursūs virōrum ingentium, nostrīs cum Gallīs pugnantibus impedimentō saepius quam ipsa tēla fuerant.   2. Aetāte properante quot gaudia discēdentia, quot dolōrēs adeuntēs aspiciō! quantō potior erit ipsa mors!

READING

Developing Reading Skills

Familiar Latin words which will help: ad, arma, caedō, centum, circum, comes, dīcō, dūcō, faciō, fugiō, nōscō, iaciō, inter, iūs, mīles, mōveō, pater, pellō, possum, prō, pudor, rapiō, rogō, stō, veniō, sacer, servus, spectō, sub, and ūnus.

English words which will help: *advent, arm, centurion, colleague, condemn, consecrate, descend, exile, implore, incarcerate, inclement, inject, injury, interrogate, intervene, judicial, militia, obsolescent, obsolete, origin, present, repel, repulse, sedition, sordid, terrify, tribunal, Tribune, unique, venial, vigil,* and *vindicate.*

Saved or Destroyed?

Postquam ad tribūnal Appī perventum est, ait Decemvir virginem aut līberam aut servam esse, itaque aut in patris manū aut in potestāte dominī; et "quoniam" inquit "quī pater dīcitur Vergīnius mīlitiae, adsertor M. Claudius Rōmae, hōc tempore est, arcessitor Vergīnius et interim virgō sequitor M.
5   Claudium." Adversus iniūriam dēcrētī multī magis fremēbant quam quisquam ūnus recūsāre audēbat, cum L. Īcilius tribūnicius amāns Vergīniae intervēnit et "Huius pudīcitiae" clāmāvit "sī vīs adferētur, ego praesentium Quirītum prō spōnsā, Vergīnius mīlitum prō ūnicā fīliā, omnēs deōrum hominumque implōrābimus fidem, neque tū istud umquam sine caede nostrī
10 faciēs!" Territus Appius prōmīsit sē Vergīnī adventum exspectātūrum, sed ūnum diem sōlum; interim Vergīniam domī patris manēre posse. Hōc dictō domum sē recēpit collēgīsque in castrīs litterās scrīpsit per quās eōs iubet Vergīniō Centūriōnī commeātum negāre; sed imprōbum cōnsilium sērum

---

2. **manū: manus,** *hand,* is the legal name for the power a father has over his daughter or a husband over his wife   3. **mīlitiae:** locative   4. **arcessitor, sequitor:** future imperatives (see Appendix)

fuit: iam enim commeātū sumptō profectus Vergīnius prīmā vigiliā erat.

Diē posterō Vergīnius sordidātus fīliam sēcum obsolētā veste comitantibus aliquot matrōnīs in Forum dēdūcit ad Appī tribūnal. Sine morā Appius, quī cum armātīs in Forum dēscenderat, dēcrētum fert quō Vergīnia M. Claudiō trādenda erit. Adsertōre virginis ā matrōnibus et aliīs circumstantibus repulsō, Appius iussit armātōs submovēre turbam et dare viam M. Claudiō. Tum Vergīnius ubi nihil usquam auxilī vīdit "Quaesō," inquit "Appī, prīmum ignōsce patriō dolōrī, sī quid inclēmentius in tē dīxī; deinde patere mē hīc cōram virgine nūtrīcem interrogāre dē illīus orīgine, sī rē vērā nōn est fīlia mea." Datā veniā sēdūcit fīliam ac nūtrīcem propter Cloācīnae ad tabernās quibus nunc "Novīs" est nōmen atque ibi ab laniō cultrō arreptō "Hōc tē ūnō quō possum" ait "modō, fīlia, in lībertātem vindicō." Pectus deinde puellae trāicit respectānsque ad tribūnal "Tē," inquit "Appī, tuumque caput sanguine hōc cōnsecrō." Tum ad mīlitēs prōfūgit, eōsque ad sēditiōnem commōvit. Sublāta est Decemvirīs potestās, quōrum aliī exsilī condemnātī sunt, Appius in carcerem iniectus est, ubi spē incīsā ante diem iūdicī suā manū mortuus est.

15

20

25

30

Shrine of Cloacina in the Roman Forum

■ READING COMPREHENSION

1. After recourse was had to Appius' tribunal, what did the Decemvir say?
2. Who was the only one who cried out in protest at the decision?   **3.** How did Appius try to prevent the arrival of Verginius?   **4.** What was the final decision of Appius about the fate of Verginia?   **5.** When Verginius saw no help anywhere, what request did he make?   **6.** What is the significance of these words: "Hōc tē ūnō quō possum modō, fīlia, in lībertātem vindicō"?
7. What threat did Verginius make to Appius?   **8.** What were the end results of Verginius' action?

---

23. Cloācīnae: A shrine or temple is often identified by the god's name in the genitive with no accompanying noun, just as we refer to Michelangelo's great church as St. Peter's.   **27. cōnsecrō:** The verb means *to dedicate to a god or gods;* if the gods are the Gods Below, the act is equivalent to a death-curse.   **28. exsilī:** genitive of the penalty; use *to* in English

LESSON 4

Gerund; Gerundive Constructions

The stadium of Domitian (now Piazza Navona). Much of modern Rome is built upon ancient foundations. The placement of the stadium seats is clear in this modern photograph.

THE PLAN OF YOUR CITY

Julius Caesar's rearrangement of the Forum was only part of a grand design for the replanning of the whole city, which had never been developed systematically, and which had been rebuilt in a very haphazard fashion after the sack by the Gauls in 390 B.C. For this he hired a Greek city planner, whose plan apparently hinged on developing the **Campus Mārtius,** which was still an uninhabited area outside the city walls, as a new civic center and connecting it to the old center of settlement (on the Caelian and Esquiline Hills) by a series of open areas. The Theatre of Pompey and the long colonnade along its north side provided a southern boundary for the new civic center. Caesar began the opening up of the connection by demolishing the slums that lay behind the **Cūria** and building the **Forum Iūlium,** a colonnaded rectangle with shops to the north and south and the Temple of **Venus Genetrīx** (the *Ancestress*) at its east end. Augustus continued the process by replacing more slums with the **Forum Augustum,** with its Temple of **Mārs Ultor** (the *Avenger*), at right angles to the **Forum Iūlium.** He also rebuilt many of the brick buildings of Rome in concrete with marble revetments, allowing him to boast that he had found a city of brick and left it a city of marble. He began the development of the **Campus Mārtius** area with the original Pantheon and the baths of Agrippa lined up along what was to be the eastern border of the area. Nero built his baths (**Thermae Nerōniānae**) along the northern border.

The Flavian emperors adhered to the same plan. Vespasian, always concerned about saving money, converted the old Central Market (**Macellum**), somewhat to the east of the Forum Augustum, into the Forum of Peace (**Forum Pācis**), so called because it contained a temple to the goddess Pax. It was notable for its library (**Bibliothēca Pācis**) which also functioned as a museum, displaying some of the treasures taken in the sack of Jerusalem. Vespasian's son Domitian removed the street which still lay between the

(Continued)

Forum Augustum and the **Forum Pācis,** interrupting the line of imperial Fora, and replaced it with the little **Forum Transitōrium,** with its Temple of Minerva. He also filled in the western edge of the Campus Martius area with a concert hall and stadium (for foot races and Greek-style games). The Flavian emperors also took advantage of the spaces created by their demolishing of Nero's Golden House to build the Colosseum and the gladiatorial school associated with it.

Trajan completed the line of connecting Fora with the huge **Forum Ulpium,** next to the **Forum Augustum,** cutting away the saddle which lay between the Quirinal and Capitoline, and adding the huge complex of shops and showrooms called the Market of Trajan, cut into the rock of the Quirinal to a depth of 38 meters. His Forum contained a Basilica and two libraries; here Hadrian later added the Temple of the Deified Trajan. All later emperors adhered to Caesar's plan, surrounding the open part of the Campus Martius with temples and other buildings. It is interesting that when Hadrian's philanthropy rebuilt the city of Athens, a similar plan was followed there, connecting the old center with a newly-developed area by a series of monumental open areas.

(*below*) **Tabernae** (shops) in Trajan's Market. The organization of levels, lanes, and shops in this great structure resembles today's up-to-date urban shopping centers.

ANCIENT ROME LIVES ON . . .

What similarities and differences are there between city planning today and city planning in the days of ancient Rome?

FORMS

GERUND

A gerund in English is a noun ending in *-ing,* made from a verb. When an English gerund is the subject or the direct object of a verb, it is represented by the Latin subjective or objective infinitive.

<table>
<tr><td>Hominibus nocēre malum est.</td><td>*Harming people is bad.*</td></tr>
<tr><td>Malus hominibus nocēre amat.</td><td>*A bad person likes harming people.*</td></tr>
</table>

For the other case uses Latin uses the future passive participle, but with an active meaning, as a gerund. Since it is used impersonally it is always neuter singular. Since it cannot be the subject, it has no nominative.

DECLENSION OF GERUNDS

	1ST CONJ.	2D CONJ.	3D CONJ.		4TH CONJ.	EŌ
NOM.	——	——	——	——	——	——
GEN.	cessandī	nocendī	cōnsulendī	moriendī	potiendī	eundī
DAT.	cessandō	nocendō	cōnsulendō	moriendō	potiendō	eundō
ACC.	cessandum	nocendum	cōnsulendum	moriendum	potiendum	eundum
ABL.	cessandō	nocendō	cōnsulendō	moriendō	potiendō	eundō

SYNTAX

GERUNDIVE CONSTRUCTION

The idea which we express in English by a gerund (the verbal noun ending in *-ing*) is expressed in Latin by a future passive participle modifying a noun; hence this construction is called gerundive (meaning gerund-like).

Nihil litterīs scrībendīs efficiēs.
You will accomplish nothing by writing a letter.

This literally means *by a letter to be written*. The idiom seems odd; but in colloquial English we sometimes use a present passive participle (which Latin doesn't have) in the same way: *Little will be accomplished by a letter being written*.

When the future passive participle is used in the gerundive construction to modify a reflexive pronoun in the genitive (**meī, nostrī, tuī, vestrī, suī**), it is always masculine singular, even if the reflexive pronoun is feminine or plural.

> Nostrī servandī causā fūgimus.
> *We fled for the purpose of saving ourselves.*
> Fēmina in agrīs suī alendī grātiā labōrābat.
> *The woman was toiling in the fields for the sake of feeding herself.*

GERUND

Since an intransitive verb can have no passive meanings, its future passive participle obviously cannot modify any noun, but must be used impersonally in the neuter singular. The future passive participle in this use is called a gerund because it resembles a neuter singular noun.

> Nihil cessandō efficiēs.　　*You will accomplish nothing by hesitating.*

Occasionally Latin will use the gerund, rather than the gerundive, even for a transitive verb, but only in the genitive or ablative. The gerund is then treated as active and takes a direct object.

> Nihil litterās scrībendō efficiēs.
> *You will accomplish nothing by writing a letter.*

A portion of the Forum of Augustus showing the remains of the Temple of Mars Ultor

Note: Neither the gerund nor the gerundive construction is ever the subject, predicate nominative, or the direct object of a verb. For these Latin uses the subjective and objective infinitive.

Litterās scrībere nihil efficiet.   *Writing a letter will accomplish nothing.*
Litterās scrībere contemnit.   *He views writing a letter with contempt.*

CASE USES OF THE GERUND AND GERUNDIVE

All of the following case uses may employ either the gerund or the gerundive construction. Some have been illustrated by the one, some by the other.

1. Genitive
a. Genitive of Possession with causā
Iter hostium morandōrum causā occupāvit.
   He seized the passage for the reason of delaying the enemy. GERUNDIVE CONSTRUCTION

b. Objective Genitive
Cōnsilium urbis occupandae cēpērunt.
   They formed the plan of seizing the city. GERUNDIVE CONSTRUCTION

c. Objective Genitive with grātiā
Patrī pārendī grātiā id fēcerat.
   He had done this for the sake of obeying his father. GERUND

2. Dative:
a. Indirect Object
Sē dedit agrīs colendīs. *He devoted himself to tilling the fields.* GERUNDIVE CONSTRUCTION

b. Dative with Intransitive Verbs
Brūtus Tarquiniīs ēiciendīs favēbat.
   Brutus was in favor of throwing the Tarquins out. GERUNDIVE CONSTRUCTION

c. Dative with Compound Verbs
Bene facere semper praestat male faciendō.
   Behaving well is always better than behaving badly. GERUND

d. Dative of Purpose
Decemvirī lēgibus scrībendīs dēlecti sunt.
   Decemvirs were chosen to write (for writing) the laws. GERUNDIVE CONSTRUCTION

e. Dative with Adjectives

> Hic locus castrīs pōnendīs idōneus est.
> *This place is suitable for pitching camp.* GERUNDIVE CONSTRUCTION

3. Accusative: Accusative of Place to Which with ad

Ad mihi nocendum vēnērunt.
> *They have come to harm (for harming) me.* GERUND

Parātiōrēs erant ad perīcula subeunda.
> *They were more prepared to undergo (for undergoing) dangers.* GERUNDIVE
CONSTRUCTION

4. Ablative:
a. Ablative of Cause

> Patris cōnsilī oblīvīscendō in perīculum cecidit.
> *She fell into danger from forgetting her father's advice.* GERUND

b. Ablative of Comparison

> Nihil referendā grātiā aequius est.
> *Nothing is fairer than returning a favor.* GERUNDIVE CONSTRUCTION

c. Ablative of Place From Which

> Ex carminibus legendīs voluptātem capiō.
> *I get pleasure from reading poems.* GERUNDIVE CONSTRUCTION

d. Ablative of Means or Instrument

> Rem auget aliīs impōnendō.
> *He increases his fortune by deceiving others.* GERUND

e. Ablative of Price

> Fēlīciter vīvere vīvendō miserē mūtāvit.
> *He exchanged living well for living unhappily.* GERUND

f. Ablative of Specification

> Latīnē loquendō nēmō eī pār est.
> *No one is his equal in speaking Latin.* GERUND

g. Ablative of Place Where

> In cōnsulendō tibi semper versor.
> *I am always occupied in looking out for your interests.* GERUND

VOCABULARY

BASIC WORDS

coma, -ae, f. *hair [of the head]; foliage [of a tree]*

mōs, mōris, m. *custom*

pāx, pācis, f. *peace*

scelus, sceleris, n. *wickedness, crime*

spatium, -ī, n. *space; distance; period*

tergum, -ī, n. *back*

victōria, -ae, f. *victory*

brevis, -e *short*

īnsignis, -e *distinguished, remarkable*

augeō, -ēre, auxī, auctum *increase (transitive)*

dēfendō, -ere, dēfendī, dēfēnsum *defend*

dēserō, -ere, dēseruī, dēsertum *desert*

Notes:
1. **Mōs maiōrum,** *the custom of our elders (i.e. ancestors)* is a Latin idiom for tradition. In the plural **mōs** sometimes means *character* or *morals.*
2. Just as **ā dextrā** and **ā sinistrā** mean *on the right* and *on the left*, **ā tergō** means *in back.*
3. **Īnsignis,** used as a substantive in the neuter plural, means *tokens, badges,* or *insignia.*

Translation Help

You have now learned four ways to express purpose in Latin: (1) the supine in the Accusative of Limit of Motion (2) the gerund or gerundive construction in the genitive with **causā** (3) the gerund or gerundive construction in the genitive with **gratiā,** and (4) the gerund or gerundive construction in the Accusative of Place to Which with **ad.**

Auxilium mihi allātum vēnit.
Auxilī mihi adferendī causā vēnit.
Auxilī mihi adferendī grātiā vēnit.
Ad auxilium mihi adferendum vēnit.
} *He came to bring me aid.*

Remember: the infinitive is not used to express purpose in Latin. Remember also that the accusative supine can be used only with a verb of motion.

44

augment	*enlarge, make greater, increase*
brevity	*the quality of being brief; concision*
comate	*hairy or tufted*
insignia	*badges, emblems, or other distinguishing marks of rank*
mores	*customs that through general observance develop the force of law*
pacific	*of a peaceful nature or disposition; tranquil, calm*
pacify	*appease; establish peace with*
spatial	*of space; happening or existing in space*

Model of the Roman Forum and the Imperial Fora: 1—**Forum Rōmānum**, 2—**Forum Iūlium**, 3—**Forum Augustum**, 4—**Forum Pācis**, 5—**Forum Transitōrium**, 6—**Forum Ulpium**

PRACTICE

A.   Explain the meaning of the following sentences:

1. He can't read a map; he has absolutely no sense of spatial relations.
2. The general never missed an opportunity to display his insignia.   3. It is very interesting to study the mores of the ancient Romans.   4. The brevity of the lawyer's summation surprised all the jurors.   5. The clerk wrote the letter to pacify the irate customer.   6. The workers were very happy when the boss said their salary would be augmented by ten percent.

B.   Identify the gerunds, then pronounce and translate each sentence:

1. Nōn omnia quaerendō reperiuntur.   2. Amīcus mortuus ab īnferīs flendō nōn reddētur.   3. Nihil efficit quī vītam agit in cessandō dubitandōque.   4. Sine spē vīvendī sē in proelium ad moriendum impulit.   5. Sē rēctē ambulāre putāns rē vērā propior erat cadendō.

C.   Identify the future passive participles in the gerundive construction; then pronounce and translate each sentence:

1. Haec omnia fēcit ad victōriam consequendam.   2. Insīgnibus ducis sumendīs mīlitibus breve spatium imposuit.   3. Rēs Rōmāna aucta est victīs adiciendīs cīvium numerō.   4. Sociōs sē propter metum dēserentīs undique vīdērunt, quamobrem ācrius pugnāvērunt suī ēripiendī causā.   5. Capite apertō Graecō mōre Cōnsul ad veterrimam Herculis āram sēdīsque deinde superōrum versus stābat nūmina auxilium rogāns ad hostīs vincendōs.

D.   Pronounce and translate these sentences, which contain gerunds, future passive participles in the gerundive construction, second periphrastics, and future passive participles as simple modifiers:

1. Officiō semper fungendum est.   2. Deī humānīs nōn contemnendī sunt.
3. Multa facienda mē domī exspectant.   4. Magister mihi dedit carmen crās legendum.   5. Poēta clārus carmen composuit armīs virōque canendīs.
6. Hūc quam celerrimē veniendō omnibus salūtī esse poteris.   7. Manibus post terga vinctīs ex urbe occīdendī tractī sunt.   8. Illa comam tam pulchram cecīdit et vēndidit suī alendī grātiā.   9. Nostrō duce absente quemadmodum pāx Rōmāna defendenda est contrā scelera improbōrum?   10. Versārī in rēbus maximīs est dissimillimum sub sōle tōtōs diēs sedendō.

E. Pronounce and translate:

1. Fugiendī cōpiam praebuit.   2. Hostīs vīcit ācriter pugnandō.   3. Auxilī ferendī causā vēnit.   4. Multa ad pecūniam faciendam ēgit.   5. Dictātor reī publicae cōnstituendae factus est.   6. Ab hostibus vincendīs domum rediit.

F. Pronounce and translate the following sentences, then rewrite each, replacing the subordinate clause with either a present active or a perfect passive participle, without changing the sentence's meaning.

1. Gracilem coniugem quam dēlexit domum dūxit.   2. Fēminās vetustiōrēs tum cum hospitis mortem dolēbant audīvī.   3. Illum quia varia signa ab imperātōre data ōstendēbat ducem adīre passī sumus.   4. Sī deās īnferās humiliter coluerimus postrēmō salūtī nōbīs erunt.   5. Aspexistisne prīmam āciem quae plūrimīs hostibus īnstābat?   6. Sī tibi parēre hunc senem coēgeris, minimō cum studiō tibi serviet.   7. Ubi pecūniam reppererat eam sorōrī caecae praebuit.   8. Quia mihi cōnsulitis vōbīs plūrēs grātiās agō.

G. Translate:

1. He was in favor of fighting.   2. I went wrong from obeying you.   3. We ran for the sake of saving ourselves.   4. He did it for the sake of pleasing the king.   5. He used to give much time to reading poems.   6. They found a place suitable for founding a city.   7. Nothing is better than living well.   8. You are like me in serving the fatherland.

FROM THE PHILOSOPHER'S HANDBOOK . . .

Timendī causa est nescīre.
Ignorance is the cause of fear.
—SENECA

List three things in the world today that young people fear. How could understanding and knowledge about these matters free them from these fears?

READING

Developing Reading Skills

These Latin words, which you already know, will help in determining the meanings of some of the new words in this passage: **arma, canō, currō, dē, diū, dō, dūcō, faciō, inter, iuvenis, mittō, mōveō, nōbilis, ob, per, possum, prō, prōdō, scelus, sedeō, stō, super,** and **vestis.**

These English words will help: *arm, atrium, barbarian, calamity, chant, commotion, denude, dissonant, erudite, exercise, intelligent, intermittent, ligament* or *ligature, mandate, nobility, occur, pallor, progress, reverberation, scintillate, station, ululation,* and *vestment.*

A Teacher Learns a Lesson

Quia Vēiī magna urbs Etrūscōrum duodecim sōlum mīlia passuum Rōmā aberant Rōmānī intellēxērunt fīnīs imperī suī illā urbe incolumī numquam augērī posse. Vēiōs ergō decem annōs sīcut Trōia obsessōs cunīculō sub terrā faciendō occupāvērunt Dictātōre Camillō duce, quī inde Faleriōs exercitum ad aliam obsidiōnem dūxit. Vidēbāturque aequē diūturnus futūrus labor ac Vēiīs; sed fortūna imperātōrī Rōmānō illō modō matūram victōriam dedit. Erat Faleriīs quīdam magister cui prīncipum līberī ērudiendī mandābantur. Is quia in pāce īnstituerat puerōs ante urbem exercendī causā prōdūcere, eō mōre per bellī tempus nihil intermissō, modo breviōribus modo longiōribus spatiīs trahendō eōs ā portā, tandem longius solitō prōgressus, inter statiōnēs hostium castraque inde Rōmāna in Praetōrium ad Camillum eōs perdūxit. Ibi scelestō facinorī scelestiōrem sermōnem addit, Faleriōs sē in manūs Rōmānīs trādidisse eīs puerīs prīncipum fīliīs in

5

10

---

7. **ērudiendī:** not the gerundive construction, since it is in the nominative; translate *to be educated*   9. **modo ... modo** = *at one time ... at another*

potestātem dēdēndis. Quae ubi Camillus audīvit, "Arma habēmus" inquit "nōn adversus eam aetātem cui etiam captīs urbibus parcitur, sed adversus armātōs. Tū scelestus ipse scelestō mūnere praebendō prōdere eōs temptāvistī quōs ego Rōmānīs artibus, virtūte opere armīs, sīcut Vēiōs vincam." Dēnūdātum deinde eum manibus post tergum inligātīs redūcendum Faleriōs puerīs trādidit, virgāsque eīs dedit quibus prōditōrem in urbem verberantēs ēgērunt. Hāc tantā animī nōbilitāte commōtī Faliscī urbem Rōmānīs trādidērunt.

In Etrūriā Rōmānī prīmum Gallīs, hominibus magnī corporis, comae flāvae, oculōrum scintillantium, barbarīs quī turbātim cum ululātibus cantibusque dissonīs vagābantur, occurrērunt. Hī apud Alliam amnem, locō quī Rōmā circā ūndecim mīlia passuum abest, cum exercitū Rōmānō pugnāvērunt quem magnā caede superāvērunt. Superstitēs aliī Vēiōs desertōs prōfūgērunt, aliī Rōmam calamitātem rettulērunt. Pavor undīque pallorque: parum vīrium cīvitātī erat ad moenia dēfendenda. Paucī mīlitēs quī Rōmae relictī erant cum Senātūs iuventūte ad arcem properābant; cēterī rūs fūgērunt; Vestālēs ignem sacrum servandum Caere portāvērunt. Seniōrēs cīvitātis prīncipēs, quī pugnāre nōn potuērunt, fugere contempsērunt, īnsignibus honōrum vestītī in suō quisque ātriō eburneīs sellīs sedēbant, mortem exspectantēs.

READING COMPREHENSION

1. Why did the Romans wish to conquer Veii?   2. After besieging it for ten years without success, how did they finally conquer it?   3. Who was the Roman commander who accomplished this feat?   4. What was the next city to be conquered?   5. How did the teacher deliver this city into the hands of the Romans?   6. What is the significance of the following words? "Arma habēmus nōn adversus eam aetātem cui etiam captīs urbibus parcitur, sed adversus armātōs. Tū scelestus ipse scelestō mūnere praebendō prōdere eōs temptāvistī quōs ego Rōmānīs artibus, virtūte opere armīs, sīcut Vēiōs vincam."   7. What did the Roman commander do to the teacher? 8. What lesson did the teacher learn?

---

17. virtūte opere armīs: Latin occasionally omits coordinating conjunctions, particularly if the meanings of the words are closely allied.   **32. eburneīs:** The higher magistrates sat upon folding stools made of or decorated with ivory, as a mark of their rank.

REVIEW 1

LESSONS 1–4

VOCABULARY DRILL

A. Give the genitive, gender, and meaning of each of the following nouns:

amāns	comes	membrum	nātus	pudor	victī
audientēs	doctī	minister	officium	scelus	victōria
cīvitās	fīnis	mora	opēs	sermō	voluptās
clāmor	īnsīgnia	mōs	pāx	spatium	
coma	littera	nāta	prōlēs	tergum	

B. Give the other nominative singular forms, and the meaning, of each of these adjectives:

absēns	brevis	humānus	improbus	īnsīgnis	mortuus
potēns					

C. Give the other principal parts, and the meaning, of each of these verbs:

agitō	augeō	dēfendō	fleō	occīdō	sequor
agō	cadō	dēserō	impellō	pellō	sūmō
āiō	caedō	ēripiō	loquor	quaerō	trahō
alō	canō	expellō	morior	rapiō	
appellō	contemnō	flectō	occidō	reddō	

DRILL ON SYNTAX

Translate:

1. Many things were to be done all at the same time.   **2.** Neither boy wanted to carry the horns found in the forest.   **3.** The younger of my sons saw your horses feeding on my grain.   **4.** Someone came to the city intending to kill the king, but was prevented from doing this.

49

LISTENING AND SPEAKING

The House of Romulus

Gnaeus and his son Titus are visiting Rome. They take a walk on the Palatine Hill and history comes alive!

TĪTUS: Quid, pater, Rōmae hodiē aspiciēmus? aut quō adīmus?

GNAEUS: Nōs in monte Palātiō ambulantēs domum Rōmulī vidēbimus. Ecce, Tīte, aedem Magnae Mātris, quae proximae domuī Rōmulī est. Hīc fuit domus et prīmī Rōmānōrum rēgis et frātris Remī.

TĪTUS: Nōnne Rōmulus, pater, ortus[1] āb Albae Longae rēgibus et quōque ab Aenēā Ascaniōque erat?

GNAEUS: Ab illīs quidem erat; cūr rogās?

TĪTUS: Haec, pater, neque aedēs neque vīlla, sed tugurium[2] multō miserius quam rēgālius est. Num domus Rōmulī, virī illīus ā deīs rēgis dēlectī, erat? Rōmulus ille in rēgiā et magnā et lautā[3] habitāre dēbēbat.

GNAEUS: Mementō, Tīte, Rōmulum et Remum infantīs[4] ab Amūliō malō ex Albā in Tiberim flūmen ēiectōs esse. Lupa[5] fera illōs in rīpā clāmantīs audīvit et servāvit. Haec erat domus fortasse[6] Faustulī, miserī pastōris, quī lupam parvulīs sīcut catulīs[7] mammās praebentem vīdit.

TĪTUS: Faustulus nūtricius[8] geminōrum erat et Rōmulus Remusque modo parvulī hīc habitābant. Sed trāns clīvum sunt aedēs maximae et lautissimae, rē vērā domus rēgī maximē idōnea. Nōnne rēgia Rōmulī erat?

GNAEUS: Certē domus secundī Rōmulī est, quī vir Rōmam iterum condēbat.

TĪTUS: Lūdisne, pater? Erat Rōmae ūnus Rōmulus sōlus quī urbem abhinc multīs saeculīs condidit!

GNAEUS: Nōlī,[9] mī fīlī, nostrī principis prīmī oblivīscī! Augustus ille ab Iūlī gente ortus post multōs annōs bellī cīvilis pācem Rōmānam cīvibus contulit et Rōmam prīmam urbem terrārum fēcit. Ille secundus Rōmulus erat et in hīs aedibus lautissimīs cum uxōre Līviā habitābat.

TĪTUS: Intellego,[10] pater; sīc Rōma maxima ab initiō minimō crēvit.

1. **orior, orīrī, ortus sum**—*to arise, rise; be descended from*

2. **tugurium, -ī, n.**—*a sod hut, a peasant's cottage.*

3. **lautus, -a, -um**—*elegant, splendid*

4. **infāns, -ntis m. & f.**—*infant, baby*

5. **lupa, -ae-, f.**—*she-wolf*

6. **fortassē**—*perhaps*

7. **catulus, -ī, m.**—*pup, whelp*

8. **nūtricius, -ī, m.**—*foster father*

9. **nōlī**—*imperative of nōlō used in prohibitions*—*don't*

10. **intellegō, -ere, intellexī, intellectum**——*to understand*

A.   Give a brief description in Latin of the founder of Rome.

B.   Choose a partner and take turns answering the following questions.

1. Ubi et Gnaeus et Tītus ambō ambulant?   2. Cuius prope aedem est domus Rōmulī?   3. Cūr Tītus hanc domum Rōmulī fuisse nōn crēdit?   4. Quis secundus Rōmulus vocātus est? 5. Cūr Augustus illō nōmine vocātus est?

The Romans of Romulus' day buried the ashes of their dead in urns that looked like the houses they lived in. Archaeologists have found the remains of such houses on the Palatine.

LESSON 5

Present Subjunctive; Hortatory Subjunctive; Jussive Subjunctive

Etruscan sarcophagus painting of a Greek soldier attacked by Amazons. His equipment is like that of Servius Tullius' army.

THE ARMY: THE MONARCHY

In the time of the Kings the army was made up entirely of patricians (**patrēs**), members of the families of the original citizens. It consisted of one legion (**legiō**) of 3000 foot soldiers (**mīlitēs**) under the command of three military Tribunes (**Tribūnī Mīlitum**). To these were added 300 elite troops (**celerēs**), the King's bodyguard, commanded by their own Tribune (**Tribūnus Celerum**) and appointed by the King. Each of the three original patrician tribes (**tribūs**), the **Ramnēs** (made up of families of Latin origin), the **Titiēs** (of Sabine origin), and the **Lucerēs** (of Etruscan origin) contributed 1000 men and chose one Tribune.

King Servius Tullius broke the power of the leading families by putting the tribes into geographical divisions and raising their number to 30 (later 35). Military service was based, however, on the census which he introduced, which divided the populace into eight ranks (**ordinēs**) based on the amount of military equipment they could provide for themselves, i.e. on income. The Senators provided commanders, the Knights (**Equitēs**) full arms and horses, and the next five classes varying amounts of infantry equipment. The lowest class was too poor to provide any military equipment, and were not counted in the census. They were called the **Prōlētāriī** because their only contribution to the war effort was the production of children (**prōlēs**). They were not required to serve in the military; if they volunteered, they were provided with equipment by the government.

The first and second lines of the army were made up of citizens of the third class, drawn up in close formation. They were equipped with helmets (**cassidēs**), cuirasses (**thōrācēs**), greaves (**ōcreae**), round shields (**clipeī**), spears (**hastae**), and short cut-and-thrust swords (**gladiī**), all of bronze, essentially the same as contemporary Greek equipment. Like the Greeks, they fought in phalanx, standing close together in a compact group, shields overlapping and spears lowered to pass between the columns. In the phalanx the soldier

(Continued)

53

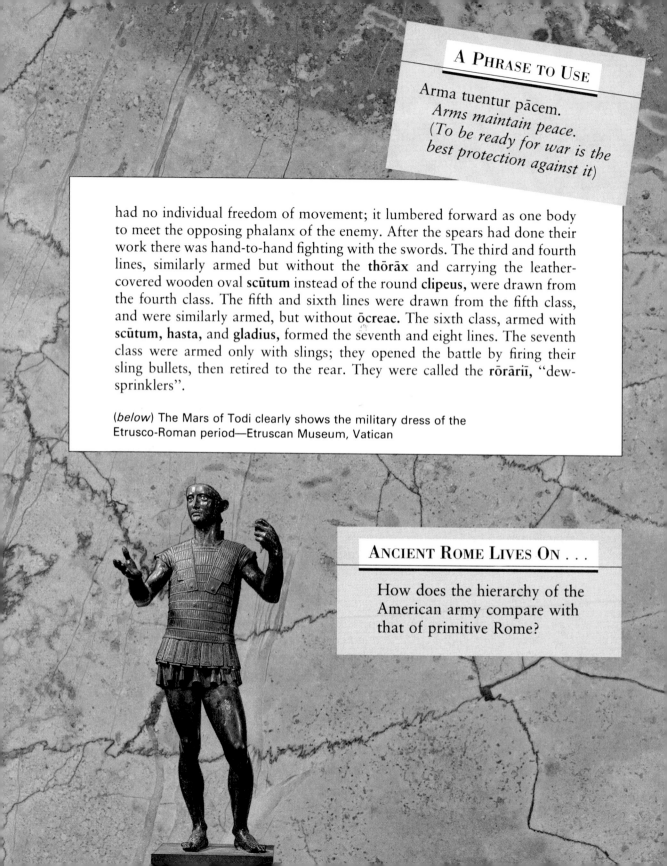

A PHRASE TO USE

Arma tuentur pācem.
Arms maintain peace.
(To be ready for war is the best protection against it)

had no individual freedom of movement; it lumbered forward as one body to meet the opposing phalanx of the enemy. After the spears had done their work there was hand-to-hand fighting with the swords. The third and fourth lines, similarly armed but without the **thōrāx** and carrying the leather-covered wooden oval **scūtum** instead of the round **clipeus**, were drawn from the fourth class. The fifth and sixth lines were drawn from the fifth class, and were similarly armed, but without **ōcreae**. The sixth class, armed with **scūtum, hasta,** and **gladius,** formed the seventh and eight lines. The seventh class were armed only with slings; they opened the battle by firing their sling bullets, then retired to the rear. They were called the **rōrāriī,** "dew-sprinklers".

(*below*) The Mars of Todi clearly shows the military dress of the Etrusco-Roman period—Etruscan Museum, Vatican

ANCIENT ROME LIVES ON . . .

How does the hierarchy of the American army compare with that of primitive Rome?

FORMS

▪ PRESENT SUBJUNCTIVE

The subjunctive is the third mood in Latin, the other two being the indicative and the imperative.

First Conjugation

The present subjunctive of the first conjugation changes the -ā of the present stem to -ē, then adds the personal endings.

PRESENT SUBJUNCTIVE, 1ST CONJUGATION

	ACTIVE		PASSIVE	
	SINGULAR	PLURAL	SINGULAR	PLURAL
1ST PERSON	vocem	vocēmus	vocer	vocēmur
2D PERSON	vocēs	vocētis	vocēris (vocēre)	vocēminī
3D PERSON	vocet	vocent	vocētur	vocentur

Second, Third, and Fourth Conjugations

The present subjunctive of the other conjugations adds -ā to the present stem, then the personal endings.

PRESENT SUBJUNCTIVE, 2D CONJUGATION

	ACTIVE		PASSIVE	
	SINGULAR	PLURAL	SINGULAR	PLURAL
1ST PERSON	habeam	habeāmus	habear	habeāmur
2D PERSON	habeās	habeātis	habeāris (habeāre)	habeāminī
3D PERSON	habeat	habeant	habeātur	habeantur

PRESENT SUBJUNCTIVE, 3D CONJUGATION

	ACTIVE		PASSIVE	
	SINGULAR	PLURAL	SINGULAR	PLURAL
1ST PERSON	ponam	ponāmus	ponar	ponāmur
2D PERSON	ponās	ponātis	ponāris (ponāre)	ponāminī
3D PERSON	ponat	ponant	ponātur	ponantur
1ST PERSON	capiam	capiāmus	capiar	capiāmur
2D PERSON	capiās	capiātis	capiāris (capiāre)	capiāminī
3D PERSON	capiat	capiant	capiātur	capiantur

PRESENT SUBJUNCTIVE, 4TH CONJUGATION

	ACTIVE		PASSIVE	
	SINGULAR	PLURAL	SINGULAR	PLURAL
1ST PERSON	audiam	audiāmus	audiar	audiāmur
2D PERSON	audiās	audiātis	audiāris (audiāre)	audiāminī
3D PERSON	audiat	audiant	audiātur	audiantur

▮ IRREGULAR VERBS

Sum and its compounds (**absum, adsum, dēsum, possum, prōsum**) have -ī instead of -ā.

A **thōrāx** worn by a Roman Centurion
—Museo della Civiltà Romana, Rome

PRESENT SUBJUNCTIVE OF SUM

	SINGULAR	PLURAL
1ST PERSON	sim	sīmus
2D PERSON	sīs	sītis
3D PERSON	sit	sint

Eō and **ferō** have normal 3d-conjugation present subjunctives: **eam, eās, eat,** etc., and **feram, ferās, ferat,** etc.

In the third and fourth conjugations the present active and passive subjunctive first person singular look just like the future active and passive indicative first person singular. The context will usually tell you which form it is.

SYNTAX

■ USE OF THE SUBJUNCTIVE

The indicative mood is used for statements and questions of fact, the imperative for commands. The subjunctive mood is used to describe unreal actions, i.e. those which are either wished for or possible. The negative adverb **nē** is always used for all the uses which express a wish; the usual negatives are used for those which express possibilities.

Hortatory Subjunctive

The present subjunctive in the first person plural is used for the idea expressed by *let's* in English:

Eamus.   *Let's go.*   Amīcōs vocēmus.   *Let's call our friends.*
Nē capiāmur.   *Let's not be captured.*

Because this idiom exhorts others to do something with the speaker, it is called the hortatory subjunctive.

Jussive Subjunctive

The present subjunctive may also be used in the second or third person, singular or plural, to give a command or suggestion. It is a little less peremptory than the imperative.

Mihi pareātis.   *You should obey me.*
Gaudeant omnēs.   *Let everyone rejoice!*

Because this subjunctive is used to bid someone do something, it is called the jussive subjunctive (**iubeō, -ēre, iussī, iussum,** *bid*).

The word *let,* used in English for third person jussives, is not the same as the *let* which means *allow.*

Discēdant.   *Let them depart! (= They should depart.)*
Eōs discēdere patere.   *Let them depart (= Allow them to depart).*

VOCABULARY

BASIC WORDS

custōs, custōdis, m. *or* f. *guard, watchman*

rīpa, -ae, f. *river bank*

saxum, -ī, n. *rock*

vultus, -ūs, m. *countenance, expression*

mortālis, -e *mortal*

vacuus, -a, -um *empty*

vagus, -a, -um *wandering, roving*

crēsco, -ere, crēvī, crētum *grow*

fallō, -ere, fefellī, falsum *deceive*

pateō, -ēre, -uī, ___ *be open; be visible; extend*

sternō, -ere, strāvī, strātum *spread out; smooth, pave; lay low, thrown down*

tegō, -ere, texī, tectum *cover, protect, roof*

Notes: 1. The perfect passive participle of **fallō** is used as an adjective: **falsus, -a -um** *false*

2. The perfect passive participle of **tegō** is used as a noun: **tectum, -ī**, n. *building (i.e. something roofed)*

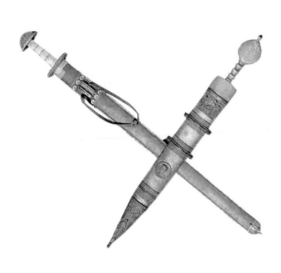

Roman military swords and armor—
Museo della Civiltà Romana, Rome

■ LEARNING ENGLISH THROUGH LATIN

consternation	*fear or anxiety that makes one feel helpless or bewildered*
fallacious	*erroneous, misleading, deceptive*
infallible	*incapable of error; not likely to fail*
mortality	*the nature of humanity as having eventually to die*
prostrate	*lying flat, prone; completely overcome*
protégé	*a person guided and helped, especially in a career, by another more influential person*
vacuity	*emptiness of mind, intelligence, interest, or thought*
vacuous	*characterized by lack of interest; inane*

▤ PRACTICE

A. Three of the words in this vocabulary are also English words. What do **strātum, vacuum,** and **vagus** mean in Latin? in English?

B. Complete each of the following sentences with a word from the above list of English derivatives:

1. They were greatly impressed with the document; they didn't know, however, that it was based on ___ reasoning. 2. They are such a ___ couple; there is no depth to them at all. 3. The citizens were ___ with grief when they read of the tragedy. 4. The infant ___ rate in that hospital is very low. 5. I know you have the highest regard for those scientists, but be careful; they aren't exactly ___. 6. Every year the Chief of Staff selects the top intern to be his ___. 7. When I saw the ___ etched on her face, I knew the news was not good.

C. Conjugate in the present subjunctive, active and (except for **possum**) passive:

1. rapiō   2. possum   3. agitō   4. augeō   5. sciō   6. trahō

D. Name the tense(s), voice, mood(s), person, and number for each of these verbs:

1. occidās, cessās, veniās   2. caedar, dēfendar, fallar   3. properēs, contemnēs, patēs   4. dēbēris, flectēris, portēris   5. placeam, crēscam, sentiam   6. trahētur, dolētur, morētur   7. agitem, optem, spērem   8. sternentur,

iuventur, augentur   9. deserāminī, persequāminī, tegāminī   10. flet, det, aget   11. neger, vocer, lauder   12. alāmus, nūntiāmus, pellāmus

E.   Translate:

1. Nē doleātis.   2. Nē morēmur.   3. Flectāris.   4. Nē occidās.
5. Moriantur.   6. Nē fallāminī.   7. Nē cadant.   8. Crēscat.   9. Augeantur.
10. Cessēmus.

F.   Pronounce and translate:

1. Spērāre aliquid dēsināmus, nam spēs caeca saepius sē ōstendit gracillimam ministram esse.   2. Nē umquam cognōscat fīlium improbissimum falsissimumque hostibus instantibus tergum vertisse et āciem dēseruisse.   3. Hostibus nōs numerō mīlitum superantibus dēfendāmus tamen rem publicam quam diūtissimē, etsī omnibus moriendum est.

G.   Translate:

1. You should lay the watchmen low without delay, for with them dead, the building, empty, will be open to every attack.   2. Let those worst of mortals not dare to believe that they excel us either in war or even in peace.
3. Let us hasten to perform the sacred duties for the most powerful gods, [the ones] destined to increase our humble state with resources and render it supreme.

FROM THE PHILOSOPHER'S HANDBOOK . . .

Quī dedit beneficium taceat; narret quī accēpit.
Let him who has done a good deed be silent;
let him who has received it tell it.

—SENECA

What does this aphorism tell you about performing and accepting good deeds? Do you make it a practice to tell others about favors you have received?

READING

Developing Reading Skills

Latin words which you have learned that may help: **aedificō, aequus, currō, dē, ferō, gravis, hostis, iaciō, in, magister, maior, opus, praetereō, rapiō, similis, sōlus,** and **stō.**

English words which may help: *adhere, atrium, august, canine, clang, concussion, create, deter, discursive, edifice, evade, excite, extrude, fraud, gravity, habit, hostile, ictus, incubate, intrepid, invade, magistrate, majesty, mandate, merganser, neglect, note, ornament, predator, preternatural, simulacrum, solitude, terrify,* and *vestige.*

The Geese Foil the Gauls

Prīmō Gallī per viās hominum vacuās discurrēbant ad praedam petendam; inde autem rūrsus ipsā sōlitūdine absterritī sēcum "In Forum" inquiunt "ac propiōra Forō loca redeāmus. Nē qua fraus hostīlis nōs vagōs excipiat." Ibi eōs, plēbis aedificiīs obserātīs, patentibus atriīs prīncipum, maior prope cunctātiō aperta quam clausa invādendī tenēbat; adeō haud aliter atque   5
venerantēs cernēbant in aedium atriīs sedentēs virōs, praeter ornātum habitumque humānō augustiōrem, maiestāte etiam quam vultus gravitāsque ōris prae sē ferēbant simillimōs dīs. Ad eōs sīcut simulācra versī ut stābant, M. Papīrius, ūnus ex eīs, dīcitur Gallō barbam suam permulcentī scīpiōne eburneō in caput incussō īram mōvisse et ab hōc occīsus esse. Sequitur   10
caedēs cēterōrum in sēdibus suīs; post prīncipum caedem nūllī deinde mortālium parcitur; tectīs dīreptīs iniciuntur ignēs. Sed arcem pugnandō nōn potuērunt capere Gallī. Āmissā igitur spē per vim atque arma subeundī obsidiōnem parant.

3. **qua** = **aliqua** after **si, nisi, num,** and **nē**   4. **prope:** adverb   6. **ornātum habitumque:** nouns   7. **maiestāte:** abl. of specification with **simillimōs**   8. **prae sē ferēbant** = *were showing* (an idiom)   9. **scīpiōne eburneō:** as a mark of distinction, men who had celebrated a triumph carried an ivory wand   13. **subeundī:** objective gen. with **spē.**

15   Vēiīs interim nōn animī tantum in diēs sed etiam vīrēs crēscēbant, Rōmānīs
eō convenientibus ex agrīs, at duce carēbant. "Nūntium" ergō inquiunt "ad
Senātōrēs Rōmam in arcem mittāmus et Senātum Dictātōrem Camillum
rogēmus." Ad eam rem Pontius Cominus, impiger iuvenis, operam pollicitus
incubāns corticī secundō Tiberī ad urbem dēfertur. Inde viā quae proxima
20 fuit ā rīpā per praeruptum eōque neglectum ab hostibus saxum in Capitōlium
ēvādit et ad magistrātūs ductus mandāta exercitūs dat, quī statim Camillum
Dictātōrem creant. Eādem dēgressus nūntius Vēiōs contendit. Sed Gallī
vestīgiō nōtātō hūmānō quā nūntius Vēiīs pervēnerat nocte sublustrī ubi
prīmō inermem viae temptandae causā praemīserant, trādentēs inde arma
25 ubi aliquid inīquī erat et trahentēs aliī aliōs, in summum ēvāsēre. Nōn
custōdēs sōlum fefellērunt sed nē canēs quidem excitābant. Anserēs nōn
fefellēre quibus sacrīs Iūnōnī in summā inopiā cibī tamen parcēbātur. Quae
rēs salūtī fuit; namque clangōre eōrum excitus M. Manlius armīs arreptīs
Gallum quī iam in summō cōnstiterat umbōne ictum dēturbat. Cuius casus
30 ubi proximōs strāvit, trepidantīs cēterōs armīsque āmissīs saxa quibus
adhaerēbant manibus amplexōs Manlius et aliī dētrūsēre.

Portrait bust of an
unknown Roman
Senator

■ READING COMPREHENSION

1. Describe what the Gauls found when, frightened by the solitude, they
went back to the Forum.   2. How did Marcus Papirius anger one of the
Gauls?   3. What was the result of his action?   4. Who was sent as a
messenger to the Senate to ask for Camillus as Dictator?   5. How did he
get there?   6. How was his route finally discovered by the Gauls?   7. In
following the route of the messenger, passing their arms along and pulling
each other up, the Gauls were able to fool the guards and the dogs; but
what didn't they fool?   8. How did this bring salvation to the Romans?

---

15. tantum: as an internal accusative this means *only.* **in diēs** = *from day to day, from one
day to the next* (an idiom)   **17. Dictātōrem Camillum:** Since the Dictatorship lasted only
for six months, Camillus had resigned his previous Dictatorship.   **20. eō:** ablative of cause
22 and 23. eādem, quā: sc. **viā**   **25. ēvāsēre** = **ēvāsērunt**; so also **dētrūsēre,** line 31

LESSON 6

Imperfect Subjunctive; Optative Subjunctive;
Adverbial Clause of Purpose

Cavalry parade, from the base of the Column of Antoninus Pius—Vatican Museum

THE ARMY: THE REPUBLIC

Rome's great general Camillus is said to have abandoned the old phalanx method of fighting and founded a much more maneuverable army. The entire army consisted of four legions (**legiōnēs**), two commanded by each of the two Consuls. Each legion consisted of 300 cavalry (**equitēs**) drawn from the wealthiest classes (**ordinēs**), and 4200 infantry (**peditēs**). The infantry consisted of four kinds of soldiers, according to age, class, and length of service. The 1200 **hastātī** ("spear-carriers," though in fact they carried no spears) were the younger men; the 1200 **prīncipēs** ("first men," though in fact they fought in the second line) were men in the prime of life; the 600 **triāriī** ("third-rankers", which they actually were) were proven veterans; and the 1200 **vēlitēs** ("light-armed") were men of the lowest classes of the census. The **equitēs** were armed with a bronze helmet (**cassis**) and cuirass (**thōrāx**), a large round shield (**clipeus**), leather greaves (**ōcreae**), and a long thrusting-spear with a point at each end (**hasta duplex**). They were divided into ten troops (**turmae**) of thirty men each, each squadron being under the command of three decurions (**Decūriōnēs**). The **hastātī** and **prīncipēs** were armed with a **cassis** with a high plume, a large wooden leather-covered oval shield (**scūtum**), a leather-and-metal corselet (**lōrīca**), **ōcreae**, a sword (**gladius**), and a heavy javelin or throwing-spear (**pīlum**). They were divided into maniples (**manipulī**) of 120 men each, each maniple being made up of two centuries (**centūriae**). Each century was under the command of a centurion (**Centūriō**); the senior centurion of the two commanded the maniple, which had its own standard (**sīgnum**). The **triāriī** were armed like the **hastātī** and **prīncipēs**, but with a thrusting-spear (**hasta**) instead of the **pīlum**. They were divided into ten maniples of 60 men each. The **vēlitēs** were armed with a leather helmet (**galea**), a small round shield (**parma**), the gladius, and several light javelins (**iacula**). They were assigned to the centuries of the other three types, twenty to a century.

(Continued)

A PHRASE TO USE

Rēs ad triāriōs rediit.
The situation has come down to
the triarii. (i.e. Things are
getting desperate.)

—LIVY

The commissioned officers were the six Military Tribunes (**Tribūnī Mīlitum**).

Attached to each Roman legion were 900 cavalry and 5000 infantry contributed by the Italian allies (**sociī**). This cavalry was divided into three squadrons (**ālae**) of 300 men each. The allied infantry was divided into twelve cohorts (**cohortēs**), ten of 420 men each, and two elite forces of 400.

In battle the maniples were drawn up checkerboard fashion. The maniples of **hastātī** formed the front rank, leaving a maniple-wide space between each two maniples. The enemy phalanx, clashing with such a line, was broken up as soldiers pressed forward into the gaps in the Roman line, leaving their flanks exposed to attacks by the **vēlitēs** attached to each maniple. Behind the gaps in the first line stood the maniples of the **prīncipēs**, who could advance through these gaps if the **hastātī** were compelled to give ground. Behind the **prīncipēs** were the **triāriī**, who waited kneeling behind their shields; if the two first ranks had to give ground, they passed through the gaps between the maniples of **triāriī**, who then held the line until the first two lines could regroup around their standards and press forward again. The allies fought alongside the Roman army in their own formation.

(*above*) Bronze **cassis**   (*below*) Tombstone relief of a cavalryman

ANCIENT ROME LIVES ON . . .

The Roman army seems to have gone through various changes over the years. What changes have the years brought to the armed forces of the United States?

FORMS

IMPERFECT SUBJUNCTIVE

The imperfect tense of the subjunctive is very easy; for all verbs it is formed by adding the personal endings to the present active infinitive.

IMPERFECT SUBJUNCTIVE

ACTIVE		PASSIVE	
SING.	PL.	SING.	PL.
1ST CONJUGATION			
vocārem	vocārēmus	vocārer	vocārēmur
vocārēs	vocārētis	vocārēris	vocārēminī
vocāret	vocārent	vocārētur	vocārentur
2ND CONJUGATION			
habērem	habērēmus	habērer	habērēmur
habērēs	habērētis	habērēris	habērēminī
habēret	habērent	habērētur	habērentur
3RD CONJUGATION			
ponerem	ponerēmus	ponerer	ponerēmur
ponerēs	ponerētis	ponerēris	ponerēminī
poneret	ponerent	ponerētur	ponerentur
caperem	caperēmus	caperer	caperēmur
caperēs	caperētis	caperēris	caperēminī
caperet	caperent	caperētur	caperentur
4TH CONJUGATION			
audīrem	audīrēmus	audīrer	audīrēmur
audīrēs	audīrētis	audīrēris	audīrēminī
audīret	audīrent	audīrētur	audīrentur
SUM			
essem	essēmus		
essēs	essētis		
esset	essent		

Since deponent verbs have no present active infinitive, one must be supplied to make their imperfect subjunctive: **morārer, morārēris, morārētur**, etc., **verērer, verērēris, verērētur**, etc., **obliviscerer, oblisciscerēris, obliviscerētur**, etc., **paterer, paterēris, paterētur**, etc., **potīrer, potīrēris, potīrētur**, etc.

Sum has an alternative imperfect subjunctive formed from its future infinitive: **forem, forēs, foret, forēmus, forētis, forent.**

Ferō and **eō** have **ferrem, ferrēs, ferret**, etc. and **īrem, īrēs, īret**, etc.

SYNTAX

■ OPTATIVE SUBJUNCTIVE

The subjunctive may be used in any person and number, in the present or imperfect tense, to express a wish. The negative adverb is always **nē**. In the present the optative (from **optō, -āre, -āvī, -ātum**, *wish*) subjunctive represents a wish which might come true (the grammarian's term is *possible of fulfillment*). In the imperfect it represents a wish which cannot come true (*impossible of fulfillment*). This distinction is hard to translate into English.

> Adsit pater!
> *If only father were here! [and he may come]*
> Adesset pater!
> *If only father were here! [but he won't be]*

The present optative is frequently, and the imperfect optative nearly always, introduced by the particle **utīnam**. There is no standard English translation for the optative; you will have to be guided by what sounds best.

> Utinam vīveret rēx!   *If only the king were alive!*
> Vīvat rēx!   *Long live the king!*
> Vīvat rēx in aeternum!   *May the king live forever!*
> Utīnam Rōmae nunc iam essem!
> *Oh, to be in Rome just now!*
> Utīnam hoc nē vērum esset!
> *Would that this were not true!*
> Deus eōs iuvet!   *God help them!*
> Ita deus mē iuvet!   *So help me god!*
> Valeās!   *Good health to you!*
> Utīnam valērēs!
> *I wish that you were in good health.*

◼ ADVERBIAL CLAUSE OF PURPOSE

The hortatory, jussive, and optative subjunctives are all independent subjunctives; i.e. they are used in principal clauses. The subjunctive also has many uses in subordinate clauses. It still, however, represents an action as wished for or possible, not real.

Since a purpose is something wished for, purpose may be expressed by the subjunctive, introduced by **ut** or **nē**. The present subjunctive is used for a present or future purpose, the imperfect for a past purpose.

> Veniō ut tē videam.   *I am coming to see you.*
> Veniam ut tē videam.   *I shall come to see you.*
> Vēnī ut tē videam.   *I have come to see you.*
> Vēnerō ut tē videam.   *I shall have come to see you.*
>
> Veniēbam ut tē vidērem.   *I was coming to see you.*
> Vēnī ut tē vidērem.   *I came to see you.*
> Vēneram ut tē vidērem.   *I had come to see you.*

VOCABULARY

BASIC WORDS

cohors, cohortis, f. (i-stem) *cohort;*
  [general's] bodyguard
ferrum, -ī, n. *iron, steel*
poena, -ae, f. *punishment*
pondus, -eris, n. *weight*
templum, -ī, n. *[sacred] precinct,*
  sanctuary

dubius, -a, -um *doubtful*
immēnsus, -a, -um *unmeasurable,*
  immense

tūtus, -a, -um *safe*

fundō, -ere, fūdī, fūsum *pour; melt;*
  spread; throw down; rout
iactō, -āre, -āvī, -ātum *throw about;*
  talk repeatedly about; boast of
impleō, -ēre, implēvī, implētum *fill up*
pendō, pendere, pependī, pēnsum *hang;*
  weigh; pay

Notes: 1. **Ferrum** is often used by metonymy for weapons; **ferrō et igne,** *with fire and sword.*
  2. Punishment was thought of as something which went from the punished to the punisher:

> Ex suō fīliō poenam sūmēbat.   *He was punishing his own son.*
> Eius fīlius poenam dabat.   *His son was being punished.*

Wall painting of Samnite soldiers, from Paestum

Building Vocabulary

1. **Impleō** is from a lost verb **pleō**, from which the adjective **plēnus** is also derived. Two other verbs are derived from this lost verb; they have the same meaning in English as **impleō**:

   compleō, -ēre, complēvī, complētum ⎫
   expleō, -ēre, explēvī, explētum ⎬ *fill up*

2. **Pendō** has a frequently-used compound:

   suspendō, -ere, suspendī, suspēnsum *hang up; suspend; keep in suspense*

■ LEARNING ENGLISH THROUGH LATIN

dubious	*ambiguous; causing doubt; questionable; vague; hesitating*
expletive	*an oath or exclamation*
implement	*to carry into effect; fulfill, accomplish*
inponderable	*unable to be conclusively determined or explained*
penal	*specifying or prescribing punishment*
ponderous	*very heavy, bulky, massive*
preponderate	*to surpass in amount, power, influence, or importance*
replete	*well-filled or plentifully supplied; stuffed with food and drink*

PRACTICE

A. Choose five words from the list of English derivatives in this lesson and write a sentence using each one.

B. **Fundō** and **pendō** both have several meanings in English, and so their derivatives cover a wide range of concepts.

1. What do the following mean, and with which meaning of **fundō** is each connected? *affusion, circumfuse, confound, confusion, diffusion, effusion, fuse, fusile, infusion, perfuse, profound, profusion, refund, refuse, suffuse, suffusion, transfusion.* **2.** What do the following mean, and with which meaning of **pendō** is each connected? *antependium, append, dependent, dispense, expense, impend, pendentive, pendulous, pendulum, pension, penthouse, perpendicular, suspend, suspense, suspension.*

C. Conjugate in the present and imperfect subjunctive, active and passive (except, of course, for **absum** and **morior**):

1. impleō   2. pendō   3. iactō   4. absum   5. sentiō   6. adeō   7. īnferō   8. morior

D. Pronounce and translate (remember that some of the independent subjunctives may be hortatory, jussive, or optative, so that more than one translation may be called for):

1. Sermōne flectātur.   2. Hostium cohors expellātur.   3. Utinam tūtior forem.   4. Crēscant artēs rūsticae.   5. Utinam loquerētur senex.   6. Plūribus voluptātibus fruar.   7. Rūrī nē diūtius cessēmus.   8. Mōre maiōrum nōbilēs semper ūtāmur.   9. Prōlī iuniōrī captīvōrum nē noceātur.   10. Īnsigne templum deae Victōriae sacrum īnstituātis.

E. Choose the correct form(s) of the verb; then pronounce and translate:

1. Hunc labōrem perfēcerat potissimum ut tibi (placuit placēret placeat). 2. Operis fīnem quam celerrimē faciāmus nē magis (morārēmur morēmur morāmur).   3. Magnum aurī pondus fūdit ut dextimē membra deī imāginis (tegat teget tegeret).   4. Solēbat vīvere simplicissimē minimam pecūniam pendēns nē comitēs eī (invidērent invident invideant).   5. Uxor in terrā aliēnā absēns litterās scrībet nē marītō ā falsō amīcō (impōnētur impōnerētur impōnātur).

(*left*) A Roman legionary at the end of the Republican period (*right*) An Etrusco-Roman warrior of the mid-Republic —reconstructions in the Museo della Civiltà Romana, Rome

F. Which Latin sentence(s) from column B correctly translate(s) each English sentence in column A?

<table>
<tr><td align="center">**A**</td><td align="center">**B**</td></tr>
</table>

A

1. I shall always despise what is worse.

2. I shall never be deceived.

3. She came to consult your interests.

4. Let them deny this if they can.

5. She came to consult you.

6. May I ever despise what is worse!

7. She has come to consult you.

8. May I never be deceived!

B

a. Vēnit ad vōs cōnsulendōs.
b. Vēnit ut vōs cōnsuleret.
c. Vēnit ut vōs cōnsulat.
d. Nē umquam fallar.
e. Vēnit ad vōbīs cōnsulendum.
f. Vēnit vestrī consulendī causā.
g. Vēnit vōbīs cōnsultum.
h. Hoc negent sī possunt.
i. Vēnit vōbīs cōnsulendī grātiā.
j. Vēnit vestrī cōnsulendī grātiā.
k. Numquam fallar.
l. Vēnit vōbīs cōnsulendī causā.
m. Eōs patere hoc negāre sī possunt.
n. Vēnit vōs cōnsultum.
o. Semper contemnam quod peius est.

Translation Help

Since in English an infinitive is the most common expression of purpose, an adverbial clause of purpose should be translated by an English infinitive wherever possible. Other translations are *in order to*, *in order that*, *so as to*, and *so that*.

Aedīs vēndidit ut pēcuniam cōnsequerētur.
  He sold his house in order to get money.
Labōrat ut līberī alantur.
  He toils in order that his children may be fed.
Celeriter currit nē capiātur.
  He is running fast so as not to be caught.
Ācriter pugnābāmus ut hostēs vincerentur.
  We were fighting fiercely so that the enemy might be conquered.

FROM THE PHILOSOPHER'S HANDBOOK . . .

Facilius per partēs in cognitiōnem tōtīus adducimur.
We are more easily led part by part to an understanding of the whole.
—SENECA

This is a good saying to remember when you feel overwhelmed by a task that lies ahead of you. Remember just to take one small part, complete it, and then turn to the next small part. Little by little everything gets accomplished, and then you can look back to a job well done.

Can you cite an example in your life of when you felt overwhelmed by something you had to do—a school project, a move to a new home, cleaning the attic? How did it get accomplished?

READING

Developing Reading Skills

Latin words you know which are, or contain, components of some of the unfamiliar words in this reading: **aequus, agō, bene, capiō, clāmō, cursus, dīgnus, dō, dubitō, emō, eximō, faciō, fundō, iaciō, imperium, laudō, loquor, māter, mittō, moneō, mōveō, pendō, pondus, stō, teneō, veniō,** and **vertō.**

English derivatives of some of the unfamiliar Latin words: *abstain, altercation, approbation, beneficial, colloquial, commerce, condemn, dubious, egress, emit, exclaim, famine, gladiator, imperative, incendiary, indignity, insolent, intervene, intolerable, laudation, matron, mercenary, migrate, momentum, monument, obscure, omen, opportune, oration, perfect, recuperate, recusant, redeem, redemption, revert, sedition, solemn,* and *transact.*

Woe to the Vanquished!

Camillus Vēiīs exercitum colligēbat ut cīvīs suōs in arce perīculō mortis ēriperet, nam Rōmānīs timōre impetūs in arcem līberātīs famēs tamen īnstābat, quae tandem quoniam nihil auxilī eīs ā Dictātōre ferēbātur vel dēdī vel redimī eōs iussit, iactantibus nōn obscūrē Gallīs haud magnā mercēde sē obsidiōnem relīctūrōs. Inde inter Q. Sulpīcium Tribūnum Mīlitum   5
et Brennum prīncipem Gallōrum colloquiō trānsacta rēs est, et mīlle pondō aurī pretium populī gentibus mox imperātūrī factum. Aurō publicō dēficiente ā mātrōnīs collātum accēpērunt ut sacrō aurō in deum aedibus abstinērētur, prō quō beneficiō post honor datus est quō eārum sīcut virōrum post mortem sollemnis laudātiō futūra erat. Reī foedissimae per sē adiecta indīgnitās est: 10
pondera ab Gallīs allāta sunt inīqua, et Tribūnō recūsante additus ab

---

6. pondō: Abl. of specification from lost 2d-declension form of **pondus; lībrārum,** *pounds,* is always to be understood when it appears. This results in the odd fact that the Roman abbreviation for **lībrārum** is **p.,** whereas our abbreviation for *pound* is *lb.*   **10. per sē:** *in itself;* we use this Latin expression in English with the same meaning

insolente Gallō ponderī gladius, audītaque intoleranda Rōmānīs vōx "Vae victīs!"

Sed dīque et hominēs prohibuēre redemptōs vīvere Rōmānōs. Nam forte
15 priusquam īnfanda mercēs perfecta est, ob altercātiōnem nōndum omnī aurō appēnsō, Dictātor intervenit auferrīque aurum dē mediō et Gallōs submovērī iubet. Suōs ferrō nōn aurō recuperāre patriam iubet. Nōn diū pugnātum est, nam prīmō concursū haud maiōre mōmentō fūsī Gallī sunt quam ad Alliam vīcerant. Nunc tamen novum perīculum urbī īnstābat, plēbe post
20 tecta urbis incēnsa cupiente migrāre Vēiōs, ut tūtiōrēs ibi vīverent. Mōvisse eōs Camillus dīcitur ōrātiōne ad contiōnem habitā, sed rem dubiam dēcrēvit vōx opportūnē ēmissa: Senātū post paulō dē hīs rēbus in Cūriā Hostilia agente cohortibusque ex praesidiīs revertentibus fortēque Forum transeuntibus, Centuriō ut in Comitium veniēbant exclāmāvit: "Sīgnifer, statue
25 sīgnum; hīc manēbimus optimē." Quā vōce audītā, et Senātus accipere sē ōmen ex Cūriā ēgressus conclāmāvit et plēbs circumfūsa approbāvit.

Paulō post īdem M. Manlius quī arcem servāverat rērum novārum cupidus plēbem ad sēditiōnem concitāvit. Capitis condemnātus est; Tribūnī eum dē Rūpe Tarpēiā dēiēcērunt; locusque īdem in ūnō homine et eximiae glōriae
30 monumentum et poenae ultimae fuit. Gēns Manlia ut huius oblīvīscerētur prohibuit Manliōs futūrōs Marcōs vocārī.

READING COMPREHENSION

1. Although the Romans had been freed from the fear of an attack on the citadel, there was still a threat. What was it?   **2.** What two choices did they have?   **3.** On what condition would the Gauls abandon the siege?
4. What deal was made between the Gauls and the Romans?   **5.** What did the matrons receive in exchange for contributing gold?   **6.** What insult was added to an already disgraceful action?   **7.** Why did the Romans not have to live as ransomed persons?   **8.** What new danger threatened the city?   **9.** What is the significance of the following? "Sīgnifer, stātue sīgnum; hīc manēbimus optimē."   **10.** After Marcus Manlius was punished, how did his family try to forget him?

---

14. prohibuēre = prohibuērunt   26. ōmen: (from **aud-men**) anything, however irrelevant, which chances to be heard during a religious ceremony, such as a Senate meeting   **28. capitis:** genitive of the penalty, *to death*   **29. in ūnō homine:** *in* with the ablative of a person often means *in the case of*

LESSON 7

Indirect Commands; Uses of nē

Sarcophagus relief depicting a battle between the Romans and the Germans. The height and reputed prowess of the Germans made them popular adversaries in battle scenes.

THE ARMY:
LATE REPUBLIC

The plebeian Marius (Consul 107–99 B.C.) made sweeping changes in the army. He opened the opportunity for military service to all classes of citizens, regardless of their census classification. This meant that so many men of little or no property enlisted voluntarily that conscriptions were no longer necessary, and the army became a group of professional soldiers rather than a citizen militia. This change seemed sensible, since it employed those who had nothing else to do. Under the old system many farms went to ruin as their proprietors were away on longer and longer campaigns. But the change was ultimately a cause of the civil wars, since the troops were loyal, not to the Senate and the magistrates, but to their general, the man who paid their salary and provided their pensions (usually in the form of farm land). As professional soldiers, the men served for much longer terms, twenty years and more; and when the wars outside Italy began to last longer, generals also might serve for more than the original one-year term, sometimes for as long as five years.

Marius also abandoned the manipular formation, which broke up the front too much, in favor of the cohort as the tactical unit. Each legion was divided into ten cohorts of 600 men each; each cohort contained three maniples of 200 men, and each maniple had two centuries of 100 men each. The three maniples of each cohort were designated as **hastātī, prīncipēs,** and **triāriī.** These terms no longer referred to position in the formation, but rather to the ranks of the Centurions commanding the centuries, the senior of the two Centurions of the **hastātī** being at the head of the cohort. A legion was drawn up with a front of four cohorts, and second and third lines of three each. The Roman cavalry and the **vēlitēs** were abolished; cavalry, archers, slingers, etc. were conscripted or enlisted among the allies of Rome outside of Italy. Within Italy the allies still served in the army; but when in 88 B.C. they received full Roman citizenship there was no longer a

(Continued)

distinction between them and the Romans of Rome itself. All legionary soldiers were issued the heavy equipment: the **galea, scūtum, pīlum,** and **gladius.** The **scūtum** was now a tall semicylindrical shield, big enough to shelter a kneeling man. It was a wooden frame covered with leather, with a hemispherical metal boss (**umbō**) in the center for warding off sling bullets and arrows; the boss had a bar behind, which served as a handle. The **pīlum** now had a metal head set in a wooden shaft, around which was wound a leather throwing-thong, to make it rotate as it flew through the air.

In Caesar's army the size of the century was reduced to 60 men, making a legion of 3600. **Lēgātī,** members of the general staff, were frequently given the command of individual legions. The Military Tribunate became an office of little importance and minor duties; it was essentially an opportunity for young aristocrats to acquire the military experience necessary to a political career.

(*above*) Roman coin of Julius Caesar with bound captives and the spoils of war   (*below*) Tombstone of a tribune of the 10th Legion.

ANCIENT ROME LIVES ON . . .

Is our Army a professional Army, like Marius', or a citizen militia, like the early republican army?

▦ SYNTAX

▦ INDIRECT COMMANDS

A command which is reported, not given directly, is expressed in Latin by **ut** or **nē** with the present or imperfect subjunctive. This is because the command is what is wished for by the person commanding, asking, or advising. In English an indirect command usually uses the infinitive.

Mē rogāvit ut discēderem.   *He asked me to leave.*

Indirect commands (which are sometimes called substantive clauses of purpose) follow verbs of commanding, asking, or advising. The case of the person commanded, asked, or advised varies according to the verb used.

Verbs of Commanding

> imperō, -āre, -āvī, -ātum   *order, command*
> mandō, -āre, -āvī, -ātum   *entrust, command, instruct*
> praecipiō, -ere, praecēpī, praeceptum   *instruct*

All three of these verbs take a dative of the person receiving the command.

Mihi $\begin{cases} \text{imperāvit} \\ \text{mandāvit} \\ \text{praecēpit} \end{cases}$ ut discēderem.   He $\begin{cases} \textit{ordered} \\ \textit{commanded} \\ \textit{instructed} \end{cases}$ *me to leave.*

Iubeō, *bid, order,* governs an infinitive phrase, not an indirect command.

Verbs of Asking

> petō, -ere, petīvī, petītum   *aim at, seek, ask*
> quaerō, -ere, quaesīvī, quaesītum   *look for, seek, ask*
> rogō, -āre, -āvī, -ātum   *ask for, ask*

Petō and **quaerō** take an Ablative of Place from Which of the person being asked; **rogō** takes an accusative of the person being asked.

$\begin{matrix} \text{Ā mē} \\ \\ \text{Mē} \end{matrix}$ $\begin{cases} \text{petit} \\ \text{quaerit} \\ \text{rogat} \end{cases}$ nē discēdam.   *He asks me not to leave.*

Verbs of Advising

> addūcō, -ere, addūxī, adductum   *lead to, influence*
> moneō, -ēre, -uī, -itum   *warn, advise*
> persuādeō, -ēre, persuāsī, persuāsum   *persuade*

Addūcō and **moneō** take an accusative of the person; **persuādeō** takes a dative of the person.

$$\begin{matrix} \text{Mē} \\ \\ \text{Mihi} \end{matrix} \left\{ \begin{matrix} \text{addūcet} \\ \text{monēbit} \\ \text{persuādēbit} \end{matrix} \right\} \text{ut discēdam.} \qquad \textit{He will} \left\{ \begin{matrix} \textit{influence} \\ \textit{warn (advise)} \\ \textit{persuade} \end{matrix} \right\} \textit{me to leave.}$$

Note: Just as in indirect statements, a third person reflexive pronoun has as its antecedent the subject of the verb governing the indirect command.

> Ā mē petīvit nē sibi nocērem.   *He asked me not to harm him.*

USES OF nē

Since negative subjunctives expressing wished-for actions (Hortatory, Jussive, Optative, Purpose Clause or Indirect Command) must always be introduced by **nē**, they cannot use any of the usual negatives. Notice the differences in the chart below:

USES OF nē

NORMAL NEGATIVE		NEGATIVE SUBJUNCTIVES EXPRESSING WISHED-FOR ACTIONS	
nec, neque	*nor, and not*	nēve	*nor, and not*
nemō	*no one*	nē quis	*not anyone*
nihil	*nothing*	nē quid	*not anything*
nōn	*not*	nē	*not*
nūllus	*no*	nē ūllus	*not any*
numquam	*never*	nē umquam	*not ever*

> Nē umquam miserī sīmus!
> *May we never be unhappy!*
> Celeriter currō nē quis mē capiat.
> *I am running fast so that no one will catch me.*
> Eīs imperāvimus nē quid facerent.
> *We ordered them to do nothing.*

Notice that the indefinite pronoun **quis** is used after **nē**, just as it is after **sī**, **nisi**, and **num**.

VOCABULARY

BASIC WORDS

crīmen, crīminis, n. *accusation*
ratiō, ratiōnis, f. *account; reasoning*
vātēs, vātis, m. or f. (not an i-
  stem) *soothsayer; bard*
vinculum, -ī, n. *bond*

cingō, -ere, cinxī, cinctum *gird*
creō, -āre, -āvī, -ātum *create; elect*
gerō, -ere, gessī, gestum *bear; wear;
  carry on*

lābor, -ī, lāpsus sum *glide, slip, fall*
orior, -īrī, ortus sum (fut. act. part.
  oritūrus) *rise, arise*
ornō, -āre, -āvī, -ātum *equip, adorn*
quiēscō, -ere, quiēvī, quiētum *rest, be
  quiet*
solvō, -ere, solvī, solūtum *loosen, untie,
  release; pay; break up;* (intrans.)
  set sail

Notes: 1. **Bellum gerere** = *wage war*. **Rēs gestae, rērum gestārum,** f. = *deeds,
        accomplishments*
        2. The perfect passive participle of **quiēscō** is used as an adjective: **quiētus, -a,
        -um** *quiet, peaceful.*

LEARNING ENGLISH THROUGH LATIN

abort   *to fail to be completed; to cut short an action because of some failure*
acquiesce   *to agree or consent, but without enthusiasm*
belligerent   *showing a readiness to fight or quarrel; warlike*
incriminate   *to accuse; to make one appear guilty*
irrational   *senseless; unreasonable*
lapse   *to backslide, to slip from a higher standard; to come to an end (said of
                 time)*
quiescent   *quiet, still, inactive*
succinct   *clearly and briefly stated, concise*

An emperor wore this symbol, called a
gorgoneion, on his armor to ward off
evil.

PRACTICE

A. The derivatives from this lesson have been used in the wrong sentences. Rewrite each sentence with a form of the correct derivative.

1. The mission was incriminating because of mechanical failure. **2.** After listening to the presentation, the boss, although dubious, lapsed to the plan. **3.** The evidence was very belligerent, but there was no real proof. **4.** Her tone was quite succinct, but I really don't think she was angry. **5.** The hospital staff was worried because the patient began to act in an aborted manner. **6.** An hour has acquiesced, and I'm still waiting for the train.

B. Fill in the correct Latin words from those listed below:

1. Neptūnus iussit ___ quiēscere. **2.** Neptūnus quaesīvit ___ ut quiēscerent. **3.** Neptūnus rogāvit ___ ut quiēscerent. **4.** Neptūnus mandāvit ___ ut quiēscerent. **5.** Neptūnus petīvit ___ ut quiēscerent. **6.** Neptūnus monuit ___ ut quiēscerent. **7.** Neptūnus imperāvit ___ ut quiēscerent. **8.** Neptūnus persuāsit ___ ut quiēscerent. **9.** Neptūnus addūxit ___ ut quiēscerent. **10.** Neptūnus praecēpit ___ ut quiēscerent.

ventōrum ventīs ventōs ad ventōs ā ventīs

The base of the Column of Trajan depicts the spoils of war—the arms and armor of the dead or defeated enemy.

C. In each of the following exercises, convert the direct statement into an indirect command governed by **imperāvit**, then pronounce and translate.

> EXAMPLE: Rēx occīditur. Imperāvit ut rēx occīderētur.
> *He ordered that the king be killed.*

1. Nihil prōmittitur.   **2.** Pudōrem sentit.   **3.** Nemō exit. **4.** Minōrēs līberōs alunt.   **5.** Vincula nōn solvuntur.   **6.** Pecūniam quam plūrimam sūmunt.   **7.** Equī nūllā herbā vēscuntur. **8.** Veterrimum rēgem mortuum flent.   **9.** Hōs versūs numquam legunt.   **10.** Illī fidem Populī Rōmānī nōn quaerunt neque petunt.

D. Change these direct commands into indirect commands, using whichever verb of *asking, commanding,* or *advising* seems most appropriate; then pronounce and translate.

> EXAMPLE: Pater mihi "Domō" inquit "statim rūs exī."
> Pater mihi mandāvit ut domō statim rūs exīrem.
> *Father ordered me to leave home for the country immediately.*

1. "Putā mē" mihi inquit "semper tuum certum comitem et amīcum." 2. "Vidēte" inquit nōbīs "illam virginem mīrā speciē in rīpā ulteriōre." 3. Magister puerīs "Numquam" inquit "oblīvīsciminī magnārum rērum gestārum Rōmānōrum priōrum."   **4.** Senior Cōnsul mīlitibus "Bellum gerite" inquit "quam ācerrimē ferrō et igne terrā marīque."   **5.** Tibi "Humō tolle" inquit "et mihi adfer illud aurī pondus in terram dē monte lapsum."

E. Change these indirect commands into direct commands, using **inquit** to govern the direct quotation; pronounce and translate.

> EXAMPLE: Pater mihi mandāvit ut domō statim rūs exīrem.
> Pater mihi "Domō" inquit "statim rūs exī."
> *Father said to me, "Leave home for the country immediately."*

1. Nōbīs imperāvit nē rēs gestās umquam iactārēmus.   **2.** Amīcō persuādet ut nōbilium partibus faveat.   **3.** Vātēs cīvitātem monuit ut dīs superīs parēret.   **4.** Pater ā fīliō petīvit ut comam faciemque coniugis futūrae aspiceret.   **5.** Magister puerīs praecēpit nē quid ulteriōris optent sed bona propiōra quaerant.

A luxurious cameo of the 4th century A.D. depicts a mounted Roman hurling a spear. Even at this late date, stirrups were not yet in use.

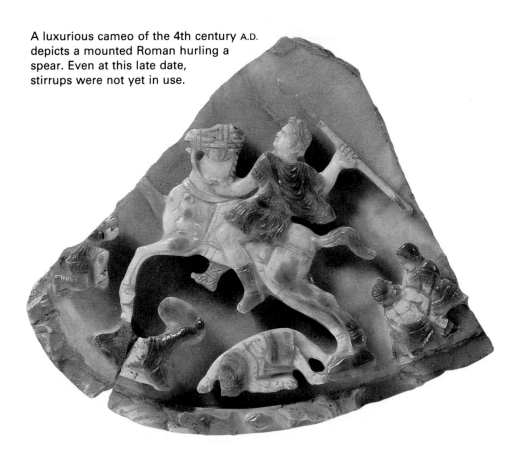

FROM THE PHILOSOPHER'S HANDBOOK . . .

Exigō ā mē nōn ut optimīs pār sim,
sed ut malīs melior.
I require myself not to be equal to the best,
but to be better than the bad.

—SENECA

What do you require of yourself?

READING

Developing Reading Skills

Latin words you know which will help with those you don't: **cingō, coniciō, crīmen, dēligō, dō, dūcō, ferō, gerō, iaciō, iuvenis, lābor, mortālis, mōveō, nōmen, ornō, prōmō, rogō, sciō, sedeō,** and **servus.**

English words which will help: *accuse, acerbity, castigate, cognomen, collapse, council, congeries, cubicle, dedicate, devote, egregious, fix, imminent, immortal, incrimination, interrogate, introduce, irritate, motion, perpetual, pestilence, prompt, relegate, religion, respond, sedation, sedition, servile, silence,* and *vast.*

Cruelty and Courage

Vīgintī annīs post M. Manlī mortem Manlius alius, L. Imperiōsus, Dictātor creātus est illā ratiōne: pestilentia ingēns orta erat, quam ad sēdandam religiō praecēpit ut clāvus in Minervae aede ā Dictātōre figerētur. Quā dē causā ab seditiōne et ā bellō quiētīs rēbus dictus est tamen L. Manlius, quī
5   etsī solvendae religiōnis ac nōn reī gerendae grātiā dēlectus erat bellum gestūrus dēlectū acerbō iuventūtem agitāvit, virgīs caesīs vel in vincula ductīs eīs quī ad nōmina nōn responderant. Quamobrem illī inditum est cognōmen Imperiōsō. Prīmum Dictātūrā abīre coāctus est, deinde diēs eī dīcitur ā M. Pompōniō Tribūnō Plēbis. Crīminī eī Tribūnus inter cētera dīxit eum vērē
10   Imperiōsum fīlium iuvenem infacundiōrem et linguā imprōmptum hāc causā rūs relēgāvisse ut opus servīle faceret. Hāc crīminātiōne irrītātus est animus omnium potius quam ipsīus iuvenis quī īnscientibus omnibus cultrō succinctus māne in urbem atque ā portā domum ad M. Pompōnium pergit.

---

3. clāvus . . . figerētur: The custom of driving nails into the temple of Minerva was probably originally a primitive method of keeping track of the years, Minerva being the goddess of numbers.   **8. diēs:** i.e. for a trial; **diēs eī dīcitur** = *he is brought to trial*   **9. crīminī eī:** double dative   **10. infacundiōrem et linguā imprōmptum:** It is interesting that the Romans thought it cruel not to allow mentally or linguistically disabled persons to lead a normal life.

Mox in cubiculum intrōductus—nam percītum īrā in patrem spēs erat
crīminis aliquid novī dēferre—omnibus abīre iussīs cultrum stringit et super
lectum stāns Pompōniō imperat ut iūret patris accūsandī causā concilium
plēbis numquam habitūrum.

Eōdem annō, seu mōtū terrae seu quā vī aliā, Forum medium specū vastō
collāpsum est in immēnsam altitūdinem, neque ea vorāgō coniectū terrae
quam prō sē quisque gerēbat explērī potuit. Vātēs interrogātī cecinērunt,
"Quid est quō plūrimum Populus Romanus potest? Mandāmus enim ut id
illī locō dētis dēdicētisque; hoc vōbīs faciendum est ut rēs publica Rōmāna
perpetua sit." Undique quaerēbant, nec quidquam reperiēbant, cum M.
Curtius, iuvenis bellō ēgregius, dubitantīs castīgāvit: "Num quid aliud
bonum magis Rōmānum est quam arma virtūsque? Ut haec sibi dēmus Īnferī
certē nōbīs imperāvērunt!" Deinde silentiō factō templa deōrum immortālium
quae Forō imminent Capitōliumque aspiciēns manūs nunc in caelum nunc
in patentīs terrae hiātūs ad Deōs Mānis porrigentem sē dēvōvit. Equō deinde
quam poterat maximē exornātō īnsidēns armātus sē in specum immīsit,
mūneraque super eum ā multitūdine virōrum ac mulierum congesta sunt.
Ille locus inde etiam hodiē Lacus Curtius vocātur.

An **eques** in armor with his
horse on a sesterce issued by
Marcus Licinius Crassus (115–
53 B.C.)—Sforza Castle, Milan

◼ READING COMPREHENSION

1. What superstition resulted in Lucius Manlius being named Dictator?
2. What name was he given because of the way he ruled?   3. Why was he
brought to trial by the Plebeian Tribune Marcus Pomponius?   4. What did
the young son of Lucius Manlius do?   5. Why did this surprise everyone?
6. What happened to the Forum?   7. What is the significance of the
following? "Quid est quō plūrimum Populus Rōmānus potest? Mandāmus
enim ut id illī locō dētis dēdicētisque; hoc vōbīs faciendum est ut rēs publica
Rōmāna perpetua sit."   8. When the Romans looked everywhere and found
nothing, what did Marcus Curtius say?   9. What did he do?   10. What
is that spot called today?

---

14. ⟨eum⟩ percītum . . . dēferre: indirect statement governed by spēs

LESSON 8

Subjunctive, Perfect System; Final Clauses; Clauses after Verbs of Fearing

(*top to bottom*) Soldiers construct a bridge and small fort; Trajan harangues his troops; the god of the Danube watches troops cross the river on a bridge of boats—Column of Trajan

CAMPS AND SIEGECRAFT

The Roman camp contributed much to Roman military success. Encampments were not adapted to the terrain. Instead, the camp always had the same plan, with streets and blocks of tents, and each group of tent-mates (**contubernālēs**) always lived at the same "address" at every encampment. An army never spent the night outside a camp; this meant that an army on the march had to build a new camp daily. The fortifications were built first of all. While some soldiers guarded the operation, the rest dug a ditch (**fossa**) along the boundaries of the camp, throwing the excavated dirt up on the inner side, forming a mound (**agger**). In this were planted the stakes (**pālī**) which the soldiers had carried with them, to make a palisade. The triple height (15–18 feet) of **fossa, agger,** and **pālī** formed what the Romans called the **vallum.**

The camp of the earlier Republic was square, 2150 Roman feet on a side, and designed to hold an army of two legions. The later camp was rectangular and somewhat smaller.

When an army had to attack a city or fortress there were three possible approaches: to get over the walls, to get under the walls, or to knock the walls down. In all cases a **vallum** was usually drawn around the place, both for a blockade and to protect the besiegers. Sometimes there were two of these, the outer one being to protect the besiegers from a relieving force. To get over the enemy walls, they usually built a causeway (**agger**) of bundles of sticks (**fascīnae**), supported at the sides by scaffolding or stone walls. This formed either a ramp rising gradually to the top of the enemy walls or a level path for rolling towers (**turrēs ambulātōriae**). The men building the **agger** were protected either by **pl. teī**, semi-circular wicker shields on wheels, or by **vīneae,** wooden or wicker sheds ten by twenty feet in size. The rolling towers were built to be higher than the walls under attack, usually ten to twenty stories (88–176 feet) high. The upper stories housed artillery

(Continued)

A PHRASE TO USE

Alea iacta est.
The die is cast. (The decision is irrevocable)

—JULIUS CAESAR

(**tormenta**), slingers (**funditōrēs**), and archers (**sagittāriī**). At the level of the top of the wall there were bridges (**sambūcae**). On the lower stories were the infantry waiting to cross the **sambūcae** and enter the fortifications. For tunneling under the walls there were **mūsculī,** long wooden sheds on wheels, which were pushed up close to the walls, under the protection of which the digging was done. These were covered with wet hides or cushions to protect them from the fire thrown down by the defenders. Walls were overthrown by the battering ram (**ariēs**), slung inside a shed to protect those who were swinging it, or by men undermining the wall under the protection of a slant-roofed wooden hide-covered shed (**testūdō**).

Roman artillery worked by torsion, rigid arms being moved by tightly twisted ropes made of women's hair. They were like giant bows which projected large arrows horizontally (**catapultae** and the smaller **scorpiōnēs**), or rocks shot at an angle of 50° (**ballistae**). The mechanical sling (**onager**) was a late invention. What we usually call a catapult, the machine which throws a missile from a long arm, was not used until the Middle Ages.

(*above*) A model of a Roman battering ram (**ariēs**)
(*below*) A battle scene from the Arch of Constantine

ANCIENT ROME LIVES ON . . .

What contrasts would a Roman soldier make between our military camps and weapons and his own?

FORMS

SUBJUNCTIVE, PERFECT SYSTEM

The subjunctive mood has four tenses: present, imperfect, perfect, and pluperfect. There is no future or future perfect. All verbs of all conjugations form the perfect and pluperfect subjunctive in the same way.

Perfect Active

The perfect active subjunctive is formed by adding **-erī-** and the personal endings to the perfect stem.

PERFECT ACTIVE SUBJUNCTIVE

1ST CONJUGATION		2D CONJUGATION		3D CONJUGATION	
vocāverim	vocāverīmus	habuerim	habuerīmus	posuerim	posuerīmus
vocāverīs	vocāverītis	habuerīs	habuerītis	posuerīs	posuerītis
vocāverit	vocāverint	habuerit	habuerint	posuerit	posuerint

3D CONJUGATION -iō VERBS		4TH CONJUGATION		SUM	
cēperim	cēperimus	audīverim	audīverīmus	fuerim	fuerīmus
cēperīs	cēperītis	audīverīs	audīverītis	fuerīs	fuerītis
cēperit	cēperint	audīverit	audīverint	fuerit	fuerint

You will notice that in the third person, singular and plural, the perfect active subjunctive is identical with the future perfect active indicative. Context will usually determine the choice.

Pluperfect Active

The pluperfect active subjunctive is formed by adding the personal endings to the perfect active infinitive.

PLUPERFECT ACTIVE SUBJUNCTIVE

1ST CONJUGATION

vocāvissem vocāvissēmus
vocāvissēs vocāvissētis
vocāvisset vocāvissent

2D CONJUGATION

habuissem habuissēmus
habuissēs habuissētis
habuisset habuissent

3D CONJUGATION

posuissem posuissēmus
posuissēs posuissētis
posuisset posuissent

**3D CONJUGATION
-iō VERBS**

cēpissem cēpissēmus
cēpissēs cēpissētis
cēpisset cēpissent

4TH CONJUGATION

audīvissem audīvissēmus
audīvissēs audīvissētis
audīvisset audīvissent

SUM

fuissem fuissēmus
fuissēs fuissētis
fuisset fuissent

Perfect and Pluperfect Passive

The perfect and pluperfect passive of the subjunctive are just like those of the indicative, except that they use the subjunctive forms of **sum.**

PERFECT PASSIVE SUBJUNCTIVE

1ST CONJUGATION

vocātus sim vocātī sīmus
vocātus sīs vocātī sītis
vocātus sit vocātī sint

2D CONJUGATION

habitus sim habitī sīmus
habitus sīs habitī sītis
habitus sit habitī sint

3D CONJUGATION

positus sim positī sīmus
positus sīs positī sītis
positus sit positī sint

**3D CONJUGATION
-iō VERBS**

captus sim captī sīmus
captus sīs captī sītis
captus sit captī sint

4TH CONJUGATION

audītus sim audītī sīmus
audītus sīs audītī sītis
audītus sit audītī sint

PLUPERFECT PASSIVE SUBJUNCTIVE

1ST CONJUGATION

vocātus essem	vocātī essēmus
vocātus essēs	vocātī essētis
vocātus esset	vocātī essent

2D CONJUGATION

habitus essem	habitī essēmus
habitus essēs	habitī essētis
habitus esset	habitī essent

3D CONJUGATION

positus essem	positī essēmus
positus essēs	positī essētis
positus esset	positī essent

-iō VERBS

captus essem	captī essēmus
captus essēs	captī essētis
captus esset	captī essent

4TH CONJUGATION

audītus essem	audītī essēmus
audītus essēs	audītī essētis
audītus esset	audītī essent

SYNTAX

FINAL CLAUSES

Subjunctive clauses introduced by **ut** and **nē** are called final clauses because they show the end (**fīnis**) at which the action of the main verb aims.

> Ut tē videam vēnī.
> *I have come to see you (I have come, to the end that I may see you).*
> Nē discēdam mē monet.
> *He warns me not to leave (He warns me, to the end that I not leave).*

CLAUSES AFTER VERBS OF FEARING

There are three kinds of final clauses in Latin: (*1*) adverbial clauses of purpose, (*2*) indirect commands, (*3*) and clauses after verbs of fearing. Since clauses which describe an action that is feared are final clauses, they must show the end aimed at, i.e. what is wished for.

Timeō nē nōbīs noceant.
I fear that they may harm us (I fear, to the end that they not harm us).
Timeō ut servēmur.
I fear that we may not be saved (I fear, to the end that we may be saved).
Timeō nē nōn servēmur.
I fear that we may not be saved (I fear, to the end that we not be not saved).

Unlike other final clauses, clauses after verbs of fearing may use perfect or pluperfect subjunctives.

Timeō nē quid perīculī ortum sit.
I fear that some danger has arisen.
Timuī nē quid perīculī ortum esset.
I feared that some danger had arisen.

Verbs of Fearing

timeō, -ēre, -uī, ____   *fear, be frightened*
vereor, -ērī, veritus sum   *fear, be worried*
metuō, -ere, metuī, metūtum   *fear, dread.*

Clauses after verbs of fearing may also be governed by other expressions of fear, e.g. **timor est, metus est.**

Timeō		I am frightened	
Vereor		I am worried	
Metuō	nē nōbīs noceant.	I dread	that they may harm us.
Timor } est mihi		I have a { fear dread	
Metus			

Roman fortifications in Britain

VOCABULARY

BASIC WORDS

agmen, agminis, n. *throng, flock; army [on the march or in marching order]*

eques, equitis, m. *horseman; (pl.) cavalry*

ordō, ordinis, f. *order, row, rank, class*

paulum, n. (defective: only nom., acc., abl. sing.) *a little*

pugna, -ae, f. *fight*

sinus, -ūs, m. *bend, fold; bay, gulf*

sors, sortis, f. (i-stem) *lot*

certō, -āre, -āvī, -ātum *contend, struggle [in rivalry], vie*

permittō, -ere, permīsī, permissum *permit*

rīdeō, -ēre, rīsī, rīsum *laugh, smile; (transitive) laugh at*

rumpō, -ere, rūpī, ruptum *break, burst*

tangō, -ere, tetigī, tactum *touch*

Notes: 1. **Paulum** is most frequently used as an internal accusative or ablative of degree of difference.

Manē paulum.   *Wait a little.*   paulō post   *a little later*

2. Because a fold of the toga hung over the chest, **sinus** also means *bosom*. It can also mean *a [bellying] sail.*

3. **Permittō**, unlike **patior**, governs a final clause, since what is permitted is an end aimed at. It takes a dative of the person.

Mihine permittēs ut eam?   *Will you permit me to go?*

LEARNING ENGLISH THROUGH LATIN

deride	*to laugh at in contempt or scorn*
derision	*contempt; ridicule*
equestrian	*having to do with horses or horsemanship*
inordinate	*immoderate, excessive, lacking restraint or moderation*
insinuate	*to hint or suggest rather than to speak outright*
rupture	*a break or breaking apart*
sinuous	*wavy, winding*
sortilege	*sorcery, black magic*
tactful	*showing a delicate perception of the right thing to say or do*
tangible	*able to be touched; tactile*

PRACTICE

A. Complete each of the following sentences with a form of a word from the derivative list in this lesson.

1. I have one hundred thousand dollars in ___ assets; the rest of my money is in stocks.   2. She is a wonderful receptionist because she is so ___ in her dealings with people.   3. The shooting down of the aircraft caused a ___ in the relations between the two countries.   4. Are you ___ that I am not honest?   5. He spoke of the incident with such ___ that it was impossible to get an objective viewpoint.   6. It is necessary to follow a long ___ pathway through the woods to locate the cabin.

B. Give the following synopses, in the indicative, subjunctive, and (where applicable) imperative:

1. **nāscor** in the 1st person singular passive   2. **creō** in the 2d person singular passive   3. **dēbeō** in the 3d person singular active   4. **veniō** in the 1st person plural active   5. **morior** in the 2d person plural passive 6. **prōsum** in the 3d person plural active

C. Give tense(s), voice, mood(s), person, and number for each form:

1. rīdēs, certēs, permittēs   2. creāris, dolēaris, nāscāris   3. implēverint, ornāverint, occiderint   4. cadam, dēbeam, metuam   5. meminerit, prōderit, cinxerit

D. Fill in the missing words from the list at the end of this exercise to complete the translation of the English sentences.

1. *We fear that rights will be denied to people of our kind.* Verēmur ___ iūra hominibus nostrī generis ___.   2. *I shall permit you to stay there for about three days.* Patiar ___ ibi trīs ferē diēs ___.   3. *I shall permit you to stay there for about three days.* Permittam ___ ___ ibi trīs ferē diēs ___.   4. *They kept asserting that we ought to leave a little before night.* Aiēbant ___ paulō ante noctem ___ esse.   5. *They kept asserting that we ought to leave a little before night, in order to see our friend.* Aiēbant ___ paulō ante noctem ___ dēbēre, ut amīcum ___.   6. *He advised us to remember our rank and not to vie with the lowest.* ___ monuit ut ___ meminissēmus ___ cum īnfimīs ___.   7. *He feared that the time was too*

short, and that he would not be useful to the state. Veritus est ___ tempus brevius ___, ___ cīvitātī nōn ___.   **8.** *She very often suffered from the fear that she was too old, and grieved that she could do little.* Saepissimē ___ labōrāvit ___ vetustior ___, doluitque ___ paulum facere ___.   **9.** *The citizenry feared that the new king born that day would not be very unlike the previous one.* Metuēbat cīvitās ___ rēx novus ___ diē nātus ___ dissimillimus ___.   **10.** *He finally began to fear that his kingdom would fall, and was scarcely able to hope that it would stand.* Postrēmō verērī ___ ___ rēgnum ___, et spērāre vix poterat ___ ___.

cadat	erat	metum	posse	sit
caderet	esse	nē	posset	stāret
cadere	esset	negābuntur	possit	stātūrum
cadet	et	negentur	priōrem	tē
certāre	id	neque	priōrī	tibi
certārēmus	illā	nēve	priōris	ut
coeperit	illō	nōbīs	prōderit	videāmus
coepit	maneās	nōs	prōdesset	vidēre
discēdendum	manēre	ordinem	prōsit	vidērēmus
discēdere	metū	ordinis	sē	

A reconstruction of a Roman catapult—West Point Museum

FROM THE PHILOSOPHER'S HANDBOOK . . .

Sēdit quī timuit nē nōn succēderet.
He who feared he would not succeed sat still.
—HORACE

Have you ever refrained from doing something because you feared failure? Was it a mistake not to try? Can you cite any example in your past life when failure was not really a tragedy?

Translation Help

Verbs of fearing may present some difficulty at first because they govern so many constructions. All three, **metuō**, **timeō**, and **vereor**, besides clauses after verbs of fearing, may take direct objects or objective infinitives. In addition, **timeō** may be used intransitively with a dative with intransitive verbs or an Ablative of Place from Which with **dē**. **Metuō** may be used absolutely, i.e. intransitively and governing no case.

Hostīs $\begin{cases} \text{metuō} \\ \text{timeō.} \\ \text{vereor} \end{cases}$ *I fear the enemy.*

Tangī metuit.   *He dreads being touched.*

Hos facere timent.   *They are afraid to do this.*

Eōs occīdere veritus est.   *He was afraid to kill them (i.e. awed by the idea).*

Sibi timuit.   *He feared for himself.*

Dē vītā timuī.   *I feared for my life.*

Ubi hostīs vīdit metuit.   *He was afraid when he saw the enemy.*

The sturdy walls of a Roman fort in England were added to in the Middle Ages to create Pevensey Castle.

Developing Reading Skills

Latin words you know which will help with those you don't: cēdō, certō, dīcō, dō, eō, eques, errō, eximō, existimō, faciō, iaciō, mīles, mittō, prīmus, rīdeō, sinus, stō, tangō, Tribūnus, veniō, vertō, vincō, and vocō.

English words which will help: *averse, collar, despoil, edict, equestrian, error, estimate, event, exhaust, explore, ictus, indicate, insinuate, intact, military, pontic, prefect, proceed, provoke, revert, sedition, silence, spoils, station, stature, tend, torque, ventral, vexation,* and *vindicate.*

Like Father, Like Son

Annō trecentēsimō et nōnāgēsimō alterō A.U.C. Gallī reversī sunt et ad pontem Anienis castra habuēre. Dictātor Rōmānus in citeriōre rīpā Anienis castra posuit. Pōns in mediō erat, neutrīs eum rumpentibus, nē timōris indicium esset. Proelia dē occupandō ponte crebra erant, quō tamen neutrī potītī sunt. Tum eximiā corporis magnitūdine in vacuum pontem Gallus   5
prōcessit et quam maximā vōce "Quem nunc" inquit "Rōma virum fortis-simum habet prōcēdat ad pugnam, ut noster duōrum ēventus ostendat gentem bellō meliōrem." Diū inter prīmōrēs iuvenum Rōmānōrum silentium fuit, quoniam et abnuere certāmen verēbantur et praecipuum sortem perīculī metuēbant; tum T. Manlius L. fīlius, quī patrem ā vexātiōne tribūniciā   10
vindicāverat, ad Dictātōrem pergit. "Sī tū permittis" inquit "ego illī bēluae ostendam mē ex eā familiā ortum quae Gallōrum agmen ex Rūpe Tarpēiā dēiēcit." Tum Dictātor "Perge, in patrem patriamque pie, et nōmen Rōmānum invictum iuvantibus dīs praestā." Adversus Gallum stolidē laetum et linguam etiam ab inrīsū exserentem prōcēdit, nēquāquam vīsū aestiman-   15

---

1. A.U.C. = **ab urbe conditā**   **2. habuēre** = **habuērunt**   **7. duōrum:** genitive because of the idea of possession in **noster:** *of us two*   **10. T. Manlius L. fīlius:** *Titus Manlius, son of Lucius Manlius;* the formal form of a Roman name

tibus hostī pār, corpus enim alterī magnitūdine eximium, alterī media mīlitāris statūra est. Sed Rōmānus scūtō scūtum īmum perculit et insinuāvit sē inter corpus armaque, et ūnō alterōque ictū ventrem hausit et in spatium ingēns labentem strāvit hostem. Iacentis inde corpus ab omnī aliā vexātiōne intactum
20 ūnō torque spoliāvit, quem collō circumdedit suō. Dehinc T. Manliō cognōmen Torquātō inditum est, quod et Manliī posterī gestūrī erant.

Īdem T. Manlius paulō post ipse Cōnsul creātus exercitum dūcēbat contrā Latīnōs seditiōnem moventīs. Quia verēbātur nē quō errōre mīlitēs cape-
25 rentur, ēdīxit nē quis extrā ordinem in hostem pugnāret. Forte inter cēterōs turmīs equitum praefectōs, quī explōrātum in omnīs partīs dīmissī erant, T. Manlius Cōnsulis fīlius ēvāsit haud procul statiōne hostium proximā, ubi quīdam Geminus eum prōvocāvit. Verēns nē virtūte carēre vidērētur, iuvenis certāmen iniit. Deinde hoste occīsō in castra ad Praetōrium ad patrem tendit.
30 "Ut mē omnēs," inquit, "pater, tuō sanguine ortum vērē ferant, prōvocātus equestria haec spolia capta ex hoste caesō portō." Sed pater fīlium āversātus contiōnem advocārī iussit.

READING COMPREHENSION

1. Why did neither the Gauls nor the Romans break down the bridge over the Anio?   2. What is the significance of the following? "Quem nunc Rōma virum fortissimum habet prōcēdat ad pugnam, ut noster duōrum ēventus ostendat gentem bellō meliōrem."   3. Who answered the challenge? 4. Describe the Gaul on the bridge.   5. What was the opinion of those evaluating the situation?   6. What did the Roman do?   7. Why was the cognomen **Torquātus** given to him?   8. What order did Titus Manlius give to his army, and why?   9. Why did his son disobey this order?   10. What did he say when he returned to camp after killing the enemy?

A Gaul wearing a torque

REVIEW 2

A. Give the genitive, gender, and meanings of these nouns:

agmen	eques	poena	rīpa	sors	vātēs
cohors	ferrum	pondus	saxum	tectum	vinculum
crīmen	ordō	pugna	sinus	templum	vultus
custōs	paulum	ratiō			

B. Give the other nominative singular forms, and the meanings, of these adjectives:

dubius	immēnsus	quiētus	tūtus	vacuus	vagus
falsus	mortālis				

C. Give the other principal parts and the meanings of these verbs:

certō	expleō	impleō	ornō	quiēscō	sternō
cingō	fallō	lābor	pateō	rīdeō	suspendō
compleō	fundō	metuō	pendō	rumpō	tangō
creō	gerō	orior	permittō	solvō	tegō
crēscō	iactō				

D. How is **utinam** used?

DRILL ON SYNTAX

Pronounce and translate:

Turbā Gallōrum variōs clāmōrēs ut nostrōs ā dextrō cornū propter metum funderent tollente, mīlitēs ā sinistrō cornū adversus hostīs simul currere coepērunt ut auxiliō comitibus forent.

LISTENING AND SPEAKING

Lacus Curtius

On the way back from their stroll on the Palatine Hill, Titus learns the interesting story of the pool of Curtius.

TĪTUS: Domus Rōmulī et aedēs Augustī, pater, mihi placēbant, sed nunc in Forum ambulēmus. Quālis locus in mediō Forō hic est? Utrum palūs[1] an lacus est? Imāginem equitis equō in specum vastum ruentis videō. Quis erat?

GNAEUS: Locus ille et virtūte et pietāte nōtissimus est, nam multīs abhinc annīs Forum medium specū vastō collāpsum est, neque vorāgō explērī potuit.

TĪTUS: Certē, pater, vel mōtus terrae, horribilis sēnsū, vel fulmen ab Iove missum specum fēcit.

GNAEUS: Manum atque opera deum hominēs rē vērā intellegere numquam possunt. Rōmānī antiquī nē rēs publica caderet timēbant, at vātēs fātidicīque interrogātī suōs cīvīs monēbant ut īnferīs dōna quam potentissima dārent. "Haec dōna," inquiunt, "vōbīs danda sunt. Sī ita fēceritis, rēs publica Rōmāna perpetua stābit."

TĪTUS: Quae rēs illa potentissima erat?

GNAEUS: Eques ille, nōmine Mārcus Curtius, dōna et virtūtem et arma fuisse dīxit. "Ut dī Rōmānīs respiciant," ait, "mē et mea arma, cassem thōrācemque et clipeum hastamque duplicem, eīs dēvōveō! Timor metusque superentur sed virtūs vincat." Ita dīcens in suum equum insiluit,[2] et in specum vastum immēnsae altitūdinis ruit.

TĪTUS: Quid dīxit, tum cum rediit?

GNAEUS: Numquam rediit, Tīte, nam nūmina eum dōnum īnferīs recēpit. Mox aquae hiātum implēvērunt, itaque hic locus inde etiam hodiē Lacus Curtius vocātur.

TĪTUS: Cīvī piō, ut rēs publica quam plurimum possit, saepissimē prō patriā moriendum est!

A. You are a guide conducting a tour group around the Roman Forum. What could you tell the group in Latin about the Lacus Curtius?

---

1. palūs, palūdis, f.— *swamp*

2. insiliō, insilīre, insiluī, insultum— *to leap upon*

B. Provide questions for the following statements.

1. Tītus in Forum Rōmānum cum patre ambulāre cupit.
2. Imāginem equitis in specum vastum ruentis videt.
3. Hominēs nesciunt, sed Gnaeus manum deōrum eum fēcisse dīxit.   4. Dōna quam potentissima danda erant.   5. Curtius sē et sua arma dōna deīs maximē idōnea fore crēdidit.

This depiction of Marcus Curtius about to plunge into the chasm is on a plaque in the Forum facing the site of the Lacus Curtius. It is also the location in the Forum where lawsuits between citizens and foreigners took place. The inscription on the back of the stone (*below*) says that it was erected by Lucius Naevius Surdinus (son of Lucius) the Praetor who heard the cases.

LESSON 9

Potential Subjunctive; Deliberative Subjunctive;
Adverbial Clause of Result

A king in his purple-dyed toga, accompanied by a slave carrying the folding
sella curūlis—Etruscan tomb painting from Tarquinia

YOUR GOVERNMENT: EARLY MONARCHY

Although we distinguish three basic periods of the development of the Roman constitution, the Monarchy, the Republic, and the Empire, the Roman government was always, until some time in the third century of our era, technically a republic (**rēs publica,** *public property* or *common wealth*). That is to say, the power to rule (**imperium**) belonged to the citizens as a whole, and was formally transferred by them to the king, the magistrates, or the emperor. The term **rēs publica,** in other words, does not describe a form, but rather a theory of government, namely that governments exist by the consent of the governed.

The imperium was symbolized by the **fascēs,** bundles of sticks with a double-bladed axe in the middle, representing the control of the citizens by corporal or capital punishment. There were twelve of these **fascēs,** each carried by an attendant called a **Lictor,** who accompanied the King. Other marks of the King's royal power were his purple-dyed toga and the **sella curūlis,** a folding stool made of or decorated with ivory. Upon the death of a king his duties were assumed by an **Interrēx,** a Senator chosen by lot, who ruled for five days and then was succeeded by another, who ruled for five days, and so on. Any **Interrēx** except the first could nominate a new King; if his choice was approved by a majority of the Senate, an assembly of all the citizens, the **Comitia Cūriāta,** was called to confer the imperium on the new King.

The Senate, which served as an advisory body to the King, was made up of the heads (**Patrēs**) of the patrician families. There were 136 Senators by the end of the monarchy. Their resolutions (**Senātūs cōnsulta**) were not binding on the King; but he usually followed their advice in order to secure the cooperation of the noble families. In matters of foreign policy, or for important changes in domestic customs, the King would consult the people as a whole, meeting as the **Comitia Cūriāta,** where the voting was Curia by

(Continued)

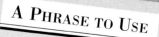

Curia. The populace was divided into three Tribes (**Tribūs**), each of which was made up of ten **Cūriae**, the **Cūria** being a group of families who fought together in time of war. The King would submit his proposal to the **Comitia Cūriāta**, in which each **Cūria** had one vote. There was no debate, just a yes-or-no vote. The decision of the majority of the **Cūriae** was not valid until it had received the approval of the Senate (**Patrum auctōritās**).

(*below*) An Etrusco-Roman bronze statue of an orator
(*below right*) **Fascēs**, the symbols of Roman magisterial authority

ANCIENT ROME LIVES ON . . .

Compare the method of granting power to rulers in our republic with that of the Romans.

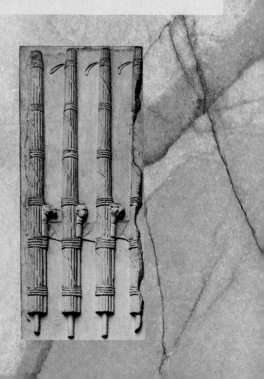

SYNTAX

◼ POTENTIAL SUBJUNCTIVE

An independent subjunctive may present an action as possible or conceivable. This use is called the potential subjunctive. The present is used for what may, might, or would happen in the present or future; the imperfect for what might have or would have happened in the past. The usual negatives (**nōn, nemō, nihil,** etc.) are used, not **nē.**

> Hoc crēdās scrīptum esse ā puerō.
> *You would (or might) think that this had been written by a child.*
> Hoc crēderēs scrīptum esse ā puerō.
> *You would (or might) have thought that this had been written by a child.*
> Hodiē vel crās discēdat.   *He may go today or tomorrow.*
> Quod vīdī neminī placēret.   *What I saw wouldn't have pleased anyone.*

◼ DELIBERATIVE SUBJUNCTIVE

An independent subjunctive in a question may represent the subject as deliberating on a course of action. This use is called the deliberative subjunctive. The present refers to present time, the imperfect to past time. The usual negatives are used.

> Quid faciam? Maneam an abeam?   *What am I to do? Should I stay, or leave?*
> Quid dīceret?   *What was he to say?*
> Nōn venīrem?   *Was I not to have come?*

INDEPENDENT SUBJUNCTIVES

The five independent subjunctives (subjunctives as verbs of principal clauses) fall into two categories, desired action and possible action.

DESIRED ACTION
Negative is **nē**:

1. Exhortation: hortatory subjunctive (1st person plural, present)
2. Order: jussive subjunctive (2d & 3d persons, singular & plural, present)
3. Wish: optative subjunctive (any person & number, present or imperfect)

Independent Subjunctives (continued)

POSSIBLE ACTION

Negative is **nōn, nemō, nihil, nūllus,** etc.

4. Possibility: potential subjunctive (any person & number, present or imperfect)
5. Deliberation: deliberative subjunctive (a question, any person & number, present or imperfect)

ADVERBIAL CLAUSE OF RESULT

The same demonstrative adjectives and adverbs which are correlative with comparative clauses (*First Year Latin,* Lesson 24) and relative clauses (*First Year Latin,* Lesson 26) may also point to an adverbial clause of result, introduced by **ut,** with its verb in the subjunctive.

Tū tālis es quālis eram ego.	*You are such as I was.*
Tu tālis es ut mihi praestēs.	*You are such as to surpass me.*
Currit tam celeriter quam tū curris.	*He runs as fast as you do.*
Currit tam celeriter ut cēterōs vincat.	{ *He runs so fast as to beat the rest.* *He runs so fast that he beats the rest.*

Because it expresses an action as possible, not wished for, an adverbial clause of result does not use **nē;** it is always introduced by **ut,** whether it is affirmative or negative.

> Tam celeriter currit ut nemō eum capiat.
> *He runs so fast that no one can catch him.*

A similar adverbial clause of purpose, expressing the action as wished for, does use **nē:**

> Celeriter currit nē quis eum capiat.
> *He runs fast so that no one may catch him.*

The demonstrative adjectives and adverbs which are often followed by an adverbial clause of result are:

Adjectives:

> tālis, -e   *such, of such a kind*
> tantus, -a, -um   *so big, so great, so much*
> tot (indeclinable)   *so many*

Adverbs:

eō, adeō	*so, to that point*
ita	*so, in such a way, to such an extent*
sīc	*so, in such a way*
tam	*so, to such an extent*
totiēns	*so many times*

Sīc modifies verbs, infinitives and participles; **tam** adjectives, participles, and adverbs. **Eō, adeō,** and **ita** modify verbs, infinitives, participles, adjectives, and adverbs.

The Curia or Roman Senate House. The present building appears much as it did after renovation during the reign of Diocletian.

VOCABULARY

BASIC WORDS

culpa, -ae, f. *blame, guilt, fault*

exemplum, -ī, n. *example*

impetus, -ūs, m. *onrush, attack*

legiō, legiōnis, f. *legion*

victor, victōris, m. *victor, conqueror*

necesse (defective adj.: only neut. nom. and acc. sing.) *necessary*

cēnseō, -ēre, -uī, cēnsum *express an opinion, vote; appraise; hold a census of*

dīscō, -ere, didicī, ___ *learn*

mīror, -ārī, -ātus sum *wonder at, admire; wonder*

queror, -ī, questus sum *complain [of], lament*

sanciō, -īre, sanxī, sanctum *make sacred [by a religious act]; make irrevocable; sanction*

quasi (adv.) *as if; as it were, sort of*

Notes: 1. In apposition with a substantive the noun **victor** has the force of an adjective, *victorious.*

> Exercitum redūxit victōrem. *He brought back his army victorious.*

2. **Necesse** is used only as a subjective complement with **sum** or an objective complement with **habeō.** The subject of **sum** or the direct object of **habeō** is often an infinitive.

> Hominī necesse est morī. *It is necessary for man to die.*
> Id facere minus necesse habeō. *I consider it less necessary to do this.*

3. **Mīror** and **queror** may be used with a direct object or an infinitive phrase.

Mīrāta est \
Questa est } fīlī facta.　　She { wondered at / complained of } her son's actions.

Mīrāta est \
Questa est } fīlium male fēcisse.　　She { was amazed / complained } that her son had behaved badly.

4. The perfect passive participle of **sanciō** is frequently used as an adjective meaning *sacred, holy, inviolable.*

■ LEARNING ENGLISH THROUGH LATIN

censure	*a condemning as wrong; strong disapproval*
culpable	*deserving blame, guilty*
exemplary	*serving as a model or example; worth imitating*
impetuous	*acting suddenly with little or no thought; rash; impulsive*
querulous	*peevish; inclined to find fault; complaining*
sacrosanct	*very sacred, holy, or inviolable*
sanctimonious	*pretending to be very holy or pious; affecting righteousness*
sanction	*authorized approval or permission*

▬ PRACTICE

A. The word *victor* has the same form in English and Latin. What other two words in the vocabulary have the same form in English? What do they mean?

B. Explain the meaning of the following sentences:

1. Throughout the whole ordeal the student's behavior was exemplary.
2. The General's sanctimonious disapproval of rest and relaxation was offensive to the soldiers. 3. When all the facts are revealed, I will be declared exculpable. 4. The laboratory was sacrosanct to the scientist.
5. Take time to think things out carefully; don't act in an impetuous manner.
6. I stood at the main entrance of the school and watched the quasi scholars hurry to their classrooms. 7. The nursing staff was having difficulty dealing with the querulous patient. 8. The teacher was very angry and said he would not sanction such an activity again.

C. Pronounce, translate, and identify each of these independent subjunctives as hortatory, jussive, optative, potential, or deliberative. In the absence of any context, more than one answer may be correct.

EXAMPLE: Flēre dēsinat.   Jussive: *Let him stop weeping.*
Optative: *May he stop weeping!*   Potential: *He may (might) stop weeping.*

1. Hocne iūs sanciāmus? 2. Hoc iūs sanciāmus. 3. Agmina nē properent.
4. Agmina nōn properent. 5. Scelusne permitterent? 6. Scelus nōn permitterent. 7. Utinam scelus nē permitterent. 8. Cohortem nē umquam dēserāmus. 9. Cohortem numquam dēserāmus. 10. Nē audeās id temptāre.

Roman magistrates in procession—a
Roman imperial relief from Germany

D. Pronounce and translate these pairs of sentences. Identify the subordinate clauses by name.

1. Tāle opus coepit quāle nēmō ante vīdit. Tāle opus coepit ut nēmō simile vīderit. **2.** Quot vātēs sortīs canunt tot sortēs variae canuntur. Tot sortēs variae canuntur ut hominēs saepissimē fallantur. **3.** Tantum clāmōrem tollēbant quantus in urbe victā audīrī solet. Tantum clāmōrem tollēbant ut omnēs urbem dēfēnsum currerent. **4.** Et vultū et sermōne prīnceps suprēmus tam hūmānus quam opibus potēns est. Et vultū et sermōne prīnceps suprēmus tam hūmānus est ut quasi humillimus exīstimētur. **5.** Quotiēns meam sortem queror totiēns dī superī aliquid peiōris mihi mittunt. Totiēns dī superī aliquid peiōris mihi mittunt ut eōs mē rīdēre putem et ulterius rogāre dubitem.

E. Pronounce and translate these pairs of sentences. Be prepared to explain the differences between them.

1. Vōs moneō hostium equitēs brevī spatiō vestrōs strātūrōs. Vōs moneō ut hostium equitēs quam prīmum sternātis. **2.** Tantum pependit ut maximam pecūniam plūrimīs dēbeat. Plūrimam pecūniam cōnsequī dēbet ut sibi crēdentibus dēbita pendat. **3.** Nōn aliter atque improbī pessimīque mentem plēbis sīc flēxit ut novās rēs agitāre exīstimārētur. Sīc ut improbī atque pessimī mentem plēbis flexit ut novās rēs agitāret.   **4.** In viam saxum ita immensum dētrāxit ut nēmō id abstrahere neque eum sequī posset. In viam saxum immensum dētrāxit nē quis id abstrahere nēve eum sequī posset. **5.** Nē morerētur metuēns rogāvit ut custōdēs ā dextrā et ā sinistrā et ā tergō sibi proximī inter comitēs ambulārent. Nē morerētur metuit adeō ut custōdēs ā dextrā et ā sinistrā et ā tergō eī proximī inter comitēs ambulāre iubērentur.

F.   Pronounce and translate:

1. Mīror hominēs tam dissimilīs amīcōs esse.   **2.** Necesse est generī hūmānō multōs cāsūs subīre.   **3.** Necessene habēs ōrnātam vestem sūmere ad rēgis aedīs itūrus?   **4.** Veterrimus mīles querēbātur iūniōrem ad Praetōrium vocātum esse priōrem quam sē.   **5.** In magnā urbe aspexit multa quae mīrātus, multa quae questus est; sed erant plūra mīranda quam querenda.

G.   Translate:

1. He considered it necessary to increase his wealth, even by harming others. **2.** That husband of yours is so thin that no one can be thinner; he is certainly the thinnest of mortals.   **3.** He performed his duties with so much care that nothing was missing from his accounts; he did this in order that no accusation would arise.

FROM THE PHILOSOPHER'S HANDBOOK . . .

Nūllus est liber tam malus
ut nōn aliquā parte prōsit.
*There is no book so bad
that it is not profitable in some part.*
—PLINY THE YOUNGER

Think of a book you have disliked but, on the other hand, have learned from. Can you apply this saying to some of the texts you have used in school?

READING

Developing Reading Skills

Latin words which may help: **ad, agō, anima, animus, ante, aspiciō, cōnstituō, Cōnsul, cum, currō, dīcō, cēdō, dīscō, ē, ex, in, īnstituō, maior, mīles, mīlle, necesse, orior, pater, pellō, petō, pius, prō, solvō, sacer, salūs, sub, tegō, verbum,** and **vocō.**

English words which may help: *abrogate, atrocious, atrocity, consular, cremate, deception, discipline, dissolve, edict, elephant, execration, extra, impunity, inspect, invade, lament, ligament, ligature, majesty, maniple, military, necessity, obedient, orbit, paling, perpetual, phalanx, proceed, proverb, recusant, repulse, restitution, salubrious, severity, specimen, spoils, structure, vain,* and *victory.*

A Profitable Punishment

Contiōne advocātā Cōnsul fīliō "Quoniam" inquit "tū, T. Manlī, neque imperium cōnsulāre neque maiestātem patriam veritus adversus ēdictum nostrum extrā ordinem in hostem pugnāstī, et dīsciplīnam mīlitārem, quā stetit ad hanc diem Rōmāna rēs, solvistī, mēque in eam necessitātem addūxistī
5 ut aut reī publicae mihi aut meī meōrumque oblīvīscendum sit, nōs cōgimur esse trīste exemplum sed in posterum salūbre. Mē quidem nōn sōlum patrius amor līberōrum sed etiam specimen istud virtūtis dēceptum vānā imāgine decoris in tē mōvet; sed quoniam aut morte tuā sancienda sunt Cōnsulum imperia aut impūnitāte in perpetuum abroganda, et esse tibi quidem, sī quid
10 in tē nostrī sanguinis est, tantam pietātem in patriam cēnseō ut nōn recūsēs dīsciplīnam mīlitārem culpā tuā lāpsam poenā restituere–ī, Lictor,

---

3. nostrum: Romans occasionally use 1st person plural for 1st person singular, especially in very formal or very informal speech. **pugnāstī:** contracted form of **pugnāvistī   4. hanc: diēs** is feminine when it refers to time in general: *to this moment, to this point in time.* **eam:** A simple demonstrative is sometimes followed by an adverbial clause of result. This usage is substandard in English: *I was that shocked I didn't know what to say.*   **11. ī, Lictor, dēligā ad pālum:** the legal formula for ordering an execution.

dēligā ad pālum." Exanimātī omnēs tam atrōcī imperiō nec aliter quam in
sē quisque dēstrictam cernentēs secūrim, metū quiēvēre. Tum repente,
postquam cervice caesā fūsus est cruor, tam līberō conquestū coortae vōcēs
sunt ut neque lāmentīs neque exsecrātiōnibus parcerētur. Spoliīs contectum 15
iuvenis corpus structō extrā vallum rogō cremātum est. Posthāc "Manliāna
imperia" in proverbī consuētūdinem vēnērunt.

Fēcit tamen atrōcitās poenae oboedientiōrem ducī mīlitem adeō ut ea
sevēritās posterīs prōdesset. Nam ubi Pyrrhus Ēpīrī rēx in Italiam cum
exercitū invāsit ut auxiliō Tarentīnīs, quī cum Rōmānīs pugnābant, esset, 20
sīc mīrātus est dīsciplīnam Rōmānam ut dīceret "Ego cum tālibus virīs brevī
orbem terrārum subigerem!" Post proelium enim quō exercitum Rōmānum
superāverat ubi corpora Rōmānōrum quī in āciē ceciderant īnspiciēbat,
omnia versa in hostīs invēnit. Hōc proeliō legiōnēs Rōmānae prīmum
phalangī Alexandrēō modō īnstructae incurrērunt, quae eīs vidēbātur quasi 25
saepēs hastārum. Septiēns manipulī sē in hastās coniēcērunt; septiēns magnā
caede repulsī sunt. Deinde vīgintī elephantī quōs rēx in copiīs suīs habēbat
in āciem Rōmānam iam dissolūtam impetum sīc fēcērunt ut hōs, quī
numquam anteā tālīs beluās aspēxerant, pavor occupāret. Post hanc Pyrrhī
victōriam, multae gentēs Italiae sociī rēgis factae sunt, quibuscum ille ad 30
quadrāgēsimum mīlliārium urbis ipsīus prōcessit.

A mosaic elephant from Ostia,
the trademark of the merchants
of Sabratha in North Africa.

■ READING COMPREHENSION

1. What punishment did the Consul order for his son?   **2.** What is the
Latin expression for this order?   **3.** How did those present react to this
punishment?   **4.** What is the significance of the phrase "Manliāna imperia"?
5. Why was this harsh punishment considered profitable?   **6.** What statement did King Pyrrhus of Epirus make about the Roman army?   **7.** What
prompted him to make this statement?   **8.** In the battle with King Pyrrhus
what two things upset the Roman army?

---

13. dēstrictam: i.e. removed from the bundle of rods in the **fascēs**. **quiēvēre** =
quiēvērunt   27. **cōpiīs**: In military idiom the plural of **cōpia** means *forces*.

LESSON 10

Consecutive Clauses; Substantive Clause of Result

Senators in procession as they attend the dedication of the Ara Pacis during the reign of Augustus—Ara Pacis, Rome

THE SERVIAN CONSTITUTION

Since there was no distinction between civil and military officers and organization, Servius Tullius' reorganization of the army had an effect on the constitution. In order to decide on the amount of military equipment each citizen could afford to provide himself with, it was necessary to hold a census. For the purpose of the census the citizenry was divided into four districts and the territory outside the city into sixteen. These districts were called Tribes (**Tribūs**), and replaced the former family-based Tribes. At the same time the division of the army into Centuries (**Centūriae**) brought into existence a new assembly of the people, the **Comitia Centūriāta,** in which each Century had one vote. It was held with the citizens in military formation in the Campus Martius. This body was timocratic, i.e., the wealthy had more voice in its decisions, whereas in the **Comitia Cūriāta** each man's vote was roughly equal to everyone else's. In the **Comitia Centūriāta** the smallest number, older men of the wealthiest classes, were assigned to 40 centuries, and the next smallest number, younger men of the same class, to another 40. The next three classes had 20 centuries each, and the next 28. The largest class of all, the **prōlētāriī**, not being in the army, had no vote. Hence the wealthy minority held a majority of votes, 100 out of 168; since the voting began with the wealthy centuries and was halted after a majority was reached, the majority of the citizens never voted at all. The **Comitia Centūriāta** took over all the functions of the **Comitia Cūriāta** except the conferring of the imperium; people stopped attending meetings of the latter, until eventually the imperium was formally conferred by thirty Lictors, each representing a **Cūria.** This practice was continued until the third century of our era.

The Senate and Comitia were advisory bodies only; legislative, judicial, and executive powers all belonged to the king. He was also the religious leader, the arbiter of morals, and the commander of the armed forces. After

(Continued)

the expulsion of the kings, the imperium and the lesser powers of the King were shared out among a number of magistrates, to keep any one person from becoming a tyrant. In case it was important to the gods to be able to deal with a King, the title was kept and assigned to the Little Sacrificing King (**Rēx Sacrificulus**), who had certain religious duties and no other powers at all. The absolute power of the King could still be granted, in time of military emergency, to the Dictator; but his term of office was limited to the six months of the campaigning season. The Consuls appointed the Dictator, who appointed his own second in command, the Master of the Horse (**Magister Equitum**). All other magistrates were elected. The **Comitia Centūriāta** elected the higher magistrates (**maiōrēs**), the Praetors, Consuls, and Censors; The **Comitia Tributa** elected the lower magistrates (**minōrēs**), the Quaestors, Aediles, and Plebeian Tribunes. All magistracies had terms of one year only, and the same office could not be held twice in ten years.

(*above*) An **antefix** (roof plaque) of the works depot of Legion XX
(*below*) The emperor Augustus depicted as a togaed Consul

ANCIENT ROME LIVES ON . . .

The United States still conducts a census every ten years. How does the purpose of this census differ from those of Ancient Rome?

SYNTAX

■ CONSECUTIVE CLAUSES

Final clauses are **ut**-clauses which show the end (**fīnis**) toward which the action of the main verb aims. Consecutive clauses are **ut**-clauses which show what naturally follows (**consequor, -ī, consecūtus sum**) upon the action of the main verb. Final clauses are introduced by **ut** or **nē**; consecutive clauses always by **ut.** There are two kinds of consecutive clause: the adverbial clause of result and the substantive clause of result.

Substantive Clause of Result

A substantive clause of result, as its name indicates, is used as a noun, and has both nominative and accusative uses.

Nominative Uses

1. Subject of these verbs:
   a. **accidit, contingit, ēvenit,** and **fit:**

   Accidit
   Contingit
   Ēvenit } ut absit. *It happens that he is away.*
   Fit   *He happens to be away.*

   b. **relinquitur** and **restat:**

   Relinquitur }
   Restat   } ut cum eō loquāmur.   *It is left for us*
                                        to speak with him.

   c. **sequitur** and **cōnsequitur:**

   Sequitur   }
   Cōnsequitur } ut grātiam referāmus. *The next thing is*
                                         to show our gratitude.

   d. **accēdit** and **additur:**

   Hūc accēdit
       additur } ut hostēs adsint.   *Added to this is the fact*
                                      that the enemy are here.

   e. **est** with **necesse, prope,** or **reliquum** as subjective complement:

   Necesse est
   Prope est   } ut pellantur.   *It is necessary*
   Reliquum est   *that they be driven away.*
                                  They are close
                                    to being driven away.
                                  It remains
                                    that they be driven away.

f. **factum est** (perfect system only) and **efficitur**:

> Factum est ut discēderent.   *They were made to leave.*
> Efficitur ut discēdant.   *Their departure is being effected.*

2. Subjunctive complement with **mōs est**:

> Mōs est hominum ut nihil satis habeant.
> *It is the way of humans never to be satisfied.*

Accusative Uses

1. Direct object of **faciō** and **efficiō**:

> Faciēmus ut discēdant.   *We shall make them leave.*
> Efficimus ut discēdant.   *We are bringing about their departure.*

2. Subject of the future active infinitive of **sum, fore**:

> Dīcit fore ut hostēs vincantur.   *He says that the enemy will be conquered.*

Note: This construction with **fore ut** is the usual way of supplying the missing future passive infinitive. A less common way is to use the accusative supine with **īrī**, an impersonal use of the present passive infinitive of **eō**.

> Dīcit hostīs victum īrī.   *He says that the enemy will be conquered.*

Here **hostīs** is the direct object of the supine **victum**. Compare the active version:

> Dīcit nōs hostīs victum īre.
> *He says that we are going to conquer the enemy.*

FROM THE PHILOSOPHER'S HANDBOOK . . .

> Tarditās et procrāstinātiō odiōsa est.
> *Delay—putting things off until*
> *tomorrow—is hateful.*
> —CICERO

Cite three examples in which procrastination caused you some difficulty either in your school life or in your personal life.

VOCABULARY

BASIC WORDS

flōs, flōris, m. *flower*
mundus, -ī, m. *the universe*
tellus, tellūris, f. *earth, land; the earth*
vulnus, vulneris, n. *wound*

honestus, -a, -um *honorable*

accidō, -ere, accidī, ___ *fall to, fall
down*; accidit *it happens, it befalls* (w.
dative of the person)
bibō, -ere, bibī, bibitum *drink* (trans. or
intrans.)
contingō, -ere, contigī, contactum *touch;
concern*; contingit *it happens, it
befalls* (w. acc. of the person)

ēveniō, -īre, ēvēnī, ēventum *come out;*
evenit *it happens, it turns out* (w. dat.
of the person)
fīō, fīerī, ___, ___ *become, be made;*
fit *it happens, it is done* (w. abl. of
specification of the person)
indicō, -āre, -āvī, -ātum *indicate; inform
against*
restō, -āre, restitī, ___ *remain behind,
be left, be left over; resist*

Notes: 1. Of the various verbs meaning *it happens*, **accidit** often refers to misfortunes,
contingit and **ēvenit** to good fortune, and **fit** to either.

2. **Fīō** has two irregularities, the passive form of its infinitive and the fact that the
-ī of its stem remains long before vowels: **fīēbam, fīam**, etc. In the present
system it replaces the passive of **faciō**, which is not used. For its perfect system
it uses the passive of **faciō**.

LEARNING ENGLISH THROUGH LATIN

contagious — *spreading from person to person*
contiguous — *touching along all or most of one side*
contingency — *dependence on chance or uncertain conditions; a possible occurrence*
efflorescent — *flowering, blooming*
imbibe — *drink; absorb*
mundane — *commonplace, everyday*
restive — *restless, unsettled; unruly, hard to control*
vulnerable — *able to be wounded or hurt in some way*

▬ PRACTICE ▬

A.　Using a derivative from this lesson, rewrite each sentence to say the same thing:

1. Let us turn from these flights of fancy to more ordinary matters.　2. I know you are thirsty, but don't drink too much after strenuous exercise. 3. When you travel be prepared for any emergency.　4. The candidate had some flaws that made him open to criticism.　5. The farm land is adjacent to the main house.　6. The landscaping was just beautiful with all the blossoming shrubs and bushes.　7. The horse was balky and refused to go forward.　8. The doctor devotes her entire practice to treating communicable diseases.

B.　Pronounce and translate:

1. Fīat pāx terrā marīque!　2. Fiet ut contrā mōrem absēns Dictātor creētur. 3. Haec voluptās, ut saepius fit, dēficere coepit et postrēmō nihil facta est. 4. Quam celeriter, ut mors propior venit, homō et vetustior et magis vacuus mente fit!

C.　Pronounce and translate:

1. Vix efficiētur ut ad alteram rīpam perveniātur.　2. Eō accessit ut ventus mareque quiēta et nāvēs tūtae essent.　3. Relinquitur ut etiam seniōrēs ad hostium impetum sustinendum nōs cingāmus.　4. Sequitur ut litterās dē īnsīgnī legiōnis victōriā ad Senātum scrībāmus.　5. Verba virī improbī quamquam falsa fēcērunt ut virgō pudōre flēret.　6. Hūc additum est ut comam falsam sūmere suā āmissā cōgerētur.　7. Mōs est hārum virginum ut flōrēs colligant et in sinū domum portent.　8. Cōnsecūtum est ut causa nostra apud Praetōrem ā dextimō homine optimē dīcerētur.

D.　Convert the subjective infinitives into substantive clauses of result, then pronounce and translate.

EXAMPLE: Hominibus morī necesse est. Necesse est ut hominēs moriantur. *It is necessary for humans to die,* or *It is necessary that humans die.*

1. Necesse erit nōbīs fīnem huius bellī facere.　2. Haud necesse erat prōlī culpam parentium indicāre.　3. Necesse erat prīncipī in hōc homine improbō exemplum facere.　4. Necesse est hīs vagīs manibus Gallōrum ūnam sōlam terram optāre et errāre dēsinere.

E. Put the verb in parentheses into the correct tense, voice, mood, person, and number; then pronounce and translate:

1. Acciderat ut nēmō meliōra (spērō). 2. Contīgit ut ille vincula rumpere (valeō). 3. Restat ut nōs ipsī urbis tēcta templaque (dēfendō). 4. Factum est ut ipsa tellūs simul (mōveō). 5. Reliquum est ut omnēs, etiam minimī, (alō). 6. Prope erat ut ā turbā inimīcōrum (occīdō). 7. Ēvēnit ut illīus pater ē pugnā victor (redeō). 8. Sīc effēcit ut ministrī sine morā officiīs (fungor).

F. Change the future passive indirect statements to future active ones.

EXAMPLE: { Dīcit fore ut hostēs vincantur. } Dīcit nōs hostīs victūrōs.
{ Dīcit hostīs victum īrī. }

1. Magister cognōvit fore ut līberī nihil diūtius doceantur. Magister cognōvit nihil diūtius līberōs doctum īrī. 2. Iūrāvit fore ut multa vulnera hostibus ā sē darentur. Iūrāvit multa vulnera hostibus ā sē datum īrī. 3. Spērāvit fore ut glōria aequa ac Caesaris ā sē acciperētur. Spērāvit glōriam aequam ac Caesaris ā sē acceptum īrī.

The reverse of the upper coin shows a man casting his ballot. The tablet bears the letter U for **utī rogās,** a favorable vote. The obverse is Vesta. The reverse of the lower coin shows a voting urn, a curule chair (magistrate's bench), and a tablet with A for **absolvō** (I acquit) and C for **condemnō.** The obverse is Liberty.

Translation Help

When the verb of the principal clause is in the present, future, or future perfect, the verb of most subordinate subjunctive clauses will be in the present or perfect. It will be in the present subjunctive if the action it describes takes place at the same time as, or later than, the action of the main verb. It will be in the perfect subjunctive if the action it describes is prior to that of the main verb.

Vereor	nē veniat.	*I fear*	*that he is coming (will come).*
Verēbor	nē vēnerit.	*I shall fear*	*that he has come.*
Veritus erō		*I shall have feared*	

When the verb of the principal clause is in the imperfect or pluperfect, the verb of a subordinate subjunctive clause will also be in the imperfect or pluperfect. It will be in the imperfect subjunctive if the action it describes takes place at the same time as, or later than, the action of the main verb. It will be in the pluperfect subjunctive if the action it describes is prior to that of the main verb.

Verēbar	nē venīret.	*I was fearing*	*that he was coming (would come).*
Veritus eram	nē vēnisset.	*I had feared*	*that he had come.*

When the verb of the principal clause is in the perfect, it will be followed by a present or perfect subjunctive if it refers to an action completed in the present. It will be followed by the imperfect or pluperfect subjunctive if it describes a past action.

Vēnī ut tē videam.   *I have come to see you.*
Vēnī ut tē vidērem.   *I came to see you.*

When the English subjunctive is used it follows the same sequence of tenses:
I have come that I may see you.
I came that I might see you.

Electoral **programmata** from Pompeii: the walls of buildings were routinely covered with these advertisements urging the election of individuals to the duumvirate and the aedileship.

READING

Developing Reading Skills

Latin words which may help: **cēdō, clāmō, cupiō, dūcō, emō, ferō, fugiō, honestus, honor, indicō, mīror, occidō, quiēscō, senex, sentiō, teneō, valeō, verbum, vertō,** and **vulnus.**

English words which may help: *abstain, admire, avert, cupidity, devastate, dilatory, exclaim, frequent, honesty, honorific, medical, occidental, proceed, proverb, quiet, redeem, respond, revert, sapience, sentence, valetudinarian, venom,* and *vulnerable.*

Postponing the Good Times

Pyrrhum bellum in Ītaliā gestūrum amīcus Cineās, homō praestantissimus sapientissimusque, rogāvit, "Ītaliā victā quid faciās?", cui rēx respondit sē effectūrum ut omnēs terrae Eurōpae occidentālis sibi cēderent. "Et cum omnium dominus eris, quid tum sequitur?" "Tum sequitur" inquit Pyrrhus "ut quiētī nōs dēmus, bibāmus, epulēmur." At Cineās "Nunc iam" inquit "sine labōre orbis vincendī quō voluptātēs tantum differs omnia haec nōn facere possīmus?" Rēgī autem decoris cupidō nōn persuāsum est nē bellum gereret. 5

Post proelium Pyrrhus ad Rōmam prōcessit, omnia ferrō igneque vastāns. Lēgātī ad Pyrrhum dē captīvīs redimendīs missī honōrificē ab eō acceptī sunt; rēx captīvōs sine pretiō reddidit. Ūnum ex lēgātīs, Fābricium, sīc admīrātus est ut eī quartam partem rēgnī suī prōmittēns temptāret facere ut ad sē trānsīret; sed ā Fābriciō contemptus est. Cineās lēgātus ā Pyrrhō ad Senātum missus petīvit ut compōnendae pācis causā rēx in urbem reciperētur. Dē quā rē postquam ad frequentiōrem Senātum referrī placuit, 10 15

---

9. ad: When the preposition is used with the accusative of a noun which has a locative, it means *toward, in the direction of,* not *to.* **15. frequentiōrem:** Foreign ambassadors were first heard by a small committee, later by the full Senate.

plēbe pācī favente, īdem Appius Claudius quī et Aquae Appiae et Viae Appiae auctor erat, sed nunc senectūte caecus propter valētūdinem oculōrum iam diū cōnsiliīs publicīs sē abstinēbat, ā quattuor fīliīs ductus vēnit in Cūriam et sententiā suā ēffecīt ut id Pyrrhō nēgarētur. Senātus ergo respondit de pāce agendum esse nōn in Italiā sed in Ēpīrō. Ad rēgem reversus Cineās dīxit sē rēgum patriam vīdisse.

Posterō annō novī Cōnsulēs contrā Pyrrhum missī sunt. Proeliō commissō, rēx vulnerātus est et vīgintī mīlia hostium caesa sunt. Hīc iterum Pyrrhus elephantōrum auxiliō vīcit, sed brevī tempore Tarentum sē recipere coactus est. Post hoc proelium dīcitur exclāmāsse: "Alia victōria tālis faciat ut in Ēpīrum sine ūllīs cōpiīs redeam!" Hinc illud "victōria Pyrrhica" in proverbī cōnsuētūdinem vēnit. Annō interiectō, Fābricius ille contrā eum cum exercitū missus est, quī castra vīcīna castrīs rēgis habuit. Ubi C. Fābriciō Cōnsulī Pyrrhī medicus quī ad eum ā rēge trānsfūgerat prōmīsit venēnum sē rēgī pretiō datūrum, vinctus ad dominum cum indiciō reductus est. Tunc rēx illum admīrātus dīxisse fertur: "Ille est Fābricius, quī difficilius ab honestāte avertī potest quam sōl ā suō cursū!"

An idealized portrait of a Hellenistic warrior wearing a wreath of victory, often thought to be Pyrrhus of Epirus

READING COMPREHENSION

1. When would Pyrrhus take his ease and "eat, drink, and be merry"?
2. What did his friend Cineas suggest?   3. Why was he unable to persuade Pyrrhus?   4. Whom did Pyrrhus try to make come over to his side by promising him one fourth of his kingdom? Did he succeed?   5. Who insisted that a peace treaty with Pyrrhus would have to be discussed in Epirus, not Italy?   6. What had he previously sponsored, and why was he no longer active?   7. What does the term "a Pyrrhic victory" mean?
8. What is the story behind the following quotation? "Ille est Fābricius, quī difficilius ab honestāte avertī potest quam sōl ā suō cursū!"

---

20. **in Ēpīrō:** They meant that they would not negotiate with him while he was on Italian soil.   21. **rēgum patriam:** A famous saying; Cineas meant that each Roman citizen acted with the same freedom as if he were a king.   25. **exclāmāsse:** contracted form of **exclāmāvisse** 26. **illud:** an adjective which modifies a quotation is in the neuter singular; translate *the famous saying*

LESSON 11

Indirect Questions

The Temple of Saturn above the Roman Forum. The basement of this building housed the **Aerārium,** the state treasury over which the **Quaestōrēs** presided.

CURSUS HONŌRUM: MAGISTRĀTŪS MINŌRĒS

In some periods by custom, and in others by law, the order in which the magistracies could be held was strictly regulated, as was the time which was supposed to pass between tenures. Only in times of emergency, as in the Hannibalic war, were these regulations violated, to allow a talented strategist to obtain a command a little earlier, or to retain it for more than a year. This order was called the **cursus honōrum**, the order of public offices. The aspiring candidate for the cursus had first to complete ten years of military service, during which he would be expected to have reached the rank of Military Tribune (**Tribūnus Mīlitum**). Since military service began at eighteen, he would be ready to run for Quaestor no younger than age twenty-eight. The Quaestors were treasury officials, collecting state revenues and paying them out on the orders of a higher magistrate. Four Quaestors served at Rome; there were eventually more of them, elected to serve in the provinces. At certain periods election to the Quaestorship carried **ex officiō** membership in the Senate; at other times Senate membership came only with the curule magistracies. After holding the Quaestorship, the politician had to wait two years before running for the Aedileship, the next step up the ladder. The **Aedīlēs,** as their name suggests, were originally in charge of the upkeep of temples; they eventually assumed responsibility for public buildings, streets, and markets. Keeping order in these places led to their gaining the power to impose fines for disturbing the peace or any offense against public order. Their most important task politically was arranging both the **lūdī** and the **mūnera gladiātōria,** for which they usually added to the allotted funds from their own pockets, hoping to win public favor for election to the higher offices. It was possible to go from the Quaestorship to the Praetorship without having been Aedile, provided that a period of five years was allowed to intervene; but most politicians did not want to miss this opportunity for good publicity. For

(Continued)

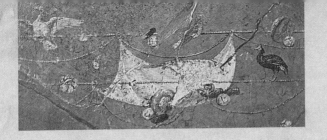

a long time Aediles were also in charge of the grain supply of the city. There were two kinds of Aediles, two Plebeian Aediles (**Aedīlēs Plēbis**) and two Curule Aediles (**Aedīlēs Cūrūlēs**) representing the people as a whole. The Curule Aediles were so called because one of the symbols of their rank was the King's **sella cūrūlis**, his folding stool made of or decorated with ivory. The Curule Aedile was the only one of the **minōrēs** who could sit on the **sella cūrūlis**, a privilege shared by all of the **maiōrēs**. Only the Curule Aedileship was regulated by the **cursus honōrum**; the Plebeian Aedileship could be held at any time and at any age, as could the Plebeian Tribunate.

The Tribunes of the Plebs (**Tribūnī Plēbis**) were the most important of the lower magistrates. There were originally two of them, later four, and eventually ten. Their functions were the protection of individual plebeians (**auxilium**), the calling of meetings of the plebs (**contiōnēs** or **concilia plēbis**), and the vetoing of legislation against the interests of the plebs (**intercessiō**). Their persons were sacrosanct, which meant that anyone who interfered with them in the performance of their duties could be fined, imprisoned, or even put to death. The Plebeian Tribunate did not bring **ex officiō** membership in the Senate, although the Tribunes were allowed to observe Senate proceedings from the doorway.

(*above*) Magistrates wooed the populace at public games with a **sparsiō**, free food and gifts dropped from ropes strung overhead   (*below*) a Roman banker

ANCIENT ROME LIVES ON . . .

In times of emergency, Roman regulations were violated. What special measures does the United States take in cases of national emergencies?

▬▬ SYNTAX ▬▬

▪ INDIRECT QUESTIONS

Questions which are reported, not quoted directly, are called indirect questions. An indirect question is introduced by an interrogative pronoun, adjective, adverb, or particle, and has its verb in the subjunctive.

Quid facit?   *What is she doing?* DIRECT
Eam rogāvī quid faceret.   *I asked her what she was doing.* INDIRECT

The first periphrastic is used to represent the future in an indirect question.

Quid faciet?   *What will she do?* DIRECT
Eam rogō quid factūra sit.   *I ask her what she will do.* INDIRECT
Eam rogāvī quid factūra esset.   *I asked her what she would do.* INDIRECT

Besides verbs of asking, indirect questions are also governed by verbs of saying, informing, knowing, and perceiving.

Mihi dīxit		*She told me*	
Mē docuit	quid faceret.	*She informed me*	what she was doing.
Scīvī		*I knew*	
Vīdī		*I saw*	

Indirect questions may also depend on verbs like **mīror** (*I wonder*), **cōnstat** (*it is established, certain, fixed*), and **certum est** (*it has been decided, resolved*), and on adjectives like **dubius** (*doubtful*).

Mīror quid faciendum sit.   *I wonder what is to be done.*

Mihi non satis cōnstat		
Mihi nōn certum est	quid faciendum sit.	*I am not sure what is to be done.*
Dubius sum		

Interrogative Words in Indirect Questions

All of the interrogative pronouns, adjectives, adverbs and particles which you have learned may introduce indirect questions. There are, however, five usages which are peculiar to indirect questions:

1. **Num** is used instead of **-ne** to introduce a yes-or-no question.

Fēlīxne es?   *Are you happy?* DIRECT
Rogāvit **num** fēlīx essēs.   *He asked if (whether) you were happy.* INDIRECT

After **num**, just as after **nē** and in conditional clauses, the indefinite pronoun and adjective **quis, quid** and **quī, qua, quod** are used for someone and anyone.

> Adestne aliquis? *Is anyone here?*
> Rogāvit num quis adesset. *He asked if there was anyone there.*

2. **Necne** replaces **annōn** in the second half of a disjunctive question.

> Utrum manēs **annōn**? *Are you staying, or not?* DIRECT
> Rogāvī utrum manērēs **necne**. *I asked if you were staying, or not.* INDIRECT

3. **Quārē** (**quā rē**, *for which reason*) is usually used instead of **cūr** for *why*.

> **Cūr** abest? *Why is he absent?* DIRECT
> Rogō **quārē** absit. *I ask why he is absent.* INDIRECT

4. **An** may sometimes introduce a single indirect question, usually in two idioms meaning *perhaps*, **haud sciō an**, *I don't know whether*, and **fors sit an** (usually written as one word, **forsitan**,) *there would be a chance that.*

> Haud sciō an ⎫
> Forsitan ⎬ hoc effectūrī sīmus. *Perhaps we shall accomplish this.*

5. **Ut**, meaning *how*, introduces indirect questions, but not after verbs of asking. Such questions differ little in meaning from indirect statements.

> Mihi dīxit frātrem discessisse. *She told me that her brother had left.*
> Mihi dīxit ut frāter discessisset. *She told me how her brother had left.*

Sī is not used to introduce an indirect question. *If* in English will be **num** or **utrum** in Latin.

> Rogāvit num mānsūrus essem. *She asked if I would stay.*
> Rogāvit utrum mānsūrus essem necne. *She asked if I would stay, or not.*

Magistrates were responsible for chariot races and other **lūdī**.

VOCABULARY

BASIC WORDS

fulmen, fulminis, n. *thunderbolt*
lapis, lapidis, m. *stone*
triumphus, -ī, m. *triumph (a solemn procession granted by the Senate to a general and his army after a victory)*

dīvēs, dīvitis *wealthy*
dīvus, -a, -um *divine; (of an emperor) deified*
levis, -e *light; trivial; fickle*

mollis, -e *soft; gentle*

cōnstō, -āre, cōnstitī, cōnstātum *consist; stand firm*; cōnstat *it is certain; it is well-known*
iungō, -ere, iūnxī, iunctum *join, unite*
memorō, -āre, -āvī, -ātum *mention*
premō, -ere, pressī, pressum *press*
taceō, -ēre, -uī, -itum *be silent* (intrans.); *be silent about* (trans.)

Notes: 1. **Iungō** and its compounds may take two accusatives with a conjunction, an acc. and a dat., or an acc. and an abl. of means or accompaniment.

Nostrum exercitum et vestrum iungēmus. TWO ACCUSATIVES
We shall unite our army and yours.

Bonae uxōrī iunctus est.
He was mated with (joined to) a good wife. DATIVE

Honōrem glōriā iūnxit.　　　ACCUSATIVE AND ABLATIVE OF MEANS
　　　　　　　　　　　　　　　He combined honor with glory.
Honōrem cum glōriā iūnxit.　ACCUSATIVE AND ABLATIVE OF ACCOMPANIMENT

2. **Premō** in compounds becomes **-primō, -primere, -pressī, -pressum**
3. The perf. pass. part. of **taceō** is used as an adj.: **tacitus, -a, -um**, *silent*

LEARNING ENGLISH THROUGH LATIN

alleviate	*to make less hard to bear; to lighten or relieve*
commemorate	*to honor the memory of; to serve as a memorial of*
dilapidated	*shabby, falling into disrepair; neglected*
levity	*lightness or gaiety; lack of seriousness*
mollify	*to soothe the temper of; to appease*
reprimand	*a severe or formal rebuke, especially by a person in authority*
reticence	*a disinclination to express one's feelings or impart information*
taciturn	*not liking to talk; silent; uncommunicative*

PRACTICE

A. Using a form of a word from the derivative list, restate each of the following sentences to say the same thing *or the direct opposite.*

1. It saddened the royal family to see their ancestral home so run down.
2. He is so loquacious that it is impossible to carry on a conversation with him.   3. The town celebrated Independence Day with a parade and fireworks display.   4. The governor established a special fund to decrease poverty in his state.   5. The principal praised the newspaper staff for the editorial.
6. The employer did everything in her power to appease the distraught workers.   7. The gravity of his manner belied the true nature of the situation.   8. Their silence was caused by their embarrassment.

B. Here are some English derivatives of **premō:** *compress, depress, express, impress, oppress, repress,* and *suppress.*

1. Using the list of prefixes in the Appendix, give the original meanings of these derivatives.   2. What are their current meanings?

C. By combining each time a clause from column **A** with a phrase or clause from column **B**, create, pronounce, and translate ten short sentences.

A	B
1. Dolet	a. quārē abeās.
2. Iubet	b. tē abīre.
3. Memorat	c. ut abeās.
4. Mīrātur	
5. Necesse est	
6. Tē rogat	
7. Tibi imperat	

D. Pronounce and translate:

1. Sciunt quālēs sītis.   2. Cognōscimus quōmodo tālia fīant.   3. Invēnistisne quō hostēs fūgissent annōn?   4. Nōvī quid potissimum fīerī cupiās.   5. Haud sciō an hāc culpā exemptī sint.   6. Sēnsērunt quemadmodum audientēs sibi inimīcī essent.   7. Facile est vidēre utrum fīlium magis amēs.   8. Bene meminī quārē tacitus dē hīs rēbus fuerim.   9. Reperīre temptābunt quantus fuerit numerus in hōc proeliō pugnantium.   10. Apud Vergilium legimus quibus labōribus Trōiānī ad Hesperiam pervēnerint.

E.   Convert each of the following indirect questions to a direct question.

EXAMPLE: Mē rogāvit quō īrem. Mihi "Quō īs?" inquit.

1. Ā Cōnsule quaeritis quandō hostīs fūsūrus sit.   **2.** Rogāvī num honestī hoc faciendum esse cēnsērent.   **3.** Līberī magistrum rogāvērunt quot mīlia passuum mundus patēret.   **4.** Nōs rogāvistī quārē diūtissimē de hōc crīmine tacuissēmus.

F.   Convert each of the following direct questions into an indirect question, governed (1) by **Rogat** and (2) by **Rogāvit**.

EXAMPLE: Puellae "Quotiēns" inquit "Rōmam adīvistī?" (1) Puellam rogat quotiēns Rōmam adīverit. (2) Puellam rogāvit quotiēns Rōmam adīvisset.

1. Amīcō "Paulumne" inquit "hīc cessābis?"   **2.** Cōnsul Cōnsulī "Quid potius" inquit "facere cupīvistī?"   **3.** Puer maior minōrī "Quandō" inquit "nātus es?"   **4.** Dīs īnferīs "Utrum opēs meae" inquit "augēbuntur annōn?"

G.   Translate:

1. I could perceive how happy you were at that time.   **2.** I don't know if the army will come back victorious.

FROM THE PHILOSOPHER'S HANDBOOK . . .

Saepe nē ūtile quidem est
scīre quid futūrum sit.
*Often it is not even advantageous
to know what will be.*
—CICERO

None of us knows what the future holds for us, and this is considered a blessing by many. On the other hand, we sometimes say, "If I had only known . . ."
Which of the two philosophies do you prefer, and why?

READING

Developing Reading Skills

Latin words which will help: **comes, Cōnsul, dēligō, iaciō, magnus, mīror, opus, ostendō, pondus, premō, socius, tantus, vestis,** and **vocō.**

English words which will help: *admire, Ag, argent, cite, coerce, comity, consular, elephant, expel, ictus, liquid, medical, oppress, ostentation, pitch, pristine, prodigy, resist, respond, Sagittarius, saline,* and *severity.*

A Stone's Throw

Fābricium quia Pyrrhō aperuit quid medicus factūrus esset rēx tantopere admīrātus est ut iterum captīvōs sine pretiō redderet omnīs novīs togīs vestītōs. Hī captīvī cōmitāte rēgis adductī sunt ut Senātuī persuādērent ut indūtiās quattuor annōrum cum Pyrrhō facerent, quī igitur in Siciliam ut adversus Pūnicōs pugnāret discessit. Sed ā Tarentīnīs revocātus post tertium   5
annum rediit. Rōmae eōdem tempore inter alia prōdigia fulmine dēiectum est in Capitōliō Summānī sīgnum, cuius caput āmissum est, nec quisquam reperīre poterat quid eō factum esset. Tantus pavor cīvitātem occupāvit ut paucī dēlectū habitō ad nōmina respondērent. Cūrius Dentātus Cōnsul omnium quī cītātī nōn responderant bona vēndidit. Tum autem cum Summānī   10
caput per Harūspicēs in ālveō Tiberis inventum est, Augurēs cecinērunt rem Rōmānam victōriam post multōs labōrēs consecūtūram.

Pyrrhus Rōmānōs necopīnantīs opprimere temptāns mīsit aliquās copiās cum elephantīs per montium angustiās, quae beluās illās sīc morātae sunt ut māne, nōn nocte, pervenīrent ita ut Cūrius eōs procul vidēret et sīc   15
parātus esset. Elephantōs petīvērunt Rōmānī sagittīs accēnsīs et doliīs ardentis picis liquidae plēnīs quae inter eōs coniecta sunt, quī igitur in rēgis castra sē recipiēbant, ubi multōs pedibus conculcātōs interfēcērunt. Pyrrhus copiīs aut interfectīs aut dēficientibus ex Italiā expulsus est et in Graeciam rediit,

---

19. dēficientibus: in a military context = deserting

20   ubi ictū lapidis ā muliere quādam iactī occīsus est. Quattuor elephantī quī restābant in Cūrī triumphō ductī sunt.

    Pyrrhō mortuō gentēs Italiae omnem spem sē Rōmānīs resistere posse āmīsērunt et in fidem Populī Rōmānī vēnērunt. Extrā quoque Italiam reliquae gentēs vidēbant quantum rēs Rōmāna posset, adeō ut Ptolemaeus Aegyptī

25   rēx societātem cum Rōmānīs iūngeret. Urbs quidem magnopere crēverat: lūstrō ā Cēnsōribus conditō cēnsa sunt cīvium capitum dūcenta septuāgintā ūnum mīlia et dūcenta vīgintī quattuor. Pristina tamen sevēritās mōrēs etiam nunc sīc coercēbat ut īdem Cēnsōrēs, ex quibus ūnus Fābricius ille erat, quendam cōnsulārem Senātū dēmōvērent quod is decem pondō argentī factī habēbat.

30   Ōstentātiō eīs temporibus tam simplex erat ut nōbilis dīves iactāre posset ūnum pōculum et ūnum salīnum ex argentō facta sibi esse.

Terra-cotta figure of a war elephant trampling a soldier

▓ READING COMPREHENSION

1. What did King Pyrrhus do out of admiration for Fabricius?   2. Influenced by the king's kindness, what did the captives persuade the Senate to do? 3. What happened to the statue of Summanus on the Capitol, and how did it affect the citizenry?   4. What did the Consul Curius Dentatus do? 5. What did the Augurs prophesy after the head was found?   6. Why were the elephant forces unsuccessful against the Romans?   7. What happened to Pyrrhus?   8. What was the result of his death?   9. Who allied himself with the Roman people?   10. How would you characterize the Roman mode of living at the time of this story?

---

29. decem: sc. **lībrārum. factī** = worked, wrought

LESSON 12

Review of Ut-Clauses; Review of Indirect Discourse

A Roman Consul, his arm raised to start the games, is surrounded by riders representing the various **factiōnes** (teams) of the Circus—Palazzo Vecchio, Florence

CURSUS HONŌRUM: MAGISTRĀTŪS MAIŌRĒS

The first of the higher magistracies, which could be held when two years had passed after the Curule Aedileship, was the Praetorship. The Praetor was the head of the state in the absence of the Consuls, and was the presiding officer in lawsuits between citizens. Later another Praetor, the **Praetor Peregrīnus,** was elected to preside over lawsuits between citizens and aliens (the other now being called the **Praetor Urbānus**). A Praetor was sometimes given command of an army when Rome had to field more than two; eventually more Praetors had to be elected to handle overseas campaigns, so that there were finally eight of them. In addition to the **sella cūrūlis,** a Praetor had the attendance of six Lictors bearing **fascēs.** In later times the Praetors served their terms at Rome, and then were given a military command, serving **prō praetōre;** such commanders are sometimes called Propraetors.

When two years had elapsed after the Praetorship, the candidate could run for Consul. He would by this time be at least in his early forties. The two Consuls were the highest officials of the government. They presided over the Senate and the two Comitia, were the commanders-in-chief of the armed forces, initiated legislation, and exercised a general supervision over the other magistrates. A Consul had the **sella cūrūlis** and twelve Lictors. He also usually followed his year in office with a military command, acting as a Proconsul, **prō cōnsule.**

Higher in honor than even the Consulship, but less in power, was the Censorship. The Censors were elected only at the time of the **lustrum,** i.e., every five years. In holding the census they also served as guardians of public morals, since they could degrade a citizen from a higher social rank to a lower one not only on the grounds of insufficient property qualification but also of immorality. They also put public contracts up for bidding. The Censors were elected from among the ex-Consuls.

ANCIENT ROME LIVES ON . . .

The two Consuls were the highest officials of the Roman government. How did their duties compare with those of the President of the United States?

(*above left*) A Commander-in-Chief receiving ambassadors—2d century relief from the Arch of Constantine   (*above*) Portrait of a late Republican Consul in his political role

SYNTAX

■ REVIEW OF UT-CLAUSES

As you have now learned, there are nine kinds of clauses which can be introduced by **ut.**

Indicative Ut-Clauses

1. Ut-Temporal Clause

Domō discessī ut sōl occidēbat. *I left home as the sun was setting.*

2. Ut-Causal Clause

Ut noctem metuī redīre cōnstituī.
As I feared the nighttime, I decided to return.

3. Ut-Comparative Clause

Sīc (ita) age ut frāter tuus. *Behave as your brother does.*

In all three of these **ut** means *as.* Ut-comparative clauses often omit the verb; they are frequently preceded by **sīc** or **ita.**

Subjunctive Ut-Clauses

1. Final Clauses
   a. Adverbial Clause of Purpose

Id fēcī ut tibi placeam. *I did it to please you.*

   b. Indirect Command (Substantive Clause of Purpose)

Ā tē petit ut sē iuvēs. *She is asking you to help her.*

   c. Clause after a Verb (or Other Expression) of Fearing

Verēbantur ut auxilium sibi adferrētur.
They were afraid that help would not be brought to them.

These are introduced by **ut** or **nē.** An indirect command is governed by a verb of *commanding, asking,* or *advising;* it may sometimes omit the **ut.**

Veniās quaerō. *I ask you to come.*

2. Consecutive Clauses
   a. Adverbial Clause of Result

Tantum erat pondus ut non portārētur.
The weight was so great that it could not be carried.

b. Substantive Clause of Result

> Accidit ut abiissent. *They happened to have gone away.*

These are always introduced by **ut**, never **nē**, although the substantive clause of result may omit the **ut**.

> Fac ad mē veniās. *See to it that you come to me.*

An adverbial clause of result is usually preceded by a word meaning *so* or *such*. A substantive clause of result is the subject or object of a verb of *happening, effecting, remaining, following, adding,* and the like.

3. Indirect Question

Always introduced by **ut**, never by **nē**, an **ut** indirect question is governed by verbs of *saying, informing, knowing,* and *perceiving* (never by verbs of asking).

> Vīdit ut sibi nōn crēderētur. *He saw how he wasn't trusted.*

Note that all but two of the subjunctive ut-clauses are substantive, and serve as the subject or direct object of particular kinds of verbs. Of the two adverbial clauses, the adverbial clause of result is usually preceded by a *so* or *such*. Hence any subjunctive **ut**-clause which is not prepared for by a particular verb or a *so* or *such* in the main clause will be an adverbial clause of purpose.

An **ut**-clause missing its verb will be ut-comparative.

An **ut**-clause missing its **ut** will be an indirect command or a substantive clause of result.

◼ REVIEW OF INDIRECT DISCOURSE

1. Indirect Statement: infinitive with accusative subject. Governed by verbs of *saying, informing, knowing, perceiving, thinking,* and *advising (warning, persuading,* etc.).

> Nōs monuērunt hostīs accēdere.
> *They warned us that the enemy were approaching.*
> Scīmus hoc factum esse. *We know that this has happened.*

2. Indirect Command: **ut** or **nē** with the subjunctive. Governed by verbs of *commanding* (except **iubeō**), *asking, advising (warning, persuading,* etc.).

> Nōs monuērunt ut hostīs fugerēmus. *They warned us to flee the enemy.*
> Ā mē quaesīvit ut ad sē venīrem. *He asked me to come to him.*

3. Indirect Question: interrogative word with the subjunctive. Governed by verbs of *asking, informing, knowing,* and *perceiving.* **Ut** indirect questions after verbs of saying are a special case.

> Scīmus quomodo hoc factum sit.   *We know how this happened.*
> Ā mē quaesīvit quārē ad sē vēnissem.
> *He asked me why I had come to him.*

Translation Help

This chart may help you to remember which kind of indirect discourse is governed by each class of verb:

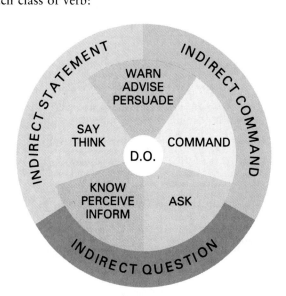

The D.O. in the center is to remind you that most of these verbs may take a direct object instead of indirect discourse.

Verbs of Saying and Informing

addō	clāmō	expōnō	narrō	queror
adiciō	cōnfirmō	ferō	negō	referō
āiō	dēmōnstrō	iactō	nūntiō	scrībō
āperiō	dīcō	indicō	oblīvīscor	taceō
canō	doceō	memorō	ōstendō	

Verbs of Knowing and Perceiving

audiō	dīscō	meminī	reperiō	videō
cernō	inveniō	nesciō	sciō	
cognōscō	legō	nōscō	sentiō	

Verbs of Thinking

cēnseō	colligō	crēdō	exīstimō	putō

Verbs of Advising (Warning, Persuading)

addūcō	moneō	persuādeō

Verbs of Commanding

imperō	mandō	praecipiō

Verbs of Asking

petō	quaerō	rogō

VOCABULARY

BASIC WORDS

aevum, -ī, n. *age*
classis, classis, f. (i-stem) *class; fleet*
fluctus, -ūs, m. *wave*
fretum, -ī, n. *sea; strait*
lūmen, lūminis, n. *light; eye*
pontus, -ī, n. *[the deep] sea*
rēmus, -ī, m. *oar*

cunctus, -a, -um *all, the whole, entire*
iustus, -a, -um *just*

dīvidō, -ere, dīvīsī, dīvīsum *divide*
perdō, -ere, perdidī, perditum *destroy; waste; lose*
voveō, -ēre, vōvī, vōtum *vow*

Notes: 1. Second-declension neuter nouns ending in **-us** (like **pontus**) are declined like masculine and feminine nouns of the 2d declension, except that the accusative singular ends in **-us,** like the nominative. They have no plurals.

2. The perfect passive participle of **voveō** is frequently used as a neuter noun: **vōtum, -ī,** n. *vow.*

■ LEARNING ENGLISH THROUGH LATIN

declassé	*lowered in social status; having lost class*
devout	*religious, pious, showing reverence*
fluctuate	*to be continually changing or varying*
illuminate	*to give light to; to make clear, explain, elucidate*
justify	*to show to be just, right, or in accord with reason*
longevity	*a long life; length of time spent in employment, service, etc.*
luminous	*giving off light; illuminated; glowing in the dark*
perdition	*ruin; complete and irreparable loss; damnation*

▬▬ PRACTICE ▬▬

A. Derivatives.

1. Make a list of as many words as possible that are derived from the following Latin words: **dīvidō, lūmen, voveō.** Use your dictionary. **2.** Show the relationship between the English word *fluctuate* and the Latin **fluctus.** **3.** A *trireme* is a warship with three banks of oars on each side. Show the Latin derivation of this word. **4.** Check the various English meanings of *classic* and *classify* and show how they are derived from the Latin **classis.**

B. Fill in the blanks:

1. Indicative ut-clauses are ___, ___, and ___ clauses. **2.** The three kinds of final clauses are ___, ___, and ___. **3.** The two kinds of consecutive clauses are ___, and ___. **4.** The ninth kind of ut-clause is ___, used only with verbs of ___. **5.** Final clauses are introduced by ___ or ___, consecutive clauses only by ___. **6.** An ut-clause without a verb will be a ___ clause. **7.** An ut-clause without the ut will be ___ or ___.

C. Identify by name the ut-clause in each sentence; then pronounce and translate.

1. Ut abeātis rogāmus. **2.** Sōl oriēbātur ut domō exībam. **3.** Celeriter currit ut cēterōs cōnsequātur. **4.** Hoc ita fac ut ego. **5.** Metuērunt ut vōta ā nūminibus audīrentur. **6.** Ut ventus nōn erat, classis rēmīs movē-bātur. **7.** Fac perveniās eādem ferē hōrā quā ego. **8.** Ā dīs īnferīs petīvit ut inimīcōs perderent. **9.** Iōvī iūsta mūnera sīc vōvit ut pater praecēperat. **10.** Fluctūs in pontō tantī erant ut nāvigāre nōn possēmus.

In art, the Senate and the Roman People (SPQR) are represented as a bearded elder and a youth wearing a toga without a tunic—Cancelleria reliefs, Vatican Museum

FROM THE PHILOSOPHER'S HANDBOOK . . .

Omnia iam fīent quae posse negābam.
Everything which I used to say could not
happen will happen now.

—OVID

As you look around your world today, can you see things happening which a few years ago you would have thought impossible? Name one that is very beneficial and one that is harmful or detrimental.

D. Tell which phrases or clauses from column **B** could follow each verb in column **A** to make a sentence.

EXAMPLE: Crēdidit could be followed by **b** and **d**.

A	B
1. Oblītus est	**a.** ut versūs legendōs in bonō lūmine pōnerem.
2. Dīscēbat	**b.** hoc aevum improbum esse.
3. Mē monuit	**c.** quid nocuisset aliquot membrīs corporis suī.
4. Mihi mandāvit	**d.** cunctum mundum ex nihilō factum esse.
5. Dē mē quaesīvit	**e.** quōmodo illīus scelus indicātum esset.
6. Mihi imperābat	**f.** nē diūtius suum cāsum dolērem.
7. Mē rogāvit	
8. Vīdit	
9. Mihi persuādēbat	
10. Exīstimāvit	

E. Match the words *to see you* in column **A** with the correct expression(s) from column **B**:

A	B
1. He has come to see you.	**a.** tē vidēre
2. He came to see you.	**b.** sē tē vidēre
3. He wants to see you.	**c.** sē tē vīsūrum
4. He wants her to see you.	**d.** tē vīsum
5. He will ask her to see you.	**e.** ad tē videndum
6. He ordered her to see you.	**f.** tuī videndī grātiā
7. He says it is good to see you.	**g.** tuī videndī causā
8. He hopes to see you.	**h.** ut tē videat
9. He promised to see you.	**i.** ut tē vidēret
10. He is afraid to see you.	
11. He is sorry to see you.	

F. Translate:

1. He instructed me to remain there a little. 2. He kept asserting that he knew everything about their customs. 3. Do you remember why they put this accusation on me? 4. Can they believe that the earth is hung upon (down from) nothing? 5. I ask of you (seek from you) that you obey me in all respects.

READING

Developing Reading Skills

Latin words which will help: **annus, arma, certō, Cōnsul, currō, dīcō, dō, ēveniō, faciō, ferō, iūstus, mare, mittō, multus, nāvis, nōmen, persuādeō, plūrēs, pugnō, quīnque, rapiō,** and **remus.**

English words which will help: *accommodate, admit, annual, apt, arm, cognomen, consulate, contention, desiccate, dissuade, event, exercise, fabricate, federal, imitate, incursion, indict, injustice, intelligent, interior, maritime, mercenary, naval, onerous, perfidious, predatory, prediction, prefect, quinquereme, substitute,* and *tempest.*

Army vs. Navy

Pyrrhus ut ē Siciliā discēdēbat dīxisse fertur sē pulchrum campum certāminī aptum Poenīs Rōmānīsque relinquere, quae praedictiō brevī explēta est. Nam quīdam mercenāriī Campānī quī sēsē Māmertīnōs vocābant ut ā rēge Syrācūsānōrum missī factī erant Messānam contendērunt, quō ut hospitēs amīcī admissī nocte perfidiōsē Messēniōs virōs occīdērunt, fēminās līberōsque et aedīs agrōsque inter sē dīvīsērunt. Poenī, quī iam cum Graecīs in Siciliā certābant, verentēs nē Māmertīnī fretum Siciliēnse nāvibus Pūnicīs clauderent, hōs expugnāre et expellere temptābant; hī igitur ā Rōmānīs ut sibi auxilium ferrent petīvēre. Rōmae Patrēs tāle bellum iniūstum fore sciēbant, cui favēbat tamen plēbs memor certāminī Pyrrhicō ēventum bonum fuisse et spērāns sē praedam multam sīc consecūtūram. Dēnique auxilium ferendum Senātus cēnsuit, postquam dē eā rē inter suādentīs ut id fieret dissuādentīsque contentiō fuit. Sīc efficitur ultimum Dīdōnis vōtum, illud "Nūllus amor populīs nec foedera suntō."

5

10

---

3. sēsē = sē   4. missī factī erant: *had been discharged;* **missum facere** is a military idiom
9. petīvēre = petīvērunt   14. suntō: Future Imperative

15   Bellum Poenīs indīctum erat; at quemadmodum pugnārētur inter classīs Pūnicās et exercitum Rōmānum? Nam Poenīs erant permultae nāvēs cīvibus armātīs ornātae, exercitus autem mercenāriōrum magnitūdine nōn tantus; exercitus Rōmānus ex cīvibus cōnstāns magnus erat, sed nūllās nāvīs habēbant—cōpiae in Siciliam nāvibus onerāriīs ā Graecīs sociīs commodātīs

20   trānsierant. Itaque quamquam facile Rōmānī Poenōs ex Siciliā interiōre expulērunt, classēs Pūnicae tamen oppida maritima nōn sōlum Siciliae sed etiam Ītaliae crebrīs incursiōnibus dīripiēbant. Rōmānī nescīvērunt quōmodo quīnquerēmis fabricārētur. Dēnique nāvem Pūnicam quam in lītus tempestāte dēlātam invēnerant imitātī sunt complūrēs fabricantēs; interim mīlitēs

25   remigiō sē exercēbant in siccō sedentēs. Classī cōnfectae praefectus est Cōnsul quī sīcut cēterī Rōmānī nescīvit nāvigāre et, quoniam cōnsulātus mūnus annuum erat, novus Cōnsul semper substituēbātur in locum eius quī dēnique intellegere coeperat quae esset ārs nāvālis. Sīc trēs classēs cunctae perditae sunt, nōn tam ab hostibus quam fluctibus tempestātibusque. Prīmae

30   classis ducī Cn. Cornēliō Scīpiōnī inditum est cognōmen Asinae ob imperītiam artis nāvālis, quā classem āmīserat.

▪ READING COMPREHENSION

1. What prophecy did Pyrrhus make that was fulfilled in a short time? **2.** What did the Campanian mercenaries call themselves? **3.** What did they do? **4.** What is the significance of the following? "Nūllus amor populīs nec foedera suntō." **5.** What was the basic military difference between the Carthaginians and the Romans? **6.** How did the Romans learn how to build a quinquereme? **7.** How did the Roman soldiers learn to row? **8.** Why did the Consuls in charge of the fleets never really learn the art of sailing? **9.** How did the Romans lose three entire fleets? **10.** What does the cognomen **Asina** mean, and why was it given to the commander of the first fleet, Gnaeus Cornelius Scipio?

REVIEW 3

LESSONS 9–12

VOCABULARY DRILL

1. Give the genitive, gender, and meaning of each of these nouns:

aevum	flōs	impetus	lūmen	rēmus	victor
classis	fluctus	lapis	mundus	tellus	vōtum
culpa	fretum	legiō	pontus	triumphus	vulnus
exemplum	fulmen				

2. Give the other nominative singular forms (or the genitive of one-termination adjectives), and the meanings, of these adjectives:

cunctus	dīvus	iūstus	mollis	necesse	sanctus
dīves	honestus	levis			

3. Give the other three principal parts, and the meanings, of these verbs:

accidō	contingō	fīō	memorō	premō	sanciō
bibō	dīscō	indicō	mīror	queror	taceō
cēnseō	dīvidō	iungō	perdō	restō	voveō
cōnstō	ēveniō				

4. What do adeō and quasī mean?

DRILL ON SYNTAX

Pronounce and translate:

1. Audīvimus quot mūnera sanctīs dīs et superīs et īnferīs praebuissēs.
2. Forsitan dīvus Iūlius, nōbīs in hāc vītā amīcus, etiam nunc nōs respectūrus sit.   3. Ā vōbis quaesīvit utrum vīnum sine aquā umquam bībissētis necne.

LISTENING AND SPEAKING

Let the Buyer Beware!

Lucretia, expecting important guests for dinner, sends Appolonia to the market. She warns her to watch the sellers very carefully to make sure she does not pay an unfair price.

1. **epulae, -ārum, f. pl.**—*feast, dinner*

2. **altilis, -is, f.**—*poultry, fattened bird*

3. **cērātus, -a, um**—*waxed* (**tabula cerata**—*waxed tablet, notepad*)

4. **sporta, -ae, f.**—*basket*

5. **lībrae, -ārum, f.pl.**—*scales*

6. **statēra, -ae, f.**—*steelyard, balance*

7. **modius, -ī, m.**—*dry measure, a peck*

8. **mensa ponderāria, -ae, f.**—*table of measures (a stone table with the standard measures cut into it to check market measures)*

LŪCRĒTIA: Licinium Duumvirum, Apollōnia, vir meus ad cēnam invītāvit et ā mē petīvit ut epulās[1] hāc nocte parēmus.

APOLLŌNIA: Accidit, domina, ut nihil in culīnā sit, nam herī dominus multōs clientīs domī hospitiō accipiēbat.

LŪCRĒTIA: Ergō tē ad Forum mittam quae holera pānemque atque piscīs altilīsque[2] emās. In tabulā cērātā[3] omnia scrīpsī.

APOLLŌNIA: Haecne sporta[4] tanta erit ut tōtum obsōnium referam?

LŪCRĒTIA: Erit; sed in Forō apud holerum vēnditōrem cavē nē pretium maius quam idōneum sit pondere vel summā holerum cōnstituat.

APOLLŌNIA: Quōmodo, domina, pretium iūstum esse sciam?

LŪCRĒTIA: Sī holera pondere vēndit, lībrās[5] vel statēram[6] spectā. Mōs est ut vēnditor malus digitum aut holera multā aquā gravia in statēram pōnat, ut sīc magnum et iniūstum pretium capiat.

APOLLŌNIA: Sī fructūs aut quicquam modiō[7] emam, quōmodo mensūrās exāminābō?

LŪCRĒTIA: In Forī angulō prō mūnicipī tabulāriō mēnsa ponderāria[8] stat. Sī modius minor tibi vidētur, fructūs vel holera in mēnsae modium pōne. Sī vēnditor bonus obsōnium bene vēndiderit, modius iūstus erit, sīn modius minor vidēbitur, aedīlem cui mēnsūrae et pondera cūrae est vocātō.

APOLLŌNIA: Nōn facile aliquid in Forō emere est, nam oculīs vigilibus opus est.

LŪCRĒTIA: Ut rectē aiunt, caveat emptor.

A. Describe in Latin what Appolonia must be careful of while shopping in the Forum, and tell how she can check the measures.

B. Answer the following questions in Latin.

1. Quem Gnaeus ad cēnam invītāvit? 2. Quantum Appolōnia in culīnā esse dīcit? 3. Ubi est mēnsa ponderāria? 4. Cui mēnsūrae et pondera cūrae sunt? 5. Cur librae vel statēra Apollōniae spectanda sunt?

Tomb relief depicting a green-grocer's shop—National Museum, Ostia

LESSON 13

Conditional Sentences

Fragment of a fresco from a building on the Palatine. Figures such as this Apollo reflect the allegories of contemporary verse writers.

YOUR LITERATURE: FIGURES OF SPEECH

I n their literature the Romans made much more common use of figures of speech than we do today. Most of these figures had been unconsciously developed, and later named, by the Greeks, so that even today we call many of them by Greek names. There are more than a hundred such names; but we will limit ourselves to a few examples.

Allegory (Greek, "an other-speaking"): A narrative in which abstract ideas figure as circumstances, events, or persons.

Alliteration (Latin, "a to-lettering"): The use of several words, consecutively or near each other, that begin with the same sound. *"Nay, for the nick of the tick of the time is a tremulous touch on the temple of terror."*

Anaphora (Greek, "a back-carrying"): The repetition of a word or phrase at the beginning of successive phrases or clauses. *"First in war, first in peace, and first in the hearts of his countrymen."*

Antithesis (Greek, "a placing opposite"): Opposition or contrast of ideas for emphasis, indicated by the positions of the contrasting words. The juxtaposition of sharply contrasting ideas in balanced or parallel words or grammatical structures. *"He for God only, she for God in him."*

Antonomasia (Greek, "a naming instead"): The substitution of an epithet or a title for a proper name, or the substitution of a personal name for a common noun. *"The Big Guy won't like that." "He's a real Benedict Arnold."*

Assonance (Latin, "a to-sounding"): Resemblance in the vowel sounds of successive or close-together words. *"Try to remember when life was so tender . . ."*

Ellipsis (Greek, "an in-leaving"): The omission of a word or words necessary to the sense. *"You'll go this way, I that."*

(Continued)

A Phrase to Use

Helluō librōrum
A bookworm (A glutton for books)

Euphemism (Greek, "a good-speaking"): The mild expression of a painful or repulsive idea. A word substituted for a taboo word. *"If anything should happen to you, this policy will take care of your loved ones."*

Hyperbole (Greek, "an over-throwing"): Exaggeration for emphasis. *"I've told you a million times, this book weighs a ton."*

Metaphor (Greek, "a bearing in exchange"): Comparison without the use of *like* or *as*. Implicit comparison or analogy. *"In the evening of life". "Her eyes are stars."*

Onomatopoeia (Greek, "a noun-making"): The formation of a word to sound like what it describes. *"Buzz, crackle"*, etc. The fitting of sound to sense in the use of words. *"The murmur of innumerable bees"*.

Rhetorical question (Greek, "an orator's question"): An affirmative statement presented in the form of a negative question, or vice versa. *"Who does not know . . .?" (= "Everyone knows . . .") "Was there ever such a man?" (= There was never such a man.)*

Simile (Latin, "a like thing"): A comparison introduced by *like* or *as* (in Latin **ut, utī, sicut, velut, velutī, quam, quot, quālis, quantus,** etc.). That to which comparison is made may be introduced by the correlative demonstrative (*so, thus, such,* etc.). *"As a duck with its eyelids, so he with his nose . . ."*

(*below*) Quintus Ennius, father of Roman epic poetry and drama

Ancient Rome Lives On . . .

Although figures of speech were used much more widely in ancient literature, examples can easily be found in modern literature. Find an example of one of these figures of speech in the Reading in this lesson.

SYNTAX

CONDITIONAL SENTENCES

As you know, conditional clauses are those introduced by some form of *if*. A sentence containing a conditional clause is called a conditional sentence.

WORDS MEANING IF

sī	*if*	sīn	
nisi	*if not, unless*	quod sī	} *but if*
etsī	*even if, although*	sīve	*or if*

sīve . . . sīve . . .
seu . . . seu . . . } *whether . . . or . . .*

Sīn is used to introduce a conditional clause following another conditional clause; otherwise **quod sī** is used.

> Sī haec manēbit, ille fēlīx erit; sīn abībit, tristis.
> *If she stays he will be happy; but if she goes he will be sad.*
> Ille fēlīx est; quod sī haec abībit, tristis erit.
> *He is happy; but if she goes he will be sad.*

In a conditional sentence the conditional clause will be referred to as *the condition,* and the principal clause *the conclusion.*

Types of Conditional Sentences

1. Indicative Conditional Sentences (You are already familiar with these, but examples are given by way of illustration.)

> Sī in urbe est apud patrem est.
> *If she is in the city she is at her father's house.*
> Sī in urbem pervēnit apud patrem est.
> *If she has arrived in the city she is at her father's house.*
>
> Sī in urbe fuit apud patrem fuit.
> *If she was in the city she was at her father's house.*
> Sī in urbem pervēnerat apud patrem fuit.
> *If she had arrived in the city she was at her father's house.*
>
> Sī in urbe crās erit apud patrem erit.
> *If she is in the city tomorrow she will be at her father's house.*

Sī in urbem crās pervēnerit apud patrem erit.
If she arrives in the city tomorrow she will be at her father's house.

Note: In English the verb of the condition is in the present tense if it is in the future or future perfect in Latin.

2. Subjunctive Conditional Sentences

   a. Should-would conditional sentences: perfect or present subjunctive in the condition, present subjunctive in the conclusion.

   Sī in urbe crās sit apud patrem sit.
   If she should be in the city tomorrow she would be at her father's house.
   Sī in urbem crās pervēnerit apud patrem sit.
   If she should arrive in the city tomorrow she would be at her father's house.

   The *if* is sometimes omitted in English: *Should she be (arrive) in the city she would be at her father's house.*

   b. Conditional sentences describing something that isn't happening or didn't happen: imperfect subjunctive in the condition and the conclusion if we are referring to the present; pluperfect subjunctive in the condition and the conclusion if we are referring to the past.

   Sī in urbe esset apud patrem esset.
   If she were in the city she would be at her father's house.
   Sī in urbe fuisset apud patrem fuisset.
   If she had been in the city she would have been at her father's house.

   The *if* is sometimes omitted in English: *Were she in the city she would be at her father's house. Had she been in the city she would have been at her father's house.*

NAMES OF CONDITIONAL SENTENCES

1. Conditional sentences using the future and/or future perfect indicative are called *Future More Vivid Conditional Sentences.*
2. Conditional sentences using the present and/or perfect subjunctive are called *Future Less Vivid Conditional Sentences.*
3. Conditional sentences using the imperfect subjunctive are called *Present Contrary-to-Fact Conditional Sentences.*
4. Conditional sentences using the Pluperfect Subjunctive are called *Past Contrary-to-Fact Conditional Sentences.*

VOCABULARY

BASIC WORDS

dignitās, dignitātis, f. *rank*
ingenium, -ī, n. *character; talent*
lacrima, -ae, f. *tear*
vulgus, -ī, n. *mob*

dulcis, -e *sweet*
iucundus, -a, -um *agreeable*
saevus, -a, -um *ferocious; cruel*

frangō, -ere, frēgī, fractum *break [to pieces]*
mereor, -ērī, -itus sum *earn, deserve*
sonō, -āre, sonuī, sonitum *[make a] sound*
vehō, -ere, vexī, vectum *transport; (passive) travel*

tandem (adv.) *at length, at last*

Notes: 1. **Vulgus** is declined like **pontus**, with an accusative singular **vulgus**, and no plural. The ablative singular is used as an adverb: **vulgō**, *publicly, commonly*.

2. The perfect participle of **mereor** is used as a noun: **meritum, -ī, n.** *merit*.

3. The ablative of means is used with the passive of **vehō**.

Equō vehitur.	*He is riding a horse.*
Nāve vehitur.	*He is coming in a ship.*

4. In questions **tandem** suggests impatience.

Quid tandem facitis?	*What on earth are you doing?* *What are you doing, pray tell?*

LEARNING ENGLISH THROUGH LATIN

dissonant	*lacking in harmony or agreement; incompatible*
divulge	*to make known, to make public; disclose, reveal*
dulcet	*soothing or pleasing to hear; sweet-sounding; melodious*
ingenious	*clever, resourceful; original and inventive*
jocund	*cheerful, pleasant, agreeable*
meritorious	*deserving reward or praise; having merit*
sonorous	*having a powerful, impressive sound; resonant*
vulgarity	*the quality of being crude, coarse, unrefined*

PRACTICE

A. A *lachrymatory* is any of the small vases found in ancient Roman sepulchers, supposed to have been used to catch the tears of mourners. Why do you suppose it is called by this name?

B. What do the following English words mean, and how are their meanings connected with that of **frangō**, from which they are all derived?

1. anfractuous   2. diffraction   3. fracas   4. fraction   5. fractious
6. fracture   7. fragile   8. fragment   9. frail   10. frangible   11. infraction   12. infringe   13. irrefragible   14. refraction   15. saxifrage

C. Pronounce and translate:

1. Sī ventus nōn esset rēmīs ūtī cōgerēmur.   2. Sī restiterīmus et hostīs expulerīmus sīcne tūtī fīāmus?   3. Nisi prīnceps sanctum vōtum solverit triumphum suprēmā victōriā nōn merēbitur.   4. Sī quis equō vehitur multō prior pervenit quam quī pedibus ambulat.   5. Sī impetum sustinēre vel flectere potuissēmus nostra legiō nōn strāta esset.   6. Sī iste amīcus honestus esset, officiīs honestē fungerētur nec falsam ratiōnem redderet.   7. Nisi Gallī vagī cornibus ācre sonuissent clāmōremque etiam peiōrem sustulissent impetum nōn metuissēmus.   8. Sīve mollibus flōribus comam tibi ornās, sīve forma vultūs tuī dulcis sine ūllīs auxiliīs aspicitur, semper mīror tē tam pulchram esse.   9. Sī quid sceleris caecī tacitīque oriēbātur dīva nūmina id per sortīs vel per vatem vel per fulmina indicābant et iustam poenam sanciēbant.   10. Huius vīta sī brevis erit ornāta decore et glōriā erit; sīn postrēmō hic domī senex quiēscat, aequus sit atque homō īnfimō locō nātus.

D. Identify any future more vivid, future less vivid, present contrary-to-fact, or past contrary-to-fact conditional sentences in C.

E. Conditional sentences are sometimes mixed, with one kind of condition and another kind of conclusion. Pronounce and translate:

1. Si quid humānum est mortāle erit.   2. Mortuus eram nisi tū mē ēripuissēs.
3. Si eum vīderim eī memorābō hoc quod mihi dīxistī.   4. Sī optimā arte opus dextimē facere didicisset opēs labōre magis augēret.   5. Etsī saxum pondere immēnsō quāsi leve esset dextrā sumpsit nōn possit per tantum flūminis spatium id conicere ut hanc rīpam tangat.

A silver plate portraying the myth of Cybele (the earth mother) and Attis. Allegorical figures decorate the outer band.

FROM THE PHILOSOPHER'S HANDBOOK . . .

Sī vīs pācem, parā bellum.
If you want peace, prepare for war.

Why would a candidate for public office consider using this saying in his or her campaign?

READING

Developing Reading Skills

Latin words which may help: **ager, arma, canō, cēdō, certō, forma, frangō, manus, mittō, nāvis,** and **vertō.**

English words which may help: *arm, auspices, condemn, convivial, corvine, deform, excogitate, intelligent, ligament, ligature, machination, mercenary, mulct, naval, pontoon, prosperous, pullet, revert,* and *successor.*

Crows and Chickens

Post Scīpiōnem Asinam victum et captum alter Cōnsul C. Duīlius sēcum putābat: "Sī certāmine nāvālī carīnās hostium rostrīs trāicere temptantēs iterum pugnāverīmus vincāmur, sīn gladiīs certābimus sine dubiō hostīs vincēmus. Mihi reperiendum est quōmodo cominus in pontō pugnētur." Ingeniōsē excōgitāvit ergō māchinātiōnem quā nāvēs inter sē iungī poterant, ponticulum clāvō ornātum quī mālō adligātus dēmittī in hostium nāvem poterat. Quia clāvus uncus rostrō avis similis mīlitibus vidēbātur, hī corvī vocātī sunt. Nāvibus sīc armātīs Poenōs proeliō nāvālī vīcit Duīlius. Ā Senātū rogātus quālem honōrem sibi prō meritīs cuperet dīxit sē Syrācūsīs aliquid iucundī vīdisse. Syrācūsānīs autem ut cēterīs Graecīs mōs erat ut post commissātiōnem iuvenēs convīvae per urbis vīcōs nocte cum fūnālibus et tībīcine canente currerent ut concentum ad cuiusdam puellae iānuam clausam facerent. Hoc Duīlius male intellegēns crēdēbat īnsīgne dīgnitātis esse. Deinde ergō per urbis viās nocte ambulāns ā tībīcine et fūnālia portantibus semper dēdūcēbātur.

Posthāc Fortūna Rōmānōs respiciēbat: Atīlius Rēgulus Cōnsul victīs nāvālī proeliō Poenīs in Āfricam cum exercitū trānsīvit. Ut aliquot proeliīs bene

5

10

15

---

2. carīnās hostium rostrīs trāicere: The metal beaks (**rostra**) of ancient warships were below the waterline, and were used to sink enemy ships by ramming.   **12. concentum ad cuiusdam puellae iānuam clausam:** a common practice among the Greeks; the serenade even had a special name, **paraclausithyron** (*beside a closed door*)

Duilius wanted to be preceded by a flute player as a sign of honor.

adversus Poenōs pugnāverat successor eī prosperē bellum gerentī ā Senātū nōn mittēbātur; id ipsum questus est per litterās ad Senātum scriptās agellum suum ā mercennāriīs dēsertum esse. Quaerente deinde Fortūnā ut magnum   20
utrīusque cāsūs exemplum in Rēgulō prōderētur, arcessitō ā Poenīs Xanthippō, Lacedaemoniōrum duce, victus proeliō et captus est. Rēs deinde ā ducibus Rōmānīs omnibus terrā marīque prosperē gestās dēformāvērunt naufragia classium. Cōnsul P. Claudius Ap. Claudī Caecī fīlius, certāmen nāvāle inceptūrus, ut auspicātus pullōs sacrōs frūmentō nōn vēscī vīdit,   25
imperāvit ut in mare iacerentur illīs verbīs, "Bibant ergō!" Itaque animī mīlitibus eius adeō dēfēcērunt ut male pugnārent, et multī interfectī sunt; classis cuncta perdita est. Claudius Rōmam reversus capitis condemnātus est. Posteā Claudia soror ā lūdīs revertēns ut turbā vulgī premēbātur saevē "Utinam frāter meus vīveret," inquit, "iterum classem duceret!" Ob eam   30
causam multa eī dicta est.

■ READING COMPREHENSION

1. What problem did Gaius Duilius have to figure out?   2. How did he solve this problem?   3. What did the term "crow" refer to?   4. What custom of the Syracusans did Duilius misunderstand and want as a mark of honor?   5. Why was the Senate not sending a successor to Regulus? 6. How did he complain about this?   7. How did Fortune exhibit in Regulus an example of both kinds of luck?   8. How did Publius Claudius react to the auspices he took before beginning his naval engagement?   9. How did this affect his soldiers' morale?   10. What happened to Claudius as a result?

---

19. **agellum ... dēsertum esse:** indirect statement governed by the idea of informing in the noun **litterās**   25. **pullōs sacrōs:** The feeding every morning of the sacred chickens was closely watched; if they refused to eat, no important undertaking, civil or military, could be done that day.

LESSON 14

Subordinate Clauses in Indirect Discourse; Conditional Sentences in Indirect Discourse

Mosaic portrait of the poet Virgil seated between the muses Clio and Melpomene. The *Aeneid* on his knee is open at the words, **"Mūsa, mihi causās memorā"**: "Muse, relate to me the reasons."

YOUR POETRY: EPIC VERSE

The major rhythms of Roman verse were established, not by a regular recurrence of accented syllables, as in English, but by arrangement of long and short syllables. A particular recurring group of long and/or short syllables is called a metrical foot. There are many different feet; but only three are used in this book:

1. THE DACTYL: a long syllable followed by two short syllables (marked — ⌣⌣)

2. THE SPONDEE: two long syllables (marked — —)

3. THE TROCHEE: a long syllable followed by a short syllable (marked — ⌣)

The various kinds of Latin poetry had their own appropriate rhythms, called meters. For example, epic was always written in dactylic hexameter (i.e. a line of six feet in a dactylic rhythm.) The Roman's favorite all-purpose meter, the elegiac couplet, alternates dactylic hexameter with dactylic pentameter (a line of five feet.)

Long Syllables

1. A syllable is long by nature if it contains a long vowel or a diphthong (**ae, au, ei, eu, oe, ui;** a vowel before a consonant **i**, as in **maior, eius, huius,** is also considered to be a diphthong).

2. A syllable is long by position if it ends in a consonant (i.e. if its vowel is followed by two or more consonants).

   a. **H** is considered to be neither a vowel nor a consonant.

   b. **Qu** and **gu** followed by a vowel are counted as one consonant each.

   c. **X** (= ks) and **z** (= dz) are counted as two consonants each.

(Continued)

Short Syllables

All syllables not long by nature or by position are short.

Common Syllables

1. **B, c, d, g, p,** or **t** followed by **l** or **r** may be treated as either two consonants or one consonant (by dividing the syllables between the two consonants). A short vowel followed by one of these combinations can make either a long or short syllable, whichever the meter requires.
2. The first person singular active personal ending **-ō** may be treated as a short vowel in verse.

Elision

A vowel, or a vowel followed by **m**, at the end of a word is usually suppressed if the following word begins with a vowel or **h**. This suppression is called elision, and the syllable is said to be elided.

Scansion

The analysis of meter is called scansion. We scan a line of verse by marking any elisions with *elision marks* (‿), marking long syllables with *macra* (—) and short syllables with *breves* (˘), and separating the feet by vertical lines.

Dactylic Hexameter

Dactylic hexameter, or epic verse, has six feet in each line. Each of the first four may be either a dactyl or a spondee; the fifth is almost always a dactyl; and the sixth is either a spondee or a trochee. A pause in the sense usually occurs in the middle of the third foot. This is called the caesura, and is marked by two vertical lines (if there is no caesura in the third foot, there may be two, one in the second and one in the fourth). Thus the pattern of dactylic hexameter is:

$$\overline{}\ \underline{\smile\smile} \mid \overline{}\ \underline{\smile\smile} \mid \overline{} \parallel \underline{\smile\smile} \mid \overline{}\ \underline{\smile\smile} \mid \overline{}\ \smile\smile \mid \overline{}\ \underline{\smile}$$

The first three verses of Dido's curse, in the Reading for this lesson, are scanned as follows:

Tum vōs | Ō Ty ri | ī ‖ stir | pem et ge nŭs | om nĕ fu | tū rum

ex er | cē te o di | īs ‖ ci ne | rī que haec | mit ti te | nost rō

mū ne ra | Nūl lus a | mor ‖ po pu | līs nec | foe de ra | sun tō

The themes of epic verse were popular subjects for decorative art. Here the Laestrygonians attack the ships of Ulysses—Vatican Library

ANCIENT ROME LIVES ON . . .

Rhythms of Roman verse were established by the arrangement of long and short syllables. What varieties of meter are found in modern poetry?

▰ SYNTAX ▰

▰ SUBORDINATE CLAUSES IN INDIRECT DISCOURSE

A subordinate clause within an indirect statement, command, or question has its verb in the subjunctive.

DIRECT STATEMENT
Mihi "Postquam ea abībit" inquit "ego eam sequar."
He says (said) to me, "After she leaves I'll follow her."

INDIRECT STATEMENT
Mihi dīcit postquam ea abeat sē eam secūtūrum esse.
He tells me that after she leaves he'll follow her.
Mihi dīxit postquam ea abīret sē eam secūtūrum esse.
He told me that after she left he'd follow her.

DIRECT COMMAND
Mihi "Postquam ego abībō" inquit "tū mē sequere."
He says (said) to me, "After I leave, you follow me."

INDIRECT COMMAND
Mē rogat ut postquam ipse abeat ego sē sequar.
He asks me to follow him after he leaves.
Mē rogāvit ut postquam ipse abīret ego sē sequerer.
He asked me to follow him after he left.

DIRECT QUESTION
Mihi "Postquam ego abībō" inquit "tūne mē sequēris?"
He says (said) to me, "After I leave, will you follow me?"

INDIRECT QUESTION
Mē rogat num postquam ipse abeat ego sē sequar.
He asks me if I'll follow him after he leaves.
Mē rogāvit num postquam ipse abīret ego sē sequerer.
He asked me if I'd follow him after he left.

If the subordinate clause is not part of the indirect statement, command, or question its verb is not changed.

DIRECT
Mihi postquam ea abiit "Ego" inquit "eam sequar."
After she left he said to me, "I shall follow her."

INDIRECT
Mihi dīxit postquam ea abiit sē eam secūtūrum esse.
He told me after she left that he would follow her.

If the clause is part of someone else's thought, however, the subjunctive must be used, even when the indirect discourse is only implied. In other words, the use of this subjunctive can tell us that the writer is reporting what was in someone else's mind.

Abiit quod patrem aspicere nōn cupiēbat.
He left because he didn't want to see his father.

Abiit quod patrem aspicere nōn cuperet.
{ *He left because, as he said, he
didn't want to see his father.
He left on the grounds that he
didn't want to see his father.* }

Note: In subordinate clauses in indirect discourse the reflexive pronoun refers back to the subject of the verb governing the indirect statement, command, or question. If the indirect discourse is only implied, the reflexive pronoun refers to the person whose thought is being expressed.

Abiit quia illa eī male faciēbat.
He left because she was treating him badly.
Abiit quia illa sibi male faceret.
He left because he felt she was treating him badly.

■ TENSES OF CLAUSES IN INDIRECT DISCOURSE

In converting an indicative subordinate clause to the subjunctive, for indirect discourse, we will often have to change the tense of the verb, as well as its mood.

INDICATIVE	SUBJUNCTIVE
Present	{ Present for present or future time
Imperfect	Imperfect for past time }
Future	
Perfect	{ Perfect for present or future time
Pluperfect	Pluperfect for past time }
Fut. Perf.	

■ CONDITIONAL SENTENCES IN INDIRECT DISCOURSE

Since the condition is a subordinate clause its verb must be in the subjunctive. Since its tense will be determined as above, there is no way to tell what kind of condition it is, simple, future, or contrary-to-fact.

When the conclusion is an indirect statement, it will have an infinitive instead of a verb.

CONCLUSIONS

DIRECT DISCOURSE VERB	INDIRECT DISCOURSE INFINITIVE
Present Indicative	Present
Imperfect Indicative Perfect Indicative Pluperfect Indicative	Perfect
Future Indicative Present Subjunctive	Future
Imperfect Subjunctive Pluperfect Subjunctive	Future with fuisse

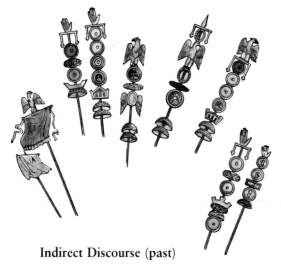

Direct Discourse:

FUTURE MORE VIVID
Sī eum vīderō salūtem dabō.
  If I see him I'll greet him.

FUTURE LESS VIVID
Sī eum vīderim salūtem dem.
  If I should see him I'd greet him.

PRESENT CONTRARY-TO-FACT
Sī eum vīderem salūtem darem.
  If I were seeing him I'd be greeting him.

PAST CONTRARY-TO-FACT
Sī eum vīdissem salūtem dedissem.
  If I had seen him I'd have greeted him.

Indirect Discourse (past)

FUTURE MORE VIVID AND FUTURE LESS VIVID
Dīxī mē sī eum vīdissem salūtem datūram.
  { *I said that if I saw him I'd greet him.*
  { *I said that if I should see him I'd greet him.*

PRESENT CONTRARY-TO-FACT
Dīxī mē sī eum vīderem salūtem datūrum fuisse.
  I said that if I were seeing him I'd be greeting him.

PAST CONTRARY-TO-FACT
Dīxī mē sī eum vīdissem salūtem datūrum fuisse.
  I said that if I had seen him I'd have greeted him.

The heroic scale of this battle scene from the Alexander mosaic matches the spirit of the epic poetry of Homer and Virgil.—Pompeii, House of the Faun

FROM THE PHILOSOPHER'S HANDBOOK . . .

Aspīrat prīmō Fortūna labōrī.
Fortune smiles upon our first effort.
—VIRGIL

Think of something you can do now with comparative ease, such as swim, tie your shoes, read a Latin sentence, or bake a cake, and think back to the first time you ever tried to do it. Did Fortune smile on your first effort? What happened? Can this also apply to your study of Indirect Discourse?

VOCABULARY

BASIC WORDS

aes, aeris, n. *copper; bronze; brass*
auris, auris, f. (i-stem) *ear*
cinis, cineris, m. *ashes*
fax, facis, f. *torch*
latus, lateris, n. *side, flank*
līmen, līminis, n. *threshold*
mōlēs, mōlis, f. (i-stem) *mass, heap;
  difficulty*

os, ossis, n. *bone*
ōtium, -ī, n. *leisure, peace*
praemium, -ī, n. *reward*

blandus, -a, -um *flattering; alluring*
niger, nigra, nigrum *black*

Note: Because the original money was made of bronze, **aes aliēnum** means *debt*.

Translation Help

Remember that in the third and fourth conjugations two forms of the future indicative are identical with two forms of the present subjunctive: the first person singular, active and passive. Likewise in all conjugations two forms of the future perfect indicative are identical with two forms of the perfect subjunctive: the third person singular and plural active. This sometimes makes it impossible to distinguish between different kinds of subordinate clauses.

Id sī inveniam tibi reddam.
> *If I find it I'll return it to you.*
> *If I should find it I would return it to you.*

Usually, however, one of the verbs will not be ambiguous.

Id sī inveniam tibi dabō. *If I find it, I'll give it to you.*
Id sī inveniam tibi dem. *If I should find it, I would give it to you.*

In indirect discourse, since all subordinate clauses must be in the subjunctive, the distinction breaks down, and context is the only guide.

Dīxī mē id sī invenīrem illī datūrum.
> *I said that if I found it I would give it to him.*
> *I said that if I should find it I would give it to him.*

■ LEARNING ENGLISH THROUGH LATIN

aural	*received through one's sense of hearing or through the ear*
bilateral	*having or involving two sides; affecting both sides equally; reciprocal*
bland	*pleasantly smooth, agreeable; mild*
blandishments	*flattery or ingratiating remarks meant to persuade*
incinerate	*to burn to ashes, burn up, cremate*
negotiate	*to confer, bargain with a view to reaching an agreement*
otiose	*useless, ineffective, superfluous*
subliminal	*below the threshold of conscious perception*

Fresco of the myth of Perseus and Andromeda, from Pompeii. The frequent depiction of Greek mythological scenes in Roman painting reflects the Romans' love of these stories, which were enhanced by the poetry of Ovid.

PRACTICE

A.   What is the meaning of the following sentences?

1. The medicine was not at all harsh; in fact it was quite bland.   2. The conference was not very worthwhile: there were just too many otiose remarks and suggestions.   3. Representatives of the two nations worked through the night to draw up a bilateral trade agreement.   4. Subliminal advertising in television and films is effective but illegal.   5. The final test in the foreign language classes stressed oral/aural skills.   6. The student council felt that it was important to negotiate the matter with the school administration. 7. Do not throw anything in the dumpster that cannot be incinerated. 8. Let's try some blandishments on them to see if they'll vote for the measure.

B.   Convert the following direct statements into indirect statements governed by **dīcit** or **negat**; then pronounce and translate.

EXAMPLE: Mihi "Dedistī mihi" inquit "quod tibi fuit." Dīcit mē sibi dedisse quod mihi fuerit.   *He says that I gave him what I had.*

1. "Nisi Cōnsulī" inquit "propior cōnstiterō vox eius aurīs meās nōn continget."   2. "Ille" inquit "qui vetustior erat nōn diūtius poterat sustinēre tantam ferrī mōlem."   3. "Sī arma" inquit "ex ferrō vel aere facta sumpsissent tot vulnera nōn acciperent."   4. "Sī ad vīllam" inquit "fretō proximam ambulēs, videās sinum minōrem quidem istō sed iucundissimum aspectū."   5. "Veritus essem" inquit "in vacuum et dēsertum templum Dīs Īnferīs sanctum īre nisi pudor mē iussisset."

C.   Convert the direct statements in B into indirect statements governed by **dīxit** or **nēgāvit**; then pronounce and translate:

EXAMPLE: Mihi "Dedistī mihi" inquit "quod tibi fuit." Dīxit mē sibi dedisse quod mihi fuisset.   *He said that I had given him what I had.*

D.   Convert the following direct commands into indirect commands governed by **rogat**; then pronounce and translate:

EXAMPLE: Mihi "Da mihi" inquit "quod tibi est." Mē rogat ut sibi dem quod mihi sit.   *He asks me to give him what I have.*

1. Tibi "Domum" inquit "venī simul atque sōl occidit."   2. Nōbīs "Maius praemium prō meritīs" inquit "huic reddite qui salūtī vōbīs fuit."

3. Mihi "Dēsine" inquit "pessima exempla ostendere nisi līberōs improbissimōs tibi esse cupis." **4.** Illī "Priusquam" inquit "ad ultimās terrās abīs veterrimum amīcum iubē valēre." **5.** "Quia saepissimē," inquit "Dī Superī, mūnera haud minima vestrīs ārīs attulī plūraque vōvī, mihi date et voluptātēs et ōtium ut quam diūtissimē illīs fruar."

E. Convert the direct commands in D into indirect commands governed by **rogāvit**; then pronounce and translate:

EXAMPLE: Mihi "Da mihi" inquit "quod tibi est." Mē rogāvit ut sibi darem quod mihi esset. *He asked me to give him what I had.*

F. Convert the following direct questions into indirect questions governed by **rogat**; then pronounce and translate:

EXAMPLE: Mihi "Dabisne mihi" inquit "quod tibi est?" Mē rogat num sibi datūrum sim quod mihi esset. *He asks me if I will give him what I have.*

1. Eīs "Nāvigāvistisne" inquit "ad Graeciam saepius quam equīs vectī estis?" **2.** Nōbīs "Quandō" inquit "dēsinētis fallere eōs quibus impōnere tam facile est?" **3.** Mihi "Cūr tantam" inquit "pecūniam semper pendis, quamobrem aes aliēnum tibi semper crēscit?" **4.** Magistrō "Nōnne sunt" inquit "in tam immēnsō mundō aliae tellūrēs ubi hominēs aliēnī vīsū habitant?" **5.** "Utrum potius cupit," inquit "sermōnem iucundum inter amīcōs mentis voluptātem, an tecta opibus plēna, quae corporī sōlī placent?"

G. Convert the direct questions in G into indirect questions governed by **rogāvit**; then pronounce and translate:

EXAMPLE: Mihi "Dabisne mihi" inquit "quod tibi est?" Mē rogāvit num sibi datūrum essem quod mihi esset. *He asked me if I would give him what I had.*

H. Pronounce and translate, trying to find ways in English to show the difference between very similar sentences:

1. Ait sē ad Ītaliam itūram ubi apud frātrem mānsūra sit quī Rōmae habitet.
2. Ait sē ad Ītaliam itūram ubi apud frātrem mānsūra sit quī Rōmae habitat.
3. Ait sē ad Ītaliam itūram ubi apud frātrem mānsūra est quī Rōmae habitat.
4. Hūc mox redībit quod sē domō abesse doleat.
5. Hūc mox redībit quod eam domō abesse dolet.

READING

Developing Reading Skills

Latin words which will help: **agō, blandus, cēdō, contrā, custōs, eō, faciō, mōveō, mūtō, nāvis, optō, orior, pēs, potēns, puer, pugnō, sacer, sentiō,** and **teneō.**

English words which will help: *adolescent, adult, blandishment, colonist, contrary, elephant, extirpate, federal, impetrate, imprecation, initial, naval, obtain, odious, odium, os, pedestrian, puerile, regress, sacrifice, sentence,* and *undulate.*

A Promise and a Curse Fulfilled

Ubi Fortūna Carthāginiēnsibus nōn iam favēbat Atīlius Rēgulus ille quī captus ā Xanthippō erat missus est ab eīs ad Senātum ut dē pāce et, sī eam nōn posset impetrāre, dē commūtandīs captīvīs ageret. Coactus est iūrāre reditūrum sē sī commūtārī captīvōs nōn placuisset. Ut Rōmam pervēnit
5 inductus in Senātum dīxit sē dēsiisse Senātōrem esse ex illā diē quā in potestātem Poenōrum vēnisset. Tum Rōmānīs persuāsit nē pācem cum Carthāginiēnsibus facerent, illōs enim tot casibus fractōs spem nūllam nisi in pāce habēre, nēve captīvōs commūtārent, nam tantī nōn esse ut tot mīlia captīvōrum propter sē ūnum et paucōs quī ex Rōmānīs captī essent
10 redderentur. Haec sententia obtinuit. In Āfricam fidē custōdītā regressus igitur saevissimīs suppliciīs periit. Mox tamen post magnum proelium nāvāle apud Lilybaeum pāx Poenīs petentibus data est, quā Poenī nōn sōlum Siciliā et Sardiniā et cēterīs īnsulīs inter Ītaliam Āfricamque dēcessērunt sed etiam omnī Hispāniā cītrā Ibērum.

---

3. posset: represents **potes** or **possīs** in direct discourse; this is implied indirect discourse, as being part of the instructions the Carthaginians gave him **5. illā diē: diēs** is feminine when it denotes an official or legal date **8. tantī:** gen. of indefinite value **11. saevissimīs:** The usual Carthaginian method of execution was by impalement, a slow death.

Sed nōndum explēta erat Dīdōnis moritūrae imprecātiō quam rēgīna apud   15
Vergilium dīxisse fertur:

> Tum vōs, Ō Tyriī, stirpem et genus omne futūrum
> exercēte odiīs, cinerīque haec mittite nostrō
> mūnera. Nūllus amor populīs nec foedera suntō.
> Exoriāre aliquis nostrīs ex ossibus ultor   20
> quī face Dardaniōs ferrōque sequēre colōnōs,
> nunc, ōlim, quōcumque dabunt sē tempore vīrēs.
> Lītora lītoribus contrāria, fluctibus undās
> imprecor, arma armīs: pugnent ipsīque nepōtēsque.

Ultor quem Elissa exoptābat Hannibal futūrus fuit, dē quō fāma est eum   25
annōrum ferē novem puerīliter blandientem patrī Hamilcarī ut ducerētur in
Hispāniam, quō exercitum traiectūrus sacrificābat, ārīs admōtum tāctīs sacrīs
iūre iūrandō adāctum sē simul atque adolēvisset hostem fore populō Rōmānō.
Hic agēns annum vīcēsimum septimum aetātis Saguntum, Hispāniae cīvitātem
Rōmānīs amīcam, oppugnāre aggressus est, id quod secundī bellī Pūnicī   30
initium fēcit. Saguntīnīs victīs Hannibal Pȳrēnaeōs montīs et Alpīs trānsiit
cum octōgintā mīlibus peditum et vīgintī mīlibus equitum et septem et
trīgintā elephantīs. Tandem tribus exercitibus Rōmānīs victīs ad Cannās in
Āpūliam pervēnit.

READING COMPREHENSION

1. Why was Regulus sent to the Senate?   2. What was he compelled to
swear?   3. What did he say when he was brought before the Senate?
4. What did he persuade the Romans *not* to do, and why?   5. When he
had kept his word, what happened to Regulus?   6. On what terms was
peace granted to the Carthaginians when they asked for it?   7. "Exoriāre
aliquis nostrīs ex ossibus ultor quī face Dardaniōs ferrōque sequēre colōnōs."
Where is this quotation from?   8. Who was the avenger Dido was longing
for destined to be?   9. What oath did he take at the age of nine?   10. What
does the following refer to? "cum octōgintā mīlibus peditum et vīgintī
mīlibus equitum et septem et trīgintā elephantīs"

---

19. suntō: Future Imperative 3d person plural   20. exoriāre = exoriāris   21. sequēre =
sequēris   24. nepōtēsque: the -que will not fit into the hexameter; in context it elides with
the next verse, which begins Haec ait   28. iūre iūrandō: iūs iūrandum is the Latin idiom
for *oath*. adāctum = adāctum esse

LESSON 15

Extended Indirect Discourse

The legendary poet Orpheus charming wild beasts with his song. The original lyres were made of tortoise shells and antelope horns—mosaic floor from Sicily

ELEGIAC AND HENDECASYLLABIC

The Romans' favorite all-purpose meter, the elegiac couplet, alternates dactylic hexameter with dactylic pentameter. A pentameter is a line of five feet, although in this case it is made up of two halves of two and a half feet each. The pentameter is made by removing the second half of the third foot and the second half of the sixth foot of the hexameter:

$$ \overline{}\smile\smile \mid \overline{}\smile\smile \mid \overline{} \parallel \overline{}\smile\smile \mid \overline{}\smile\smile \mid \overline{} $$

The first two feet can be either dactyls or spondees; the two full feet of the second half are always dactyls. A word always ends at the caesura in the middle. The elegiac couplet was the favorite meter for graffiti; for example, when Nero was building the Golden House, which was spreading over more and more of the city, the following couplet appeared everywhere:

> Rōma fit ūna domus. Vēiōs migrāte, Quirītēs,
> Sī nōn et Vēiōs occupat illa domus!

This is scanned:

> Rō ma fit | ū na do | mus ‖ Vē | iōs mig | rā te, Qui | rī tēs,
> Sī nōn | et Vē | iōs ‖ oc cu pat | il la do | mus

You might like to translate and scan a favorite graffito found in several places in Pompeii:

> Admīror, pariēs, tē nōn cecidisse ruīnā,
> Quī tot scriptōrum taedia sustineās!

A mediaeval elegiac couplet is supposed to represent the speeches of Cain and Abel. It is a curiosity because the pentameter has the same words as the hexameter (in reverse order), yet it is of course shorter by two half-feet. If you memorize it it will help you remember about common syllables.

(Continued)

A PHRASE TO USE

Poēta nāscitur, nōn fit.
The poet is born, not made.

Sacrum pingue dabō; nōn macrum sacrificābō.
  Sacrificābo macrum; nōn dabo pingue sacrum.

$$\overline{}\ \overline{}\ |\ \overline{}\ \cup\ \cup\ |\ \overline{}\ \overline{}\ ||\ \overline{}\ |\ \overline{}\ \overline{}\ |\ \overline{}\ \cup\ \cup\ |\ \overline{}\ \overline{}$$

Sac rum | pin gue da | bō || nōn | mac rum | sac ri fi | cā bō.

$$\overline{}\ \cup\ \cup\ |\ \overline{}\ \cup\ \cup\ |\ \overline{}\ ||\ \overline{}\ \cup\ \cup\ |\ \overline{}\ \cup\ \cup\ |\ \overline{}$$

  Sac ri fi | cā bo ma | crum || nōn da bo | pin gue sa | crum.

Another popular meter, often used for epigrams and other witty poems, is the hendecasyllabic (11-syllable) verse, also called the Phalaecean, made up of the same three kinds of feet as the others, spondee, dactyl, and trochee.

$$\overline{}\ \overline{}\ |\ \overline{}\ \cup\ \cup\ |\ \overline{}\ \cup\ |\ \overline{}\ \cup\ |\ \underset{=}{\overline{}}\ \cup$$

The poet Catullus uses hendecasyllables to complain to his friend Furius that the storm which threatens his country place comes from a mortgage, not a wind:

> Fūrī, vīllula nostra nōn ad Austrī
> flātūs opposita est neque ad Favōnī
> nec saevī Boreae aut Apēliōtae,
> vērum ad mīlia quīndecim et ducentōs—
> ō ventum horribilem atque pestilentem!

The first verse is scanned as follows. You may wish to practice on the others.

$$\overline{}\ \overline{}\ |\ \overline{}\ \cup\ \cup\ |\ \overline{}\ \cup\ |\ \overline{}\ \cup\ |\ \overline{}\ \overline{}$$

Fū rī | vīl lu la | nos tra | nōn ad | Aus trī

(*below*) Cupid, shown here with the attributes of Bacchus, represents the trials and delights of love, the predominant themes of elegiac poetry.

ANCIENT ROME LIVES ON . . .

Scribbling on public surfaces was quite common in Roman times. Where do we find such graffiti today?

SYNTAX

EXTENDED INDIRECT DISCOURSE

Latin authors use indirect discourse much more frequently than is common in modern American English, sometimes indirectly reporting speeches which go on for pages. Any verb which governs indirect discourse may introduce such a passage, and when the discourse changes from statement to command or question, no new verb is provided. To make a less awkward translation it is usually necessary to render such speeches as direct discourse in English. Therefore it is useful to know how to convert longer speeches in direct discourse to indirect, and vice versa.

EXTENDED INDIRECT DISCOURSE

DIRECT DISCOURSE	INDIRECT DISCOURSE
Indicative Statement Potential Subjunctive	Indirect Statement
Imperative Jussive Subjunctive Hortatory Subjunctive Optative Subjunctive	Indirect Command
Indicative Question Deliberative Subjunctive	Indirect Question
Indicative Subordinate Clause Subjunctive Subordinate Clause	Subjunctive Subordinate Clause

TENSES IN INDIRECT DISCOURSE

Since all verbs in indirect discourse are in the subjunctive, there are only four tenses to choose from, instead of six. The choice is further restricted by the fact that the present and perfect subjunctive can be used only when the action of the sentence is in the present or future (primary sequence), and the imperfect and pluperfect only when the action is in the past (secondary sequence). The choice between the present and the perfect, or between the imperfect and the pluperfect, is determined by the nature of the action: if it is or was already completed at the time of the sentence, the perfect or pluperfect must be used; otherwise the present or imperfect must be used. Study the following paraphrase of Dido's curse, in both direct and indirect discourse:

Dīdō "Tum vōs," inquit, "Ō Tyriī, prōlem et omne genus futūrum agitāte inīmicitiīs, cinerīque haec mittite nostrō mūnera. Sit nūllus amor populīs nec amīcitia. Oriāris aliquis nostrīs ex ossibus quī face Dardaniōs ferrōque sequēris fugientīs, nunc, ōlim, quōcumque dabunt sē tempore vīrēs. Nōnne erunt lītora lītoribus contrāria, fluctibus fluctūs, arma armīs? Pugnābunt ipsīque nepōtēsque."

Dīdō ā Tyriīs petīvit ut prōlem eius et omne genus futūrum agitārent inīmicitiīs, cinerīque ea mitterent suō mūnera. Nē esset ūllus amor populīs nēve amīcitia. Orīrētur aliquis suīs ex ossibus quī face Dardaniōs ferrōque sequerētur fugientīs, tunc, ōlim, quōcumque darent sē tempore vīrēs. Num lītora futūra nōn essent lītoribus contrāria, fluctibus fluctūs, arma armīs? Pugnātūrōs ipsōsque nepōtēsque.

Dido said, "Then you, O Tyrians, harass with enmities his descendants and all his race to be, and send my ashes these funeral gifts. May the nations have no love nor friendship. May someone arise from my bones, you who will pursue the fleeing Dardanians with fire and sword, now, some day, at whatever time the strength will present itself. Will not shores be opposed to shores, waves to waves, arms to arms? They themselves will fight, and so will their descendants."

Dido begged the Tyrians to harass with enmities his descendants and all his race to be, and to send her ashes those funeral gifts. ⟨She prayed that⟩ the nations should have no love nor friendship ⟨and that⟩ someone arise from her bones who would pursue the fleeing Dardanians with fire and sword, then, some day, at whatever time the strength would present itself. ⟨She asked⟩ if shores would not be opposed to shores, waves to waves, arms to arms ⟨and said that⟩ they themselves would fight, and so would their descendants.

A detailed mosaic in tiny tesserae of doves, birds sacred to Venus— Capitoline Museum, Rome

VOCABULARY

BASIC WORDS

cultus, -ūs, m. *adornment, dress;
education; reverence*
digitus, -ī, m. *finger; toe*
dīvitiae, -ārum, f. *wealth, riches*
fūnus, fūneris, n. *funeral*
iūdex, iūdicis, m. *juryman, judge*
sacerdōs, sacerdōtis, m. or f. *priest,
priestess*
spīritus, -ūs, m. *breath; life; spirit;
courage*

commūnis, -e *common, shared*
superbus, -a, -um *haughty, arrogant*

experior, -īrī, expertus sum *test;
experience*
gignō, -ere, genuī, genitum *beget; give
birth to*
licet, -ēre, licuit, licitum *it is permitted*
(w. dat. and infin.)

Notes: 1. **Cultus,** when it means *adornment* or *dress,* refers to clothing, hair style,
accessories—all of what we colloquially call "a get-up."

2. *Licet* is given in the 3d person because it is always used impersonally

Mihi īre licuit.
I was permitted to go (To go was permitted to me).

FROM THE PHILOSOPHER'S HANDBOOK . . .

Struit īnsidiās lacrimīs
cum fēmina plōrat.
*When a woman weeps,
she is setting traps with her tears.*
—DIONYSIUS CATO

What is meant by this statement? Do you believe it is true?

■ LEARNING ENGLISH THROUGH LATIN

adjudicate	*to serve as a judge*
communal	*shared by all; public*
congenital	*existing as such at birth*
digit	*a finger or toe; any numeral from 0 to 9 (so called because they can be counted on one's fingers)*
funereal	*gloomy, dismal; suitable for a funeral*
illicit	*prohibited, unauthorized, unlawful*
judicious	*having sound judgment, wise and careful*
progeny	*lineage, descendants, offspring*

▬ PRACTICE ▬

A. Show the relationship of the following words to the Latin **commūnis, -e**: *commune, communicable, communicate, communion, communism, community*.

B. Show the relationship of the following words to the Latin **spīritus, -ūs, m.**: *spirit, spirited, spiritual, spirituous*.

C. In law, the exclusive right of the eldest son to inherit his father's estate is called *primogeniture*. Show the Latin derivation of this word.

D. Sophonisba's appeal, lines 18–31 of the Reading "A Prisoner's Last Wish" would read as follows in direct discourse:

"Deī et tua virtūs" inquit "effēcērunt ut omnia quidem in mē possīs; sed sī captīvae apud dominum vītae mortisque suae vōcem supplicem mittere licet, sī genua, sī victrīcem attingere dextram, precor quaerōque per maiestātem rēgiam in quā paulō ante ego quoque fuī, per gentis Numidārum nōmen quod tibi cum Syphāce commūne fuit, per huius rēgiae deōs quōs spērō tē acceptūrōs meliōribus omnibus quam Syphācem hinc mīserint, hanc veniam supplicī dēs ut ipse quodcumque feret animus dē captīvā tuā statuās neque mē in cuiusquam Rōmānī superbum et crūdēle arbitrium venīre sinās. Sī nihil aliud quam Syphācis uxor fuissem, tamen Numidae atque in eādem mēcum Āfricā genitī magis quam aliēnigenae et externī fidem experīrī optārem; vidēs quid Carthāginiēnsī ab Rōmānō timendum sit. Sī nūllā rē aliā potes, morte mē vindicā ab Rōmānōrum arbitriō. Āfricaene grātiā commūnis parentis hoc beneficium mihi dabis?"

Now convert the following passage of indirect discourse into direct discourse, using **inquit** as the governing verb.

Eques iūdicēs rogāvit ut sē audīrent: crīmen quod ille (*change to iste*) inimīcus suus sibi intulisset falsum esse. Ubi ille esset tum cum cēterī eius (*change to huius*) ordinis ferē cunctī prō patriā pugnārent (*change to 1st person*)? Ōstenderet ille sibi vulnera illīus, sī ūlla habēret. Sē autem postquam hostēs saevum impetum et in latus et in tergum fēcissent, tum cum tellūs sangine nigra esset et quāsī tecta corporibus membrīsque suōrum (*use nostrōrum*) quae lātē longēque per campum strāta essent, omnia perīcula expertum esse nec pugnāre cessāvisse.

E. Convert the following passage of direct discourse into indirect discourse, beginning **Rēgīnam virum rogāvit.** (See example in **D.**)

Rēgīna virō "Cūr mē relīquistī?" inquit, "Nōnne potuistī aliquam moram dare? Ego tē ex flūctibus tum cum maris perīculīs labōrābās ēripuī, tuōs sociōs aluī, tibi rēgnum meum dīvīsī. Cūr tacēs? Loquere mihi, sī potes. Saepissimē mihi fidem prōmīsistī; iam nunc tē honestum esse dēmōnstrā. Homo quī honestus vocārī merētur amīcōs non fallit; amāns fēminae quam dīligit nōn impōnit. Vidē meās lacrimās quae semel modo virum flēvī atque hīc manē."

F. Translate into Latin:

The teacher said to the young man, "What do you want most [importantly] for yourself? Riches? Believe me: becoming wealthy is not the highest good of human life, which has been given to man so that he may aim at higher ends. How will resources be useful to your bones and ashes at that time when our common fate will befall you? After your funeral your immense house, your haughty style (*cultus*), so many gold coins will be worth nothing. You were wrong wishing for riches; henceforth seek things which are healthful to the heart, mind, and spirit."

G. Convert the above passage (in F) of direct discourse into indirect discourse.

Greco-Roman mosaic of dolphins. Such decor was frequently employed on the floors of luxurious houses—Roman Quarter, Delos

READING

Developing Reading Skills

Latin words which will help: **aliēnus, arma, bene, cōnstituō, currō, emō, faciō, ferō, gignō, instituō, maior, māter, necesse, rēx, socius, tangō,** and **victor.**

English words which will help: *anular, arbitrate, arm, benefit, cruel, external, extract, genuflect, imprecation, majesty, matrimony, necessary, offer, omen, redeem, regal, respond, society, statute, suppliant,* and *venial.*

A Prisoner's Last Wish

Proeliō apud Cannās Cōnsulēs ambō victī sunt, ē quibus ūnus occīsus est. Occīsa quoque sunt mīlitum quadrāgintā mīlia, ita ut rēs Rōmāna paene perīret. Hannibal cōpiam captīvōs redimendī obtulit Rōmānīs, quī respond-ērunt eōs cīvīs quī armātī capī potuissent nōn esse necessāriōs. Hōs omnīs
5 captīvōs ille posteā variīs suppliciīs interfēcit, et trīs modiōs ānulōrum aureōrum Carthāginem mīsit quōs manibus Equitum et Senātōrum mortuō-rum dētrāxerat.

Annō decimō tertiō postquam in Ītaliam Hannibal vēnit P. Cornēlius Scīpiō Cōnsul creātus est, quī posterō annō in Āfricam missus est. Ibi
10 societātem facere temptāvit cum Syphāce rēge Numidārum Massaesȳlōrum, cui contrā Poenōs pugnantī Scīpiōnis pater auxiliō fuerat. Syphāx autem ut amōre pulcherrimae Pūnicae Sophonisbae raptus erat quam postquam in mātrimōnium dūxit socius Poenōrum factus est. Scīpiō ergō societātem fēcit cum Masinissā rēge Numidārum Massȳlōrum cui Syphāx Poenōrum auxiliō
15 rēgnī partem cēperat. Auxiliō Rōmānōrum Masinissa Syphācem vīcit et in vinculīs Cirtam oppidum rēgium Massaesȳlōrum rettulit. Sophonisba vīsō procul marītō victō vinctōque Masinissae in ipsō līmine occurrit et dīxit deōs et illīus virtūtem effēcisse ut ille omnia quidem in sē posset; sed sī captīvae apud dominum vītae mortisque suae vōcem supplicem mittere

A Roman bust of an African prisoner—Djemila, Algeria

licēret, sī genua, sī victrīcem attingere dextram, sē precārī quaerereque per   20
maiestātem rēgiam in quā paulō ante ipsa quoque fuisset, per gentis
Numidārum nōmen quod illī cum Syphāce commūne fuisset, per eius rēgiae
deōs quōs spērāret illum acceptūrōs meliōribus ōminibus quam Syphācem
inde mīsissent, eam veniam supplicī daret ut ipse quodcumque ferret animus
dē captīvā ipsīus statueret nēve sē in cuiusquam Rōmānī superbum et crūdēle   25
arbitrium venīre sineret. Sī nihil aliud atque Syphācis uxor fuisset, sē tamen
Numidae atque in eādem sēcum Āfricā genitī magis quam aliēnigenae et
externī fidem experīrī optātūram fuisse; illum vidēre quid Carthāginiēnsī ab
Rōmānō timendum esset. Sī nūllā rē aliā posset, morte sē vindicāret ab
Rōmānōrum arbitriō. Num Āfricae grātiā commūnis parentis id beneficium   30
sibi daret?

READING COMPREHENSION

1. What battle, because of the great number of casualties, nearly brought
Rome to an end?   2. What opportunity did Hannibal offer the Romans?
3. After they refused, what did Hannibal do?   4. Why did Syphax, the
king of the Massaesylian Nomads, become an ally of Carthage?   5. Who
was the king of the Massylian Nomads?   6. What happened to Syphax?
7. What did Sophonisba mean by saying, "Sī genua, sī victrīcem attingere
dextram . . . "?   8. What was the prisoner's last wish?

---

20. genua: It was customary for a suppliant to embrace the knees of the person of whom he
or she was asking mercy.   **24. ut:** introducing a substantive clause of result in apposition
with **veniam. ferret animus:** *his mind might bring forth* = *he might think of*

LESSON 16

Volō, Nōlō, Mālō, Edō; Prohibitions

This 3d century mosaic shows an allegory of the month of March. In front of a statue of Mars, three cult-followers are tanning a wild boar hide—Museo Borghese, Rome

IF YOU LIVED IN ANCIENT ROME . . .

YOUR CALENDAR

Roman time measurement may seem difficult to us. The first day of the month was called **Kalendae** (from the verb **calāre**, *to summon*), the day on which the Pontifices called an assembly of the People (**Comitia Calāta**) to announce the new moon, from which the other days were reckoned. The halfway point of the month, the full moon, was called **Īdūs** (related to the verb **dīvidere**, *to divide*). The eighth day before the Ides was called **Nōnae** (meaning *ninth*; but the Romans counted both ends of a series). The Nones fell on the seventh of March, May, July, and October, and on the fifth of the other months. The Ides fell on the fifteenth of March, May, July, and October, and on the thirteenth of the other months.

The days within a month were numbered by counting backward from the next named day, so that March 11, for example, would be expressed as "the fifth day before the Ides." The idiom is **ante diem quīntum Īdūs Mārtiōs**, the name of the month being an adjective modifying **Īdūs.** Such a phrase is usually abbreviated; this one would be **a.d.V.Īd. Mārt.**

A.d.V Īd.Mārt. imperātōrī novissimus diēs erat.
March 11 was the commander's last day.

All the dates of the second half of a month are thus identified by the name of the next month: e.g. December 25 would be called **a.d.VII Kal.Iān.**

The day before one of the named days is **prīdiē Kalendās, prīdiē Nōnās, prīdiē Īdūs** (abbreviated **pr.Kal., pr.Nōn., pr.Īd.**); the day before that is **a.d.III Kal., a.d.III Nōn., a.d.III Īd.**, again because the Romans counted both ends of a series. May 30 would be **a.d.III Kal.Iūn.**

In a leap year (leap years were instituted by Julius Caesar) February 24 was counted twice: in other words it was **a.d.VI Kal.Mārt.** for two days in a row. To avoid confusion, the second one would be **a.d.VI Kal.Mārt.bīs.**

The names of the months are all adjectives: **Iānuārius, -a, -um; Februārius;**

(Continued)

185

A PHRASE TO USE

ad Kalendās Graecās
(*at the Greek Kalends*) Since this
term was used only by the Romans,
at the Greek Kalends is an emphatic
way of saying "*never!*"

-a, -um; Mārtius, -a, -um; Aprīlis, -e; Māius, -a, -um; Iūnius, -a, -um; Quīntīlis, -e (later Iūlius, -a, -um); Sextīlis, -e (later Augustus, -a, -um); September, Septembris, Septembre; Octōber, Octōbris, Octōbre; November, Novembris, Novembre; December, Decembris, Decembre; and Mercēdōnius, -a, -um (a month inserted occasionally, before the Julian Calendar, when the 355-day year got too much out of synchronization with the seasons). The numbered months reflect the early times before King Numa Pompilius added January and February to the year.

Year dates are given by naming the two Consuls of that year in an ablative absolute:

> Hoc factum est Kalendīs Sextīlibus Caesare et Bibulō Cōnsulibus.
> *This happened on 1 August, 56 B.C.*

The abbreviation would be **Caesare Bibulō Coss.** This system of identifying years is much less convenient than numbering them; but until the Romans figured out, toward the end of the Republic, that the city had been founded in 753 B.C., they had nothing to date from. Even after that, conservatism made them stick, in official dating, to the names of Consuls.

The Romans had two kinds of week. In the religious week the days were named after the sun, moon, and planets: **diēs Sōlis, diēs Lūnae, diēs Mārtis, diēs Mercūriī, diēs Iōvis, diēs Veneris,** and **diēs Sāturni.** Besides this seven-day religious week there was also an eight-day commercial week, which the Romans, counting both ends, called a nine-day week. A market would be held in any market town every eighth day; the market was called **nūndīnae, -ārum, f.,** from **novem + diēs.** The days of the nundinal week were not named, but each one was identified in any community by the name of the nearby town where market was held on that day.

(*above*) A fragment of a Roman calendar on stone from Amiternum—Museo Romano, L'Aquila   (*left*) A Roman calendar with months numbered in the Greek manner; days of the week; and the signs of the zodiac   (*below*) The sun god in his chariot surrounded by the zodiac signs by which the Romans often marked the passage of the seasons

ANCIENT ROME LIVES ON . . .

"Beware the Ides of March" is an expression often quoted today that comes to us from the time of Julius Caesar. What does it mean?

FORMS

VOLŌ, NŌLŌ, MĀLŌ, AND EDŌ

Volō, velle, voluī, ____ (*wish, be willing*) and its compounds nōlō, nōlle, nōluī, ____ (*not wish, be unwilling*) and mālō, mālle, māluī, ____ (*wish more, wish rather*) and edō, ēsse, ēdī, ēsum (*eat*) are all irregular in the present system.

CONJUGATION OF VOLO, NOLO, MALO, AND EDO

INDICATIVE

PRESENT

volō	volumus	nōlō	nōlumus	mālō	mālumus	edō	edimus
vīs	vultis	nōn vīs	nōn vultis	māvīs	mavultis	ēs	ēstis
vult	volunt	nōn vult	nōlunt	māvult	mālunt	ēst	edunt

IMPERFECT

volēbam	volēbāmus	nōlēbam	nōlēbāmus	mālēbam	mālēbāmus	edēbam	edēbāmus
volēbās	volēbātis	nōlēbās	nōlēbātis	mālēbās	mālēbātis	edēbās	edēbātis
volēbat	volēbant	nōlēbat	nōlēbant	mālēbat	mālēbant	edēbat	edēbant

FUTURE

volam	volēmus	nōlam	nōlēmus	mālam	mālēmus	edam	edēmus
volēs	volētis	nōlēs	nōlētis	mālēs	mālētis	edēs	edētis
volet	volent	nōlet	nōlent	mālet	mālent	edet	edent

SUBJUNCTIVE

PRESENT

velim	velīmus	nōlim	nōlīmus	mālim	mālīmus	edim	edīmus
velīs	velītis	nōlīs	nōlītis	mālīs	mālītis	edīs	edītis
velit	velint	nōlit	nōlint	mālit	mālint	edit	edint

Subjunctive Continued

IMPERFECT

vellem	vellēmus	nōllem	nōllēmus	māllem	māllēmus	ederem	ēssēmus
vellēs	vellētis	nōllēs	nōllētis	māllēs	māllētis	ēssēs	ēssētis
vellet	vellent	nōllet	nōllent	māllet	māllent	ēsset	ēssent

IMPERATIVE

PRESENT

——	——	nōlī	nōlīte	——	——	ēs	ēste

PARTICIPLE

volēns	nōlēns	——	edēns

These four verbs are all regular in the perfect system.

SYNTAX

■ VOLŌ AND ITS COMPOUNDS

Like other verbs of wishing (e.g. **cupiō**), **volō**, **nōlō**, and **mālō** may take a direct object, an objective infinitive, or an infinitive phrase—i.e. accusative, infinitive, or both.

Hoc volō.   *I want this.*

Hoc facere volō.   *I want to do this.*

Tē hoc facere volō.   *I want you to do this.*

Hoc nōlō.   *I don't want this.*

Hoc facere nōlō.   *I don't want to do this.*

Tē hoc facere nōlō.   *I don't want you to do this.*

Hoc mālō.   *I prefer this.*

Hoc facere mālō.   *I prefer to do this.*

Tē hoc facere mālō.   *I prefer you to do this.*

Mālō, as a compound of **magis** and **volō,** often has a **quam.**

Hoc malō quam illud.   *I want this more than that.*
Hoc facere malō quam illud.   *I want to do this rather than that.*
Tē hoc facere malō quam illud.   *I want you to do this rather than that.*

In the present or imperfect potential subjunctive **volō** and its compounds are more often followed by a substantive clause of result without the **ut.**

Velim hoc faciās.   *I'd like you to do this.*
Nōllem hoc facerēs.   *I wouldn't have wanted you to do this.*
Mallem hoc facerēs.   *I would have preferred you to have done this.*

PROHIBITIONS

A negative command is called a prohibition. Sometimes a prohibition is expressed by the imperative with **nē:** but two other idioms are far more common, the present infinitive with **nōlī** or **nōlīte** and the second person present subjunctive with **cavē** or **cavēte.**

Nōlī
Nōlīte } eī crēdere. }   (*Be unwilling to trust him.*)   } *Do not trust him.*

Cavē eī crēdās.
Cavēte eī crēdātis. }   (*Beware you should trust him.*)

A prohibition in indirect discourse, however, is an ordinary negative indirect command.

Mē monuit nē eī crēderem.   *She warned me not to trust him.*

FROM THE PHILOSOPHER'S HANDBOOK . . .

Volō, nōn valeō.
I am willing but unable.
Velle est posse.
To be willing is to be able.

Which of these two sayings comes closer to your own philosophy?

VOCABULARY

BASIC WORDS

fās (defective: nom. and acc.sing. only), n. *divine law, that which is permitted by the gods*; **fās est** *it is right, it is permitted, it is lawful*

furor, furōris, m. *madness*

audāx, audācis *rash, foolhardy, daring*

integer, integra, integrum *whole, unharmed, sound; innocent*

turpis, -e *ugly, disgraceful*

caveō, -ēre, cāvī, cautum *guard against, beware of*

complector, -ī, complexus sum *embrace*

concēdō, -ere, concessī, concessum (intrans.) *retire, withdraw; give in;* (trans.) *give up*

nūbō, -ere, nūpsī, nuptum *be married*

pariō, -ere, peperī, partum *give birth to; obtain*

spīrō, -āre, -āvī, -ātum *breathe*

velut (adv.) *as, just as; just as if*

Notes: 1. **Fās est** is usually used with a supine or an infinitive.

Hoc fās est dictū.	*This is lawful to say.*
Fās est hoc dīcere.	*It is lawful to say this.*

2. The perfect passive participle of **caveō** is used as an adjective meaning *cautious, careful*.

3. The perfect passive participle of **nūbō** is used in the feminine as a noun meaning *bride*.

LEARNING ENGLISH THROUGH LATIN

audacious	*bold, daring, fearless*
benevolent	*kindly, charitable*
malevolent	*wishing evil or harm to others; malicious*
nefarious	*very wicked; villainous*
obese	*very fat, stout, corpulent*
viper	*a poisonous snake; a malevolent or spiteful person*
volition	*conscious or deliberate decision; using one's will*
voluntary	*of one's own free choice*

Translation Help

Because Roman society contained so many social classes, Latin has a number of ways of expressing commands and prohibitions, from the most peremptory to the most polite. It is not always easy in translating to preserve the tone of the original. Here are the different ways of saying *Do this* and *Don't do this*, arranged in descending order of politeness:

POTENTIAL SUBJUNCTIVE WITH SUBSTANTIVE CLAUSE OF RESULT

Velim hoc faciās.
I'd like you to do this.

Nōlim hoc faciās.
I wouldn't like you to do this.

JUSSIVE SUBJUNCTIVE

Hoc faciās.
You should (might) do this.

Nē hoc faciās.
You should not do this.

IMPERATIVE

Hoc fac.
Do this.

Cavē hoc faciās.
Nōlī hoc facere.
Don't do this.

JUSSIVE SUBJUNCTIVE IN THE PERFECT

Hoc fēcerīs.
See that this is done right now.

Nē hoc fēcerīs.
You'd better not have done this.

This use of the jussive in the perfect is confined to the 2d person singular.

Romans, like Orientals, used the abacus for arithmetic calculations.

PRACTICE

A. Some Latin expressions are used also in English, and can be found in an English dictionary. Check your dictionary for the English use of: *caveat*, *nolle prosequi*, *noli-me-tangere*, and *nolo contendere*.

B. In zoology the term designating a species of animal that normally bears more than one offspring is *multiparous*. Show the Latin derivation of this word.

C. What would the meanings of the terms *oviparous* and *viviparous* be?

D. What English words are derived from the Latin **nūbō, -ere, nūpsī, nūptum,** *be married?*

E. Give a synopsis, in the active voice, of

1. volō in the 1st person singular.   2. nōlō in the second person singular.
3. mālō in the 3d person plural.   4. edō in the 2d person plural.

F. Pronounce and translate:

1. Esse fēlīcēs volunt.   2. Esse illud nōlēbant.   3. Illud mālent quam hoc.
4. Vellem hoc concēderent.   5. Nōlim id experiāris.

G. Translate:

1. They didn't want to eat this.   2. Do you want us to eat this?   3. I'd rather you ate this.   4. I'd like him to eat this.   5. Whether willing or unwilling he will be compelled to eat this.

H. Pronounce and translate:

1. Istī nūbere nōlī.   2. Cavē istī nūbās.   3. Istī nē nūbās.   4. Nōlim istī nūbās.   5. Istī nē nūpserīs.

I. If you were an ancient Roman, how would you tell, or ask, the following people not to break your finger?

1. The Emperor?   2. Your father?   3. A friend?   4. Another friend?
5. A slave?

J.   Pronounce and translate:

1. Velīsne mihi permittere ut tē complectar?   2. Forsitan ēsse quod hostēs dedērunt cautī nōlint.   3. Māllem eum invenīrēs tūtum integrumque sine hīs vulneribus.   4. Tantus furor rēgīnam occupāverat ut morī māllet quam sine virō vīvere.   5. Hic sacerdōs tam audax est ut edit quod sacerdōtī nōn licet ēsse.   6. Dux equitibus imperāvit ut dextrum cornū adīrent quod latus suīs patēre nōllet.   7. Sacerdōs dicit fās esse in illum populum bellum īnferre quī iūs gentium rūperit.   8. In ipsō līmine cum face stābat viam ad portam digitō indicāns, seu voluī seu nōluī sequendus.   9. In urbe vīdī ut cīvēs parvās avīs cum ipsīs ossibus vulgō ēssent, turpe et vīsū et audītū. 10. Vir fortis cum novā nuptā in terram ulteriōrem trāns montīs concēdere mālet quam hīc manēre ubi alere quod haec pepererit vix poterit.

A Roman calendar stone marking the zodiac signs, number of days in the month, day length, and important festivals

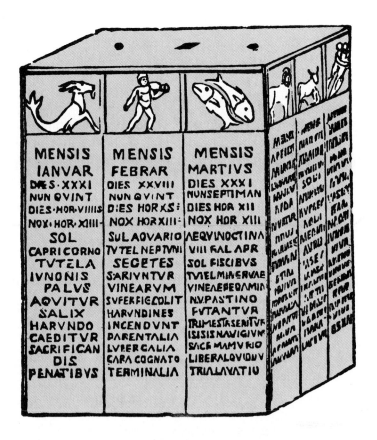

Developing Reading Skills

Latin words which will help: **blandus, caveō, certus, cor, custōs, dō, dūcō, emō, exeō, fidēs, flōs, fundō, grātus, iuvenis, lābor, māter, miser, nūbō, orior, potēns, putō, rēx, socius, spīritus, spīrō,** and **vertō.**

English words which will help: *afflict, arbitrate, avert, blandishment, certain, confound, confuse, constant, consume, custody, exhaust, exit, federal, fidelity, impeccable, incautious, insane, intemperate, matron, misery, nuptial, oration, precipitous, pristine, prolapse, prudent, regal, society, solace, stultify, tabernacle, trepidation,* and *venom.*

An Unusual Wedding Gift

Sophonisbae forma erat īnsīgnis et flōrentissima aetās. Itaque ut modo genua modo dextram complectēns nē cui Rōmānō trāderētur fidem petēbat, propiusque blanditiās iam ōrātiō erat quam precēs, nōn in misericordiam modo prōlāpsus est animus victōris sed, ut est genus Numidārum in Venerem praeceps, amōre captīvae victor volēns captus est. Prōmissō datō incēpit   5
reputāre sēcum ipse quemadmodum prōmissī fidem praestāret. Tandem ab Amōre audāx mūtuātur cōnsilium: nūptiās in eum ipsum diem parārī repente iussit, nē quid Scīpiō agere vellet velut in captīvam in eam quae Masinissae iam nupta foret. Nūptiīs clam Scīpiōnem factīs Sȳphax in Praetōrium ad Scīpiōnem inductus est. Scīpiōnī quaerentī quārē nōn societātem sōlum   10
noluisset Rōmānam sed ultrō bellum intulisset peccāsse quidem sēsē atque īnsānīsse fatēbātur, sed nōn tum dēmum ubi arma adversus Populum Rōmānum cēpisset; id fuisse exitum suī furōris, nōn prīncipium; tum sē īnsānīsse, tum foedera omnia ex animō ēiēcisse, cum Carthāginiēnsem

---

6. sēcum ipse: the intensive in the nominative following the reflexive gives it emphasis: *to himself in private*   **9. nupta foret:** subjunctive because it is part of Masinissa's thought (implied indirect discourse)   **11. peccāsse.** contracted form of **peccāvisse. sēsē** = **sē**   **12. īnsānīsse:** contracted form of **īnsānīvisse**

15 mātrōnam domum accēpisset. Illīs nuptiālibus facibus rēgiam ārsisse suam;
illam Furiam omnibus blanditiīs animum suum āvertisse. Perditō tamen atque
adflīctō sibi hoc in miseriīs sōlātī esse, quod in omnium hominum inimīcissimī
sibi domum ac Penātēs eandem Furiam trānsiisse vidēret. Neque prūden-
tiōrem neque cōnstantiōrem Masinissam quam sē esse, etiam iuventūte
20 incautiōrem; certē stultius illum atque intemperantius eam quam sē dūxisse.
Scīpiō verēns ergō nē Masinissa idem atque Sӯphax faceret imperāvit ut
Sophonisba Rōmam captīva cum coniuge pristinō mitterētur. Masinissae
hoc audientī lacrimae obortae sunt. Ex Praetōriō in tabernāculum suum
confūsus concessit, ubi cum crebrō suspīritū et gemitū aliquantum temporis
25 consumpsit, ingentī ad postrēmum ēditō gemitū fidum ē servīs vocāvit sub
cuius custōdiā rēgiō mōre ad incerta Fortūnae venēnum erat, et mixtum in
pōculō ferre ad Sophonisbam iussit ac simul nūntiāre Masinissam māluisse
prīmam eī fidem praestāre, sed quoniam sibi eius arbitrium quī possent
adimerent, sē secundam fidem praestāre nē vīva in potestātem Rōmānōrum
30 venīret. Memor duōrum rēgum quibus nūpta fuisset sibi ipsa cōnsuleret.
Ubi hunc nūntium ac simul venēnum ferēns minister ad Sophonisbam
vēnerat "Accipiō" inquit "nūptiāle mūnus, neque ingrātum, sī nihil maius
vir uxōrī praestāre potuit. Hoc tamen nūntiā: melius mē moritūram fuisse,
sī nōn in fūnere meō nūpsissem." Et acceptum pōculum nūllō trepidātiōnis
35 sīgnō datō impavidē hausit.

▪ READING COMPREHENSION

1. How did Sophonisba's blandishments and supplications affect Masinissa?
2. What foolhardy plan did he devise to fulfill his promise to her, and why?
3. What reason did Syphax give to Scipio for not only refusing an alliance
with Rome but even making unprovoked war on her?   4. Although ruined
and cast down, what comfort did Syphax have?   5. Fearing that Masinissa
might do the same thing as Syphax, what decision did Scipio make?   6. How
did Masinissa react to this decision?   7. What did he order his slave to
do?   8. How did Sophonisba accept the wedding gift, and what message
did she send back to Masinissa?

---

17. quod: quod with the indicative may mean *the fact that;* such a clause is called a quod-
substantive clause. Why is **vidēret** subjunctive here?   **20. dūxisse:** sc. **in mātrimōnium;**
dūcere is often used to mean *marry,* with the rest of the phrase being understood.   **26. rēgiō
mōre:** Kings usually kept some painless poison by them to keep from falling alive into the
hands of their enemies.   **28. quī:** supply an antecedent: *those who*

VOCABULARY DRILL

A. Give the genitive (if any), gender, and meaning of each noun:

aes	dīgnitās	furor	līmen	ōtium
auris	dīvitiae	ingenium	meritum	praemium
cinis	fās	iūdex	mōlēs	sacerdōs
cultus	fax	lacrima	nupta	spīritus
digitus	fūnus	latus	os	vulgus

B. Give the other nominative singular forms (or the genitive, for adjectives of one termination), and the meaning, of each adjective:

audax	cautus	dulcis	iūcundus	superbus
blandus	commūnis	integer	saevus	turpis

C. Give the other principal parts and the meanings of these verbs:

caveō	experior	licet	pariō	spīrō
complector	frangō	mereor	sonō	vehō
concēdō	gignō	nūbō		

DRILL ON SYNTAX

Translate the participles in these sentences as conditions or conclusions.

1. Fulmen ā sinistrā audītum vox deum haud dubia esse ā vātibus cēnseātur.
2. Nostrā cohorte in prīmā aciē cīvitātem dēfendente legiō maximā cum glōriā ē pugnā ēvēnisset.   3. Hic dīves plūrimum potest et sē cēterīs meliōrem cēnset, ridendus tamen sī opēs perdiderit.   4. Cōnsule seniōre absente nostrī quī iuniōrem contemnunt nōn adducentur ut ad proelium sē cingant.   5. In numerō animārum dubiō vīdī lūmine umbram miserae rēgīnae, quiētae modo sī improbus amor cor eius nōn iactāvisset.

LISTENING AND SPEAKING

Becoming Educated

Titus' parents are providing him with a good education and so, like many Roman boys, he is studying oratory and literature. He prefers oratory and the power of speaking to memorizing poetry.

LŪCRĒTIA: Fuistīne, Tīte, hodiē apud magistrum Hortēnsium?

TĪTUS: Fuī, māter, et ōrātiōnem dē Catilīnae coniūrātiōne habuī. Ego partīs Catōnis, Mārcus Cicerōnis, et Hortēnsius Caesaris ēgit. Ars ōrātōria et vīs dīcendī mihi maximē placent.

LŪCRĒTIA: Librumne in tuā manū videō? Quid nunc faciendum est?

TĪTUS: Magister nōbīs imperāvit ut prīmōs versūs Vergilī Aenēidos discāmus et memoriā teneāmus. Fābulam Aenēae ā Vergiliō tam bene narrātam dīligō, at cūr versūs memoriā mihi tenendī erunt, sī carmen facile in librō legere poterō?

LŪCRĒTIA: Vergilius ille nōtissimus et clārissimus poētārum Rōmānōrum est, cuius carmina rēs gestās virōrum patriae cecinērunt. Pater Mūcius, sī multīs ante annīs versūs carminum nōn didicisset, vir doctus nunc nōn habērētur.

TĪTUS: Magister meus nōs sī paucōs de versibus dē Vergiliō et Horātiō bene sciāmus, facile carmina aliēna legere et dīcere posse dīxit.

LŪCRĒTIA: Ars carminum dīcendōrum dōnum magistrōrum est. Sī carmina bene dīcēs, semper hospēs carus apud virōs doctissimōs et potentissimōs eris. Ut versūs bene dīcās, mētra et nūmerī memoriā tenenda sunt; quamobrem Hortensius ut versūs discās tē rogāvit. Dīc mihi aliquōs.

TĪTUS: Arma virumque canō, Trōiae quī prīmus ab ōrīs, Ītaliam fātō profugus Lāvīniaque vēnit lītora. . . . Difficile est, māter, plūrēs tibi crās mē dictūrum spērō.

A. Give a brief summary in Latin of the advice and encouragement Lucretia gives her son.

B. An English-speaking guest is interested in the conversation between Lucretia and Titus. An interpreter asks the following questions, hears the answers, then translates them for the guest. Act out this scenario.

1. Apud quem Tītus hodiē fuit?   **2.** Quīd Tītus apud Hortēnsium fēcit?   **3.** Cūr Tītus versūs carminum memoriā tenēre nōn cupit?   **4.** Quālis Tītus, sī versūs bene discet, esse habēbitur?   **5.** Quae memoriā hominī tenenda sunt ut versūs bene dīcat?

A boy and his teacher—Louvre Museum, Paris

LESSON 17

Review of Impersonal Constructions

A portrait of the conservative consul and dictator Sulla, whose civil war with the forces of Marius typified the disturbances which eventually brought down the Republic

YOUR HISTORY: LATE REPUBLIC

The military successes of the 2d century B.C. brought changes to the Roman state with which the government was little prepared to cope. If you had lived in Italy at the end of this century, you would have noticed the gradual loss of small farms, the enlargement of the army, the difficulty in placing veterans in jobs and a rising gap between rich and poor, citizen and non-citizen. The two Gracchi brothers, Tiberius and Gaius, from the patrician Sempronius family, proposed land reform legislation and colonization proposals aimed at reversing the expansion of large scale agricultural holdings in the hands of a few and the increase of urban poor in Rome. Conservative senatorial forces and the people—alarmed at Gaius' attempts to extend citizenship to the Italians—combined to crush the brothers in disturbances which led to their assassinations. These incidents ushered in a century of civil wars and political upheaval which you might have found quite frightening to live through.

Buffeted by these forces from within, Rome found herself threatened by Gallic invasion from the north. Fortunately, the Roman military produced an effective middle-class commander, Gaius Marius, who successfully quelled the threat.

No sooner had the Gallic threat been dispatched, than the Italians rose in arms (90 B.C.) seeking the citizenship so long denied them. The Romans "won" this war as much by acquiescing to Italian demands for citizenship as by defeating them in the field. A second commander, L. Cornelius Sulla, a patrician, distinguished himself in this war, was elected consul in 88 B.C. and given a foreign command against Mithridates, King of Pontus. Rivalry between Sulla and Marius over the command initiated a bloody civil war between the factions supporting the two men. If you had been on the wrong side at any time, you might have found yourself with a price on your head as an enemy of the state and your family might have lost its estates and

(Continued)

finances. Sulla hastily settled the war with Mithridates, established a dictatorship, and rewrote the constitution in favor of the Senate and the patricians.

In the years following Sulla, Gnaeus Pompeius, a general with no prior patrician connections, amassed a string of stunning victories against slaves, rebels, and pirates in the West and East. If you had been one of Pompey's soldiers or even a middle-class Roman patriot, you might well have approved of Pompey's modest nickname, "the Great." Conservative patricians resented the general's power and moved to limit his influence. Pompey, however, turned to other frustrated politicians, Julius Caesar and Marcus Crassus, and formed a political association known as the First Triumvirate which dominated the political scene from 60 to 50 B.C. This arrangement provided Caesar with a consulship and a command in Gaul which he turned into the conquest of what is now France and a famous military career. After the death of Crassus, open rivalry broke out between the two remaining leaders. In 49 B.C. the conservatives in the Senate won the day politically and ordered Caesar to lay down his command. As a follower of Caesar you would have supported his treasonous decision to cross the Rubicon river into Italy and to make war upon the senatorial forces led by Pompey. Although Pompey's army rapidly fled Italy, Caesar's highly trained forces overwhelmed it in Greece (49 B.C.), and Pompey was later killed. Caesar returned to Rome and established himself as dictator for life.

(*below*) Pompey the Great on a coin he issued in 49 B.C.

ANCIENT ROME LIVES ON . . .

Do the army and generals play powerful roles in any modern country as they did in ancient Rome?

SYNTAX

■ REVIEW OF IMPERSONAL CONSTRUCTIONS

A verb is said to be used impersonally when it cannot have a noun or pronoun subject. Impersonal uses fall into four categories, (1) those in which the verb can have no subject, (2) those in which the verb has an infinitive subject, (3) those in which the verb has an infinitive phrase for its subject, and (4) those in which the verb has a clause for its subject.

Impersonal Verbs with no Subject

Intransitive verbs are used in the passive in the third person singular to describe an action without stating or implying a subject. In the passive of the perfect system and in the second periphrastic the participle is in the neuter.

> Nunc quiēscitur. *Now there is rest.*
> Diū et ācriter pugnābātur. *Fierce fighting was going on for a long time.*
> Ad montīs perventum est. *The mountains were arrived at.*
> Patrī parendum est. *Father is to be obeyed.*

There are also a few active verbs which have no subject. They all describe emotions, and take a direct object of the person feeling the emotion and a genitive of the person or thing causing the emotion. These verbs overlap somewhat in their meanings. They are all regular second-conjugation verbs, except that they always appear in the third person singular.

miseret, -ēre, -uit, ____ (*pity, compassion, distress*)
> Scīpiōnem Sophonisbae nōn miseruit. *Scipio did not pity Sophonisba.*

paenitet, -ēre, -uit, ____ (*repentance, regret, displeasure*)
> Eum huius cōnsilī paenitēbit. *He will regret this plan.*

piget, -ēre, -uit, ____ (*disgust, annoyance, regret, shame*)
> Mē piget sceleris tuī. *I am disgusted at your wickedness.*

pudet, -ēre, -uit, ____ (*shame*)
> Cōnsulem suī fīlī pudēbat. *The Consul was ashamed of his own son.*

taedet, -ere, -uit, ____ (*loathing, disgust, weariness*)
> Rēgīnam lūminis taedet. *The queen is weary of the daylight.*

Impersonal Verbs with Infinitive Subjects

All five of the verbs listed on page 203 may have infinitives as subjects.

Eum hoc fēcisse paenitēbit.   *He will regret having done this.*
Mē piget scelus tuum vidēre.   *I am disgusted to see your wickedness.*
Rēgīnam vīvere taedet.   *The queen is weary of living.*

The impersonal verb **decet, -ēre, -uit, ___**, *it is becoming*, also has an infinitive subject and a direct object of the person.

Tē deceat hoc facere.   *It would become you to do this.*

The impersonal verb **licet**, *it is permitted*, and the passive of **videō** when it is used impersonally to mean *it seems best*, have an infinitive subject, but a dative of the person.

Tibi īre licēbit.   *You will be permitted to go.*
Mihi īre vīsum est.   *It seemed best to me to go.*

Impersonal Verbs with Infinitive Phrases as Subject

The impersonal verbs **cōnstat**, *it is established*, and **oportet, -ēre, -ui, ___**, *it is proper, it is necessary*, have infinitive phrases for subjects.

Cōnstat eum patrem occīdisse.
It is well known that he killed his father.
Mē īre oportet.   *I should (must) go.*

Oxen lay out the furrow for a new colony in the 1st century B.C.

Impersonal Verbs with Clauses as Subject

A verb which governs a subordinate clause may be used impersonally in the passive.

Mīlitī imperātum est ut pugnāret. *The soldier was ordered to fight.*
Ab Hannibale quaeritur ut abīret. *Hannibal was asked to leave.*
Effectum est ut abīret. *He was made to leave.*

An active verb which has a substantive clause of result for its subject also belongs to this classification.

Ut abessēs accidit. *You happened to be away.*
Restat ut hoc faciāmus. *It remains for us to do this.*

VOCABULARY

BASIC WORDS

fōns, fontis, m. (i-stem) *spring, source; fountain*
foris, -is, f. (i-stem) *door*
iugum, -ī, n. *yoke; [mountain] ridge*
pecus, pecoris, n. *herd, flock*
tenebrae, -ārum, f. *darkness, obscurity*
vitium, -ī, n. *fault, defect, vice*

antīquus, -a, -um *ancient, previous; old-fashioned*
ignōtus, -a, -um *unknown*
nimius, -a -um *too great, too much, excessive*
plērusque, plēraque, plērumque *the larger part of, the majority of*
tener, tenera, tenerum *tender, delicate*

cieō, -ēre, cīvī, citum *arouse; summon*

Notes: 1. From the same root as **foris** comes the locative **forīs**, meaning *outdoors, out-of-doors, out, outside, not at home.* The corresponding accusative of limit of motion, **forās**, means *[to] out, [to] outdoors.*

2. **Nimius** and **plērusque** are used very frequently as internal accusatives.

Nōlī eī nimium crēdere. *Don't trust her too much.*
Labōrem praemium plērumque sequitur.
A reward generally (for the most part) follows effort.

3. The perfect passive participle of **cieō**, **citus, -a, -um,** is used as an adjective meaning *quick, speedy.*

LEARNING ENGLISH THROUGH LATIN

antiquated	*old-fashioned, out of date, obsolete*
citation	*a summons to appear before a court of law; a formal statement honoring a person in public with an award*
impudent	*shamelessly bold or disrespectful, insolent, impertinent*
incite	*to stir up, rouse, urge to action*
resuscitate	*to revive, bring back to life*
solicitous	*showing care, attention, or concern*
tenebrous	*dark, gloomy*
vitiate	*to make faulty; spoil, corrupt*

PRACTICE

A. Derivatives.

1. An *antiquarian* deals in rare old books and an *antiquary* is a person who collects and studies relics and ancient works of art. Show the Latin derivation of these two words.   2. *Nimiety* is a word meaning excess or redundancy. What is its Latin derivation?   3. *Oscitancy* means drowsiness, dullness, or apathy. It comes from two Latin words meaning "to move the mouth". What are these two Latin words, and what does mouth movement have to do with the meaning of oscitancy?   4. *Jugate, jugular, jugum, conjugate,* and *subjugate* are all derived from the Latin **iugum, -ī,** n. Look up the meaning of each of these words.

B. Find a possible subject for each sentence from the list below, or say if the verb can have no subject.

1. Caveātur.   2. Cōnstat.   3. Tē decet.   4. Tibi licet.   5. Oportet. 6. Nōbīs permissum est.   7. Nōbīs persuādēbitur.   8. Nōs vitī piget. 9. Tēne pudet?   10. Tibi vidēbātur.

iūs iurandum ridēre   vōs tacēre   ut pecūniam pendāmus

C. Pronounce and translate:

1. Dubitābātur quid faciendum esset.   2. Hostium impetibus nōn cēdendum est.   3. Mē taedet istōrum verbōrum blandōrum.   4. Utrum tibi persuāsum est annōn?   5. Nōnne vōs paenitet hunc honestum indicāvisse?

D. Translate:

1. I must go away. (two ways)   2. I ought to go away. (two ways)

E. Pronounce and translate:

1. Sī aquam vīs ad fontem ambulandum erit.   2. Ut vātī nōn crēdēbātur itum est ad sortīs.   3. Quemadmodum tuō amīcō invidētur cui omnibus rēbus praestātur?   4. Mē piget istīus cultūs; comam aliter compōnere tē decēret.   5. Agminī nostrōrum sīc instābātur ut ad castra redeundum esset. 6. Hīc tam bene vīvitur ut mē eōrum quī alibi habitant misereat.   7. Sī magistrō parēbitur et bene serviētur, ad alteram rīpam citō perveniētur. 8. Ut victōriae nūntius vulgō audiēbātur ad Rostra undique volātum est. 9. Crīmine patris dignitātī nōn nocēbātur quoniam omnēs culpam alterī esse scīvērunt.   10. Ut clāmor ad aurīs pervēnit sēnsī ad cohortis ducem mihi currendum esse.

F. Translate:

1. We are permitted to go outdoors.   2. We are permitted to go outdoors (another way).   3. He happened to have broken a bone.   4. In how many hours will the departure be?   5. Isn't he ashamed of having stolen the flock?   6. If she marries him, will there be rejoicing?   7. Which one is favored, this one or that one?

From the Philosopher's Handbook . . .

Assiduus ūsus ūnī reī deditus
et ingenium et artem saepe vincit.
*Constant practice devoted to one subject
often outdoes both intelligence and skill.*
—CICERO

Can you explain this saying in relation to the study of Latin? Can it also be applied to sports?

READING

Developing Reading Skills

Latin words which will help: **cernō, Cōnsul, dīcō, dō, dominus, finis, iterum, nōmen, orior, sentiō, trahō,** and **valeō.**

English words which will help: *cognomen, consulate, debilitate, decree, delete, domination, finish, formidable, reiteration, minatory, oriental, prevail, protract, respond, sentence, terrify, vase,* and *venom.*

And There Were Wars . . .

Post Scīpiōnis et Masinissae victōriam in Āfricā Hannibalī imperātum est ā Carthāginiēnsibus ut ex Ītaliā redīret. Ita annō decimō septimō Ītalia ab Hannibale līberāta est. Sed Hannibalis nōmen tanta formīdō plūs ūnō saeculō mānsit ut mātres nūtrīcēsque puerōs improbōs terrēre temptantēs illīs verbīs
5 "Hannibal ad portās!" ūterentur. Scīpiō Hannibalque duo peritissimī fortissimīque ducēs tandem convēnērunt proeliō quod apud Zamam commissum est, ā quō ille victor discessit. Post hoc proelium pax facta est; Scipiōnī inditum est cognōmen alterum Āfricānō. Fīnītō Pūnicō bellō, secūtum est bellum Macedonicum contrā Philippum rēgem, et Lacedaemonium contrā
10 Nābidem, quibus bellīs omnēs Graeciae cīvitātēs sociī et amīcī Populī Rōmānī factae sunt. Deinde secutum est bellum Syriacum contrā Antiochum rēgem, quōcum Hannibal Carthāgine fugiēns sē iūnxerat. Nāvālī proeliō cum Hannibale pugnatum est quī vāsa anguibus plēna tormentīs in nāvīs coniciēns Rōmānōrum sociōs terruit, sed victus tamen est. Post hoc bellum ā quō
15 Rōmānī victōrēs discessērunt Hannibal ad Bīthȳniam fūgit quō Rōmānīs persequentibus sē venēnō interfēcit.

Nunc omnēs ferē partēs orbis terrārum orientālis in fidem Populī Rōmānī sē contulerant. In Austrī partibus Carthāgō quamquam dēbilis post bellum

---

5. Hannibal ad portās: In just the same way, in the Nineteenth Century, English nursemaids would threaten naughty children with *Boney* (Napoleon Bonaparte). **10. sociī et amīcī:** a technical term for an alliance whereby a nation kept its internal autonomy but surrendered its foreign policy decisions to Rome

Portrait bust supposed to be that of Scipio Africanus

erat reī Rōmānae tamen minitārī aliquibus Senātōribus vidēbātur, in prīmīs
M. Porciō Catōnī illī, qui in Senātū sententiam rogātus semper respondēbat,   20
quācumque dē rē agēbātur, "Delenda est Carthāgō!" Iterātiō, ut plērumque
fit, praevalēbat: vīsum est Senātuī ergō bellum indīcere quod brevī confectum
est. Post hoc bellum igitur et bella Numidicum et Hispānicum dominātiō
Rōmāna undīque patēbat exceptīs partibus ad Septentriōnem, ex quibus
Cimbrī et Teutonēs aliaeque Germānōrum et Gallōrum gentēs Italiae   25
minābantur, multōsque Rōmānōrum exercitūs iam fūdērunt. Ingēns fuit
Rōmae timor nē iterum Gallī urbem occupārent. Ergō quīdam C. Marius
quī nepōtem Masinissae in Numidiā vīcerat Cōnsul iterum est creātus
bellumque eī contrā Cimbrōs et Teutonēs dēcrētum est; bellōque prōtractō,
eī tertius et quartus cōnsulātus dēlātus est. In proeliō cum Teutonibus ad   30
Aquās Sextiās ducenta mīlia hostium cecīdit, octōgintā mīlia cēpit, inter
quōs eōrum regēm Teutobudum; propter quod meritum absēns quīntum
Cōnsul creātus est.

READING COMPREHENSION

1. What is the meaning of the expression "Hannibal ad portās!"   2. In
what battle did the two most skilled and courageous generals, Hannibal
and Scipio meet, and who was victorious?   3. List three wars that followed
the Second Punic War.   4. In Rome's Syrian War against King Antiochus,
how did Hannibal terrify the Roman allies?   5. How did Hannibal die?
6. What is the significance of the expression "Delenda est Carthāgō"?
7. The Roman empire now stretched everywhere except in areas to the
north. Who were threatening the Romans from this territory?   8. Who
was elected Consul and assigned the war against these tribes? How many
terms did he serve?

---

19. in prīmīs: sometimes written imprīmīs, *especially*

LESSON 18

Cum Clauses; Dum and Dōnec Clauses

The Emperor Vespasian (right) is welcomed to Rome by his son, Domitian. The sculptor has given us a good portrait of the hard-bitten former general—Vatican Museum

YOUR HISTORY: EARLY EMPIRE

D espite the political strife of the late Republic, the strength of the Roman military provided the city-state with an empire that stretched from Mesopotamia to the Atlantic. Even as a die-hard republican, you might have wondered how officials elected for a single year could cope with such responsibilities. But tradition ran strongly in Rome against a return to monarchy.

Thus, you might have supported the murder of Caesar by Marcus Brutus, Cassius, and other senators offended by what they saw as his monarchical aspirations. The assassination initiated another period of civil wars first between the republicans and those loyal to Caesar—Marc Antony, Lepidus, and Caesar's young heir, Octavian—and eventually between Marc Antony and Octavian. The defeat of Antony finally ended the civil strife. The exhausted Romans turned to Octavian—now hailed as Augustus—to provide peace.

The reign of Augustus established an autocratic empire instead of a republic dominated by a narrow class of wealthy nobles. To make the transition acceptable to Roman tradition, Augustus assumed republican titles and powers and proclaimed that he shared power on an equal basis with the Senate, but he, his descendants, and later dynasties personally controlled the army, on which real power rested.

Tiberius, Augustus' stepson, established the hereditary and monarchical nature of imperial rule. The erratic Caligula was murdered by the imperial guard when the army lost confidence in his regime. Claudius bribed the guards to spare his life and support his claims to the throne. He proved a competent administrator who vastly increased the role of freedmen in administering the growing imperial bureaucracy. As a member of an old Roman family, you might have resented the growing power of these up-start ex-slaves in the government. Claudius was poisoned by his last wife,

(Continued)

211

A PHRASE TO USE

Mē duce tūtus eris.
Under my leadership you will be
safe.

who wished to ensure the claims of her own son, Nero, to the throne. If you had lived in the first five years of Nero's reign, you probably would have looked back along with most Romans on the "*quīnquennium*" as the best years of the century. But as the young emperor grew to majority, he lost his wisest advisors and control over his armies. The year 69 A.D. saw four different army commanders assume imperial power briefly. Vespasian emerged victorious from this threat to imperial rule and established the Flavian dynasty, which was carried on by his two sons, Titus and Domitian. The first emperor to come directly from the army and the middle class, Vespasian was a tough soldier, a shrewd accountant, and a hard-minded administrator with much common sense and ready wit. Titus, though popular, was short lived, and Domitian, little trained for rule, became so autocratic and paranoid that he feared intellectuals and philosphers and persecuted them. He was eventually assassinated by his own household who became increasingly frightened for their own safety.

Since Domitian had no heir, the Senate chose as ruler an elderly and respected senator, Nerva, who established the sequence of the "five good emperors." The following four, Trajan, Hadrian, Antoninus Pius and Marcus Aurelius, each came to the throne as an heir chosen by his predecessor. However, Marcus Aurelius' unwise choice of his son Commodus began the return to the murderous dynastic changes of the Late Empire.

(*below*) A coin showing Domitian, who reigned from 81–96 A.D.

ANCIENT ROME LIVES ON . . .

Does the feeling of class consciousness so prevalent throughout Roman history have any counterpart today?

SYNTAX

CUM CLAUSES

Besides the **cum** temporal clause which you have already learned, there are three other kinds of clauses introduced by the conjunction **cum: cum** circumstantial, **cum** causal, and **cum** concessive.

Cum Temporal Clause

Cum with the indicative defines the time at which something happens; **cum** is translated *when*. A correlative **tum** is often found in the principal clause.

> Tum cum bellum gerebātur Rōmā aberam.
> *At the time when the war was going on I was away from Rome.*

> Eum cum vēnerit māter complectētur.
> *When he comes (will have come) his mother will embrace him.*

Cum Circumstantial Clause

Cum with a past tense of the subjunctive defines the circumstances under which an action took place. **Cum** is translated *when*.

> Cum bellum gererētur Rōmā abesse mē puduit.
> *I was ashamed to be away from Rome when the war was going on.*

Cum Causal Clause

Cum with the subjunctive defines the cause of some action. **Cum** is translated *since*.

> Id difficile nōn est, cum tantum equitibus valeāmus.
> *This is not difficult, since we are so strong in cavalry.*

Cum Concessive Clause

Cum with the subjunctive defines something in spite of which some action takes place. **Cum** is translated *although;* there is often a **tamen** in the principal clause.

> Cum prīmī ordinēs cecidissent, tamen ācerrimē reliquī pugnābant.
> *Although the first ranks had fallen, still the others were fighting very fiercely.*

Cum . . . Tum . . .

When the correlatives **cum** and **tum** are used, with the cum clause preceding the **tum,** they can be translated *not only . . . but also . . .* or *as . . . so especially. . . .* The **cum** clause is technically **cum** temporal, and so has its verb in the indicative.

> Cum multa perīcula caveō, tum hoc in prīmīs.
> *Just as I am on guard against many dangers,*
> *so I especially watch out for this one.*
> Cum difficile est, tum nē aequum quidem.
> *Not only is it difficult, but it is also not even fair.*

■ DUM AND DŌNEC CLAUSES

The adverbial conjunctions **dum** and **dōnec,** both of which technically introduce temporal clauses, have a number of different meanings:

1. **Dum** with the present indicative means *while.* If the action is in the past, the present indicative is translated as an imperfect.

> Hoc dum narrat forte audīvī.
> *I happened to hear this while he was telling it.*
> Dum haec geruntur iūdicēs pervēnērunt.
> *The jury arrived while these things were going on.*

2. **Dum** with the present or imperfect subjunctive means *until,* in a clause implying expectancy. Normal negatives are used.

> Mānsī dum illa redīret. { *I waited until she should return.*
> { *I waited for her to return.*

3. **Dōnec** with the perfect indicative means *until,* in a clause describing an actual event.

> Mānsī dōnec illa rediit. *I waited until she returned.*

4. **Dum** and **dōnec** with any tense of the indicative both mean *as long as.*

> Dum anima est spēs esse dīcitur.
> *As long as there is life there is said to be hope.*
> Dōnec tibi grātus eram rēge fēlīcior fuī.
> *As long as I was pleasing to you I was happier than a king.*

5. **Dum** with the subjunctive means *provided that,* in a clause implying a proviso. The negative is **nē.**

> Faciat ut placet dum nē cui noceat.
> *Let him do as he likes, provided that he harm no one.*

VOCABULARY

BASIC WORDS

aeger, aegra, aegrum *sick, ill*
maestus, -a, -um *sad, sorrowful*
merus, -a, -um *pure; mere*

dīvertō, -ere, dīvertī, dīversum *turn away, turn in a different direction*
dōnō, -āre, -āvī, -ātum *present*
repetō, -ere, repetīvī, repetītum *demand back again, seek to recover; renew, begin again*

spargō, -ere, spārsī, spārsum *scatter, sprinkle*

adhūc (adv.) *thus far, till now*
frūstrā (adv.) *in vain*
praetereā (adv.) *besides that, in addition*
quondam (adv.) *once; sometime*
usque (adv.) *continuously; all the way*

Notes:
1. The adverb of **aeger, aegrē,** means *painfully, with difficulty, scarcely.*

2. **Merus,** modifying **vīnum** understood, makes a noun **merum, -ī,** n., meaning *wine not mixed with water.*

3. The participle of **dīvertō, dīversus, -a, -um,** is also used as an adjective meaning *hostile* or *different.*

4. Like *present* in English, **dōnō** may govern either of two constructions, a dative of the person and an accusative of the thing, or an accusative of the person and an ablative of the thing.

   Mātrī flōrēs dōnāvit.   *He presented flowers to his mother.*
   Mātrem flōribus dōnāvit.   *He presented his mother with flowers.*

5. In compounds **spargō** becomes **-spergō, -ere, -spersī, spersum.**

LEARNING ENGLISH THROUGH LATIN

aspersion	*a damaging or disparaging remark; slander; innuendo*
condone	*overlook [an offense]; pardon, forgive*
divers	*several, various*
diverse	*different, dissimilar*
diversion	*distraction of attention; a pastime or amusement*
frustrate	*to prevent from achieving an objective; foil, baffle*
intersperse	*to scatter among other things; to put here and there at intervals*
sparse	*thinly spread or distributed; not dense or crowded*

Translation Help

It is not hard to translate **cum** clauses and **dum** and **dōnec** clauses from Latin to English.

cum + indicative   *when*

cum + subjunctive   { *when* / *since* / *although* }

dum + indicative
dōnec + indicative
dum + subjunctive   { *while* / *as long as* }   } depending on context

{ *until* / *provided that* }

▀▀ PRACTICE ▀▀

A. Fill in each blank with a form of one of the derivatives presented in this lesson.

1. I am so ___; I cannot solve any of these problems.   2. Although the candidate was very popular, the crowds who came to see him were quite ___.   3. You are casting ___ on my friend's character, and I cannot condone this.   4. The lawn was beautiful, with groups of daffodils ___ among the ivy and other ground cover.   5. I will not ___ these activities any longer.   6. There are ___ opportunities to improve yourself; you have only to take advantage of them.   7. There were all sorts of ___ aboard ship; you would never have been bored.   8. Their opinions on the matter were very ___; he was very positive, but she was very negative.

B. Which adverbial conjunctions introduce temporal clauses in Latin?

C. Which adverbial conjunctions introduce causal clauses in Latin?

D.   With what kind of verb does **dum** mean

1. while?   2. until?   3. as long as?   4. provided that?

E.   In each sentence change the subordinate clause to a cum-clause; then pronounce and translate:

1. Simul ac puerum genuit iucunda vōtum solvit.   2. Quod poenam turpem experīrī nōlēbat suam tellūrem repetīvit.   3. Ut domō cum comitibus exībam lūmen concēdēns vagum vīdī.   4. Rēx ille quamquam hūmānus erat aiēbat sē deum haud mortālem esse.   5. Tuus fīlius quoniam puer tenerō aevō est equō Rōmam vehī nōn poterit.   6. Ut mortuī cinis nec hic nec alibi reperīrī potest hodiē nōn fiet fūnus.   7. Omnēs mīrātī sumus ubi immēnsum pondus lapidum parvōrum dē vacuō caelō quondam lāpsum est. 8. Quia iste inimīcus superbus in hōc tectō tē nōn quaeret forsitan tūtior hīc futūra sīs.

F.   In each sentence change the participial phrase to a cum-clause; then pronounce and translate:

1. Pecūniā inter omnīs commūniter dīvīsā nēmō iam maestus erat.   2. Rem suam in diēs augēns aiēbat tamen sibi parum opum esse.

G.   Pronounce and translate:

1. Cum aevum mortāle hominem premit comam prīmum deinde ratiōnem perdit.   2. Vōbīscum bibēmus dum aqua addātur, cum merum bibere nōs nimium pigeat.   3. Duo dicta Rōmāna vulgō nōta sunt "Dum vīvimus vīvāmus!" et "Dum spīrō spērō."   4. Metuō ut quiētī hīc in limine paulum maneant dum nōs ad pugnam cingāmus.   5. Nōn audiēmus utrum mūnera frūstrā vōverīmus necne dōnec vātēs canet quid nūmina voluerint.   6. Cum fluctūs in pontō immēnsī essent usque in fretum tamen rēmīs ūtendō pervenīre temptābāmus.   7. Dum furor virum potentiōrem ferrō reddēbat vincula rumpere et custōdēs velut fulmen sternere valēbat.   8. Dōnec dubia erat num quid dīceret adhūc tacita morābātur; deinde cum antīquī spīritūs meminisset audacter locūta est.   9. Cum omnibus rēbus īnsīgnis tum pugnā saevissimus est: plūs potest ūnō digitō quam cēterī ambābus manibus valent. 10. Ibi cessāvī ut paulum quiēscerem dōnec immēnsum saxum dē montis iugō lāpsum est, ā quō aegrē mē membrīs intergrīs ēripuī.

The famous statue of Augustus as Commander-in-Chief from the imperial villa at Prima Porta. The sculptor is fully versed in the classicizing style introduced by the emperor.

FROM THE PHILOSOPHER'S HANDBOOK . . .

Excitābat fluctūs in simpulō.
He was stirring up billows in a ladle.

—CICERO

Can you cite an English proverb that says the same thing? What do they both mean? Can you see any relevance to any event in Roman history?

READING

Julius Caesar:
Complex and Compelling

C. Iūlius Caesar, quī ab Iūlō Veneris nepōte nōbile genus dūcēbat, nātus est annō sescentēsimō quīnquāgēsimō secundō a.u.c., eōdem quō Marius mātris frāter Teutonēs apud Aquās Sextiās cecīdit, id quod initium temporum certāminis inter Populārēs Optimātēsque sīgnāvit, quōrum hōs L. Cornēlius Sulla, illōs C. Marius et posteā L. Cornēlius Cinna dūcēbant. Annum agēns octāvum decimum patrem āmīsit; sequentibus Cōnsulibus Flāmen Diālis dēstinātus Cornēliam Cinnae quater Cōnsulis fīliam dūxit uxōrem, ex quā illī mox Iūlia nāta est; neque ut repūdiāret compellī ā Dictātōre Sullā ūllō modō potuit. Quārē ex sacerdōtiō et uxōris dōte et gentīliciīs hērēditātibus

5

---

2. a.u.c.: abbreviation for **ab urbe conditā**   **6. sequentibus Cōnsulibus:** *with the next people being Consuls = in the next year*   **8. Dictātōre:** not the old republican 6-month office, but a new office of indefinite duration for setting up a new constitution, **Dictātor Reī Publicae Cōnstituendae**

Remains of the Temple of Venus Genetrix, dedicated by Julius Caesar to his divine ancestress

10   multātus dīversārum partium habēbātur, ita ut etiam discēdere ē mediō et
prope per singulās noctīs commūtāre latēbrās cōgerētur sēque ab inquī-
sītōribus pecūniā redimeret, dōnec per quōsdam amīcōs veniam impetrāvit.
Satis cōnstat Sullam, cum dēprecantibus amīcissimīs et ornātissimīs virīs
aliquamdiū dēnegāsset atque illī pertināciter contenderent, expugnātum
15   tandem prōclāmāsse sīve dīvīnitus sīve aliquā coniectūrā: "Vincite et vōbīs
eum habētōte, dum modo sciātis eum quem incolumem tantopere cupitis
aliquandō Optimātium partibus, quās mēcum simul dēfendistis, exitiō
futūrum; nam Caesarī multī Mariī īnsunt."

---

10. partium: in the plural **pārs** can mean *a [political] party*   **14. dēnegāsset =**
dēnegāvisset   **15. prōclāmāsse = prōclāmāvisse**   **16. habētōte:** Future Imperative

Stīpendia prīma in Asiā contrā Mīthridātem fēcit M. Thermī Praetōris
contuberniō, ā quō in expugnātiōne Mytilēnārum corōnā cīvicā dōnātus est.   20
Meritus est et sub Servīliō Isauricō in Ciliciā, sed brevī tempore; nam Sullae
morte compertā Rōmam properē rediit ut cursum honōrum inciperet.
Cornēlium Dolabellam cōnsulārem et triumphālem repetundārum postulāvit,
sed frūstrā; quō absolūtō Rhodum sēcēdere cōnstituit, et ad dēclīnandam
invidiam et ut per ōtium ac requiem Apollōniō Molōnī clārissimō tunc   25
dīcendī magistrō operam daret. Hūc dum transit ā praedōnibus captus est
mānsitque apud eōs non sine summā indīgnātiōne prope quadrāgintā diēs
cum ūnō medicō et cubiculāriīs duōbus, nam servōs cēterōs initiō statim ad
expediendās pecūniās dīmīserat ut redimerētur. Numerātīs deinde quin-
guāgintā talentīs expositus in lītore nōn morātus est sed ē vestīgiō classe   30
dēductā persecūtus abeuntīs est ac redactōs in potestātem suppliciō quod
saepe illīs minātus inter iocum erat adfēcit. Sed in ulcīscendō ingenium adeō
lēne erat ut hōs pirātās quōs suffīxurum sē crucī ante iurāverat iugulārī
prius iubēret, deinde suffīgī.
    Ā tribūnātū mīlitum quī prīmus Rōmam reversō per suffragia populī   35
honor obtigit mox usque eō prōgressus est ut Quaestor creārētur. Quaestor
Iūliam amitam uxōremque Cornēliam dēfunctās laudāvit ē mōre prō Rostrīs,
et in amitae quidem laudātiōne dē eius ac patris suī utrāque orīgine dīxit
esse in genere et sanctitātem rēgum, cum eōrum māter fīlia Mārcī Rēgis
fuisset, et caerimōniam deōrum, cum pater ā Venere orīginem dūxisset.   40

▌ READING COMPREHENSION

1. From whom did Julius Caesar trace his noble line?   2. When was he
born?   3. Whom did he marry?   4. Who considered him to be a member
of the opposition party and constantly pursued him?   5. How did he finally
obtain pardon?   6. Under what circumstances did he earn his first military
pay?   7. When did he begin his political career in Rome?   8. What
happened when he decided to withdraw to Rhodes?   9. What did he do
after he paid his ransom?   10. What service did he perform as Quaestor?

---

20. corōnā cīvicā: a military decoration, a garland of oak leaves, awarded for saving the life
of a Roman citizen in battle   **22. cursum honōrum:** The aspiring politician would first try
to attract public attention by winning some sensational legal case.   **23. repetundārum:**
genitive of the charge or penalty. **A lēx dē rēbus repetundīs** or **rērum repetundārum** (using
an archaic form of the gerundive future passive participle) was a law on extortion, allowing
provincials to sue a governor for recovery of property which he had wrongfully seized.   **30. ē
vestīgiō:** *from the footprint* is a picturesque Roman way of saying *on the spot*

LESSON 19

Relative Clause of Characteristic; Relative
Clause of Purpose; Relative Clause of Result

This beardless youth in a classical exomis is a Roman depiction of Christ as the Good
Shepherd. Christianity quickly took root in Rome in the 1st century.

YOUR LIFE: EARLY EMPIRE

A Roman citizen's life during the Empire as established by Augustus was by and large a good and prosperous one. The less autocratic emperors successfully enlisted the cooperation of educated nobility in the administration, which was reinforced by freedmen from many different backgrounds.

If you lived in the provinces, this prosperity brought: a central and unified administration; improved and secure communication, trade and travel; and a fairly tolerant acceptance of different local traditions. Indeed, had you resided in the eastern realms of the Empire, you might have worshipped the figure of the emperor as a god. The reluctance of the Romans to grant citizenship dramatically changed under imperial rule and by the late 2d century and early 3d century A.D., you would have almost certainly been a Roman citizen even though you lived in a distant province.

Administratively and culturally this spread of **Rōmānitās** (*Roman-ness*) was accomplished by the famous system of Roman roads which linked Roman colonies and seats of administration in cities and towns. However, not all provincials accepted Roman rule gladly. Though usually tolerant of local custom and tradition, Roman insistence on allegiance to the emperor in deified form and reverence for Rome personified as a goddess ran counter to the fervently held monotheistic beliefs of the Jews and the rapidly increasing numbers of Christians. If you had been in Jerusalem during these times, you might have participated in the serious rebellions and equally severe repressions of A.D. 66–77, 115–117, and 132–135. Though early Christians were thought of as a Jewish sect and protected by law, they were quickly perceived to be something quite different which was misunderstood to be mysterious and thus potentially dangerous. Christians kept to themselves, avoided civic responsibilities, and worshipped privately, maintaining a network of local associations. This privacy and secrecy ran counter to the

(Continued)

223

public nature of traditional pagan worship and engendered much mistrust and dislike of Christians. Apart from isolated government persecutions under Claudius, Nero and other emperors of this period, government policy tended toward moderation. However, insistence on abjuring the faith and sacrificing to the emperor forced numerous martyrdoms among the devout. As an early Christian, your willingness to run the risk of death for your beliefs weeded out the faint-hearted and resulted in an ever stronger religion.

With the exception of Trajan, who pursued astonishingly successful military campaigns, Roman foreign policy was essentially conservative and defensive. But massive movements of peoples on the outskirts of the Empire in central Europe and the near east meant that the Roman armies had to call for more and more help from barbarian settlers on the borders. During the last decades of the "good emperors", wars on the northern and eastern borders became a constant drain of men, money, and resources.

With the death of Marcus Aurelius, the throne passed to his son Commodus, an incompetent autocrat who styled himself a Hercules. He rapidly destroyed the respect which had surrounded the imperial office during his predecessors' rules. His eventual assassination brought a return to dynastic struggles and civil war.

(*below*) The Emperor Commodus in the guise of Hercules

ANCIENT ROME LIVES ON . . .

What basic freedoms that we take for granted were not evident in some periods of Roman history?

SYNTAX

■ RELATIVE CLAUSE OF CHARACTERISTIC

A relative clause which, instead of adding some fact about the substantive it modifies, tells what is characteristic of it, has its verb in the subjunctive. Such a clause is called a relative clause of characteristic.

Indicative (ordinary relative clause)
    Mārcus nōn est is quī hoc fēcit.   *Marcus is not the one who did this.*

Subjunctive (relative clause of characteristic)

Mārcus nōn est is quī hoc fēcerit.
{
Marcus is not one who would have done this.
Marcus is not the kind of person to have done this.
}

Relative clauses of characteristic are potential in nature. Hence a safe translation will be *who (which) is (was) of such a kind as. . . .* This will seldom be your final version, but it will lead you reliably to the proper concept. Here is an example:

Face tē dōnābo quae tē in tenebrīs iuvet.
    I shall present you with a torch which is of such a kind as to help you in the dark > I shall present you with a torch to help you in the dark.

Look at the following relative clauses of characteristic and determine how each translation was arrived at. Notice that a relative clause of characteristic can express almost any idea which the subjunctive can express: cause, concession, proviso, purpose, and result.

Ille nōbīs nocet quī hostibus auxiliō sit.
    He harms us by aiding the enemy. CAUSE
Errāvī quī nōn mānsissem.   *I was wrong not to have stayed.* CAUSE
Maesta erat quae patrem āmīsisset.
    She was sad at having lost her father. CAUSE
Lūcius fēlīx est quī dīves sit.
    Lucius is lucky in that he is wealthy. CAUSE

Ego quī herī modo Rōmam pervēnerim multa tamen iam vīdī.
    Even though I arrived in Rome only yesterday, I have still seen many things already. CONCESSION

Cunctam pecūniam tibi mīsī quam quidem invēnerim.
    I have sent you all my money—at least all I could find. PROVISO

Hīc sunt carmina quae legās.   *Here are poems for you to read.* PURPOSE
Semper erant quī aliter cēnsērent.
   There were always some to vote the other way. PURPOSE
Sōlus erās quī mē pervenientem complectereris.
   You were the only one to embrace me when I arrived. PURPOSE

Maiōrēs arborēs caedēbant quam quās ferre mīles posset.
   They were cutting down trees too large for a soldier to be able to carry.
   RESULT
Eius ingenium tāle est quod victīs parcat.
   His nature is such as to spare the conquered. RESULT
Nihil vīdī quod timērem.   *I didn't see anything to be afraid of.* RESULT
Tū is nōn es quī hoc nesciās.
   You are not the kind of person not to know this. RESULT
Quis est quem huius factī nōn pudeat?
   Who is there who wouldn't be ashamed of this deed? RESULT

Relative Clause of Characteristic with Dīgnus and Idōneus

When it is necessary to state that someone or something is worthy of, or suitable for, some action, a relative clause of characteristic is used instead of the ablative of specification or the dative with adjectives.

Quīntus honōre dīgnus est.   *Quintus is worthy of the honor.*
Quīntus dīgnus est quī audiātur.
   Quintus is worthy of being heard (worth hearing, worthy to be heard).
Haec legiō proeliō idōnea est.   *This legion is suitable for battle.*
Haec legiō idōnea est quae pugnet.
   This legion is suitable for fighting (fit to fight).

The treasury of Petra, Jordan, 2d century A.D. In the high Roman Empire an international style of Greco-Roman architecture prevailed throughout a network of prosperous provinces.

■ RELATIVE CLAUSES OF RESULT AND PURPOSE

In construing sentences we usually distinguish relative clauses of result and purpose (see examples, p. 226) from the other relative clauses of characteristic.

A relative clause of result may be used instead of an adverbial clause of result when there is no word meaning *so* or *such* in the principal clause, or when the word meaning *so* or *such* is an adjective, i.e. is, **tālis, tantus,** or **tot.**

The relative clause of purpose indicates the purpose of the substantive it modifies. The adverbial clause of purpose indicates the purpose of the verb it modifies.

> Mīlitēs mīsit quī terrae nātūram cognōscerent.
> *He sent soldiers who were to learn the nature of the terrain.*
> Mīlitēs mīsit ut terrae nātūram cognōsceret.
> *He sent soldiers so that he might learn the nature of the terrain.*

Although these two sentences are different in meaning, either may be translated *He sent soldiers to learn the nature of the terrain.*

When a purpose clause contains a comparative, it is nearly always a relative clause of purpose introduced by **quō** (abl. of degree of difference).

> Tantī oculī, cāra mea, mihi sunt quō melius tē videam.
> *I have such big eyes the better to see you, my dear.*
> Adeāmus ad Rōstra quō facilius Cōnsulem audiāmus.
> *Let's go up to the Rostra to hear the Consul more easily.*

FROM THE PHILOSOPHER'S HANDBOOK . . .

Trahimur omnēs laudis studiō.
We are all led on by our eagerness for praise.
—CICERO

Do you think that giving people praise has a beneficial or detrimental effect? What rulers or heroes of ancient Rome do you feel were led on by an eagerness for praise?

VOCABULARY

BASIC WORDS

arbor, arboris, f. *tree*

ōsculum, -i, n. *kiss*

amplus, -a, -um *ample, large; important*

placidus, -a, -um *placid*

rapidus, -a, -um *seizing; violent; rapid*

cūrō, -āre, -āvī, -ātum *care for, take
care of*

fingō, -ere, fīnxī, fictum *mold; imagine,
invent*

īrāscor, -ī, īrātus sum *become angry*

lūdō, -ere, lūsī, lūsum *play; tease;
deceive*

supersum, superesse, superfuī, superfutūrus
be over and above; be left, survive

surgō, -ere, surrēxī, surrectum *stand up,
rise; grow*

suprā (adv. and prep. w. acc.) *above*

Notes: 1. The fact that **arbor** is feminine may help you to remember that all names of
trees are also feminine, regardless of declension.
2. **Ōsculum** literally means little mouth.
3. **Lūdō** may be used transitively or intransitively.

A leopard from a Roman mosaic of a
gladiatorial scene. Tradition has
exaggerated the stories of Christians
"thrown to the lions."

LEARNING ENGLISH THROUGH LATIN

allude	*to refer to in a casual or indirect way*
amplify	*to make larger or stronger; to develop more fully*
arboretum	*a place where many trees and shrubs are grown for study or exhibition*
collusion	*a conspiracy; a secret agreement for an illegal or fraudulent purpose*
effigy	*a crude image or representation of a disliked person*
feign	*to fabricate, pretend, simulate*
irascible	*quick-tempered, easily angered, irritable*
ludicrous	*absurd, ridiculous, causing laughter because of absurdity*

PRACTICE

A. The vocabulary in this lesson provides a wealth of English derivative material. Look up the meaning of each of the following words and name the Latin word in this lesson from which it is derived.

1. ample **2.** arboriculture **3.** curator **4.** placidity **5.** feint **6.** irate
7. resurgence **8.** supraliminal **9.** surge **10.** fictitious

B. Pronounce and translate:

1. Fēmina est quam amās. **2.** Fēmina est quam amēs. **3.** Fēmina tālis est quam amēs. **4.** Fēmina tālis est quālem amās. **5.** Fēmina idōnea est quam amēs.

C. Translate:

1. These verses are worth reading. **2.** He was wrong to do that. **3.** They killed such enemies as they found. **4.** We shall walk faster to arrive more quickly. **5.** If only someone were here to take care gently of this sick mind!

D. Pronounce and translate:

1. Multa mihi discenda sunt quō opus facilius cōnficerem. **2.** Huius mundī nātūra tālis est quae rēs dīversissimās pariat. **3.** Dulcissima carmina canit quaedam avis cuius vox quāsī humānum sonet. **4.** Quālis est quī suam amplam gentem dē deīs ēvēnisse vultū nōn ridente iactet? **5.** Parvam puellam cui pater graviter īrāscerētur sūmpserat māter et in sinū servābat ōsculaque dabat. **6.** Sunt quī inimīcōs persequendī causā pudōrem ita dēserant ut cuncta faciant quōrum eōs pudēre dēbeat. **7.** Exemplī grātiā mundum fingāmus in quō spatium nōn modo in trīs sed in quattuor partīs crēscat vel trahātur. **8.** Vōs quī falsē et leviter nōbīscum ēgerītis dīgnī estis quī hōc bellō moriāminī; supersint autem illī honestī iūstīque. **9.** Ille quī litterās post longam moram modo accēpisset nescīvit num necesse esset sociōs addūcere ut latus nostrum in proeliō tegerent. **10.** Nē post mortem quidem hostis maximī placidus quiēvit, sed - id quod fās nōn est - mīlitēs mīsit quī illīus cinerem ossaque in rapidō flūmine spargerent, nē humō tegerentur.

E. Translate the following sentences six different ways (with the supine, three uses of the gerund or gerundive construction, adverbial clause of purpose, and relative clause of purpose):

1. He sent soldiers to collect the money.   **2.** Men will come to serve the king.

F. Translate each of these sentences in as many ways as possible:

1. Men are here to serve the king.   **2.** He ordered me to serve the king. **3.** It is easy to serve the king, but difficult to collect the money.   **4.** He asked me to collect the money.   **5.** He sent the soldiers to collect more money.

The removal of the temple menorah from Jerusalem after ruthless suppression of the Jewish revolt by Vespasian—From The Arch of Titus, Rome

READING

Developing Reading Skills

Latin words which will help: **agō, animum, aspiciō, cadō, cēdō, cōnstituō, currō, dīcō, diēs, dō, dūcō, faciō, faveō, fundō, legō, lūdō, māter, memorō, mulier, nihil, nūllus, orior, ōsculum, parō, petō, potēns, praetereā, pratereō, Praetor, putō, respiciō, urbs, veniō, vertō,** and **vetus.**

English words which will help: *abundant, accomodate, apparatus, attest, attribute, basilica, ceremony, colleague, competitor, conciliate, descend, dignity, edition, favor, gladiator, impetrate, introduce, joke, largesse, matrimony, memorable, nil, opinion, orient, osculation, pact, pontificate, portico, predator, predict, preternatural, profuse, pullet, repudiate, revert, signature, structure, suspicion, urbane,* and *veteran.*

An Active Life

In Cornēliae locum Caesar Pompēiam dūxit Q. Pompēī fīliam L. Sullae nepōtem, quam post sex annīs repudiāvit opīnātus intrōdūxisse P. Clōdium muliebrī veste in Bonae Deae caerimōniās, dīcēns cum quīdam eum sīc agere suspiciōne modo quererentur oportēre Caesaris uxōrem suprā suspiciōnem esse. Quaestōrī Ulterior Hispānia obvēnit ubi cum Gādīs vēnisset animadversā   5
apud Herculis templum Magnī Alexandrī imāgine ingemuit quasī eum ignāviae suae taedēret quod nihildum ā sē memorābile actum esset in aetāte quā Alexander orbem terrārum subēgisset. In Hispāniā autem prīmum Gallīs tālibus populīs occurrit inter quālīs magnā potestāte potītūrus erat.

Rōmam reversus et Aedīlis Curūlis creātus praeter Comitium ac Forum   10
basilicāsque etiam Capitōlium ornāvit porticibus ad tempus exstrūctīs in quibus abundante rērum cōpiā pārs apparātūs expōnerētur. Vēnātiōnēs

---

3. caerimōniās: These were held at the house of Caesar as Pontifex Maximus and presided over by his wife with the assistance of the Vestals; men were rigorously excluded.   **12. abundante ... cōpiā:** ablative absolute. **apparātūs:** Before giving the games the Aediles used to display in the Forum the scenery, costumes, parade armor, etc. which were to be used, as a kind of advertisement.

A bust of Pompey the Great. As long as Pompey was married to Caesar's daughter Julia, the smoldering tensions between the two generals failed to burst into flame; with her death, civil war became imminent.

lūdōsque ēdidit quibus adiēcit etiam gladiātōrium mūnus, ita ut in aes aliēnum grāviter incideret. Conciliātō populī favōre, duōbus post annīs
15 pontificātum maximum petīvit nōn sine prōfusissimā largitiōne, in quā reputāns magnitūdinem aeris aliēnī cum māne ad comitia dēscenderet praedīxisse mātrī ōsculantī fertur domum sē nisi Pontificem Maximum nōn reversūrum. Atque potentissimōs duōs competitōrēs multumque et aetāte et dīgnitāte antecedentīs superāvit. Posterō annō Praetor creātus est. Itaque
20 quod cursum honōrum explēret reliquum erat sōlum ut Cōnsul fieret; Senātuī autem et Optimātibus plērīsque nōn placuit ut quī rēs novās peteret.

Eōdem annō quō praetūram Caesar consecūtus est Cn. Pompēius ab oriente victor rediit quō quīnque annīs anteā profectus erat ut praedōnēs Mīthridātemque subigeret. Senātōribus īrātus quī nollent aut sancīre cōn-

---

21. ut quī: followed by a relative clause of characteristic, this means *as being the kind of person who would* . . . **22. Cn. Pompēius:** He had been sent by the Senate, at the urging of Cicero, to finish the war against Mithridates and rid the Mediterranean of pirates; he had been most successful, having found land for the pirates and turned them into small farmers. The Senate, however, jealous of his popularity, delayed ratifying his settlements and giving his veterans the usual pension (a piece of public land to farm).

stitūtiōnēs eius in oriente aut veterānīs eius agrōs dōnāre pactus est cum 25
M. Liciniō Crassō dīvitissimō Rōmānōrum, quī magnās pecūniās Caesarī
commodāverat spērāns sē per eum potestatem in rē publicā consecutūrum.
Crassus Populāribus partibus, Pompēius Optimātibus Senātuīque faverat,
sed hic, quī nihil ā Senātū impetrāre posset, ad Populārīs trānsīvit. Per Crassī
dīvitiās effectum est ut Caesar Cōnsul creārētur, quī deinde lēgem tulit quā 30
Pompēiō Hispānia, Crassō Bellum Parthicum, sibi Gallia minor prōvincia
tribuerētur. Eōdem annō Pompēiō Iūliam fīliam in mātrimōnium dedit; ipse
Calpurniam dūxit L. Calpurnī Pīsōnis fīliam Populārium fautōris. Caesaris
collēga M. Calpurnius Bibulus quī cotīdiē pullōs sacrōs frūmentum ēsse
nōlle nūntiāret acta Caesaris omnia inrita facere temptābat, sed frūstrā adeō 35
ut nonnūllī urbānōrum, cum aliquid per iocum testandī grātiā sīgnārent,
nōn Caesare et Bibulō, sed Iūliō et Caesare Cōnsulibus actum scrīberent,
utque vulgō mox ferrentur hī versūs:

> Nōn Bibulō quiddam nūper sed Caesare factumst,
> nam Bibulō fierī Cōnsule nīl meminī. 40

Posterō annō Crassus Caesarque in prōvinciās prōfectī sunt; Pompēius
Rōmae mānsit, imperiō in Hispāniā per lēgātōs fungēns.

▪ READING COMPREHENSION

1. What is the meaning of the phrase "oportēre Caesaris uxōrem suprā suspiciōnem esse"? 2. Why did Caesar groan when he noticed a statue of Alexander the Great at the sanctuary of Hercules? 3. How did Caesar fall heavily into debt? 4. What is the meaning of the phrase "domum sē nisi Pontificem Maximum nōn reversūrum"? 5. What one thing was left to complete Caesar's political career? 6. Why was Gnaeus Pompey angry with the Senators? 7. What did he do? 8. When Caesar became Consul, what law did he bring in? 9. Name Caesar's three wives. 10. What is the meaning of the following elegiac couplet?

> Non Bibulō quiddam nūper sed Caesare factumst,
> nam Bibulō fierī Cōnsule nīl meminī.

---

31. Parthicum: The Parthians, who had revived the defunct Persian empire, seemed a threat to the Roman empire's eastern borders; there was constant disagreement over the control of Armenia, for example. **minor:** Crassus and Pompey were both gaining large armies by assuming assignments where wars were going on; Caesar, without their political, military, or economic power, dared ask only for a pacified area where there was little chance of war. **39. Bibulō:** sc. **Cōnsule. factumst = factum est;** when the verb **sum** elides with a preceding word it is **sum's** opening vowel which is suppressed

LESSON 20

Uses of Quīn; Quōminus Clauses

An elaborate **aureus** shows Constantius Chlorus being welcomed to London. His successful exploits enabled his son Constantine quickly to claim the title of **Caesar**.

YOUR HISTORY: LATE EMPIRE

After the civil wars which disrupted the Empire following the assassination of Commodus, Septimius Severus, a military usurper, gained the throne. Severus established a family dynasty, which owed all its power to the support of the soldiers. In an effort to make the government into a military monarchy, he entrusted soldiers with as many civil duties as military ones, in part to entice men to a career that was becoming increasingly less attractive.

The result of Severan militarism was an increasingly clear-cut class system. Senators, equestrians, municipal aristocrats and soldiers were **honestiōrēs** who enjoyed greater rights and privileges before the law than **humiliōrēs,** the lower classes. High taxation and the return of agriculture to large holdings reduced mobility between the classes. The death of Alexander Severus in 235 A.D. ushered in a half century of internal anarchy and foreign invasion. The "soldier emperors", as these men were called, ruled briefly and ended violently. Of the 26 emperors of the period only one died a quiet death. (One was even captured by barbarians, put to death and stuffed like a prized wild animal after a hunt!)

A brief respite from the steady decline of Roman power came during the reigns of Claudius II and Aurelian who stamped out plots against the throne and had the foresight to build huge fortifications around the city of Rome. If you lived during the last quarter of the third century, your despair over the previous reigns might well have turned to guarded confidence, for Diocletian, a man of lowly birth who rose to the throne through the army, devised creative answers to the problems threatening the Empire. He first established the tetrarchy, the rule of four, by dividing the Empire into four regions. He then appointed a co-ruler and styled this man and himself as **Augustī.** In addition, two vice emperors and heirs to the **Augustī** were styled as **Caesarēs.** Each man was supreme in his own region. It looked as if the

(Continued)

problems of administering a far-flung empire and ensuring proper succession were solved. However, Diocletian underestimated the attractions of power. By 310 A.D. there were five competing **Augustī** and no **Caesarēs**! Eventually Constantine defeated the other contenders and adopted Christianity. The concept of the emperor as a ruler by the grace of God rather than by the will of Senate or army became a forerunner of medieval monarchical rule.

Constantine established a new Imperial capital at Constantinople near the entrance to the Black Sea. Although he ruled a united realm as sole emperor, the Empire was redivided by his sons and subsequent successors. By 286 A.D. Milan replaced Rome as the capital of the West and in 402 A.D. the capital was moved again to Ravenna. After Theodosius the Great proclaimed Christianity the state religion and moved to stamp out paganism, the divided empire began to follow two distinct courses. The East, which had maintained Greek language and culture during centuries of Roman administration, awoke to form a strong and distinctly Greek Christian rule whose history lasted to the fifteenth century as the Byzantine Empire. The history of the West after Theodosius is one of successive barbarian invasions by Visigoths, Huns, and Vandals. Although the West was thus fragmented into an increasingly divided and rural culture, the legacy of Roman rule had forever changed the pattern of language, law, and custom in Western Europe.

(*below*) The Romans battling the Dacians—Arch of Constantine

ANCIENT ROME LIVES ON . . .

Do you see any resemblance between the attitudes of the **humiliōrēs** and that of serfs in the Middle Ages? Are there any such attitudes today?

SYNTAX

USES OF QUĪN

Quīn is an adverb made from the old neuter ablative singular, **quī,** of the interrogative and relative pronouns **quis, quid** and **quī, quae, quod,** to which has been added an **-n** representing a negative. Its basic meaning is *by which (or by what) . . . not.* It can introduce a direct statement, question, or command, or a relative clause of characteristic.

Introducing Statements

With a statement **quīn** represents what is usually called the corroborative *why.* This kind of *why* does not ask a question, but introduces an additional proof of what has been said. It is often accompanied by *even* (**etiam.**)

> Trīstissimus vidēbātur; quīn etiam lacrimās dēmittēbat.
> *He seemed very sad; why, he was even weeping.*

Introducing Questions

With a question **quīn** means *why not.* A **quīn** question is often equivalent to a command.

> Quīn id accipis?   *Why aren't you taking it? = Here, take it.*
> Quīn abīs?   *Why aren't you leaving? = Get out of here.*

Introducing Commands

With a command **quīn** means *why don't you?*

> Quīn mihi id redde.   *Give it back to me, why don't you?*

Introducing Relative Clauses of Characteristics

With a relative clause of characteristic **quīn** can be either nominative (= **quī nōn,** *who . . . not*) or ablative (= **quō nōn,** *by which not*). Here are some examples of its use as a nominative; note that it follows either a negative or a question in the principal clause:

> Nēmō nostrum est quīn id sciat.   *There is none of us who wouldn't know this.*
> Quis est quīn hoc sciat?   *Who is there who wouldn't know this?*
> Nēmō fuit mīlitum quīn vulnus recēpisset.
> *There was not one of the soldiers but had received a wound.*

In the nominative **quīn** is particularly common with relative clauses of result:

> Quis est tam fortis quīn hoc metuat?
> *Who is brave enough not to dread this?*

> Nēmō erat adeō cautus quīn auxiliō Praetōrī esse vellet.
> *No one was so cautious as to be unwilling to help the Praetor.*
> Nihil tam difficile est quīn quaerendō cognōscī possit.
> *Nothing is so difficult but that it could be learned by asking* (here **quīn** = **quod nōn**).

The ablative use of **quīn** follows negative verbs of *hindering, resisting, refusing, doubting,* and *delaying,* and some phrases with **sum, possum,** and **absum.** Some verbs and phrases of these kinds are:

contineō	*restrain*	nōn multum abest	
fallō	*escape the notice of*	paulum abest	} *it is not far*
moror	*delay*	facere nōn possum	*I cannot but*
praetereō	*neglect*	fierī nōn potest	
dubitō	*doubt*	efficī nōn potest	} *it cannot be*
impediō	*hinder*		
recūsō	*refuse*	nōn dubium est	*there is no doubt*

Mīlitēs continērī nōn poterant quīn in urbem inrumperent.
The soldiers could not be restrained from bursting into the city.

Caesarem nōn fefellit quīn hostēs per tenebrās discēdere temptārent.
It did not escape Caesar's notice that the enemy were trying to leave in the dark.

Nōn morandum cēnsuit quīn in aciē certāret.
He thought he had better not delay fighting it out in a pitched battle.

Praeterīre nōn potuī quīn scrīberem ad tē.   *I could not neglect writing to you.*

Nōn dubitābat quīn eī crēderēmus.   *He did not doubt that we believed him.*

Amīcōs impedīre nōn potuimus quīn ad alterās partīs trānsīrent.
We could not stop our friends from switching to the other party.

Nōn recūsābunt quīn nōbīscum pugnent.   *They will not refuse to fight us.*

Nōn multum āfuit quīn castrīs expellerentur.
They came near being driven out of the camp.

Paulum āfuit quīn rēgem interficeret.   *He just missed killing the king.*

Facere nōn possum quīn tē amem.
I can't help loving you. I cannot but love you.

Fierī nūllō modō poterat quīn captīvīs parcerētur.
It was out of the question that the captives should not be spared.

Effici nōn potest quīn hoc memorem.
Nothing can prevent my mentioning this.

Nōn erat dubium quīn illum huius paenitēret.
There was no doubt that he regretted this.

■ QUŌMINUS CLAUSES

Verbs of *hindering* and *refusing,* when they are not negative or in questions, are followed by relative clauses of characteristic introduced by **quōminus,** *by which the less,* instead of by **quīn,** *by which not.* This word is a fusion of **quō** (abl. of degree of difference) and **minus** (comparative adverb), "by which the less", so such a clause is really a relative clause of purpose.

Amīcōs impedīre potuimus quōminus ad alterās partīs trānsīrent.
We were able to stop our friends from switching to the other party.

Recūsābunt quōminus nōbīscum pugnent.
They will refuse to fight us.

═══ VOCABULARY ═══

BASIC WORDS

nemus, nemoris, n. *grove*
ratis, -is, f. (i-stem) *raft; vessel*
vertex, verticis, m. *whirlpool, whirlwind; top [of the head]*
____, vicis, f. (no nom. sing. or gen. plur.) *interchange, alternation*

assiduus, -a, -um *constant, steady*
dēnsus, -a, -um *close together, dense*
fessus, -a, -um *tired*
sēcūrus, -a, -um *carefree; secure*

niteō, -ēre, -uī, ____ *shine, glitter*
terō, -ere, trīvī, trītum *rub; wear out*
ūrō, -ere, ussī, ūstum *burn* (transitive)

namque (conj.) *for indeed*

Note: Vicem, vice, in vicem (invicem), and **ad vicem** all mean *in place [of], instead [of].*
Per **vicēs** and **in vicēs** both mean *alternately, in turn, by turns.*

By the third century, external threats to Rome were so serious that the Emperor Aurelian commissioned protective walls for the city.

◼ LEARNING ENGLISH THROUGH LATIN

assiduous	*done with constant and careful attention; diligent*
contrite	*penitent; feeling deep sorrow or remorse*
detriment	*anything that causes damage or injury*
inpediment	*obstacle, obstruction, anything that impedes*
tribulation	*great misery or distress; affliction; trial*
trite	*no longer having originality, novelty, or freshness*
vicarious	*endured or performed by one person in place of another; involving imagined participation in another's experience*
vicissitude	*unpredictable changes that can occur in life; varying circumstances; ups and downs*

Translation Help

Almost the only difficulty in translating Latin is the number of verbs which govern different constructions than their English counterparts: clauses instead of infinitives; datives or ablatives instead of accusatives, etc. You may find it helpful, before moving on to the translation of real, not "made" Latin, to make some kind of list of the verbs you have learned with whatever unexpected constructions they govern. A sample list follows on the following page. You may find some other arrangement more convenient, and each person's own list will no doubt be different from everyone else's.

VERBS GOVERNING SPECIAL CONSTRUCTIONS

GENITIVE	DATIVE			ABLATIVE
meminī	accēdō	crēdō	parcō	careō
miseret	addō	dēsum	pareō	concēdō
oblīvīscor	adferō	faveō	persuādeō	dōnō
paenitet	adiciō	imperō	placeō	fruor
piget	adsum	impōnō	praecipiō	fungor
potior	auferō	īnstō	praestō	potior
pudet	cēdō	licet	prōsum	prohibeō
taedet	committō	noceō	serviō	ūtor
	cōnsulō	nūbō	timeō	vēscor

INFINITIVE		INFINITIVE PHRASE			
audeō	nōlō	audiō	doleō	moneō	referō
cessō	optō	canō	exīstimō	negō	reperiō
coepī	paenitet	cēnseō	ferō	nesciō	sciō
cōnstituō	parō	cernō	fingō	nōlō	scrībō
dēbeō	piget	clāmō	fleō	nōscō	sentiō
decet	possum	cognōscō	gaudeo	nūntiō	spērō
dēsinō	properō	cōgō	iactō	oportet	taceō
dīscō	pudet	colligō	inveniō	ōstendō	trādō
dubitō	soleō	cōnfirmō	iubeō	patior	videō
incipiō	taedet	cōnstat	iūrō	persuādeō	volō
licet	temptō	dēmōnstrō	legō	prōhibeō	vōveō
mālō	timeō	dīcō	mālō	prōmittō	
metuō	valeō	dīscō	memorō	putō	
miseret	volō	doceō	mīror	queror	

FINAL CLAUSE	CONSECUTIVE CLAUSE	INDIRECT QUESTION		QUĪN/QUŌMINUS CLAUSE
addūcō	accidit	cernō	nōscō	contineō
caveō	cōnsequitur	cognōscō	ōstendō	dubitō
imperō	contingit	dēmōnstrō	petō	fallō
metuō	cūrō	dīcō	quaerō	impediō
moneō	efficiō	dīscō	reperiō	moror
permittō	ēvenit	doceō	rogō	recūsō
persuādeō	faciō	inveniō	sciō	
petō	fit	legō	scrībō	
praecipiō	restat	mīror	sentiō	
quaerō	sequitur	narrō	taceō	
rogō		nesciō	videō	
timeō				
vereor				

PRACTICE

A. Derivatives

1. *Vertex* is an English word as well as a Latin word. What does it mean? **2.** Show the connection between the English words *impediment* and *impedimenta*. **3.** There is a Latin ablative absolute which is a commonly-used English expression. The participle is from the verb **vertō**; the noun is in this lesson. What is the expression? **4.** What was the original literal meaning of words like *viceroy*, *vice-president*, and *vice-chairman*?

B. Look up the meanings of the English words *adust*, *triturate*, and *uredo*, and show their connections to Latin words in this lesson.

C. Pronounce and translate:

1. Quid eō fieret sī nēmō esset quīn eī nocēre vellet? **2.** Audītus nūntius illōs impedīvit quōminus mīlitēs mitterent quī rēgem occīderent. **3.** Quis est quīn sciat quemadmodum amor ut fax pectus ūrat? **4.** Quīn abīte in

FROM THE PHILOSOPHER'S HANDBOOK . . .

Lēgum servī sumus
ut līberī esse possīmus.
*We are slaves of the laws
in order that we may be free.*
—CICERO

This statement seems very self-contradictory. Is there any particular law which you are always very careful to obey? How does this make you free?

malam rem quī nōs aere invicem aurī dōnāverītis.   5. Dōnec sōlī in īnsulā manēbāmus nihil nōs impedīvit quīn essēmus quidquid invēnissēmus.   6. Quīn rogās illōs sub sōle ambulandō fessōs ut hīc in nemore quiēscant?   7. Nōn mē fallit quīn tū post tergum meum meō amantī nūbere velīs.   8. Mōs est quibusdam Graecīs ut vītās improbās vīvant; quīn etiam merum assiduē bibunt.   9. Ut agrō carēre coeperat facere nōn poterat quīn cunctās arborēs dēnsī nemoris occīderet.   10. Quaerit utrum quisquam valeat tantum quīn pondus tam grave portāns nimium fessus fīat necne.

D.   Tell how many clauses there are in each sentence in C, say which ones are principal clauses, and identify the subordinate clauses by name.

E.   Translate:

1. If I should see him I'd hinder him from leaving.   2. I was very close to dying, if someone hadn't rescued me.   3. They will by no means refuse to permit us to summon the allies.   4. He departed on the grounds that he didn't want to be compelled to refuse to be helpful to us.   5. Surely you won't delay presenting the woman with money with which to feed her little ones?   6. Who can doubt that with father as steersman we shall cross the river on the raft free from care?   7. He was growing so angry that he could not be restrained from dragging the hair down from the top of his own head.   8. I wouldn't want you to neglect taking care of the flowers in the sacred precinct, for indeed if you don't bring them water they won't grow.   9. My girl's beauty shines above the rest as the sun shines above the earth; why, I even become blind when I look at her.   10. There is no doubt that the well-worn way is the safe way, but if you want to find anything new you have to go along an unknown route.

F.   Pronounce and translate:

1. Metuimus nē quōminus iūs iūrandum nōbīs dent recūsent nēve praetereā nōs in proeliō dēserant.   2. Vulgō surgente nōn multum aberat quīn quīdam ex īmō populō ad vicem nōbilium rērum potīrentur.   3. Fīerī nōn potest quīn mē tuī miserēret memorem ut lūdēns Fortūna in vicēs nōs mortālīs fēlīcēs maestōsque reddat.   4. Eī dīxī tē recūsātūrum quīn eum adeās etsī magnam pecūniam et multa praetereā tibi dōnāverit.   5. Efficī nōn poterat quīn iter factūrī inter sē dīverterentur, cum alius per mare, alius per terram īre mallet.

READING

Developing Reading Skills

Latin words which will help: **aequus, aliēnus, annus, cēdō, Cōnsul, emō, eō, faciō, ferō, fidēs, fugiō, māter, mōlēs, ordō, petō, putō, quīnque, stō, trahō, vertō,** and **volō.**

English words which will help: *affect, aggression, alienate, circuit, confident, consulate, convert, extract, fabricate, imperfect, iniquity, intercede, intercession, intrude, matrimony, minatory, offer, ordain, petition, pontoon, progress, quinquennial, regress, resilient, revert, status, tend, tuba, veto, vindicate,* and *voluntary.*

The Die is Cast!

Nemō est quīn sciat Caesarem prōvinciam minōrem bellīs ciendīs maiōrem reddidisse. Gessit novem annīs quibus in imperiō fuit haec ferē: omnem Galliam quae saltū Pȳrēnaeō Alpibusque et monte Cebennā, flūminibus Rhēno ac Rhodanō, continētur patetque circuitū ad bis et trīciēns centum
5   mīlia passuum in prōvinciae formam redēgit. Germānōs quī trāns Rhēnum incolunt prīmus Rōmānōrum ponte fabricātō aggressus maximīs adfēcit clādibus; aggressus est et Britannōs ignōtōs anteā superātīsque pecūniās et obsidēs imperāvit.

    Cum secundō annō imperī inimīcī eius minārentur sē eum postulātūrōs
10   ademptūrōsque eī exercitūs Crassum Pompēiumque in urbem prōvinciae suae Lūcam extractōs addūxit ut dētrūdendī inimīcōs causā cōnsulātum peterent, effēcitque per utrumque ut in quīnquennium sibi imperium prōrogārētur. Pompēius autem quī Caesaris victōriīs invidēret abaliēnārī coeptus erat adeō ut Iūliae amor sōlus illum impedīret quōminus hunc Crassumque

---

4. bis et trīciēns centum: two times and thirty times a hundred = 3,200

relinqueret et ad Optimātīs redīret. Duōbus post annīs Iūlia mortua est; 15
Caesar ad retinendam autem Pompēī necessitūdinem ac voluntātem Octāviam
sorōris suae nepōtem in matrimōnium obtulit sibique fīliam eius uxōrem
petīvit, sed nūllō modō fierī potuit quīn Pompēius sē cum Senātū iungeret,
praecipuē cum Crassus in Bellō Parthicō occīsus esset.

Caesar per Tribūnōs Plēbis ad populum tulit ut absentī sibi cum imperī 20
tempus explērī coepisset petītiō cōnsulātūs darētur, nē eā causā imperfectō
adhūc bellō dēcēderet. Pompēī exercitibus cōnfīsō Senātuī placuit Caesarem
revertī iubēre priusquam tempus imperī explētum esset, id quod Tribūnī M.
Antōnius et Q. Cassius vetuērunt. Senātus cum intercessiōnem minimī fēcit
tum Tribūnōs confugere coēgit. 25

Caesar trānsierat in Citeriōrem Galliam Ravennaeque substitit bellō
vindicātūrus sī quid dē Tribūnīs Plēbis intercēdentibus prō sē gravius ā
Senātū cōnstitūtum esset. Cum ergō sublātam Tribūnōrum intercessiōnem
ipsōsque urbe cessisse nūntiātum esset prōgressus ad Rubicōnem flūmen,
quī prōvinciae eius fīnis erat, paulum cōnstitit, ac reputāns quantum 30
mōlīrētur conversus ad proximōs "Etiam nunc" inquit "regredī possumus;
quod sī ponticulum trānsierimus omnia armīs agenda erunt." Dubitantī
ōstentum tāle factum est: quīdam eximiā magnitūdine et formā apparuit,
quī raptā ab mīlite tubā prōsiluit ad flūmen et ingentī spiritū classicum
exorsus pertendit ad alteram rīpam. Tum Caesar "Eātur" inquit "quō 35
deōrum ōstenta et inimīcōrum inīquitās vocat. Iacta ālea est." Sīc Bellum
Cīvīle coeptum est.

Post bellum Rōmam reversus Caesar incipiēbat sē convertere ad ordinan-
dum reī publicae statum, cum occīsus est quod rēgem sē facere vellet ā
quibusdam Senātōribus, inter quōs M. Cassius et sibi amīcissimus M. Iūnius 40
Brūtus, quem inruentem vidēns fertur dīxisse, "Et tū, Brūte?" Cum Senātus
ad Theātrum Pompēī convenīret, Caesar tribus et vīgintī plāgīs confossus
cecidit ad pedēs imāginis inimīcī magnī.

Scrīpserat Caesar complūrīs librōs, inter quōs Commentāriōs dē Bellō
Gallicō, quōrum aliquot partēs hinc sequuntur. 45

---

21. imperfectō bellō: Another reason for the request was no doubt the fact that Caesar could
not be prosecuted while he was either out of the country or holding office; he would have
been vulnerable campaigning in Rome.   **24. minimī:** genitive of indefinite value
28. cōnstitūtum esset: subjunctive as representing part of Caesar's thought, hence not
necessarily past contrary-to-fact; what kind of condition is most likely to have been in
Caesar's mind?   **32. armīs:** Since a military command could not be brought within the
borders of Italy, Caesar, if he crossed with his army, would be declaring war on his own
country.

This imperial portrait of Julius Caesar suggests a man of strict discipline, but with a sense of humor.

■ READING COMPREHENSION

1. List the accomplishments of Caesar during the nine years he was in command.   **2.** How did he get his command extended by five years? **3.** How did he try to keep from losing Pompey's friendship?   **4.** Why did Caesar propose to the people that he be allowed to run for Consul in absentia?   **5.** What did the Senate decide about this issue?   **6.** Who vetoed this decision, and what happened?   **7.** What is the significance of the following statement? Tum Caesar "Eātur" inquit "quō deōrum ōstenta et inimīcōrum inīquitās vocat. Iacta ālea est."   **8.** Why was Caesar killed? **9.** "Et tū, Brūte?" has often been quoted. Under what circumstances has this quotation been used?   **10.** What is the title of the best-known book written by Caesar?

REVIEW 5

A. Give the genitive, gender, and meaning of each noun:

arbor	iugum	pecus	tenebrae	vicis
fōns	nemus	ratis	vertex	vitium
foris	ōsculum			

B. Give the other nominative singular forms and the meaning of each adjective:

aeger	citus	ignōtus	nimius	rapidus
amplus	dēnsus	maestus	placidus	sēcūrus
antīquus	dīversus	merus	plērusque	tener
assiduus	fessus			

C. Give the other principal parts and the meaning of each verb:

cieō	fingō	lūdō	repetō	surgō
cūrō	impediō	niteō	spargō	terō
dōnō	īrāscor	recūsō	supersum	ūrō

D. Give the meanings of the following adverbs:

adhūc	forās	frūstrā	praetereā	suprā
aegrē	forīs	invicem	quondam	usque

DRILL ON SYNTAX

Translate into Latin:

1. The soldier was commanded to perform his duty. **2.** Brides are, for the most part, persuaded to throw their flowers. **3.** Do not despise the Senate, for every time there is a meeting your interests are consulted.

LISTENING AND SPEAKING

Women in History

Mucia is a forerunner of young women in the twentieth century who question their place in society and want to exert more influence. How would young women today react to Lucretia's philosophy?

MŪCIA: Frāter Tītus, māter, apud Hortensium magistrum saepe it, sed domī mihi praecipiendum est. Cūr domī mihi manendum est?

LŪCRĒTIA: Nōnne bene docta numerīs linguīsque et Graecā et Latīnā es? Multa ex illīs quae fēmina scīre dēbet domī discuntur, et magistrī quī modōs mōrēsque Forī et Cūriae sciunt ratiōnem aedium familiaeque instituere saepe nōn possunt.

MŪCIA: At, māter, multō auxiliō patrī in laterāriā es, et semper ratiōnēs ad nummum cōnficis. Num domī illās facere didicistī?

LŪCRĒTIA: Ego puella cum mātre patreque linguās et numerōs ratiōnēsque dīscēbam. Vir quam plurimum in Forō et negōtiō possit; vīrēs fēminārum domī et in familiā manent. Decora publica fēminae nōn petimus, nam nostra iam sunt.

MŪCIA: Rē vērā, māter, rectē dīcere vidēris; cūr tamen fēminae nōn sunt quae terrās sīcut principēs Rōmānī regēbant?

LŪCRĒTIA: Oblivīscerisne fābulārum quās tibi dē fēminīs nōtissimīs praeteritīs narrāvī? Mementō Dīdōnis, rēgīnae Carthāginis, quae Aenēam miserē amābat, et Boudicēae magnā virtūte, dominae Britannōrum, quī cum Rōmānīs paucīs ante annīs pugnābant, et tandem Cleopātrae formā pulcherrimā, quae nōn sōlum Egyptōs sed etiam Jūlium Caesarem et Mārcum Antōnium regēbat.

MŪCIA: Rēgīnae nōtissimae rē vērā illae erant, sed Dīdō misera amōre fuit; Boudicēam Rōmānī superāvērunt, et Cleopātra sē interfēcit.

LŪCRĒTIA: Fēminae Rōmānae domī semper rēxērunt, sīcut Līvia, uxor principis prīmī Augustī. Fēmina illa virum regēbat. Dīc mihi uter terrās mariaque rē vērā regēret!

MŪCIA: Intellegō, mater; verbum sat sapientī.

A.   Present an oral reading of the dialogue.

B.   Relay race: The class must be divided into two teams. A moderator will ask the following questions first of one team and then of the other. Those who do not answer correctly must sit down. The team with the greater number of people standing at the end of a given time wins the race.

1. Ubi et ā quō Tītus Mūciaque docentur?   **2.** Quid māter magistrōs scīre dicit?   **3.** Ubi Lūcrētia multō auxiliō virō est? **4.** Cūr fēminae Rōmānae decora publica nōn petunt?   **5.** Uter terrās mariaque rēgēbat, Augustus an Līvia?

Livia, wife of Augustus— Louvre Paris. Livia, the powerful materfamilias of Augustus' household, was reputed to have plotted the accession of her own son, Tiberius, over Augustus' descendants.

Commentāriī dē Bellō Gallicō

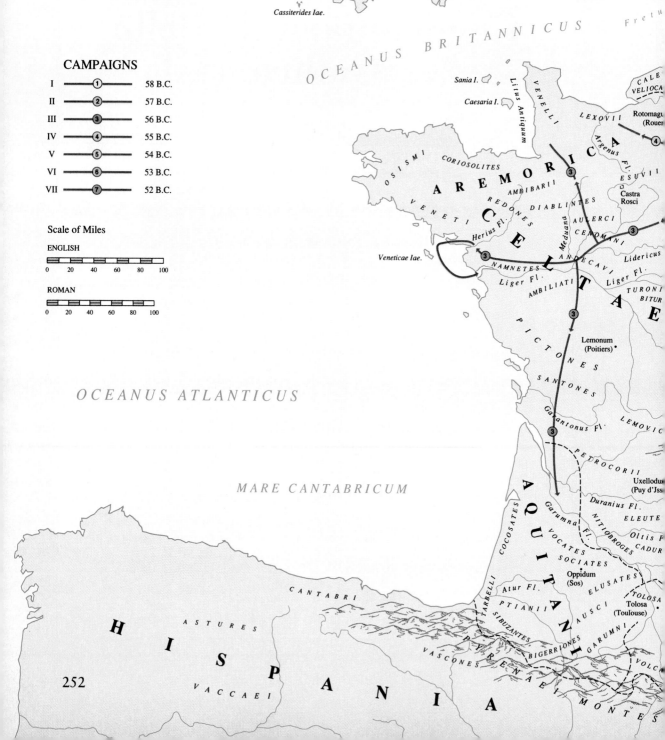

Caesar's Gallic Campaigns

CAMPAIGNS

I	①	58 B.C.
II	②	57 B.C.
III	③	56 B.C.
IV	④	55 B.C.
V	⑤	54 B.C.
VI	⑥	53 B.C.
VII	⑦	52 B.C.

Scale of Miles

ENGLISH

0   20   40   60   80   100

ROMAN

0   20   40   60   80   100

OCEANUS ATLANTICUS

MARE CANTABRICUM

BRITANNIA

TRINOBANT
CASSI
• St. Alban
Londiniu
ANCALITES
CANTIUM
(KENT)
SEGONTIACI
BIBROC
Tamesis Fl.
Vectis I.

Cassiterides Iae.

OCEANUS BRITANNICUS   *Fretu*

Sania I.
Caesaria I.
Litus Antiquum
VENELLI
LEXOVII
Rotomagu
(Rouen)
CALE
VELIOCA
Argenus Fl.
ESUVII
Castra
Rosci
AREMORICA
OSISMI
CORIOSOLITES
AMBIBARII
REDONES
DIABLINTES
AULERCI
CENOMANI
Meduana
ANDECAVI
Lidericus
CELTAE
VENETI
Herius Fl.
NAMNETES
Liger Fl.
Liger Fl.
TURONI
BITUR
AMBILIATI
Veneticae Iae.
PICTONES
Lemonum
(Poitiers) •
SANTONES
LEMOVIC
Garantonus Fl.
PETROCORII
Uxellodu
(Puy d'Jss
Duranius Fl.
ELEUTE
AQUITANI
Garumna Fl.
NITIOBROGES
Oltis F
CADUR
COCOSATES
VOCATES
SOCIATES
Oppidum
(Sos)
ELUSATES
TOLOSA
Tolosa
(Toulouse)
Atur Fl.
AUSCI
TARBELLI
PTIANII
SIBUZATES
BIGERRIONES
GARUMNI
VASCONES
VOLC
PYRENAEI MONTES

CANTABRI

ASTURES

HISPANIA

VACCAEI

252

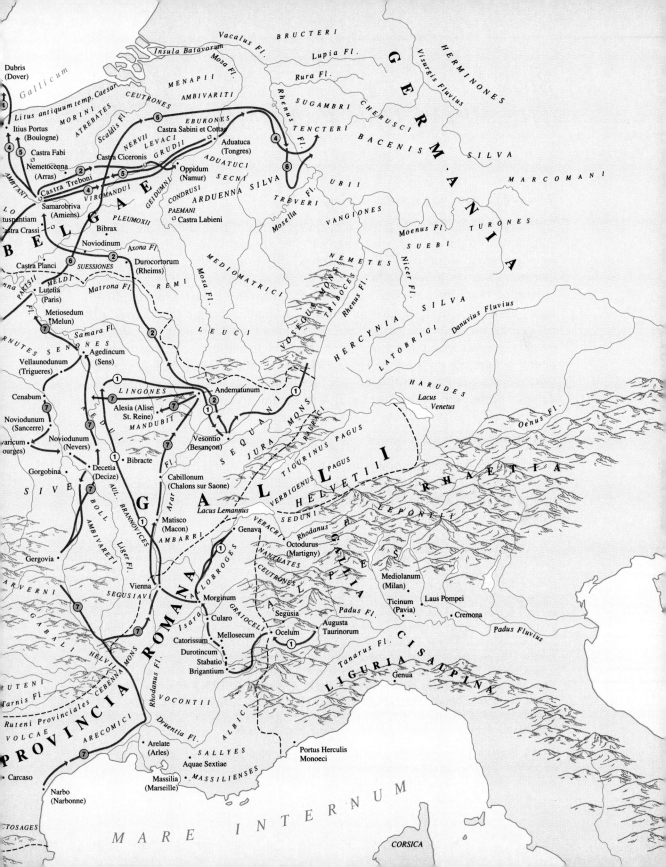

Book 1
THE HELVETIAN CAMPAIGN

1. The Divisions and Peoples of Gaul

Gallia est omnis dīvīsa in partīs trīs, quārum ūnam incolunt Belgae, aliam Aquītānī, tertiam, quī ipsōrum linguā Celtae, nostrā Gallī appellantur. Hī omnēs linguā, īnstitūtīs, legibus inter sē differunt. Gallōs ab Aquītānīs Garumna flūmen, ā Belgīs Matrona et Sēquana dīvidit.

5   Hōrum omnium fortissimī sunt Belgae, proptereā quod ā cultū atque hūmānitāte Prōvinciae longissimē absunt, minimēque saepe mercātōrēs ad eōs commeant, atque ea, quae ad effēminandōs animōs pertinent, important; proximīque sunt Germānīs, quī trāns Rhēnum incolunt, quibuscum continenter bellum gerunt. Quā dē causā Helvētiī quoque reliquōs Gallōs virtūte
10   praecēdunt, quod ferē cotīdiānīs proeliīs cum Germānīs contendunt, cum aut suīs fīnibus eōs prohibent, aut ipsī in eōrum fīnibus bellum gerunt.

2. Orgetorix

Apud Helvētiōs longē nōbilissimus fuit et dītissimus Orgetorīx. Is, M. Messālā et M. Pīsōne cōnsulibus, rēgnī cupiditāte inductus coniūrātiōnem nōbilitātis fēcit, et cīvitātī persuāsit, ut dē fīnibus suīs cum omnibus cōpiīs exīrent.

---

1.   **1. omnis:** *as a whole.* **dīvīsa:** a participle, here used as a predicate adjective with **est**—*is divided.* **trīs:** The three geographical divisions of Gaul were (1) Aquitania, in the southwest; (2) Belgium, in the northeast; and (3) the large central area occupying what is now most of modern France.   **2. Aquītānī:** sc. **incolunt.** (eī) **quī:** *those who.* **ipsōrum:** *their own.* **nostrā:** sc. **linguā**   **3. linguā:** ablative of specification—i.e., *in respect to language,* etc. **īnstitūtīs:** *customs.* **inter sē:** *among themselves*   **4. Garumna flūmen:** *the Garonne;* **Matrona:** *the Marne*   **5. proptereā quod:** *because.* **cultū atque hūmānitāte:** *civilization and culture*   **6. mercātōrēs:** Roman merchants had penetrated into nearly every part of Gaul.   **7. ea:** *those things.* **effēminandōs animōs:** *weakening their courage*   **9. Quā dē causā:** *For this reason*   **10. praecēdunt:** *surpass*   **11. suīs ... eōs ... ipsī ... eōrum:** Note Caesar's use of pronouns. The Helvetians keep them (**eōs**) i.e., the rest of the Germans, from their (**suīs**) lands, or they themselves (**ipsī**) wage war in their (**eōrum**) lands.

2.   **2. Messālā ... cōnsulibus:** i.e., in 61 B.C.   **3. nōbilitātis:** *among the nobility.* **ut exīrent:** *to emigrate;* an indirect command

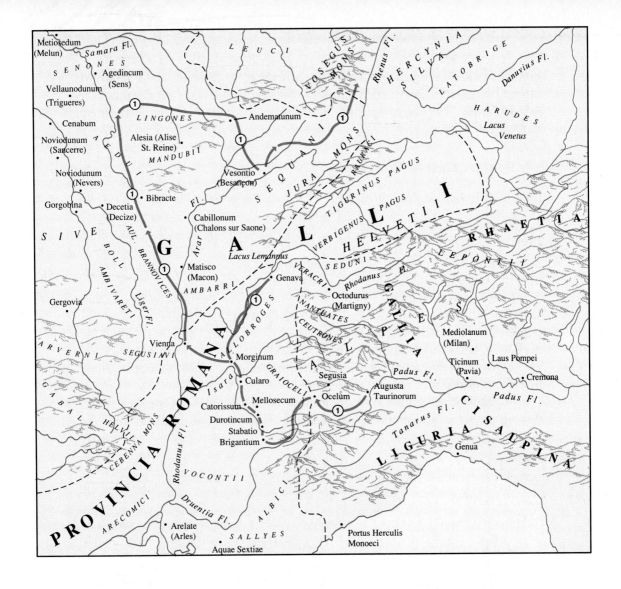

Id facilius eīs persuāsit, quod undique locī nātūrā Helvētiī continentur: 5
ūnā ex parte flūmine Rhēnō, lātissimō atque altissimō, quī agrum Helvētium
ā Germānīs dīvidit; alterā ex parte monte Iūrā altissimō, quī est inter
Sēquanōs et Helvētiōs; tertiā, lacū Lemannō et flūmine Rhodanō, quī
Prōvinciam nostram ab Helvētiīs dīvidit. Hīs rēbus fīēbat ut et minus lātē
vagārentur et minus facile fīnitimīs bellum īnferre possent; quā ex parte 10

---

5. **id:** (*to do*) *this;* a pronominal direct object   7. **monte Iūrā:** *the Jura range*   8. **lacū**
Lemannō: *Lake Geneva*   9. **ut . . . vagārentur:** a substantive result clause, after **fīēbat**
10. **fīnitimīs:** dative with **īnferre**—*on their neighbor.* **quā ex parte:** *for this reason*

hominēs bellandī cupidī magnō dolōre afficiēbantur. Prō multitūdine autèm hominum et prō glōriā bellī atque fortitūdinis angustōs sē finīs habēre arbitrābantur, quī in longitūdinem mīlia passuum CCXL, in lātitūdinem CLXXX patēbant.

3. Orgetorix Forms a Conspiracy

Hīs rēbus adductī et auctōritāte Orgetorīgis permōtī cōnstituērunt comparāre ea quae ad profiscīscendum pertinērent, iūmentōrum et carrōrum quam maximum numerum coemere, sēmentēs quam maximās facere, ut in itinere cōpia frūmentī suppeteret, cum proximīs cīvitātibus pācem et amīcitiam cōnfīrmāre. Ad eās rēs cōnficiendās biennium sibi satis esse exīstimāvērunt; in tertium annum profectiōnem lēge cōnfīrmant.

Ad eās rēs cōnficiendās Orgetorīx dēligitur. Is sibi lēgātiōnem ad cīvitātēs suscēpit. In eō itinere persuādet Casticō, Catamantāloedis fīliō, Sēquanō, ut rēgnum in cīvitāte suā occupāret, quod pater ante habuerat; itemque persuādet Dumnorīgī Aeduō, frātrī Dīviciācī, quī eō tempore prīncipātum in cīvitāte obtinēbat ac maximē plēbī acceptus erat, ut idem cōnārētur, eīque fīliam suam in mātrimōnium dat.

Illīs cōnfīrmat sē suae cīvitātis imperium obtentūrum, atque suīs cōpiīs suōque exercitū illīs rēgna conciliātūrum. Hāc ōrātiōne adductī, inter sē

---

11. bellandī: a gerund; genitive case with cupidī, which is nominative. Prō . . . hominum: *Considering the large number of people.* It is estimated that there were about 263,000 people in Switzerland at that time. Today there are over two million.   12. angustōs: with finīs
14. CLXXX: sc. mīlia passuum—The actual distance is about 80 miles. The error may be due to a mistake on the part of a scribe in copying the manuscript.

3.   1. cōnstituērunt: sc. Helvētiī as subject, modified by the participles adductī and permōtī
2. ea: *those things;* object of comparāre. pertinērent: subjunct. in a relative clause of characteristic—*such things as would have to do with their departure*   3. ut . . . suppeteret: a purpose clause   6. in . . . annum: *for the third year;* i.e., 59 B.C.   6. cōnfīrmant: historical present; translate by the perfect—*they set*   7. ad cīvitātēs: i.e., to the neighboring states—the Sequani and the Aedui. Orgetorix wanted to secure the power in the state of the Helvetians, and persuade Casticus and Dumnorix to seize the thrones in their states.   10. quī: Dumnorix   11. plēbī acceptus: *popular with the common people.* idem cōnārētur: *to make the same attempt*   13. Illīs: *to them*—i.e., to Casticus and Dumnorix. obtentūrum: sc. esse; Caesar frequently omits esse in fut. act. and perf. pass. infin.   14. rēgna: i.e., Sequanian and Aeduan   inter . . . dant: i.e., *they swore mutual fidelity*

fidem et iūs iūrandum dant, et rēgnō occupātō per trīs potentissimōs ac   15
firmissimōs populōs sēsē tōtīus Galliae imperium obtinēre posse spērant.

4. The Conspiracy Fails

Ea rēs est Helvētiīs per indicium ēnūntiāta. Mōribus suīs Orgetorīgem ex
vinculīs causam dīcere coēgērunt; oportēbat eum damnātum igne cremārī.

   Diē cōnstitūtā Orgetorīx ad iūdicium omnem suam familiam, ad hominum
mīlia decem, undique coēgit, et omnīs clientīs obaerātōsque suōs, quōrum
magnum numerum habēbat, eōdem condūxit; per eōs, nē causam dīceret,   5
sē ēripuit. Cum cīvitās ob eam rem incitāta armīs iūs suum exsequī cōnārētur,
multitūdinemque hominum ex agrīs magistrātūs cōgerent, Orgetorīx mortuus
est. Helvētiī autem arbitrantur ipsum sē interfēcisse.

5. The Helvetians Prepare to Migrate

Post eius mortem nihilō minus Helvētiī id, quod cōnstituerant, facere
cōnantur, ut ē fīnibus suīs exeant. Ubi iam sē ad eam rem parātōs esse
arbitrātī sunt, oppida sua omnia, numerō ad duodecim, vīcōs ad quadrin-
gentōs, reliqua prīvāta aedificia incendunt. Frūmentum omne, praeter quod
sēcum portātūrī erant, combūrunt, ut domum reditiōnis spē sublātā parātiōrēs   5
ad omnia perīcula subeunda essent; trium mēnsium molita cibāria sibi
quemque domō efferre iubent. Persuādent Rauracīs et Tulingīs et Latobrīgīs
fīnitimīs ūtī, oppidīs suīs vīcīsque exūstīs, ūnā cum eīs proficīscantur. Boiōs,
quī trāns Rhēnum incoluerant et in agrum Nōricum trānsierant Nōreiamque
oppugnārant, ad sē sociōs recipiunt.   10

---

4.   **1. per indicium:** i.e., through informers. **Mōribus suīs:** *according to their customs*
2. causam dīcere: *to plead his case.* **damnātum:** *if condemned*   **3. Diē:** diēs is usually
masculine, except when it means an appointed time, as it does here. **familiam:** *household,*
including slaves. **ad:** with numbers, *about*   **4. clientēs obaerātōsque:** these persons were in
various ways under obligation to Orgetorix, and bound to support him.   **5. nē . . . dīceret:**
from pleading his case   **6. iūs . . . exsequī:** *to assert its rights*—i.e., bring Orgetorix to trial
7. mortuus est: *died*   **8. ipsum sē:** ipsum is the subject, and sē the object of **interfēcisse.**

5.   **2. ut . . . exeant:** a substantive clause in apposition with **id**   **5. portātūrī erant:** *they
intended to take.* **spē sublātā:** *with hope . . . removed*   **6. subeunda:** gerundive of **subeō.**
trium . . . cibāria: *a three month's supply of ground grain*   **8. ūtī** = **ut. eīs:** i.e., the
Helvetians   **9. agrum Nōricum:** *The territory of the Norici,* in what is now part of Austria.
10. oppugnārant = **oppugnāverant**   **sociōs:** in apposition with **Boiōs**

Sarcophagus with a scene from the Gallic invasion of Italy in 290 B.C. The Gauls are wearing the torques which gave Manlius Torquatus his cognomen. The Gauls of Caesar's day, being somewhat more civilized, were more disciplined in battle.

6. The Helvetians Decide to Go through the Roman Province

Erant omnīnō itinera duo, quibus itineribus domō exīre possent: unum per Sēquanōs, angustum et difficile, inter montem Iūram et flūmen Rhodanum, quā vix singulī carrī dūcerentur; mōns autem altissimus impendēbat, ut facile perpaucī eōs prohibēre possent; alterum per Prōvinciam nostram, 5 multō facilius atque expedītius, proptereā quod inter fīnīs Helvētiōrum et Allobrogum, quī nūper pācātī erant, Rhodanus fluit, isque nōn nūllīs locīs vadō trānsītur.

Extrēmum oppidum Allobrogum proximumque Helvētiōrum fīnibus est

---

6. **1. omnīnō:** *only,* literally, *in all.* **itineribus:** need not be translated. **possent:** subjunc. in a relative clause of characteristic—*by which they would be able.* **unum** (iter): through the Pas de l'Ecluse at the southern end of the Jura Range **3. quā:** *by which way.* **dūcerentur:** subjunc. in a relative clause of characteristic—*could be drawn.* **ut . . . possent:** a result clause **4. alterum:** sc. iter. **per Prōvinciam nostram:** the Roman province south of Gaul, which had belonged to Rome for over sixty years. By this route, the migration of the Helvetians would be through a comparatively level and peaceful country. **5. facilius atque expedītius:** both mean *easier,* modifying **iter,** understood. **6. nūper:** *recently;* three years before this, the Allobroges had rebelled against the Romans and been subdued. **isque:** *and this* (the Rhone)

Genāva. Ex eō oppidō pōns ad Helvētiōs pertinet. Allobrogibus sēsē vel persuāsūrōs exīstimābant, vel vī coāctūrōs, ut per suōs fīnēs eōs īre paterentur. Omnibus rēbus ad profectiōnem comparātīs diem dīcunt, quā diē ad rīpam Rhodanī omnēs conveniant. Is diēs erat a. d. v Kal. Apr., L. Pīsōne, A. Gabīniō cōnsulibus.   10

7. Caesar Hurries to Geneva

Caesarī cum id nūntiātum esset, eōs per Prōvinciam nostram iter facere cōnārī, mātūrat ab urbe proficīscī et, quam maximīs potest itineribus, in Galliam ulteriōrem contendit et ad Genāvam pervenit. Prōvinciae tōtī quam maximum potest mīlitum numerum imperat (erat omnīnō in Galliā ulteriōre legiō ūna); pontem, quī erat ad Genāvam, iubet rescindī.   5

Ubi dē eius adventū Helvētiī certiōrēs factī sunt, lēgātōs ad eum mittunt nōbilissimōs cīvitātis, quī dīcerent, sibi esse in animō sine ūllō maleficiō iter per Prōvinciam facere, proptereā quod nūllum aliud iter habērent; sē rogāre ut sibi licēret eius voluntāte id facere. Caesar, quod memoriā tenēbat L. Cassium cōnsulem occīsum exercitumque eius ab Helvētiīs pulsum et sub   10 iugum missum, concēdendum nōn putābat; neque exīstimābat hominēs inimīcō animō, datā facultāte per Prōvinciam itineris faciendī, ab iniūriā et maleficiō temperātūrōs. Tamen, ut spatium intercēdere posset, dum mīlitēs, quōs imperāverat, convenīrent, lēgātīs respondit, diem sē ad dēliberandum sūmptūrum; sī quid vellent, ad Īd. Aprīl. reverterentur.   15

---

9. **Genāva:** the old part of Geneva today is on the south side of the Rhone; the modern city is on the north.   10. **suōs:** i.e., of the Allobroges. **eōs:** the Helvetians. **paterentur:** *to allow,* from **patior**   11. **dīcunt:** *they fixed.* **quā diē:** *on which*   12. **conveniant:** *they were to gather* (rel. purpose). **a.d. V. Kal. Apr.:** ante diem quīntum Kalendās Aprīlīs— *the fifth day before the Kalends of April,* i.e., *March 28, 58* B.C.

7.   1. **Caesarī:** Caesar was in Rome when he heard that the Helvetians planned to migrate through the Roman province. He arrived in the vicinity of Geneva in 8 days.   2. **quam . . . itineribus:** *as fast as he could travel;* literally, *by the longest possible marches*   3. **ad:** *to the vicinity of*   4. **imperat:** *he levied upon*   5. **legiō:** the famous Tenth. **ad:** *at.* **rescindī:** *to be cut down.* It was a wooden bridge; today a stone bridge spans the Rhone at about the same place.   7. **quī dīcerent:** a relative clause of purpose. **sibi . . . animō:** *that it was their intention*   10. **occīsum:** sc. **esse;** also with **pulsum, missum,** and **concēdendum. sub iugum missum:** *made to walk under the yoke* (an arch of spears), as a sign of submission. This defeat took place in 107 B.C.   11. **concēdendum:** *this should be granted*   13. **temperātūrōs (esse):** *would refrain from.* **ut . . . posset:** *in order to gain time.* **dum:** *until;* introducing a clause of anticipation   14. **diem:** *time;* literally, *a day or two;* actually they had to wait for two weeks for his reply; this gave Caesar time to strengthen his defenses.   15. **ad Īd. Aprīl.:** *about the Ides (13th) of April.* **reverterentur:** subjunc. in an indirect command

8. Caesar Fortifies the South Bank of the Rhone

Intereā eā legiōne, quam sēcum habēbat, mīlitibusque, quī ex Prōvinciā convēnerant, ā lacū Lemannō, quī in flūmen Rhodanum īnfluit, ad montem Iūram, quī fīnīs Sēquanōrum ab Helvētiīs dīvidit,—mīlia passuum XIX— mūrum in altitūdinem pedum sēdecim fossamque perdūcit. Eō opere perfectō
5 praesidia dispōnit, castella commūnit, ut Helvētiōs trānsīre cōnantīs prohibēre possit.

Ubi ea diēs, quam cōnstituerat cum lēgātīs, vēnit, et lēgātī ad eum revertērunt, negat sē mōre et exemplō populī Rōmānī posse iter ūllī per Prōvinciam dare; et, sī vim facere cōnentur, sē eōs prohibitūrum ostendit.
10 Helvētiī, eā spē dēiectī, aliī, nāvibus iūnctīs ratibusque complūribus factīs, flūmen trānsīre cōnantur; aliī vadīs Rhodanī, quā minima altitūdō flūminis erat, nōn numquam interdiū, saepius noctū, perrumpere cōnantur. Sed operis mūnītiōne et mīlitum concursū et tēlīs repulsī hōc cōnātū dēstitērunt.

9. The Sequani Allow the Helvetians to Pass

Relinquēbātur ūna via per Sēquanōs, quā, Sēquanīs invītīs, propter angustiās īre nōn poterant. Hīs cum suā sponte persuādēre nōn possent, lēgātōs ad Dumnorīgem Aeduum mittunt, ut, eō dēprecātōre, ā Sēquanīs impetrārent. Dumnorīx grātiā et largītiōne apud Sēquanōs plūrimum poterat, et Helvētiīs
5 erat amīcus, quod ex eā cīvitāte Orgetorīgis fīliam in mātrimōnium dūxerat. Ille autem cupiditāte rēgnī adductus novīs rēbus studēbat, et quam plūrimās cīvitātēs suō beneficiō obstrictās habēre volēbat. Itaque rem suscipit, et ā Sēquanīs impetrat, ut per fīnīs suōs Helvētiōs īre patiantur, atque perficit ut obsidēs inter sēsē dent: Sēquanī, nē itinere Helvētiōs prohibeant; Helvētiī,
10 ut sine maleficiō et iniūriā trānseant.

---

8.   5. castella: *redoubts*   8. negat sē ... posse *he said that he could not.* iter: *permission to go*   10. dēiectī: *disappointed.* aliī ... aliī: *some ... others.* nāvibus iūnctīs: *i.e., by making a pontoon bridge*   11. quā: adverb, *where*

9.   1. ūna via: this was along the north bank of the Rhone. Sēquanīs invītīs: *if the Sequani were unwilling*   2. suā sponte: *by their own efforts.* They did not themselves possess sufficient influence, so it was necessary to use Dumnorix, an Aeduan, as mediator.   3. eō dēprecātōre: *by his intercession.* impetrārent: *they might gain their request*   4. plūrimum poterat: *was very powerful;* plūrimum is used as an adverb.   6. novīs rēbus: *a revolution;* dative with studeō   7. obstrictās: *under obligation*   9. obsidēs: *hostages*—usually prominent people, men, women, or children, who were held as a guarantee of good faith

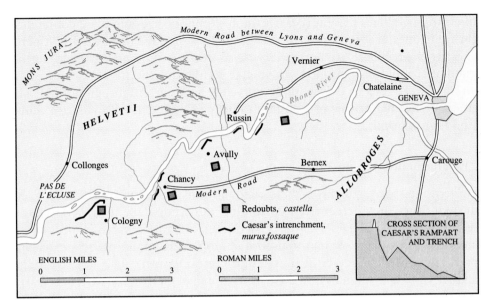

Caesar's fortification of the south bank of the Rhone

10. Caesar Crosses the Alps

Caesarī renūntiātur, Helvētiīs esse in animō per agrum Sēquanōrum et
Aeduōrum iter in Santonum fīnīs facere, quī nōn longē ā Tolōsātium fīnibus
absunt, quae cīvitās est in Prōvinciā. Id sī fieret, intellegēbat magnō cum
perīculō Prōvinciae futūrum, ut hominēs bellicōsōs, populī Rōmānī inimīcōs,
locīs patentibus maximēque frūmentāriīs fīnitimōs habēret. Ob eās causās   5
eī mūnītiōnī, quam fēcerat, T. Labiēnum lēgātum praefēcit; ipse in Italiam
magnīs itineribus contendit duāsque ibi legiōnēs cōnscrībit, et trīs, quae
circum Aquileiam hiemābant, ex hībernīs ēdūcit et, quā proximum iter in

10.   **1. Helvētiīs . . . animō:** *that the Helvetians intended*   **2. Santonum:** *the Santones*
were a people in southwestern Gaul. The Helvetians planned to settle in their lands.
Tolōsātium: *the Tolosates* were part of the **Provincia Romana,** about 120 miles away from
the Santones.   **3. quae cīvitās:** *a state which*   **4. hominēs bellicōsōs:** i.e., the Helvetians
5. locīs: dat. with **fīnitimōs**   **6. mūnītiōnī:** dative with **praefēcit. Labiēnum:** *Labienus,* one
of Caesar's ablest officers in the whole Gallic campaign   **7. contendit:** *hurried;* Caesar
realized that he could not stop the Helvetians with his small army, so he hurried back to
Cisalpine Gaul, enlisted two new legions, and brought back three others that had wintered
near Aquileia. The two new legions were the XIth and XIIth; the other three were the VIIth,
VIIIth, and IXth. These, with the Xth that was near Geneva, gave him six full legions.

ulteriōrem Galliam per Alpīs erat, cum hīs quīnque legiōnibus īre contendit.
Ibi Ceutronēs et Graiocelī et Caturīgēs locīs superiōribus occupātīs itinere
exercitum prohibēre cōnantur. Hīs pulsīs complūribus proeliīs, ab Ocelō,
quod est oppidum citeriōris prōvinciae extrēmum, in fīnīs Vocontiōrum
ulteriōris prōvinciae diē septimō pervenit; inde in Allobrogum fīnīs, ab
Allobrogibus in Segūsiāvōs exercitum dūcit. Hī sunt extrā Prōvinciam trāns
Rhodanum prīmī.

11. The Aedui Ask for Protection

Helvētiī iam per angustiās et fīnīs Sēquanōrum suās cōpiās trādūxerant, et
in Aeduōrum fīnīs pervēnerant eōrumque agrōs populābantur. Aeduī, cum
sē suaque ab eīs dēfendere nōn possent, lēgātōs ad Caesarem mittunt quī
auxilium rogent: Ita sē omnī tempore dē populō Rōmānō meritōs esse, ut,
paene in cōnspectū exercitūs nostrī, agrī eōrum vāstārī, līberī in servitūtem
abdūcī, oppida expugnārī nōn dēbuerint. Eōdem tempore Ambarrī, necessāriī
et cōnsanguineī Aeduōrum, Caesarem certiōrem faciunt, sēsē, dēpopulātīs
agrīs, nōn facile ab oppidīs vim hostium prohibēre. Item Allobrogēs, quī
trāns Rhodanum vīcōs possessiōnēsque habēbant, fugā sē ad Caesarem
recipiunt, et dēmōnstrant, sibi praeter agrī solum nihil esse reliquī. Quibus
rēbus adductus Caesar sibi nōn exspectandum esse statuit, dum, omnibus
fortūnīs sociōrum cōnsūmptīs, in Santonōs Helvētiī pervenīrent.

12. Caesar Destroys One Division of the Helvetians

Flūmen est Arar, quod per fīnīs Aeduōrum et Sēquanōrum in Rhodanum
īnfluit, incrēdibilī lēnitāte, ita ut oculīs iūdicārī nōn possit in utram partem

---

9. per Alpīs: probably through the Mt. Genèvre pass   **12. extrēmum (oppidum):** from the point of view of Rome

11.   **1. iam:** It took Caesar about 50 days to go to Cisalpine Gaul, obtain reinforcements, and overtake the Helvetians. Meanwhile the emigrants had crawled slowly along a distance of 100 miles from the Pas de l'Ecluse. It was now about June 7th.   **2. eōrum:** i.e., the fields of the Aedui   **3. sē suaque:** *themselves and their property*   **4. Ita . . . esse:** (saying that) *they had always deserved so well of the Roman people*   **6. dēbuerint:** the perfect tense is sometimes used in clauses of result to emphasize the result; the regular sequence would subordinate it.   **7. dēpopulātīs:** *having been laid waste;* in this case the deponent verb has a passive meaning in the ablative absolute.   **10. sibi . . . reliquī:** *that they had nothing left except the bare ground*   **11. sibi . . . esse:** *that he ought not to wait;* a passive periphrastic

12.   **1. Arar:** *the Saône,* which flows into the Rhone at the modern city of Lyons   **2. lēnitāte:** ablative of description. **partem:** *direction.*

fluat. Id Helvētiī ratibus ac lintribus iūnctīs trānsībant. Ubi per explōrātōrēs Caesar certior factus est, Helvētiōs iam trīs partīs cōpiārum id flūmen trādūxisse, et quārtam ferē partem citrā flūmen Ararim reliquam esse, dē   5 tertiā vigiliā cum legiōnibus tribus ē castrīs profectus, ad eam partem pervēnit, quae nōndum flūmen trānsierat. Eōs impedītōs et inopīnantīs aggressus, magnam partem eōrum concīdit; reliquī sēsē fugae mandārunt atque in proximās silvās abdidērunt. Is pāgus appellābātur Tigurīnus; nam omnis cīvitās Helvētia in quattuor pāgōs dīvīsa est.   10

Hic pāgus ūnus, cum domō exīsset, patrum nostrōrum memoriā L. Cassium cōnsulem interfēcerat et eius exercitum sub iugum mīserat. Ita sīve cāsū sīve cōnsiliō deōrum immortālium, ea pars cīvitātis Helvētiae, quae īnsignem calamitātem populō Rōmānō intulerat, prīnceps poenās persolvit. Quā in rē Caesar nōn sōlum pūblicās, sed etiam prīvātās iniūriās ultus est, quod   15 Tigurīnī eōdem proeliō eius socerī L. Pīsōnis avum, L. Pīsōnem lēgātum, interfēcerant.

Chapters 13–20

Caesar then built a bridge over the Saône, and led his army across. The Helvetians sent envoys to him, but Caesar refused their suggestions for peace. The Aedui, who were supposedly friendly to Caesar, and were to supply him with much grain, secretly held back their provisions. Thereafter the Helvetians marched westward, and Caesar followed about five miles behind, building a new camp each night.

21. Caesar Plans an Attack on the Helvetians

Eōdem diē ab explōrātōribus certior factus hostīs sub monte cōnsēdisse mīlia passuum ab ipsīus castrīs octō, mīsit explōrātōrēs, quī cognōscerent

---

3. trānsībant: When Caesar arrived, the Helvetians were still crossing the river. It is estimated that it took twenty days to cross.   **5. citrā:** i.e., on the east side of the river. **dē:** *in*
8. mandārunt = mandāvērunt   9. Is pāgus: i.e., the **quarta pars,** which Caesar annihilated
11. memoriā: *within the memory*   **12. interfēcerat:** in 107 B.C. See Chapter 7.   **14. prīnceps**
... persolvit: *was the first to pay the penalty*   **15. ultus est:** *avenged;* from **ulcīscor**

21.   1. Eōdem diē: probably about June 17, *the same day,* that Caesar had held interviews with Dumnorix and Diviciacus about grain supplies. **sub:** *at the foot of.* The hill was near Bibracte in the Loire valley.

The Gauls had also invaded Asia Minor (the Galatians were Gauls.) This sculpture of a dying Gaul, identified by the torque around his neck, comes from the Great Altar of Pergamum.

the dying Gaul
—Hel

quālis esset nātūra montis et quālis in circuitū ascēnsus. Renūntiātum est ascēnsum esse facilem. Dē tertiā vigiliā Titum Labiēnum lēgātum cum duābus legiōnibus et eīs ducibus, quī iter cognōverant, summum iugum montis ascendere iubet; quid suī cōnsilī sit, ostendit. Ipse dē quārtā vigiliā eōdem itinere, quō hostēs ierant, ad eōs contendit equitātumque omnem ante sē mittit. P. Cōnsidius, quī reī mīlitāris perītissimus habēbātur et in exercitū L. Sullae et posteā in M. Crassī fuerat, cum explōrātōribus praemittitur.

22. Caesar's Plan Fails

Prīmā lūce, cum summus mōns ā Labiēnō tenērētur, ipse ab hostium castrīs nōn longius mīlle et quīngentīs passibus abesset, neque (ut posteā ex captīvīs

---

3. **in circuitū:** *on the other side;* he hoped to be able to attack the enemy camp from two sides at the same time.   5. **ducibus:** *as guides*   6. **cōnsilī:** a partitive genitive; *what his plan was.* **dē quārtā vigiliā:** i.e., about 2 A.M.   8. **habēbātur:** *was considered*

22.   1. **Prīmā lūce:** 4 A.M. **tenērētur:** Labienus was above and in back of the Helvetian camp, unknown to the enemy.   2. **passibus:** ablative of comparison with **longius**

comperit) aut ipsīus adventus aut Labiēnī cognitus esset, Cōnsidius equō
admissō ad eum accurrit, dīcit montem, quem ā Labiēnō occupārī voluerit,
ab hostibus tenērī; id sē ā Gallicīs armīs atque īnsignibus cognōvisse. Caesar   5
suās cōpiās in proximum collem subdūcit, aciem īnstruit.

Labiēnus, ut eī erat praeceptum ā Caesare nē proelium committeret, nisi
ipsīus cōpiae prope hostium castra vīsae essent, ut undique ūnō tempore in
hostīs impetus fieret, monte occupātō nostrōs exspectābat proeliōque abstinēbat. Multō dēnique diē per explōrātōrēs Caesar cognōvit, et montem ā   10
suīs tenērī et Helvētiōs castra mōvisse et Cōnsidium, timōre perterritum,
quod nōn vīdisset prō vīsō renūntiāsse. Eō diē, quō cōnsuērat intervāllō,
hostēs sequitur et mīlia passuum tria ab eōrum castrīs castra pōnit.

23. Caesar Turns toward Bibracte

Postrīdiē eius diēī, quod omnīnō bīduum supererat, cum exercituī frūmentum
mētīrī oportēret, et quod ā Bibracte, oppidō Aeduōrum longē maximō et
cōpiōsissimō, nōn amplius mīlibus passuum XVIII aberat, reī frūmentāriae
prōspiciendum exīstimāvit; iter ab Helvētiīs āvertit ac Bibracte īre contendit.

Ea rēs per fugitīvōs L. Aemilī, decuriōnis equitum Gallōrum, hostibus   5
nūntiātur. Helvētiī, seu quod timōre perterritōs Rōmānōs discēdere ā sē
exīstimārent, seu quod eōs rē frūmentāriā interclūdī posse cōnfīderent,
commūtātō cōnsiliō atque itinere conversō, nostrōs ā novissimō agmine
īnsequī ac lacessere coepērunt.

---

3. **equō admissō**: *at full gallop*   4. **voluerit**: subj. in indirect discourse; perfect tense.   5. **id
sē**: id is object, and sē subject of **cognōvisse** in indirect discourse after **dīcit**.   6. **subdūcit**:
withdrew. He still did not know that Considius was mistaken.   7. **eī . . . praeceptum**: *he
had been ordered*   8. **ipsīus**; i.e., Caesar's   10. **Multō diē**: *late in the day*—after the
Helvetians had continued their march to the west   12. **prō vīsō**: *as seen*. **quō . . . intervāllō**:
at the usual distance—about five or six miles. **cōnsuērat** = **cōnsuēverat**

23.   1. **Postrīdiē eius diēī**: *On the following day*. **supererat**: *was left;* from **supersum**. **cum**:
before   2. **Bibracte**: ablative singular; most names of towns ending in -e have the ablative
singular in -e, as well as the nominative and accusative singular. Bibracte was the capital
city of the Aedui, situated on a high plateau, now called Mt. Beuvray. It is generally believed
that Caesar wrote up the accounts of the Gallic war in this town in the winter of 52–51
B.C., after defeating Vercingetorix in the climactic battle described in Book 7.   4. **prōspiciendum
(esse)**: *that he ought to provide for*   5. **fugitīvōs**: *run away slaves*. **equitum Gallōrum**: *the
Roman army used Gallic horsemen*   6. **seu, seu**: *either, or*   7. **existimārent**: **quod** causal
clauses take the indicative when the reason is given on the authority of the speaker, and the
subjunctive when the reason is given on the authority of another.   8. **ā novissimō agmine**:
at the rear

24. Both Sides Prepare to Fight

Postquam id animum advertit, cōpiās suās Caesar in proximum collem
subdūcit equitātumque, quī sustinēret hostium impetum, mīsit. Ipse interim
in colle mediō triplicem aciem īnstrūxit legiōnum quattuor veterānārum. In
summō iugō duās legiōnēs, quās in Galliā citeriōre proximē cōnscrīpserat,
et omnia auxilia collocāvit. Intereā sarcinās in ūnum locum cōnferrī et eum
locum ab hīs, quī in superiōre aciē cōnstiterant, mūnīrī iussit. Helvētiī cum
omnibus suīs carrīs secūtī, impedīmenta in ūnum locum contulērunt; ipsī
cōnfertissimā aciē, reiectō nostrō equitātū, phalange factā, sub prīmam
nostram aciem successērunt.

25. The Helvetians Are Forced Back

Caesar, prīmum suō equō deinde equīs omnium ex cōnspectū remōtīs—ut,
aequātō omnium perīculō, spem fugae tolleret—cohortātus suōs, proelium
commīsit. Mīlitēs, ē locō superiōre pīlīs missīs, facile hostium phalangem
perfrēgērunt. Eā disiectā, gladiīs dēstrictīs in eōs impetum fēcērunt.

Gallīs magnō ad pugnam erat impedīmentō quod, plūribus eōrum scūtīs
ūnō ictū pīlōrum trānsfīxīs et colligātīs, cum ferrum sē īnflexisset, neque
pīla ēvellere neque, sinistrā impedītā, satis commodē pugnāre poterant.
Itaque multī scūtum manū ēmittere et nūdō corpore pugnāre praeoptābant.
Tandem vulneribus dēfessī, pedem referre, et, quod mōns suberat circiter
mīlle passuum spatiō, eō sē recipere coepērunt.

----

24. **1. id:** *this,* i.e., that the Helvetians were now pursuing him. **animum advertit** =
animadvertit, *noticed.* **collem:** the hill above Armecy, about eighteen miles south of Bibracte
3. in . . . mediō: *halfway up the hill.* **triplicem:** *triple;* the four legions were drawn up in
three lines, the first and second to do the fighting, and the third held in reserve. The veterans
were put in the first line. **veterānārum:** i.e., the VII, VIII, IX, and Xth legions   **5. auxilia:**
the auxiliaries, usually non-Roman archers and slingers. **sarcinās:** *packs,* which each soldier
carried on the march. They contained personal belongings, food rations, and cooking utensils.
They were tied up in a bundle, and fastened to a pole, which was carried over the shoulder.
7. impedīmenta: *the heavy baggage,* of the whole army   **8. phalange:** *the phalanx,* or close
formation in which those in front held their shields in front of them, overlapping each other,
and those behind held their shields over their heads

25. **1. suō equō:** sc. **remōtō omnium:** *of all (the officers)*   **2. spem . . . tolleret:** i.e., they
had to fight or die; there could be no escape on horseback.   **3. superiōre:** *higher;* the Roman
missiles fell with more force, since the enemy was advancing up the hill. The **pīlīs,** *javelins,*
could be hurled effectively from fifty to sixty feet.   **4. Eā:** sc. **phalange. disiecta:** *broken up*
5. Gallīs: dative of reference. **impedīmentō:** dative of purpose   **6. trānsfīxīs et colligātīs:**
pierced and pinned together   **7. sinistrā:** sc. **manū**   **8. ēmittere:** *to let go.* **nūdō:**
unprotected   **9. pedem referre:** *to retreat*

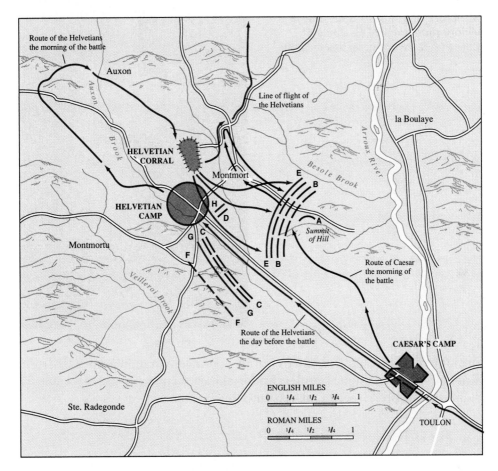

Plan of Caesar's first battle with the Helvetians

A Fortification built by the 10th and 11th Legions   **B-B** Roman triple line, 1st position   **C-C** 1st and 2nd Roman lines, 2nd position   **D** 3rd Roman line, 2nd position   **E-E** Helvetians, 1st position   **F-F** Helvetians, 2nd position **G-G** Helvetians, 3rd position, attacking again   **H** Boii and Tulingi

Captō monte et succēdentibus nostrīs, Boiī et Tulingī, quī hominum mīlibus circiter XV agmen hostium claudēbant et novissimīs praesidiō erant, ex itinere nostrōs ab latere apertō aggressī sunt. Id cōnspicātī Helvētiī, quī

---

11. Captō: *reached*   **12. agmen claudēbant:** *were bringing up the rear.* **novissimīs praesidiō:** double dative; *to protect the rear*   **13. ex itinere:** i.e., without stopping to rest or reform their lines. **apertō:** *exposed* (i.e., the right, since the shields were on the left arm)

Sculpture of a captive Gaul from a victory monument. The Gauls of Caesar's day wore breeches in battle.

in montem sēsē recēperant, rūrsus īnstāre et proelium redintegrāre coepērunt.

15 Rōmānī bipertītō signa intulērunt; prīma et secunda aciēs, ut victīs ac summōtīs resisteret; tertia, ut venientīs sustinēret.

26. The Helvetians Are Defeated

Ita ancipitī proeliō diū atque ācriter pugnātum est. Diūtius cum sustinēre nostrōrum impetūs nōn possent, alterī sē, ut coeperant, in montem recēpērunt, alterī ad impedīmenta et carrōs suōs sē contulērunt. Nam hōc tōtō proeliō, cum ab hōrā septimā ad vesperum pugnātum esset, āversum hostem vidēre

5 nēmō potuit. Ad multam noctem etiam ad impedīmenta pugnātum est, proptereā quod prō vāllō carrōs obiēcerant et ē locō superiōre in nostrōs venientīs tēla coniciēbant, et nōn nūllī inter carrōs rotāsque matarās ac trāgulās subiciēbant nostrōsque vulnerābant. Diū cum esset pugnātum,

---

15. signa intulērunt: *advanced.* **victīs ac summōtīs:** the Helvetians. **venientīs:** The Boiī and Tulingī

26. 1. pugnātum est: *the battle raged* **2. alterī, alterī:** *the one division* (the Helvetians), *the other* (the Boii and Tulingi) **4. cum:** *although.* **hōrā septimā:** *midday.* **āversum:** *turned in flight* **5. Ad . . . noctem:** *until late at night* **6. ē locō superiōre:** i.e., from the top of the rampart of carts

impedīmentīs castrīsque nostrī potītī sunt. Ibi Orgetorīgis fīlia atque ūnus ē
fīliīs captus est.

Ex eō proeliō circiter hominum mīlia cxxx superfuērunt, quī nūllam
partem noctis itinere intermissō, in fīnīs Lingonum diē quārtō pervēnērunt.
Nam nostrī et propter vulnera mīlitum et propter sepultūram occīsōrum
trīduum morātī, eōs sequī nōn potuērunt. Caesar ad Lingonēs litterās
nūntiōsque mīsit, nē eōs frūmentō nēve aliā rē iuvārent. Ipse trīduō intermissō
cum omnibus cōpiīs eōs sequī coepit.

27. The Helvetians Ask for Peace

Helvētiī omnium rērum inopiā adductī lēgātōs dē dēditiōne ad eum mīsērunt.
Quī cum eum in itinere convēnissent sēque eius ad pedēs prōiēcissent
flentēsque pācem petīssent, eōs in eō locō, quō tum erant, suum adventum
exspectāre iussit. Eō postquam Caesar pervēnit, obsidēs, arma, servōs, quī
ad eōs perfūgerant, poposcit.

Dum ea conquīruntur et cōnferuntur, nocte intermissā, circiter hominum
mīlia VI eius pāgī, quī Verbigenus appellātur, sīve timōre perterritī, sīve spē
salūtis inductī, prīmā nocte ē castrīs Helvētiōrum ēgressī ad Rhēnum fīnīsque
Germānōrum contendērunt.

28. The Terms of Surrender

Quod ubi Caesar resciit, imperāvit hīs, quōrum per fīnīs ierant, utī eōs
conquīrerent et redūcerent; eōs reductōs in hostium numerō habuit; reliquōs
omnēs, obsidibus, armīs, perfugīs trāditīs, in dēditiōnem accēpit. Helvētiōs,
Tulingōs, Latobrīgōs in fīnīs suōs, unde erant profectī, revertī iussit; et,
quod omnibus frūgibus āmissīs domī nihil erat, quō famem tolerārent,
Allobrogibus imperāvit, ut eīs frūmentī cōpiam facerent; ipsōs oppida
vīcōsque, quōs incenderant, restituere iussit.

---

9. impedīmentīs castrīsque: ablative with **potior**   **11. superfuērunt:** *survived* **12. Lingonum:**
the Lingones, about seventy miles north of the battle site   **15. nē iuvārent:** *(ordering them)
not to help them.* **nēve = et nē**

27.   **2. Quī cum:** *When these* (envoys)   **3. eōs:** i.e., the Helvetians   **6. ea:** i.e., the
obsidēs, arma, and **servī**   **8. ēgressī:** *setting out*

28.   **1. Quod:** *this;* i.e., that some of the Helvetians had fled to the Rhine. **utī = ut**   **2. eōs
reductōs:** *those who were brought back* (to Caesar). **in . . . habuit:** *he treated as enemies—*
by killing them or selling them off into slavery   **5. frūgibus āmissīs:** They had destroyed
their grain before leaving home. **quō tolerārent:** *with which to stave off,* (rel.
purpose)   **6. facerent:** *provide*   **ipsōs:** (the Helvetians) *themselves*

Id eā maximē ratiōne fēcit, quod nōluit eum locum, unde Helvētiī discesserant, vacāre nē propter bonitātem agrōrum Germānī, quī trāns Rhēnum incolunt, ē suīs fīnibus in Helvētiōrum fīnēs trānsīrent et fīnitimī Galliae prōvinciae Allobrogibusque essent. Aeduīs permīsit, ut in fīnibus suīs Boiōs collocārent; quibus illī agrōs dedērunt, quōsque posteā in parem iūris lībertātisque condiciōnem recēpērunt.

10

Roman troops fighting with barbarians—a 2d century relief from the Arch of Constantine, Rome

8. eā ... ratiōne: *for this reason especially*   9. vacāre: *to be unoccupied*   12. ut ... collocārent: The Aedui wanted to bring the Boii into their state to strengthen them against the rival Sequani. in parem ... condiciōnem: i.e., the Boii would have equal legal rights with the Aedui

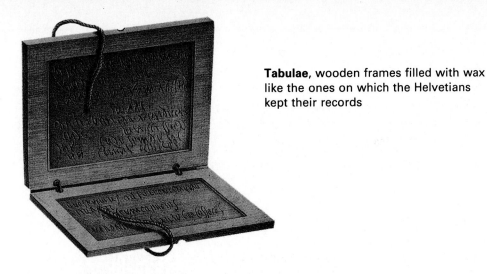

Tabulae, wooden frames filled with wax like the ones on which the Helvetians kept their records

29. The Helvetian Roster

In castrīs Helvētiōrum tabulae, litterīs Graecīs cōnfectae, repertae sunt et ad Caesarem relātae, quibus in tabulīs nōminātim ratiō cōnfecta erat, quī numerus domō exīsset eōrum quī arma ferre possent, et item sēparātim puerī, senēs mulierēsque. Quōrum omnium summa erat Helvētiōrum mīlia CCLXIII, Tulingōrum mīlia XXXVI, Latobrīgōrum XIV, Rauracōrum XXIII, Boiōrum XXXII; ex hīs, quī arma ferre possent, ad mīlia nōnāgintā duo.

Summa omnium fuit ad mīlia CCCLXVIII. Eōrum, quī domum rediērunt, cēnsū habitō, ut Caesar imperāverat, repertus est numerus mīlium C et X.

5

Chapters 30–54

> *After the defeat of the Helvetians, Caesar marched north to negotiate with a tribe of Germans, under their king Ariovistus, who had recently crossed into Gaul, and threatened to seize a large part of the Gallic territory. After negotiations failed, the two armies made camp, and prepared to fight a battle, near modern Ostheim. Each day Caesar led out his troops to offer battle, but the Germans stayed in camp. Finally Caesar forced a battle and defeated the Germans, killing all but a few.*

---

29.   1. tabulae: *lists.* **cōnfectae:** *written*   **2. nōminātim:** *by name*   **3. sēparātim:** *under separate heads*   **4. summa:** *total;* a noun. Also in line 7. **quī** = **eī quī**   **8. cēnsū habitō:** *a census having been taken.* According to Caesar's figures, less than one third of the original number returned home.

Book 2
THE CAMPAIGN AGAINST THE BELGIANS 57 B.C.

1. The Belgians Form a Conspiracy

Cum esset Caesar in citeriōre Galliā, ita utī suprā dēmōnstrāvimus, crēbrī ad eum rūmōrēs afferēbantur, litterīsque item Labiēnī certior fīēbat, omnīs Belgās (quam tertiam esse Galliae partem dīxerāmus) contrā populum Rōmānum coniūrāre obsidēsque inter sē dare.

5 Coniūrandī hae erant causae: prīmum, quod verēbantur nē, omnī pācātā Galliā, ad eōs exercitus noster addūcerētur; deinde, quod ab nōn nūllīs Gallīs sollicitābantur. Ex hīs aliī, ut Germānōs diūtius in Galliā versārī nōluerant, ita populī Rōmānī exercitum hiemāre atque inveterāscere in Galliā molestē ferēbant; aliī mōbilitāte et levitāte animī novīs imperiīs studēbant.
10 Ab nōn nūllīs etiam sollicitābantur, quod in Galliā ā potentiōribus atque eīs, quī ad condūcendōs hominēs facultātēs habēbant, vulgō rēgna occupābantur, quī minus facile eam rem imperiō nostrō cōnsequī poterant.

2. Caesar Marches towards Belgium

Hīs nūntiīs litterīsque commōtus, Caesar duās legiōnēs in citeriōre Galliā novās cōnscrīpsit, et, initā aestāte, Q. Pedium lēgātum mīsit, quī in ulteriōrem

---

1. **1. Cum . . . Galliā:** Caesar spent the winter of 58–57 B.C. in Cisalpine Gaul, performing administrative duties. **ita utī:** *just as.* **suprā:** *above,* i.e., at the end of Book 1 **2. Labiēnī:** *from Labienus,* who was in command of the winter camp near Vesontio **3. quam:** refers to **Belgās,** but is in the singular on account of **partem. dīxerāmus:** in the first chapter of Book 1 **4. inter sē:** *to each other* **5. verēbantur:** *they (the Belgians) were afraid.* A verb of fearing is followed by the subjunctive with **nē,** *that (lest),* and **ut,** *that . . . not* **6. Galliā:** Celtic Gaul is meant here, not Gaul as a whole. **8. inveterāscere:** *was becoming established.* **9. molestē ferēbant:** *they were annoyed.* **imperiīs:** dative with **studeō** **11. quī . . . habēbant:** *who had the means of hiring men.* **rēgna:** *power*

2. **1. duās legiōnēs:** the XIIIth and XIVth. Caesar now had a total of eight legions, or about 30,000 men. **2. initā aestāte:** i.e., of 57 B.C.

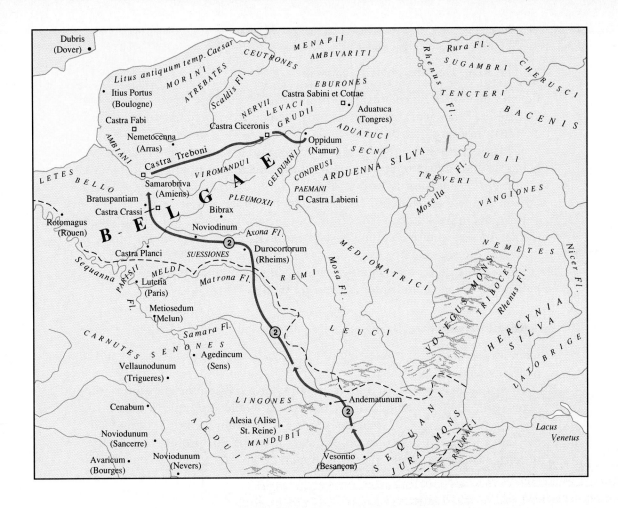

Galliam eās dēdūceret. Ipse, cum prīmum pābulī cōpia esse inciperet, ad
exercitum vēnit. Dat negōtium Senonibus reliquīsque Gallīs, quī fīnitimī
Belgīs erant, utī ea, quae apud eōs gerantur, cognōscant sēque dē hīs rēbus
certiōrem faciant.

    Hī cōnstanter omnēs nūntiāvērunt manūs cōgī, exercitum in ūnum locum
condūcī. Tum vērō exīstimāvit sē dēbēre ad eōs statim proficīscī. Rē
frūmentāriā comparātā, castra movet diēbusque circiter quīndecim ad fīnīs
Belgārum pervenit.

        5

        10

---

3. cum prīmum: *as soon as.* The indicative is more common with **cum prīmum;** the subjunctive
here emphasizes the circumstances.   **5. ea:** *those things;* object of **cognōscant. sē:** Caesar.
The reflexive in an indirect command refers to the subject of the verb governing it.
7. cōnstanter: *repeatedly, consistently*

3. The Remi Declare Their Friendship

Eō cum dē imprōvīsō celeriusque omnī opīniōne vēnisset, Rēmī, quī proximī Galliae ex Belgīs sunt, ad eum lēgātōs Iccium et Andecumborium, prīmōs cīvitātis, mīsērunt, quī dīcerent:

Sē in fidem atque in potestātem populī Rōmānī sē suaque omnia permittere; 5 neque sē cum Belgīs reliquīs cōnsēnsisse neque contrā populum Rōmānum coniūrāvisse, parātōsque esse et obsidēs dare et imperāta facere et eum in oppida recipere et frūmentō cēterīsque rēbus iuvāre.

Reliquōs omnīs Belgās in armīs esse, Germānōsque quī cis Rhēnum incolerent sēsē cum hīs coniūnxisse. Tantum esse eōrum omnium furōrem, 10 ut nē Suessiōnēs quidem, frātrēs cōnsanguineōsque suōs (quī eōdem iūre et īsdem lēgibus ūterentur, ūnum imperium ūnumque magistrātum cum ipsīs habērent), ab hāc coniūrātiōne dēterrēre possent.

4. The Origins of the Belgians

Cum ab hīs quaereret, quae cīvitātēs quantaeque in armīs essent et quid in bellō possent, sīc reperiēbat:

Plērōsque Belgās esse ortōs ā Germānīs, atque Rhēnum antīquitus trāductōs, propter locī fertilitātem ibi cōnsēdisse, Gallōsque, quī ea loca incol-5 erent, expulisse. Eōs esse sōlōs quī patrum nostrōrum memoriā, omnī Galliā vexātā, Teutonōs Cimbrōsque intrā suōs fīnis ingredī prohibērent; quā ex rē fierī, utī eārum rērum memoriā magnam sibi auctōritātem magnōsque spīritūs in rē mīlitārī sūmerent.

Dē eōrum numerō sē omnia comperisse Rēmī dīcēbant, proptereā quod, 10 propinquitātibus affīnitātibusque coniūnctī, quantam quisque multitūdinem in commūnī Belgārum conciliō ad id bellum pollicitus esset, cognōscerent.

Bellovacōs et virtūte et auctōritāte et hominum numerō plūrimum valēre; hōs posse cōnficere centum mīlia armātōrum, pollicitōs esse ex eō numerō sexāgintā mīlia, tōtīusque bellī imperium sibi postulāre.

---

3. **1. Eō:** *there*—i.e., to the territory of the Belgians. **Rēmī:** a state loyal to the Romans **3. dīcerent:** The remainder of the chapter is in indirect discourse after **dīcerent.** **4. sē suaque omnia:** *themselves and all their possessions;* direct object of **permittere** **8. cis:** *on this side of;* i.e., the west **11. īsdem** = **eīsdem. magistrātum:** *government.* **ipsīs:** the Remi

4. **1. hīs** = **Rēmīs. quaereret:** sc. Caesar. **quid possent:** *what strength they had* **3. ortōs ā Germānīs:** The Belgians were of both German and Celtic stock. **6. Teutonōs … prohibērent:** *kept the Teutons and Cimbri from invading their country* **7. fierī:** *the result was.* **memoriā:** ablative of cause **8. spīritūs:** *pride;* accusative plural **10. propinquitātibus affīnitātibusque:** *by the ties of blood relationship and intermarriage* **11. ad:** *for* **12. virtūte:** ablative of specification **13. cōnficere:** *muster*

Suessiōnēs suōs esse fīnitimōs; eōs fīnīs lātissimōs ferācissimōsque agrōs 15
possidēre. Apud eōs fuisse rēgem nostrā etiam memoriā Dīviciācum, tōtīus
Galliae potentissimum, quī cum magnae partis hārum regiōnum, tum etiam
Britanniae imperium obtinuisset; nunc esse rēgem Galbam; ad hunc propter
iūstitiam prūdentiamque summam tōtīus bellī omnium voluntāte dēferrī;
eōs oppida habēre numerō XII, pollicērī quīnquāgintā mīlia armātōrum; 20
totidem pollicērī Nerviōs, quī maximē ferī inter ipsōs habērentur longissi-
mēque abessent; quīndecim mīlia pollicērī Atrebātēs, Ambiānōs decem mīlia,
Morinōs XXV mīlia, Menapiōs VII mīlia, Caletōs X mīlia, Veliocassēs et
Viromanduōs totidem, Aduatucōs XVIIII mīlia; Condrūsōs, Eburōnēs,
Caerōsōs, Paemānōs (quī ūnō nōmine Germānī appellantur), arbitrārī sē 25
posse cōnficere ad XL mīlia.

5. Caesar Camps North of the Aisne River

Caesar, Rēmōs cohortātus, omnem senātum ad sē convenīre prīncipumque
līberōs obsidēs ad sē addūcī iussit. Quae omnia ab hīs dīligenter ad diem
facta sunt.

Ipse Dīviciācum Aeduum magnopere cohortātus docet, quantō opere
necesse sit manūs hostium distinērī, nē cum tantā multitūdine ūnō tempore 5
cōnflīgendum sit. Id fierī posse, sī suās cōpiās Aeduī in fīnēs Bellovacōrum
intrōdūxerint et eōrum agrōs populārī coeperint. Hīs mandātīs eum ab sē
dīmittit.

Postquam omnēs Belgārum cōpiās in ūnum locum coāctās ad sē venīre
vīdit, atque ab eīs quōs mīserat explōrātōribus et ab Rēmīs cognōvit, eās 10
iam nōn longē abesse, exercitum flūmen Axonam, quod est in extrēmīs
Rēmōrum fīnibus, trādūcere mātūrāvit atque ibi castra posuit. Quae rēs et
latus ūnum castrōrum rīpīs flūminis mūniēbat, et ea, quae post eum erant,
tūta ab hostibus reddēbat, et efficiēbat ut commeātūs ab Rēmīs reliquīsque
cīvitātibus sine perīculō ad eum portārī possent. 15

---

17. **cum, tum:** *not only, but also*   19. **summam:** a noun, *the chief command*   20. **eōs:** the
Suessiones   21. **totidem:** *the same number*—50,000 armed men. **ipsōs:** i.e., the Belgians.
habērentur: *were considered*   24. **totidem:** i.e., 10,000 men   25. **ūnō:** *the same.* **arbitrārī
sē:** i.e., the Remi thought that the Condrusi, etc., would furnish about 40,000 men. The
total number of men promised for the war was just under 300,000.

5.   2. **Quae omnia:** *All of these things.* **ad diem:** *on time*   4. **Dīviciācum:** *Diviciacus, the
Aeduan*, not the other one (Chapter 4, l. 16). **quantō opere:** *how greatly*   5. **distinērī:** *to
be kept apart*   6. **nē cōnflīgendum sit:** *so that he would not have to fight*   11. **Axonam:**
the Aisne River. **in extrēmīs finibus:** about eight miles north of modern Rheims   12. **Quae
rēs:** *This maneuver*   13. **latus:** accusative, object of **mūniēbat**

In eō flūmine pōns erat. Ibi praesidium pōnit et in alterā parte flūminis Quīntum Titūrium Sabīnum lēgātum cum sex cohortibus relinquit; castra in altitūdinem pedum duodecim vāllō fossāque duodēvīgintī pedum mūnīrī iubet.

6. The Belgians Attack the Town of Bibrax

Ab hīs castrīs oppidum Rēmōrum, nōmine Bibrax, aberat mīlia passuum octō. Id ex itinere magnō impetū Belgae oppugnāre coepērunt. Aegrē eō diē sustentātum est.

Gallōrum eadem atque Belgārum oppugnātiō est haec: Ubi, circumiectā
5 multitūdine hominum tōtīs moenibus, undique in mūrum lapidēs iacī coeptī sunt, mūrusque dēfēnsōribus nūdātus est, testūdine factā portās succēdunt mūrumque subruunt. Quod tum facile fīēbat. Nam cum tanta multitūdō lapidēs ac tēla conicerent, in mūrō cōnsistendī potestās erat nūllī.

Cum fīnem oppugnandī nox fēcisset, Iccius Rēmus, summā nōbilitāte et
10 grātiā inter suōs, quī tum oppidō praeerat, ūnus ex eīs, quī lēgātī dē pāce ad Caesarem vēnerant, nūntium ad eum mittit: nisi subsidium sibi summittātur, sēsē diūtius sustinēre nōn posse.

7. The Belgians March toward Caesar

Eō dē mediā nocte Caesar, īsdem ducibus ūsus, quī nūntiī ab Icciō vēnerant, Numidās et Crētās sagittāriōs et funditōrēs Baleārēs subsidiō oppidānīs

---

16. **in alterā parte:** *on the other* (or south) *side*   18. **in altitūdinem:** *to a height.* Translate with **vāllō. vāllō:** *the rampart,* about 12 feet high. **fossā:** *the ditch,* about 18 feet wide at the top

6.   1. **hīs castrīs:** this camp of Caesar's on the north bank of the Aisne River has been excavated. Much of our information about the size and shape of Caesar's camps has been obtained from this site.   2. **ex itinere:** *on the march;* i.e., they expected to capture the town quickly without much interruption to their march towards the Romans.   3. **sustentātum est:** impersonal passive; *the defense was maintained*   4. **eadem atque:** *the same as.* **oppugnātiō:** *the method of storming*   5. **coeptī sunt:** the passive form is used, instead of **coepērunt,** when the complementary infinitive is passive.   6. **testūdine:** *a testudo,* literally, *tortoise*—a close formation of men holding their shields over their heads   7. **subruunt:** *undermine*   8. **in mūrō ... nūllī:** *no one had a chance of standing on the wall;* **nūllī** is dative of possession with **erat.**   9. **Rēmus:** one of the Remi   11. **nisi etc.:** (saying that) *unless help was sent*

7.   1. **Eō:** *there,* i.e., to Bibrax. **dē:** *just after, during*   2. **Numidās:** *Numidian* from Numidia, in northern Africa.   **Crētās:** *Cretan,* from the island of Crete. **Baleārēs:** *Balearic,* from the Balearic Islands east of Spain

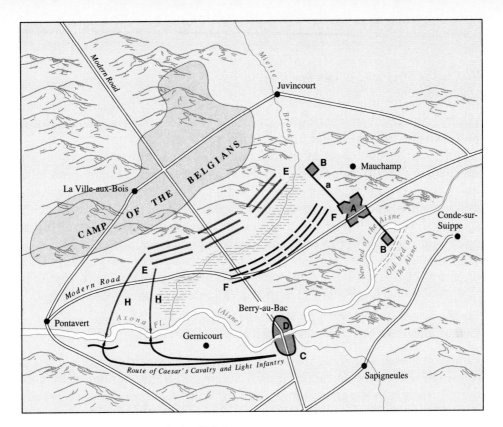

Plan of Caesar's battle with the Belgians

BATTLE OF AISNE:　**A**　Caesar's camp (Chap. 5; Chap. 7; Chap. 8)　**a, b** Trenches, **fossae** (Chap. 8)　**B, B** Redoubts, **castella** (Chap. 8)　**C** Redoubt at the south end of the bridge, **castellum,** held by Q. Titurius Sabinus (Chap. 5; Chap. 9)　**D** Guard at the north end of the bridge, **praesidium** (Chap. 5)　**E–E** The Belgians in battle order (Chap. 8)　**F–F** The six legions in battle order (Chap. 8)　**H–H** Probable routes taken by the Belgians to the fords at the Aisne, where they were met by Caesar's light-armed troops and cavalry (Chap. 9).

mittit; quōrum adventū et Rēmīs cum spē dēfēnsiōnis studium prōpugnandī accessit, et hostibus eādem dē causā spēs potiendī oppidī discessit.

　Itaque paulisper apud oppidum morātī agrōsque Rēmōrum dēpopulātī, omnibus vīcīs aedificiīsque, quō adīre potuerant, incēnsīs, ad castra Caesaris omnibus cōpiīs contendērunt et ā mīlibus passuum minus duōbus castra posuērunt; quae castra, ut fūmō atque ignibus significābātur, amplius mīlibus passuum octō in lātitūdinem patēbant. 5

---

3. prōpugnandī: *for taking the offensive*　**4. accessit:** *was added.* **hostibus:** dative of separation with **discessit**　**5. morātī:** sc. **hostēs**　**7. cōpiīs:** sc. **cum**; with the ablative of accompaniment, **cum** is sometimes omitted in military expressions. **ā mīlibus ... duōbus:** *less than two miles away*

8. Caesar Strengthens His Position

Caesar prīmō et propter multitūdinem hostium et propter eximiam opīniōnem virtūtis proeliō abstinēre statuit; cotīdiē tamen equestribus proeliīs, quid hostis virtūte posset et quid nostrī audērent, experiēbātur.

Ubi nostrōs nōn esse īnferiōrēs intellēxit, locō prō castrīs ad aciem
5 īnstruendam nātūrā opportūnō atque idōneō, ab utrōque latere eius collis, ubi castra posita erant, trānsversam fossam obdūxit circiter passuum quadringentōrum, et ad extrēmās fossās castella cōnstituit, ibique tormenta collocāvit. Eās mūnītiōnēs īnstituit nē, cum aciem īnstrūxisset, hostēs propter multitūdinem ab lateribus pugnantēs suōs circumvenīre possent.

10 Hōc factō, duābus legiōnibus quās proximē cōnscrīpserat in castrīs relictīs, ut, sī opus esset, subsidiō dūcī possent, reliquās sex legiōnēs prō castrīs in aciē cōnstituit. Hostēs item suās cōpiās ex castrīs ēductās īnstrūxerant.

9. The Belgians Try to Cross the River

Palūs erat nōn magna inter nostrum atque hostium exercitum. Hanc sī nostrī trānsīrent, hostēs exspectābant; nostrī autem, sī ab illīs initium trānseundī fieret, ut impedītōs aggrederentur, parātī in armīs erant. Interim proeliō equestrī inter duās aciēs contendēbātur. Ubi neutrī trānseundī initium faciunt,
5 secundiōre equitum proeliō nostrīs, Caesar suōs in castra redūxit.

Hostēs prōtinus ex eō locō ad flūmen Axonam contendērunt, quod esse post nostra castra dēmōnstrātum est. Ibi, vadīs repertīs, partem suārum cōpiārum trādūcere cōnātī sunt, eō cōnsiliō, ut, sī possent, castellum, cui praeerat Quīntus Titūrius lēgātus, expugnārent pontemque interscinderent;
10 sī minus potuissent, agrōs Rēmōrum populārentur, quī magnō nōbīs ūsuī ad bellum gerendum erant, commeātūque nostrōs prohibērent.

---

8. **1. eximiam opīniōnem:** *excellent reputation* **2. quid hostis . . . posset:** *what the enemy could do* **4. locō . . . idōneō:** *since the place was naturally well suited,* etc. **prō:** *in front of* **7. ad . . . fossās:** *at the ends of the trenches.* **tormenta:** The term **tormenta** (*tension machines*) includes the catapult, which shot long arrows, and the ballista, which hurled stones. **11. subsidiō:** dative of purpose

9. **1. Palūs:** *a swamp,* or *marshy ground* near the Miette Brook, about two miles below the bridge. Caesar's lines faced north towards this marsh; the Belgians were encamped on higher ground on the other side of the marsh. **2. illīs:** the Belgians **4. neutrī:** *neither side;* plural because the Belgians and Romans are plural **5. secundiōre:** *more favorable.* **nostrīs:** dative with **secundiōre** **8. eō cōnsiliō:** *with this plan;* i.e. to encircle and capture the bridge. **sī possent,** and **sī . . . potuissent,** represent respectively a future and future perfect in direct discourse **10. minus = nōn**

10. Caesar Stops the Belgians

Caesar, certior factus ab Titūriō, omnem equitātum et levis armātūrae Numidās, funditōrēs sagittāriōsque pontem trādūcit atque ad eōs contendit. Ācriter in eō locō pugnātum est. Hostīs impedītōs nostrī in flūmine aggressī magnum eōrum numerum occīdērunt; per eōrum corpora reliquōs audācis- simē trānsīre cōnantīs multitūdine tēlōrum reppulērunt; prīmōs, quī trān- sierant, equitātū circumventōs interfēcērunt.

Hostēs, ubi et dē expugnandō oppidō et dē flūmine trānseundō spem sē fefellisse intellēxērunt, neque nostrōs in locum inīquiōrem prōgredī pugnandī causā vīdērunt, atque ipsōs rēs frūmentāria dēficere coepit, concilium convocāvērunt. In eō conciliō cōnstituērunt, optimum esse, domum suam quemque revertī, et, quōrum in fīnēs prīmum Rōmānī exercitum intrōdūx- issent, ad eōs dēfendendōs undique convenīre, ut potius in suīs quam in aliēnīs finibus dēcertārent et domesticīs cōpiīs reī frūmentāriae ūterentur. Ad eam sententiam cum reliquīs causīs haec quoque ratiō eōs dēdūxit, quod Dīviciācum atque Aeduōs finibus Bellovacōrum appropinquāre cognōverant. Hīs persuādērī, ut diūtius morārentur neque suīs auxilium ferrent, nōn poterat.

5

10

15

11. The Belgians Retreat

Eā rē cōnstitūtā, secundā vigiliā magnō cum strepitū ac tumultū castrīs ēgressī, nūllō certō ōrdine neque imperiō, cum sibi quisque prīmum itineris locum peteret et domum pervenīre properāret, fēcērunt ut cōnsimilis fugae profectiō vidērētur. Hāc rē statim Caesar per speculātōrēs cognitā, īnsidiās veritus, quod, quā dē causā discēderent, nōndum perspexerat, exercitum equitātumque castrīs continuit. Prīmā lūce cōnfirmātā rē ab explōrātōribus, omnem equitātum, quī novissimum agmen morārētur, praemīsit.

5

---

10. **1. Titūriō:** Quintus Titūrius Sabinus, who was in command of Caesar's garrison at the bridge **7. spem ... fefellisse:** *that they had been disappointed in their hope*—of both capturing the town and crossing the river **8. in locum inīquiōrem:** i.e., the marshy ground **9. ipsōs:** *them* (the Belgians) **10. optimum esse:** *that it was best* **11. quemque:** *for each (state).* **quōrum:** the antecedent is **eōs** in the next line **13. ūterentur:** *they could make use of*

11. **1. strepitū:** *noise;* ablative of manner **2. ēgressī:** *leaving.* **nūllō ... imperiō:** i.e., they did not march out in line, or in any particularly military order, and no officers were giving orders. **3. fēcērunt ... vidērētur:** *they made their departure seem* etc. **4. speculātōrēs:** *spies;* Caesar had scouts constantly watching the enemy.

Model of a pile bridge, with bundles of branches resting on logs, built by Caesar to cross from Gaul to Germany

Hīs Quīntum Pedium et Lūcium Aurunculeium Cottam lēgātōs praefēcit; Titum Labiēnum lēgātum cum legiōnibus tribus subsequī iussit. Hī novissimōs adortī et multa mīlia passuum prōsecūtī, magnam multitūdinem eōrum fugientium concīdērunt. Nam cum eī ab extrēmō agmine cōnsisterent fortiterque impetum nostrōrum mīlitum sustinērent, priōrēs, exaudītō clāmōre, perturbātīs ōrdinibus, omnēs in fugā sibi praesidium pōnēbant. Ita sine ūllō perīculō tantam eōrum multitūdinem nostrī interfēcērunt, quantum fuit diēī spatium; sub occāsum sōlis dēstitērunt sēque in castra, ut erat imperātum, recēpērunt.

12. Noviodunum Surrenders to Caesar

Postrīdiē eius diēī Caesar, prius quam sē hostēs ex terrōre ac fugā reciperent, in fīnīs Suessiōnum, quī proximī Rēmīs erant, exercitum dūxit et magnō itinere ad oppidum Noviodūnum contendit. Id ex itinere oppugnāre cōnātus,

---

11. cum: *whereas.* **cōnsisterent:** *were making a stand*   **12. priōrēs:** *the ones in front*
14. tantam multitūdinem quantum: *as large a multitude as*

12.   **1. prius quam ... reciperent:** *before the enemy could recover from their terror and flight;* a clause of anticipation   **3. Noviodūnum:** the capital city of the Suessiones, near the modern Soissons

quod vacuum ab dēfēnsōribus esse audiēbat, propter lātitūdinem fossae mūrīque altitūdinem, paucīs dēfendentibus, expugnāre nōn potuit. Castrīs mūnītīs, vīneās agere, quaeque ad oppugnandum ūsuī erant, comparāre coepit.

Interim omnis ex fugā Suessiōnum multitūdō in oppidum proximā nocte convēnit. Celeriter vīneīs ad oppidum āctīs, aggere iactō turribusque cōnstitūtīs, magnitūdine operum, quae neque vīderant ante Gallī neque audīverant, et celeritāte Rōmānōrum permōtī lēgātōs ad Caesarem dē dēditiōne mittunt et, petentibus Rēmīs ut cōnservārentur, impetrant.

13. The Bellovaci Surrender to Caesar

Caesar, obsidibus acceptīs prīmīs cīvitātis atque ipsīus Galbae rēgis duōbus fīliīs, armīsque omnibus ex oppidō trāditīs, in dēditiōnem Suessiōnēs accēpit exercitumque in Bellovacōs dūcit. Quī cum sē suaque omnia in oppidum Brātuspantium contulissent, atque ab eō oppidō Caesar cum exercitū circiter mīlia passuum quīnque abesset, omnēs maiōrēs nātū, ex oppidō ēgressī, manūs ad Caesarem tendere et vōce significāre coepērunt, sēsē in eius fidem ac potestātem venīre neque contrā populum Rōmānum armīs contendere. Item, cum ad oppidum accessisset castraque ibi pōneret, puerī mulierēsque ex mūrō, passīs manibus, suō mōre pācem ab Rōmānīs petiērunt.

14. Diviciacus Confers with Caesar

Prō hīs Dīviciācus (nam post discessum Belgārum, dīmissīs Aeduōrum cōpiīs, ad eum reverterat) facit verba:

Bellovacōs omnī tempore in fidē atque amīcitiā cīvitātis Aeduae fuisse; impulsōs ab suīs prīncipibus,—quī dīcerent, Aeduōs ā Caesare in servitūtem redāctōs omnēs indignitātēs contumēliāsque perferre,—et ab Aeduīs dēfēcisse

---

6. vīneās agere: to bring up movable sheds; so-called because of their resemblance to vine covered arbors **9. aggere iactō:** an agger having been thrown up; i.e., a roadway to the town wall, made by throwing earth and brush into the trenches. **turribus:** towers, also movable, and affording an elevation from which weapons could be thrown **12. petentibus Rēmīs:** at the request of the Remi

13. **1. obsidibus:** as hostages—in apposition with **prīmīs** and **fīliīs** **5. maiōrēs nātū:** the older men **6. vōce significāre:** i.e., they did not speak Latin, but they made their meaning clear **9. passīs:** outstretched; from **pandō, -ere, pandī, passum**

14. **1. Prō:** in behalf of. **hīs:** the Bellovaci. **Dīviciācus:** the Aeduan **2. eum:** Caesar. **facit verba:** spoke. The rest of the chapter is in indirect discourse. **5. dēfēcisse:** the subject is Bellovacōs, modified by **impulsōs.**

et populō Rōmānō bellum intulisse. Quī eius cōnsilī prīncipēs fuissent, quod intellegerent quantam calamitātem cīvitātī intulissent, in Britanniam profūgisse.

Nōn sōlum Bellovacōs, sed etiam prō hīs Aeduōs petere, ut suā clēmentiā
10   ac mānsuētūdine in eōs ūtātur. Quod sī fēcerit, eum Aeduōrum auctōritātem apud omnīs Belgās amplificātūrum quōrum auxiliīs atque opibus, sī qua bella inciderint, sustinēre cōnsuērint.

15. Caesar Spares the Bellovaci

Caesar, honōris Diviciācī atque Aeduōrum causā, sēsē eōs in fidem receptūrum et cōnservātūrum dīxit; et quod erat cīvitās magnā inter Belgās auctōritāte atque hominum multitūdine praestābat, sescentōs obsidēs poposcit. Hīs trāditīs omnibusque armīs ex oppidō collātīs, ab eō locō in fīnīs
5   Ambiānōrum pervēnit; quī sē suaque omnia sine morā dēdidērunt.

Eōrum fīnēs Nerviī attingēbant; quōrum dē nātūrā mōribusque Caesar cum quaereret, sīc reperiēbat:

Nūllum aditum esse ad eōs mercātōribus; nihil patī vīnī reliquārumque rērum ad lūxuriam pertinentium īnferrī, quod hīs rēbus relanguēscere animōs
10   eōrum et remittī virtūtem exīstimārent; esse hominēs ferōs magnaeque virtūtis; increpitāre atque incūsāre reliquōs Belgās, quī sē populō Rōmānō dēdidissent patriamque virtūtem prōiēcissent; cōnfirmāre, sēsē neque lēgātōs missūrōs neque ūllam condiciōnem pācis acceptūrōs.

16. Caesar Marches against the Nervii

Cum per Nerviōrum fīnīs trīduum iter fēcisset, inveniēbat ex captīvīs, Sabim flūmen ā castrīs suīs nōn amplius mīlibus passuum x abesse; trāns id flūmen omnīs Nerviōs cōnsēdisse, adventumque ibi Rōmānōrum exspectāre ūnā

---

6. **quī:** *Those who.* **prīncipēs:** *ring-leaders*   9. **clēmentiā ac mānsuētūdine:** ablative with **ūtor**   10. **eum:** Caesar   11. **sī qua:** *if any, whatsoever*   12. **cōnsuērint:** contracted form of **cōnsuēverint**

15.   1. **eōs:** the Bellovaci   4. **collātīs:** from **cōnferō**   6. **quōrum:** i.e., of the Nervii 8. **mercātōribus:** dative of possession   **patī:** sc. **eōs** (**Nerviōs**) as subject. **vīnī,** and **rērum,** partitive genitive with **nihil**   9. **pertinentium:** agrees with **rērum;** *which pertain to.* **rēbus:** ablative of cause   10. **eōrum:** i.e., *of the other Gauls*   11. (**eōs**) **increpitāre atque incūsāre:** *they* (the Nervii) *reproached and accused*   12. **patriam:** adjective

16.   1. **Sabim:** *the Sambre;* Caesar was approaching from the north side of this river. 2. **trāns id flūmen:** i.e., on the south side   3. **ūnā cum:** *together with*

cum Atrebātibus et Viromanduīs, fīnitimīs suīs; ab hīs etiam Aduatucōrum cōpiās exspectārī atque esse in itinere; mulierēs, eōsque quī per aetātem ad pugnam inūtilēs vidērentur, in eum locum coniectōs esse, quō propter palūdēs exercituī aditus nōn esset.

17. The Nervii Plan to Attack

Hīs rēbus cognitīs explōrātōrēs centuriōnēsque praemittit, quī locum idōneum castrīs dēligant. Eō tempore complūrēs ex dēditīciīs Belgīs reliquīsque Gallīs ūnā cum Caesare iter faciēbant. Quīdam ex hīs, ut posteā ex captīvīs cognitum est, cōnsuētūdine itineris nostrī exercitūs perspectā, nocte ad Nerviōs pervēnērunt, atque hīs dēmōnstrārunt, inter singulās legiōnēs impedīmentōrum magnum numerum intercēdere; neque esse quicquam negōtī, cum prīma legiō in castra vēnisset reliquaeque legiōnēs magnum spatium abessent, hanc sub sarcinīs adorīrī; quā pulsā impedīmentīsque dīreptīs, futūrum esse ut reliquae cōnsistere nōn audērent.

Adiuvābat etiam eōrum prōpositum quī rem dēferēbant, quod Nerviī antīquitus, cum equitātū nihil possent, quō facilius fīnitimōrum equitātum impedīrent, sī praedandī causā ad eōs vēnissent, eius modī cōnsilium cēperant: Tenerīs arboribus incīsīs atque īnflexīs, et rubīs sentibusque interiectīs, saepīs dēnsās fēcerant, quae fīrmissimum mūnīmentum praebērent. Hīs rēbus cum iter agminis nostrī impedīrētur, nōn omittendum sibi cōnsilium Nerviī exīstimāvērunt.

18. The Romans Camp on a Hill

Locī nātūra quem nostrī castrīs dēlēgerant, erat haec. Collis, ab summō aequāliter dēclīvis, ad flūmen Sabim, quod suprā nōmināvimus, vergēbat.

---

5. **per aetātem:** *by reason of their age*   6. **quō** = ad quem locum

17.   4. **cōnsuētūdine . . . . perspectā:** *having observed the order of marching of our army*
5. **dēmōnstrārunt** = dēmōnstrāvērunt   6. **neque . . . negōtī:** *and that there would be no difficulty*   8. **hanc:** *this* (first legion). **sub sarcinīs:** i.e., while the men were still carrying their marching packs. **quā** = hāc legiōne   9. **futūrum esse ut:** *the result would be that;* followed by a substantive clause of result   10. **Adiuvābat,** etc.: the subject is the **quod** clause, and **prōpositum** is the object. *The proposal . . . was favored by the circumstance that . . .* **eōrum:** the antecedent of **quī**   11. **cum . . . possent:** *since their cavalry was not strong.* **quō:** used to introduce a purpose which contains a comparative (**facilius**)   12. **cēperant:** *had formed*   13. **tenerīs:** *young.* The trees were cut into on one side, and then bent over. The branches grew out thickly, forming a hedge. **rubīs sentibusque:** *brambles and briar bushes*—planted in between the branches of the bent trees, to provide a thicker hedge.

Ab eō flūmine parī acclīvitāte collis nāscēbātur adversus huic et contrārius, passūs circiter ducentōs īnfimus apertus, ab superiōre parte silvestris, ut nōn facile intrōrsus perspicī posset. Intrā eās silvās hostēs in occultō sēsē continēbant; in apertō locō secundum flūmen paucae statiōnēs equitum vidēbantur. Flūminis erat altitūdō pedum circiter trium.

19. The Nervii Make a Sudden Attack

Caesar, equitātū praemissō, subsequēbātur omnibus cōpiīs; sed ratiō ōrdōque agminis aliter sē habēbat, ac Belgae ad Nerviōs dētulerant. Nam quod hostibus appropinquābat, cōnsuētūdine suā Caesar sex legiōnēs expedītās dūcēbat; post eās tōtīus exercitūs impedīmenta collocārat; inde duae legiōnēs, quae proximē cōnscrīptae erant, tōtum agmen claudēbant praesidiōque impedīmentīs erant.

Equitēs nostrī cum funditōribus sagittāriīsque flūmen trānsgressī, cum hostium equitātū proelium commīsērunt. Illī identidem in silvās sē recipiē-bant, ac rūrsus ex silvā in nostrōs impetum faciēbant. Nostrī autem longius quam ad silvās hostēs cēdentīs īnsequī nōn audēbant. Interim legiōnēs sex quae prīmae vēnerant opere dīmēnsō castra mūnīre coepērunt.

Ubi prīma impedīmenta nostrī exercitūs ab eīs, quī in silvīs abditī latēbant, vīsa sunt, subitō omnibus cōpiīs prōvolāvērunt impetumque in nōstrōs equitēs fēcērunt. Hīs facile pulsīs ac prōturbātīs, incrēdibilī celeritāte ad flūmen dēcucurrērunt, ut paene ūnō tempore et ad silvās et in flūmine et iam in manibus nostrīs hostēs vidērentur. Eādem autem celeritāte adversō colle ad nostra castra atque eōs, quī in opere occupātī erant, contendērunt.

---

18. **3. parī acclīvitāte:** *with like slope.* **nāscēbātur:** *arose* **4. apertus:** *open;* i.e., cleared for about 200 paces from the river; above this it was thickly wooded. **6. secundum flūmen:** *along the river;* **secundum** is a preposition. **statiōnēs:** *pickets*

19. **1. equitātū praemissō:** i.e., for a preliminary testing skirmish. **ratiō ōrdōque:** *the marching order.* Because they were nearing the enemy, Caesar changed the arrangement of his march, leading off with the six legions, following this with the heavy baggage of the whole army, and finally placing the two new legions at the rear. He had previously put the baggage of each legion directly behind that legion, and that is what the escaped prisoners had reported to the Nervii. **2. aliter . . . ac:** *was different from that which* **4. collocārat:** contracted form for **collocāverat. duae legiōnēs:** the XIIIth and XIVth **8. Illī:** the enemy's cavalry **11. dīmēnsō:** *laid out*—from **dīmetior.** This deponent verb sometimes has a passive meaning in an ablative absolute. **12. prīma impedīmenta:** *the first part of the heavy baggage*—appearing behind the six legions. The enemy mistook this for the baggage of the leading legion. **latēbant:** *were hiding* **14. Hīs:** i.e., the Roman cavalry **16. in manibus nostrīs:** *upon us.* **adversō colle:** *up the opposite hill,* where the Romans were building their camp

The Romans drew their cavalry and light-armed foot soldiers (archers and slingers) from their allies.

20. Caesar Acts Quickly

Caesarī omnia ūnō tempore erant agenda: vēxillum prōpōnendum (quod erat īnsigne, cum ad arma concurrī oportēret); mīlitēs ab opere revocandī; eī, quī paulō longius aggeris petendī causā prōcesserant, arcessendī; aciēs īnstruenda; mīlitēs cohortandī; signum tubā dandum. Quārum rērum magnam partem temporis brevitās et incursus hostium impediēbat.

Hīs difficultātibus duae rēs erant subsidiō: scientia atque ūsus mīlitum, quī, superiōribus proeliīs exercitātī, sibi praescrībere poterant quid fierī oportēret; et quod Caesar ab opere singulīsque legiōnibus singulōs lēgātōs discēdere, nisi mūnītīs castrīs, vetuerat. Hī propter propinquitātem et

5

---

20.   **1. erant agenda:** *had to be done.* The situation was serious for the Romans, who were caught completely by surprise. **prōpōnendum:** sc. **erat;** also **erat** (or **erant**) with the following gerundives—**revocandī, arcessendī, īnstruenda, cohortandī,** and **dandum.** The best translation for these passive periphrastics in past time is, *had to be . . .* The omission of the verb **erat** suggests the emphasis on speed. **vēxillum:** *the flag;* i.e., the signal for arming   **3. aggeris:** *material* (for the rampart)   **4. signum:** *the signal,* to begin fighting   **6. scientia atque ūsus:** *the knowledge and experience*   **7. superiōribus:** *earlier*   **8. singulīs:** *respective.* **singulōs:** *the individual*   **9. nisi . . . castrīs:** *until the camp was finished*

10 celeritātem hostium nihil iam Caesaris imperium exspectābant, sed per sē, quae vidēbantur, administrābant.

21. Caesar Encourages His Men

Caesar, necessāriīs rēbus imperātīs, ad cohortandōs mīlitēs dēcucurrit et forte ad legiōnem decimam dēvēnit. Mīlitēs nōn longiōre ōrātiōne cohortātus est quam utī suae prīstinae virtūtis memoriam retinērent, neu perturbārentur animō, hostiumque impetum fortiter sustinērent. Deinde, quod nōn longius
5 hostēs aberant quam quō tēlum adigī posset, proelī committendī signum dedit. Atque in alteram partem item cohortandī causā profectus, pugnantibus occurrit. Temporis tanta fuit exiguitās hostiumque tam parātus ad dīmicandum animus, ut nōn modo ad īnsignia accommodanda, sed etiam ad galeās induendās scūtīsque tegimenta dētrahenda tempus dēfuerit. Quam quisque
10 ab opere in partem cāsū dēvēnit et quae prīma signa cōnspexit, ad haec cōnstitit, nē in quaerendīs suīs pugnandī tempus dīmitteret.

22. The Romans Are Taken by Surprise

Quibus ex rēbus īnstrūctus est exercitus magis ut locī nātūra dēiectusque collis et necessitās temporis, quam ut reī mīlitāris ratiō atque ōrdō postulābat. Dīversae legiōnēs, aliae aliā in parte, hostibus resistēbant, atque, saepibus dēnsissimīs interiectīs, prōspectus impediēbātur. Neque certa subsidia col-
5 locārī, neque quid in quāque parte opus esset prōvidērī, neque ab ūnō omnia imperia administrārī poterant. Itaque in tantā rērum inīquitāte ēventūs variī sequēbantur.

23. The Roman Camp Is Left Unprotected

Legiōnis nōnae et decimae mīlitēs, ut in sinistrā parte aciēī cōnstiterant, Atrebātēs cursū exanimātōs ac lassitūdine oppressōs celeriter ex locō superiōre in flūmen compulērunt, et eōs trānsīre cōnantīs īnsecūtī, gladiīs magnam

---

10. **nihil** = **nōn**   11. **vidēbantur:** *seemed best*

21.   3. **quam utī,** etc.: *than that they should remember* . . .   5. **quō . . . posset:** *as far as a javelin could be thrown*   6. **pugnantibus:** sc. **suīs;** dative with **occurrō**   9. **dēfuerit:** the perfect tense is sometimes used in a result clause, instead of the more regular imperfect, to emphasize the actuality of the result. **Quam . . . in partem:** *to whatever place*   10. **quae . . . signa:** *whatever standards*   11. **suīs:** sc. **signīs;** i.e., there was not time enough to find their regular places, so they could not afford to lose any time.

22.   1. **Quibus ex rēbus:** *For these reasons*   3. **aliae . . . parte:** *some in one place, others in another*   4. **certa:** *at fixed points;* on account of the thick hedges, Caesar could not see where reinforcements were needed.

partem eōrum impedītam interfēcērunt. Ipsī trānsīre flūmen nōn dubitāvērunt et, in locum inīquum prōgressī, rūrsus resistentīs hostīs in fugam coniēcērunt. 5

Item aliā in parte dīversae duae legiōnēs, ūndecima et octāva, prōflīgātīs Viromanduīs ex locō superiōre, in ipsīs flūminis rīpīs proeliābantur.

At tōtīs ferē castrīs ā fronte et ā sinistrā parte nūdātīs, cum in dextrō cornū legiō duodecima et, nōn magnō ab eā intervāllō, septima cōnstitisset, omnēs Nerviī cōnfertissimō agmine duce Boduognātō, quī summam imperī 10 tenēbat, ad eum locum contendērunt; quōrum pars ab apertō latere legiōnēs circumvenīre, pars summum castrōrum locum petere coepit.

24. The Situation Is Desperate

Eōdem tempore equitēs nostrī levisque armātūrae peditēs, quī cum eīs ūnā fuerant (quōs prīmō hostium impetū pulsōs dīxeram), cum sē in castra reciperent, adversīs hostibus occurrēbant ac rūrsus aliam in partem fugam petēbant. Itemque cālōnēs, quī ab decumānā portā ac summō iugō collis nostrōs victōrēs flūmen trānsīsse cōnspexerant, praedandī causā ēgressī, cum 5 respexissent et hostīs in nostrīs castrīs versārī vīdissent, praecipitēs fugae sēsē mandābant. Simul eōrum, quī cum impedīmentīs veniēbant, clāmor fremitusque oriēbātur, aliīque aliam in partem perterritī ferēbantur.

Quibus omnibus rēbus permōtī sunt equitēs Trēverī, quōrum inter Gallōs virtūtis opīniō est singulāris, quī auxilī causā ā cīvitāte ad Caesarem missī 10 vēnerant. Cum enim multitūdine hostium castra nostra complērī, legiōnēs premī et paene circumventās tenērī, cālōnēs, equitēs, funditōrēs, Numidās dissipātōs in omnīs partīs fugere vīdissent, dēspērātīs nostrīs rēbus, domum contendērunt; Rōmānōs pulsōs superātōsque, castrīs impedīmentīsque eōrum hostīs potītōs, cīvitātī renūntiāvērunt. 15

---

23.   **4. impedītam:** *hindered,* in trying to cross the river. **Ipsī:** the Romans on the left wing **5. inīquum:** the Romans were now pursuing the enemy uphill   **7. in ipsīs rīpīs:** *right on the banks*   **8. nūdātīs:** *exposed;* or unprotected. As the IXth and Xth legions on the left wing, and the VIIIth and XIth in the center, had followed the retreating enemy down to the river, the camp was left with few defenders.   **10. cōnfertissimō:** *very compact.* **summam imperī:** *the chief command*   **11. quōrum:** i.e., the Nervii

24.   **1. levis armātūrae:** genitive of description; referring to the archers and slingers **2. pulsōs:** sc. esse   **3. adversīs:** *face to face*   **4. cālōnēs:** *the camp-servants*—drivers, servants of the officers, etc., many of them slaves. **decumānā portā:** *the rear gate,* of the Roman camp   **5. ēgressī:** *coming out*—thinking that the Romans had won the battle, and that they could collect booty   **6. versārī:** *moving about*   **8. ferēbantur:** *fled*   **9. Trēverī:** a Belgian tribe; most of Caesar's cavalry came from this state. When they saw the Romans losing the battle on the right wing, they took off for home.   **10. opīniō:** *reputation* **11. legiōnēs premī:** the VIIth and XIIth were being hard pressed.   **12. Numidās:** African archers in the Roman army

25. Difficulties on the Right Wing

Caesar ab decimae legiōnis cohortātiōne ad dextrum cornū profectus est,
ubi suōs urgērī atque, signīs in ūnum locum collātīs, duodecimae legiōnis
cōnfertōs mīlitēs sibi ipsōs ad pugnam esse impedīmentō vīdit. Quārtae
cohortis omnēs centuriōnēs occīsī erant, signiferōque interfectō, signum
āmissum erat; reliquārum cohortium omnēs ferē centuriōnēs aut vulnerātī
aut occīsī erant, atque in hīs prīmipīlus P. Sextius Baculus, fortissimus vir,
multīs gravibusque vulneribus erat cōnfectus, ut iam sē sustinēre nōn posset.
Reliquī erant tardiōrēs et nōn nūllī ab novissimīs, dēsertō locō, proeliō
excēdēbant ac tēla vītābant. Hostēs neque ā fronte ex īnferiōre locō subeuntēs
intermittēbant et ab utrōque latere īnstābant. Caesar ubi rem esse in angustō
vīdit, neque ūllum esse subsidium, quod summittī posset,—scūtō ab novissimīs ūnī mīlitī dētrāctō, quod ipse eō sine scūtō vēnerat, in prīmam aciem
prōcessit et, centuriōnibus nōminātim appellātīs, reliquōs cohortātus, mīlitēs
signa īnferre et manipulōs laxāre iussit, quō facilius gladiīs ūtī possent.
Cuius adventū, spē illātā mīlitibus ac redintegrātō animō, cum prō sē quisque
in cōnspectū imperātōris etiam in extrēmīs suīs rēbus operam nāvāre cuperet,
paulum hostium impetus tardātus est.

26. Help from the Tenth Legion

Caesar, cum septimam legiōnem, quae iūxtā cōnstiterat, item urgērī ab hoste
vīdisset, tribūnōs mīlitum monuit, ut paulātim legiōnēs sēsē coniungerent et
conversa signa in hostēs īnferrent. Quō factō, cum aliīs aliī subsidium ferrent,
neque timērent nē āversī ab hoste circumvenīrentur, audācius resistere ac
fortius pugnāre coepērunt.

Interim mīlitēs legiōnum duārum, quae in novissimō agmine praesidiō

---

25.   **1. decimae legiōnis:** i.e., on the left wing   **2. urgērī:** *hard pressed.* **collātīs:** from
cōnferō   **3. sibi esse impedīmentō:** i.e., they were getting in each other's way   **4. signum:**
standard   **6. prīmipīlus:** *the chief centurion*   **7. cōnfectus:** *exhausted*   **8. novissimīs:** *the
rear*   **10. in angustō:** *in a critical condition*   **11. scūtō ... dētrāctō:** *taking a shield from
a soldier at the rear;* we see Caesar rushing into the fight to inspire the soldiers to fight more
fiercely.   **13. nōminātim:** *by name;* Caesar knew the names of all the officers in the army.
14. signa inferre: *to advance.* **manipulōs laxāre:** *to open up the ranks;* they had been too
crowded together to fight effectively with swords.   **16. operam nāvāre:** i.e., to give a good
account of himself, in the sight of the general

26.   **1. septimam legiōnem:** on the extreme right wing   **2. sēsē coniungerent:** the two
legions on the right wing had been fighting separately.   **3. conversa ... īnferrent:** *to face
about and charge the enemy.* **aliīs aliī:** *each to the other*   **4. āversī:** *from the rear*   **6. legiōnum
duārum:** the XIIIth and XIVth, which were bringing up the rear of the marching column

A commander addressing his troops—2d century relief from the Arch of Constantine, Rome. The standards bear the eagle, the symbol of the legion, and the decorations won by each legion or any of its soldiers.

impedīmentīs fuerant, proeliō nūntiātō, cursū incitātō, in summō colle ab hostibus cōnspiciēbantur; et Titus Labiēnus castrīs hostium potītus et ex locō superiōre cōnspicātus quae rēs in nostrīs castrīs gererentur, decimam legiōnem subsidiō nostrīs mīsit. Quī cum ex equitum et cālōnum fugā cognōvissent quō in locō rēs esset, quantōque in perīculō et castra et legiōnēs et imperātor versārētur, nihil ad celeritātem sibi reliquī fēcērunt.   10

27. The Nervii Are Wiped Out

Hōrum adventū tanta rērum commūtātiō est facta, ut nostrī, etiam quī vulneribus cōnfectī prōcubuissent, scūtīs innīxī proelium redintegrārent; cālōnēs, perterritōs hostīs cōnspicātī, etiam inermēs armātīs occurrerent; equitēs vērō, ut turpitūdinem fugae virtūte dēlērent, omnibus in locīs pugnandō sē legiōnāriīs mīlitibus praeferrent.   5

---

8. **potītus:** *after gaining possession of;* with the ablative. Labienus looked back and saw the Nervii in the Roman camp.   10. **Quī:** *These soldiers* (of the Tenth Legion)   12. **nihil . . . fēcērunt:** literally, *they left themselves nothing undone in regard to speed;* i.e., they returned with all possible speed; **reliquī** is partitive genitive with **nihil.**

27.   1. **etiam quī:** *even those who*   2. **scūtīs innīxī:** *leaning on their shields*   3. **etiam inermēs:** *even though unarmed.* **armātīs:** sc. **hostibus**   5. **sē praeferrent:** *outdid;* with the dative

At hostēs etiam in extrēmā spē salūtis tantam virtūtem praestitērunt, ut, cum prīmī eōrum cecidissent, proximī iacentibus īnsisterent atque ex eōrum corporibus pugnārent. Hīs dēiectīs et coacervātīs cadāveribus, quī supererant, ut ex tumulō, tēla in nostrōs coniciēbant et pīla intercepta remittēbant. Nōn nēquīquam tantae virtūtis hominēs ausī sunt trānsīre lātissimum flūmen, ascendere altissimās rīpās, subīre inīquissimum locum; quae facilia ex difficillimīs animī magnitūdō redēgerat.

28. The Nervii Surrender

Hōc proeliō factō et prope ad internecionēm gente ac nōmine Nerviōrum redāctō, maiōrēs nātū, quōs ūnā cum puerīs mulieribusque in aestuāria ac palūdēs coniectōs dīxerāmus, hāc pugnā nūntiātā, cum victōribus nihil esse impedītum, victīs nihil tūtum arbitrārentur, omnium quī supererant cōnsēnsū lēgātōs ad Caesarem mīsērunt sēque eī dēdidērunt. In commemorandā cīvitātis calamitāte ex sescentīs ad trēs senātōrēs, ex hominum mīlibus sexāgintā vix ad quīngentōs quī arma ferre possent, sēsē redāctōs esse dīxērunt. Quōs Caesar, ut in miserōs ac supplicēs ūsus misericordiā vidērētur, dīligentissimē cōnservāvit, suīsque fīnibus atque oppidīs ūtī iussit, et fīnitimīs imperāvit ut ab iniūriā et maleficiō sē suōsque prohibērent.

Chapters 29–35

After the surrender of the Nervii, many other states of northern and northwestern Gaul surrendered to Caesar. Also, some envoys came to him from the German states across the Rhine. In Rome, when the news of these conquests reached the people, a thanksgiving was proclaimed for fifteen days.

---

6. **praestitērunt:** *displayed*   7. **iacentibus:** *those who had fallen*   8. **quī supererant:** *those who survived*   9. **ut ex tumulō:** *as from a mound.* **intercepta;** *which they picked up.*   **Nōn nēquīquam:** *not in vain;* i.e., because of their great courage   11. **ex:** *instead of*

28.   1. **internecionēm:** *annihilation*   3. **victōribus . . . tūtum:** *that there was no obstacle in the way of the victors, and no safety for the conquered*   5. **commemorandā:** *telling*   8. **ūsus misericordiā:** *to have shown pity*

Book 3
THE CAMPAIGN
AGAINST THE VENETI

Among the states which surrendered to Caesar in the fall of 57 B.C., were the Veneti, on the western coast of what is now Brittany. These people were seafaring, and had a large fleet of ships. Caesar made preparations during the winter to assemble and build a fleet of his own. In the spring of 56 B.C. he led his main army across the northern part of Gaul to attack the Veneti, who had surrendered but then revolted. As soon as Caesar approached, his enemy disappeared, and sailed away to another garrison. But when Caesar's fleet arrived, Decimus Brutus defeated the Veneti in a naval battle, and the whole nation was compelled to surrender. Further operations during this campaign were conducted by Sabinus and Cotta, two of Caesar's generals, against the Venelli, and by Crassus against the Aquitanians. Caesar also proceeded against the Morini, in the extreme north. After this highly successful campaign, he established his legions in winter quarters among the coastal states which he had conquered during the summer.

A warship with the
steersman in the stern

Book 4
THE FIRST
EXPEDITION TO BRITAIN

Chapters 1–19

Caesar's next move was against the Germans, some of whom had crossed the Rhine, and were settling in states of Gaul. To prevent them from continuing this practice, he decided to cross the Rhine by building a bridge. He completed this bridge in ten days, and devastated the lands of the Sugambri. He returned across his bridge, and destroyed it.

20. Caesar Prepares to Invade Britain

Exiguā parte aestātis reliquā, Caesar, etsī in hīs locīs (quod omnis Gallia ad septentriōnēs vergit) mātūrae sunt hiemēs, tamen in Britanniam proficīscī contendit, quod omnibus ferē Gallicīs bellīs hostibus nostrīs inde summin-istrāta auxilia intellegēbat; et, sī tempus annī ad bellum gerendum dēficeret,

5　tamen magnō sibi ūsuī fore arbitrābātur, sī modo īnsulam adīsset, genus hominum perspexisset, loca, portūs, aditūs cognōvisset; quae omnia ferē Gallīs erant incognita. Neque enim temerē, praeter mercātōrēs, illō adit quisquam, neque eīs ipsīs quicquam praeter ōram maritimam atque eās regiōnēs, quae sunt contrā Galliās, nōtum est. Itaque vocātīs ad sē undique

10　mercātōribus, neque quanta esset īnsulae magnitūdō, neque quae aut quantae nātiōnēs incolerent, neque quem ūsum bellī habērent aut quibus īnstitūtīs ūterentur, neque quī essent ad maiōrum nāvium multitūdinem idōneī portūs, reperīre poterat.

20.　**1. Exiguā . . . reliquā:** *it was late July, 55* B.C. **omnis . . . vergit:** *all of Gaul lies to the north*　**3. quod . . . intellegēbat:** The real reason may have been Caesar's desire to invade Britain for the first time. The recorded history of Britain virtually begins with this account. **4. sī:** *even though*　**7. illō:** *there, to that place*　**9. contrā:** *opposite.* **Galliās:** i.e., **Belgae** and **Celtae**　**10. quanta esset:** This and the following indirect questions depend on **reperīre,** line 13.

21. Volusenus Is Sent to Get Information

Ad haec cognōscenda, prius quam perīculum faceret, idōneum esse arbitrātus Gaium Volusēnum cum nāve longā praemittit. Huic mandat ut, explōrātīs omnibus rēbus, ad sē quam prīmum revertātur. Ipse cum omnibus cōpiīs in Morinōs prōficīscitur, quod inde erat brevissimus in Britanniam trāiectus. Hūc nāvīs undique ex fīnitimīs regiōnibus et, quam superiōre aestāte ad Veneticum bellum effēcerat classem, iubet convenīre.

Interim cōnsiliō eius cognitō et per mercātōrēs perlātō ad Britannōs, ā complūribus īnsulae cīvitātibus ad eum lēgātī veniunt, quī polliceantur obsidēs dare atque imperiō populī Rōmānī obtemperāre. Quibus audītīs, līberāliter pollicitus hortātusque, ut in eā sententiā permanērent, eōs domum remittit; et cum eīs ūnā Commium, quem ipse, Atrebātibus superātīs, rēgem ibi cōnstituerat, cuius et virtūtem et cōnsilium probābat et quem sibi fidēlem esse arbitrābātur, cuiusque auctōritās in hīs regiōnibus magnī habēbātur, mittit. Huic imperat, quās possit, adeat cīvitātēs hortēturque ut populī Rōmānī fidem sequantur, sēque celeriter eō ventūrum nūntiet.

Volusēnus, perspectīs regiōnibus omnibus, quantum eī facultātis darī potuit, quī nāve ēgredī ac sē barbarīs committere nōn audēret, quīntō diē ad Caesarem revertitur, quaeque ibi perspexisset, renūntiat.

5

10

15

22. The Morini Surrender

Dum in hīs locīs Caesar nāvium parandārum causā morātur, ex magnā parte Morinōrum ad eum lēgātī vēnērunt, quī sē dē superiōris temporis cōnsiliō excūsārent, quod, hominēs barbarī et nostrae cōnsuētūdinis imperītī, bellum populō Rōmānō fēcissent, sēque ea, quae imperāsset, factūrōs pollicērentur. Hoc sibi Caesar satis opportūnē accidisse arbitrātus, quod neque post tergum hostem relinquere volēbat, neque bellī gerendī propter annī tempus facultātem habēbat, neque hās tantulārum rērum occupātiōnēs

5

---

21.   2. **nāve longā:** *a galley,* or *warship* propelled by oars   4. **trāiectus:** *crossing.* The place Caesar sailed from was probably Portus Itius, the modern Boulogne. The crossing is about 30 miles at this point.   5. **quam:** the antecedent is **classem**, line 6.   9. **imperiō:** dative after **obtemperāre**, *obey.* **Quibus:** neuter   11. **Commium:** direct object of **mittit**   13. **magnī:** *of great importance*   14. **Huic:** *him* (Commius). **adeat:** sc. **ut**   16. **quantum . . . potuit:** *as far as opportunity could be provided to one . . .*   17. **quī . . . audēret:** criticism of the way Volusenus carried out his mission. He was expected to land in Britain and bring back information.

22.   2. **dē cōnsiliō:** *for their conduct*—i.e., in the previous year, described in Book 3. They had failed to send ambassadors about peace.   3. **imperītī:** *unfamiliar with;* taking the genitive   7. **facultātem:** *opportunity.* **tantulārum rērum:** *such trifling matters*—as waging war with the Morini, when he was about to sail to Britain

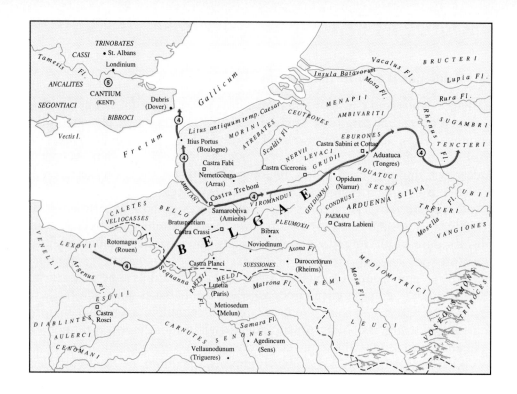

Britanniae antepōnendās iūdicābat, magnum eīs numerum obsidum imperat. Quibus adductīs, eōs in fidem recēpit.

10   Nāvibus circiter LXXX onerāriīs coāctīs contrāctīsque, quot satis esse ad duās trānsportandās legiōnēs exīstimābat, quod praetereā nāvium longārum habēbat, quaestōrī, lēgātīs praefectīsque distribuit. Hūc accēdēbant XVIII onerāriae nāvēs, quae ex eō locō ā mīlibus passuum VIII ventō tenēbantur, quō minus in eundem portum venīre possent; hās equitibus distribuit.

15   Reliquum exercitum. Q. Titūriō Sabīnō et L. Auruncāleiō Cottae lēgātīs in Menapiōs atque in eōs pāgōs Morinōrum, ā quibus ad eum lēgātī nōn vēnerant, dūcendum dedit; P. Sulpicium Rūfum lēgātum cum eō praesidiō, quod satis esse arbitrābātur, portum tenēre iussit.

23. Caesar Sails to Britain

Hīs cōnstitūtīs rēbus, nactus idōneam ad nāvigandum tempestātem, tertiā

---

11. quod ... nāvium longārum: *the warships which*   **12. Hūc accēdēbant:** *There were in addition to these*   **13. ā:** adverb, *away*   **14. quō minus ... possent:** *from being able to reach the same port.* The cavalry transports were held up by the wind at Ambleteuse, eight Roman miles up the coast from Portus Itius.   **17. dūcendum:** *to be led*

23.   1. nactus: *finding;* from **nancīscor. tempestātem:** *weather*

ferē vigiliā nāvīs solvit, equitēsque in ulteriōrem portum prōgredī et nāvīs cōnscendere et sē sequī iussit. A quibus cum paulō tardius esset administrā- tum, ipse hōrā diēī circiter quārtā cum prīmīs nāvibus Britanniam attigit atque ibi in omnibus collibus expositās hostium cōpiās armātās cōnspexit. Cuius locī haec erat nātūra, atque ita montibus angustīs mare continēbātur, utī ex locīs superiōribus in lītus tēlum adigī posset. Hunc ad ēgrediendum nēquāquam idōneum locum arbitrātus, dum reliquae nāvēs eō convenīrent, ad hōram nōnam in ancorīs exspectāvit.

Interim lēgātīs tribūnīsque mīlitum convocātīs, et quae ex Volusēnō cognōvisset, et quae fierī vellet, ostendit, monuitque ut ad nūtum et ad tempus omnēs rēs ab eīs administrārentur. Hīs dīmissīs, et ventum et aestum ūnō tempore nactus secundum, datō signō et sublātīs ancorīs, circiter mīlia passuum septem ab eō locō prōgressus, apertō ac plānō lītore nāvīs cōnstituit.

24. The Britons Resist His Landing

At barbarī, cōnsiliō Rōmānōrum cognitō, praemissō equitātū et essedāriīs, quō plērumque genere in proeliīs ūtī cōnsuērunt, reliquīs cōpiīs subsecūtī nostrōs nāvibus ēgredī prohibēbant. Erat ob hās causās summa difficultās, quod nāvēs propter magnitūdinem nisi in altō cōnstituī nōn poterant; mīlitibus autem, ignōtīs locīs, impedītīs manibus, magnō et gravī onere armōrum oppressīs simul et dē nāvibus dēsiliendum et in flūctibus cōnsis- tendum et cum hostibus erat pugnandum; cum illī aut ex āridō aut paulum in aquam prōgressī, omnibus membrīs expedītī, nōtissimīs locīs, audācter tēla conicerent et equōs īnsuēfactōs incitārent. Quibus rēbus nostrī perterritī, atque huius omnīnō generis pugnae imperītī, nōn eādem alacritāte ac studiō, quō in pedestribus ūtī proeliīs cōnsuērant, ūtēbantur.

---

2. nāvīs solvit: *he set sail;* this was on the night of August 25, 55 B.C. **ulteriōrem portum:** i.e., the port of Ambleteuse; see note on line 14, chapter 22   **3. Ā quibus,** etc.: The cavalry were slow in carrying out Caesar's orders. **tardius:** *too slowly.* **esset administrātum:** impersonal **4. hōrā . . . quārtā:** at about 9 A.M., August 26th   **5. collibus:** i.e., the Dover cliffs. The natives had heard of Caesar's preparations, and were waiting for him in large numbers. **9. ad hōram nōnam:** until about three o'clock in the afternoon   **11. ad nūtum:** i.e., instantly **13. secundum:** *favorable.* **sublātīs ancorīs:** *weighing anchors*   **14. apertō lītore:** There was a level beach here suitable for landing.

24.   1. essedāriīs: *charioteers;* the method of fighting from chariots is described in Chapter 33.   **2. quō genere:** *a kind of fighter which*   **5. mīlitibus:** dative of agent with **dēsiliendum** (**erat**): i.e., the soldiers had to jump.   **6. oppressīs:** agrees with **mīlitibus**   **7. cum illī:** *while they* (the Britons)   **8. expedītī:** *light armed;* contrasting with the Romans (**impedītīs manibus**)   **9. īnsuēfactōs:** *well trained*—to go into the water

25. The Romans Succeed in Landing

Quod ubi Caesar animadvertit, nāvēs longās, quārum speciēs erat barbarīs
inūsitātior, paulum removērī ab onerāriīs nāvibus et rēmīs incitārī et ad
latus apertum hostium cōnstituī, atque inde fundīs, sagittīs, tormentīs hostīs
prōpellī ac summovērī iussit; quae rēs magnō ūsuī nostrīs fuit. Nam et
5   nāvium figūrā et rēmōrum mōtū et inūsitātō genere tormentōrum permōtī
barbarī cōnstitērunt ac paulum modo pedem rettulērunt.

Atque nostrīs mīlitibus cunctantibus, maximē propter altitūdinem maris,
quī decimae legiōnis aquilam ferēbat, obtestātus deōs, ut ea rēs legiōnī
fēlīciter ēvenīret, "Dēsilīte," inquit, "commīlitōnēs, nisi vultis aquilam
10 hostibus prōdere; ego certē meum reī pūblicae atque imperātōrī officium
praestiterō." Hoc cum vōce magnā dīxisset, sē ex nāve prōiēcit atque in
hostīs aquilam ferre coepit. Tum nostrī cohortātī inter sē, nē tantum dēdecus
admitterētur, ūniversī ex nāve dēsiluērunt. Hōs item ex proximīs nāvibus
cum cōnspexissent, subsecūtī hostibus appropinquārunt.

26. The Romans Rout the Enemy

Pugnātum est ab utrīsque ācriter. Nostrī tamen, quod neque ōrdinēs servāre
neque fīrmiter īnsistere neque signa subsequī poterant, atque alius aliā ex
nāve, quibuscumque signīs occurrerat, sē aggregābat, magnopere perturbā-
bantur; hostēs vērō, nōtīs omnibus vadīs, ubi ex lītore aliquōs singulārēs ex
5   nāve ēgredientīs cōnspexerant, incitātīs equīs, impedītōs adoriēbantur, plūrēs
paucōs circumsistēbant, aliī ab latere apertō in ūniversōs tēla coniciēbant.

Quod cum animadvertisset Caesar, scaphās longārum nāvium, item
speculātōria nāvigia mīlitibus complērī iussit et, quōs labōrantīs cōnspexerat,
hīs subsidia summittēbat. Nostrī simul in āridō cōnstitērunt, suīs omnibus

---

25.   **1. Quod:** *this;* i.e., that his men were holding back   **2. inūsitātior:** *quite unfamiliar.*
The **nāvēs longae** were longer and narrower, and propelled by oars.   **3. latus apertum:** i.e.,
the enemy's right flank. **tormentīs:** *artillery* on the Roman ships   **8. quī:** sc. **is**—*he who;*
i.e., the standard bearer   **11. praestiterō:** *I shall have performed* (my duty)   **12. dēdecus:**
disgrace; i.e., losing the standard to the enemy   **13. ex . . . nāvibus:** *those on the nearest
ships*

26.   **1. ōrdinēs servāre:** *to keep the ranks*   **2. īnsistere:** *to stand up* (in the water)
3. quibuscumque signīs: *whatever standards.* **sē aggregābat:** *joined*   **4. aliquōs singulārēs:**
some (of the Romans) *by themselves*   **7. scaphās:** the small boats, carried on the galleys
8. speculātōria nāvigia: *spy-boats;* both these and the **scaphae** were small, and could come
in close to shore. **quōs:** the antecedent is **hīs**   **9. simul** = **simul atque,** *as soon as*

cōnsecūtīs, in hostīs impetum fēcērunt atque eōs in fugam dedērunt; neque   10
longius prōsequī potuērunt, quod equitēs cursum tenēre atque īnsulam
capere nōn potuerant. Hoc ūnum ad prīstinam fortūnam Caesarī dēfuit.

27. The Britons Ask for Peace

Hostēs proeliō superātī, simul atque sē ex fugā recēpērunt, statim ad
Caesarem lēgātōs dē pāce mīsērunt; obsidēs sēsē datūrōs, quaeque imperāsset
factūrōs pollicitī sunt. Ūnā cum hīs lēgātīs Commius Atrebās vēnit, quem
suprā dēmōnstrāveram ā Caesare in Britanniam praemissum. Hunc illī ē
nāve ēgressum, cum ad eōs ōrātōris modō Caesaris mandāta dēferret,   5
comprehenderant atque in vincula coniēcerant; tum proeliō factō remīsērunt.
In petendā pāce, eius reī culpam in multitūdinem contulērunt et propter
imprūdentiam ut ignōscerētur petīvērunt.

   Caesar questus, quod, cum ultrō (in continentem lēgātīs missīs) pācem ab
sē petīssent, bellum sine causā intulissent, ignōscere sē imprūdentiae dīxit   10
obsidēsque imperāvit; quōrum illī partem statim dedērunt, partem ex
longinquiōribus locīs arcessītam paucīs diēbus sēsē datūrōs dīxērunt. Intereā
suōs remigrāre in agrōs iussērunt, prīncipēsque undique convenīre et sē
cīvitātēsque suās Caesarī commendāre coepērunt.

28. Caesar's Cavalry Transports Are Driven Back

Hīs rēbus pāce cōnfirmātā, diē quārtō postquam est in Britanniam ventum,
nāvēs XVIII (dē quibus suprā dēmōnstrātum est), quae equitēs sustulerant,
ex superiōre portū lēnī ventō solvērunt. Quae cum appropinquārent Britanniae et ex castrīs vidērentur, tanta tempestās subitō coorta est, ut nūlla
eārum cursum tenēre posset, sed aliae eōdem, unde erant profectae, refer-   5
rentur, aliae ad īnferiōrem partem īnsulae, quae est propius sōlis occāsum,

---

12. **capere:** *reach*

27.   3. **Atrebās:** one of the Atrebates   4. **Hunc:** Commius. **illī:** the Britons   5. **ōrātōris
modō:** *in the manner of an envoy*   6. **remīsērunt:** sc. **eum**   7. **in multitūdinem contulērunt:**
they laid upon the people   8. **ut ignōscerētur:** *that they be forgiven;* impersonal in Latin
9. **questus:** *complaining;* from **queror. quod intulisset:** subjunc. because Caesar the author
is quoting Caesar the general.

28.   1. **est ventum:** *they came*—an impersonal use of **veniō**   3. **superiōre portū:** Ambleteuse, where the cavalry was still trying to sail in order to join Caesar   4. **castrīs:** i.e., the
Roman camp in Britain. This happened on the morning of August 30. **nūlla:** sc. **nāvis**
6. **īnferiōrem partem:** *lower part;* i.e., to the southwest

magnō cum perīculō dēicerentur; quae tamen, ancorīs iactīs, cum flūctibus
complērentur, necessāriō adversā nocte in altum prōvectae continentem
petiērunt.

29. Caesar's Fleet Is Damaged by a Storm

Eādem nocte accidit ut esset lūna plēna, quī diēs maritimōs aestūs maximōs
in Ōceanō efficere cōnsuēvit, nostrīsque id erat incognitum. Ita ūnō tempore
et longās nāvīs, quibus Caesar exercitum trānsportandum cūrāverat, quāsque
in āridum subdūxerat, aestus complēverat, et onerāriās, quae ad ancorās
5   erant dēligātae, tempestās afflīctābat, neque ūlla nostrīs facultās aut admin-
istrandī aut auxiliandī dabātur.

    Complūribus nāvibus frāctīs, reliquae cum essent (fūnibus, ancorīs reli-
quīsque armāmentīs āmissīs) ad nāvigandum inūtilēs, magna, id quod necesse
erat accidere, tōtīus exercitūs perturbātiō facta est. Neque enim nāvēs erant
10   aliae, quibus reportārī possent, et omnia deerant, quae ad reficiendās nāvīs
erant ūsuī; et, quod omnibus cōnstābat, hiemārī in Galliā oportēre, frūmentum in hīs locīs in hiemem prōvīsum nōn erat.

30. The Britons Plan to Revolt

Quibus rēbus cognitīs, prīncipēs Britanniae, quī post proelium ad Caesarem
convēnerant, inter sē collocūtī, cum equitēs et nāvīs et frūmentum Rōmānīs
dēesse intellegerent, et paucitātem mīlitum ex castrōrum exiguitāte cognōscerent (quae hōc erant etiam angustiōra, quod sine impedīmentīs Caesar

---

7. **dēicerentur:** *were driven.* **cum** (before **flūctibus**): *since.* After they had dropped anchors, they found that they were being swamped, so they weighed anchors again, and sailed back to the continent.   8. **adversā nocte:** *in the face of the* (coming) *night*

29.   1. **quī diēs:** *a time* (of the month) *which*   2. **nostrīs ... incognitum:** The Romans apparently knew little about the connection between high tides and the full moon. There is very little tide in the Mediterranean.   3. **longās nāvīs:** object of **complēverat. cūrāverat:** *had arranged for*   4. **āridum:** *dry land*   7. **frāctīs:** *wholly wrecked*   9. **perturbātiō:** *panic.* The soldiers were not prepared for spending the winter in Britain, and there seemed to be no way to get the army back to the continent.   11. **omnibus cōnstābat:** *it was clear to all* 12. **in hīs locīs:** i.e., in Britain. No grain supply had been provided, since they had expected to winter in Gaul.

30.   1. **prīncipēs:** subject of **dūxērunt,** line 5   4. **hōc:** *for this reason*

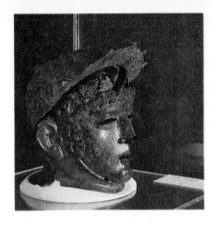

Funerary mask of a soldier with a bronze helmet (cassis, see p. 65)—British Museum. Such masks were kept by the dead man's family or buried with the body if it wasn't cremated.

legiōnēs trānsportāverat), optimum esse dūxērunt, rebelliōne factā, frūmentō commeātūque nostrōs prohibēre et rem in hiemem prōdūcere, quod, hīs superātīs aut reditū interclūsīs, nēminem posteā bellī īnferendī causā in Britanniam trānsitūrum cōnfīdēbant. Itaque rūrsus, coniūrātiōne factā, paulātim ex castrīs discēdere ac suōs clam ex agrīs dēdūcere coepērunt. 5

31. Caesar Suspects the Britons

At Caesar, etsī nōndum eōrum cōnsilia cognōverat, tamen et ex ēventū nāvium suārum et ex eō, quod obsidēs dare intermīserant, fore id, quod accidit, suspicābātur. Itaque ad omnīs cāsūs subsidia comparābat. Nam et frūmentum ex agrīs cotīdiē in castra cōnferēbat et, quae gravissimē afflīctae erant nāvēs, eārum māteriā atque aere ad reliquās reficiendās ūtēbātur et, quae ad eās rēs erant ūsuī, ex continentī comportārī iubēbat. Itaque, cum summō studiō ā mīlitibus administrārētur, XII nāvibus āmissīs, reliquīs ut nāvigārī commodē posset, effēcit. 5

---

5. optimum . . . dūxērunt: *thought that the best thing to do was.* **rebelliōne factā:** *to renew hostilities;* they had agreed to peace terms (Chapter 27), but changed their minds after the storm. **6. rem:** *campaign.* **hīs:** i.e., the Romans now in Britain **9. castrīs:** i.e., the Roman camp. **suōs:** i.e., those Britons who had been sent back to the fields

31. **1. ēventū:** i.e., what had happened **2. ex eō, quod:** *from the fact that.* **fore** = **futūrum esse** **3. suspicābātur:** *he suspected that that would happen which did happen—* the Britons did not surrender after seeing Caesar's damaged fleet. **ad omnīs cāsūs:** *for every emergency* **4. quae nāvēs, eārum** = **eārum nāvium quae.** **afflīctae:** *damaged* **5. māteriā:** *timber.* **aere:** *bronze*—used for the beaks and part of the frame of the ships. **reliquās:** *the rest* of the ships, which were not so badly damaged

32. The Britons Attack the VIIth Legion

Dum ea geruntur, legiōne ex cōnsuētūdine ūnā frūmentātum missā, quae appellābātur septima, neque ūllā ad id tempus bellī suspīciōne interpositā, cum pars hominum in agrīs remanēret, pars etiam in castra ventitāret,—eī, quī prō portīs castrōrum in statiōne erant, Caesarī nūntiāvērunt, pulverem maiōrem quam cōnsuētūdō ferret in eā parte vidērī, quam in partem legiō iter fēcisset. Caesar id, quod erat, suspicātus, aliquid novī ā barbarīs initum cōnsilī, cohortīs, quae in statiōnibus erant, sēcum in eam partem proficīscī, ex reliquīs duās in statiōnem cohortīs succēdere, reliquās armārī et cōnfestim sēsē subsequī iussit.

Cum paulō longius ā castrīs prōcessisset, suōs ab hostibus premī atque aegrē sustinēre et, cōnfertā legiōne, ex omnibus partibus tēla conicī animadvertit. Nam quod, omnī ex reliquīs partibus dēmessō frūmentō, pars ūna erat reliqua, suspicātī hostīs hūc nostrōs esse ventūrōs, noctū in silvīs dēlituerant; tum dispersōs, dēpositīs armīs, in metendō occupātōs subitō adortī, paucīs interfectīs, reliquōs incertīs ōrdinibus perturbāverant, simul equitātū atque essedīs circumdederant.

33. The War Chariots of the Britons

Genus hoc est ex essedīs pugnae. Prīmō per omnīs partīs perequitant et tēla coniciunt, atque ipsō terrōre equōrum et strepitū rotārum ōrdinēs plērumque perturbant; et cum sē inter equitum turmās īnsinuāvērunt, ex essedīs dēsiliunt et pedibus proeliantur. Aurīgae interim paulātim ex proeliō excēdunt, atque ita currūs collocant ut, sī illī ā multitūdine hostium premantur, expedītum ad suōs receptum habeant. Ita mōbilitātem equitum, stabilitātem peditum

---

32.   1. **frūmentātum:** *to get grain;* a supine, used with a verb of motion (**missā**) to express purpose   2. **neque . . . interpositā:** There had been no reason so far for Caesar to be suspicious of the good faith of the Britons.   3. **ventitāret:** *kept coming;* the frequentative form of **veniō. eī:** the soldiers of the Xth legion   5. **maiōrem . . . ferret:** *more than usual.* **partem:** *direction*   6. **aliquid novī cōnsilī:** *namely that some new plan.* **cōnsilī** is a partitive genitive. **initum:** sc. **esse**   8. **reliquās:** sc. **cohortīs.** Caesar ordered the two cohorts which were on guard duty to go immediately to help the seventh legion; two others were to take their places on guard duty, and the remaining six cohorts were to arm themselves and follow quickly. **armārī:** middle voice   15. **incertīs:** *in disorder*

33.   2. **equōrum:** i.e., caused by the horses. **ōrdinēs:** *ranks of the enemy*   4. **Aurīgae:** *the drivers.* Each chariot had a driver and several warriors. After the warriors had thrown their weapons, they dismounted, and the drivers withdrew the chariots to a safe distance, and waited to pick up any warriors in difficulty.   6. **receptum:** *a means of retreat*

in proeliīs praestant, ac tantum ūsū cotīdiānō et exercitātiōne efficiunt, utī in dēclīvī ac praecipitī locō incitātōs equōs sustinēre et brevī moderārī ac flectere, et per tēmōnem percurrere et in iugō īnsistere, et sē inde in currūs citissimē recipere cōnsuēverint.   10

34. The Britons Prepare to Attack

Quibus rēbus perturbātīs nostrīs tempore opportūnissimō Caesar auxilium tulit; namque eius adventū hostēs cōnstitērunt, nostrī sē ex timōre recēpērunt. Quō factō, ad lacessendum hostem et ad committendum proelium aliēnum esse tempus arbitrātus, suō sē locō continuit et, brevī tempore intermissō, in castra legiōnēs redūxit.   5

Dum haec geruntur, nostrīs omnibus occupātīs, quī erant in agrīs reliquī, discessērunt. Secūtae sunt continuōs complūrīs diēs tempestātēs, quae et nostrōs in castrīs continērent et hostem ā pugnā prohibērent.

Interim barbarī nūntiōs in omnīs partīs dīmīsērunt paucitātemque nostrōrum mīlitum suīs praedicāvērunt et, quanta praedae faciendae atque in   10 perpetuum suī līberandī facultās darētur, sī Rōmānōs castrīs expulissent, dēmōnstrāvērunt. Hīs rēbus celeriter magnā multitūdine peditātūs equitātūsque coāctā, ad castra vēnērunt.

35. The Britons Are Routed

Caesar, etsī idem, quod superiōribus diēbus acciderat, fore vidēbat, ut, sī essent hostēs pulsī, celeritāte perīculum effugerent, tamen nactus equitēs circiter XXX, quōs Commius Atrebās, dē quō ante dictum est, sēcum trānsportāverat, legiōnēs in aciē prō castrīs cōnstituit. Commissō proeliō, diūtius nostrōrum mīlitum impetum hostēs ferre nōn potuērunt ac terga   5 vertērunt. Quōs tantō spatiō secūtī, quantum cursū et vīribus efficere potuērunt, complūrīs ex eīs occīdērunt; deinde, omnibus longē lātēque aedificiīs incēnsīs, sē in castra recēpērunt.

---

7. praestant: *exhibit*   **8. incitātōs:** *at full speed.* **sustinēre:** *to control.* **brevī:** *quickly*

34.   1. Caesar picks up the story from the end of Chapter 32. **rēbus:** ablative of means 3. **aliēnum:** *unfavorable*   6. **quī:** *those who*   11. **suī līberandī:** *of freeing themselves,* from Roman domination

35.   1. **idem fore:** *that the same thing would happen*   6. **tantō spatiō . . . quantum:** *as far as.* **secūtī:** sc. **nostrī**

36. Caesar Returns to Gaul

Eōdem diē lēgātī ab hostibus missī ad Caesarem dē pāce vēnērunt. Hīs Caesar numerum obsidum, quem ante imperāverat, duplicāvit, eōsque in continentem addūcī iussit, quod, propinquā diē aequinoctī īnfīrmīs nāvibus hiemī nāvigātiōnem subiciendam nōn exīstimābat.

5   Ipse, idōneam tempestātem nactus, paulō post mediam noctem nāvīs solvit; quae omnēs incolumēs ad continentem pervēnērunt; sed ex eīs onerāriae duae eōsdem portūs, quōs reliquae, capere nōn potuērunt, et paulō īnfrā dēlātae sunt.

37. Roman Soldiers Attacked by the Morini

Quibus ex nāvibus cum essent expositī mīlitēs circiter trecentī atque in castra contenderent, Morinī, quōs Caesar in Britanniam proficīscēns pācātōs relīquerat, spē praedae adductī, prīmō nōn ita magnō suōrum numerō circumstetērunt ac, sī sēsē interficī nōllent, arma pōnere iussērunt. Cum illī, 5 orbe factō, sēsē dēfenderent, celeriter ad clāmōrem hominum circiter mīlia sex convēnērunt. Quā rē nūntiātā, Caesar omnem ex castrīs equitātum suīs auxiliō mīsit.

    Interim nostrī mīlitēs impetum hostium sustinuērunt atque amplius hōrīs quattuor fortissimē pugnāvērunt, et, paucīs vulneribus acceptīs, complūrīs 10 ex hīs occīdērunt. Posteā vērō quam equitātus noster in cōnspectum vēnit, hostēs, abiectīs armīs, terga vertērunt magnusque eōrum numerus est occīsus.

38. Caesar Punishes the Morini

Caesar posterō diē Titum Labiēnum lēgātum cum eīs legiōnibus, quās ex Britanniā redūxerat, in Morinōs, quī rebelliōnem fēcerant, mīsit. Quī cum propter siccitātēs palūdum, quō sē reciperent, nōn habērent, omnēs ferē in potestātem Labiēnī pervēnērunt.

---

36.   **3. propinquā diē aequinoctī:** *the period of the equinox being near.* Caesar sailed back to the continent about the middle of September.   **4. hiemī:** *stormy weather;* dative after **subiciendam. subiciendam** (esse): *ought to be exposed*   **5. tempestātem:** *weather*   **7. eōsdem portūs:** *the same harbors*—Portus Itius and Ambleteuse, from which they had sailed. **quōs:** *as*   **8. īnfrā:** i.e., down the coast to the south

37.   **1. Quibus ex nāvibus:** the two **onerāriae** mentioned in line 7, chapter 36. **expositī:** *landed*   **4. pōnere:** *lay down.* **illī:** i.e., the Romans   **10. ex hīs:** i.e., of the enemy. **Posteā quam** = Postquam

38.   **3. siccitātēs:** *dryness;* plural form with singular meaning. **quō sē reciperent:** *a place to which they might retreat*

During a Roman Thanksgiving (**supplicātiō**), worshippers were allowed to approach the figures of the gods, garland them with flowers, and even offer them food— fresco from Herculaneum

At Q. Titūrius et L. Cotta lēgātī, quī in Menapiōrum fīnīs legiōnēs   5
dūxerant, omnibus eōrum agrīs vāstātīs, frūmentīs succīsīs, aedificiīs incēnsīs,
quod Menapiī sē omnēs in dēnsissimās silvās abdiderant, sē ad Caesarem
recēpērunt. Caesar in Belgīs omnium legiōnum hīberna cōnstituit.

Hīs rēbus gestīs, ex litterīs Caesaris diērum vīgintī supplicātiō ā senātū
dēcrēta est.   10

---

9. diērum vīgintī supplicātiō: After the second campaign in Gaul, a fifteen-day thanksgiving had been decreed.

Book 5
THE ATTACK
ON CICERO'S CAMP

Chapters 1–37

During the winter of 55–54 B.C. Caesar employed his legions in building 600 transports for the coming expedition to Britain. They were built a little shallower than usual, so that they could be more easily beached. They were also wider, which enabled them to carry heavier cargoes and more horses. When Caesar reached the army in the spring, these transports together with 28 war galleys were almost ready to be launched.

In July, leaving Labienus in Gaul with three legions, Caesar sailed to Britain with five legions and 2000 horsemen. Owing to the size of his expedition his landing was not opposed. He marched inland and took a British stronghold. Again his ships were damaged by a storm, but he was able to repair most of them and had Labienus build others in Gaul. He briefly describes the geography and customs of the Britons. After again defeating the Britons, Caesar crossed the Thames River and took the stronghold of the British commander Cassivellaunus. Meanwhile the Britons in Kent attacked Caesar's naval camp and were defeated. Consequently Cassivellaunus offered to surrender. Caesar took hostages and brought all his forces safely back to Gaul.

In the fall of 54 B.C. Caesar distributed his legions in widely separated winter camps in northern Gaul. One legion under Labienus was quartered among the Treveri. Another, under Quintus Cicero, was quartered among the Nervii. One and a half legions were stationed among the Eburones, under the joint command of Sabinus and Cotta. This camp was attacked first, by Ambiorix, the chief of the Eburones, who had been a friend of Caesar's three years before. Sabinus and Cotta disagreed as to what the Romans should do,

Sabinus arguing that they should leave their camp and join another one, and Cotta strongly opposing this idea. A council of officers was called, and Sabinus forced Cotta to yield.

So the Romans left their camp with all their baggage. When they had gone down into a valley, the Gauls appeared on all sides of them and attacked. Sabinus asked for a conference with Ambiorix, but was treacherously killed. Then the Gauls killed most of the Romans, including Cotta. The rest of the Romans killed themselves, except a few, who escaped to Labienus' camp with news of the disaster.

38. Ambiorix Incites the Nervians to Revolt

Hāc victōriā sublātus, Ambiorīx statim cum equitātū in Aduatucōs, quī erant eius rēgnō fīnitimī, proficīscitur; neque noctem neque diem intermittit, peditātumque sēsē subsequī iubet. Rē dēmōnstrātā Aduatucīsque concitātīs, posterō diē in Nerviōs pervenit hortāturque nē suī in perpetuum līberandī atque ulcīscendī Rōmānōs prō eīs, quās accēperint, iniūriīs occāsiōnem dīmittant; interfectōs esse lēgātōs duōs magnamque partem exercitūs interīsse dēmōnstrat; nihil esse negōtī, subitō oppressam legiōnem, quae cum Cicerōne hiemet, interficī; sē ad eam rem profitētur adiūtōrem. Facile hāc ōrātiōne Nerviīs persuādet.

5

39. The Nervii Ask for Help from Their Neighbors

Itaque cōnfestim dīmissīs nūntiīs ad Ceutronēs, Grudiōs, Levācōs, Pleumoxiōs, Geidumnōs, quī omnēs sub eōrum imperiō sunt, quam maximās possunt manūs cōgunt, et dē imprōvīsō ad Cicerōnis hīberna advolant, nōndum ad eum fāmā dē Titūrī morte perlātā.

---

38. **1. Hāc victōriā sublātus:** *Elated by this victory*—over Sabinus and Cotta **3. Rē:** i.e., what they had achieved **5. ulcīscendī Rōmānōs:** *of punishing the Romans;* a rare use of the gerund with an object **6. lēgātōs:** *lieutenant generals*—Sabinus and Cotta **7. nihil . . . negōtī:** *that there would be no difficulty*

39. **4. Titūrī:** Sabinus. His full name was Quintus Titurius Sabinus.

Huic quoque accidit, quod fuit necesse, ut nōn nūllī mīlitēs, quī lignātiōnis mūnītiōnisque causā in silvās discessissent, repentīnō equitum adventū interciperentur. Hīs circumventīs, magnā manū Eburōnēs, Nerviī, Aduatucī atque hōrum omnium sociī et clientēs legiōnem oppugnāre incipiunt. Nostrī celeriter ad arma concurrunt, vāllum cōnscendunt. Aegrē is diēs sustentātur, quod omnem spem hostēs in celeritāte pōnēbant atque, hanc adeptī victōriam, in perpetuum sē fore victōrēs cōnfīdēbant.

40. The Romans Fight All Day and Work All Night

Mittuntur ad Caesarem cōnfestim ā Cicerōne litterae, magnīs prōpositīs praemiīs, sī pertulissent; obsessīs omnibus viīs, missī intercipiuntur. Noctū ex māteriā, quam mūnītiōnis causā comportāverant, turrēs admodum CXX excitantur incrēdibilī celeritāte; quae deesse operī vidēbantur, perficiuntur. Hostēs posterō diē, multō maiōribus coāctīs cōpiīs, castra oppugnant, fossam complent. Eādem ratiōne, quā prīdiē, ā nostrīs resistitur.

Hoc idem reliquīs deinceps fit diēbus. Nūlla pars nocturnī temporis ad labōrem intermittitur; nōn aegrīs, nōn vulnerātīs facultās quiētis datur. Quaecumque ad proximī diēī oppugnātiōnem opus sunt, noctū comparantur; multae praeūstae sudēs, magnus mūrālium pīlōrum numerus īnstituitur; turrēs contabulantur, pinnae lōrīcaeque ex crātibus attexuntur. Ipse Cicerō, cum tenuissimā valētūdine esset, nē nocturnum quidem sibi tempus ad quiētem relinquēbat, ut ultrō mīlitum concursū ac vōcibus sibi parcere cōgerētur.

41. The Nervii Propose a Conference

Tunc ducēs prīncipēsque Nerviōrum, quī aliquem sermōnis aditum causamque amīcitiae cum Cicerōne habēbant, colloquī sēsē velle dīcunt. Factā

---

5. **Huic quoque:** *to him* (Cicero) *also; just as had happened to Sabinus and Cotta.* **lignātiōnis . . . causā:** *for the sake of getting timber for the fortification* 9. **sustentātur:** *they held out.* 10. **adeptī:** *if they gained;* from **adipiscor.**

40. 1. **ad Caesarem:** Caesar was at this time at Samarobriva, the modern Amiens. 2. **sī pertulissent:** *if they reached him.* **missī:** *the messengers* 8. **intermittitur:** *was left unused* 9. **opus:** *necessary* 10. **praeūstae:** *burned at the ends*—to harden them 11. **contabulantur:** *were provided with platforms.* **pinnae . . . crātibus:** screens of interwoven branches—for the protection of the men hurling weapons 12. **cum . . . esset:** *although he was in very poor health* 13. **ultrō:** *actually.* **vōcibus:** *pleas*

41. 1. **aliquem . . . aditum:** *some claim to talk with him,* since they had met him before.

Models of Roman siege machines: **turris ambulātōria** with **ariēs, testūdō, vīnea,** and **pluteus** (see pp. 87–88)

potestāte, eadem, quae Ambiorīx cum Titūriō ēgerat, commemorant: omnem esse in armīs Galliam; Germānōs Rhēnum trānsīsse; Caesaris reliquōrumque hīberna oppugnārī. Addunt etiam dē Sabīnī morte; Ambiorīgem ostentant fideī faciendae causā. Errāre eōs dīcunt, sī quicquam ab hīs praesidī spērent, quī suīs rēbus diffīdant; sēsē tamen hōc esse in Cicerōnem populumque Rōmānum animō, ut nihil nisi hīberna recūsent, atque hanc inveterāscere cōnsuētūdinem nōlint; licēre illīs per sē incolumibus ex hībernīs discēdere et, quāscumque in partīs velint, sine metū proficīscī. 10

    Cicerō ad haec ūnum modo respondit: Nōn esse cōnsuētūdinem populī Rōmānī, accipere ab hoste armātō condiciōnem; sī ab armīs discēdere velint, sē adiūtōre ūtantur lēgātōsque ad Caesarem mittant; spērāre, prō eius iūstitiā, quae petierint, impetrātūrōs.

---

5. ostentant: *point to*   **6. fideī faciendae causā:** *as proof.* **quicquam:** *any at all;* stronger than quid. **hīs quī:** *men who*   **7. in:** *towards*   **8. nihil nisi hīberna:** The Nervii claim that they will do anything for Caesar and the Romans except allow them to keep their winter camps in their lands.   **9. per sē:** *as far as they were concerned*

42. The Enemy Renew the Attack

Ab hāc spē repulsī Nerviī vāllō pedum X et fossā pedum XV hīberna cingunt. Haec et superiōrum annōrum cōnsuētūdine ā nōbīs cognōverant et, quōsdam dē exercitū nactī captīvōs, ab hīs docēbantur; sed nūllā ferrāmentōrum cōpiā, quae esset ad hunc ūsum idōnea, gladiīs caespitēs circumcīdere,
5 manibus sagulīsque terram exhaurīre cōgēbantur. Quā quidem ex rē hominum multitūdō cognōscī potuit; nam minus hōrīs tribus mīlium passuum III in circuitū mūnītiōnem perfēcērunt. Reliquīs diēbus turrīs ad altitūdinem vāllī, falcēs testūdinēsque, quās īdem captīvī docuerant, parāre ac facere coepērunt.

43. The Enemy Set Fire to the Huts in the Roman Camp

Septimō oppugnātiōnis diē, maximō coortō ventō, ferventīs fūsilī ex argillā glandīs fundīs et fervefacta iacula in casās, quae mōre Gallicō strāmentīs erant tēctae, iacere coepērunt. Hae celeriter ignem comprehendērunt et ventī magnitūdine in omnem locum castrōrum distulērunt. Hostēs maximō clā-
5 mōre, sīcutī partā iam atque explōrātā victōriā, turrīs testūdinēsque agere et vāllum ascendere coepērunt.

At tanta mīlitum virtūs atque ea praesentia animī fuit ut, cum undique flammā torrērentur maximāque tēlōrum multitūdine premerentur, suaque omnia impedīmenta atque omnīs fortūnās cōnflagrāre intellegerent, nōn
10 modo dēmigrandī causā dē vāllō dēcēderet nēmō, sed paene nē respiceret quidem quisquam, ac tum omnēs ācerrimē fortissimēque pugnārent.

Hic diēs nostrīs longē gravissimus fuit; sed tamen hunc habuit ēventum, ut eō diē maximus numerus hostium vulnerārētur atque interficerētur, ut sē sub ipsō vāllō cōnstīpāverant, recessumque prīmīs ultimī nōn dabant.
15 Paulum quidem intermissā flammā, et quōdam locō turrī adāctā et

---

42. **1. pedum X:** *ten feet high;* genitive of measure. **pedum XV:** *fifteen feet wide* (at the top)   **3. exercitū:** sc. Rōmānō. **nūllā cōpiā:** *there being no supply;* ablative absolute **4. caespitēs:** *sod*   **5. sagulīs:** *in their cloaks.* **exhaurīre:** *to carry out*   **8. falcēs:** wooden poles, or beams, with a hook-shaped iron in the end, used to tear down the enemy's walls. **testūdinēs:** *movable sheds,* under which the soldiers might work in safety

43. **1. ferventīs ... glandīs:** *red hot balls of molded clay*—thrown with slings (**fundīs**) which must have been lined with metal   **2. casās:** *huts.* **strāmentīs ... tēctae:** *were thatched.* They would catch fire very quickly.   **3. Hae:** *These huts*   **5. partā:** *gained;* from **pariō.** **explōrātā:** *secured.* **agere:** *to move up*   **8. torrērentur:** *they were being scorched*   **9. fortūnās:** *their personal possessions*   **10. dēmigrandī causā:** *to move his belongings.* **paene nē respiceret quidem quisquam:** *hardly anyone even looked around*   **13. ut:** *since*   **14. cōnstīpāverant:** *they had crowded in*   **15. turrī:** an enemy tower

contingente vāllum, tertiae cohortis centuriōnēs ex eō, quō stābant, locō recessērunt suōsque omnīs remōvērunt, nūtū vōcibusque hostīs, sī introīre vellent, vocāre coepērunt; quōrum prōgredī ausus est nēmō. Tum ex omnī parte lapidibus coniectīs dēturbātī, turrisque succēnsa est.

44. Two Brave Centurions

Erant in eā legiōne fortissimī virī, centuriōnēs quī prīmīs ōrdinibus appropinquārent, T. Pullō et L. Vorēnus. Hī perpetuās inter sē contrōversiās habēbant, uter alterī anteferrētur, omnibusque annīs dē locō summīs simultātibus contendēbant. Ex hīs Pullō, cum ācerrimē ad mūnītiōnēs pugnārētur, "Quid dubitās," inquit, "Vorēne? Aut quem locum tuae probandae virtūtis exspectās? Hic diēs dē nostrīs contrōversiīs iūdicābit." Haec cum dīxisset, prōcēdit extrā mūnītiōnēs, quaeque pars hostium cōnfertissima est vīsa, in eam irrumpit.   5

Nē Vorēnus quidem sēsē vāllō continet, sed omnium veritus exīstimātiōnem, subsequitur. Mediocrī spatiō relictō, Pullō pīlum in hostīs immittit   10
atque ūnum ex multitūdine prōcurrentem trāicit; quō percussō et exanimātō, hunc scūtīs prōtegunt hostēs, in illum ūniversī tēla coniciunt neque dant prōgrediendī facultātem. Trānsfīgitur scūtum Pullōnī et verūtum in balteō dēfīgitur. Āvertit hic cāsus vāgīnam et gladium ēdūcere cōnantī dextram morātur manum, impedītumque hostēs circumsistunt. Succurrit inimīcus illī   15
Vorēnus et labōrantī subvenit.

Ad hunc sē cōnfestim ā Pullōne omnis multitūdō convertit; illum verūtō trānsfīxum arbitrantur. Gladiō comminus rem gerit Vorēnus atque ūnō interfectō reliquōs paulum prōpellit; dum cupidius īnstat, in locum dēiectus īnferiōrem concidit. Huic rūrsus circumventō subsidium fert Pullō, atque   20
ambō incolumēs, complūribus interfectīs, summā cum laude sēsē intrā mūnītiōnēs recipiunt.

Sīc fortūna in contentiōne et certāmine utrumque versāvit, ut alter alterī inimīcus auxiliō salūtīque esset, neque dīiūdicārī posset, uter utrī virtūte anteferendus vidērētur.   25

---

19. dēturbātī (sunt): *the enemy were driven off*

44.   1. quī ... appropinquārent: *were getting close to the first rank* (of centurions)
3. uter: *as to which of the two.* **dē locō:** *for the position*—of first centurion   **5. Quid:** *Why.*
quem locum: i.e., *what better opportunity*   **9. Nē Vorēnus quidem:** *Nor did Vorenus either.*
exīstimātiōnem: *opinion;* i.e., *what everyone would think of him, if Pullo went and he stayed
behind*   **11. exanimātō:** *stunned*   **15. inimīcus:** *his rival.* **illī:** *notice how Pullo and Vorenus
are referred to by different pronouns.*   **19. dēiectus:** *stumbling*   **23. alter alterī:** *each ...
to the other*

A Roman fort (a permanent camp) in Britain, on the English Channel

45. A Message Reaches Caesar

Quantō erat in diēs gravior atque asperior oppugnātiō,—maximē quod, magnā parte mīlitum cōnfectā vulneribus, rēs ad paucitātem dēfēnsōrum pervēnerat,—tantō crēbriōrēs litterae nūntiīque ad Caesarem mittēbantur; quōrum pars dēprehēnsa, in cōnspectū nostrōrum mīlitum cum cruciātū necābātur.

Erat ūnus intus Nervius, nōmine Verticō, locō nātus honestō, quī ā prīmā obsidiōne ad Cicerōnem perfūgerat suamque eī fidem praestiterat. Hic servō spē lībertātis magnīsque persuādet praemiīs, ut litterās ad Caesarem dēferat. Hās ille in iaculō illigātās effert et Gallus inter Gallōs sine ūllā suspīciōne versātus ad Caesarem pervenit. Ab eō dē perīculīs Cicerōnis legiōnisque cognōscitur.

45. 1. Quantō gravior, tantō crēbriōrēs: *The more desperate, the more frequently.* in diēs: *each day*   4. quōrum: *of these* (messengers). dēprehēnsa: *intercepted*   6. intus: *in the camp* (of Cicero). prīmā: *the beginning of*   7. praestiterat: *had shown.* Hic: *This man* (Vertico). servō: *a slave of his*   9. illigātās: *tied,* or concealed in some way on the javelin. The plan succeeded, and Caesar was informed of the attack on Cicero's camp.   10. versātus: *moving about*

46. Caesar Acts Quickly

Caesar, acceptīs litterīs hōrā circiter ūndecimā diēī, statim nūntium in Bellovacōs ad M. Crassum quaestōrem mittit, cuius hīberna aberant ab eō mīlia passuum XXV; iubet mediā nocte legiōnem proficīscī celeriterque ad sē venīre. Exit cum nūntiō Crassus. Alterum ad C. Fabium lēgātum mittit, ut in Atrebātium fīnīs legiōnem addūcat, quā sibi iter faciendum sciēbat. Scrībit Labiēnō, sī reī pūblicae commodō facere posset, cum legiōne ad fīnīs Nerviōrum veniat. Reliquam partem exercitūs, quod paulō aberat longius, nōn putat exspectandam; equitēs circiter CCCC ex proximīs hībernīs cōgit.

47. Help Arrives from Other Winter Camps

Hōrā circiter tertiā ab antecursōribus dē Crassī adventū certior factus, eō diē mīlia passuum XX prōcēdit. Crassum Samarobrīvae praeficit legiōnemque eī attribuit, quod ibi impedīmenta exercitūs, obsidēs cīvitātum, litterās pūblicās frūmentumque omne, quod eō tolerandae hiemis causā dēvexerat, relinquēbat. Fabius, ut imperātum erat, nōn ita multum morātus, in itinere cum legiōne occurrit.

Labiēnus, interitū Sabīnī et caede cohortium cognitā, cum omnēs ad eum Trēverōrum cōpiae vēnissent, veritus nē, sī ex hībernīs fugae similem profectiōnem fēcisset, hostium impetum sustinēre nōn posset,—praesertim quōs recentī victōriā efferrī scīret,—litterās Caesarī remittit, quantō cum perīculō legiōnem ex hībernīs ēductūrus esset; rem gestam in Eburōnibus perscrībit; docet omnīs equitātūs peditātūsque cōpiās Trēverōrum tria mīlia passuum longē ab suīs castrīs cōnsēdisse.

---

46. **1. hōrā . . . ūndecimā:** *about 5 P.M.* **2. aberant:** Crassus' camp was 25 miles south of Samarobriva; Fabius' was the same distance to the north. **4. cum nūntiō:** i.e., as soon as the message reached him **6. sī . . . posset:** i.e., if consistent with the best interest of the state **7. veniat:** indirect command, *that he should come*

47. **1. antecursōribus:** *scouts,* who ran ahead. Caesar had left Samarobriva without waiting for Crassus to arrive, but he left orders for him to stay there and guard the supplies. **adventū:** *approach* **3. litterās:** *documents* **6. occurrit:** *met him* (Caesar), as arranged. **7. Labiēnus:** Caesar had advised Labienus that he should decide for himself whether or not he should try to help Cicero, and Labienus decided that it was too risky. **10. quōs . . . scīret:** causal, *since he knew that they. . . quantō,* etc.: *explaining how dangerous it would be* **12. perscrībit:** *he described in detail*—the things that had happened to Cotta and Sabinus. When Caesar heard this, he let his hair and beard grow long, swearing not to shave again until he had avenged this defeat.

48. Cicero Receives a Message from Caesar

Caesar, cōnsiliō eius probātō, etsī opīniōne trium legiōnum dēiectus ad duās redierat, tamen ūnum commūnis salūtis auxilium in celeritāte pōnēbat. Vēnit magnīs itineribus in Nerviōrum fīnīs. Ibi ex captīvīs cognōscit, quae apud Cicerōnem gerantur, quantōque in perīculō rēs sit. Tum cuidam ex equitibus Gallīs magnīs praemiīs persuādet, utī ad Cicerōnem epistulam dēferat.

Hanc Graecīs cōnscrīptam litterīs mittit, nē, interceptā epistulā, nostra ab hostibus cōnsilia cognōscantur. Sī adīre non possit, monet ut trāgulam cum epistulā ad āmentum dēligātā intrā mūnītiōnem castrōrum abiciat. In litterīs scrībit, sē cum legiōnibus profectum celeriter affore; hortātur, ut prīstinam virtūtem retineat. Gallus perīculum veritus, ut erat praeceptum, trāgulam mittit.

Haec cāsū ad turrim adhaesit, neque ā nostrīs bīduō animadversa tertiō diē ā quōdam mīlite cōnspicitur, dēmpta ad Cicerōnem dēfertur. Ille perlēctam in conventū mīlitum recitat maximāque omnīs laetitiā afficit. Tum fūmī incendiōrum procul vidēbantur; quae rēs omnem dubitātiōnem adventūs legiōnum expulit.

49. The Gauls Turn on Caesar

Gallī, rē cognitā per explōrātōrēs, obsidiōnem relinquunt, ad Caesarem omnibus cōpiīs contendunt. Haec erant armāta circiter mīlia LX. Cicerō, datā facultāte, Gallum ab eōdem Verticōne, quem suprā dēmōnstrāvimus, repetit, quī litterās ad Caesarem dēferat; hunc admonet, iter cautē dīligenterque faciat; perscrībit in litterīs hostīs ab sē discessisse omnemque ad eum multitūdinem convertisse. Quibus litterīs circiter mediā nocte Caesar allātīs suōs facit certiōrēs, eōsque ad dīmicandum animō cōnfirmat.

Posterō diē lūce prīmā movet castra; et circiter mīlia passuum quattuor prōgressus, trāns vallem et rīvum multitūdinem hostium cōnspicātur. Erat magnī perīculī rēs tantulīs cōpiīs inīquō locō dīmicāre; tum, quoniam

---

48.   **1. opīniōne dēiectus:** *disappointed in his expectation;* he had hoped for three legions, but Labienus did not come with his   **6. Hanc:** *this letter.* **Graecīs litterīs:** *in Greek letters;* but the contents of the letter were in Latin.   **7. adīre:** *get through* (to Cicero)   **8. āmentum:** *thong,* or *strap,* for hurling the javelin   **12. Haec:** *This javelin,* which was lodged in the wood of a tower.   **13. dēmpta:** *when taken down*   **14. fūmī:** of villages burned by Caesar

49.   **1. rē:** i.e., Caesar's approach   **3. Gallum:** i.e., *another slave*   **5. sē:** *him* (Cicero). **eum:** *him* (Caesar); notice how much clearer the Latin is than the English.   **10. tantulīs cōpiīs:** *with such small forces;* he had about 7,000 men, whereas the enemy had 60,000.

Prisoners of war being brought to a commander—2d century relief from the Arch of Constantine

obsidiōne līberātum Cicerōnem sciēbat, aequō animō remittendum dē celeritāte exīstimābat. Cōnsēdit et, quam aequissimō potest locō, castra commūnit, atque haec, (etsī erant exigua per sē, vix hominum mīlium septem, praesertim nūllīs cum impedīmentīs), tamen angustiīs viārum, quam maximē potest, contrahit, eō cōnsiliō, ut in summam contemptiōnem hostibus veniat. Interim, speculātōribus in omnīs partīs dīmissīs, explōrat, quō commodissimē itinere vallem trānsīre possit. 15

50. Caesar Plans a Surprise

Eō diē parvulīs equestribus proeliīs ad aquam factīs, utrīque sēsē suō locō continent: Gallī, quod ampliōrēs cōpiās, quae nōndum convēnerant, exspectābant; Caesar, sī forte timōris simulātiōne hostis in suum locum ēlicere posset, ut citrā vallem prō castrīs proeliō contenderet; sī id efficere nōn posset, ut, explōrātīs itineribus, minōre cum perīculō vallem rīvumque 5 trānsīret.

Prīmā lūce hostium equitātus ad castra accēdit proeliumque cum nostrīs equitibus committit. Caesar cōnsultō equitēs cēdere sēque in castra recipere iubet; simul ex omnibus partibus castra altiōre vāllō mūnīrī portāsque obstruī atque in hīs administrandīs rēbus quam maximē concursārī et cum 10 simulātiōne agī timōris iubet.

---

13. haec ... contrahit: Caesar reduced the width of the streets, and made the whole camp as small as possible, in order to make the enemy think that he had fewer men than he did.

50. 2. ampliōrēs cōpiās: *more troops;* even though they outnumbered Caesar by more than eight to one! **3. suum locum:** *his own ground* **4. ut:** translate this word before **si** in line 3. **8. cōnsultō:** *on purpose* **10. concursārī:** *to rush around*—to give the enemy the impression that they were panic-stricken **11. agi:** *to act*

51. The Gauls Are Routed

Quibus omnibus rēbus hostēs invītātī cōpiās trādūcunt aciemque inīquō locō cōnstituunt; nostrīs vērō etiam dē vāllō dēductīs, propius accēdunt et tēla intrā mūnītiōnem ex omnibus partibus coniciunt, praecōnibusque circummissīs prōnūntiārī iubent, seu quis Gallus seu Rōmānus velit ante hōram tertiam ad sē trānsīre, sine perīculō licēre; post id tempus nōn fore potestātem.

Ac sīc nostrōs contempsērunt, ut, obstrūctīs in speciem portīs singulīs ōrdinibus caespitum, quod eā nōn posse intrōrumpere vidēbantur, aliī vāllum manū scindere, aliī fossās complēre inciperent. Tum Caesar, omnibus portīs ēruptiōne factā equitātūque ēmissō, celeriter hostīs in fugam dat, sīc utī omnīnō pugnandī causā resisteret nēmō, magnumque ex eīs numerum occīdit atque omnīs armīs exuit.

52. Caesar Inspects Cicero's Camp

Longius prōsequī veritus, quod silvae palūdēsque intercēdēbant neque etiam parvulō dētrīmentō illōrum locum relinquī vidēbat, omnibus suīs incolumibus cōpiīs eōdem diē ad Cicerōnem pervēnit. Īnstitūtās turrīs, testūdinēs mūnītiōnēsque hostium admīrātur; legiōne prōductā cognōscit, nōn decimum quemque esse reliquum mīlitem sine vulnere; ex hīs omnibus iūdicat rēbus, quantō cum perīculō et quantā cum virtūte rēs sint administrātae. Cicerōnem prō eius meritō legiōnemque collaudat; centuriōnēs singillātim tribūnōsque mīlitum appellat, quōrum ēgregiam fuisse virtūtem testimōniō Cicerōnis cognōverat. Dē cāsū Sabīnī et Cottae certius ex captīvīs cognōscit.

Posterō diē, cōntiōne habitā, rem gestam prōpōnit, mīlitēs cōnsōlātur et cōnfīrmat; quod dētrīmentum culpā et temeritāte lēgātī sit acceptum, hōc aequiōre animō ferendum docet, quod, beneficiō deōrum immortālium et virtūte eōrum expiātō incommodō, neque hostibus diūtina laetitia neque ipsīs longior dolor relinquātur.

---

51.   **1. invītātī:** *lured on*   **2. (hostēs) accēdunt:** *came nearer;* after the Romans came down from their walls   **6. in speciem:** *for show, merely.* **singulīs . . . caespitum:** *each with a single thickness of sod*   **9. ēruptiōne:** *a sally;* the slight barrier of sod was flung aside, and the Romans burst out of the gates, surprising the enemy.

52.   **1. neque . . . relinquī:** *and that no opportunity remained for (inflicting) even a trifling loss upon them*   **4. nōn decimum quemque:** *not one in ten—had escaped without injuries*   **8. appellat:** *called by name;* he apparently knew many of the officers by name, and praised them individually.   **11. dētrīmentum:** *the defeat*—i.e., at the camp of Sabinus and Cotta. This was not a defeat for the army as much as poor judgment on the part of one general, Sabinus. **hōc . . . quod:** *for the reason that*   **13. eōrum:** i.e., the soldiers to whom he is speaking   **14. ipsīs:** *to them* (the Romans)

Book 6
GALLIC AND GERMAN CUSTOMS

Chapters 1–10

During the winter Caesar more than made up for the losses he had sustained by recruiting two new legions and obtaining the loan of another from Pompey. He took the field earlier than usual, and by his rapid movements quickly stamped out revolts among the Nervii, Senones, and Carnutes. He then ravaged the country of the Menapii and reduced them to submission.

Meanwhile Labienus was again attacked by the Treveri, but by the pretense of fear he drew them into an unfavorable position and defeated them. Caesar now joined forces with him and at once started on a second expedition into Germany.

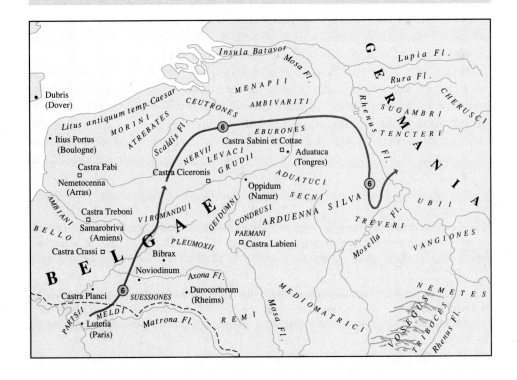

11. Party Strife among the Gauls

Quoniam ad hunc locum perventum est, nōn aliēnum esse vidētur dē Galliae
Germāniaeque mōribus et, quō differant hae nātiōnēs inter sēsē, prōpōnere.

In Galliā nōn sōlum in omnibus cīvitātibus atque in omnibus pāgīs
partibusque, sed paene etiam in singulīs domibus factiōnēs sunt, eārumque
5   factiōnum prīncipēs sunt quī summam auctōritātem eōrum iūdiciō habēre
exīstimantur, quōrum ad arbitrium iūdiciumque summa omnium rērum
cōnsiliōrumque redeat.

Idque eius reī causā antīquitus īnstitūtum vidētur, nē quis ex plēbe contrā
potentiōrem auxilī egēret; suōs enim quisque opprimī et circumvenīrī nōn
10 patitur, neque, aliter sī faciat, ūllam inter suōs habet auctōritātem. Haec
eadem ratiō est in summā tōtīus Galliae; namque omnēs cīvitātēs in partīs
dīvīsae sunt duās.

12. Changes in Leadership among the Gauls

Cum Caesar in Galliam vēnit, alterīus factiōnis prīncipēs erant Aeduī, alterīus
Sēquanī. Hī cum per sē minus valērent, quod summa auctōritās antīquitus
erat in Aeduīs magnaeque eōrum erant clientēlae, Germānōs atque Ariovis-
tum sibi adiūnxerant eōsque ad sē magnīs iactūrīs pollicitātiōnibusque
5   perdūxerant.

Proeliīs vērō complūribus factīs secundīs, atque omnī nōbilitāte Aeduōrum
interfectā, tantum potentiā antecesserant, ut magnam partem clientium ab
Aeduīs ad sē trādūcerent, obsidēsque ab eīs prīncipum fīliōs acciperent, et
pūblicē iūrāre cōgerent, nihil sē contrā Sēquanōs cōnsilī initūrōs, et partem
10 fīnitimī agrī per vim occupātam possidērent, Galliaeque tōtīus prīncipātum
obtinērent. Quā necessitāte adductus, Dīviciācus auxilī petendī causā Romam
ad senātum profectus, īnfectā rē redierat.

Adventū Caesaris factā commūtātiōne rērum, obsidibus Aeduīs redditīs,
veteribus clientēlīs restitūtīs, novīs per Caesarem comparātīs, quod hī, quī

---

11.   **1. perventum est:** *we have reached*—in the narrative. **nōn aliēnum:** *not out of place*
6. summa . . . rērum: *the final decision in all matters*   **7. redeat:** *is referred*   **8. antīquitus:**
an adverb   **9. auxilī:** genitive with **egeō,** which normally takes the ablative—*be in want of
help.* **quisque:** *each chief.* **circumvenīrī:** *to be deceived*   **11. ratiō:** *system*

12.   **2. Hī:** *the latter*   **3. clientēlae:** *dependencies,* i.e., the states that were subject to them
4. iactūrīs: *expense*   **7. antecesserant:** *they* (the Sequani) *had surpassed them* (the Aedui)
11. Dīviciācus: the leader of the Aedui   **12. īnfectā rē:** *without accomplishing his
purpose*

sē ad eōrum amīcitiam aggregāverant, meliōre condiciōne atque aequiōre   15
imperiō sē ūtī vidēbant, reliquīs rēbus eōrum grātiā dignitāteque amplificātā,
Sēquanī prīncipātum dīmīserant.

In eōrum locum Rēmī successerant; quōs quod adaequāre apud Caesarem
grātiā intellegēbātur, eī, quī propter veterēs inimīcitiās nūllō modō cum
Aeduīs coniungī poterant, sē Rēmīs in clientēlam dicābant. Hōs illī dīligenter   20
tuēbantur; ita et novam et repente collēctam auctōritātem tenēbant. Eō tum
statū rēs erat, ut longē prīncipēs habērentur Aeduī, secundum locum dignitātis
Rēmī obtinērent.

13. Classes of the People in Gaul

In omnī Galliā eōrum hominum, quī aliquō sunt numerō atque honōre,
genera sunt duo; nam plēbs paene servōrum habētur locō, quae nihil audet
per sē, nūllī adhibētur cōnsiliō. Plērīque, cum aut aere aliēnō aut magnitūdine
tribūtōrum aut iniūriā potentiōrum premuntur, sēsē in servitūtem dicant
nōbilibus; quibus in hōs eadem omnia sunt iūra quae dominīs in servōs.   5
Sed dē hīs duōbus generibus alterum est druidum, alterum equitum. Illī
rēbus dīvīnīs intersunt, sacrificia pūblica ac prīvāta prōcūrant, religiōnēs
interpretantur; ad eōs magnus adulēscentium numerus disciplīnae causā
concurrit, magnōque hī sunt apud eōs honōre. Nam ferē dē omnibus
contrōversiīs pūblicīs prīvātīsque cōnstituunt; et, sī quod est admissum   10
facinus, sī caedēs facta, sī dē hērēditāte, dē fīnibus contrōversia est, īdem
dēcernunt, praemia poenāsque cōnstituunt; sī quī aut prīvātus aut populus
eōrum dēcrētō nōn stetit, sacrificiīs interdīcunt. Haec poena apud eōs est
gravissima. Quibus ita est interdictum, hī numerō impiōrum ac scelerātōrum
habentur, hīs omnēs dēcēdunt, aditum sermōnemque dēfugiunt, nē quid ex   15
contāgiōne incommodī accipiant, neque hīs petentibus iūs redditur neque
honōs ūllus commūnicātur.

Hīs autem omnibus druidibus praeest ūnus, quī summam inter eōs habet
auctōritātem. Hōc mortuō, aut, sī quī ex reliquīs excellit dignitāte, succēdit,

---

15. eōrum: i.e., of the Aedui   16. ūtī: *were enjoying*   18. quōs . . . intellegēbātur: *because
it was realized that they stood equally high* (with the Aedui) *in Caesar's favor*   20. dicābant:
i.e., pledged   21. Eō: with statū, *such*

13.   1. aliquō numerō: *of any account*   5. quibus sunt: *they have.* in hōs: *over them*
6. Illī: *They,* the Druids   10. sī quod facinus: *if any crime*   13. interdīcunt: *they exclude
him*   14. Quibus est interdictum, hī: *those who are excluded.* numerō: sc. in   16. incommodī:
genitive of the whole with quid   17. honōs = honor

Stonehenge, a Druid temple in Britain

20   aut, sī sunt plūrēs parēs, suffrāgiō druidum dēligitur; nōn numquam etiam
armīs dē prīncipātū contendunt. Hī certō annī tempore in fīnibus Carnutum,
quae regiō tōtīus Galliae media habētur, cōnsīdunt in locō cōnsecrātō. Hūc
omnēs undique (quī contrōversiās habent) conveniunt eōrumque dēcrētīs
iūdiciīsque pārent.

25   Disciplīna in Britanniā reperta atque inde in Galliam trānslāta esse
exīstimātur; et nunc quī dīligentius eam rem cognōscere volunt plērumque
illō discendī causā proficīscuntur.

---

25. reperta: *to have originated*. Caesar is wrong in this statement, though at the time of
Caesar, the Druids were stronger in Britain than in Gaul.   **27. illō:** adverb, *there*, to Britain

14. Beliefs of the Druids

Druidēs ā bellō abesse cōnsuērunt neque tribūta ūnā cum reliquīs pendunt; mīlitiae vacātiōnem, omniumque rērum habent immūnitātem. Tantīs excitātī praemiīs, et suā sponte multī in disciplīnam conveniunt et ā parentibus propinquīsque mittuntur. Magnum ibi numerum versuum ēdiscere dīcuntur. Itaque annōs nōn nūllī vīcēnōs in disciplīnā permanent. Neque fās esse 5 exīstimant ea litterīs mandāre, cum in reliquīs ferē rēbus, pūblicīs prīvātīsque ratiōnibus, Graecīs litterīs ūtantur. Id mihi duābus dē causīs īnstituisse videntur, quod neque in vulgus disciplīnam efferrī velint, neque eōs quī discunt, litterīs cōnfīsōs, minus memoriae studēre; quod ferē plērīsque accidit, ut praesidiō litterārum dīligentiam in perdiscendō ac memoriam 10 remittant.

In prīmīs hoc volunt persuādēre, nōn interīre animās, sed ab aliīs post mortem trānsīre ad aliōs; atque hōc maximē ad virtūtem excitārī putant, metū mortis neglēctō. Multa praetereā dē sīderibus atque eōrum mōtū, dē mundī ac terrārum magnitūdine, dē rērum nātūrā, dē deōrum immortālium 15 vī ac potestāte disputant et iuventūtī trādunt.

15. The Knights

Alterum genus est equitum. Hī, cum est ūsus atque aliquod bellum incidit (quod ante Caesaris adventum ferē quotannīs accidere solēbat, utī aut ipsī iniūriās īnferrent aut illātās prōpulsārent), omnēs in bellō versantur; atque eōrum ut quisque est genere cōpiīsque amplissimus, ita plūrimōs circum sē ambactōs clientēsque habet. Hanc ūnam grātiam potentiamque nōvērunt. 5

---

14. 3. **praemiīs:** *privileges* 4. **ēdiscere:** *to learn by heart* 6. **cum:** *although* 7. **Graecīs litterīs:** i.e., Greek characters, in which they wrote their own (Celtic) language. Inscriptions of that kind have come down to us. 9. **minus ... studēre:** *pay too little attention (to)* 10. **praesidiō:** *through reliance (on)* 12. **persuādēre:** *to teach* 15. **mundī:** *the universe*

15. 1. **cum est ūsus:** *whenever there is need.* Notice the indicative and cf. **cum,** 16. 10. 3. **illātās:** sc. **iniūriās**—*attacks on them* 5. **ambactōs:** *retainers.* These retainers were hired servants, inferior to the **clientēs,** who were dependents, or followers.

16. Human Sacrifices

Nātiō est omnis Gallōrum admodum dēdita religiōnibus; atque ob eam causam [quī sunt affectī graviōribus morbīs, quīque in proeliīs perīculīsque versantur, aut prō victimīs hominēs immolant aut sē immolātūrōs vovent, administrīsque ad ea sacrificia druidibus ūtuntur, quod, prō vītā hominis
5 nisi hominis vīta reddātur, nōn posse deōrum immortālium nūmen plācārī arbitrantur; pūblicēque eiusdem generis habent īnstitūta sacrificia. Aliī immānī magnitūdine simulācra habent, quōrum contexta vīminibus membra vīvīs hominibus complent; quibus succēnsīs, circumventī flammā exanimantur hominēs. Supplicia eōrum, quī in furtō aut in latrōciniō aut aliquā noxiā
10 sint comprehēnsī, grātiōra dīs immortālibus esse arbitrantur; sed cum eius generis cōpia dēfēcit, etiam ad innocentium supplicia dēscendunt.

17. Gods of the Gauls

Deum maximē Mercurium colunt. Huius sunt plūrima simulācra; hunc omnium inventōrem artium ferunt, hunc viārum atque itinerum ducem, hunc ad quaestūs pecūniae mercātūrāsque habēre vim maximam arbitrantur. Post hunc Apollinem et Mārtem et Iovem et Minervam. Dē hīs eandem ferē,
5 quam reliquae gentēs, habent opīniōnem: Apollinem morbōs dēpellere, Minervam operum atque artificiōrum initia trādere, Iovem imperium caelestium tenēre, Mārtem bella regere. Huic, cum proeliō dīmicāre cōnstituērunt, ea, quae bellō cēperint, plērumque dēvovent; cum superāvērunt, animālia capta immolant reliquāsque rēs in ūnum locum cōnferunt. Multīs
10 in cīvitātibus hārum rērum exstrūctōs tumulōs locīs cōnsecrātīs cōnspicārī licet; neque saepe accidit ut quispiam, neglēctā religiōne, aut capta apud sē occultāre aut posita tollere audēret, gravissimumque eī reī supplicium cum cruciātū cōnstitūtum est.

---

16.   **1. religiōnibus:** *to rites*   **3. prō:** *as;* i.e., they sacrificed not animals, but humans. **4. vītā hominis . . . hominis vīta:** the ABBA word order ("chiasmus") is used to bring out the contrast between the person who is to live and the one to die.   **7. simulācra:** *figures,* or *images* in human form, made out of wicker work (**vīminibus**), and filled with living men

17.   **1. Mercurium:** *Mercury* and the other gods mentioned here were Celtic gods, with Gallic names, whom Caesar identifies with the Roman gods of the same attributes.   **2. ferunt:** *they declare*   **4. Post hunc:** sc. **colunt.**   **6. operum atque artificiōrum initia:** *the fundamentals of arts and crafts.* **trādere = docēre**   **8. quae . . . cēperint:** *whatever spoils they may take in war*—they dedicate to Mars   **11. capta:** *spoils,* object of **occultāre**   **12. posita:** *things deposited*

18. Other Customs of the Gauls

Gallī sē omnīs ab Dīte patre prōgnātōs praedicant idque ab druidibus prōditum dīcunt. Ob eam causam spatia omnis temporis nōn numerō diērum, sed noctium fīniunt; diēs nātālīs et mēnsium et annōrum initia sīc observant, ut noctem diēs subsequātur.

In reliquīs vītae īnstitūtīs hōc ferē ab reliquīs differunt, quod suōs līberōs,   5
nisi cum adolēvērunt ut mūnus mīlitiae sustinēre possint, palam ad sē adīre nōn patiuntur, fīliumque puerīlī aetāte in pūblicō in cōnspectū patris assistere turpe dūcunt.

19. Marriages and Funerals

Virī, quantās pecūniās ab uxōribus dōtis nōmine accēpērunt, tantās ex suīs bonīs, aestimātiōne factā, cum dōtibus commūnicant. Huius omnis pecūniae coniūnctim ratiō habētur frūctūsque servantur; uter eōrum vītā superāvit, ad eum pars utrīusque cum frūctibus superiōrum temporum pervenit.

Virī in uxōrēs, sīcutī in līberōs, vītae necisque habent potestātem; et cum   5
pater familiae, illūstriōre locō nātus, dēcessit, eius propinquī conveniunt et, dē morte sī rēs in suspīciōnem venit, dē uxōribus in servīlem modum quaestiōnem habent et, sī compertum est, igne atque omnibus tormentīs excruciātās interficiunt.

Fūnera sunt prō cultū Gallōrum magnifica et sūmptuōsa; omniaque quae   10
vīvīs cordī fuisse arbitrantur in ignem īnferunt, etiam animālia; ac paulō suprā hanc memoriam servī et clientēs, quōs ab eīs dīlēctōs esse cōnstābat, iūstīs fūneribus cōnfectīs, ūnā cremābantur.

---

18.   **1. Dīte patre:** *father Pluto*, god of the Underworld   **2. prōditum (esse):** *has been handed down*   **3. noctium:** This seems logical to Caesar, because night, like all things black, belongs to the gods of the Lower World in Roman practice. Among the Gauls, the notion that night was the source of day probably corresponds to the idea that death was the source of life (Chapter 14).   **7. assistere:** *to appear*   **8. turpe dūcunt:** *they consider it disgraceful*

19.   **1. pecūniās:** *property;* among primitive people, usually cattle   **2. cum . . . commū-nicant:** *they add to the dowry*   **3. frūctūs:** *profits*, or *income.* **uter . . . superāvit:** *whichever of them outlives the other*   **7. dē uxōribus quaestiōnem habent:** *they examine his wives under torture*—as was done among the Romans in the case of slaves   **8. sī compertum est:** *if they are found guilty*   **11. cordī fuisse:** *were dear to*   **12. suprā . . . memoriam:** *before our time*   **13. iūstīs . . . cōnfectīs:** *after the regular funeral was finished*

A deer hunt—mosaic from the imperial palace at Piazza Armerina, Sicily

20. Talking about the State Forbidden

Quae cīvitātēs commodius suam rem pūblicam administrāre exīstimantur,
habent lēgibus sānctum, sī quis quid dē rē pūblicā ā fīnitimīs rūmōre aut
fāmā accēperit, utī ad magistrātum dēferat nēve cum quō aliō commūnicet,
quod saepe hominēs temerāriōs atque imperītōs falsīs rūmōribus terrērī et
5   ad facinus impellī et dē summīs rēbus cōnsilium capere cognitum est.
Magistrātūs, quae vīsa sunt, occultant, quaeque esse ex ūsū iūdicāvērunt,
multitūdinī prōdunt. Dē rē pūblicā nisi per concilium loquī nōn concēditur.

21. Customs of the Germans

Germānī multum ab hāc cōnsuētūdine differunt. Nam neque druidēs habent,
quī rēbus dīvīnīs praesint, neque sacrificiīs student. Deōrum numerō eōs
sōlōs dūcunt quōs cernunt et quōrum apertē opibus iuvantur, Sōlem et
Vulcānum et Lūnam; reliquōs nē fāmā quidem accēpērunt.
5   Vīta omnis in vēnātiōnibus atque in studiīs reī mīlitāris cōnsistit; ā parvīs
labōrī ac dūritiae student.

---

20.   1. **commodius:** *to greater advantage* (than the rest)   2. **habent . . . sānctum:** i.e.,
have laws that provide. **sī quis quid:** *if anyone (hears) anything*   6. **quae vīsa sunt:** *what
seems best.* **ex ūsū:** *of advantage*

21.   3. **dūcunt:** *they reckon*   4. **Vulcānum:** i.e., fire

22. No Private Property

Agrī cultūrae nōn student, maiorque pars eōrum vīctūs in lacte, cāseō, carne cōnsistit. Neque quisquam agrī modum certum aut fīnīs habet propriōs; sed magistrātūs ac prīncipēs in annōs singulōs gentibus cognātiōnibusque hominum, quīque ūnā coiērunt, quantum et quō locō vīsum est agrī attribuunt atque annō post aliō trānsīre cōgunt.   5

Eius reī multās afferunt causās: nē, assiduā cōnsuētūdine captī, studium bellī gerendī agrī cultūrā commūtent; nē lātōs fīnīs parāre studeant, potentiōrēsque humiliōrēs possessiōnibus expellant; nē accūrātius ad frīgora atque aestūs vītandōs aedificent; nē qua oriātur pecūniae cupiditās, quā ex rē factiōnēs dissēnsiōnēsque nāscuntur; ut animī aequitāte plēbem contineant,   10 cum suās quisque opēs cum potentissimīs aequārī videat.

Chapters 23 and 24 deal with German Frontiers.

25. The Hercynian Forest

Huius Hercyniae silvae, quae suprā dēmōnstrāta est, lātitūdō novem diērum iter expedītō patet; nōn enim aliter fīnīrī potest, neque mēnsūrās itinerum nōvērunt. Oritur ab Helvētiōrum et Nemetum et Rauracōrum fīnibus, rēctāque flūminis Dānuvī regiōne pertinet ad fīnīs Dācōrum et Anartium; hinc sē flectit sinistrōrsus, dīversīs ā flūmine regiōnibus, multārumque   5 gentium fīnīs propter magnitūdinem attingit; neque quisquam est huius Germāniae quī sē aut adīsse ad initium eius silvae dīcat, cum diērum iter LX prōcesserit, aut, quō ex locō oriātur, accēperit; multaque in eā genera ferārum nāscī cōnstat, quae reliquīs in locīs vīsa nōn sint; ex quibus quae maximē differant ā cēterīs et memoriae prōdenda videantur, haec sunt.   10

---

22. 2. modum: *amount* **3. gentibus ... hominum:** *to clans and groups of kinsmen* **4. quō locō vīsum est:** *where they think best.* **agrī:** with **quantum** **5. annō post:** *a year later.* **aliō:** adverb **7. parāre:** *to obtain* **8. accūrātius** *with too great care* **10. aequitāte:** *contentment*

25. 1. lātitūdō: *width,* from north to south **2. expedītō:** *for a man traveling light* (without luggage). **fīnīrī:** *be measured* **3. Oritur:** *It starts* **4. rēctā ... regiōne:** *straight along the Danube* **6. huius Germāniae:** *of this part of Germany* **10. memoriae prōdenda (esse):** *to deserve to be recorded*

26. Strange Kinds of Animals: Unicorn Reindeer

Est bōs cervī figūrā, cuius ā mediā fronte inter aurīs ūnum cornū exsistit, excelsius magisque dērēctum hīs, quae nōbīs nōta sunt, cornibus; ab eius summō sīcut palmae rāmīque lātē diffunduntur. Eadem est fēminae marisque nātūra, eadem fōrma magnitūdōque cornuum.

27. Elk and Moose

Sunt item quae appellantur alcēs. Hārum est cōnsimilis caprīs figūra et varietās pellium, sed magnitūdine paulō antecēdunt mutilaeque sunt cornibus et crūra sine nōdīs articulīsque habent, neque quiētis causā prōcumbunt, neque, sī quō afflīctae cāsū concidērunt, ērigere sēsē aut sublevāre possunt.
5 Hīs sunt arborēs prō cubīlibus; ad eās sē applicant, atque ita paulum modo reclīnātae quiētem capiunt. Quārum ex vēstīgiīs cum est animadversum ā vēnātōribus quō sē recipere cōnsuērint, omnēs eō locō aut ab rādīcibus subruunt aut accīdunt arborēs, tantum ut summa speciēs eārum stantium relinquātur. Hūc cum sē cōnsuētūdine reclīnāvērunt, īnfirmās arborēs pon-
10 dere afflīgunt.

28. Wild Oxen

Tertium est genus eōrum, quī ūrī appellantur. Hī sunt magnitūdine paulō īnfrā elephantōs, speciē et colōre et figūrā taurī. Magna vīs eōrum est et magna vēlōcitās, neque hominī neque ferae quam cōnspexērunt parcunt. Hōs studiōsē foveīs captōs interficiunt. Hōc sē labōre dūrant adulēscentēs
5 atque hōc genere vēnātiōnis exercent; et quī plūrimōs ex hīs interfēcērunt, relātīs in pūblicum cornibus, quae sint testimōniō, magnam ferunt laudem. Sed assuēscere ad hominēs et mānsuēfierī nē parvulī quidem exceptī possunt. Amplitūdō cornuum et figūra et speciēs multum ā nostrōrum boum cornibus differt. Haec studiōsē conquīsīta ab labrīs argentō circumclūdunt atque in
10 amplissimīs epulīs prō pōculīs ūtuntur.

---

26.   **1. bōs:** This has been thought by some to be the reindeer, glimpsed from the side, so that its two antlers (which grow quite close together) appear to be one. **fronte:** *forehead*
2. hīs cornibus: *than those horns*; ablative of comparison   **3. sīcut:** *so to speak.* **fēminae marisque:** *of the female and the male*

27.   **1. alcēs:** *elk*   **2. mutilae:** *broken-looking*   **3. crūra . . . articulīs:** *legs without nodes or joints.* **quiētis:** *sleep*   **5. Hīs sunt:** *They use.* **sē applicant:** *they lean against*   **8. subruunt:** *they uproot.* **accīdunt:** *cut into.* **tantum ut:** *only in such a way that.* **summa speciēs:** *the exact appearance*

28.   **1. ūrī:** *wild ox* (bos primigenius), the ancestor of domestic cattle. It was finally hunted to extinction in the 17th century   **4. foveīs:** *in pits*   **7. nē . . . exceptī:** *not even if caught when young*   **9. ab labrīs:** *at the edges,* or *rims*   **10. prō pōculīs:** *for drinking horns*

Book 7
THE STORY
OF VERCINGETORIX

Caesar had been in Gaul six years. He had conquered the country and annexed it as a province of Rome. Yet he had by no means won the allegiance of the Gallic states. Hitherto he had succeeded in holding them under control by shrewdly playing faction against faction and by suppressing scattered revolts through the superiority of his army. But the Gauls had not lost all hope of expelling the Roman invader. What they had lacked thus far was a truly great commander, under whom they could unite to do battle against a common enemy. Now at last in the seventh year there appeared among them an inspiring leader, who combined unusual military ability with great personal magnetism. This was the Arvernian nobleman, Vercingetorix.

During the winter of 53–52 B.C. the city of Rome was greatly disturbed by political dissensions and street riots. Thinking that these troublous conditions would detain Caesar in Northern Italy, many chiefs of Gaul secretly met and conspired against him. The Carnutes began the rebellion by massacring the Roman citizens at Cenabum. News of this outbreak soon reached Gergovia, capital city of the Arverni, the home of Vercingetorix. He at once appealed to the patriotism of his people and persuaded them to take part in this movement for the freedom of Gaul. Numerous other states quickly followed the example set by the Arverni. A large army was assembled and the supreme command was given to Vercingetorix. His first step was to send a force to invade the Roman Province and attack Narbo.

Roused by these alarming reports, Caesar moved with lightning speed. He first went to Narbo and provided for the protection of the Province. Then with a small force he crossed the Cévennes Mountains through snow six feet deep, and suddenly descended upon the Arverni. He thereby forced Vercingetorix, who was farther north among the Bituriges, to return for the relief of his own people.

Now came Caesar's opportunity. Leaving his forces in the command of Brutus to devastate the Arvernian district, he dashed to the river Rhone, up the Saône, through the Aedui, into the country of the Lingones, where two of his legions were wintering. Then stationing two legions at Agedincum to guard the heavy baggage, in quick succession he captured Vellaunodunum, Cenabum, and Noviodunum, and marched toward Avaricum.

These disasters convinced Vercingetorix that there was only one way to cope with the Romans. He called a council and set forth his plan. It called for the utmost self-sacrifice on the part of his countrymen. They must burn their houses, their barns, their villages,—even their towns, and thus cut off Caesar's supplies. The only alternative was to be conquered, and that meant death for the warriors and captivity for their wives and children. To this staggering appeal the Gauls responded in a spirit of noble patriotism, and soon the countryside was ablaze in every direction. But the Bituriges could not bear to see their splendid capital Avaricum destroyed. They insisted that it was impregnable, and pled so piteously that at last Vercingetorix yielded against his better judgment.

Dispatching Labienus with four legions to put down a revolt in the valley of the Seine, Caesar with the six remaining legions laid siege to Gergovia. But the Aedui were threatening to rebel, and he hurried away to win them back to their allegiance. In his absence Vercingetorix made a furious attack upon the Roman camp, and Caesar returned just in time to save it from capture.

The situation now caused Caesar deep anxiety, for his forces were widely separated, and the rebellion was rapidly gaining in strength. He attempted to surprise the enemy, but the attack—though successful at first—was eventually repulsed with severe losses. A few days later Caesar abandoned the siege and marched north into the country of the Aedui, only to find that they too had joined the rebellion. He was hemmed in on every side, and his supplies were falling short. Marching day and night, at length he reached the Loire, and having crossed its swollen stream, once more confounded his enemies by his speed. Labienus, who had defeated the Parisii and returned to Agedincum, was summoned, and with the arrival of his legions Caesar's united army resumed operations in more hopeful spirit.

An idealized portrait of
Vercingetorix

But the disaster to the Romans at Gergovia had already had its effect. All the states of Celtic and Belgic Gaul except three, the Remi, Lingones, and Treveri, were now included in the Great Rebellion.

Vercingetorix was made Commander-in-Chief. He assembled an army, and his cavalry attacked the Roman army, but were routed by the German cavalry that Caesar had obtained. Vercingetorix was forced to withdraw his army to the town of Alesia, where he built a walled camp. Caesar surrounded the camp and town with an elaborate eleven-mile fortification, while Vercingetorix summoned all Gaul to help him. Caesar then made an outer wall, with defenses facing out, to defend against Gauls coming to relieve the siege, as the Gauls gathered an enormous army and headed for Alesia. The Gauls in Alesia were in the meantime starving, and a man named

Critognatus suggested that they eat those who were unable to fight. In the end, however, the elders, the women, and the children were driven out of the town, and Caesar refused to let them through his lines. Then the Gallic army of relief arrived, but was defeated in two attacks on Caesar's forces. Finally this army made a surprise attack on the Romans from the outside while Vercingetorix attacked from the inside, and a critical battle ensued in which Caesar ultimately defeated both Gallic forces. Vercingetorix surrendered, and most of his men were given to the Roman soldiers as booty.

Plutarch describes the scene at Vercingetorix's surrender. Caesar was seated on a tribunal erected well within his fortified lines when forth from the city gate came Vercingetorix, clad in armor, mounted upon a splendidly adorned horse. Riding around the tribunal, he dismounted, put off his armor, and then took his place at the feet of his conqueror. For a time there was profound silence. At length Caesar gave an order, and a guard quietly led the Gallic chieftain away.

Vercingetorix was sent to Rome, where he remained a prisoner for six years. At Caesar's triumph in 46 B.C. he marched in the procession, and then with several other noble captives was slain in sacrifice to the gods of Rome. Yet, in spite of this sad fate, he won a glorious name in history as a high-minded patriot and martyr to the cause of Gallic freedom. Today his statue crowns the heights of ancient Alesia, and the people of France respect and honor him as the first of their great national heroes.

The modern statue of Vercingetorix on the site of Alesia in France

A Brief Anthology of
Latin Readings

About the Author NEPOS

Cornelius Nepos was born about 100 B.C. in Cisalpine Gaul, probably at Ticinum (modern Pavia), and died about 25 B.C.

He took up his residence at Rome early in life and seems to have had an independent fortune because he was able to devote his whole attention to literary pursuits. He took no part in politics, which was unusual for a man in his position, but he was on friendly terms with the outstanding politicians as well as with the famous literary men of his day. In fact, the famous poet Catullus dedicated his book of poems to him.

We know through references of other writers that he wrote in several different areas of literature, but unfortunately, most of his work has been lost. The only surviving work is part of a collection of short biographies entitled *Dē Virīs Illūstribus*. This text consisted of at least sixteen books. The biographies were arranged in classes or groups with two books for each group. The first book included distinguished men from foreign nations, mostly Greece, and the second book treated distinguished men from Rome. One book, *Dē Excellentibus Ducibus Exterārum Gentium ("On Outstanding Foreign Military Commanders")* we have in its entirety. It is from this book that we have the biography of Alcibiades, perhaps the most remarkable man of all Greece.

The style of Nepos is simple and pleasing. His vocabulary is limited, and as a rule he expresses himself in short sentences. Although he was a contemporary of Julius Caesar, his Latin is not so strictly classical as that of the author of *"The Gallic Wars."* He sometimes has a poetic coloring to his writing that is missing in the writing of Caesar. When Nepos occasionally attempts long sentences, it soon becomes evident that he is not comfortable with a complicated style, and at times he even becomes careless, especially in the omission of pronouns. As a general rule, however, his style is very clear, and thus he is an appropriate author for students who are beginning to read Latin.

Selections from *ALCIBIADES*

BACKGROUND

Alcibiades was an Athenian general whose treachery helped cause the defeat of Athens in the Peloponnesian War—the war between Athens and Sparta 431–404 B.C. He persuaded Athens to attack the Peloponnesian League in 418 B.C. and Sicily in 415 B.C. Both attacks failed. When the citizens of Athens accused him of destroying the sacred images of the god Hermes, he was ordered to a hearing but escaped to Sparta and helped the Spartans aid the Sicilians.

1. The Outstanding Virtues and Vices of Alcibiades

Alcibiadēs, Clīniae fīlius, Athēniēnsis. In hōc nātūra quid efficere possit vidētur experta; cōnstat enim inter omnīs, quī dē eō memoriae prōdidērunt, nihil illō fuisse excellentius vel in vitiīs vel in virtūtibus. Nātus in amplissimā cīvitāte summō genere, omnium aetātis suae multō fōrmōsissimus, ad omnīs rēs aptus cōnsilīque plēnus (namque imperātor fuit summus et marī et terrā) disertus, ut in prīmīs dīcendō valēret, quod tanta erat commendātiō ōris atque ōrātiōnis, ut nēmō eī posset resistere; dīves; cum tempus posceret, labōriōsus, patiēns; līberālis, splendidus nōn minus in vītā quam vīctū; affābilis, blandus, temporibus callidissimē serviēns: īdem, simul ac sē remīserat neque causa suberat quā rē animī labōrem perferret, lūxuriōsus, dissolūtus, intemperāns reperiēbātur, ut omnēs admīrārentur in ūnō homine tantam esse dissimilitūdinem tamque dīversam nātūram.

5

10

---

1. 1. **Clīnias, -ae** m.: *Clinias,* father of Alcibiades. **In hōc:** *In the case of this man.* **nātūra:** subject of both **possit** and **vidētur experta (esse)** 9. **temporibus serviēns:** *adapting to circumstances* 10. **neque causa suberat:** *and there was no underlying reason*

One of many ancient portraits of the philosopher Socrates

2. The Youth of Alcibiades

Ēducātus est in domō Periclī, ērudītus ā Sōcrate. Socerum habuit Hippōnīcum, omnium Graecā linguā loquentium dītissimum, ut, sī ipse fingere vellet, neque plūra bona comminīscī neque maiōra posset cōnsequī, quam vel nātūra vel fortūna tribuerat.

---

2. **1. in domō Periclī:** Alcibiades was born about 450 B.C., and his father died in 447 B.C. Pericles, Alcibiades' cousin, was the greatest Greek statesman of the period 460–430 B.C. ("The Periclean Age"). **ērudītus:** in the informal manner of Socrates, known to us from the dialogues and *Apology* of Plato **2. sī vellet . . . posset:** subjunctives in a past contrary-to-fact condition, where the imperfect sometimes appears instead of the pluperfect; *If he had wished, he would not have been able . . .* **3. comminīscī:** from **comminīscor** *to invent, think of*

3. Alcibiades Suspected of Knocking Down the Herms (415 B.C.)

Bellō Peloponnēsiō hūius cōnsiliō atque auctōritāte Athēniēnsēs bellum
Syrācūsānīs indīxērunt. Ad quod gerendum ipse dux dēlēctus est, duo
praetereā collēgae datī, Nīciās et Lāmachus. Id cum parārētur, prius quam
classis exīret, accidit ut ūnā nocte omnēs Hermae, quī in oppidō erant
Athēnīs, dēicerentur praeter ūnum. Hoc cum appārēret nōn sine magnā   5
multōrum cōnsēnsiōne esse factum, quae nōn ad prīvātam, sed ad pūblicam
rem pertinēret, magnus multitūdinī timor est iniectus nē qua repentīna vīs
in cīvitāte exsisteret, quae lībertātem opprimeret populī.

Hoc maximē convenīre in Alcibiadem vidēbātur, quod et potentior et
māior quam prīvātus exīstimābātur; multōs enim līberālitāte dēvinxerat,   10
plūrīs etiam operā forēnsī suōs reddiderat. Quā rē fīēbat ut omnium oculōs,
quotiēnscumque in pūblicum prōdīsset, ad sē converteret neque eī pār
quisquam in cīvitāte pōnerētur. Itaque nōn sōlum spem in eō habēbant
maximam, sed etiam timōrem, quod et obesse plūrimum et prōdesse poterat.
Aspergēbātur etiam īnfāmiā, quod in domō suā facere mystēria dīcēbātur—   15
quod nefās erat mōre Athēniēnsium—idque nōn ad religiōnem, sed ad
coniūrātiōnem pertinēre exīstimābātur.

4. Alcibiades Accused of Sacrilege

Hōc crīmine in cōntiōne ab inimīcīs compellābātur. Sed īnstābat tempus ad
bellum proficīscendī. Id ille intuēns neque ignōrāns cīvium suōrum cōnsuētūdinem postulābat ut, sī quid dē sē agī vellent, potius dē praesente quaestiō
habērētur, quam absēns invidiae crīmine accūsārētur. Inimīcī vērō ēius
quiēscendum in praesentia, quia nocērī eī nōn posse intellegēbant, et illud   5
tempus exspectandum dēcrēvērunt quō exīsset, ut absentem aggrederentur;
itaque fēcērunt. Nam postquam in Siciliam eum pervēnisse crēdidērunt,
absentem, quod sacra violāsset, reum fēcērunt.

---

3. **2. Syrācūsānī, -ōrum** m.: *The Syracusans* (in Sicily) **4. Hermae:** busts of the god
Hermes, each resting on a square pillar **8. quae ... opprimeret:** relative characteristic
clause, *violence of the sort that would ...* **9. convenīre in:** *to point to* (lit. *to suit*).
11. suōs: *his friends* **13. pōnerētur:** *was considered* **15. mystēria:** refers to the Eleusinian
Mysteries, secret rites of rebirth and immortality which were said to bring great joy

4. **2. cōnsuētūdinem:** i.e. their way of humbling the great **3. dē (sē) praesente:** *about
him in his presence* **4. invidiae crīmine:** *on a charge arising from malice* **5. quiēscendum:**
supply **sibi esse** (passive periphrastic). **nocērī eī nōn posse:** *he could not be harmed* **8. quod
... violāsset:** subjunctive because it shows the enemies' reason, not the author's. **reum
fēcērunt:** *they prosecuted him* (**reus** means *defendant*)

A bronze herm from Africa

Quā dē rē cum eī nūntius ā magistrātū in Siciliam missus esset, ut domum
10 ad causam dīcendam redīret, essetque in magnā spē prōvinciae bene admin-
istrandae, nōn pārēre nōluit et in trirēmem, quae ad eum dēportandum erat
missa, ascendit. Hāc Thūriōs in Italiam vectus, multa sēcum reputāns dē
immoderātā cīvium suōrum licentiā crūdēlitāteque ergā nōbilīs, ūtilissimum
ratus impendentem vītāre tempestātem, clam sē ab custōdibus subdūxit et
15 inde Thēbās vēnit. Postquam autem sē capitis damnātum bonīs pūblicātīs
audīvit, et, id quod ūsū vēnerat, Eumolpidās sacerdōtēs ā populō coāctōs
ut sē dēvovērent, ēiusque dēvōtiōnis quō testātior esset memoria, exemplum
in pīlā lapideā incīsum esse positum in pūblicō, Lacedaemonem dēmigrāvit.
Ibi, ut ipse praedicāre cōnsuērat, nōn adversus patriam, sed inimīcōs suōs
20 bellum gessit, quī īdem hostēs essent cīvitātī; nam cum intellegerent sē
plūrimum prōdesse posse reī pūblicae, ex eā ēiēcisse plūsque īrae suae quam
ūtilitātī commūnī pāruisse. Itaque hūius cōnsiliō Lacedaemoniī cum Perse
rēge amīcitiam fēcērunt, deinde Decelēam in Atticā mūniērunt praesidiōque
ibi perpetuō positō in obsidiōne Athēnās tenuērunt. Eiusdem operā Iōniam
25 ā societāte āvertērunt Athēniēnsium. Quō factō multō superiōrēs bellō esse
coepērunt.

---

9. ut . . . redīret: depends on nūntius, *message*   10. ad causam dīcendam: *to plead his case.*
prōvinciae: *his mission.*   11. nōn pārēre: *to disobey*   12. Thūriī, -ōrum, m.: *Thurii,* a
town in southern Italy. sēcum *to himself* (a common idiom)   15. capitis: *on a capital charge*
16. id quod ūsū vēnerat: *as had actually happened.* Eumolpidae, -ārum, m.: the
priests of Demeter   17. dēvōtiōnis: depends on memoria. testātior: *better attested to.*
18. Lacedaemōn, -onis, f.: *Sparta*   20. sē: Alcibiades   21. ēiēcisse: the subject is inimīcōs
suōs (understood)   22. Perse rēge: Darius II (423–404 B.C.)   23. Decelēam: a town near
Marathon, controlling the road by which the grain supply from the north reached Athens.
So the maneuver was brilliant and effective. Attica, -ae, f.: the district of Greece that included
Athens   24. Iōnia, -ae f.: *west coast of Asia Minor.*

5. Alcibiades Goes to Asia Minor

Neque vērō hīs rēbus tam amīcī Alcibiadī sunt factī quam timōre ab eō
aliēnātī; nam cum ācerrimī virī praestantem prūdentiam in omnibus rēbus
cognōscerent, timuērunt nē cāritāte patriae ductus aliquandō ab ipsīs dēficeret
et cum suīs in grātiam redīret. Itaque tempus ēius interficiendī quaerere
īnstituērunt. Id Alcibiadēs diūtius cēlārī nōn potuit; erat enim eā sagācitāte   5
ut dēcipī nōn posset, praesertim cum animum attendisset ad cavendum.
Itaque ad Tissaphernem, praefectum rēgis Darīī, sē contulit. Cūius cum in
intimam amīcitiam pervēnisset et Athēniēnsium male gestīs in Siciliā rēbus,
opēs senēscere, contrā Lacedaemoniōrum crēscere vidēret, initiō cum Pīs-
andrō praetōre, quī apud Samum exercitum habēbat, per nūntiōs colloquitur   10
et dē reditū suō facit mentiōnem. Is enim erat eōdem quō Alcibiadēs sēnsū,
populī potentiae nōn amīcus et optimātium fautor. Ab hōc dēstitūtus prīmum
per Thrasybūlum ab exercitū recipitur praetorque fit apud Samum; post
suffrāgante Thērāmene populī scītō restituitur parīque absēns imperiō
praeficitur simul cum Thrasybūlō et Thērāmene.   15

Hōrum in imperiō tanta commūtātiō rērum facta est, ut Lacedaemoniī,
quī paulō ante victōrēs viguerant, perterritī pācem peterent. Victī enim erant
quīnque proeliīs terrestribus, tribus nāvālibus, in quibus ducentās nāvīs
trirēmīs āmīserant, quae captae in hostium vēnerant potestātem. Alcibiadēs
simul cum collēgīs recēperat Iōniam, Hellēspontum, multās praetereā urbīs   20
Graecās, quae in ōrā sitae sunt Asiae, quārum expūgnārant complūrīs, in
hīs Byzantium, neque minus multās cōnsiliō ad amīcitiam adiūnxerant, quod
in captōs clēmentiā fuerant ūsī. Ita praedā onustī, locuplētātō exercitū,
maximīs rēbus gestīs Athēnās vēnērunt.

---

5.   **1. sunt factī:** the subject is the Spartans, as in the last sentence   **2. virī:** genitive
5. cēlārī: *to be kept ignorant of* (**Cēlō** *conceal from* in the passive may keep one of its two
accusatives.) **eā:** *such*   **7. Tissaphernēs, is,** m.: *Tissaphernes,* a Persian governor   **8. in**
Siciliā: the Sicilian expedition was totally defeated and its leaders put to death in 413 B.C.
9. contrā: adverb. **Lacedaemoniōrum:** supply **opēs. Pisander, -drī,** m.: *Pisander,* an Athenian
general   **10. Samum:** the island of Samos was the chief naval base of Athens at this time
(411 B.C.)   **11. is:** i.e. Pisander. Pisander thought that Alcibiades could arrange for Persian
help for the aristocratic party at Athens. **quō:** after **eōdem:** *as*   **12. hōc:** Pisander.
13. Thrasybūlum: Thrasybulus was one of the ten generals for the year. **post:** adverb
14. suffrāgante Thērāmene: *on the motion of Theramenes,* (in the assembly at Athens).
restituitur: i.e. to citizenship   **17. pācem peterent:** 409 B.C. They were turned down   **20–**
23. These victories, somewhat exaggerated by Nepos, made safe the grain route from the
Black Sea   **20. recēperat:** notice the force of re-. **Hellēspontus, -ī,** m.: *the Hellespont,* strait
north of the Aegean Sea   **22. Byzantium, -ī,** n.: *Byzantium* (Istanbul)   **23. in:** *towards*

6. Alcibiades' Triumphant Return to Athens (407 B.C.)

Hīs cum obviam ūniversa cīvitās in Pīraeum dēscendisset, tanta fuit omnium exspectātiō vīsendī Alcibiadis, ut ad ēius trirēmem vulgus cōnflueret, proinde ac sī sōlus advēnisset. Sīc enim populō erat persuāsum, et adversās superiōrēs et praesentīs secundās rēs accidisse ēius operā. Itaque et Siciliae āmissum et
5   Lacedaemoniōrum victōriās culpae suae tribuēbant, quod tālem virum ē cīvitāte expulissent. Neque id sine causā arbitrārī vidēbantur; nam postquam exercituī praeesse coeperat, neque terrā neque marī hostēs parēs esse potuerant. Hic ut ē nāvī ēgressus est, quamquam Thērāmenēs et Thrasybūlus eīsdem rēbus praefuerant simulque vēnerant in Pīraeum, tamen ūnum omnēs
10   illum prōsequēbantur, et, id quod numquam anteā ūsū vēnerat nisi Olympiae victōribus, corōnīs laureīs taeniīsque vulgō dōnābātur. Ille lacrimāns tālem benevolentiam cīvium suōrum accipiēbat, reminīscēns prīstinī temporis acerbitātem.

Postquam in urbem vēnit, cōntiōne advocātā sīc verba fēcit ut nēmō tam
15   ferus fuerit quīn ēius cāsum lacrimārit inimīcumque eīs sē ostenderit quōrum operā patriā pulsus fuerat, proinde ac sī alius populus, nōn ille ipse quī tum flēbat, eum sacrilegī damnāsset. Restitūta ergō huic sunt pūblicē bona, eīdemque illī Eumolpidae sacerdōtēs rūrsus resacrāre sunt coāctī, quī eum dēvōverant, pīlaeque illae, in quibus dēvōtiō fuerat scrīpta, in mare praecip-
20   itātae.

7. New Disfavor for Alcibiades

Haec Alcibiadī laetitia nōn nimis fuit diūturna. Nam cum eī omnēs essent honōrēs dēcrētī tōtaque rēs pūblica domī bellīque trādita, ut ūnīus arbitriō gererētur, et ipse postulāsset ut duo sibi collēgae darentur, Thrasybūlus et Adīmantus, neque id negātum esset, classe in Asiam profectus, quod apud
5   Cȳmēn minus ex sententiā rem gesserat, in invidiam recidit; nihil enim eum nōn efficere posse dūcēbant. Ex quō fiēbat ut omnia minus prōsperē gesta

---

6.   **1. hīs:** depends on **obviam. Pīraeus, ī,** m.: *Piraeus,* the port of Athens   **2. proinde ac sī:** *just as if,* a contrary-to-fact comparison   **3. Sīc:** *of this,* referring to **adversās** (**rēs**), etc. **populō erat persuāsum:** *the nation was convinced*   **4. āmissum:** *loss* (a noun)   **10. ūsū vēnerat:** See 4. 16.   **15. quīn** (**quī** + **nē**): *that he did not.* **lacrimārit = lacrimāverit:** perfect subjunctive   **17. sacrilegī:** *for sacrilege* (genitive).

7.   **2. bellī:** locative   **4. apud Cȳmēn:** Alcibiades was near Cyme, in Asia Minor, helping Thrasybulus, but his fleet was off Notium near Ephesus. It was engaged in a battle contrary to orders and was defeated (406 B.C.).   **5. minus ex sententiā:** *not as they wished*

The Acropolis, citadel of Athens

culpae tribuerent, cum aut eum neglegenter aut malitiōsē fēcisse loquerentur, sīcut tum accidit; nam corruptum ā rēge capere Cȳmēn nōluisse arguēbant. Itaque huic maximē putāmus malō fuisse nimiam opīniōnem ingenī atque virtūtis; timēbātur enim nōn minus quam dīligēbātur, nē secundā fortūnā magnīsque opibus ēlātus tyrannidem concupīsceret. Quibus rēbus factum est ut absentī magistrātum abrogārent et alium in ēius locum substituerent.

Id ille ut audīvit, domum revertī nōluit et sē Chersonēsum contulit ibique tria castella commūniit manūque collēctā prīmus Graecae cīvitātis in Thrāciam introiit, glōriōsius exīstimāns barbarōrum praedā locuplētārī quam Grāiōrum. Quā ex rē crēverat cum fāmā tum opibus magnamque amīcitiam sibi cum quibusdam rēgibus Thrāciae pepererat.

10

15

---

9. **huic ... malō:** double dative, *a source of trouble to him.* **maximē:** with **huic fuisse.**
12. **magistrātum:** his appointment as general. In fact, it was election time and ten new generals were appointed for the year.   13. **Chersonēsus, -ī** f.: *The Chersonese,* a peninsula in the North Aegean Sea   14. **prīmus:** supply **civis.** (**Prīmus** in the nominative is usually translated *(was) the first to.*) Others had been to Thrace earlier, but with **introiit** Nepos is probably referring to penetration well into the interior.   15. **locuplētārī:** the middle (reflexive) use of the passive form, *to enrich himself*   16. **cum ... tum:** *not only ... but also*
17. **pepererat:** from **pariō** *to bear, bring forth, obtain*

8. Alcibiades' Advice to the Athenians Is Refused (405 B.C.)

Neque tamen ā cāritāte patriae potuit recēdere. Nam cum apud Aegos flūmen Philoclēs, praetor Athēniēnsium, classem cōnstituisset suam neque longē abesset Lȳsander, praetor Lacedaemoniōrum, quī in eō erat occupātus ut bellum quam diūtissimē prōdūceret, quod ipsīs pecūnia ā rēge suppedi-
5 tābātur, contrā Athēniēnsibus exhaustīs praeter arma et nāvīs nihil erat super, Alcibiadēs ad exercitum vēnit Athēniēnsium ibique praesente vulgō agere coepit: sī vellent, sē coāctūrum Lȳsandrum dīmicāre aut pācem petere; Lacedaemoniōs eō nōlle classe cōnflīgere, quod pedestribus cōpiīs plūs quam nāvibus valērent; sibi autem esse facile Seuthem, rēgem Thrācum, addūcere
10 ut eum terrā dēpelleret; quō factō necessāriō aut classe cōnflīctūrum aut bellum compositūrum. Id etsī vērē dictum Philoclēs animadvertēbat, tamen postulāta facere nōluit, quod sentiēbat sē Alcibiade receptō nūllīus mōmentī apud exercitum futūrum et, sī quid secundī ēvēnisset, nūllam in eā rē suam partem fore, contrā ea, sī quid adversī accidisset, sē ūnum eius dēlīctī
15 futūrum reum. Ab hōc discēdēns Alcibiadēs "Quoniam," inquit, "victōriae patriae repūgnās, illud moneō, nē iūxtā hostem castra habeās nautica; perīculum est enim nē immodestiā mīlitum vestrōrum occāsiō dētur Lȳsandrō vestrī opprimendī exercitūs." Neque ea rēs illum fefellit; nam Lȳsander cum per speculātōrēs comperisset vulgum Athēniēnsium in terram praedātum
20 exīsse nāvīsque paene inānīs relīctās, tempus reī gerendae nōn dīmīsit eōque impetū bellum tōtum dēlēvit.

9. Alcibiades Withdraws to Asia Minor Again

At Alcibiadēs, victīs Athēniēnsibus nōn satis tūta eadem loca sibi arbitrāns, penitus in Thrāciam sē suprā Propontidem abdidit, spērāns ibi facillimē suam fortūnam occulī posse. Falsō. Nam Thrācēs, postquam eum cum magnā pecūniā vēnisse sēnsērunt, īnsidiās fēcērunt; ea quae apportārat
5 abstulērunt, ipsum capere nōn potuērunt. Ille cernēns nūllum locum sibi

---

8.   **1. patriae:** objective genitive. **Aegos flūmen:** *Aegospotami,* a river in the Chersonese **2. neque longē:** about five miles, at Lampsacus, across the Hellespont   **3. in eō erat occupātus ut . . . prōdūceret:** *was intent on prolonging*   **5. contrā:** (See 5, 9.) **erat super =** supererat, with dative   **6. vulgō:** *the soldiers*   **8. eō . . . quod:** *for the reason that*   **12. Alcibiade receptō:** translate with *if* an ablative absolute depending on a future verb   **13. quid secundī:** *anything successful*   **18. Neque ea rēs illum fefellit:** *and he was not wrong in this* **19. praedātum:** supine   **21. dēlēvit:** *ended*

9.   **2. Propontis, idis,** f.: *the Propontis,* a sea northeast of the Aegean

tūtum in Graeciā propter potentiam Lacedaemoniōrum ad Pharnabāzum in Asiam trānsiit, quem quidem adeō suā cēpit hūmānitāte, ut eum nēmō in amīcitiā antecēderet. Namque eī Grÿnium dederat, in Phrygiā castrum, ex quō quīnquāgēna talenta vectīgālis capiēbat. Quā fortūnā Alcibiadēs nōn erat contentus neque Athēnās victās Lacedaemoniīs servīre poterat patī. Itaque ad patriam līberandam omnī ferēbātur cōgitātiōne. Sed vidēbat id sine rēge Perse nōn posse fierī, ideōque eum amīcum sibi cupiēbat adiungī neque dubitābat facile sē cōnsecūtūrum, sī modo ēius conveniendī habuisset potestātem. Nam Cÿrum frātrem eī bellum clam parāre Lacedaemoniīs adiuvantibus sciēbat; id sī aperuisset, magnam sē initūrum grātiam vidēbat.

10

15

10. Plans to Kill Alcibiades (404 B.C.)

Hoc cum mōlīrētur peteretque ā Pharnabāzō ut ad rēgem mitterētur, eōdem tempore Critiās cēterīque tyrannī Athēniēnsium certōs hominēs ad Lÿsandrum in Asiam mīserant, quī eum certiōrem facerent, nisi Alcibiadem sustulisset, nihil eārum rērum fore ratum, quās ipse Athēnīs cōnstituisset; quā rē, sī suās rēs gestās manēre vellet, illum persequerētur. Hīs Lacō rēbus commōtus statuit accūrātius sibi agendum cum Pharnabāzō. Huic ergō renūntiat quae rēgī cum Lacedaemoniīs essent, nisi Alcibiadem vīvum aut mortuum sibi trādidisset. Nōn tulit hunc satrapēs et violāre clēmentiam quam rēgis opēs minuī māluit.

5

Itaque mīsit Susamithrēn et Bagaeum ad Alcibiadem interficiendum, cum ille esset in Phrygiā iterque ad rēgem comparāret. Missī clam vīcīnitātī, in quā tum Alcibiadēs erat, dant negōtium ut eum interficiant. Illī cum ferrō aggredī nōn audērent, noctū līgna contulērunt circā casam in quā quiēscēbat eamque succendērunt, ut incendiō cōnficerent, quem manū superārī posse diffīdēbant. Ille autem ut sonitū flammae est excitātus, etsī gladius eī erat

10

15

---

6. **Pharnabazus, -i,** m.: governor of northwest Asia Minor   7. **hūmānitāte:** *culture and manners*   8. **Phrygia, -ae,** f.: district of northwest Asia Minor   9. **quīnquāgēna talenta:** the distributive numeral means 50 each year. A talent was worth several thousand modern dollars.   11. **ferēbātur:** *he was moved*   12. **rēge:** now Artaxerxes II (404–358 B.C.), son of Darius II   13. **ēius conveniendī:** *of meeting him*   14. **frātrem:** (of Artaxerxes)   15. **initūrum:** *would gain*

10.   2. **Critiās:** principal member of the "Thirty Tyrants," the government set up in Athens by Lysander and the Spartans after the defeat of Athens in 404 B.C. **certōs:** *reliable* 5. **persequerētur:** indirect command *he should . . .* **Lacō:** *the Spartan,* i.e. Lysander   7. **renūntiat:** here, *renounced.* **quae:** *the agreement which*   8. **Nōn tulit hunc:** *did not resist him* 10. **Susamithres** and **Bagaeus** were Persians.   11. **vīcīnitātī:** *to the (residents of the) neighborhood*   12. **Illī:** *the residents*

subductus, familiāris suī subālāre tēlum ēripuit. Namque erat cum eō quīdam ex Arcadiā hospes, quī numquam discēdere voluerat. Hunc sequī sē iubet et id quod in praesentiā vestīmentōrum fuit arripuit. Hīs in īgnem coniectīs flammae vim trānsiit. Quem ut barbarī incendium effūgisse vīdērunt, tēlīs

20 ēminus missīs interfēcērunt caputque eius ad Pharnabāzum rettulērunt. At mulier quae cum eō vīvere cōnsuērat muliebrī suā veste contēctum aedificī incendiō mortuum cremāvit, quod ad vīvum interimendum erat comparātum. Sīc Alcibiadēs annōs circiter quadrāgintā nātus diem obiit suprēmum.

11. The Superlative Abilities of Alcibiades

Hunc īnfāmātum ā plērīsque trēs gravissimī historicī summīs laudibus extulērunt: Thūcȳdidēs, quī eiusdem aetātis fuit, Theopompus, post aliquantō nātus, et Tīmaeus; quī quidem duo maledicentissimī nēsciō quō modō in illō ūnō laudandō cōnsentiunt. Namque ea, quae suprā scrīpsimus, dē eō

5 praedicārunt atque hoc amplius: cum Athēnīs, splendidissimā cīvitāte, nātus esset, omnīs splendōre ac dīgnitāte superāsse vītae; postquam inde expulsus Thēbās vēnerit, adeō studiīs eōrum īnservīsse ut nēmō eum labōre corporisque vīribus posset aequiperāre—omnēs enim Boeōtiī magis firmitātī corporis quam ingenī acūminī serviunt;—eundem apud Lacedaemoniōs, quōrum

10 mōribus summa virtūs in patientiā pōnēbātur, sīc dūritiae sē dedisse, ut parsimōniā victūs atque cultūs omnīs Lacedaemoniōs vinceret; fuisse apud Thrācas, hominēs vīnolentōs rēbusque veneriīs dēditōs: hōs quoque in hīs rēbus antecessisse; vēnisse ad Persās, apud quōs summa laus esset fortiter vēnārī, lūxuriōsē vīvere: hōrum sīc imitātum cōnsuētūdinem, ut illī ipsī eum

15 in hīs māximē admīrārentur. Quibus rēbus effēcisse ut, apud quōscumque esset, prīnceps pōnerētur habērēturque cārissimus. Sed satis dē hōc; reliquōs ōrdiāmur.

---

16. subālāre tēlum: probably a dagger (**subālāre** means *worn under the arm*)   **18. vestīmentōrum:** partitive with **id quod:** *whatever clothing*   **21. (eum) contēctum:** *covered him and . . .*   **23. quadrāgintā:** Alcibiades was probably over 45, since the date was 404 B.C. **diem obiit suprēmum:** *met his final hour*

11.   **1. īnfāmātum:** has concessive force: *although discredited*   **2. Theopompus, Tīmaeus:** Greek historians, born about 25 and 50 years respectively after the death of Alcibiades   **3. quī . . . duo:** *these (last) two*. **nēsciō quō modō:** *somehow*   **5. cum:** from **cum** to **cārissimus** (line 16) is an indirect statement, of which **Alcibiadem** is the understood subject   **8. Boeōtiī:** Thebes was in Boeotia, northwest of Athens. The sophisticated Athenians generally considered the Boeotians slow-witted rustics. The subsequent references to the Spartans, Thracians, and Persians also reflect the accepted stereotypes.   **14. imitātum:** infinitive in indirect statement   **16. hōc:** m.   **17. ōrdiāmur:** hortatory subjunctive

About the Author OVID

Publius Ovidius Naso was born in 43 B.C., and so came of age at about the time that the Emperor Augustus was setting about his tasks of reconstructing the Roman government and reforming Roman religion and morals. The Roman constitution, shaky since the second century B.C., had collapsed completely during the bloody civil wars of the first century. Family life, among the upper classes, had suffered almost as seriously: the birth rate had declined, divorce was common, social life was lively but vicious. The traditional Roman religion, the bulwark of the state, no longer commanded the devotion of the educated class. To support his program of reconstruction and reform, Augustus enlisted the support of the writers of his time—and they were great writers: among them were Vergil, Horace, and Livy.

Hence Ovid lived and wrote at a time which marked the height of Roman literary achievement, but though he was a brilliant poet himself he was not drawn into the group of writers whose work bolstered the new regime. Much as he admired their work, his literary tastes and his talents were quite different. He described the brilliant but corrupt and frivolous society of his day, praising the polish and cultivation of urban life, and scorning the old-fashioned rustic gravity and simplicity which Augustus was trying to foster. His *Amores,* a group of love poems, and particularly the *Ars Amatoria,* three books of instruction in the Art of Love, treated flirtations and adulteries in a lighthearted manner very much out of tune with the emperor's program of reform.

In 8 A.D. Augustus banished Ovid to a remote town on the shores of the Black Sea, where the climate was cold and inhospitable, and where the barbarian inhabitants spoke no Latin and little Greek. From here Ovid wrote the *Tristia,* a series of poems addressed to the imperial family begging

(Continued)

for pardon, and *Epistulae ex Ponto,* verse letters to various friends at Rome. He died in exile in 17 A.D.

His epic, the *Metamorphoses,* was his greatest work. It is the story of all the transformations of gods or humans to other forms, from the creation of the universe to the deification of Julius Caesar in 42 B.C. The construction of the poem is very complex—many of the stories are told by characters in other stories or presented in the form of flashbacks—and the mood constantly shifts from grave to happy; but it is so expertly put together that the smooth flow of the narrative is never broken.

Ancient bust supposed to be a portrait of Ovid—Uffizi Gallery, Florence

DAEDALUS AND ICARUS

BACKGROUND

King Minos of Crete had employed the Athenian Daedalus to build a labyrinth, in which he kept the Minotaur. After Daedalus had shown Ariadne, the daughter of King Minos, how to help Theseus escape from the labyrinth, Minos, in anger, would not allow him to return to Athens by ship. And so Daedalus made wings for himself and his son Icarus, to enable them to fly over the sea.

Daedalus intereā, Crētēn longumque perōsus
exsilium tāctusque locī nātālis amōre,
clausus erat pelagō. "Terrās licet," inquit, "et undās
obstruat, at caelum certē patet: ībimus illāc.   186
Omnia possideat, nōn possidet āera Mīnōs."
Dīxit, et ignōtās animum dīmittit in artīs,
nātūramque novat. Nam pōnit in ordine pennās,
ā minimā coeptās, longam breviōre sequente,   190
ut clīvō crēvisse putēs. Sīc rustica quondam
fistula disparibus paulātim surgit avēnīs.
Tum līnō mediās et cērīs adligat īmās,
atque ita compositās parvō curvāmine flectit,
ut vērās imitētur avīs. Puer Īcarus ūnā   195
stābat et, ignārus sua sē tractāre perīcla,
ōre renīdentī modo quās vaga mōverat aura

---

183. Crētēn: Greek accusative. **perōsus:** *hating,* [perōdī]   **184. locī nātālis:** i.e., Athens
185. licet: *although*   **186. obstruat:** *he* (Minos) *may shut off*   **187. possideat:** concessive
subjunctive: *though he may hold.* **āera:** Greek accusative singular   **189. novat:** *he makes
anew;* i.e., he improves upon nature   **191. ut . . . putēs:** *so that you might suppose they
had grown on a slope*   **192. fistula:** *the Pan's pipe,* made of reeds (**avēnīs**) of different
lengths, so as to give tones of different pitch   **193. līnō, cērīs:** He fastened the lower ends
of the feathers with wax, and tied the broader part of the wings with thread.   **195. ūnā:**
nearby   **196. ignārus:** introduces the indirect statement that follows. **sua perīcla**
(= **perīcula**): i.e., the means of his own destruction   **197. ōre renīdentī:** *with beaming face.*
modo . . . modo: *now . . . now*

captābat plūmās, flāvam modo pollice cēram
mollībat, lūsūque suō mīrābile patris
impediēbat opus. Postquam manus ultima coeptō 200
imposita est, geminās opifex lībrāvit in ālās
ipse suum corpus, mōtāque pependit in aurā.
   Īnstruit et nātum, "Mediō" que "ut līmite currās,
Īcare," ait, "moneō, nē, sī dēmissior ībis,
unda gravet pennās, sī celsior, ignis adūrat. 205
Inter utrumque volā; nec tē spectāre Boōtēn
aut Helicēn iubeō strictumque Ōrīonis ēnsem.
Mē duce carpe viam." Pariter praecepta volandī
trādit et ignōtās umerīs accommodat ālās.
   Inter opus monitūsque genae maduēre senīlēs, 210
et patriae tremuēre manūs. Dedit oscula nāto
nōn iterum repetenda suō, pennīsque levātus
ante volat comitīque timet, velut āles, ab altō
quae teneram prōlem prōdūxit in āera nīdō;
hortāturque sequī damnōsāsque ērudit artīs, 215
et movet ipse suās et nātī respicit ālās.
Hōs aliquis, tremulā dum captat harundine piscīs,
aut pastor baculō stīvāve innīxus arātor,
vīdit et obstipuit, quīque aethera carpere possent
crēdidit esse deōs. Et iam Iūnōnia laevā 220
parte Samos (fuerant Dēlosque Parosque relictae),
dextra Lebinthos erat fēcundaque melle Calymnē,
cum puer audācī coepit gaudēre volātū,
dēseruitque ducem, caelīque cupīdine tāctus

---

198. pollice: from **pollex,** *thumb*   **199. mollībat:** old form of **molliēbat**   **200. manus ultima:** i.e., the finishing touches. **coeptō:** *on his work*   **201. opifex:** i.e., Daedalus   **204. nē:** introduces the purpose of **currās,** which in turn is an ind. command depending on **moneō.** **dēmissior:** *too low*   **205. ignis:** i.e., the sun   **206. Boōtēn:** Boötes (the Plowman), Helice (the Big Dipper) and Orion are the most striking constellations in the northern heavens. **208. Pariter:** *at the same time*   **210. maduēre = maduērunt**   **211. tremuēre = tremuērunt** **212. nōn . . . repetenda:** *never again to be repeated*   **213. comitī:** *for his companion,* i.e., Icarus. **velut . . . nīdō:** a simile, comparing Daedalus to a bird   **215. damnōsās artīs:** *the fatal art* (of flight)   **217. harūndine:** i.e., fishing rod   **218. innīxus:** *leaning on*—with both **baculō** and **stīvā**   **220. Iūnōnia:** Samos was sacred to Juno. The course of their flight was towards Asia Minor; they had flown north over the Cyclades (Delos, etc.) before turning east.

Pompeian fresco of the flight of Daedalus

altius ēgit iter. Rapidī vīcīnia sōlis 225
mollit odōrātās, pennārum vincula, cērās.
Tābuerant cērae: nūdōs quatit ille lacertōs,
rēmigiōque carēns nōn ūllās percipit aurās;
ōraque caeruleā patrium clāmantia nōmen
excipiuntur aquā, quae nōmen trāxit ab illō. 230
At pater īnfēlix, nec iam pater, "Īcare," dīxit,
"Īcare," dīxit, "ubi es? quā tē regiōne requīram?"
"Īcare," dīcēbat. Pennās adspēxit in undīs;
dēvōvitque suās artīs, corpusque sepulcrō
condidit; et tellūs ā nōmine dicta sepultī. 235

Metamorphoses, viii. 183–235

---

225. Rapidī: *burning, consuming*   **226. odōrātās:** i.e., from the melting   **227. Tābuerant:** *began to melt.* **nūdōs (alīs):** *stripped of his wings*   **228. rēmigiō carēns:** *lacking the 'oarage' (of his wings).* **percipit:** *catches,* in such a way as to be supported   **230. nōmen:** the waters west and south of Samos were called the Icarian Sea. **trāxit:** *drew,* i.e, *took*   **231. nec iam:** *no longer*   **232. requīram:** deliberative subjunctive, *should I look for?*   **234. dēvōvit:** *cursed*   **235. tellūs:** the island Icaria, west of Samos

PYRAMUS AND THISBE

> **BACKGROUND**
>
> Pyramus and Thisbe lived in Babylon, in adjoining houses. They fell
> in love, but their parents forbade their marriage. The story is parodied
> by Shakespeare in *A Midsummer Night's Dream*.

Pȳramus et Thisbē, iuvenum pulcherrimus alter,   55
altera quās oriēns habuit praelāta puellīs,
contiguās tenuēre domōs, ubi dīcitur altam
coctilibus mūrīs cīnxisse Semīramis urbem.
Nōtitiam prīmōsque gradūs vīcīnia fēcit;
tempore crēvit amor. Taedae quoque iūre coissent,   60
sed vetuēre patrēs: quod nōn potuēre vetāre,
ex aequō captīs ārdēbant mentibus ambō.
Cōnscius omnis abest: nūtū signīsque loquuntur;
quōque magis tegitur, tēctus magis aestuat ignis.
Fissus erat tenuī rīmā, quam dūxerat ōlim   65
cum fieret, pariēs domuī commūnis utrīque.
Id vitium nūllī per saecula longa notātum—
quid nōn sentit amor?—prīmī vīdistis, amantēs,
et vōcis fēcistis iter; tūtaeque per illud
murmure blanditiae minimō trānsīre solēbant.   70
    Saepe, ubi cōnstiterant hinc Thisbē, Pȳramus illinc,
inque vicēs fuerat captātus anhēlitus ōris,
"Invide," dīcēbant, "pariēs, quid amantibus obstās?

---

56. **praelāta**: *the loveliest*; i.e., preferred before. **puellīs**: dative with compound, **praeferō**
57. **tenuēre** = **tenuērunt** 58. **coctilibus**: *of burnt brick.* **Semīramis**: the wife of Ninus, and
the founder of Babylon 60. **Taedae iūre coissent**: *They would have joined in lawful
wedlock.* 61. **(id) quod**: *that which* 62. **ex aequō captīs**: *equally enslaved* 63. **Cōnscius**:
witness; i.e., go-between 64. **quōque** = **et quō. quō magis, magis**: *the more . . . the more*;
quō is ablative of degree of difference 65. **Fissus erat**: *had been cracked.* The wall (**pariēs**)
was common to both houses. **dūxerat**: *it had received* 66. **fieret**: *it was being built* 67. **Id
vitium**: *this defect.* **nūllī**: dative of agent 68. **prīmī . . . amantēs**: *you lovers were the first
to see* 69. **iter**: *a passage* 72. **in vicēs**: *in turn* 73. **Invide**: *Hateful*; vocative. **quid**: *why*

Quantum erat, ut sinerēs tōtō nōs corpore iungī,
aut, hoc sī nimium, vel ad ōscula danda patērēs? 75
Nec sumus ingratī: tibi nōs dēbēre fatēmur
quod datus est verbīs ad amīcās trānsitus aurīs."
Tālia dīversā nēquīquam sēde locūtī,
sub noctem dīxēre "Valē," partīque dedēre
ōscula quisque suae nōn pervenientia contrā. 80

    Postera nocturnōs aurōra remōverat ignīs,
sōlque pruīnōsās radiīs siccāverat herbās:
ad solitum coiēre locum. Tum murmure parvō
multa prius questī, statuunt ut nocte silentī
fallere custōdēs foribusque excēdere temptent, 85
cumque domō exierint, urbis quoque tēcta relinquant;
nēve sit errandum lātō spatiantibus arvō,
conveniant ad busta Ninī lateantque sub umbrā
arboris. Arbor ibī niveīs uberrima pōmīs
ardua mōrus erat, gelidō contermina fontī. 90
Pacta placent; et lūx, tardē discēdere vīsa,
praecipitātur aquīs et aquīs nox exit ab īsdem.

    Callida per tenebrās, versātō cardine, Thisbē
ēgreditur fallitque suōs, adopertaque vultum
pervenit ad tumulum dictāque sub arbore sēdit. 95
Audācem faciēbat amor. Venit ecce recentī
caede leaena boum spūmantīs oblita rictūs,
dēpositūra sitim vīcīnī fontis in undā.
Quam procul ad lūnae radiōs Babylōnia Thisbē
vīdit, et obscūrum trepidō pede fūgit in antrum, 100
dumque fugit, tergō vēlāmina lapsa relīquit.
Ut lea saeva sitim multā compescuit undā,
dum redit in silvās, inventōs forte sine ipsā
ōre cruentātō tenuīs laniāvit amictūs.

---

74. erat: *it would be;* for the imperfect subjunctive   **75. vel.** *even.* **patērēs:** *that you would open far enough*   **80. nōn pervenientia:** (kisses) *that did not go through*   **81. ignīs:** *stars* (by "metonymy")   **83. coiēre:** *they came together*   **87. nēve sit errandum:** *so that they will not miss each other.* **spatiantibus:** *they, as they walked,* dative of agent with **errandum.** **88. conveniant:** depends on **statuunt** (line 84). **busta Ninī:** *the tomb of Ninus*   **90. contermina:** *near to*   **91. lūx:** *daylight*   **93. Callida:** *slyly*   **94. adoperta vultum:** *with her face covered*   **95. dictā:** *agreed upon*   **96. recentī . . . rictūs:** *a lioness whose foaming jaws were smeared* (**oblita**) *from the recent slaughter of cattle*   **98. dēpositūra:** *in order to quench*   **103. sine ipsā:** *without* (Thisbe) *herself*   **104. amictūs:** here refers to *the veil*

Fresco of Pyramus and Thisbe—from the outdoor dining room of Loreius Tiburtinus in Pompeii

Sērius ēgressus, vestīgia vīdit in altō   105
pulvere certa ferae tōtōque expalluit ōre
Pȳramus. Ut vērō vestem quoque sanguine tīnctam
repperit, "Una duōs," inquit, "nox perdet amantīs;
ē quibus illa fuit longā dignissima vītā,
nostra nocēns anima est. Ego tē, miseranda, perēmī,   110
in loca plēna metūs quī iussī nocte venīrēs,
nec prior hūc vēnī. Nostrum dīvellite corpus,
et scelerāta ferō cōnsūmite vīscera morsū,
O quīcumque sub hāc habitātis rūpe leōnēs!
Sed timidī est optāre necem." Vēlāmina Thisbēs   115
tollit et ad pactae sēcum fert arboris umbram;
utque dedit nōtae lacrimās, dedit ōscula vestī,
"Accipe nunc," inquit, "nostrī quoque sanguinis haustūs!"

---

105. **Sērius:** *too late*   109. **ē quibus:** *of whom*   110. **nostra,** *my.* **nocēns:** *guilty, at fault*
111. **iussī venīrēs:** *(I who) told you to come;* prose construction would be an infinitive phrase
113. **scelerāta vīscera:** *guilty flesh*   115. **timidī:** *it is (the part) of a coward* **Thisbēs:** genitive
singular   117. **nōtae vestī:** *to (Thisbe's) well-known veil*

Quōque erat accīnctus, dēmīsit in īlia ferrum;
nec mora, ferventī moriēns ē vulnere trāxit   120
et iacuit resupīnus humō. Cruor ēmicat altē,
nōn aliter quam cum vitiātō fistula plumbō
scinditur, et tenuī strīdente forāmine longās
ēiaculātur aquās atque ictibus āera rumpit.
Arboreī fētūs adspergine caedis in ātram   125
vertuntur faciem, madefactaque sanguine rādīx
purpureō tingit pendentia mōra colōre.
    Ecce, metū nōndum positō, nē fallat amantem,
illa redit iuvenemque oculīs animōque requīrit,
quantaque vītārit nārrāre perīcula gestit.   130
Utque locum et vīsā cognōscit in arbore fōrmam,
sīc facit incertam pōmī color: haeret an haec sit.
Dum dubitat, tremebunda videt pulsāre cruentum
membra solum, retrōque pedem tulit, ōraque buxō
pallidiōra gerēns exhorruit aequoris instar,   135
quod tremit, exiguā cum summum stringitur aurā.
Sed postquam remorāta suōs cognōvit amōrēs,
percutit indignōs clārō plangōre lacertōs,
et laniāta comās amplexaque corpus amātum
vulnera supplēvit lacrimīs, flētumque cruōrī   140
miscuit, et gelidīs in vultibus ōscula fīgēns,
"Pȳrame," clāmāvit, "quis tē mihi cāsus adēmit?
Pȳrame, respondē! tua tē cārissima Thisbē
nōminat: exaudī vultūsque attolle iacentīs!"
Ad nōmen Thisbēs oculōs ā morte gravātos   145
Pȳramus ērēxit, vīsāque recondidit illā.

---

119. Quōque = **Et quō.** The antecedent of **quō** is **ferrum** **120. trāxit**: the object is still
ferrum **122. nōn aliter quam cum**: *just as when*, a common way of starting a simile. **vitiātō
. . . plumbō**: *a water-pipe with a weak spot in the lead* **123. tenuī . . . forāmine**: *by a small
hissing opening* **124. ictibus . . . rumpit**: *cleaves the air with its spurting* **125. Arboreī
fētūs**: *the berries on the tree.* The myth explains the dark color of the mulberry. **127. mōra**:
mulberries **128. nē fallat amantem**: *so as not to disappoint her lover* **130. vītārit** =
vītāverit. gestit: *is eager* **131. Utque . . . sīc**: *and though . . . yet* **132. haeret**:
she doubts **133. tremebunda**: *the quivering (limbs)* **134. solum**: *ground.* **ōra . . . pallidiōra**:
her face paler than boxwood **135. exhorruit**: *she shivered.* **aequoris instar**: *like
the sea* **136. summum**: *its surface.* **stringitur**: *is ruffled* **138. indignōs**: *undeserving* (of
the pain) **139. laniāta comās**: *tearing her hair* **140. vulnera**: plural for singular; so also
vultibus (141) and **vultūs** (144) **142. quis** = **quī**, modifying **cāsus. mihi**: *from me* **146. vīsā
illā**: *having looked upon her.* **recondidit**: *closed them again*

A bronze lioness from a sculpture
of the goddess Cybele

    Quae postquam vestemque suam cognōvit et ēnse
vīdit ebur vacuum, "Tua tē manus," inquit, "amorque
perdidit, īnfēlīx! Est et mihi fortis in ūnum
hoc manus; est et amor: dabit hīc in vulnera vīrīs.   150
Persequar exstīnctum, lētīque miserrima dīcar
causa comesque tuī. Quīque ā mē morte revellī
heu sōlā poterās, poteris nec morte revellī!
Hoc tamen ambōrum verbīs estōte rogātī,
Ō multum miserī, meus illīusque parentēs,   155
ut quōs certus amor, quōs hōra novissima iūnxit,
compōnī tumulō nōn invideātis eōdem.
At tū, quae rāmīs arbor miserābile corpus
nunc tegis ūnīus, mox es tēctūra duōrum,
signa tenē caedis, pullōsque et lūctibus aptōs   160
semper habē fētūs, geminī monimenta cruōris."
    Dīxit, et aptātō pectus mūcrōne sub īmum,
incubuit ferrō, quod adhūc ā caede tepēbat.
Vōta tamen tetigēre deōs, tetigēre parentīs;
nam color in pōmō est, ubi permātūruit, āter,   165
quodque rogīs superest, ūnā requiēscit in urnā.

Metamorphoses, iv. 55–166

---

148. **ebur:** *ivory scabbard*   149. **in ūnum hoc:** *for this one deed*   150. **in:** *for*   151. **exstīnctum:** sc. **tē**   152. **Quīque** = **Et tū quī**   153. **sōlā:** with **morte**, line 152. **nec:** *not even*   154. **hoc ... rogātī:** *Grant in this (matter) the prayers of both of us.* 155. **multum:** adverbial   156. **quōs:** *we whom.* **novissima:** *final*   157. **nōn invideātis:** *do not begrudge*   158. **quae arbor** = **arbor quae**   159. **duōrum:** sc. **corpora**   164. **tetigēre** = **tetigērunt.**   165. **color āter:** The fruit of the common mulberry is black when ripe 166. **rogīs:** *from the funeral pyres*

ORPHEUS AND EURYDICE

BACKGROUND
Soon after Orpheus and Eurydice were married, Eurydice was bitten by a serpent and died. Orpheus penetrated the shadows of the Lower World to bring her back, and he moved Pluto and Proserpina to grant his request, but only on the condition that he not look behind him until he reached the Upper World.

Note: *In the following selection the macrons have been omitted. In learning meter, the final step is scanning lines without macrons.*

Inde per immensum, croceo velatus amictu,
aethera digreditur Ciconumque Hymenaeus ad oras
tendit, et Orphea nequiquam voce vocatur.
Adfuit ille quidem, sed nec sollemnia verba
nec laetos vultus nec felix attulit omen.   5
Fax quoque quam tenuit lacrimoso stridula fumo
usque fuit, nullosque invenit motibus ignis.
Exitus auspicio gravior. Nam nupta per herbas
dum nova Naiadum turba comitata vagatur,
occidit, in talum serpentis dente recepto.   10
 Quam satis ad superas postquam Rhodopeïus auras
deflevit vates, ne non temptaret et umbras,
ad Styga Taenaria est ausus descendere porta,

---

1. inde: from Crete, where the wedding of Iphis and Ianthe had just taken place **2. aethera:** accusative singular, modified by **immensum. Ciconum:** *The Cicones were a people in Thrace* **3. Orphea:** an adjective. **nequiquam:** *in vain*—because the marriage ended in tragedy **4. ille:** Hymen, god of marriage **quidem:** *to be sure* **6. Fax:** *the torch,* an attribute of Hymen. **stridula:** *sputtering*—a bad omen **7. usque** *always.* **motibus:** *by swinging* **8. nupta nova:** the nymph Eurydice **10. occidit:** *fell dead* **11. Rhodopeius vates:** Orpheus; Rhodope was a mountain in Thrace, the home of Orpheus. **12. ne non = ut,** *so as not to leave untried.* **et:** adverb, *even* **13. Styga:** accusative singular. **Taenaria porta:** a cavern on the promontory of Taenarus at the southern end of the Peloponnesus

perque levis populos simulacraque functa sepulcro
Persephonen adiit inamoenaque regna tenentem
umbrarum dominum; pulsisque ad carmina nervis 15
sic ait: "O positi sub terra numina mundi,
in quem recidimus, quicquid mortale creamur!
si licet et, falsi positis ambagibus oris,
vera loqui sinitis, non huc, ut opaca viderem
Tartara, descendi, nec uti villosa colubris 20
terna Medusaei vincirem guttura monstri.
Causa viae est coniunx, in quam calcata venenum
vipera diffudit, crescentisque abstulit annos.
Posse pati volui, nec me temptasse negabo: 25
vicit Amor. Supera deus hic bene notus in ora est:
an sit et hic, dubito. Sed et hic tamen auguror esse;
famaque si veteris non est mentita rapinae,
vos quoque iunxit Amor. Per ego haec loca plena timoris,
per Chaos hoc ingens vastique silentia regni, 30
Eurydices, oro, properata retexite fata!
Omnia debemus vobis, paulumque morati,
serius aut citius sedem properamus ad unam.
Tendimus huc omnes, haec est domus ultima; vosque
humani generis longissima regna tenetis. 35
Haec quoque, cum iustos matura peregerit annos,
iuris erit vestri: pro munere poscimus usum.
Quod si fata negant veniam pro coniuge, certum est
nolle redire mihi: leto gaudete duorum."

---

14. levis: i.e., because they were mere shadows. **simulacra . . . sepulcro:** *forms that have found a tomb*—i.e., been buried **15. adiit:** the second i is long here, though normally short (diastole) **16. dominum:** Pluto. **ad:** *in accompaniment to.* **nervis:** i.e., the strings of the lyre **17. O:** with **numina** **18. recidimus:** see note on **adiit** (line 15). **quicquid . . . creamur** *all of us who are created mortal* **19. falsi oris:** *of deceptive speech* **22. Medusaei monstri:** i.e., the three-headed Cerberus; Hercules had bound Cerberus and taken him to the Upper World. **25. pati:** *to endure* (the loss of Eurydice) **26. supera ora:** *the world above,* i.e., the earth **28. rapinae:** refers to the carrying off of Proserpina by Pluto **29. vos:** Pluto and Proserpina. **Per:** *By* (used in oaths). **30. Chaos:** neuter acc. sing. **31. Eurydices:** genitive singular. **retexite:** *spin backwards*—referring to the Fates, who spin the threads of life **33. citius:** *sooner* **36. Haec quoque:** *She too* **37. iuris vestri:** *in your power* . . . **pro . . . usum:** i.e., I ask the enjoyment of her presence—as a loan, not a gift **38. Quod si:** *But if.* **veniam:** *favor.* **certum est mihi:** *I am resolved*

Talia dicentem nervosque ad verba moventem   40
exsangues flebant animae; nec Tantalus undam
captavit refugam, iacuitque Ixionis orbis,
nec carpsere iecur volucres, urnisque vacarunt
Belides, inque tuo sedisti, Sisyphe, saxo.
Tunc primum lacrimis victarum carmine fama est   45
Eumenidum maduisse genas. Nec regia coniunx
sustinet oranti, nec qui regit ima, negare;
Eurydicenque vocant. Umbras erat illa recentis
inter, et incessit passu de vulnere tardo.
Hanc simul et legem Rhodopeius accipit Orpheus,   50
ne flectat retro sua lumina, donec Avernas
exierit vallis: aut irrita dona futura.
    Carpitur acclivis per muta silentia trames,
arduus, obscurus, caligine densus opaca.
Nec procul afuerunt telluris margine summae: 55
hic, ne deficeret, metuens, avidusque videndi,
flexit amans oculos—et protinus illa relapsa est.
Bracchiaque intendens prendique et prendere captans,
nil nisi cedentis infelix arripit auras.
Iamque iterum moriens non est de coniuge quicquam   60
questa suo: quid enim nisi se quereretur amatam?
supremumque "Vale", quod iam vix auribus ille
acciperet, dixit, revolutaque rursus eodem est.

                        Metamorphoses, x. 1–63.

---

41. Tantalus: His punishment was to be placed in water up to his chin; as soon as he stooped
to take a drink, the water retreated.   **42. iacuit:** *lay still*   **Ixionis:** Ixion was bound to a
revolving fiery wheel.   **43. iecur:** the *liver* of Tityus, fed upon by vultures, and growing
again as fast as it was consumed. **urnis:** ablative of separation with **vacarunt. vacarunt** =
vacaverunt   44. Belides: the granddaughters of Belus, the Danaids, whose punishment was
to carry water in a jug with holes in the bottom of it. **Sisyphe:** Sisyphus' punishment was to
roll a huge stone up a hill.   **46. Eumenidum:** the Furies, implacable goddesses of vengeance
47. sustinet = **potest. qui:** *he who.*   **48. Eurydicen:** acc. sing.   **50. Hanc et legem:** *her and
the condition*   **51. lumina:** *eyes*, by metonymy. **Avernas:** *of the Underworld*   **52. irrita:** *in
vain*   **55. afuerunt:** the e is short, though regularly long (systole)   **56. deficeret:** sc. Eurydice
58. captans: *eagerly reaching*   **60. non est quicquam questa:** *she made no complaint*
61. nisi: with **se amatum:** *except that.* **quereretur:** deliberative subjunc., *was she to complain
about*   **62. supremum Vale:** *a last farewell;* treated as a noun

About the Author MARTIAL

It is through the writings of Martial (Marcus Valerius Martial) that we get most of our knowledge of Roman society in the second half of the first century A.D.

Martial was born about 40 A.D. in Bilbilis, a Roman colony in Spain which was perched on a rock above the Salo River. Some historians feel that the rugged scenery of his birthplace had a deep effect on him and fostered his capacity for descriptive writing. He was a freeborn Roman citizen and in his youth he made his way to Rome and attached himself to various patrons who would enable him to make his living as a poet. While there Martial received various imperial favors, but since he often pleaded poverty, his talent for spending seems to have been equaled by his capacity for earning.

His first two works were undistinguished, and his fame has really always rested on the twelve books of epigrams, the last of which was published in about 102 A.D.

As his renown grew, Martial became acquainted with the famous literary people of his day—great men whose works are read to this day—Quintilian, Pliny the Younger, Juvenal, and Seneca, to mention a few.

Martial has been accused of having two great faults—excessive adulation and obscenity. It is said that he indulged in excessive flattery of the "higher-ups", especially the emperor Domitian, and he seems to have cringed before men of influence and wealth. However, it may have been the only way for a literary person to survive in the Rome of that era. His other fault was less offensive than it could have been because it was expressed with such wit, charm, literary craftsmanship, and human sympathy. When all is said and done, the greatest tribute to this man is that centuries later, he is quoted, translated, and imitated by many of the world's great writers. He is, in fact, the foremost writer of the epigram. However, in his stress on the simple joys of life, and in his prescriptions for happiness and contentment, we are reminded a great deal of the earlier poet Horace and his sentiments in *The Satires* and *Odes*.

(Continued)

The meters used by Martial in all the selections that follow, except for the first one, are the elegiac couplet and the hendecasyllabic (eleven-syllable) line which have been presented in Lesson 15.

The epigrams of Martial were often read as part of the entertainment after a meal such as the one depicted here. The woman holding the silver ladle has been chosen by the other guests to mix wine with water for the postprandial drinking. She is accompanied by a flute player.

EPIGRAMS

BACKGROUND

Martial wrote over 1500 epigrams which taken together give us valuable information on the everyday life of his time. An epigram is a short poem with a witty or satirical message. It consists of two parts. The first part introduces the subject and the second part gives the message which is often a surprise and sometimes not revealed until the very last word.

Petit Gemellus nuptiās Marōnillae
et cupit et īnstat et precātur et dōnat.
Adeōne pulchra est? Immo foedius nīl est.
Quid ergō in illā petitur et placet? Tussit. *I.10*

Ō mihi post nūllōs, Iūlī, memorande sodālīs,
   sī quid longa fidēs cānaque iūra valent,
bis iam paene tibī cōnsul trīcēsimus īnstat,
   et numerat paucōs vix tua vīta diēs.
Nōn bene distuleris videās quae posse negārī,   5
   et sōlum hoc dūcās, quod fuit, esse tuum.
Exspectant cūraeque catēnātīque labōrēs,
   gaudia nōn remanent, sed fugitīva volant.
Haec utrāque manū complexūque adsere tōtō:
   saepe fluunt īmō sīc quoque lapsa sinū.   10
Nōn est, crēde mihi, sapientis dīcere 'Vīvam':
   sēra nimis vīta est crastina: vīve hodiē. *I.15*

I.10.   **4. Tussit:** Wealthy older people, especially sick ones, were considered desirable spouses. Notice how Martial saves the point till the last word.

I.15   **3. cōnsul:** year; The year was named for its consuls.   **4. vīta:** i.e., remaining (enjoyable) life   **5. distuleris:** from **differō**, *put off.* This subjunc. (and **ducās**) is potential, *you cannot.* **videās quae** = **quae videās**   **6. dūcās:** *can consider*   **7. catēnātī:** *continual* **10. fluunt:** i.e., *escape*   **11. sapientis:** *the act of a wise man*   **12. crastina:** *tomorrow's*

Sī meminī fuerant tibi quattuor, Aelia, dentēs:
  expulit ūna duōs tussis et ūna duōs.
Iam sēcūra potes tōtīs tussīre diēbus:
  nīl istīc quod agat tertia tussis habet.   *I.19*

Nōn amo tē, Sabidī, nec possum dīcere quā rē;
  hoc tantum possum dīcere, nōn amo tē.   *I.32*

Āmissum nōn flet cum sōla est Gellia patrem;
  sī quis adest, iussae prōsiliunt lacrimae.
Nōn lūget quisquis laudārī, Gellia, quaerit;
  ille dolet vērē quī sine teste dolet.   *I.33*

Quem recitās meus est, ō Fīdentīne, libellus:
  sed male cum recitās, incipit esse tuus.   *I.38*

Nūper erat medicus, nunc est vispillo Diaulus:
  quod vispillo facit, fēcerat et medicus.   *I.47*

A slave bringing food to a banquet—
mosaic floor from Carthage

I.19.   3. **sēcūra:** *safe(ly)*   4. **istīc:** *there.* **quod agat:** *to shake out*

I.32   1. **amo:** Martial often shortens the second syllable of iambic (u—) words   2. **tantum:** *only.* Compare to this poem Thomas Brown to Dr. John Fell, Dean of Christ Church, Oxford: "I do not love thee, Dr. Fell. The reason why I cannot tell; but this alone I know full well, I do not love thee Dr. Fell" (about 1680).

I.33.   2. **prōsiliunt:** *leap forth*

I.38   1. **libellus:** *little book*   2. **tuus:** i.e., it is unrecognizable as mine

I.47.   1. **vispillo, -ōnis:** *undertaker*   2. **quod:** i.e., *making funerals possible.* **facit, fēcerat:** the subject is still Diaulus

Vīcīnus meus est manūque tangī
dē nostrīs Novius potest fenestrīs.
Quis nōn invideat mihī putetque
hōrīs omnibus esse mē beātum,
iunctō cuī liceat fruī sodāle?   5
Tam longē est mihi quam Terentiānus,
quī nunc Nīliacam regit Syēnēn.
Nōn convīvere, nec vidēre saltem,
nōn audīre licet, nec urbe tōtā
quisquam est tam prope tam proculque nōbīs.   10
Mīgrandum est mihi longius vel illī.
Vīcīnus Noviō vel inquilīnus
sit, sī quis Novium vidēre nōn vult.   *I.86*

Nē valeam, sī nōn tōtīs, Deciāne, diēbus
   et tēcum tōtīs noctibus esse velim.
Sed duo sunt quae nōs disiungunt mīlia passum:
   quattuor haec fīunt, cum reditūrus eam.
Saepe domī nōn es; cum sīs, quoque saepe negāris: 5
   vel tantum causīs vel tibi saepe vacās.
Tē tamen ut videam, duo mīlia nōn piget īre:
   ut tē nōn videam, quattuor īre piget.   *II.5*

"Thāida Quīntus amat." "Quam Thāida?" "Thāida luscam."
   Ūnum oculum Thāis nōn habet, ille duōs.   *II.8*

I.86.   **2. Novius:** subject of **est** and **potest**   **3. invideat:** *would envy*   **5. iunctō:** *so close*
6. mihi: *from me* (cf. **nobis,** line 10)   **7. Nīliacam Syēnēn:** (the town of) Syene on the Nile.
Greek accusative   **8. convīvere:** *to dine with him*   **12. inquilīnus:** fellow-lodger

II.5   **1. Nē valeam:** a wish (optative)   **3. disiungunt:** *separate.* **passum = passuum.**
4. reditūrus: *planning to return*   **5. negāris:** *you are said not to be* (by the doorkeeper)
6. causīs: *for legal business.* **vacās:** *you have time*   **8. nōn videam:** *fail to see.* The last
couplet balances the second couplet, while the first and third contrast.

II.8.   **1. Thāida:** Greek accus. of Thāis. **luscam:** *one-eyed*   **2. nōn habet:** *lacks.* **ille dūos:**
figuratively speaking

A patrician dining, attended by his servants. The servant on the left holds a wine pitcher and strainer. A wine flask with its cloth covering sits on the floor.

Tū Sētīna quidem semper vel Massica pōnis.
   Pāpyle, sed rūmor tam bona vīna negat;
dīceris hāc factus caelebs quater esse lagōnā:
   nec putō nec crēdō, Pāpyle, nec sitiō.   *IV.69*

Thāis habet nigrōs, niveōs Laecānia dentīs.
   Quae ratiō est? Emptōs haec habet, illa suōs.   *V.43*

IV.69.   **1. Sētīna, Massica:** sc. vīna. These wines were famous. **pōnis:** *you serve*   **3. caelebs, -ibis,** m., *widower.* **quater:** *four times.* **lagōnā:** bottle   **4. sitiō, -īre:** *be thirsty*

V.43.   **2. Emptōs:** from **emō,** *buy*

Crās tē victūrum, crās dīcis, Postume, semper.
  Dīc mihi, crās istud, Postume, quando venit?
Quam longē crās istud, ubi est? aut unde petendum?
  Numquid apud Parthōs Armeniōsque latet?
Iam crās istud habet Priamī vel Nestoris annōs.   5
  Crās istud quantī, dīc mihi, posset emī?
Crās vīvēs? Hodiē iam vīvere, Postume, sērum est:
  ille sapit quisquis, Postume, vīxit herī.   *V.58*

Nōn dōnem tibi cūr meōs libellōs,
ōrantī totiēns et exigentī,
mīrāris, Theodōre? Magna causa est:
dōnēs tū mihi nē tuōs libellōs.   *V.73*

"Cinnam," Cinname, tē iubēs vocārī.
Nōn est hic, rogō, "Cinna" barbarismus?
Tū sī Fūrius ante dictus essēs,
"Fur" istā ratiōne dīcerēris.   *VI.17*

Lōtus nōbīscum est, hilaris cēnāvit, et īdem
  inventus māne est mortuus Andragorās.
Tam subitae mortis causam, Faustīne, requīris?
  In somnīs medicum vīderat Hermocratēn.   *VI.53*

V.58.   **1. victūrum:** from **vīvō**   **4. Numquid** = **Num**, expecting "no." **Parthōs Armeni-ōsque:** examples of faraway nations   **5. Priamī, Nestoris:** Priam, King of Troy, and Nestor, King of Pylos, examples of the very old   **6. quantī:** *for how much,* gen, of value   **8. vīxit herī:** notice how Martial effectively "frames" the poem with this phrase and the contrasting phrase **crās victūrum** (line 1) in chiastic (ABBA) word order. Compare the last couplet.

V.73.   **1. cūr:** begins first clause (cf. **nē**, line 4)   **2. ōrantī, exigentī:** with **tibi;** both are concessive. **exigō, -ere:** *demand*   **4.** Note the balance with line 1.

VI.17.   **1. Cinnam:** an aristocratic Roman name. Cinnamus was a Greek name. **2. barbarismus:** *barbarism* or *error in speech*   **4. Fūr:** *thief*

VI.53.   **1. Lōtus est:** from **lavō:** *he bathed.* **hilaris:** *cheerfully.* **īdem:** *all the same* **2. Andragorās:** Greek masc. nom. sing.

Nūbere vīs Prīscō: nōn mīror, Paula; sapīstī.
  Dūcere tē nōn vult Prīscus: et ille sapit.   *IX.5*

Iam senior Lādōn Tiberīnae nauta carīnae
  proxima dīlectīs rūra parāvit aquīs.
Quae cum saepe vagus premeret torrentibus undīs
  Thȳbris et hībernō rumperet arva lacū,
ēmeritam puppim, rīpā quae stābat in altā,   5
  implēvit saxīs opposuitque vadīs.
Sīc nimiās āvertit aquās. Quis crēdere posset?
  Auxilium dominō mersa carīna tulit.   *X.85*

Difficilis facilis, iūcundus acerbus es īdem:
  nec tēcum possum vīvere nec sine tē.   *XII.46*

Saepe rogāre solēs quālis sim, Prīsce, futūrus,
  sī fīam locuplēs simque repente potēns.
Quemquam posse putās mōrēs narrāre futūrōs?
  Dīc mihi, sī fīās tū leō, quālis eris?   *XII.92*

Roman mosaic of a lion—from
Tunisia

IX.5.   **1. Nūbere** (with dat.) is used for women, **dūcere** (line 2) for men. **vīs:** verb   **2. et:** adverb, *too*

X.85.   **1. Lādōn:** Greek nom. masc. sing. **Tiberīnae carīnae:** of a ship on the Tiber River (**Thȳbris,** line 4)   **2. parāvit:** *bought*   **3. Quae: rūra. torrentibus:** *rushing*   **4. hībernō:** *wintry*   **5. ēmeritam:** *retired*   **6. vadīs:** *(in the way of) the water*

XII.46.   **1. iūcundus:** *pleasant.* **acerbus:** *unpleasant.* **īdem:** *at the same time*

XII.92.   **2. locuplēs, -ētis:** *rich*

About the Author PLAUTUS

Twenty-one plays of Rome's most popular writer of comedies, Titus Maccius Plautus (about 254–184 B.C.) have been preserved. These vary greatly in tone and treatment, but they are all **fabulae palliatae**, adaptations of Greek comedy. It is obvious however, from his masterful use of the Latin language that Plautus did more than merely translate his Greek models. In fact his plays differ in many ways from the few surviving examples of Athenian New Comedy and from the comedies of his Roman successor, Terence, who seems to have followed the Greek originals much more closely. In the Greek plays and in those of Terence the characters behave like real people in real situations; and so the plays have a serious tone not usually found in Plautus, who is usually willing to sacrifice plausibility for the sake of getting a laugh.

Although Plautus' plays all supposedly take place in Greek settings, he shows no interest in local color, and even pokes fun occasionally at playwrights who do try to make their plays authentically Greek. He frequently mentions purely Roman customs, and sometimes introduces references to current events. In fact, he does not seem to be much concerned with dramatic illusion. His characters actually interrupt the action to address the audience or individual spectators; they may also break into song.

Because of the use of masks in New Comedy, there is a tendency for the characters to become standardized; and Plautus carries this trend still further. The clever slave, the foolish old man, the braggart warrior, the love-sick youth, the saucy young girl, the cynical old maidservant, etc., appear in play after play with little difference except a change of name. This use of stock characters undoubtedly helped to make Plautus' plays popular; the audience would be able to identify immediately what sort of person each character was, without the trouble of following subtleties of characterization. Plautus' characters do not really develop in the course of the play. For example, in the *Aulularia* when Euclio, a worthy but poor old gentleman, is made suddenly wealthy by finding a pot of gold, we are not shown any sympathetic details of the gradual effect such an event would have on his character; he merely suddenly becomes the typical Old Miser, a type to be laughed at.

The frequent pathos of New Comedy is almost entirely absent from Plautus' plays; situations which in real life would be pathetic are funny in Plautus. We would undoubtedly feel some sympathy for an old man cheated by his own son or for an old woman whose husband has left her for a young girl; but in Plautus these characters are figures of fun.

Although Plautus' methods may sometimes shock our sense of dramatic convention, we cannot help but admire his use of the Latin language—in this he is unsurpassed. He is a master of witty invective and clever repartee, or epigrams and plays on words. His comedies are in verse, and hence the language is necessarily somewhat artificial; yet he nevertheless convincingly captures the tone and rhythm of real conversation. However unreal the characters may be, Plautus' dialogue must be close to the way the Romans really spoke.

You will find Plautus' Latin very different from that of Caesar. There is much more flexibility in his syntax: for example, words which normally govern the subjunctive may take an infinitive, and vice versa. And the conversations are, like real conversations, often somewhat elliptical: What do you think of my actions? becomes **Quid factis?** in context. Nevertheless Plautus is fairly easy to read, because his language is much closer to a natural mode of expression than more formal Latin, and because the liveliness of his style holds the reader's attention.

Because of his early date, texts of Plautus show several differences in spelling from later Latin; in the following selections these have been made to conform with the forms which you are used to.

A mosaic showing masks of a courtesan and a clever slave

Scenes from *AULULARIA*

BACKGROUND

"The Pot of Gold," called 'Aulularia' in Latin, is the story of a miser, named Euclio, who discovers a pot of gold buried within his house, and is constantly worried that some one will find out that he has it. He has a daughter named Phaedria, who has been wronged by Lyconides, a young gentleman of Athens. In the following scene, the uncle of Lyconides, an old gentleman named Megadorus, asks Euclio for the hand of his daughter. Euclio is suspicious, thinking that Megadorus must have learned about his discovery. The scene is Athens, a street on which are the houses of Euclio and Megadorus.

SETTING OF THE PLAY

The stage in Roman comedy represented a street running from the marketplace (stage left) to the harbor or countryside (stage right); consequently it was wide but not deep. Along the back wall of the stage were three doorways, representing three houses, or two houses and a temple, on the other side of the street.

Note: *In this selection the macrons have been omitted in order to train you to read without these aids. The standard examinations of the College Entrance Examination Board do not use macrons in any passages in the examinations.*

The costumes for *Aulularia* resembled this scene from an unknown comedy with similar stock characters. The foolish old man on the left (like Megadorus) is restraining an angry old man (like Euclio), while on the right a young wastrel (like Lyconides) confers with his clever slave (like Strobilus).

Scene 1

MEGA. Salvus atque fortunatus, Euclio, semper sis.

EUCL. Di te ament, Megadore.

MEGA. Quid tu? rectene atque ut vis vales?

EUCL. *(aside)* Non temerarium est, ubi dives blande appellat pauperem. Iam
hic homo aurum scit me habere, eo me salutat blandius.   5

MEGA. Aisne tu te valere?

EUCL. Pol ego haud perbene a pecunia.

MEGA. Pol si est animus aequus tibi, sat habes qui bene vitam colas.

EUCL. *(aside, frightened)* Anus hercle huic indicium fecit de auro, perspicue
palam est, cui ego iam linguam abscidam atque oculos effodiam domi.   10

MEGA. Quid tu solus tecum loquere?

EUCL. Meam pauperiem queror. Virginem habeo grandem, dote cassam
atque inlocabilem, neque eam queo locare cuiquam.

MEGA. Tace, bonum animum habe, Euclio. Dabitur, adiuvabere a me. Dic,
si quid est, impera.   15

ECUL. *(aside)* Nunc petit, cum pollicetur. Inhiat aurum ut devoret. Altera
manu fert lapidem, panem ostentat altera. Nemini credo, qui large
blandus est dives pauperi.

MEGA. Paucis, Euclio, est quod te volo de communi re appellare mea et tua.

EUCL. *(aside)* Ei misero mihi! Aurum mi intus harpagatum est. Nunc eam   20
rem vult, scio, mecum adire ad pactionem. Verum intervisam domum.

Euclio hurries toward his house.

MEGA. Quo abis?

EUCL. Iam ad te revertar; nunc est quod visam domum. *(Exits)*

MEGA. Credo edepol, ubi mentionem fecero de filia, ut mihi despondeat, se   25
a me derideri rebitur. Neque illo quisquam est alter hodie ex paupertate
parcior.

Re-enter Euclio

---

1. 1. **fortunatus:** *lucky.* **sis:** *may you be,* optative subjunc.; so also **ament** 1.2. **3. Quid
tu?:** i.e., What about you? 4. **temerarium:** *without a reason* 7. **Pol:** *By Pollux, By golly.*
a: *with respect to* 8. **sat** = **satis.** **qui** = **quo,** *(the means) with which* 9. **Anus:** *The old
woman,* Euclio's slave Staphyla. **perspicue:** *obviously* 10. **palam est:** *it is clear.* **effodiam:**
I will dig out 11. **loquere** = **loqueris** 12. **virginem:** *unmarried daughter.* **dote cassam:**
without a dowry 13. **inlocabilem:** *unable to be married,* because of a lack of a dowry.
locare cuiquam: i.e., find her a husband 14. **Dabitur:** sc. **pecunia. adiuvabere** = **adiuvaberis**
15. **si quid est:** i.e., if you need anything 16. **altera . . . altera:** i.e., as one would lure and
kill an animal 19. **Paucis:** sc. **verbis. est quod** *there is something which* 20. **Ei:** *Ah, woe.*
mi = **mihi. harpagatum:** *hooked* 21. **adire ad pactionem:** *to make a deal.* **verum:** *but.*
intervisam: *I'll go look.* 24. **quod visam:** *something to see to* 26. **rebitur:** *he will think;*
[**reor**]. **illo:** ablative of comparison

EUCL. *(aside)* Di me servant, salva res est. Salvum est si quid non perit.
30   Nimis male timui. Priusquam intro redii, exanimatus fui. *(To Megadorus)*
    Redeo ad te, Megadore, si quid me vis.

MEGA. Habeo gratiam. Quaeso, quod te percontabor, ne te pigeat proloqui.

EUCL. Dum ne quid perconteris quod non lubeat proloqui.

MEGA. Dic mihi, quali me arbitraris genere prognatum?

35 EUCL. Bono.

MEGA. Quid fide?

EUCL. Bona.

MEGA. Quid factis?

EUCL. Neque malis neque improbis.

40 MEGA. Aetatem meam scis?

EUCL. Scio esse grandem, item ut pecuniam.

MEGA. Certe edepol te civem sine malitia semper sum arbitratus et nunc
    arbitror.

EUCL. *(aside)* Aurum huic olet.

45   *(aloud)* Quid nunc me vis?

MEGA. Quoniam tu me et ego te qualis sis scio, quae res recte vertat mihique
    tibique tuaeque filiae, filiam tuam mihi uxorem posco. Promitte hoc
    fore.

EUCL. *(whining)* Heia, Megadore, haud decorum facinus facis, ut inopem
50   atque innoxium abs te atque abs tuis inrideas. Nam de te neque re neque
    verbis merui ut faceres quod facis.

MEGA. Neque edepol ego te derisum venio, neque derideo, neque dignum
    arbitror.

EUCL. Cur igitur poscis meam natam tibi?

55 MEGA. Ut propter me tibi sit melius mihique propter te et tuos.

---

*Euclio finally agrees to the marriage, and the two men make plans
to have the marriage feast. Megadorus undertakes to pay for the
feast and he goes off to buy provisions and hire cooks.*

---

29. res: i.e., the money. **si quid:** *whatever*   **30. Nimis male:** *too much*   **31. me:** *of me,* abl.
so also **me.** l. 45.   **32. percontabor:** *I shall ask.* **ne . . . proloqui:** *that you not be reluc-
tant to speak out about;* **pigeat,** like **lubeat** in l. 33, is an impersonal verb   **36. Quid:** sc.
arbitraris   **44. huic olet:** *smells to him;* i.e., he has got a whiff of   **46. vertat:** *and may
this matter turn out well;* optative subjunc.   **47. hoc fore:** *that this will happen*   **49. Heia:**
Now, now. **haud decorum facinus:** *an unkind deed*   **50. innoxium abs te:** i.e., *who has
never harmed you.* **abs. se** note on **a,** l. 7.   **52. derisum:** *to make fun of;* supine, used with
verbs of motion to express purpose. **neque dignum arbitror:** *nor do I think it fitting*

Scene 2

An hour has elapsed, and the slave of Megadorus, named Pythodicus,
comes in bringing two cooks, Anthrax and Congrio, two music girls,
attendants with provisions, and two lambs.

PYTHO. Postquam obsonavit erus et conduxit coquos tibicinasque has apud
    forum, edixit mihi ut dispertirem obsonium hic bifariam.

ANTHR. Me quidem hercle, dicam tibi, non divides. Si tu totum me vis ire,
    operam dabo.

PYTHO. Sed erus nuptias hodie faciet. 5

ANTHR. Cuius ducit filiam?

PYTHO. Vicini huius Euclionis senis e proximo. Ei adeo obsoni hinc iussit
    dimidium dari, cocum alterum itidemque alteram tibicinam.

ANTHR. Nempe huc dimidium dicis, dimidium domum?

PYTHO. Nempe sicut dicis. 10

ANTHR. Quid? Hic non poterat de suo senex obsonari filiae nuptiis?

PYTHO. Vah!

ANTHR. Quid negoti est?

PYTHO. Quid negoti sit rogas?
    Pumex non aeque est aridus atque hic est senex. 15

ANTHR. Aisne tandem?

PYTHO. Ita est ut dixi. Tute existima:
    quin divum atque hominum clamat continuo fidem, suam rem periisse
    seque eradicari, de suo tigillo fumus si qua exit foras. Quin cum it
    dormitum, follem obstringit ob gulam. 20

ANTHR. Cur?

PYTHO. Ne quid animae forte amittat dormiens. At scisne etiam quomodo?
    Aquam hercle plorat, cum lavat, profundere. Quin ipsi pridem tonsor

---

2.   **1. obsonavit:** *bought provisions.* **erus:** *my master* (Megadorus)   **2. dispertirem:** *divide*
3. hercle: *by Hercules!*   **7. e proximo:** *from next door.* **adeo:** *in fact*   **8. alterum:** *one of*
the two   **9. huc:** *here*—to Euclio's house   **11. de suo:** *at his own expense*   **12. Vah!:**
Bah!   **13. negoti:** partitive genitive with **quid**   **15. Pumex:** A pumice stone. **aridus:** i.e.,
miserly. **atque:** *as*   **16. tandem:** *tell me*   **17. Tute:** Tu + the intensive enclitic -te—*you*
yourself   **18. quin:** *why he . . .* **divum:** *of the gods;* genitive plural, for **divorum**   **19. si**
qua: *if in any way;* Euclio hates to lose even the smoke from his fire   **20. dormitum:** *to*
sleep; supine. **follem . . . gulam:** *he ties a bag over his jaws*   **23. plorat:** *he objects to*

A comic actor gets into character by contemplating his mask, that of the love-sick young man. He will also play the courtesan and clever slave whose masks sit on the table.

unguis dempserat: collegit, omnia abstulit praesegmina. Sescenta sunt
25   quae memorem, si otium sit. Sed uter vestrorum est celerior?
ANTHR. Ego, et multo melior.
PYTHO. Cocum ego, non furem, rogo.
ANTHR. Cocum ergo dico.
PYTHO. *(to Congrio)* Quid tu ais?
30 CONGR. Sic sum ut vides.
PYTHO. *(to Anthrax)* Tace nunc iam tu, atque agnum hinc uter est pinguior
   cape atque abi intro ad nos.
ANTHR. Licet.
PYTHO. Tu, Congrio, quem reliquit agnum, eum sume, atque abi intro illuc,
35   et vos illum sequimini. Vos ceteri ite huc ad nos.
CONGR. Hercle! iniuria dispertivisti: pinguiorem agnum isti habent.
PYTHO. At nunc tibi dabitur pinguior tibicina. I cum illo, Phrugia. Tu,
   autem, Eleusium, huc intro abi ad nos.

*Later in the play, Strobilus, the slave of Lyconides who had wronged
Euclio's daughter, spies for his master to find out where Euclio hides
his pot of gold. By climbing a tree in the grove of Silvanus, he
watches the old man while he is trying to conceal the pot. Then
after Euclio has gone, he digs up the pot to take to his master. Then
Euclio discovers its loss.*

---

24. dempserat: *had cut.* **Sescenta:** 600 is used to mean a large number—*thousands of things*
25. quae memorem: *which I could tell you.* **sit:** the present subjunctive in a present contrary
to fact condition, normally the imperfect   **31. uter:** here used as a relative (not interrogative)
pronoun—*whichever of the two*   **33. Licet:** used colloquially to indicate assent—*O.K.*
36. iniuria: abl. as adverb, *unfairly*   **37. Phrugia, Eleusium:** the names of the flute-girls

Scene 3

EUCL. *(running wildly back and forth)*

Perii, interii, occidi. Quo curram? Quo non curram?

Tene, tene—Quem? Quis?

Nescio, nil video, caecus eo, atque equidem quo eam aut ubi sim aut qui sim nequeo cum animo certum investigare.   5

(To the audience) Obsecro vos ego, mi auxilio, oro, obtestor, sitis et hominem demonstretis, quis eam abstulerit?

Quid est? Quid ridetis? Novi omnis, scio fures esse hic complurīs, qui vestitu et creta occultant sese atque sedent quasi sint frugi. Quid ais tu?

(pointing to a spectator) Tibi credere certum est, nam esse bonum ex   10
vultu cognosco.

Hem, nemo habet horum? Occidisti. Dic igitur, quis habet? Nescis? Heu, me miserum, misere perii, male perditus, pessime ornatus eo. Tantum gemiti et mali maestitiaeque hic dies mihi obtulit, famem et pauperiem. Perditissimus ego sum omnium in terra. Nam quid mihi opus est vita,   15
qui tantum auri perdidi, quod custodivi sedulo? Ego me defraudavi animumque meum geniumque meum. Nunc alii laetificantur meo malo et damno. Pati nequeo.

In the following scene, Lyconides has decided to confess to Euclio that he has wronged his daughter and wants to marry her.

There is much confusion over the Latin word **illam** (line 12 in Scene 4), which means *her* (*Phaedria*) to Lyconides, and *it* (*the pot*) to Euclio.

---

3.   **4. caecus eo:** *I am going blind.*   **5. certum:** *for certain.* **investigare:** *to tell*   **7. demonstretis:** both the direct object, **hominem**, and the indirect question, **quis . . . abstulerit**, depend on this verb—*show me the man, show me who stole it* (the pot)   **8. Novi:** *I know*   **9. vestitu et creta:** i.e., in dapper clothes. Chalk was rubbed on the woolen toga to make it whiter. **frugi:** *honest;* dative of purpose, used as an indeclinable adjective   **10. certum est:** *I have made up my mind.*   **12. nemo horum:** *none of these*—the spectators. **Occidisti:** *You have killed me;* i.e., I'm done for   **13. me miserum:** *poor me!* accusative of exclamation **ornatus:** *rewarded*   **14. gemiti:** gen. sing., for **gemitus**   **15. opus est:** *is the need,* or *use*   **16. sedulo:** *carefully.* **me defraudavi:** *I have deprived myself*   **17. genium:** *pleasures* **laetificantur:** *are making merry*   **18. damno:** *at (my) expense*

Scene 4

EUCL. *(hearing the sound of a voice)* Quis homo hic loquitur?

LYCO. *(stepping forward)* Ego sum miser.

EUCL. Immo ego sum, et misere perditus, cui tanta mala maestitudoque
obtigit.

5 LYCO. Animo bono es.

EUCL. Quo, obsecro, pacto esse possum?

LYCO. Quia id facinus, quod tuum sollicitat animum, id ego feci, et fateor.

EUCL. Quid ego ex te audio?

LYCO. Id quod verum est.

10 EUCL. Quid ego de te merui, adulescens, mali, quam ob rem ita faceres
meque meosque perditum ires liberos?

LYCO. Deus impulsor mihi fuit, is me ad illam inlexit.

EUCL. Quo modo?

LYCO. Fateor peccavisse et me culpam commeritum scio. Id adeo te oratum
15 venio ut animo aequo ignoscas mihi.

EUCL. Cur id ausus es facere, ut id quod non tuum esset tangeres?

LYCO. Quid vis fieri? Factum est illud: fieri infectum non potest. Deos credo
voluisse; nam nisi vellent, non fieret, scio.

EUCL. Quid ergo meam me invito tetigisti?

20 LYCO. Quia vini vitio atque amoris feci.

EUCL. Homo audacissime! Nimis vile est vinum et amor, si ebrio atque
amanti impune facere quod lubeat licet.

LYCO. Quin tibi ultro supplicatum venio ob meam stultitiam.

EUCL. Non mihi homines placent qui quando male fecerunt purgant. Tu
25 illam sciebas non tuam esse. Non tactam oportuit.

LYCO. Ergo quia tangere ausus sum, haud causificor quin eam ego habeam
potissimum.

---

4. **2. Ego sum miser:** *It's I, an unhappy man.* But Euclio takes him to mean '*I am unhappy*'.
3. mala: neuter nominative plural, used as a noun   **4. obtigit:** singular, agreeing with the
nearer of two subjects   **5. es:** *be* (imperative)   **10. mali:** partitive genitive with **quid. quam
ob rem:** etc., a relative clause of characteristic   **11. perditum ires:** **eo,** with a supine,
you would go to destroy; freely, *you would try to ruin*   **12. Deus:** *A demon.* **impulsor:**
instigator. **inlexit:** *lured (me) on*   **14. oratum:** supine, *to beg*   **16. ut ... tangeres:**
substantive clause in apposition with **id**   **19. Quid:** *why?*   **21. audacissime:** vocative **Nimis
vile:** *too cheap*   **22. impune:** *without punishment.* **quod lubeat:** *what he may please*
23. Quin: *Why, even.* **supplicatum:** supine, *to entreat*   **25. (eam) tactam (esse)**   **26. haud
causificor:** *I have no objection*   **27. potissimum:** *in preference to others*

EUCL. Tune me invito habeas meam?

LYCO. Haud te invito postulo; sed meam esse oportere arbitror. Quin tu 30
iam invenies, inquam, meam illam esse oportere, Euclio.

EUCL. Iam quidem, hercle, te ad praetorem rapiam nisi refers.

LYCO. Quid tibi ego referam?

EUCL. Quod rapuisti meum.

LYCO. Rapui ego tuum? unde? aut quid id est? 35

EUCL. Ita te amabit Iuppiter ut tu nescis.

LYCO. Nisi quidem tu mihi quid quaeras dixeris.

EUCL. Aulam auri, inquam, te reposco, quam tu confessus es mihi te
abstulisse.

LYCO. Neque edepol ego dixi neque feci.

EUCL. Negas? 40

LYCO. Pernego immo. Nam ego neque aurum neque aula quae sit scio nec
novi.

EUCL. Illam quam ex Silvani luco abstuleras, refer. Dimidiam tecum potius
partem dividam. Tam etsi fur mihi es, molestus non ero. I vero, refer.

LYCO. Tu non sanus es qui furem me voces. Ego te, Euclio, de alia re rescisse 45
censui quod ad me attinet. Magna est res quam ego tecum otiose, si
otium est, cupio loqui.

EUCL. Age nunc loquere quid vis.

LYCO. Filiam ex te tu habes.

EUCL. Immo ecce illam domi. 50

LYCO. Audi nunc iam. Qui homo culpam admisit in se, nullus est tam parvi
preti, cum pudeat, quin purget se. Nunc te obtestor, Euclio, ut si quid
ego erga te imprudens peccavi aut natam tuam, ut mihi ignoscas, eamque
uxorem mihi des, ut leges iubent.

EUCL. Ei mihi, quod ego facinus ex te audio? 55

LYCO. Cur eiulas, quem ego avum feci ut esses filiae nuptiis? Nam tua nata
peperit. Ea re repudium remisit avunculus causa mea.

---

29. Quin: see line 23   **31. ad praetorem:** *to the praetor;* i.e., the judge   **35. Ita . . . nescis:**
As you are ignorant, so will Jupiter love you; i.e., God bless your innocence.   **36.** sc. **nescio:**
from **nescis** in line 35, *I am ignorant if you won't tell,* etc.   **43. abstuleras,** from **aufero**
44. molestus non ero: *I won't make any trouble.* **I,** imperative of **eo**   **45. rescisse = rescivisse**
46. ad me attinet: *concerns me.* **otiose:** i.e., when you have time   **48. Age:** *Come*   **49. ex**
te: *of your own:* i.e., not adopted   **51. Qui homo nullus est = Est nullus homo qui. culpam**
admisit in se: *has committed a sin.* **tam parvi preti:** *of so little value*   **52. cum pudeat:** *when*
he is ashamed. **quin purget se:** *that he does not apologize.* **si quid . . . peccavi:** *if I have*
committed any sin   **56. esses:** sc. **avus.** **57. peperit:** from **pario,** *has borne (a child).* **Ea re**
etc.: *Therefore my uncle has broken off his engagement for my sake.*

EUCL. Perii oppido. Ita mihi ad malum malae res plurimae se adglutinant!
Ibo intro, ut quid huius verum sit sciam.

60

Exit into house

LYCO. (*after a pause*) Haec propemodum iam esse in vado salutis res videtur.
(*looking around*) Nunc servum esse ubi dicam meum Strobilum non
reperio. Etiam hic opperiar paulisper. Postea intro hunc subsequar. Nunc
interim spatium ei dabo exquirendi meum factum ex natae nutrice anu.

65

Ea rem novit.

Enter Strobilus

STROB. Di immortales, quibus et quantis me donatis gaudiis! Quadrilibrem
aulam auro onustam habeo. Quis me est ditior? Quid me Athenis nunc
magis quisquam est homo cui di sint propitii?

70

LYCO. Certo enim ego vocem hic loquentis mihi audire visus sum.

(*catching a glimpse of Strobilus' face*)

STROB. (*aside*) Hem, erumne aspicio meum?

LYCO. (*aside*) Videone ego hunc servum meum?

STROB. (*aside*) Ipse est.

75

LYCO. (*aside*) Haud alius est.

STROB. (*aside*) Congrediar. (*moves toward Lyconides*)

LYCO. (*aside*) Contollam gradum. Credo ego illum, ut iussi, eam anum
adiisse, huius nutricem virginis.

STROB. (*aside*) Quin ego illi me invenisse dico hanc praedam? Igitur orabo

80

ut me manu emittat. Ibo atque eloquar. Repperi. . . .

LYCO. Quid repperisti?

STROB. Non quod pueri clamitant in faba se repperisse.

LYCO. Iamne autem, ut soles, deludis? (*pretends to start to leave*)

STROB. Ere, mane, loquar iam, ausculta.

85

LYCO. Age ergo loquere.

STROB. Repperi hodie, ere, divitias nimias.

LYCO. Ubinam?

---

58. oppido: adverb, *completely.* se adglutinant: *attach themselves* 61. Haec propemodum
etc., *It does look as if this matter is now almost in the shallow water of safety;* i.e., we are
getting out of trouble. 62. ubi dicam: *any place where I can say* 63. opperiar: *I'll wait*
64. spatium: *time.* exquirendi: i.e., to inquire about. nutrice anu: *the old nurse* 68. Quid:
how 69. magis: with propitii 72. Hem: *Aha!* 77. Contollam gradum: *I'll go meet him.*
79. Quin ego: *Why do I not . . .* 80. manu emittat: *set me free* 82. faba: *a bean.* It is
not clear just what boys found in a bean. 83. deludis: *are you fooling me?* 84. ausculta:
imperative, *listen* 87. Ubinam = Ubi

Painting of a comic mask of a foolish old man

STROB. Quadrilibrem, inquam, aulam auri plenam.

LYCO. Quod ego facinus audio ex te? (*aside*) Euclioni hic seni surripuit. Ubi
id est aurum? 90

STROB. In arca apud me. Nunc volo me emitti manu.

LYCO. Egone te emittam manu, scelerum cumulatissime?

STROB. (*crestfallen, then starting to laugh*) Abi, ere, scio quam rem geras.
Lepide hercle animum tuum temptavi. Iam ut eriperes parabas. Quid
faceres, si repperissem? 95

LYCO. Non potes probavisse nugas. I, redde aurum.

STROB. Reddam ego aurum?

LYCO. Redde, inquam, ut huic reddatur.

STROB. Unde?

LYCO. Quod modo confessus es esse in arca. 100

STROB. Soleo hercle ego garrire nugas.

LYCO. Non te habere dicis aurum?

STROB. Ita loquor.

*The rest of the play is lost, except for a few fragments. It can be
assumed that Strobilus returned the pot of gold to Lyconides, and
that he in turn returned it to Euclio, who then gave his daughter to
Lyconides, together with the pot of gold for a wedding present.*

---

92. cumulatissime: vocative, *you heap (of crimes)*   **94. Quid . . . repperissem?:** a contrary
to fact condition, *What would you do if I had found it?*   **96. probavisse nugas:** i.e., *convince
me that you were joking*   **98. huic,** *to him (Euclio)*   **101. garrire nugas,** *to talk nonsense*

About the Author LIVY

Livy's real name was Titus Livius and he was born in what is now known as Padua in northern Italy. He received a good local education and was well versed in Greek and Latin literature. His one burning desire as a youth was to write history and so, very early in life, he went to Rome for this purpose. He lived in Rome during the reign of Augustus who became his friend and patron.

His **Historiae ab Urbe Condita** (*History from the Founding of the City*) relates Roman history from the founding of Rome until the death of Drusus in 9 B.C. It took him more than forty years to write this masterpiece which consisted of 142 books. The work may have been organized and published in sets of five books. It is estimated that the entire project would fill twenty-four modern texts of 300 pages each. The **Historiae** became known through summaries and abridgements (many of which are still available), and Livy was an instant success in his own lifetime. The work became very famous and was widely quoted.

Livy used a psychological approach and made the many wars and politics of the time more interesting by focusing on the emotions of various personalities during dramatic situations. Like all historians of the ancient world, he wrote the speeches he attributes to others so he could better illustrate their psychology. Even when original speeches were available, he never used them.

As an historian, critics feel he was too chauvinistic and romantic. Although he most likely tried to be truthful, he is accused of abandoning accuracy to achieve a special literary effect. However, in spite of this criticism, all agree that his description of the historical and political events of Rome is more vivid than that of any other author, his full and flowing Latin style is unparalleled, and his work is even today considered a valuable historical source.

HORATIUS AT THE BRIDGE

BACKGROUND

Lars Porsena of Clusium attacks Rome after the expulsion of the kings in an effort to restore the Tarquins as kings of Rome. Horatius holds the bridge against the Etruscans of Porsena.

Porsena Rōman infestō exercitū vēnit. Nōn umquam aliās ante tantus terror senātum invāsit.

Cum hostēs adessent, prō sē quisque in urbem ex agrīs dēmigrant, urbem ipsam saepiunt praesidiīs. Alia mūrīs, alia Tiberī obiectō vidēbantur tūta: pōns sublicius iter paene hostibus dedit, nī ūnus vir fuisset, Horātius Cocles;   5 id mūnīmentum illō diē fortūna urbis Rōmānae habuit. Quī positus forte in statiōne pontis, cum captum repentīnō impetū Iāniculum atque inde citātōs dēcurrere hostīs vīdisset trepidamque turbam suōrum arma ōrdinēsque relinquere, reprehendēns singulōs, obsistēns obtestānsque deum et hominum fidem testābātur nēquīquam desertō praesidiō eōs fugere; sī trānsitum ponte   10 ā tergō relīquissent, iam plūs hostium in Palātiō Capitōliōque quam in Iāniculō fore. Itaque monēre, praedīcere ut pontem ferrō, ignī, quācumque vī possint, interrumpant: sē impetum hostium, quantum corpore ūnō posset obsistī, exceptūrum. Vādit inde in prīmum aditum pontis, īnsignīsque inter cōnspecta cēdentium pugnae terga obversīs comminus ad ineundum proelium   15 armīs ipsō mīrāculō audāciae obstupefēcit hostīs. Duōs tamen cum eō pudor tenuit, Sp. Larcium ac T. Herminium, ambōs clārōs genere factīsque.

---

1. aliās: adv. *previously*   **4. alia . . . alia:** *some parts . . other parts.* **Tiberī obiectō:** abl. abs., *by the barrier of the Tiber*   **5. pōns sublicius:** *the wooden bridge* (the first bridge erected in Rome connecting the Janiculum with Rome)   **6. Quī:** *He* (lit. *who*) i.e. Horatius   **7. citātōs dēcurrere:** *were charging down at a run*   **10. trānsitum ponte:** *a passage across the bridge*   **12. monēre, praedīcere:** historical infinitives: *he warned, he commanded*   **13. quantum corpore ūnō posset obsistī:** *as far as it could be withstood by a single body*   **15. cōnspecta:** with **terga**; *among the backs of those seen.* **pugnae:** dative (with **cēdentium**, *yielding to the fight*); translate: *withdrawing from the fight.* **obversīs . . . armīs:** *with weapons opposed for joining battle hand to hand*

Father Tiber shown with Romulus and Remus, symbols of Rome

Cum hīs prīmam perīculī procellam et quod tumultuōsissimum pugnae erat parumper sustinuit; deinde eōs quoque ipsōs exiguā parte pontis relictā
20 revocantibus quī rescindēbant cēdere in tūtum coēgit. Circumferēns inde trucēs mināciter oculōs ad procerēs Etrūscōrum nunc singulōs prōvocāre, nunc increpāre omnīs: servitia rēgum superbōrum, suae lībertātis immemorēs aliēnam oppugnātum venīre. Cunctātī aliquamdiū sunt, dum alius alium, ut proelium incipiant, circumspectant. Pudor deinde commōvit aciem, et clā-
25 mōre sublātō undique in ūnum hostem tēla coniciunt. Quae cūncta cum in obiectō scūtō haesissent, neque ille minus obstinātus ingentī pontem obtinēret gradū, iam impetū cōnābantur dētrūdere virum, cum simul fragor ruptī pontis, simul clāmor Rōmānōrum alacritāte perfectī operis sublātus, pavōre subitō impetum sustinuit. Tum Coclēs "Tiberīne pater," inquit, "tē sancte
30 precor, haec arma et hunc mīlitem propitiō flūmine accipiās." Ita sīc armātus in Tiberim dēsiluit multīsque superincidentibus tēlīs incolumis ad suōs trānāvit, rem ausus plūs fāmae habitūram ad posterōs quam fideī. Grāta ergā tantam virtūtem cīvitās fuit: statua in comitiō posita; agrī quantum ūnō diē circumarāvit datum. Prīvāta quoque inter pūblicōs honōrēs studia
35 ēminēbant; nam in magnā inopiā prō domesticīs copiīs ūnusquisque eī aliquid, fraudāns sē ipse victū suō, contulit.

18. quod ... erat: *what was the stormiest (moment) of the battle*   **19. ipsos:** refers to Larcius and Herminius   **20. revocantibus:** abl. abs: (eīs) revocantibus quī   **21. prōvocāre, increpāre:** historical infinitives   **22. servitia ... venīre:** indirect statement: (saying) *that they as slaves of haughty kings unmindful of their own liberty were coming to overthrow that of others*   **23. oppugnātum:** supine   **33. ergā:** *for*   **34. prīvāta ... studia:** *private support*   **35. prō domesticīs copiīs:** *proportionate to his own domestic means*

MUCIUS SCAEVOLA

BACKGROUND

Mucius Scaevola undertakes to enter the camp of the Etruscans to kill Porsena. However, he has never seen Porsena and kills the king's secretary instead. When captured, he wins Porsena's admiration by showing remarkable bravery as he puts his hand in a flame and burns it off.

Expugnātūrum sē urbem spem Porsena habēbat, cum C. Mūcius, adulēscēns nōbilis, cui indignum vidēbātur populum Rōmānum servientem cum sub rēgibus esset nūllō bellō nec ab hostibus ūllīs obsessum esse, līberum eundem populum ab īsdem Etrūscīs obsidērī quōrum saepe exercitūs fūderit,—itaque magnō audācīque aliquō facinōre eam indignitātem vindicandam 5 ratus, prīmō suā sponte penetrāre in hostium castra cōnstituit; dein metuēns, nē, sī cōnsulum iniussū et ignārīs omnibus īret, forte dēprehēnsus ā custōdibus Rōmānīs retraherētur ut trānsfuga, fortūnā tum urbis crīmen adfirmante, senātum adit. "Trānsīre Tiberim," inquit, "patrēs, et intrāre, sī possim, castra hostium volō, nōn praedō nec populātiōnum in vicem ultor: maius, 10 sī dī iuvant, in animō est facinus." Adprobant patrēs. Abditō intrā vestem ferrō proficīscitur. Ubi eō vēnit, in cōnfertissimā turbā prope rēgium tribūnal cōnstitit. Ibi cum stīpendium mīlitibus forte darētur, et scrība cum rēge sedēns pārī ferē ōrnātū multa ageret eumque mīlitēs vulgō adīrent, timēns sciscitārī uter Porsena esset, nē ignōrandō rēgem sēmet ipse aperīret quis 15 esset, quō temerē trāxit fortūna facinus, scrībam prō rēge obtruncat. Vādentem inde, quā per trepidam turbam cruentō mucrōne sibi ipse fēcerat

---

1. cum C. Mūcius: the verb is **cōnstituit** (6)   **2. cui indignum ... fūderit:** *"to whom it seemed shameful that the Roman people in their servitude when they were under the kings were not besieged in any war nor by any enemy, the very same people should be besieged by the same Etruscans whose armies they had routed"*   **5. vindicandum:** understand **esse** in a passive periphrastic in indirect statement   **6. ratus** *thinking* (i.e. Mucius)   **8. fortūnā ... adfirmante:** *ill fortune of the city then confirming the charge* (that the hardships of the siege would lead to desertion)   **10. in vicem:** *in retaliation*   **15. sēmet** = **sē**   **16. quō ... facinus:** *where fortune at random directed his action*

An Etruscan aristocrat—figure from
the top of a terra-cotta cinerary urn

viam, cum concursū ad clāmōrem factō comprehēnsum rēgiī satellitēs
retrāxissent, ante tribūnal rēgis dēstitūtus, tum quoque inter tantās fortūnae
20 minās metuendus magis quam metuēns, "Rōmānus sum," inquit, "cīvis; C.
Mūcium vocant. Hostis hostem occidere voluī, nec ad mortem minus animī
est quam fuit ad caedem: et facere et patī fortia Rōmānum est. Nec ūnus
in tē ego hōs animōs gessī; longus post mē ōrdō est idem petentium decus.
Proinde in hoc discrīmen, si iuvat, accingere, ut in singulās hōrās capite
25 dīmicēs tuō, ferrum hostemque in vestibulō habeās rēgiae. Hoc tibi iuventūs
Rōmāna indīcimus bellum. Nūllam aciem, nūllum proelium timuerīs; ūnī
tibi et cum singulīs rēs erit." Cum rēx simul īrā īnfēnsus perīculōque
conterritus circumdarī ignīs minitābundus iubēret nisi exprōmeret properē
quās īnsidiārum sibi minās per ambāgēs iaceret, "Ēn tibi," inquit, "ut sentiās
30 quam vīle corpus sit iīs quī magnam glōriam vident," dextramque accēnsō
ad sacrificium fōculō inicit. Quam cum velut aliēnātō ab sēnsū torrēret
animō, prope attonitus mīrāculō rēx cum ab sēde suā prōsiluisset āmovērīque
ab altāribus iuvenem iussisset, "Tū vērō abī," inquit, "in tē magis quam in
mē hostilia ausus. Iubērem macte virtūte esse, sī prō meā patriā ista virtūs
35 stāret; nunc iūre bellī līberum tē intactum inviolātumque hinc dīmittō."

19. dēstitūtus: *left alone*   21. nec ad mortem . . . caedem: *nor have I less courage for death
than I had for murder*   23. hōs animōs gessī: *have this resolution*   24. Proinde . . .
accingere: *Accordingly, if you think it worth your while, gird yourself against this peril.*
accingere *is the present middle imperative singular.* capite tuō: *for your life*   26. timuerīs:
perfect subjunctive as hortatory   28. circumdarī ignīs minitābundus iubēret: *threateningly
ordered him to be thrown into the flames*   29. per ambāgēs: *in riddles*   31. velut aliēnātō
ab sēnsū animō: *as if his spirit were insensitive to feeling*   34. iubērem macte virtūte esse:
I should order it be said, 'Well done' for your courage.

THE CHARACTER OF HANNIBAL

BACKGROUND
Hannibal was a famous general and statesman of Carthage. He was able to defeat armies much larger than his own and overcome great handicaps because of his great leadership ability and excellent military strategy. He had a strong personality and always instilled confidence in his army even under the poorest of conditions.

Missus Hannibal in Hispāniam prīmō statim adventū omnem exercitum in sē convertit; Hamilcarem iuvenem redditum sibi veterēs mīlitēs crēdere; eundem vigōrem in vultū vimque in oculīs, habitum ōris līneāmentaque intuērī. Deinde brevī effēcit ut pater in sē minimum mōmentum ad favōrem conciliandum esset. Numquam ingenium idem ad rēs dīversissimās, pārendum atque imperandum, habilius fuit. Itaque haud facile discernerēs, utrum imperātōrī an exercituī cārior esset; neque Hasdrubal alium quemquam praeficere malle, ubi quid fortiter ac strēnuē agendum esset, neque mīlitēs aliō duce plus cōnfīdere aut audēre. Plūrimum audāciae ad perīcula capessenda, plūrimum cōnsilī inter ipsa perīcula erat. Nūllō labōre aut corpus fatīgārī aut animus vincī poterat. Calōris ac frīgoris patientia pār; cibī pōtiōnisque dēsīderiō nātūrālī, nōn voluptāte modus fīnītus; vigiliārum somnīque nec diē nec nocte discrīmināta tempora; id, quod gerendīs rēbus superesset, quiētī datum; ea neque mollī strātō neque silentiō accersīta; multī saepe mīlitārī sagulō opertum humī iacentem inter custōdiās statiōnēsque mīlitum cōnspexērunt. Vestītus nihil inter aequālīs excellēns; arma atque equī cōnspiciēbantur. Equitum peditumque īdem longē prīmus erat; prīnceps in proelium ībat, ultimus consertō proeliō excēdēbat. Hās tantās

5

10

15

---

1. **in sē convertit:** *turned towards himself, won over*   2. **Hamilcarem:** *Hamilcar,* Hannibal's father, had died. He had been much respected by his troops. **crēdere . . . intuērī:** historical infinitives   4. **mōmentum:** lit. *impulse.* Translate here *influence*   7. **Hasdrubal:** Hannibal's brother-in-law and commander of Carthaginian troops in Spain   8. **malle . . . confīdere . . . audēre:** historical infinitives. **ubi:** *whenever*   9. **aliō duce:** *under any other leader*   11. **cibī . . . modus fīnītus:** *the amount of his food and drink was determined*   13. **discrīmināta:** *divided up*   14. **accersīta** = **arcessīta**   16. **inter aequālīs excellēns:** *remarkable among (that of) his fellows*

An ancient portrait head thought to be Hannibal

virī virtūtēs ingentia vitia aequābant, inhūmāna crūdēlitās, perfidia plūs quam Pūnica, nihil vērī, nihil sanctī, nūllus deum metus. nūllum iūs iūrandum, nūlla religiō. Cum hāc indole virtūtum atque vitiōrum trienniō sub Hasdrubale imperātōre meruit nūllā rē, quae agenda videndaque magnō futūrō ducī esset, praetermissā.

20

---

19. perfidia plūs quam Pūnica: The Romans put no trust in Punic good faith.   **22. meruit:** *served*

HANNIBAL CROSSES THE RHONE

BACKGROUND

In 219 B.C. Rome declared war on Carthage—The Second Punic War. Very early in the war Hannibal astonished the Romans with his daring military maneuvers. In addition to troops and horses, he also utilized elephants because they could shatter enemy lines like tanks in modern warfare.

Iamque omnibus satis comparātīs ad trāiciendum terrēbant ex adversō hostēs omnem rīpam equitēs virīque obtinentēs. Quōs ut āverteret, Hannōnem, Bomilcaris fīlium, vigiliā prīmā noctis cum parte cōpiārum, maximē Hispānīs, adversō flūmine īre iter ūnīus diēī iubet, et ubi prīmum possit, quam occultissimē traiectō amnī circumdūcere agmen, ut, cum opus factō sit, 5 adoriātur ab tergō hostīs. Ad id datī ducēs Gallī ēdocent inde mīlia quinque et vīgintī ferē suprā parvae īnsulae circumfūsum amnem lātiōre, ubi dīvi-dēbātur, eōque minus altō alveō trānsitum ostendere. Ibi raptim caesa māteria ratēsque fabricātae in quibus equī virīque et alia onera trāicerentur. Hispānī sine ūllā mōle in ūtrēs vestibus coniectīs ipsī caetrīs superpositīs 10 incubantēs flūmen trānāvēre. Et alius exercitus ratibus iūnctīs trāiectus, castrīs prope flūmen positīs, nocturnō itinere atque operis labōre dēfessus quiēte ūnīus diēī reficitur intentō duce ad cōnsilium opportūnē exsequendum. Posterō diē profectī ex locō ēditō fumō significant sē trānsīsse et haud procul

---

1. hostēs: is the subject of **terrēbant**; **equitēs virīque** are in apposition with **hostēs**. **āverteret:** the understood subject is Hannibal, as also with **iubet** below **3. Hispānīs:** Spaniards were preferred for such a task as they were particularly trained in swimming rivers in the fashion here described. **4. adversō flūmine:** *up river* **5. traiectō amnī:** *having crossed the stream.* **cum opus factō sit:** *when there was need for the action* **6. Ad id . . . ostendere:** *The Gauls assigned as guides for this showed him that almost twenty-five miles from there up river (**supra**) the stream, flowing around a small island, with a wider river-bed where it was divided and for that reason shallower, offered a crossing.* **9. fabricātae:** understand **sunt**. **trāicerentur:** a relative clause of purpose **10. sine ūllā mōle:** *without any trouble.* **caetra, -ae, f.:** *a small, light shield* **11. alius exercitus:** *the rest of the force* (i.e. of Hanno's group) **13. intentō duce . . . exsequendum:** *their leader intent on carrying out his plan at the proper time*

Hannibal's elephants crossing the Rhone on rafts

15 abesse. Quod ubi accēpit Hannibal, nē temporī dēesset dat signum ad
    trāiciendum. Iam parātās aptatāsque habēbant pedes lintrīs, eques ferē
    propter equōs nāvīs.
        Elephantōrum trāiciendōrum varia cōnsilia fuisse crēdō, certē variat
    memoria actae reī. Quīdam congregātīs ad rīpam elephantīs trādunt ferō-
20 cissimum ex iīs inrītātum ab rectōre suō, cum refugientem in aquam nantem
    sequerētur, trāxisse gregem ut quemque impetus ipse flūminis in alteram
    rīpam raperet. Cēterum magis cōnstat ratibus trāiectōs; id ut tūtius cōnsilium
    ante rem foret, ita actā rē ad fidem prōnius est.

---

15. nē tempore dēesset: *not to miss the opportunity*   16. lintrīs: *skiffs*   17. nāvīs: *large
boats*   18. cōnsilia: *ideas*   19. actae reī: *of the actual event*. **Quīdam:** *certain (authors)*
20. rectōre: *the keeper.*   21. sequerētur: the elephant is the subject   22. **Cēterum:** *but.*
trāiectōs = eōs trāiectōs esse. ut-foret: *as . . . would be* (potential subjunctive)

382

Appendix

FORMS

NOUNS

FIRST DECLENSION

	SINGULAR	PLURAL
NOM.	puella, *a girl*	puellae, *girls*
GEN.	puellae, *of a girl* or *girl's*	puellārum, *of girls* or *the girls'*
DAT.	puellae, *to* or *for a girl*	puellīs, *to* or *for the girls*
ACC.	puellam, *a girl*	puellās, *the girls*
ABL.	puellā, *by, with, from a girl*	puellīs, *by with, from the girls*

Nouns of the first declension are feminine, except nouns denoting males, which are masculine. The dative and ablative plural of **fīlia** is **fīliābus**, and of **dea** is **deābus**.

SECOND DECLENSION

Second declension nouns in **-us, -er,** or **-ir** are masculine; those in **-um** are neuter. **Fīlius,** proper names in **-ius,** and nouns in **-ium** usually, have **-ī** (not **-ii**) in the gen. sing., with the accent on the penult, as **fī'lī, Vale'rī, auxi'lī.**

SINGULAR

NOM.	amīcus	puer	ager	vir
GEN.	amīcī	puerī	agrī	virī
DAT.	amīcō	puerō	agrō	virō
ACC.	amīcum	puerum	agrum	virum
ABL.	amīcō	puerō	agrō	virō
VOC.	amīce			

PLURAL

NOM.	amīcī	puerī	agrī	virī
GEN.	amīcōrum	puerōrum	agrōrum	virōrum
DAT.	amīcīs	puerīs	agrīs	virīs
ACC.	amīcōs	puerōs	agrōs	virōs
ABL.	amīcīs	puerīs	agrīs	virīs

	SINGULAR	PLURAL	SINGULAR	PLURAL
NOM.	bellum, N.	bella	fīlius, M.	fīliī
GEN.	bellī	bellōrum	fīlī	fīliōrum
DAT.	bellō	bellīs	fīliō	fīliīs
ACC.	bellum	bella	fīlium	fīliōs
ALB.	bellō	bellīs	fīliō	fīliīs
VOC.			fīlī	

VOCATIVE CASE

The vocative is the case of direct address. *Its ending is like the nominative.*

EXCEPTIONS: In the singular of second decl. nouns in **-us** the vocative ends in **-e**, as: **serve,** *O slave.* The vocative sing. of **fīlius** and proper names of the second decl. in **-ius** end in **-ī** (not **-ie**) with the accent on the penult, as: **fī′lī,** *O son;* **Vale′rī,** *O Valerius.*

THIRD DECLENSION

CONSONANT STEMS

SINGULAR

NOM.	mīles, M.	pater, M.	dux, M.
GEN.	mīlitis	patris	ducis
DAT.	mīlitī	patrī	ducī
ACC.	mīlitem	patrem	ducem
ABL.	mīlite	patre	duce

PLURAL

NOM.	mīlitēs	patrēs	ducēs
GEN.	mīlitum	patrum	ducum
DAT.	mīlitibus	patribus	ducibus
ACC.	mīlitēs	patrēs	ducēs
ABL.	mīlitibus	patribus	ducibus

	SINGULAR	PLURAL	SINGULAR	PLURAL
NOM.	flūmen, N.	flūmina	corpus, N.	corpora
GEN.	flūminis	flūminum	corporis	corporum
DAT.	flūminī	flūminibus	corporī	corporibus
ACC.	flūmen	flūmina	corpus	corpora
ABL.	flūmine	flūminibus	corpore	corporibus

	I STEMS	
	SINGULAR	

NOM.	hostis, M.	caedēs, F.	urbs, F.
GEN.	hostis	caedis	urbis
DAT.	hostī	caedī	urbī
ACC.	hostem	caedem	urbem
ABL.	hoste	caede	urbe

	PLURAL	

NOM.	hostēs	caedēs	urbēs
GEN.	hostium	caedium	urbium
DAT.	hostibus	caedibus	urbibus
ACC.	hostīs (-ēs)	caedīs (-ēs)	urbīs (-ēs)
ABL.	hostibus	caedibus	urbibus

	SINGULAR	PLURAL	SINGULAR	PLURAL
NOM.	mare, N.	maria	animal, N.	animalia
GEN.	maris	marium	animālis	animālium
DAT.	marī	maribus	animālī	animālibus
ACC.	mare	maria	animal	animālia
ABL.	marī	maribus	animālī	animālibus

-i stems include:

1. Masculines and feminines in **-is** and **-ēs** not increasing in the genitive, as **nāvis, caedēs.**
2. Neuters in **-e, -al,** and **-ar,** as **mare, animal, calcar.**
3. Monosyllables whose base ends in two consonants, as **pars, part-is; nox, noct-is.**
4. Nouns whose base ends in **-nt** or **-rt,** as **cliēns, client-is; cohors, cohort-is.**
   (**Turris** and some proper names in **-is** have **-im** in the acc. sing., as: **turrim, Tiberim.**)

FOURTH DECLENSION

	SINGULAR	

NOM.	frūctus, M.	cornu, N.	domus, F.
GEN.	frūctūs	cornūs	domūs (domī, LOC.)
DAT.	frūctuī	cornū	domuī, domō
ACC.	frūctum	cornū	domum
ABL.	frūctū	cornū	domō, domū

PLURAL

NOM.	frūctūs	cornua	domūs
GEN.	frūctuum	cornuum	domuum, domōrum
DAT.	frūctibus	cornibus	domibus
ACC.	frūctūs	cornua	domōs, domūs
ABL.	frūctibus	cornibus	domibus

Fourth declension nouns in **-us** are masculine and those in **ū** are neuter, except **manus** and **domus,** which are feminine.

FIFTH DECLENSION

	SINGULAR	PLURAL	SINGULAR	PLURAL
NOM.	diēs, M.	diēs	rēs, F.	rēs
GEN.	diēī	diērum	reī	rērum
DAT.	diēī	diēbus	reī	rēbus
ACC.	diem	diēs	rem	rēs
ABL.	diē	diēbus	rē	rēbus

The ending of the gen. and dat. sing. is **-eī**, instead of **-ēī**, when a consonant precedes, as: **reī, fideī, speī**. Fifth declension nouns are feminine, except **diēs,** which is usually masculine in the singular, and always in the plural.

IRREGULAR NOUNS

	SINGULAR	PLURAL	SINGULAR	PLURAL
NOM.	deus, M.	deī, diī, dī	vīs, F.	vīrēs
GEN.	deī	deōrum, deum	vīs	vīrium
DAT.	deō	deīs, diīs, dīs	vī	vīribus
ACC.	deum	deōs	vim	vīrēs (-īs)
ABL.	deō	deīs, diīs, dīs	vī	vīribus

ADJECTIVES

FIRST AND SECOND DECLENSION

	SINGULAR			PLURAL		
NOM.	malus, M.	mala, F.	malum, N.	malī, M.	malae, F.	mala, N.
GEN.	malī	malae	malī	malōrum	malārum	malōrum
DAT.	malō	malae	malō	malīs	malīs	malīs
ACC.	malum	malam	malum	malōs	malās	mala
ABL.	malō	malā	malō	malīs	malīs	malīs
VOC.	male					

THIRD DECLENSION

THREE ENDINGS

	SINGULAR			PLURAL		
NOM.	celer, M.	celeris, F.	celere, N.	celerēs, M.	celerēs, F.	celeria, N.
GEN.	celeris	celeris	celeris	celerium	celerium	celerium
DAT.	celerī	celerī	celerī	celeribus	celeribus	celeribus
ACC.	celerem	celerem	celere	celerēs (-īs)	celerēs (-īs)	celeria
ABL.	celerī	celerī	celerī	celeribus	celeribus	celeribus

TWO ENDINGS

	SINGULAR		PLURAL	
NOM.	brevis, M. F.	breve, N.	brevēs, M. F.	brevia, N.
GEN.	brevis	brevis	brevium	brevium
DAT.	brevī	brevī	brevibus	brevibus
ACC.	brevem	breve	brevēs (-īs)	brevia
ABL.	brevī	brevī	brevibus	brevibus

ONE ENDING

	SINGULAR		PLURAL	
NOM.	audāx, M. F.	audāx, N.	audācēs, M. F.	audācia, N.
GEN.	audācis	audācis	audācium	audācium
DAT.	audācī	audācī	audācibus	audācibus
ACC.	audācem	audāx	audācēs (-īs)	audācia
ABL.	audācī	audācī	audācibus	audācibus

IRREGULAR ADJECTIVES

	SINGULAR			PLURAL		
NOM.	sōlus, M.	sōla, F.	sōlum, N.	sōlī, M.	sōlae, F.	sōla, N.
GEN.	sōlīus	sōlīus	sōlīus	sōlōrum	sōlārum	sōlōrum
DAT.	sōlī	sōlī	sōlī	sōlīs	sōlīs	sōlīs
ACC.	sōlum	sōlam	sōlum	sōlōs	sōlās	sōla
ABL.	sōlō	sōlā	sōlō	sōlīs	sōlīs	sōlīs
VOC.	sōle					

Other adjectives declined like **sōlus** are: **alius, alter, ūllus, nūllus, uter, uterque, neuter, tōtus, ūnus.**

PRESENT PARTICIPLE

	MASC.	FEM.	NEUT.	MASC.	FEM.	NEUT.
NOM.		regēns		regentēs		regentia
GEN.		regentis			regentium	
DAT.		regentī			regentibus	
ACC.	regentem		regēns	regentēs (-īs)		regentia
ABL.		regente (-ī)			regentibus	

Present participles, when used as participles or substantives, have **-e** in the abl. sing.; when used as adjectives, they have **-ī**.

COMPARISON OF ADJECTIVES

POSITIVE	REGULAR COMPARATIVE	SUPERLATIVE
lātus, -a, -um	lātior, lātius	lātissimus, -a, -um
fortis, forte	fortior, fortius	fortissimus, -a, -um
miser, -era, erum	miserior, miserius	miserrimus, -a, -um
ācer, ācris, ācre	ācrior, ācrius	ācerrimus, -a, -um,
facilis, facile	facilior, facilius	facillimus, -a, -um

Adjectives in **-er** have **-rimus** in the superlative. Six adjectives in **-lis** have **-limus** in the superlative,—**facilis, difficilis, similis, dissimilis, humilis,** and **gracilis.**

Comparison of Adjectives Continued

POSITIVE	IRREGULAR COMPARATIVE	SUPERLATIVE
bonus, *good*	melior, *better*	optimus, *best*
malus, *bad*	peior, *worse*	pessimus, *worst*
magnus, *great*	maior, *greater*	maximus, *greatest*
parvus, *small*	minor, *smaller*	minimus, *smallest*
{ multus, *much*	——, plus, *more*	plūrimus, *most*
{ multī, *many*	plūrēs, plūra, *more*	plūrimī, *very many*
idōneus, *suitable*	magis idōneus	maximē idōneus
exterus, *outer*	exterior	extrēmus *or* extimus
īnferus, *below*	īnferior	īnfimus *or* īmus
posterus, *following*	posterior	postrēmus *or* postumus
superus, *above*	superior	suprēmus *or* summus
(cis, citrā)	citerior, *hither*	citimus
(in, intrā)	interior, *inner*	intimus
(prae, prō)	prior, *former*	prīmus
(prope)	propior, *nearer*	proximus
(ultrā)	ulterior, *farther*	ultimus

COMPARISON OF ADVERBS

POS.	COMP.	SUPERL.	POS.	COMP.	SUPERL.
lātē	lātius	lātissimē	bene	melius	optimē
aegrē	aegrius	aegerrimē	male	peius	pessimē
fortiter	fortius	fortissimē	magnopere	magis	maximē
ācriter	ācrius	ācerrimē	parum	minus	minimē
facile	facilius	facillimē	multum	plūs	plūrimum
			diū	diūtius	diūtissimē

DECLENSION OF COMPARATIVES

SINGULAR

NOM.	lātior, M. F.		lātius, N. ——		plūs, N.
GEN.		lātiōris	——		plūris
DAT.		lātiōrī	——		
ACC.	lātiōrem		lātius	——	plūs
ABL.		lātiōre	——		plūre

PLURAL

NOM.	lātiōrēs		lātiōra	plūrēs	plūra
GEN.		lātiōrum		plūrium	
DAT.		lātiōribus		plūribus	
ACC.	lātiōrēs		lātiōra	plūrēs (-īs)	plūra
ABL.		lātiōribus		plūribus	

NUMERALS

	MASC.	FEM.	NEUT.	MASC.	FEM.	NEUT.
NOM.	ūnus	ūna	ūnum	duo	duae	duo
GEN.	ūnīus	ūnīus	ūnīus	duōrum	duārum	duōrum
DAT.	ūnī	ūnī	ūnī	duōbus	duābus	duōbus
ACC.	ūnum	ūnam	ūnum	duōs, duo	duās	duo
ABL.	ūnō	ūna	ūnō	duōbus	duābus	duōbus

			SINGULAR	PLURAL
NOM.	trēs, M. F.	tria, N.	mīlle, ADJ.	mīlia, NOUN, N.
GEN.		trium	mīlle	mīlium
DAT.		tribus	mīlle	mīlibus
ACC.	trēs (trīs)	tria	mīlle	mīlia
ABL.		tribus	mīlle	mīlibus

	ROMAN	CARDINALS	ORDINALS
1	I	ūnus, -a, -um, *one*	prīmus, *first*
2	II	duo, duae, duo, *two*	secundus, *second*
3	III	trēs, tria, *three*	tertius, *third*
4	IIII *or* IV	quattuor	quārtus
5	V	quīnque	quīntus
6	VI	sex	sextus
7	VII	septem	septimus
8	VIII	octō	octāvus
9	VIIII *or* IX	novem	nōnus
10	X	decem	decimus
11	XI	ūndecim	ūndecimus
12	XII	duodecim	duodecimus
13	XIII	tredecim	tertius decimus
14	XIIII *or* XIV	quattuordecim	quārtus decimus
15	XV	quīndecim	quīntus decimus
16	XVI	sēdecim	sextus decimus
17	XVII	septendecim	septimus decimus

Numerals Continued

	ROMAN	CARDINALS	ORDINALS
18	XVIII	duodēvīgintī	duodēvīcēsimus
19	XVIIII *or* XIX	ūndēvīgintī	ūndēvīcēsimus
20	XX	{ vīgintī	{ vīcēsimus
21	XXI	{ vīgintī ūnus ūnus et vīgintī	{ vīcēsimus prīmus ūnus et vīcēsimus
30	XXX	trīgintā	trīcēsimus
40	XXXX *or* XL	quadrāgintā	quadrāgēsimus
50	L	quīnquāginta	quīnquāgēsimus
60	LX	sexāgintā	sexāgēsimus
70	LXX	septuāgintā	septuāgēsimus
80	LXXX	octōgintā	octōgēsimus
90	LXXXX *or* XC	nōnāgintā	nōnāgēsimus
100	C	centum	centēsimus
101	CI	centum (et) ūnus	centēsimus (et) prīmus
200	CC	ducentī, -ae, -a	ducentēsimus
300	CCC	trecentī, -ae, -a	trecentēsimus
400	CCCC	quadringentī, -ae, -a	quadringentēsimus
500	D	quīngentī, -ae, -a	quīngentēsimus
600	DC	sescentī, -ae, -a	sescentēsimus
700	DCC	septingentī, -ae, -a	septingentēsimus
800	DCCC	octingentī, -ae, -a	octingentēsimus
900	DCCCC	nōngentī, -ae, -a	nōngentēsimus
1000	M	mīlle	mīllēsimus
2000	MM	duo mīlia	bis mīllēsimus

PRONOUNS

PERSONAL AND REFLEXIVE

SINGULAR

NOM.	ego	tū	——
GEN.	meī	tuī	suī
DAT.	mihi	tibi	sibi
ACC.	mē	tē	sē *or* sēsē
ABL.	mē	tē	sē *or* sēsē

PLURAL

NOM.	nōs	vōs	——
GEN.	nostrum *or* nostrī	vestrum *or* vestrī	suī
DAT.	nōbīs	vōbīs	sibi
ACC.	nōs	vōs	sē *or* sēsē
ABL.	nōbīs	vōbīs	sē *or* sēsē

DEMONSTRATIVE

SINGULAR

NOM.	hic, M.	haec, F.	hoc, N.	ille, M.	illa, F.	illud, N.
GEN.		huius			illīus	
DAT.		huic			illī	
ACC.	hunc	hanc	hoc	illum	illam	illud
ABL.	hōc	hāc	hōc	illō	illā	īllō

PLURAL

NOM.	hī	hae	haec	illī	illae	illa
GEN.	hōrum	hārum	hōrum	illōrum	illārum	illōrum
DAT.		hīs			illīs	
ACC.	hōs	hās	haec	illōs	illās	illa
ABL.		hīs			illīs	

SINGULAR

NOM.	is, M.	ea, F.	id, N.	īdem, M.	eadem, F.	idem, N.
GEN.		eius			eiusdem	
DAT.		eī			eīdem	
ACC.	eum	eam	id	eundem	eandem	idem
ABL.	eō	eā	eō	eōdem	eādem	eōdem

PLURAL

NOM.	eī *or* iī	eae	ea	eīdem / iīdem	eaedem	eadem
GEN.	eōrum	eārum	eōrum	eōrundem	eārundem	eōrundem
DAT.		eīs *or* iīs			eīsdem *or* īsdem	
ACC.	eōs	eās	ea	eōsdem	eāsdem	eadem
ABL.		eīs *or* iīs			eīsdem *or* īsdem	

INTENSIVE

	SINGULAR			PLURAL		
NOM.	ipse, M.	ipsa, F.	ipsum, N.	ipsī, M.	ipsae, F.	ipsa, N.
GEN.		ipsīus		ipsōrum	ipsārum	ipsōrum
DAT.		ipsī		ipsīs	ipsīs	
ACC.	ipsum	ipsam	ipsum	ipsōs	ipsās	ipsa
ABL.	ipsō	ipsā	ipsō	ipsīs	ipsīs	

RELATIVE

	SINGULAR			PLURAL		
NOM.	quī, M.	quae, F.	quod, N.	quī, M.	quae, F.	quae, N.
GEN.		cuius		quōrum	quārum	quōrum
DAT.		cui		quibus		
ACC.	quem	quam	quod	quōs	quās	quae
ABL.	quō	quā	quō	quibus		

INTERROGATIVE

SINGULAR

NOM.	quis, M. F.		quid, N.
GEN.		cuius	
DAT.		cui	
ACC.	quem		quid
ABL.		quō	

The plural of the interrogative pronoun **quis** is like the plural of the relative **quī**. The interrogative adjective is declined throughout like the relative **quī**, as: **quī deus,** *what god?* **quae via,** *what road?* **quod dōnum,** *what gift?*

INDEFINITE

SINGULAR

NOM.	aliquis, M. F.		aliquid, N.
GEN.		alicuius	
DAT.		alicui	
ACC.	aliquem		aliquid
ABL.		aliquō	

PLURAL

NOM.	aliquī, M.	aliquae, F.	aliqua, N.
GEN.	aliquōrum	aliquārum	aliquōrum
DAT.		aliquibus	
ACC.	aliquōs	aliquās	aliqua
ABL.		aliquibus	

SINGULAR

NOM.	quīdam, M.	quaedam, F.	quiddam, N.
GEN.		cuiusdam	
DAT.		cuidam	
ACC.	quendam	quandam	quiddam
ABL.	quōdam	quādam	quōdam

PLURAL

NOM.	quīdam, M.	quaedam, F.	quaedam, N.
GEN.	quōrundam	quārundam	quōrundam
DAT.		quibusdam	
ACC.	quōsdam	quāsdam	quaedam
ABL.		quibusdam	

The adjective form has **quoddam,** n., instead of **quiddam.**

	SINGULAR		SINGULAR	
NOM.	quisque, M. F.	quidque, N.	quisquam, M. F.	quicquam
GEN.	cuiusque		cuiusquam	
DAT.	cuique		cuiquam	
ACC.	quemque	quidque	quemquam	quicquam
ABL.	quōque		quōquam	
	(PLURAL RARE)		(PLURAL LACKING)	

The adjective form of **quisque** is **quisque, quaeque, quodque. Quisquam** is used chiefly in negative sentences, and in questions implying a negative answer.

REGULAR VERBS

FIRST CONJUGATION

PRINCIPAL PARTS: portō, portāre, portāvī, portātum
STEMS: portā-, portāv-, portāt-

ACTIVE VOICE		PASSIVE VOICE	

INDICATIVE
PRESENT

I carry, am carrying		*I am carried*	
portō	portāmus	portor	portāmur
portās	portātis	portāris	portāminī
portat	portant	portātur	portantur

IMPERFECT

I carried, was carrying		*I was carried*	
portābam	portābāmus	portābar	portābāmur
portābas	portābātis	portābāris	portābāminī
portābat	portābant	portābātur	portābantur

FUTURE

I shall (will) carry		*I shall (will) be carried*	
portābō	portābimus	portābor	portābimur
portābis	portābitis	portāberis	portābiminī
portābit	portābunt	portābitur	portābuntur

PERFECT

I have carried, I carried		*I have been (was) carried*	
portāvī	portāvimus	portātus (-a, -um) { sum / es / est }	portātī (-ae, -a) { sumus / estis / sunt }
portāvistī	portāvistis		
portāvit	portāvērunt		

PLUPERFECT

I had carried		*I had been carried*	
portāveram	portāverāmus	portātus (-a, -um) { eram / erās / erat }	portātī (-ae, -a) { erāmus / erātis / erant }
portāverās	portāverātis		
portāverat	portāverant		

FUTURE PERFECT

I shall have carried						
portāverō	portāverimus		erō		erimus
portāveris	portāveritis	portātus	eris	portātī	eritis
portāverit	portāverint	(-a, -um)	erit	(-ae, -a)	erunt

I shall have been carried

SUBJUNCTIVE
PRESENT

portem	portēmus	porter	portēmur
portēs	portētis	portēris	portēminī
portet	portent	portētur	portentur

IMPERFECT

portārem	portārēmus	portārer	portārēmur
portārēs	portārētis	portārēris	portārēminī
portāret	portārent	portārētur	portārentur

PERFECT

portāverim	portāverīmus		sim		sīmus
portāverīs	portāverītis	portātus	sīs	portātī	sītis
portāverit	portāverint	(-a, -um)	sit	(-ae, -a)	sint

PLUPERFECT

portāvissem	portāvissēmus		essem		essēmus
portāvissēs	portāvissētis	portātus	essēs	portātī	essētis
portāvisset	portāvissent	(-a, -um)	esset	(-ae, -a)	essent

IMPERATIVES
PRESENT

Carry   *Be carried*

portā	portāte	portāre	portāminī

FUTURE

You shall carry   *You shall be carried*

portātō	portātōte	portātor	——
portātō	portāntō	portātor	portantor

INFINITIVES

PRES.	portāre, *to carry*	portārī, *to be carried*
PERF.	portāvisse, *to have carried*	portātus esse, *to have been carried*
FUT.	portātūrus esse, *to be about to carry*	portātum īrī, *to be about to be carried*

First Conjugation Continued

PARTICIPLES

PRES.	portāns, -antis, *carrying*	PERF.	portātus, -a, -um, *having been carried*
FUT.	portātūrus, -a, -um, *about to carry*	FUT.	portandus, -a, -um, *to be carried*, etc.
	GERUND		SUPINE
GEN.	portandī, *of carrying*	ACC.	portātum, *to carry*
DAT.	portandō, *for carrying*	ABL.	portātū, *to carry*
ACC.	portandum, *carrying*		
ABL.	portandō, *by carrying*		

SECOND CONJUGATION

PRINCIPAL PARTS: moneō, monēre, monuī, monitum
STEMS: monē-, monu-, monit-

ACTIVE VOICE		PASSIVE VOICE	

INDICATIVE
PRESENT

moneō	monēmus	moneor	monēmur
monēs	monētis	monēris	monēminī
monet	monent	monētur	monentur

IMPERFECT

monēbam	monēbāmus	monēbar	monēbāmur
monēbās	monēbātis	monēbāris	monēbāminī
monēbat	monēbant	monēbātur	monēbantur

FUTURE

monēbō	monēbimus	monēbor	monēbimur
monēbis	monēbitis	monēberis	monēbiminī
monēbit	monēbunt	monēbitur	monēbuntur

PERFECT

monuī	monuimus	monitus (-a, -um) {	sum / es / est	monitī (-ae, -a) {	sumus / estis / sunt
monuistī	monuistis				
monuit	monuērunt				

PLUPERFECT

monueram	monuerāmus	monitus (-a, -um) {	eram / erās / erat	monitī (-ae, -a) {	erāmus / erātis / erant
monuerās	monuerātis				
monuerat	monuerant				

FUTURE PERFECT

monuerō	monuerimus	monitus (-a, -um)	{ erō eris erit	monitī (-ae, -a)	{ erimus eritis erunt
monueris	monueritis				
monuerit	monuerint				

SUBJUNCTIVE
PRESENT

moneam	moneāmus	monear	moneāmur
moneās	moneātis	moneāris	moneāminī
moneat	moneant	moneātur	moneantur

IMPERFECT

monērem	monērēmus	monērer	monērēmur
monērēs	monērētis	monērēris	monērēminī
monēret	monērent	monērētur	monērentur

PERFECT

monuerim	monuerīmus	monitus (-a, -um)	{ sim sīs sit	monitī (-ae, -a)	{ sīmus sītis sint
monuerīs	monuerītis				
monuerit	monuerint				

PLUPERFECT

monuissem	monuissēmus	monitus (-a, -um)	{ essem essēs esset	monitī (-ae, -a)	{ essēmus essētis essent
monuissēs	monuissētis				
monuisset	monuissent				

IMPERATIVES
PRESENT

monē	monēte	monēre	monēminī

FUTURE

monētō	monētōte	monētor	——
monētō	monentō	monētor	monentor

INFINITIVES

PRES.	monēre	monērī
PERF.	monuisse	monitus esse
FUT.	monitūrus esse	monitum īrī

PARTICIPLES

PRES.	monēns, -entis	PERF.	monitus, -a, -um
FUT.	monitūrus, -a, -um	FUT.	monendus, -a, -um

Second Conjugation Continued

GERUND		SUPINE	
GEN.	monendī	ACC.	monitum
DAT.	monendō	ABL.	monitū
ACC.	monendum		
ABL.	monendō		

THIRD CONJUGATION

PRINCIPAL PARTS: dūcō, dūcere, dūxī, ductum
STEMS: dūc-, dūx-, duct-

ACTIVE VOICE		PASSIVE VOICE	

INDICATIVE
PRESENT

dūcō	dūcimus	dūcor	dūcimur
dūcis	dūcitis	dūceris	dūciminī
dūcit	dūcunt	dūcitur	dūcuntur

IMPERFECT

dūcēbam	dūcēbāmus	dūcēbar	dūcēbāmur
dūcēbās	dūcēbātis	dūcēbāris	dūcēbāminī
dūcēbat	dūcēbant	dūcēbātur	dūcēbantur

FUTURE

dūcam	dūcēmus	dūcar	dūcēmur
dūcēs	dūcētis	dūcēris	dūcēminī
dūcet	dūcent	dūcētur	dūcentur

PERFECT

dūxī	dūximus	ductus (-a, -um)	sum / es / est	ductī (-ae, -a)	sumus / estis / sunt
dūxistī	dūxistis				
dūxit	dūxērunt				

PLUPERFECT

dūxeram	dūxerāmus	ductus (-a, -um)	eram / erās / erat	ductī (-ae, -a)	erāmus / erātis / erant
dūxerās	dūxerātis				
dūxerat	dūxerant				

FUTURE PERFECT

dūxerō	dūxerimus	ductus (-a, -um)	erō / eris / erit	ductī (-ae, -a)	erimus / eritis / erunt
dūxeris	dūxeritis				
dūxerit	dūxerint				

SUBJUNCTIVE
PRESENT

dūcam	dūcāmus	dūcar	dūcāmur
dūcās	dūcātis	dūcāris	dūcāminī
dūcat	dūcant	dūcātur	dūcantur

IMPERFECT

dūcerem	dūcerēmus	dūcerer	dūcerēmur
dūcerēs	dūcerētis	dūcerēris	dūcerēminī
dūceret	dūcerent	dūcerētur	dūcerentur

PERFECT

dūxerim	dūxerīmus	ductus (-a, -um)	sim / sīs / sit	ductī (-ae, -a)	sīmus / sītis / sint
dūxerīs	dūxerītis				
dūxerit	dūxerint				

PLUPERFECT

dūxissem	dūxissēmus	ductus (-a, -um)	essem / essēs / esset	ductī (-ae, -a)	essēmus / essētis / essent
dūxissēs	dūxissētis				
dūxisset	dūxissent				

IMPERATIVES
PRESENT

dūc[1]	dūcite	dūcere	dūciminī

FUTURE

dūcitō	dūcitōte	dūcitor	—
dūcitō	dūcuntō	dūcitor	dūcuntor

INFINITIVES

PRES.	dūcere	dūcī
PERF.	dūxisse	ductus esse
FUT.	ductūrus esse	ductum īrī

PARTICIPLES

PRES.	dūcēns, -entis	PERF.	ductus, -a, -um
FUT.	ductūrus, -a, -um	FUT.	dūcendus, -a, -um

Third Conjugation Continued

	GERUND		SUPINE
GEN.	dūcendī	ACC.	ductum
DAT.	dūcendō	ABL.	ductū
ACC.	dūcendum		
ABL.	dūcendō		

FOURTH CONJUGATION

PRINCIPAL PARTS: audiō, audīre, audīvī, audītum
STEMS: audī-, audīv-, audīt-

ACTIVE VOICE			PASSIVE VOICE	

INDICATIVE
PRESENT

audiō	audīmus	audior	audīmur
audīs	audītis	audīris	audīminī
audit	audiunt	audītur	audiuntur

IMPERFECT

audiēbam	audiēbāmus	audiēbar	audiēbāmur
audiēbās	audiēbātis	audiēbāris	audiēbāminī
audiēbat	audiēbant	audiēbātur	audiēbantur

FUTURE

audiam	audiēmus	audiar	audiēmur
audiēs	audiētis	audiēris	audiēminī
audiet	audient	audiētur	audientur

PERFECT

audīvī	audīvimus	audītus, (-a, -um)	sum es est	audītī (-ae, -a)	sumus estis sunt
audīvistī	audīvistis				
audīvit	audīvērunt				

PLUPERFECT

audīveram	audīverāmus	audītus, (-a, -um)	eram erās erat	audītī (-ae, -a)	erāmus erātis erant
audīverās	audīverātis				
audīverat	audīverant				

FUTURE PERFECT

audīverō	audīverimus	audītus, (-a, -um)	erō eris erit	audītī, (-ae, -a)	erimus eritis erunt
audīveris	audīveritis				
audīverit	audīverint				

SUBJUNCTIVE
PRESENT

audiam	audiāmus	audiar	audiāmur
audiās	audiātis	audiāris	audiāminī
audiat	audiant	audiātur	audiantur

IMPERFECT

audīrem	audīrēmus	audīrer	audīrēmur
audīrēs	audīrētis	audīrēris	audīrēminī
audīret	audīrent	audīrētur	audīrentur

PERFECT

audīverim	audīverīmus	audītus,	sim	audītī,	sīmus
audīverīs	audīverītis	(-a, -um)	sīs	(-ae, -a)	sītis
audīverit	audīverint		sit		sint

PLUPERFECT

audīvissem	audīvissēmus	audītus,	essem	audītī,	essēmus
audīvissēs	audīvissētis	(-a, -um)	essēs	(-ae, -a)	essētis
audīvisset	audīvissent		esset		essent

IMPERATIVES
PRESENT

audī	audīte	audīre	audīminī

FUTURE

audītō	audītōte	audītor	——
audītō	audiuntō	audītor	audiuntor

INFINITIVES

PRES.	audīre	audīrī
PERF.	audīvisse	audītus esse
FUT.	audītūrus esse	audītum īrī

PARTICIPLES

PRES.	audiēns, -entis		PERF.	audītus, -a, -um
FUT.	audītūrus, -a, -um		FUT.	audiendus, -a, -um

GERUND / SUPINE

GEN.	audiendī		ACC.	audītum
DAT.	audiendō		ABL.	audītū
ACC.	audiendum			
ABL.	audiendō			

THIRD CONJUGATION VERBS IN -IŌ

PRINCIPAL PARTS: capiō, capere, cēpī, captum
STEMS: capi-, cēp-, capt-

<table>
<tr><td colspan="2">ACTIVE VOICE</td><td colspan="2">PASSIVE VOICE</td></tr>
</table>

INDICATIVE
PRESENT

capiō	capimus	capior	capimur
capis	capitis	caperis	capiminī
capit	capiunt	capitur	capiuntur

IMPERFECT

capiēbam, etc.	capiēbar, etc.

FUTURE

capiam	capiēmus	capiar	capiēmur
capiēs	capiētis	capiēris	capiēminī
capiet	capient	capiētur	capientur

PERFECT

cēpī, etc.	captus sum, etc.

PLUPERFECT

cēperam, etc.	captus eram, etc.

FUTURE PERFECT

cēperō, etc.	captus erō, etc.

SUBJUNCTIVE
PRESENT

capiam	capiāmus	capiar	capiāmur
capiās	capiātis	capiāris	capiāminī
capiat	capiant	capiātur	capiantur

IMPERFECT

caperem, etc.	caperer, etc.

PERFECT

cēperim, etc.	captus sim, etc.

PLUPERFECT

cēpissem, etc.	captus essem, etc.

IMPERATIVES
PRESENT

cape	capite	capere	capimini

FUTURE

capitō	capitōte	capitor	——
capitō	capiuntō	capitor	capiuntor

INFINITIVES

PRES.	capere	capī
PERF.	cēpisse	captus esse
FUT.	captūrus esse	captum īrī

PARTICIPLES

PRES.	capiēns, -entis	PERF.	captus, -a, -um
FUT.	captūrus, -a, -um	FUT.	capiendus, -a, -um

GERUND | | SUPINE

GEN.	capiendī	ACC.	captum
DAT.	capiendō	ABL.	captū
ACC.	capiendum		
ABL.	capiendō		

DEPONENT VERBS

Deponent verbs are passive in form, active in meaning. They are inflected in all conjugations as follows:

FIRST CONJUGATION

PRINCIPAL PARTS: cōnor, cōnārī, cōnātus sum
STEMS: cōnā-, cōnāt-

PRESENT		INDICATIVE	IMPERFECT
cōnor	cōnāmur	cōnābar	cōnābāmur
cōnāris	cōnāminī	cōnābāris	cōnābāminī
cōnātur	cōnantur	cōnābātur	cōnābantur

First Conjugation Continued

FUTURE

I shall try

cōnābor	cōnābimur
cōnāberis	cōnābiminī
cōnābitur	cōnābuntur

PERFECT		PLUPERFECT		FUTURE PERFECT	
I have tried		*I had tried*		*I shall have tried*	
cōnātus (-a, -um)	sum es est	cōnātus (-a, -um)	eram erās erat	cōnātus (-a, -um)	erō eris erit
cōnātī (-ae, -a)	sumus estis sunt	cōnātī (-ae, -a)	erāmus erātis erant	cōnātī (-ae, -a)	erimus eritis erunt

SUBJUNCTIVE

PRESENT	IMPERFECT
cōner	cōnārer
cōnēris	cōnārēris
cōnētur	cōnārētur
cōnemur	cōnārēmur
cōnēminī	cōnārēminī
cōnentur	cōnārentur

PERFECT		PLUPERFECT	
cōnātus (-a, -um)	sim sīs sit	cōnātus (-a, -um)	essem essēs esset
cōnātī (-ae, -a)	sīmus sītis sint	cōnātī (-ae, -a)	essēmus essētis essent

PRESENT IMPERATIVES

cōnāre, *try*	cōnāminī, *try*

INFINITIVES	GERUND

PRES.	cōnārī, *to try*	GEN.	cōnandī, *of trying*
PERF.	cōnātus esse, *to have tried*	DAT.	cōnandō, *for trying*
FUT.	cōnātūrus esse, *to be about to try*	ACC.	cōnandum, *trying*
		ABL.	cōnandō *by trying*

PARTICIPLES		SUPINE	

PRES.	cōnāns, -antis, *trying*	ACC.	cōnātum, *to try*
FUT. ACT.	cōnātūrus, *about to try*	ABL.	cōnātū, *to try*
PERF.	cōnātus, *having tried*		
FUT. PASS.	cōnandus, *necessary to be tried,*		
	or as Gerundive, *trying*		

CONJ. II.	vereor, verērī, veritus sum
CONJ. III.	sequor, sequī, secūtus sum
-IOR VERB.	patior, patī, passus sum
CONJ. IV.	potior, potīrī, potītus sum

INDICATIVE

PRES.	vereor	sequor	patior	potior
IMP.	verēbar	sequēbar	patiēbar	potiēbar
FUT.	verēbor	sequar	patiar	potiar
PERF.	veritus sum	secūtus sum	passus sum	potītus sum
PLUP.	veritus eram	secūtus eram	passus eram	potītus eram
FUT. P.	veritus erō	secūtus erō	passus erō	potītus erō

SUBJUNCTIVE

PRES.	verear	sequar	patiar	potiar
IMP.	verērer	sequerer	paterer	potīrer
PERF.	veritus sim	secūtus sim	passus sim	potītus sim
PLUP.	veritus essem	secūtus essem	passus essem	potītus essem

PRESENT IMPERATIVE

SING.	verēre	sequere	patere	potīre
PL.	verēminī	sequiminī	patiminī	potīminī

INFINITIVES

PRES.	verērī	sequī	patī	potīrī
PERF.	veritus esse	secūtus esse	passus esse	potītus esse
FUT.	veritūrus esse	secūtūrus esse	passūrus esse	potītūrus esse

PARTICIPLES

PRES.	verēns, -entis	sequēns, -entis	patiēns, -entis	potiēns, -entis
FUT. ACT.	veritūrus	secūtūrus	passūrus	potītūrus
PERF.	veritus	secūtus	passus	potītus
FUT. PASS.	verendus	sequendus	patiendus	potiendus

GERUND

GEN.	verendī, etc.	sequendī, etc.	patiendī, etc.	potiendī, etc.

First Conjugation Continued

SUPINE

ACC.	veritum	secūtum	passum	potītum
ABL.	veritū	secūtū	passū	potītū

SEMIDEPONENT VERBS

Four verbs, which are active in the present system, become deponents in the perfect system, and are called semideponents. They are:

audeō, audēre, ausus sum, *dare*

fīdō, fīdere, fīsus sum, *trust*

gaudeō, gaudēre, gāvīsus sum, *rejoice*

soleō, solēre, solitus sum, *be accustomed*

IRREGULAR VERBS

SUM, *BE*

PRINCIPAL PARTS: sum, esse, fuī, futūrus

INDICATIVE

PRESENT		IMPERFECT		FUTURE	
sum	sumus	eram	erāmus	erō	erimus
es	estis	erās	erātis	eris	eritis
est	sunt	erat	erant	erit	erunt

PERFECT		PLUPERFECT		FUTURE PERFECT	
fuī	fuimus	fueram	fuerāmus	fuerō	fuerimus
fuistī	fuistis	fuerās	fuerātis	fueris	fueritis
fuit	fuērunt	fuerat	fuerant	fuerit	fuerint

SUBJUNCTIVE

PRESENT		IMPERFECT		PERFECT	
sim	sīmus	essem	essēmus	fuerim	fuerīmus
sīs	sītis	essēs	essētis	fuerīs	fuerītis
sit	sint	esset	essent	fuerit	fuerint

PLUPERFECT		PRESENT IMPERATIVES	
fuissem	fuissēmus	es	este
fuissēs	fuissētis		
fuisset	fuissent		

INFINITIVES		PARTICIPLE
PRES.	esse	
PERF.	fuisse	
FUT.	futūrus esse or fore	futūrus

POSSUM, *BE ABLE*

PRINCIPAL PARTS: possum, posse, potuī,

	INDICATIVE		SUBJUNCTIVE	
PRES.	possum	possumus	possim	possīmus
	potes	potestis	possīs	possītis
	potest	possunt	possit	possint
IMP.	poteram		possem	
FUT.	poterō			
PERF.	potuī		potuerim	
PLUP.	potueram		potuissem	
FUT. P.	potuerō			

INFINITIVES

PRES.	posse	PERF.	potuisse

FERŌ *BEAR, BRING*

PRINCIPAL PARTS: ferō, ferre, tulī, lātum

	ACTIVE VOICE		PASSIVE VOICE	
		INDICATIVE		
PRES.	ferō	ferimus	feror	ferimur
	fers	fertis	ferris	feriminī
	fert	ferunt	fertur	feruntur
IMP.	ferēbam		ferēbar	
FUT.	feram		ferar	
PERF.	tulī		lātus sum	
PLUP.	tuleram		lātus eram	
FUT. P.	tulerō		lātus erō	

Ferō Bear, Bring Continued

SUBJUNCTIVE

PRES.	feram	ferar
IMP.	ferrem	ferrer
PERF.	tulerim	lātus sim
PLUP.	tulissem	lātus essem

PRESENT IMPERATIVES

fer	ferte	ferre	feriminī

INFINITIVES

PRES.	ferre	ferrī
PERF.	tulisse	lātus esse
FUT.	lātūrus esse	lātum īrī

PARTICIPLES

PRES.	ferēns, -entis	PERF.	lātus
FUT.	lātūrus	FUT.	ferendus

	GERUND		SUPINE
GEN.	ferendī, etc.	ACC.	lātum
		ABL.	lātū

EŌ, GO

PRINCIPAL PARTS: eō, īre, īvī *or* iī, itum

	INDICATIVE			SUBJUNCTIVE	
PRES.	eō	īmus	eam	eāmus
	īs	ītis	eās	eātis
	it	eunt	eat	eant
IMP.	ībam		īrem	
FUT.	ībō			
PERF.	īvī *or* iī		īverim *or* ierim	
PLUP.	īveram *or* ieram		īvissem *or* īssem	
FUT. P.	īverō *or* ierō			

	PRESENT IMPERATIVES		INFINITIVES	
ī	īte	PRES.	īre
		PERF.	īvisse *or* īsse
		FUT.	itūrus esse
		PASSIVE PRES.	īrī

PARTICIPLES		GERUND	
PRES.	iēns, euntis	GEN.	eundi, etc.
FUT.	itūrus		
PERF.	itum (impers.)		
FUT.	eundus		

EDŌ, EAT

PRINCIPAL PARTS edō, ēsse, ēdī, ēsum

	INDICATIVE			SUBJUNCTIVE	
PRES.	edō	edimus		edim	edīmus
	ēs	ēstis		edīs	edītis
	ēst	edunt		edit	edint
IMP.	edēbam	edēbāmus		ederem	ēssēmus
	edēbās	edēbātis		ēssēs	ēssētis
	edēbat	edēbant		ēsset	ēssent
FUT.	edam				
PERF.	ēdī			ēderim	
PLUP.	ēderam			ēdissem	
FUT. PERF.	ēderō				

PRESENT IMPERATIVES		PARTICIPLES		GERUND
ēs	ēste	edēns		edendī, etc.
			ēsus	
		ēsūrus	edendus	

VOLŌ, NŌLŌ, MĀLŌ

PRINCIPAL PARTS volō, velle, voluī, *be willing, wish* nōlō, nōlle, nōluī, *be unwilling* mālō, mālle, māluī, *prefer*

INDICATIVE

PRES.	volō	nōlō	mālō
	vīs	nōn vīs	māvīs
	vult	nōn vult	māvult
	volumus	nōlumus	mālumus
	vultis	nōn vultis	māvultis
	volunt	nōlunt	mālunt
IMP.	volēbam	nōlēbam	mālēbam
FUT.	volam	nōlam	mālam

Volō Nōlō, Mālō Continued

PERF.	voluī		nōluī		māluī
PLUP.	volueram		nōlueram		mālueram
FUT. P.	voluerō		nōluerō		māluerō

SUBJUNCTIVE

PRES.	velim	velīmus	nōlim	nōlīmus	mālim	mālīmus
	velīs	velīs	nōlīs	nōlītis	mālīs	mālītis
	velit	velint	nōlit	nōlint	mālit	mālint
IMP.	vellem		nōllem			mallem
PERF.	voluerim		nōluerim			māluerim
PLUP.	voluissem		nōluissem			māluissem

PRESENT IMPERATIVES

	——	nōlī	nōlīte	——

INFINITIVES

PRES.	velle	nōlle	mālle
PERF.	voluisse	nōluisse	māluisse

PARTICIPLE

PRES.	volēns, -entis	nōlēns, -entis	——

CONTRACTED FORMS

Perfects in **-āvī** and **-ēvī** (as well as other tenses in the perfect system) are sometimes contracted, losing **-ve-** before **-r**, and **-vi-** before **-s**, as: **oppugnārunt** for **oppugnāvērunt, cōnsuērat** for **cōnsuēverat**.

Perfects in **-īvī** may lose **-vi-** before **-s**, as: **audīssem** for **audīvissem**.

In poetry, the third person plural of the perfect indicative active frequently ends in **-ēre**, instead of **-ērunt**. Also the second person singular passive may end in **-re**, instead of **-ris**, in the present, imperfect and future tenses.

The forms **forem, forēs**, etc., are frequently used in place of **essem, essēs**, etc.

SYNTAX

PARTS OF SPEECH

Noun ⎫
Pronoun ⎬ Substantives
Adjective ⎭
Adverb

Preposition
Particle
Verb
Infinitive

Participle
Gerund
Supine
Interjection

SYNTAX OF SUBSTANTIVES

APPOSITION

A noun used to describe another substantive is said to be its APPOSITIVE, or to be used in apposition with it. An appositive must refer to the same person or thing as the substantive to which it applies, and must also be in the same case. In Latin it usually follows its substantive. Latin does not use the genitive for apposition, as English does in an expression like *the city of Boston* or *the state of Indiana*.

> Hecuba rēgīna terram Graeciam spectat.
> *Queen Hecuba looks at the land of Greece.*

CASES OF SUBSTANTIVES

NOMINATIVE

The SUBJECT of a verb (i.e. the person, place, or thing about which something is said) is in the nominative case.

A noun used with a linking verb such as **sum** or the passive of a factitive verb (a verb of naming, making, or choosing) is in the nominative. Such a noun is called a PREDICATE NOMINATIVE, or PREDICATE NOUN, or SUBJECTIVE COMPLEMENT.

> Asia est prōvincia.   *Asia is a province.*
> Fīlia vocābātur Helena.   *The daughter used to be called Helen.*

VOCATIVE

The vocative case is used for speaking directly to someone. A noun in the vocative always denotes the person being spoken to. In Latin the vocative comes not (as in English) at the beginning or end of a sentence, but just after the beginning, usually in second or third place.

> Quō Vergilī ambulās?   *Virgil, where are you walking to?*
> Esne bone amīce in vīllā?   *Are you in the farmhouse, my good friend?*

GENITIVE

The genitive case is used to show possession. The English translation of the GENITIVE OF POSSESSION uses *'s* or *s'*, or a prepositional phrase with *of*.

> agricolae vīlla   *the farmer's farmhouse, the farmhouse of the farmer*
> agricolārum vīllae   *the farmers' farmhouse, the farmhouses of the farmers*

The genitive of the personal and reflexive pronouns is not used to show possession. Instead we use the possessive adjectives **meus, noster, tuus, vester,** and **suus.** A possessive adjective may be joined to a genitive of possession by a coordinating conjunction.

> Haec domus mea et uxōris est.   *This house is my wife's and mine.*

When *of* in English implies advantage or disadvantage it is rendered by the Dative of Reference in Latin.

> Vīllam meō amīcō occupant.   *They are seizing my friend's farmhouse.*

A PREDICATE GENITIVE is used with the verb **sum** to indicate function or duty.

> Bonī hominis est deīs parēre.
> *It is <the part> of a good man to obey the gods.*
> Errāre hominis est, deī ignōscere.
> *To err is human (of a man), to forgive divine (of a god).*

A word which implies a part or portion of a whole person, thing, or group may be used with a genitive to indicate the whole. This genitive is called the GENITIVE OF THE WHOLE (or PARTITIVE GENITIVE). The English translation of this genitive uses the preposition *of.*

> Pars urbis occupāta est.   *Part of the city has been seized.*
> Multae nāvium ad īnsulam nāvigant.
> *Many of the ships are sailing to the island.*

Many phrases made up of a noun of quantity (e.g. **mīlia, nihil, parum, plūs,** and **satis**) and a Partitive Genitive in Latin are translated as a noun modified by an adjective in English.

> decem mīlia mīlitum   *ten thousand soldiers*
> nihil aquae   *no water*   plūs aurī   *more gold*
> parum frūmentī   *too little grain*   satis amōris   *enough love*

This construction is also common with **quid, aliquid,** etc.

> Quid consilī cēpit?   *What plan did he make?*

Plēnus and other adjectives of fullness and emptiness may be construed with the Genitive of the Whole. The same is true of verbs of filling and emptying.

> Flūmen aquae plēnum est.   *The stream is full of water.*
> Eum implēvit temeritātis suae.   *She filled him with her own rashness.*

Some adjectives (e.g. **cēterī, extrēmus, īmus, medius, omnis, reliquus,** and **summus**) already contain a partitive idea in their meaning, and so they do not need a genitive to express it.

> Ad extrēmum oppidum ambulō.   *I'm walking to the end of the town.*
> In mediā silvā stat.   *She is standing in the middle of the forest.*

When a noun is the name of an action, it may be accompanied by a noun in the genitive telling who or what receives the action. Because this person or thing would be the direct object if the action noun were a verb, this use is called the OBJECTIVE GENITIVE.

> Puellam amō.　*I love the girl.*
> Meus amor puellae magnus est.　*My love for the girl is great.*

Grātia in the ablative, following an Objective Genitive, means *for the sake.*

> Iovis grātiā　*for Jupiter's sake*

The Objective Genitive may also be used with certain adjectives, e.g. **cupidus** (*desirous*) and **memor** (*mindful*).

> Cum laudis cupidus tum honōris memor erat.
> *Just as he was eager for praise, so especially he remembered his honor.*

The Objective Genitive differs from all other genitives in that it cannot always be translated with *of.*

> Fugam malōrum narrāvit.　*He told of his flight from evils.*

An Objective Genitive, rather than an accusative, is construed with **potior** and with verbs of remembering and forgetting.

> Patriae memorēs, maiōrum virtūtis numquam oblīvīscēbāmur.
> *Remembering our fatherland, we were never forgetful of the courage of our ancestors.*
> Mementōte nostrī!　*Remember us!*

Quality may be denoted by the Genitive of Description.

> vir magnae virtūtis　*a man of great courage*

This genitive is used when in English a noun of quality (e.g. *courage*) is modified by an adjective (e.g. *great*). When the noun is not modified by an adjective (as in *a man of courage*), simply translate **vir fortis**, *a brave man.*

Definite measurements, using numerals, are expressed by the Genitive of Measure.

> amnis decem pedum　*a ten-foot river*

The genitive of nouns and adjectives of quantity is used with **sum** and **faciō** as the Genitive of Indefinite Value.

> Servus parvi est.　*The slave is of little value.*
> Tua verba nihilī faciō.　*I consider your words worth nothing.*

The Genitive of the Charge or Penalty is used with verbs of accusing, condemning, or acquitting.

> Eum caedis arguēbant.　*They were accusing him of murder.*
> Capitis damnātus est.　*He was condemned to death.*

> Eum pecūniae condemnāvērunt.　*They sentenced him to pay a fine.*

DATIVE

With verbs or other expressions of giving, saying, showing, and the like, the dative indicates to whom or to what something is given, said, shown, etc., the Indirect Object. English uses the preposition *to* or no preposition at all, depending on the word order.

Rēgīnae fābulam narrābat.
{ *He was telling a story to the queen.*
He was telling the queen a story.

Equum vocant dōnum deīs.   *They call the horse a gift to the gods.*

Some verbs may be construed with either this dative or the Accusative of Place to Which, depending on how much actual motion is intended in the verb.

Nūntium rēgī mīsit.   *He sent the king a message.*
Nūntium ad rēgem mīsit.   *He sent a message to the king.*

Many verbs compounded with certain prefixes may take an indirect object (the DATIVE WITH COMPOUND VERBS), which completes the meaning of the prefix, rather than that of the verb itself.

Cēterīs malīs dolor accessit.   *To the rest of the evils grief was added.*
Hic illī praestat.   *This man is better than that one.*
Legiōnī praeest.   *He is at the head of the Legion.*

Certain verbs, such as **crēdō, faveō, invideō, noceō, parcō, pareō, placeō,** and **serviō** (and verbs of similar meanings), take an indirect object in Latin (the DATIVE WITH INTRANSITIVE VERBS) instead of a direct object, as in English.

Tibi crēdō.   *I believe you.*   Tibi crēditur.   *You are believed.*
Eī nōn nocēbant.   *They were not harming him.*

The DATIVE OF REFERENCE may be used with any verb to show to whose advantage or disadvantage the action of the verb is performed. The English translation uses the preposition *for* or no preposition at all.

Meō amīcō vīllam aedificant.
{ *They are building a farmhouse for my friend.*
They are building my friend a farmhouse.

When *of* or *from* in English implies advantage or disadvantage it may be rendered by the Dative of Reference in Latin.

Vīllam meō amīcō occupant.
{ *They are seizing the farmhouse from my friend.*
They are seizing my friend's farmhouse.

Cōnsulō, metuō, timeō, and **vereor** may be used with a Dative of Reference in addition to, or instead of, a direct object.

Tē cōnsulit.   *He consults you.*   Tibi cōnsulit.   *He consults your interests.*
Tibi timeō.   *I fear for you.*   Perīculum tibi timeō.   *I fear danger for you.*

The DATIVE OF PURPOSE is used to show what the noun serves as, its purpose or its result.

Hoc auxiliō praebet.   *He offers this as (for) an aid.*

The six nouns most commonly used in this construction are:

auxiliō   *as (for) an aid (a help)*   impedimentō   *as (for) a hindrance*
cordī   *for a heart (dear)*   salūtī   *as (for) a salvation*
cūrae   *for a care (worry)*   ūsuī   *as (for) a use (advantage)*

The Dative of Purpose is usually coupled with a Dative of Reference. This construction is called the DOUBLE DATIVE.

<blockquote>
Hoc mihi auxiliō est.   *This serves as a help to me.*

Hoc mihi impedīmentō est.   *This acts as a hindrance to me.*

Fīlius patrī cūrae erat.   { *The son was a worry to his father.*
                          { *The father was worried about his son.*
</blockquote>

The DATIVE WITH ADJECTIVES is used to complete or extend the meaning of an adjective.

<blockquote>
Rōmānī Āfricānīs dissimilēs sunt.   *The Romans are unlike the Africans.*

Poenī Trōiānīs amīcī sunt.   *The Carthaginians are friendly to the Trojans.*

Dōnec grātus eram tibi fēlīx eram.

As long as I was pleasing to you I was happy.
</blockquote>

The DATIVE OF POSSESSION is used with **sum**. The possessor is put into the dative; the thing possessed is the subject of the verb *to be* and is in the nominative.

<blockquote>
Puerō equus est.   *The boy has a horse.*
</blockquote>

Dēsum is used with the Dative of Possession to show lack of possession.

<blockquote>
Puerō equus dēest.   *The boy does not have a horse.*
</blockquote>

The DATIVE OF AGENT may be used (instead of the ablative with **ā, ab**) to express agency with any passive participle. It is the usual construction with the future passive participle, unless the participle itself governs a dative.

<blockquote>
Deī aliēnī acceptī rēgī nostrō erant.

Foreign gods had been welcomed by our king.

Hoc mihi faciendum erat.   *I ought to have done this.*

Patrī ā tē parendum est.   *You must obey your father.*
</blockquote>

ACCUSATIVE

One of the uses of the accusative case is to indicate the DIRECT OBJECT of an active transitive verb, infinitive, or participle, or of a transitive deponent verb, infinitive, or participle, or of a supine.

Some verbs, e.g. **doceō** and **rogō**, may have a direct object of the person, a direct object of the thing, or both (the DOUBLE ACCUSATIVE).

<blockquote>
Rēgem rogāvit.   *He asked (questioned) the king.*

Pecūniam rogāvit.   *He asked for money.*

Rēgem pecūniam rogāvit.   *He asked the king for money.*
</blockquote>

When verbs which take a Double Accusative are in the passive, either the person or the thing may become the subject; the other remains in the accusative as a RETAINED OBJECT.

<blockquote>
Rēx pecūniam rogātus est.   *The king was asked for money.*

Pecūnia rēgem rogāta est.   *Money was asked for from the king.*
</blockquote>

The neuter accusative of adjectives, pronouns, and the nouns **nihil, parum, paulum, plūs**, and **satis** may be used to modify an idea which is in the verb. This INTERNAL ACCUSATIVE is used with transitive, intransitive, and even modal verbs. If the verb is transitive and active it will also have a direct object.

> Multa errat.   *He makes many mistakes.*
> Plūrimum potest.   *He has the most ability.*
> Prīmum mātrem valēre iussit.   *He said his first goodbye to his mother.*
> Mihi ista nihil nocent.   *Your actions do me no harm.*
> Plūs valeō quam tū.   *I have more strength than you.*
> Ego tē multum, tū mē parum dīligis.
>   *I have much love for you, and you have too little for me.*
> Tē nōn satis aspiciō.   *I don't see you enough.*

The ACCUSATIVE OF EXCLAMATION is normal in Latin.

> Ō malam Trōiānōrum fortūnam!   *Ah, the evil fortune of the Trojans!*

A factitive verb (a verb of naming, making, or choosing) may take, in addition to its Direct Object, a second accusative called the PREDICATE ACCUSATIVE or OBJECTIVE COMPLEMENT.

> Fīliam vocō Helenam.   *I call my daughter Helen.*

The SUBJECT, and hence also the SUBJECTIVE COMPLEMENT, OF AN INFINITIVE are in the accusative case.

> Mē abīre iussit.   *He bade me go away.*
> Lūcium esse amīcum meum optō.   *I wish Lucius to be my friend.*
> Lūcius sē fore amīcum meum promittit.   *Lucius promises to be my friend.*

The ACCUSATIVE OF EXTENT OF SPACE, without a preposition, is used to answer the question *How far?*

> Quīngentōs passūs ambulābit.   *He will walk five hundred paces.*
> Oppidum ab amne DCCCC pedēs iacet.   *The town lies 900 feet from the river.*

The ACCUSATIVE OF DURATION OF TIME, without a preposition, is used to answer the question *How long?*

> Eam trīs hōrās exspectāvimus.   *We waited for her for three hours.*

Nouns which have a locative case, as well as the supine, indicate place to which by the ACCUSATIVE OF LIMIT OF MOTION (without a preposition).

Domum venit.   *He comes home.*   Rōmam venimus.   *We are coming to Rome.*
> Urbem spectātum vēnit.   *He has come to look (towards looking) at the city.*

The ACCUSATIVE OF PLACE TO WHICH is used with prepositions to answer the question *Where to?*

> Quō nāvigātis? Ad Graeciam nāvigāmus.
>   *Where are you sailing to? We are sailing to Greece.*

With a verb of motion the Accusative of Place to Which is used instead of the Ablative of Place Where.

> Ad oppidum in Asiam nāvigat.   *She is sailing to a town in Asia.*

Some verbs may be construed with either the Accusative of Place to Which or the Dative of Indirect Object, depending on how much motion is intended in the verb.

> Nūntium ad rēgem mīsit.   *He sent a message to the king.*
> Nūntium rēgī mīsit.   *He sent the king a message.*

The use of a person as a means or instrument is shown by the ACCUSATIVE OF SECONDARY AGENT with the preposition **per**.

> Bellum per lēgātōs nūntiāvimus.   *We announced the war by means of legates.*

An accusative which sums up a whole idea is called an ACCUSATIVE IN APPOSITION WITH A CLAUSE.

> Hostēs, id quod nōbīs magnō impedīmentō erat, ducem nostrum occīderant.
> *The enemy had killed our leader, an action which was very disadvantageous to us.*

ABLATIVE PROPER (THE *FROM* ABLATIVE)

With a verb of separation, when no motion is implied, *from* is expressed by the ABLATIVE OF SEPARATION, without a preposition.

> Servum timōre līberāvimus.   *We freed the slave from fear.*
> Hostīs urbe prohibuimus.   *We kept the enemy from the city.*
> Aquā carēmus.   *We lack water.*

When separation is not implied by the verb, the preposition **sine** or the adverb **procul** is used with the Ablative of Separation.

> Sine aquā sumus.   *We are without water.*
> Vīlla procul urbe est.   *The farmhouse is some distance from the city.*

When motion from, rather than separation, is implied, *from* is expressed by the Ablative of Place from Which. If advantage or disadvantage is emphasized more than either separation or motion from, the Dative of Reference is used.

The ABLATIVE OF SOURCE, without a preposition, is used with words implying parentage to designate the begettor or bearer.

> Ō nāte deā!   *O goddess-born!*
> Eam servā suā nātam et servam appellāvit.
> *He called her a slave and a daughter of his slave.*

The ABLATIVE OF CAUSE is used without a preposition.

> Amōre vestrī id fēcimus.   *We did it from (because of, for the) love of you.*

Nouns which have a locative case indicate place from which by the ABLATIVE OF PLACE FROM WHICH WITHOUT A PREPOSITION.

> Domō venit.   *He comes from home.*
> Rōmā venimus.   *We are coming from Rome.*

When a noun which is to be compared with another noun is in the nominative or accusative, comparison *(than)* may be expressed by the ABLATIVE OF COMPARISON (without a preposition) instead of a comparative clause with **quam**.

Iuvenem celeriōrem Lūciō numquam vīdī.
I have never seen a young man swifter than Lucius.
(Compare **celeriōrem quam Lūcium**)

Perīculum est maius spē omnium. *The danger is greater than everyone hoped.*
(Compare **maius quam omnēs spērāvērunt**)

The ABLATIVE OF PLACE FROM WHICH is used with the prepositions **ā, ab, ābs, dē, ē,** and **ex** to answer the question *Where from?*

Unde nāvigātis? Ā Graeciā nāvigāmus.
Where are you sailing from? We are sailing from Greece.

When *from* in English implies advantage or disadvantage it is rendered by the Dative of Reference in Latin.

With **paucī, quīdam,** and cardinal numerals, the partitive idea is expressed by the PARTITIVE ABLATIVE OF PLACE FROM WHICH with **dē, ē,** or **ex.**

Paucī dē nāvibus nāvigant. *Few of the ships are sailing.*
Quaedam dē nāvibus nāvigant. *Some of the ships are sailing.*
Decem ex nāvibus nāvigant. *Ten of the ships are sailing.*

With a passive verb the person by whom the action is performed is expressed by the ABLATIVE OF PERSONAL AGENT with the preposition **ā** (**ab, ābs**), since the Romans thought of the action as coming *from* the agent.

Poēta fābulam narrat. *The poet is telling a story.*
Fābula ā poēta narrātur. *A story is being told by the poet.*

INSTRUMENTAL/CIRCUMSTANTIAL ABLATIVE
(THE *WITH* ABLATIVE)

The means by which, or the instrument with which, something is done is expressed by the ABLATIVE OF MEANS, without a preposition. The English translation usually uses *with* or *by*, but it can also use any English preposition which in context implies *by means of.*

Deōrum auxiliō Graecōs superābimus.
With (or By) the help of the gods we shall defeat the Greeks.
Fabulam paucīs verbīs narrābō. *I shall tell the story in a few words.*
Ad Asiam equō volābat. *He was speeding to Asia on a horse.*

Plēnus and other adjectives of fullness and emptiness may be construed with the Ablative of Means. The same is true of verbs of filling and emptying.

Flūmen aquā plēnum est. *The stream is filled with water.*
Pōcula vīnō compleāmus. *Let us fill our cups with wine.*

The idiom **opus est** with an Ablative of Means means *there is need.*

Pecūniā opus est. *Money is needed.*
Mihi pecūniā opus est. *I need money.*

With the Ablative of Means the means or instrument must not be a person; if it is, the Accusative of Secondary Agent is used instead. The deponent verbs **fruor,**

fungor, potior, ūtor, and **vēscor** are construed with an Ablative of Means rather than a direct object.

> Aedibus potīta erat.   *She had gotten possession of the house.*
> Meā pecūniā ūtēbāris.   *You were using my money.*

The same construction is used when the passive of **vehō** means *ride.*

> Equō vehitur.   *She is riding a horse.*

With verbs of buying, selling, and exchanging, the means of payment is expressed by the ABLATIVE OF PRICE.

> Agrum magnā pecūniā vēndidit.   *He sold the land for a large sum of money.*
> Agrum vīllā mūtāvit.   *He exchanged the field for a farmhouse.*

The ABLATIVE OF DEGREE OF DIFFERENCE, without a preposition, is used to answer the question *By how much?* It is used with **post** and **ante** (both as adverbs and as prepositions), and with the comparative and superlative degrees of adjectives.

> Multīs ante annīs vēnit.   *He came many years ago.*
>   (before or after by many years)
> Multīs post annīs vēnit.   *He came many years later.*
> Iūlia est multō altior quam Tullia.   *Julia is much taller than Tullia.*
> Iūlia est multō altissima puellārum.   *Julia is much the tallest of the girls.*

The ABLATIVE OF SPECIFICATION is used, without a preposition, to answer the question *With respect to what?* The preposition *in* is usually used to translate this construction into English. However, when this ablative is used with the adjective **dīgnus** (*worthy*), the English uses the preposition *of.*

> Herculī virtūte cēdō.   *I yield to Hercules in courage.*
> Hecuba nōmine modo rēgīna est.   *Hecuba is queen only in name.*
> Aenēās laude dīgnus est.   *Aeneas is worthy of praise.*

With the Genitive of Measure the dimension is specified by an Ablative of Specification.

> amnis quīnquāgintā pedum lātitūdine   *a river fifty feet wide (broad)*

The ablative of the supine is always an Ablative of Specification.

> Hoc nōn modo foedum vīsū sed etiam audītū est.
> *This is ugly not only to see (with respect to seeing),*
> *but even to hear about (with respect to hearing).*

Quality may be denoted by the ABLATIVE OF DESCRIPTION,

> vir magnā virtūte   *a man of great courage*

The ablative of description is used when in English a noun of quality (e.g. *courage*) is modified by an adjective (e.g. *great*). When the noun is not modified by an adjective (as in *a man of courage*), simply translate **vir fortis,** *a brave man.*

The circumstances under which an action occurs are often expressed by the ABLATIVE ABSOLUTE, a substantive in the ablative modified by a participle. Since **sum** has no present participle, an Ablative Absolute may also consist of two substantives or a substantive and an adjective.

> Hostibus nōs persequentibus cessāre nōn possumus.
> *With the enemy pursuing us we cannot pause.*
> Auxiliō nōbīs allātō servābimur.
> *If help is brought to us we shall be saved.*
> Caesare duce hostīs vincēmus.
> *Caesar being our leader we shall conquer the enemy.*
> Etrūscīs inimīcīs ad montīs nōn perveniētur.
> *Since the Etruscans are unfriendly the mountains will not be reached.*

The ABLATIVE OF ACCOMPANIMENT is used with the preposition **cum.**

> Agricola cum nautīs nāvigat. *The farmer is sailing with the sailors.*
> Cum sociīs hostīs superābimus.
> *With (accompanied by) our allies we shall overcome the enemy.*

The ABLATIVE OF MANNER is used with or without the preposition **cum.** If the noun expressing the manner is not modified by an adjective, **cum** must be used.

> Verba cum cūrā parāvit. *He prepared his words with care.*

If the noun is modified by an adjective, the **cum** may be omitted; if it is used the order must be adjective—**cum**—noun.

> Verba magnā cūrā parāvit.
> Verba magnā cum cūrā parāvit. } *He prepared his words with great care.*

LOCATIVE ABLATIVE (THE *IN-ON-AT* ABLATIVE)

The ABLATIVE OF TIME WHEN, without a preposition, is used to answer the question *When?*

> Quartā hōrā veniet. *He will come at the fourth hour.*

The ABLATIVE OF TIME WITHIN WHICH, without a preposition, is used to answer the question *Within what period?*

> Quattuor hōrīs veniet. *He will come within four hours.*

The ABLATIVE OF PLACE WHERE is used with the prepositions **in, prae, prō,** and **sub** to answer the question *Where?*

> Ubi estis? In Graeciā sumus. *Where are you? We are in Greece.*

The Ablative of Place Where, when the noun is modified by **tōtus,** often omits the proposition.

> Ignēs tōtā urbe vidēbantur. *Fires were seen all over the city.*

The preposition is omitted also in the phrase **terrā marīque,** *by land and sea.* With a verb of motion the Accusative of Place to Which is used instead of the Ablative of Place Where.

> Ad oppidum in Asiam nāvigat. *She is sailing to a town in Asia.*

LOCATIVE

The locative case, which is confined to names of cities, towns, and small islands, and the nouns **animus, domus, foris, humus, mīlitia,** and **rūs,** answers the question *At what place?* Other nouns use the Ablative of Place Where.

Domī est. *She is at home.*   In aedibus est. *She is in the house.*

SYNTAX OF PRONOUNS

AGREEMENT OF PRONOUNS

The substantive for which a pronoun stands is called its antecedent. A pronoun agrees with its antecedent in gender, number, and person. It takes its case, just as a noun does, from its use in the sentence.

Helena ubi eam vīdī laeta vīsa est. *Helen seemed happy when I saw her.*
Ego quoque quī eam vīdī laetus eram. *I who saw her was also happy.*
Si castra posuerint ea capiēmus. *If they pitch a camp we shall take it.*
Hī sunt eī quōrum urbem vīdimus. *These are the people whose city we saw.*

USES OF PRONOUNS

The antecedent of a reflexive pronoun is normally the subject of the clause in which it is found.

Tē laudās. *You praise yourself.*   Sē laudant. *They praise themselves.*

In indirect discourse, however, the reflexive refers to the subject of the verb governing the indirect statement, question, or command.

Virgō eum rogāvit quārē sibi nocēre vellet.
 The girl asked him why he wanted to harm her.
Rēx eīs imperāvit ut ad sē venīrent.
 The king ordered them to come to him.

When different personal pronouns are used together, the first person takes precedence over the second, and the second person over the third, both in word order and in determining the person of the verb.

Ego et tū (*or* vōs) discessimus. *You and I left.*
Tū et is discessistī. *You and he left.*

The demonstrative antecedent of the relative pronoun is often omitted, and must be supplied.

Quī bonum amīcum invēnit fēlīx est.
 He who has found a good friend is fortunate.
Quam amat nōn relinquet. *He will not abandon the one he loves.*
Quod facitis mē nōn iuvat. *That which you are doing does not please me.*

If the relative pronoun introduces a principle clause, rather than a relative clause, it serves as a conjunction + a demonstrative.

Erant ignēs in hostium arce, quōs simul atque vīdī ad amīcōs nūntium mīsī.
 There were fires on the enemy citadel, and as soon as I saw them
 I sent a message to my friends.

■ SYNTAX OF ADJECTIVES

AGREEMENT OF ADJECTIVES

An adjective agrees with the substantive it modifies in gender, number, and case.

> Ager est magnus.   *The field is large.*
> Via est magna.   *The road is large.*
> Perīculum est magnum.   *The danger is great.*
> Agrum magnum spectat.   *She looks at the large field.*
> Viam magnam spectat.   *He looks at the large road.*

If one adjective modifies nouns of different genders, it is masculine plural if the nouns refer to persons, neuter plural if to things.

> Silva et via magnae sunt.   *The forest and the road are large.*
> Silva et ager magna sunt.   *The forest and the field are large.*
> Fēminae et puellae sunt miserae.   *The women and girls are unhappy.*
> Puerī et puellae sunt miserī.   *The boys and girls are unhappy.*

USES OF ADJECTIVES

An adjective which modifies a substantive is either attributive or predicative. An ATTRIBUTIVE ADJECTIVE merely gives additional information about the substantive it modifies; the sentence would still be a sentence without it.

> Agricola miser ambulat in magnam vīllam.
> *The unhappy farmer is walking into the large farmhouse.*

A PREDICATIVE ADJECTIVE (used usually with the verb *to be* or the passive of a factitive verb) makes a statement about the noun it modifies; if it is removed the meaning of the sentence is radically changed.

> Vīlla magna, at agricola miser est.
> *The farmhouse is large, yet the farmer is unhappy.*
> Ille fēlīx vocātur.   *That man is called lucky.*

Without the verb *to be* or a passive factitive verb, word order may make an adjective predicative.

> Puerī laetī domum vēnērunt.   *The happy boys came home.*
> Puerī domum vēnērunt laetī.   *The boys came home happy.*

A SUBSTANTIVE ADJECTIVE has no substantive to modify, but it is used as a noun itself.

> Nōlīte cum malīs ambulāre.   *Do not walk with the wicked.*
> Bonī moriuntur juvenēs.   *The good die young.*
> Bona virī occupāvērunt.   *They seized the man's goods.*

■ SYNTAX OF VERBS

AGREEMENT OF VERBS

A verb must agree with its subject in person and number. If subjects differ in person, the verb will be in the first person if one of the subjects is first person. If there is no first person subject, but there is one in the second person, the verb will be in the second person. If there is more than one subject the verb is plural if the subjects are connected by any form of *and*; but it will agree with the nearest subject when the subjects are connected by *or* or *nor*.

> Ego et tū ambulābāmus.   *You and I were walking.*
> Ego et ille ambulābāmus.   *He and I were walking.*
> Tū et ille ambulābātis.   *You and he were walking.*
> Nauta nāvigat.   *The sailor is sailing.*
> Nautae nāvigant.   *The sailors are sailing.*
> Nautae nāvigāmus.   *We sailors are sailing.*
> Vir et puer nāvigant.   *The man and the boy are sailing.*
> Nec vir nec puerī nāvigant.   *Neither the man nor the boys are sailing.*
> Nec virī nec puer nāvigat.   *Neither the men nor the boy is sailing.*

Two singular subjects may have a singular verb if they are thought of as parts of a single idea, or if the second subject is a correction or clarification of the first.

> Bellum et caedēs dīs nōn placet.
> *The slaughter in war does not please the gods.*
> *War, or rather killing, does not please the gods.*

In the passive of the perfect system, the participial part of the verb agrees with its subject in gender, as well as in number and person.

> Puer vocātus est.   *The boy was (has been) called.*
> Puellae vocātae erant.   *The girls had been called.*
> Vocātus (*or* vocāta) erō.   *I shall have been called.*

IMPERSONAL VERBS   See pp. 203–205.

INDEPENDENT SUBJUNCTIVE

There are five uses of the independent subjunctive: the hortatory and the jussive (p. 57), the optative (p. 67), and the potential and the deliberative (p. 105).

■ SUBORDINATE CLAUSES

Every verb is contained in a clause; clauses are either principal or subordinate.

SUBSTANTIVE CLAUSES

The two chief kinds of substantive clause are the **quod**-substantive (**quod** with the indicative) and the substantive clause of result (**ut** with the subjunctive).

> Hoc tantum mē iuvat quod tū mihi crēdis.
> *Only this comforts me, the fact that you believe me.*
> Huic accēdit ut pecūniā careāmus.
> *Added to this is the fact that we lack money.*

RELATIVE CLAUSES

Relative clauses are clauses which serve as adjectives. They are introduced by relative pronouns, adjectives, and adverbs.

>Stābō ego in eō locō ubi tū stās.
>*I shall stand in that place where you are standing.*

A relative clause may modify an understood antecedent.

Quod facitis nōn mē iuvat.   *That which you are doing does not please me.*
Quī bene vīvit fēlīx erat.   *He who lives well will be happy.*

A relative clause may serve as a principal clause.

>Erant ignēs in hostium arce, quōs simul atque vīdī ad amīcōs nūntium mīsī.
>*There were fires on the enemy citadel, and as soon as I saw them
>I sent a message to my friends.*

An indefinite relative clause (one introduced by a pronoun, adjective, or adverb of the **quisquis** or **quīcumque** pattern), because it has no definite antecedent, often serves as a substantive, rather than an adjective, clause.

Fac quidquid vīs.   *Do whatever you wish.*
Quaecumque virgō adest ille amat.   *He loves whatever girl is present.*

SUBJUNCTIVE RELATIVE CLAUSES   See pp. 225–227 and 237–239.

TEMPORAL CLAUSES

Temporal clauses are adverbial clauses which answer the question *When?* They are introduced by **cum, dōnec, dum, postquam, ubi,** and **ut**. The verb is normally in the indicative; for exceptions, see p. 214.

>Eum vīdistī ubi ex vīllā discēdēbat.
>*You saw him when he was leaving the farmhouse.*
>Eum tum vīdistī cum ex vīllā discēdēbat.
>*You saw him at that time when he was leaving the farmhouse.*
>Eum vīdistī postquam ex vīllā discessit.
>*You saw him after he left the farmhouse.*

CAUSAL CLAUSES

Causal clauses, introduced by **cum** (subjunctive; see p. 213), **quia, quod, quoniam,** and **ut** (indicative), are adverbial clauses answering the question *Why?*

Ut aqua dēest hinc discēdēmus.   *As there is no water, we shall leave this place.*
Hoc fēcit quia eam amāvit.   *He did this because he loved her.*

CONCESSIVE CLAUSES

The two chief concessive clauses are **quamquam** clauses (indicative) and **cum** clauses (subjunctive; see p. 213).

>Quamquam tē amō, tē relinquere oportet.
>*Although (However much) I love you I must still leave you.*

CONDITIONAL CLAUSES   See pp. 153–154, 165–166.

COMPARATIVE CLAUSES

Comparative clauses, introduced by **atque** (**ac**), **quam**, **tamquam**, **sīcut**, and **ut**, express a comparison.

> Simul atque dux advēnit impetum fēcimus.
> *As soon as the leader arrived we charged.*
> Hoc sīc fac ut ego faciō.   *Do this just as I do it.*
> Esne tam laetus quam ego sum?   *Are you as happy as I am?*

Used with the comparative degree of an adjective or adverb, the comparative clause is always introduced by **quam**, and is usually elliptical, consisting only of the word being compared, in the same case as the word with which it is being compared. This is quite different from the English idiom.

> Nūllīus virginis pulchriōris quam illīus meminī.
> *I remember no maiden more beautiful than she.*
> Rēgī multō clāriōrī quam tibi paret.
> *He obeys a king much more famous than you.*
> Vīllam altiōrem quam lātiōrem vīdī.   *I saw a farmhouse higher than <it was> wide.*

A **quam**-comparative clause may contain a superlative and some form of **possum**; but the verb is often omitted.

> Hoc fac quam optimē potes.   *Do this as best you can.*
> Hoc fac quam optimē.   *Do this as well as possible.*

A comparative clause is introduced by **atque** (**ac**) when the comparison is made with **aliud** and its adverbs, with **īdem**, and with the adverbs **aequē**, **pariter**, **similiter** and **dissimiliter**, and **simul**.

> Nihil aliud ac nūmen hoc facere potuit.
> *Nothing other than divine power could have done this.*
> Lingua Graeca aliter atque Latīna scrībitur.
> *The Greek language is written differently from (otherwise than) the Latin.*
> Hoc idem atque illud est.   *This is the same as that.*
> Patriam amō aequē ac tū.   *I love our country as much (equally) as you do.*

CUM CLAUSES   See pp. 213–214.

DUM AND DŌNEC CLAUSES   See pp. 214 and 216.

QUĪN AND QUŌMINUS CLAUSES   See pp. 237–239.

UT-CLAUSES   See pp. 138–139.

There are three indicative **ut**-clauses: **ut**-temporal, **ut**-causal, and **ut**-comparative. The **ut**-comparative often has no verb expressed.

> Domō discessī ut sōl occidēbat.   *I left home as the sun was setting.*
> Ut noctem metuī redīre cōnstituī.
> *As I feared the nighttime I decided to return.*
> Sīc (ita) age ut frāter tuus.   *Behave as your brother does.*

There are three kinds of subjunctive **ut**-clauses: final clauses, consecutive clauses, and indirect questions. There are three final clauses (p. 91): the adverbial clause of purpose (p. 68), the indirect command (pp. 78–79), and the clause after a verb (or other expression) of fearing (pp. 91–92). The indirect command may omit the **ut**. There are two consecutive clauses (p. 117): the adverbial clause of result (pp. 106–107), and the substantive clause of result (pp. 117–118). The substantive clause of result may omit the **ut**. The indirect question introduced by **ut** is a less formal way of reporting a statement (p. 129).

INDIRECT DISCOURSE   See pp. 139–140, 164–166, and 177–178

The three kinds of indirect discourse are the indirect statement (see Infinitive Phrase, below), the indirect command (pp. 78–79), and the indirect question (pp. 128–129). Subordinate clauses in indirect discourse require the subjunctive (pp. 164–166).

SYNTAX OF THE INFINITIVE

The COMPLEMENTARY INFINITIVE is used with modal verbs, i.e. verbs which describe not the action but the mode of the action, and which need an infinitive to complete their meaning. Such verbs are **audeō**, **possum**, and **soleō**.

Hoc facere audeō.	*I dare to do this.*
Hoc facere possum.	*I can do this.*
Hoc facere soleō.	*I usually do this.*

Many verbs which in the active voice govern an Infinitive Phrase need a Complementary Infinitive when they are in the passive.

Abīre iussus sum.   *I was ordered to go away.*
Puerī domum īre prohibēbuntur.   *The boys will be prevented from going home.*
Pulchra esse dīcitur.   *She is said to be beautiful.*
Pulchra esse exīstimātur.   *She is thought to be beautiful.*

Some intransitive verbs, e.g. **cesso**, **dubitō**, and **valeō**, may take a Complementary Infinitive.

Discēdere cessāvit.	*He hesitated to leave.*
Stāre nōn valeō.	*I am not strong enough to stand.*

The SUBJECTIVE or OBJECTIVE INFINITIVE, used as a verbal noun in the neuter nominative or accusative singular, may be the subject or the direct object of a verb.

Amō carmina legere.   *I like reading poems.*
Mihi placet carmina legere.   *It pleases me to read poems.*
Carmina legere mihi grātum est.   *Reading poems is pleasant to me.*
Mē carmina legere docuit.   *He taught me to read poems.*

Verbs of hoping, promising, and swearing are followed by the Infinitive Phrase, not the Objective Infinitive, as they are in English.

Mē hoc factūrum spērō.   *I hope to do this.*
Mē hoc factūrum promittō.   *I promise to do this.*
Mē hoc factūrum iūrō.   *I swear to do this.*

Some verbs, e.g. **cōgō**, **doleō**, **gaudeō**, **iubeō**, **mīror**, **prohibeō**, and **queror**, verbs of wishing, verbs of swearing, hoping, and promising, and verbs of saying, thinking, knowing, perceiving, informing, warning, advising, and persuading may be followed by an INFINITIVE PHRASE, i.e. an infinitive with an accusative subject.

Mē abīre iussit.   *He bade me go away.*
Tē hoc facere cupit.   *She wants you to do this.*
Puerōsne domum īre patientur?   *Will they allow the boys to go home?*
Lūcium esse amīcum meum optō.   *I wish Lucius to be my friend.*
Tē hoc fēcisse gaudet.   *She is glad that you have done this.*
Puerōs domum īre prohibēbunt.   *They will prevent the boys from going home.*
Lūcius sē fore amīcum meum promittit.   *Lucius promises to be my friend.*
Id vērum esse nūntiant.   *They report that this is true.*

The INFINITIVE OF EXCLAMATION, with subject accusative, may be used independently. It is often introduced by an interrogative word.

Mēne hoc audīre!   *That I should hear this!*

The HISTORICAL INFINITIVE, with its subject in the nominative, may be used independently to replace a verb in rapid or emotional narration.

Tunc montēs mōvērī, arborēs cadere, ruere tecta.
Then—mountains moving!—trees falling!—collapse of buildings!

SYNTAX OF PARTICIPLES

The syntax of participles is the same as that of adjectives, except that participles govern all the constructions that their verbs govern: direct object, indirect object, infinitive construction, etc. See p. 6. When the future active participle is used as a predicate adjective with the verb **sum**, the construction is called the active (or first) periphrastic. The passive (or second) periphrastic is the use of the future passive participle in the same construction. See pp. 17–18. The future passive participle, modifying a substantive, may also be used in the gerundive construction. See pp. 39–42.

SYNTAX OF THE GERUND

The gerund is the future passive participle used impersonally, but with an active meaning. See pp. 39–42.

SYNTAX OF THE SUPINE

The accusative of the supine is always the accusative of limit of motion and can be used only with a verb of motion; the ablative is always the ablative of specification with the noun **fās** or an adjective. In Latin these replace some uses of the infinitive in the other Indo-European languages. The accusative supine with the impersonal passive of **eō** provides a substitute for the missing future passive infinitive. In the accusative the supine may have a direct object.

Urbem spectātum vēnit.   *He has come to look at the city.*
Dīcit hostīs victum īrī.   *He says that the enemy will be conquered.*
Quid bonum erit factū?   *What will be a good thing to do?*
Hoc facile est inceptū, difficile confectū.   *This is easy to begin but hard to finish.*

Word Formation

PREFIXES

On Adjectives (assimilated forms in parentheses)

co-, com-, con- — *completely, very*
dī-, dis-, (dif-) — *not*
ē-, ex-, (ef-) — *completely, very*
in-, (im-) — *not*
per- — *completely, very*
prae- — *completely, very*
sub- — *somewhat*

On Verbs (assimilated forms in parentheses)

ā-, ab-, abs-, au- — *from, off, away*
ad-, (ac-, af-, ag-, al-, am-, an-, ap-, ar-, as-,
    at-) — *to, toward, in addition*
ante- — *before, forward*
co-, com-, con- — *together, forcibly*
dē- — *down, completely*
dī, dis-, (dif-) — *apart, away, in another
    direction*
ē-, ex-, (ef-) — *out, completely*
in-, (il-, im-, ir-) — *in, on, into, onto*
inter-, (intel-) — *between, at interval, to pieces*
ob-, obs-, (oc-, of-, om-, op-, os-) — *towards,
    to meet, in opposition to*
per-, (pel-) — *through, completely*
por- — *forth, forward*
prae- (English *pre-*) — *ahead, beforehand*
prō- — *forth, forward*
re-, red-, (ret-) — *back, again*
sē- — *apart, to another place*
sub-, (suc-, suf-, sug-, sum-, sup-, sur-, sus-) —
    *under, secretly, up from under, to the aid
    of*
trā-, trāns- — *across, over, through and through*

SUFFIXES

Making nouns from nouns

Denoting the office or function of, or a collected
body of:
   -ātus, -ātūs, m. — *-ate*
Denoting the quality of a noun (English *-ness, -
dom, -hood, -ship):*
   -mōnia, -mōniae, f. — *-mony*
   -mōnium, -mōnī, n. — *-mony*
   -tās, -tātis, f. — *-ty*
   -tūs, -tūtis, f. — *-ty*
Denoting a thing connected with something:
   -āria, -āriae, f.
Denoting the place where something is found,
made, or sold:
   -āria, -āriae, f.
   -ārium, -ārī, n. — *-arium*
Denoting the person who deals with something:
   -ārius, -ārī, m. — *-ary*
Meaning the place where something grows:
   -ētum, -ētī, n. — *-et, -etum*
Meaning the act or practice of "*-izing*":
   -isma, -ismatis, n. — *ism*
Meaning one who (*–izes*):
   -ista, istae, m. — *-ist*
Diminutive, meaning small or little:
   -culus, -culī, m. — *-cle, -cule, -culus*
   -cula, -culae, f. — *-cle, -cule*
   -culum, -culī, n. — *-cle, -cule*
   -ellus, -ellī, m. — *-el, -le*
   -ella, -ellae, f. — *-elle, -le*
   -ellum, -ellī, n. — *-el, -le*
   -ōlus, -ōlī, m. — *-ole, -olus*
   -ōla, -ōlae, f. — *-ole*
   -ōlum, -ōlī, n. — *-ole*
   -ulus, -ulī, m. — *-le, -ule*

(Suffixes continued)
-ula, -ulae, f. — *-le*, *-ule*
-ulum, -ulī, n. — *-le*, *-ule*
Meaning the bearer of:
-fer, -ferī, m. — *-fer*
Denoting something associated with the noun:
-āticum, -āticī, n. — *-age*

Making adjectives from nouns:

Meaning provided with, having:
-ātus, -āta, -ātum — *-ate*
-tus, -ta, -tum — *-t*, *-te*
Meaning full of:
-idus, -ida, -idum — *-id*
-lēns, -lentis — *-lent*
-lentus, -lenta, -lentum — *-lent*
-ōsus, -ōsa, -ōsum — *-ose*, *-ous*
Meaning belonging to:
-ānus, -āna, -ānum — *-an*, *-ane*
-ārius, -āria, -ārium — *-ary*
-āticus, -ātica, -āticum — *-atic*
-ēnus, -ēna, -ēnum — *-ene*
-ernus, -erna, -ernum — *-ern*, *-erne*, *-ern⟨al⟩*
-icus, -ica, -icum — *-ic*
-īnus, -īna, -īnum — *-in*, *-ine*
-nus, -na, -num — *-n*, *-n⟨al⟩*, *-ne*
-ter, -tris, -tre — *-ter*, *-tri⟨an⟩*
-ticus, -tica, -ticum — *-tic*
-timus, -tima, -timum — *-time*
-tris, -tre — *-ter*, *-tri⟨an⟩*
-urnus, -urna, -urnum — *-urn*, *-urne*, *-urn⟨al⟩*
Meaning connected with:
-āticus, -ātica, -āticum — *-atic*
-icus, -ica, -icum — *-ic*
-ticus, -tica, -ticum — *-tic*
Meaning pertaining to:
-ālis, -āle — *-al*, *-ale*
-āris, -āre — *-ar*, *-ary*
-īlis, -īle — *-il*, *-ile*
Meaning bearing:
-fer, -fera, -ferum — *-ferous*
-ferus, -fera, -ferum — *-ferous*
Meaning making:
-ficus, -fica, -ficum — *-fic*
Meaning made of:
-āceus, -ācea, -āceum — *-aceous*

-eus, -ea, -eum — *-eous*
-icius, -icia, -icium — *-icious*
Meaning coming from:
-āneus, -ānea, -āneum — *-aneous*, *-ane⟨an⟩*
-ānus, -āna, -ānum — *-an*, *-ane*
-ēnus, -ēna, -ēnum — *-ene*
-eus, -ea, -eum — *-eous*
-īnus, -īna, -īnum — *-in*, *-ine*
-ius, -ia. -ium — *-ious*
-nus, -na, -num — *-n*, *-ne*

Making verbs from nouns:

Meaning to be or perform whatever the noun means:
-iō, -īre, -īvī, -ītum (on i- stems) — _____, *-ite*
-ō, -āre, -āvī, -ātum — _____, *-ate*
-uō, -uere, -uī, -ūtum (on 4th-declension nouns) — _____, *-ute*
Meaning to be bearing, or the bearer of:
-ferō, -ferāre, -ferāvī, -ferātum — *-ferate*
Meaning to make:
-ficō, -ficāre, -ficāvī, -ficātum — *-ficate*, *-fice*, *-fy*
Meaning to "–ize":
-izō, -izāre, -izāvī, -izātum — *-ize*

On Adjectives: Making nouns from adjectives

Denoting the quality of an adjective (English *-ness*, *-dom*, *-hood*):
-ia, -iae, f. — *-y*
-iēs, -iēī, f. — *-y*
-mōnia, -mōniae, f. — *-mony*
-mōnium, -mōnī, n. — *-mony*
-tās, -tātis, f. — *-ty*
-tia, -tiae, f. — *-ce*, *-cy*, *-ty*
-tiēs, -tiēī, f. — *-ty*
-tūdō, -tūdinis, f. — *-tude*
-tūs, -tūtis, f.
Denoting something associated with the adjective:
-āticum, -āticī, n. — *-age*
Meaning the act or practice of "–izing":
-isma, -ismatis, n. — *-ism*

Meaning one who "–izes":
   -ista, -istae, m. — *-ist*

Making adjectives from adjectives:

Meaning making:
   -ficus, -fica, -ficum — *-fic*
Meaning connected with:
   -āticus, -ātica, -āticum — *-atic*
   -icus, -ica, -icum — *-ic*
   -ticus, -tica, -ticum — *-tic*
Diminutive, meaning small or slightly:
   -culus, -cula, -culum
   -ellus, -ella, -ellum
   -ōlus, -ōla, -ōlum
   -ulus, -ula, -ulum

Making verbs from adjectives:

Meaning to be or perform whatever the adjective means:
   -ō, -āre, -āvī, -ātum — *-ate*
   iō, -īre, -īvī, -ītum (on i-stems) — ____, *-ite*
Meaning to make:
   -ficō, -ficāre, -ficāvī, -ficātum — *-ficate, -fice, -fy*
Meaning to "–ize":
   -izō, -izāre, -izāvī, -izātum — *-ize*

On verbs: Making nouns from verbs

Denoting the action of the verb:
   -āticum, -āticī, n. — *-age*
   -iō, -iōnis, f.* — *-ion*
   -ium, -ī, n.* — *-y*
   -or, -ōris, m. — *-or*
   -siō, -siōnis, f. — *-sion*
   -sūra, -sūrae, f. — *-sure*
   -sus, -sūs, m.* — *-se*
   -tiō, -tiōnis, f. — *-tion*
   -tūra, -tūrae, f. — *-ture*
   -tus, -tūs, m.* — *-t, -te*
Denoting the means or instrument of the action:
   -āticum, -āticī, n. — *-age*
   -brum, -brī, n. — ____
   -bula, -bulae, f. — *-ble, -bule*
   -bulum, -bulī, n. — *-ble, -bule*

   -crum, -crī, n. — *-cher, -cre*
   -culum, -culī, n. — *-cle, -cule*
   -men, -minis, n. — *-me, -men, -ment*
   -mentum, -mentī, n. — *-ment*
   -mōnia, -mōniae, f. — *-mony*
   -mōnium, -mōnī, n. — *-mony*
   -trum, -trī, n. — *-ter, -trum*
   -ula, -ulae, f. — *-le, -ule*
Denoting the result of the action:
   -āticum, -āticī, n. — *-age*
   -men, -minis, n. — *-me, -men, -ment*
   -mentum, -mentī, n. — *-ment*
Denoting the abstract quality of the verb:
   -or, -ōris, m. — *-or*
   -sus, -sūs, m.* — *-se*
   -tus, -tūs, m.* — *-t, -te*
Naming the doer or agent of the action:
   -sor, -sōris, m. — *-sor*
   -tor, -tōris, m. — *-tor*
   -trīx, -trīcis, f. — *-tress, -trix*
Denoting the place where the action is performed:
   -tōrium, -tōrī, n. — *-torium, -tory*

Making adjectives from verbs:

Meaning making:
   -ficus, -fica, -ficum — *-fic*
Meaning connected with the action:
   -āticus, -ātica, -āticum — *-atic*
   -icus, -ica, -icum — *-ic*
   -ticus, -tica, -ticum — *-tic*
Meaning pertaining to the action:
   -sōrius, -sōria, -sōrium — *-sory*
   -tōrius, -tōria, -tōrium — *-tory*
Meaning having an aggressive tendency to ____:
   -āx, -ācis — *-acious*
Meaning performing or able to perform the action of the verb:
   -bundus, -bunda, -bundum — *-bund*
   -cundus, -cunda, -cundum — *-cund*
   -ēns, -entis — *-ent*
   -idus, -ida, -idum — *-id*

---

* These may also become concrete in their meaning.

-īvus, -īva, -īvum — *-ive*
-ndus, -nda, -ndum — *-nd*
-ns, -ntis — *-nt*
-uus, -ua, -uum — *-uous*

Meaning receiving or able the action of the verb:

    -bilis, -bile — *-bile, -ble*
    -ilis, -ile — *-ile, -le*
    -īvus, īva, -ivum — *-ive*
    -tilis, -tile — *-tile, -tle*
    -uus, -ua, -uum — *-uous*

Making verbs from verbs:

Meaning to make:

    -ficō, -ficāre, -ficāvī, -ficātum — *-ficate, -fice, -fy*

Inceptive, meaning to begin, become, be in the process of:

    -scō, -scere, ____, ____ — *-ish, -sce*

Iterative, meaning to do continually or repeatedly:

    -itō, -itāre, -itāvī, -itātum — *-itate*
    -sō, -sāre, -sāvī, -sātum — *-sate, -se*
    -tō, -tāre, -tāvī, -tātum — *-tate*

Diminutive, meaning to do feebly or slightly:

    -illō, -iiāre, -illāvī, -illātum — *-illate*

Meditative, meaning to do eagerly:

    -essō, -essere, -essīvī, -essītum

Desiderative, meaning to desire to do:

    -suriō, -surīre, -surīvī, -surītum
    -turiō, -turīre, -turīvī, -turītum

GLOSSARY OF PROPER NAMES

A

Aduatucī, -ōrum, m. *the Aduatuci* (a Belgic tribe)

Aedīlēs, Aedīlum, m. *Aediles, Ediles* (magistrates originally in charge of the upkeep of the temples, who later assumed responsibility for public buildings, streets, and markets

Aeduus, -a, -um *Aeduan*

Aegyptī, -ōrum, m. *the Egyptians*

Aegyptus, -ī, f. *Egypt*

Aemilius, -ī, m. *Aemilius* (a Decurion of the Gallic cavalry)

Aequī, -ōrum, m. *the Aequians* (a tribe east of Rome)

Āfrica, -ae, f. *[North] Africa*

Āfricānus, -a, -um *African, Africanus* (as a Roman **cognōmen,** granted to Scipio, the conquerer of Hannibal)

Āfricus, -a, -um *African*

Āfricus, -ī, m. *Africus* (the southwest wind)

Agrippa, -ae, m. *Agrippa* (a Roman **cognōmen**)

Albānus, -a, -um *Alban, of Alba*

Alexander, Alexandrī, m. *Alexander* (a Greek name); Alexander the Great

Alexandrēus, -a, -um *of Alexander [the Great]*

Algidus, -ī, m. *Algidus* (a mountain in Latium)

Allia, -ae, f. *the Allia* (a tributary of the Tiber)

Allobrogēs, -um, m. (acc. **Allobrogās**) *the Allobrogians* (a Gallic people)

Alpēs, Alpium, f. *Alps*

Alpīnus, -a, -um *Alpine*

Ambarrī, -ōrum, m. *the Ambarri* (a tribe near the Saone River)

Ambiānī, -ōrum, m. *the Ambiani* (a small state in Belgium)

Ambiorīx, -īgis, m. *Ambiorix* (chief of the Eburones)

Aniō, Aniēnis, m. *the Anio* (a tributary of the Tiber)

Antiochus, -ī, m. *Antiochus* (name of 13 kings of Syria)

Antōnius, -a, -um *Antony, Antonius, Antonia, Antonian, of the Antonian family* (a Roman **nōmen gentīle;** Marc Antony was the Triumvir)

Ap. abbreviation of *Appius*

Apollō, -inis, m. *Apollo*

Apollōnius, -ī, m. *Apollonius* (a Greek name)

Appius, -ī, m. *Appius* (a Roman **praenōmen**)

Apr. = *Aprīlis*

Aprīlis, -e *April*

Āpūlia, -ae, f. *Apulia* (a part of Italy just northwest of the "heel")

Aquae Sextiae, Aquārum Sextiārum, f. *Aquae Sextiae* (a small town of Gaul, north of what is now Marseilles)

Aquileia, -ae, f. *Aquileia* (a city at the head of the Adriatic)

Aquītānia, -ae, f. *Aquitania* (one of the divisions of Gaul)

Arar, -is, (acc., **-im**) *the Arar* (now the Saone)

Argos (only nom. and acc.), n. *Argos* (in the Peloponnesus)

Asia, -ae, f. *Asia; Asia Minor*

Asina, -ae, m. *Asina* (from **asina, -ae,** f., "ass," a Roman **cognōmen** given to Cornelius Asina, Consul in 260 B.C.)

Athēnae, -ārum, f. *Athens*

Athēniēnsis, -e *Athenian, of Athens*

Atīlius, -a, -um *Atilius, Atilia, Atilian, of the Atilian family* (a Roman **nōmen gentīle**)

Atlās, -antis, m. *Atlas*

Atrebās, -ātis, m. *an Atrebatian* (a Belgic tribe)

Augur, Auguris, m. or f. *Augur* (an official soothsayer)

Aurunculeius, -ī, m. *Aurunculeius, Aurunculeia, Aurunculeian* (a Roman **nōmen gentīle;** L. Aurunculeius Cotta was a lieutenant of Caesar)

Auster, Austrī, m. *Auster* (the South Wind)

Avernus, -a, -um *Avernian* (belonging to Lake Avernus, in the Lower World)

Axona, -ae, f. *the Aisne* (a river)

B

Babylōnius, -a, -um *Babylonian*

Baculus, -ī, m. *Baculus* (a Roman **cognōmen**; P. Sextius Baculus was one of Caesar's centurions)

Baleāris, -e *Balearic, of the Balearic Islands*

Balventius, -a, um *Balventius, Balventia* (a Roman **nōmen gentīle**; T. Balventius was a centurion)

Belgae, -ārum, m. *the Belgians*

Belgium, -ī, n. *Belgium*

Bellovacī, -ōrum, m. *the Bellovaci* (a Belgic tribe)

Bibracte, -is, m. *Bibracte* (capital of the Aedui)

Bibrax, -actis, n. *Bibrax* (a town of the Remi)

Bibulus, -a, -um *Bibulus* ("Thirsty", a Roman **cognōmen**; L. Calpurnius Bibulus was Caesar's colleague in his consulship)

Bīthȳnia, -ae, f. *Bithynia* (a country of Asia Minor)

Boduognātus, -ī, m. *Boduognatus* (a leader of the Nervii)

Boiī, -ōrum, m. *the Boii*

Bona Dea, Bonae Deae, f. *Bona Dea, Good Goddess* (a euphemistic name for Fauna, a mysterious goddess whose rituals were performed by women only)

Boōtēs, -ae, m. *Bootes,* the Ploughman

Brennus, -ī, m. *Brennus, Bran* (a Gallic name or title)

Britannī, -ōrum, m. *the Britons*

Britannia, -ae, f. *Britain*

Britannicus, -a, -um *British*

C

C. abbreviation of Gaius

Caecus, -a, -um *Caecus, the Blind* (a Roman **cognōmen**)

Caere, n. (indeclinable) *Caere* (an old town of the Etruscans)

Caesar, Caesaris, m. *Caesar* (a Roman **cognōmen**)

Caletī, -ōrum, also **Caletēs, -um, m.** *the Caletes* (a tribe near the mouth of the Seine)

Calpurnius, -a, -um *Calpurnius, Calpurnia, Calpurnian, of the Calpurnian family* (a Roman **nōmen gentīle**; a Calpurnia was a wife of Julius Caesar)

Calymnē, -ēs, f. *Calymne* (an island in the Aegean)

Camillus, -ī, m. *Camillus* (a Roman **cognōmen**)

Campānia, -ae, f. *Campania* (a district in southern Italy)

Campānus, -a, -um *Campanian, of Campania*

Campus Mārtius, Campī Mārtiī, m. *Campus Martius, Field of Mars* (a plain in Rome along the Tiber, where the elections were held)

Cannae, -ārum, f. *Cannae* (a small town in Apulia, where Hannibal defeated the Romans in 216 B.C.)

Capitōlium, -ī, n. *Capitolium* (one of the two peaks of the Capitoline Hill, the other being the Arx; also, the temple of Jupiter, Juno, and Minerva on the hill)

Carnutēs, -um, m. *the Carnutes* (a people in central Gaul)

Carthāginiēnsis, -e *Carthaginian*

Carthāgō, Carthāginis, f. *Carthage*

Cassius, -a, -um *Cassius, Cassia, Cassian, of the Cassian family* (a Roman **nōmen gentīle**; C. Cassius Longinus was one of the conspirators against Caesar; Lucius Cassius Longinus was Consul in 107 B.C.)

Casticus, -ī, m. *Casticus* (a prominent Sequanian)

Catamantaloedis, -is, m. *Catamantaloedis* (a leader of the Sequani)

Catō, Catōnis, m. *Cato* (a Roman **cognōmen**; M. Porcius Cato, the Censor; M. Porcius Cato Uticensis, grandson of Cato the Censor)

Caturīgēs, -um, m. *the Caturiges*

Cebenna, -ae, f. *the Cebenna range* (mountains in Gaul, now the Cevennes)

Celtae, -ārum, m. *the Celts* (inhabitants of central Gaul)

Cēnsor, Cēnsōris, m. *Censor* (a magistrate charged with assigning citizens to their proper financial classes and with the policing of morals)

Cerēs, -eris, f. *Ceres* (goddess of agriculture)

Ceutronēs, -um, m. *the Ceutrones* (a people in the eastern part of the Province, or a Belgic people)

Chaos, (abl., **Chaō**), n. *Chaos, the Lower World; Darkness*

Charōn, Charontis, m. *Charon*

Cicerō, -ōnis, m. *Cicero* (a Roman **cognōmen**; M. Tullius Cicero was the orator and statesman; Q. Tullius Cicero, brother of the orator, was one of Caesar's generals)

Cilicia, -ae, f. *Cilicia* (a country of southern Asia Minor)

Cimbrī, -ōrum, m. *the Cimbrians* (a German tribe)

Cincinnātus, -a, -um *Cincinnatus* ("Curly", a Roman **cognōmen**; L. Quinctius Cincinnatus was called from his plough to be dictator at Rome)

Cineās, Cineae, m. *Cineas* (a Greek name; an envoy of Pyrrhus)

Cinna, -ae, m. *Cinna* (a Roman **cognōmen**; Cornelius Cinna was an associate of Marius)

Cirta, -ae, f. *Cirta* (capital of the Massaesylian Nomads)

Cisalpīnus, -a, -um *Cisalpine* (i.e. on this side of the Alps)

Claudius, -a, -um *Claudius, Claudia, Claudian, of the Claudian family* (a Roman **nōmen gentīle**; Appius Claudius, one of the decemvirs)

Cloācīnus, -a, -um *of the Cloaca* noun, **Cloācīna, -ae,** f., **Cloacina,** the goddess of the stream, who had a small shrine in the Forum to repay her for the burial of her stream)

Clōdius, -a, -um *Clodius, Clodia, Clodian, of the Clodian family* (a Roman **nōmen gentīle**)

Cn. abbreviation of *Gnaeus*

Cocles, -itis, m. *Cocles* (a Roman **cognōmen**; Horatius Cocles defended the Pons Sublicius)

Cominus, -ī, m. *Cominus* (a Roman cognōmen)

Comitium, -ī. n. *the Comitium* (a place in the Forum where assemblies were held)

Commius, -ī, m. *Commius* (as Atrebatian, a friend of Caesar)

Cōnsidius, -a, -um *Considius, Considia, Considian* (a Roman **nōmen gentīle**; P. Considius was an officer in Caesar's army)

Cōnsul, Cōnsulis, m. *Consul* (one of the two chief magistrates at Rome)

Corinthus, -ī, f. *Corinth* (a city in Greece)

Corinthius, -a, -um *of Corinth, Corinthian*

Coriolānus, -a, -um *of Corioli, Coriolanus* (as a Roman **cognōmen**)

Coriolī, -ōrum, m. *Corioli* (a town of the Volsci)

Cornēlius, -a, -um *Cornelius, Cornelia, Cornelian, of the Cornelian family* (a Roman **nōmen gentīle**)

Cotta, -ae, m. *Cotta* (a Roman cognōmen)

Crassus, -a, -um *Crassus* ("Solid", a Roman **cognōmen**; M. Licinius Crassus was the triumvir with Caesar and Pompey; P. Licinius Crassus, son of the triumvir, was an officer of Caesar in Gaul; M. Licinius Crassus, son of the triumvir, was a Quaestor in Caesar's army in Gaul)

Crāstinus, -ī, m. *Crastinus* ("Tomorrow", a Roman **cognōmen**; a centurion in Caesar's army)

Crēta, -ae, f. *Crete*

Cūria, -ae, f. *Curia, Senate-House*

Cūrius, -a, -um *Curius, Curia, Curian, of the Curian family* (a Roman **nōmen gentīle**)

Curtius, -a, -um *Curtius, Curtia, Curtian, of the Curtian family* (a Roman **nōmen gentīle**) **Lacus Curtius** (a sacred place in the Forum)

D

D., *abbreviation for* **Decimus**

Daedalus, -ī, m. *Daedalus*

Dardanius, -a, -um *Dardanian (Trojan), of Dardanus* (a son of Jupiter, one of the founders of the Trojan race)

Dea Bona see **Bona Dea**

December, -bris, -bre *December*

Decemvir, Decemvirī, m. *Decemvir* (member of a Board of Ten)

Decimus, -ī, m. *Decimus* (a Roman praenōmen)

Decius, -a, um *Decius, Decia, Decian* (a Roman **nōmen gentīle**)

Dēlos, -ī, f. *Delos* (an island in the Aegean Sea)

Delphī, -ōrum, m. *Delphi* (famed for its oracle of Apollo)

Delphicus, -a, -um *Delphic, of Delphi*

Dentātus, -a, -um *Dentatus* ("Toothy", a Roman cognōmen)

Dī Mānēs, Deum Mānium, m. *the Manes* (mysterious gods of the Lower World or of the dead; tombstones are dedicated to the Manes—always plural—of the dead person)

Diālis see **Flāmen Diālis**

Dictātor, Dictātōris, m. *Dictator* (a official with power to override the constitution, appointed for a six-month term)

Dictātūra, -ae. f. *Dictatorship*

Dīdō, Dīdōnis, f. *Dido* (nickname of Elissa)

Diēs Sōlis, Diēs Lūnae, Diēs Mārtis, Diēs Mercūriī, Diēs Iōvis, Diēs Veneris Diēs Sāturnī *Sunday, Monday, Tuesday, Wednesday, Thursday, Friday, Saturday.*

Dīs, Dītis, m. *Dis* (also called Pluto, the god of the Lower World)

Dolabella, -ae, m. *Dolabella* (a Roman cognōmen)

Domitius, -a, um *Domitius, Domitia, Domitian* (a

Roman **nōmen gentīle**; one of Caesar's officers was a Domitius)

Druidēs, -um, m. *Druids*

Duīlius, -a, -um *Duilius, Duilia, Duilian, of the Duilian family* (a Roman **nōmen gentīle**; C. Duilius was a Roman commander)

Dumnorīx, -īgis, m. *Dumnorix* (an Aeduan noble)

E

Eburōnēs, -um, m. the *Eburones* (a tribe in Belgium)

Elissa, -ae, f. *Elissa, Eliza* (founder and queen of Carthage)

Ēpīrus, -ī, f. *Epirus* (a country of Greece, part of modern Albania)

Eporēdorīx, -īgis, m. *Eporedorix* (a prominent Aeduan)

Etrūria, -ae, f. *Etruria* (a country northwest of Rome)

Etrūscus, -a. -um *Etruscan*

Eucliō, -ōnis, m. *Euclio*

Eumenides, -um, f. the *Eumenides, the Furies*

Eurōpa, -ae, f. *Europe*

Eurus, -ī, m. *Eurus* (the east wind)

Eurydicē, -ēs, f. *Eurydice* (wife of Orpheus)

F

Fābricius, -a, -um *Fabricius, Fabricia, Fabrician, of the Fabrician family* (a Roman **nōmen gentīle**; C. Fabricius Luscinus fought against Pyrrhus)

Faleriī, -ōrum, m. *Falerii* (a city of the Etruscans, north of Rome)

Falīscus, -a, -um *Faliscan, of Falerii*

Februārius, -a, -um *February*

Falīscus, -a, -um *Faliscan, of Falerii*

Flāmen Diālis, Flāminis Diālis, m. the *Flamen Dialis* (a priest of Jupiter)

Fortūna, -ae, f. *Fortuna, Fortune (goddess of Fortune)*

Forum, -ī, n. *Forum*

Furia, -ae, f. *a Fury (the Furies were avenging goddesses who drove people to madness)*

G

Gādēs, -ium, f. *Gades* (a town in the southwest of Spain, now Cadiz)

Gāius, -ī, m. *Gaius* (a Roman **praenōmen**); *abbreviated C.*

Galba, -ae, m. *Galba* (a Roman **cognōmen**)

Gallia, -ae, f. *Gaul*

Gallia Citerior, Galliae Citeriōris, f. *Hither Gaul* (a Roman province, now north Italy)

Gallicus, -a, -um *Gallic, of Gaul*

Gallus, -a, um *Gallic, of Gaul;* (as substantive) *a Gaul*

Garumna, -ae, f. *Garumna* (the Garonne River, in southern France)

Geidumnī, -ōrum, m. the *Geidumni* (a Belgic people near the Nervii)

Geminus, -a, -um *Geminus* ("Twin", a Roman **cognōmen**)

Genāva, -ae, f. *Geneva*

Germānia, -ae, f. *Germany*

Germānus, -a, -um *German*

Gnaeus, -ī, m. *Gnaeus* (a Roman praenōmen); abbreviated Cn.

Graecia, -ae, f. *Greece.* **Magna Graecia,** southern Italy

Graecus, -a, -um *Greek*

Graī, -ōrum, m. *The Greeks*

Graiocelī, -ōrum, m. the *Graioceli* (a Gallic people in the Alps)

Grudiī, -ōrum, m. the *Grudii* (a Belgic people)

H

Hamilcar, Hamilcaris, m. *Hamilcar* (Carthaginian general in the 1st Punic War, father of Hannibal)

Hannibal, Hannibalis, m. *Hannibal* (Carthaginian general in the 2nd Punic War)

Haruspex, Haruspicis, m. *Haruspex* (Etruscan soothsayer)

Hasdrubal, -alis, m. *Hasdrubal* (a brother of Hannibal; another Hasdrubal was a general in command at the siege of New Carthage)

Helicē, -es, f. *Helice* (the constellation of the Great Bear)

Helvētius, -a, -um *Helvetian*

Herculēs, Herculis, m. *Hercules, Heracles* (a hero of great strength)

Hercynius, -a, -um *Hercynian* (of a forest in southern Germany)

Hibernia, -ae, f. *Hibernia* (Ireland)

Hispānia, -ae, f. *Hispania, Spain* (including what is now Portugal)

Hispānia Ulterior, Hispāniae Ulteriōris, f. *Outer Spain* (a Roman province in southern and western Spain)

Hispānicus, -a, -um *Spanish*

Hispāniēnsis, -e *Spanish*

Horātius, -a, um *Horatius, Horatia, Horatian* (a Roman **nōmen gentīle**; Horatius Cocles defended the bridge against the Etruscans; Q. Horatius Flaccus is the Latin name of the poet Horace; the Horatii triplets fought against the Curiatii; M. Horatius Pulvillus was Consul in 509 B.C.)

Hostīlius, -a, -um *Hostilian, of [Tullus] Hostilius* (Tullus Hostilius was the third king of Rome)

I

Iāniculum, -ī, n. *the Janiculum* (a hill in Rome)

Iānuārius, -a, -um *January*

Ibērus, -ī, m. *Iber, Iberus* (a river of Spain, now called Ebro)

Īcarus, -ī, m. *Icarus* (son of Daedalus)

Īcilius, -a, -um *Icilius, Icilia, Icilian, of the Icilian family* (a Roman **nōmen gentīle**)

Īd., abbreviation for *Īdūs*

Īdūs, Īduum, f. *the Ides* (the fifteenth day or the middle of the month)

Illyricum, -ī, n. *Illyricum* (on the east coast of the Adriatic)

Imperiōsus, -a, -um *Imperiosus* ("Tyrannical", a Roman cognōmen)

Īnsubrēs, -ium, m. *the Insubrians* (Gauls dwelling south of the Alps)

Iō! interj. *hurrah!*

Isauricus, -a, -um *Isauricus* (a **cognōmen** assumed by P. Servilius Vatia, the conqueror of the Isaurians in Cilicia)

Ītalia, -ae, f. *Italy*

Ītalicus, -a, -um *of Italy, Italian*

Italus, -a, -um *of Italy, Italian*

Iūlius, -a, -um *Julius, Julia, Julian, of the Julian family* (a Rōman **nomen gentīle**; Julia, daughter of Caesar and wife of Pompey)

Iūlus, -ī, m. *Iulus* (son of Aeneas)

Iūnius, -a, -um *June*

Iūnō, -ōnis, f. *Juno, wife of Jupiter*

Iūnōnius, -a, -um *sacred to Juno; of Juno*

Iuppiter, Iovis, m. *Jupiter, Jove (chief of the gods)*

Iūra, -ae, f. *Jura mountains* (in eastern France)

K

Kal., Kalendae

Kalendae, -ārum, f. *Calends* (the first day of the month)

L

L. abbreviation of *Lūcius*

Labiēnus, -a, um *Labienus, Labiena, Labienan* (a Roman **nōmen gentīle**; Titus Labienus was one of Caesar's ablest officers)

Lacedaemonius, -a, -um *Lacedaemonian, Laconian, Spartan*

Lacōnia, -ae, f. *Laconia*

Lacus Curtius, Lacūs Curtī, m. *Lacus Curtius* (the name of a sacred area in the Forum)

Larēs, -um, m. *the Lares* (household gods, deified spirits of the place)

Latīnus, -a, -um *of Latium, Latin*

Latium, -ī, n. *Latium* (the region around Rome)

Latobrīgī, -ōrum, m. *the Latobrigi* (a people near the Helvetii)

Lebinthus, -ī, f. *Lebinthos* (an island in the Aegean)

Lemannus, -ī, m. *[Lake Leman] Lake Geneva*

Lēthaea, -ae, f. *Lethea (wife of Olenos)*

Lēthē, -ēs, f. *[River] Lethe (in the underworld)*

Levācī, -ōrum, m. *the Levaci (a Belgic tribe)*

Licinius, -a, -um *Licinius, Licinia, Licinian, of the Licinian family* (a Roman **nōmen gentīle**; P. Licinius Crassus was Consul in 171 B.C.)

Lictor, Lictōris, m. *a Lictor* (one of the fasces-bearing attendants on a king or curule magistrat)

Liger, -eris, m. *the Liger* (in central Gaul, now the Loire river)

Lilybaeum, -ī, n. *Lilybaeum* (a town on the westernmost promontory of Sicily)

Lingones, -um [acc., ēs or as], m. *the Lingones* (a Gallic state west of the Sequani)

Līvius, -ī, m. *Livius, Livy, Livia, Livian* (a Roman nōmen gentīle; T. Livy was a Roman historian)

Lūca, -ae, f. *Luca* (a town of Etruria, now Lucca)

Lūcānius, -ī, m. *Lucanius* (a Roman cognōmen; Q. Lucanius was a Centurion)

Lūcius, -ī, m. *Lucius* (a Roman praenōmen); abbreviated L.

Lugotorīx, -īgis, m. *Lugotorix* (a British chief)

M

M. abbreviation of *Mārcus*

Macedonia, -ae, f. *Macedonia* (a country north of Greece)

Macedonicus, -a, -um *Macedonian*

Magnēsia, -ae, f. *Magnesia* (a city in Asia Minor)

Māmertīnus, -a, -um *Mamertine, of Mars*

Mānlius, -a, -um *Manlius, Manlia, Manlian, of the Manlian family* (a Roman nōmen gentīle; T. Manlius Torquatus slew a Gallic champion in single combat; Cn. Manlius Volso was Consul in 189 B.C.)

Mārcius, -a, -um *Marcius, Marcia, Marcian, of the Marcian family* (a Roman nōmen gentīle)

Mārcus, -ī, m. *Marcus* (a Roman praenōmen)

Marius, -a, -um *Marius, Maria, Marian, of the Marian family* (a Roman nōmen gentīle; L. Marius defeated Jugurtha and later opposed Sulla)

Mārs, Mārtis, m. *Mars* (god of the growing grain and of war)

Masinissa, -ae, m. *Masinissa* (a king of the Massylian Nomads)

Massaesȳlus, -a, -um *Massaesylian* (of western Numidia)

Massȳlus, -a, -um *Massylian* (of eastern Numidia)

Matrona, -ae, f. *the Matrona* (now the Marne river)

Maurētania, -ae. f. *Mauretania* (in north Africa, modern Morocco)

Medūsaeus, -a, -um *Medusa-like*

Megadōrus, -ī, m. *Megadorus*

Menapiī, -ōrum, m. *the Menapii* (a Belgic tribe)

Menēnius, -a, -um *Menenius, Menenia, Menenian, of the Menenian family* (a Roman nōmen gentīle)

Mercēdōnius, -a, -um *Mercedonius* (a month inserted occasionally, before the Julian calendar, when the 355-day year got too much out of synchronization with the seasons)

Mercurius, -i, m. *Mercury*

Messāna, -ae, f. *Messana, Messene* (modern Messina, a town of Sicily)

Messēnius, -a, -um *Messenian, of Messene* (Messana)

Mīlētus, -ī, f. *Miletus* (a city in Asia Minor)

Minerva, -ae, f. *Minerva* (daughter of Jupiter, goddess of wisdom, war-strategy and arts and crafts, especially weaving)

Mīnōs, -ōis, m. *Minos* (king of Crete; judge in the Lower World)

Mīthridātēs, Mīthridātis, m. *Mithridates VI* (king of Pontus, 135–63)

Molō, Molōnis, m. *Molo* (a Greek rhetorician, teacher of Caesar and Cicero)

Morinī, -ōrum, m. *the Morini* (a Belgic tribe)

Mysia, -ae, f. *Mysia* (a country in Asia Minor)

Mytilēnae, -ārum, f. *Mytilene* (Greek city, capital of the island of Lesbos)

N

Nābis, Nābidis, m. *Nabis* (a king of Sparta)

Nāis, -idos, f. *a Naiad* (water nymph)

Narbō, -ōnis, m. *Narbo* (a city in the Province, modern Narbonne)

Nemetēs, -um, m. *the Nemetes* (a Germanic tribe)

Neptūnius, -a, -um *of Neptune*

Neptūnus, -ī, m. *Neptune* (god of the sea)

Nēreis, -idis, f. *Nereid, daughter of Nereus* (a sea nymph)

Nervius, -ī, m. a *Nervian*; pl., *the Nervii* (a tribe in Belgium)

Nōnae, -ārum, f. *the Nones* (ninth day before the Ides)

November, -bris, -bre *November*

Noviodūnum, -ī, n. *Noviodunum*

Numantia, -ae, f. *Numantia* (a city in Spain)

Numida, -ae, m. a *Nomad, a Numidian* (archers of the Roman army)

Numidia, -ae, f. *Numidia* (the country of the Nomads in North Africa)

Numidicus, -a, -um, *Numidian*

O

Ōceanus, -ī, m. *the Ocean, the great sea or body of water*

Ocelum, -ī, n. *Ocelum* (a city in northern Italy)

Octāvius, -a, -um *Octavius, Octavia, Octavian, of the Octavian family* (a Roman **nōmen gentīle**)

Octōber, bris, -bre *October*

Olympus, -ī, m. *[Mt.] Olympus*

Optimātēs, -ium, m. *Optimates* (the aristocratic party of the late republic)

Orcus, -ī, m. *Orcus* (the Lower World)

Orgetorix, -īgis, m. *Orgetorix* (a Helvetian nobleman)

Ōrīon, -īonis, m. *Orion* (a constellation)

Orpheus, -ī, m. *Orpheus* (a Thracian bard)

Ōstia, -ae, f. *Ostia* (seaport at the mouth of the Tiber)

P

P. abbreviation of *Pūblius*

Palātīnus, -a, -um *Palatine*

Palātium, -ī, n. *the Palatine Hill*

Papīrius, -a, -um *Papirius, Papiria, Papirian, of the Papirian family* (a Roman **nōmen gentīle**; L. Papirius Cursor was a general in the second Samnite war)

Parīsiī, -ōrum, m. *the Parisii* (a Gallic tribe on the Seine)

Paros, -ī, f. *Paros* (one of the Cyclades islands)

Parthicus, -a, -um *Parthian*

Patrēs, Patrum, m. *the Fathers (Senators)*

Peloponnēsus, -ī, f. *the Peloponnesus* (southern Greece)

Penātēs, -ium, m. (i-stem) *Penates* (gods of the household)

Persae, -ārum, m. *the Persians*

Persephōnē, -ēs, f. *Proserpine* (goddess of the Lower World)

Persicus, -a, -um *Persian*

Petrosidius, -ī, m. *Petrosidius* (a **cognōmen**; L. Petrosidius was a brave standard-bearer)

Philippus, -ī, m. *Philip* (name of several kings of Macedon)

Pictonēs, -um, m. *the Pictones* (a Gallic tribe south of the Loire)

Pīsō, Pīsōnis, m. *Piso* (a Roman **cognōmen**)

Pleumoxiī, -ōrum, m. *the Pleumoxii* (a Belgic tribe near the Nervii)

Plutōn, -ōnis, m. *Pluto* (a Greek name for Dis)

Poenus, -a, -um *Phoenician; Carthaginian*

Pompēius, -a, -um *Pompeius, Pompey, Pompeia, Pompeian, of the Pompeian family* (a Roman **nōmen gentīle**); C. Pompeius Magnus is known as Pompey the Great)

Pompōnius, -a, -um *Pomponius, Pomponia, Pomponian, of the Pomponian family* (a Roman **nōmen gentīle**)

Pontifex Maximus, Pontificis Maximī, m. *the Pontifex Maximus* (high priest at Rome, president of the College of Pontifices)

Pontius, -a, -um *Pontius, Pontia, Pontian* (a Samnite and Roman **nōmen gentīle**; C. Pontius was a general in Second Samnite war)

Pontus, -ī, m. *Pontus* (a country north of the Black Sea)

Populārēs, -ium, m. *Populares* (the popular party of the late republic)

Porcius, -a, -um *Porcius, Porcia, Porcian, of the Porcian family* (a Roman **nōmen gentīle**)

Porsena, -ae, m. *Porsena* (an Etruscan name; Lars Porsena was king of Clusium)

Praetor, Praetōris, m. *Praetor* (the magistrate just below a Consul in rank)

Praetōrium, -ī, n. *Praetorium (a Roman general's headquarters)*

Proserpina, -ae, f. *Proserpina* (wife of Pluto)

Ptolemaeus, -ī, m. *Ptolemy* (the name of a general of Alexander and of his descendants, the Macedonian kings of Egypt)

Publius, -ī, m. *Publius* (a Roman **praenōmen**); abbreviation P.

Pullō, -ōnis, m. *Pullo* (a Roman **cognōmen** borne by one of Caesar's Centurions)

Pūnicus, -a, -um *Punic, Carthaginian*

Pȳramus, -ī, m. *Pyramus* (lover of Thisbe)

Pyrēnaeī [montēs] *the Pyrenees [Mountains]*

Pȳrēnaeus, -a, -um *Pyrenaean*

Pyrrhicus, -a, -um *Pyrrhic, of Pyrrhus*

Pyrrhus, -ī, m. *Pyrrhus* (a king of Epirus)

Pȳthia, -ae, f. *Pythia* (a priestess of Apollo)

Q

Q. abbreviation of *Quintus*

Quaestor, Quaestōris, m. *Quaestor* (one of the officials in charge of the public treasury, below the Aediles in rank)

Quīnctius, -a, -um *Quinctius, Quinctia, Quinctian, of the Quinctian family* (a Roman **nōmen gentīle**; Titus Quinctius was a Roman general)

Quīntīlis, -e *Quintilis* (the original name of July)

Quīntus, -ī, m. *Quintus* (a Roman praenōmen); abbreviation Q.

Quirītēs, Quirītum m. *Quirites* (a term for Roman citizens in their civic, non-military, character)

R

Racīlius, -a, -um *Racilius, Racilia, Racilian, of the Racilian family* (a Roman **nōmen gentīle**)

Rauracī, -ōrum, m. *the Rauraci* (a Celtic people in Gaul)

Ravenna, -ae, f. *Ravenna* (a town of Hither Gaul)

Redonēs, -um, m. *the Redones* (a people in northern Gaul)

Rēgulus, -ī, m. *Regulus* ("Little King", a Roman cognōmen; M. Atilius Regulus was a Roman general in the First Punic War)

Rēmī, -ōrum, m. *the Remi* (a Gallic tribe near modern Rheims)

Rēmus, -ī, m. *a Remus* (one of the Remi)

Rēx, Rēgis, m. *Rex* ("King", a cognōmen assumed by the gēns Mārcia as being descended from King Ancus Marcius)

Rhadamanthus, -ī, m. *Rhadamanthus* (judge in the Lower World)

Rhēnus, -ī, m. *the Rhine*

Rhodanus, -i, m. *the Rhone*

Rhodopēius, -a, -um *Rhodopeian, Thracian*

Rhodus, -ī, f. *Rhodes*

Rōma, -ae, f. *Rome*

Rōmānus, -a, -um *Roman, of Rome*

Rōmulus, -ī, m. *Romulus (first king of Rome)*

Rubicō, Rubicōnis, m. *the Rubicon* (a small river marking the boundary between Hither Gaul and Italy)

Rūfus, -ī, m. *Rufus* ("Red", a Roman **cognōmen**; P. Sulpicius Rufus was one of Caesar's officers)

Rūpēs Tarpēia, Rūpis Tarpēiae, f. *the Tarpeian Rock* (a cliff of the Capitoline Hill from which those convicted of treason were thrown)

S

Sabīnus, -a, -um *Sabine, of the Sabines*

Sabīnus, -i, m. see **Titurius**

Sabis, -is, m. *the Sabis* (now the Sambre River, in Belgium)

Saguntīnus, -a, -um *Saguntine, Zacynthan, of Saguntum (Zacynthos)*

Saguntum, -ī, n. *Saguntum, Zacynthos* (a Greek colony on the east coast of Spain)

Salmydessus, -ī, m. *Salmydessus* (a town in Thrace)

Samarobrīva, -ae, f. *Samarobriva* (a city of the Ambiani, modern Amiens)

Samos, -ī, f. *Samos* (an island in the Aegean Sea)

Santonēs, -um, or **Santonī, -ōrum,** m. *the Santones* (a tribe on the seacoast, north of the Garonne)

Sardinia, -ae, f. *Sardinia*

Sāturnus, -ī, m. *Saturn* (an old Latin god)

Scaevola, -ae, m. *Scaevola* ("Lefty", a Roman **cognōmen**; C. Mucius Scaevola burned off his right hand)

Scīpiō, Scīpiōnis, m. *Scipio* ("Staff [of a triumphātor]", a Roman cognōmen; Scipio Africanus Major defeated Hannibal at Zama, 201 B.C.; Africanus Minor destroyed Carthage in 146 B.C.)

Scythicus, -a, -um *Scythian*

Segusiāvī, -ōrum, m. *the Segusiavi* (a Gallic tribe)

Semīramis, -idis, f. *Semiramis* (queen of Assyria)

Senātor, Senātōris, m. *Senator*

Senātus, -ūs, m. *the Senate*

Senonēs, -um, m. *the Senones* (a people of central Gaul)

September, -bris, -bre *September*

Septentriō, Septentriōnis, m. *Septentrio* (a northern constellation, also called Ursa Major)

Sēquana, -ae, f. *Sequana* (the Seine river)

Sēquanī, -ōrum, m. *the Sequanians (a Gallic people west of the Jura range)*

Sēquanus, -a, -um *Sequanian*

Ser. Abbreviation for *Servius*

Servīlius, -a, -um *Servilius, Servilia, Servilian, of the Servilian family* (a Roman **nōmen gentīle**)

Sicilia, -ae, f. *Sicily*

Siciliēnsis, -e *Sicilian* (**Fretum Siciliēnse,** the *straits of Messina*)

Siculus, -a, -um *Sicilian*

Sīgnifer, Sīgniferī, m. *Signifer, Standard-Bearer*

Sophonisba, -ae, f. *Sophonisba* (a Carthaginian noblewomen, known for her beauty)

Sp. *abbreviation for Spurius*

Spurius, -ī, m. *Spurius* (a Roman **praenomen**); abbreviation Sp.

Styx, Stygis, f. *[the river] Styx (in the Lower World)*

Suebī, -ōrum, m. *the Suebi* (the Swabians, a German tribe)

Suessiōnēs, -um, m. *the Suessiones,* (a Belgic tribe; modern Soissons)

Sulla, -ae, m. *Sulla* (a Roman **cognōmen;** L. Cornelius Sulla was Dictator 82–79 B.C.; P. Cornelius Sulla, nephew of the Dictator, was one of Caesar's officers)

Sulpicius, -a, -um *Sulpicius, Sulpicia, Sulpician, of the Sulpician family* (a Roman **nōmen gentīle;** P. Sulpicius was Consul in 279 B.C.; one of Caesar's officers was also called Sulpicius)

Summānus, -ī, m. *Summanus* (an old Roman god of night lightning)

Syphāx, Syphācis, m. *Syphax* (a king of the Massaesylian Nomads)

Syrācūsae, -ārum, f. *Syracuse* (a Greek city of Sicily)

Syrācūsānus, -a, -um *Syracusan, of Syracuse*

Syria, -ae, f. *Syria* (a country in Asia at the eastern end of the Mediterranean)

Syriacus, -a, -um *Syrian*

Syrius, -a, -um *Syrian*

T

T., abbreviation for *Titus*

Taenarius, -a, -um *of Taenarum*

Taenarum or **Taenarus, -ī,** m. *Taenarus* (a promontory in Greece)

Tantalus, -ī, m. *Tantalus* (father of Pelops and Niobe)

Tarentum, -ī, n. *Tarentum* (a Greek town of southern Italy)

Tarentīnus, -a, -um *Tarentine, of Tarentum*

Tartarus, -ī, m. *Tartarus* (the part of the Lower World where evildoers were punished)

Tectosagēs, -um m. *the Tectosages* (a tribe near the Hercynian forest)

Teutobodus, -ī, m. *Teutobodus* (a king of the Teutons)

Teutonēs, -um, m. *the Teutons* (a German tribe)

Theātrum, Theātrī, n. **Pompeī** *Theatre of Pompey* (Built by Pompey from the spoils of the Mithridatic War, it included a colonnaded park and a Curia)

Thēbae, -arum, f. *Thebes*

Thēbānī, -ōrum, m. *Thebans*

Thermōdōn, -dontis, m. *the Thermodon* (a river in Pontus)

Thermus, -ī, m. *Thermus* (a Roman **cognōmen**)

Thessalia, -ae, f. *Thessaly, in northeastern Greece*

Thisbē, -ēs, f. *Thisbe* (a Babylonian maiden, loved by Pyramus)

Thrācēs, -um, m. *Thracians*

Thracia, -ae, f. *Thrace* (a country in northern Greece)

Ti. Abbreviation for *Tiberius*

Tiberis, Tiberis, m. (i-stem: acc. **Tiberim,** abl. **Tiberī**) *the Tiber*

Ticīnus, -ī, m. *the Ticinus River*

Tigurīnus, -ī, m. *Tigurian, of the Tigurian division* (one of the four divisions of the Helvetians)

Titūrius, -ī, m. *Titurius, Tituria, Titurian* (a Roman **nōmen gentīle;** Q. Titurius Sabinus, one of Caesar's officers)

Titus, -ī, m. *Titus* (a Roman **praenōmen,** abbreviation T.)

Tolōsātēs, -ium, m. *the Tolosates* (a tribe near modern Toulouse)

Torquātus, -a, -um *Torquatus* ("Wearing a Torque", a Roman **cognōmen;** T. Manlius Torquatus took a torque (neck chain) from the gigantic Gaul he killed)

Trānsalpinus, -a, -um *Transalpine (beyond the Alps)*

Trebōnius, -ī, m. *Trebonius, Trebonia, Trebonian* (a Roman **nōmen gentīle;** C. Trebonius was one of Caesar's officers)

Trēverī, -ōrum, m. *the Treveri* (a Belgic people near the Rhine)

Trēverus, -a, -um *Treveran, of the Treveri*

Tribūnus Mīlitum, Tribūnī Mīlitum, m. *Tribune of Soldiers, Military Tribune* (a commissioned rank in the army)

Tribūnus Plēbis, Tribūnī Plebis, m. *Tribune of the Plebs, Plebeian Tribune* (an official elected to protect the interests of the plebeians)

Trōia, -ae, f. *Troy*

Trōiānus, -a, -um *Trojan*

Tulingī, -ōrum, m. *the Tulingi* (a German tribe north of the Helvetians)

Tyrius, -a, -um *Tyrian, of Tyre*

U

Ubiī, -ōrum, m. *the Ubii* (a German tribe)

Ulterior Hispānia see **Hispania Ulterior**

V

Valerius, -ī, m. *Valerius, Valeria, Valerian* (a Roman **nōmen gentīle**)

Vēiī, -ōrum, m. *Veii* (a town of the Etruscans, near Rome)

Veliocassēs, -ium, m. *the Veliocasses* (a state north of the Sequana)

Venetī, -ōrum, m. *the Veneti* (a Gallic tribe on the west coast)

Veneticus, -a, -um *Venetan, of the Veneti*

Venus, Veneris, f. *Venus* (goddess of love and female charm)

Verbigenus, -ī, m. *Verbigen* (a canton of the Helvetians)

Vercellae, -ārum, f. *Vercellae* (a town in northern Italy)

Verginius, -a, -um *Verginius, Verginia, Verginian, of the Verginian family* (a Roman **nōmen gentīle**)

Verticō, -ōnis, m. *Vertico* (one of the Nervii)

Vesta, -ae, f. *Vesta* (goddess of the hearth)

Vestālis, -e *Vestal, of Vesta*

Veturius, -a, -um *Veturius, Veturia, Veturian, of the Veturian family* (a Roman **nōmen gentīle**; a Veturia was Coriolanus' mother; T. Veturius was Consul in 321 B.C.)

Viromanduī, -ōrum, m. *the Viromandui* (a Belgic people)

Vocontiī, -ōrum, m. *the Vocontii* (a Gallic tribe)

Volcānus, -ī, m. *see* **Vulcānus**

Volscī, -ōrum, m. *the Volscians* (a highland tribe southeast of Rome)

Volumnius, -a, -um *Volumnius, Volumnia, Volumnian, of the Volumnian family* (a Roman **nōmen gentīle**; a Volumnia was Coriolanus' wife)

Volusēnus, -ī, m. *Volusenus, Volusena, Volusenan* (a Roman **nōmen gentīle**; C. Volusenus was a tribune in Caesar's army)

Vorēnus, -ī, m. *Vorenus* (a Roman **cognōmen**; a Vorenus was a centurion in Caesar's army)

Vulcānus, -ī, m. *Vulcan, god of fire*

X

Xanthippus, -ī, m. *Xanthippus* (a Greek name; a general of the Lacedaemonians)

Z

Zama, -ae, f. *Zama* (a town of Numidia; scene of the victory of Scipio over Hannibal)

LATIN–ENGLISH VOCABULARY

Words which appear in the Lesson Vocabularies are followed by the number of the Lesson in which each occurs. Those which should have been mastered in *First Year Latin* have a I added. If a word is derived from a word already known, the known word follows in parentheses. If the new word has an English derivative which is close to it in meaning, it will be indicated. If the derivative is also a translation, it is not given in the parentheses.

A

ā, ab, abs (prep. w. abl.) *from, away from, by;* (of time) *since, from, after.* (as an adverb) *away* I

ab See **ā, ab, abs**

abaliēnō, -āre, -āvī, -ātum (aliēnus) *separate, alienate, estrange*

abdicō, -āre, -āvī, -ātum (ABDICATE) *renounce, deny, refuse;* (w. reflexive & abl. of separation) *abdicate, resign*

abdō, -ere, abdidī, abditum *hide*

abdūcō, -ere, abdūxī, abductum (dūcō, ABDUCT) *lead away; withdraw; abduct*

abeō, abīre, abiī (abīvī), **abitum** *go away, depart* I

abiciō, -ere, abiēcī, abiectum (iaciō, ABJECT) *throw away, throw, cast*

abnuō, -ere, abnuī, abnuitum or **-nūtum** *[shake or toss the head to] refuse, deny*

abrogō, -āre, -āvī, -ātum (rogō) *repeal, annul, abrogate, take from*

abs see **ā, ab, abs**

abscīdō, -ere, abscīdī, abscīsum (caedō) *cut off*

absēns, absentis *absent, being absent* 1

absolvō, -ere, absolvī, absolūtum (solvō, ABSOLUTION) *free, acquit, absolve; finish*

absterreō, -ēre, -uī, -itum *frighten away, frighten off*

abstineō, -ēre, -uī, abstentum (teneō, ABSTAIN) *hold back from, keep away from, hold off; keep away, refrain from, abstain* (w. abl. of place from which or abl. of separation)

abstrahō, -ere, abstrāxī, abstractum *drag away* 2

absum, abesse, āfuī, āfutūrus *be away, be absent, be free from, be wanting* I

abundō, -āre, -āvī, -ātum (ABUNDANT) *overflow, abound, have in abundance*

ac See **atque.**

accēdō, -ere, accessī, accessum *go to, go toward, approach, advance; be added, undertake* I

accendō, -ere, accendī, accensum *kindle, set on fire*

acceptus, -a, -um (accipiō) *acceptable, welcome*

accidō, -ere, accidī *fall to, fall down;* impers., **accidit** *it happens, it befalls* (w. dat. of the person) 10

accingō, -ere, accīnxī, accīnctum (cingō) *gird up*

accipiō, -ere, accēpī, acceptum *receive, accept; learn, listen* I

acclīvis, -e *sloping upward, rising*

acclīvitās, acclīvitātis, f. *slope, ascent* (ACCLIVITY)

accommodō, -āre, -āvī, -ātum *fit to, put on, adjust; accommodate*

accūrātē, adv. (cūrō, ACCURATE) *carefully*

accurrō, -ere, accurrī, accursum (currō) *run to, come up*

accūsō, -āre, -āvī, -ātum (causa) *accuse*

ācer, ācris, ācre *sharp, fierce, keen, shrill, bitter* I

acerbitās, acerbitātis, f. (ACERBITY) *bitterness*

acerbus, -a, -um (ACERB) *bitter, rough, severe, harsh*

aciēs, -ēī, f. *sharp edge; straight line; eyeshot; line of battle* I

acūmen, acūminis, n. (ACUMEN) *keenness, sharpness*

ad (prep. w. acc.) *to, towards, up to; at, near; for, approximately* (with numbers) I

adaequō, -āre, -āvī, -ātum (aequus, ADEQUATE) *equal*

addō, -ere, addidī, additum *put to, add* I

addūcō, -ere, addūxī, adductum *lead to, bring to; induce, influence* 7

adeō (adv.) *so, to that point, to such an extent* 9

adeō, adīre, adiī (adīvī), **aditum** *go to, approach* (trans.) I

adferō, adferre, attulī, allātum (also **afferō**) *bring up;* (w. dat.) *bring to, bring, report; cause, present; allege, assign;* **vim afferre,** *offer violence* I

adficiō, -ere, adfēcī, affectum (faciō, AFFECT) *influence, affect; punish; weaken; afflict, visit with*

adfirmō, -āre, āvī, -atum *confirm, affirm*

adflīgō, -ere, adflīxī, adflīctum (AFFLICTION) *strike, damage, injure; discourage*

adglūtinō, -āre, -āvī, -ātum (AGGLUTINATION) *glue, pile up, attach*

adhaereō, -ēre, adhaesī, adhaesum (ADHESIVE) *cling to, stick to*

adhibeō, -ēre, -uī, -itum (habeō) *summon, invite, offer; use, apply*

adhūc (adv.) *thus far, till now, hitherto, as yet, still* 18

adiciō, -ere, adiēcī, adiectum (iaciō, ADJECTIVE) *throw, add to, join to* I

adigō, -ere, adēgī, adactum (agō) *drive to, compel, constrain; cast, hurl;* **iūre iūrandō adigere** *put on oath*

adimō, -ere, adēmī, ademptum (emō) *take away; cut off*

adipīscor, -ī, adeptus (ADEPT) *gain, secure, obtain*

aditus, -ūs, m. (adeō, ADIT) *approach, access, entrance*

adiungō, -ere, adiūnxī, adiūnctum (iungō, ADJUNCT) *join to, add to, win over*

adiūtor, adiūtōris, m. (iuvō) *helper, advocate*

adiuvō, -āre, adiūvī, adiūtum (iuvō, ADJUTANT) *help, aid, assist*

adligō, -āre, -āvī, -ātum *tie to, bind to, fasten to*

administer, administrī, m. (minister, ADMINISTER) *assistant; priest, minister*

administrō, -āre, -āvī, -ātum (minister) *render assistance, manage, administer*

admīror, -ārī, -ātus sum (mīror) *wonder, be amazed; wonder at, admire*

admittō, -ere, admīsī, admissum (mittō) *let go; admit, receive; commit;* **equō admissō** *with his horse at full speed*

admodum, adv. (modus) *very, exceedingly, quite*

admoneō, -ēre, -uī, -itum (moneō) *remind, warn, admonish*

admoveō, -ēre, admōvī, admōtum (moveō) *bring to, move toward, apply; bring near*

adolēscō, -ere, adolēvī, adultum (ADOLESCENT) *come to maturity, grow up*

adoperiō, -īre, adoperuī, adopertum (āperiō) *cover*

adorior, -īrī, adortus sum (orior) *rise against, attack, assail*

adprobō see **approbō**

adserō, -ere, adseruī, adsertum *grasp*

adsertor, adsertōris, m. *claimant, (one who asserts that another is free or a slave)*

adspergō, adsperginis, f. (spargō) *spray, sprinkling*

adspiciō, -ere, adspexī, adspectum See **aspiciō**

adsum, adesse, adfuī, adfutūrus *be present;* (w. dat.) *be present at, be present to help* I

adulēscēns, adulēscentis, (ADOLESCENT) *young, as a noun,* m. or f. *young man, young woman*

adūrō, -ere, adussī, adustum (ūrō) *scorch, singe*

adveniō, -īre, advēnī, adventum (veniō, ADVENT) *come to, arrive*

adventus, -ūs, m. (veniō, ADVENT) *arrival, coming*

adversus, -a, -um (vertō) *turned toward, facing, opposite; adverse, unfavorable, unsuccessful.* **adversō colle,** *up the hill.* **in adversum ōs,** *full in the face*

adversus (prep. w. acc.) *against, opposed to, opposite to* I

advertō, -ere, -vertī, -versum (vertō, ADVERT) *turn (to), direct*

advocō, -āre, -āvī, -ātum (vocō, ADVOCATE) *summon, call in*

advolō, -āre, -āvī, -ātum (volō) *fly towards, dash up to*

aedēs see **aedis**

aedificium, -ī, n. (aedificō, EDIFICE) *building, house*

aedificō, -āre, -āvī, -ātum (aedis + faciō, EDIFY) *build, construct* I

aedis or **aedēs, aedis,** f. (i-stem) *building, temple;* (plural) *house* I

aeger, aegra, aegrum *sick, ill* 18

aegrē (adv.) *painfully, with difficulty, scarcely;* **aegrē ferre,** *to be annoyed at, take hard* 18

aequālis, -e (aequus) *equal, contemporary*

aequāliter, adv. (aequus) *evenly, uniformly*

aequinoctium, -ī, n. (aequus + nox) *the equinox*

aequiperō, -āre, -āvī, -ātum (aequus) *equal*

aequitās, aequitātis, f. (aequus) *fairness, justice, equity*; animī aequitās, *calmness, equanimity*

aequō, -āre, -āvī, -ātum (aequus) *level, make equal, equate, equalize*

aequor, aequoris, n. *the sea*

aequus, -a, -um *fair, just; level, calm; equal; favorable*; aequō animō, *calmly, with equanimity* 1

āēr, āeris, (aec. āera) m. *air*

aes, aeris, n. *copper, brass, bronze; money*; aes aliēnum *debt* 14

aestās, aestātis, f. *summer*

aestimātiō, aestimātiōnis, f. (aes, exīstimō, ESTIMATION) *evaluation*

aestimō, -āre, -āvī, -ātum (aes, exīstimō) *estimate, assess, evaluate*

aestuārium, -ī, n. (ESTUARY) *tidal marsh, marsh*

aestuō, -āre, -āvī, -ātum *boil, seethe, roll in waves*

aestus, -ūs, m. *heat; tide*

aetās, aetātis, f. *age, lifetime; time* 1

aeternus, -a, -um *eternal, everlasting, perpetual* 1

aethēr, aetheris, m. *upper air; ether*

aevum, -ī, n. *age* 12

affābilis, -e (AFFABLE) *congenial*

afferō See adferō

afficiō, -ere, affēcī, affectum (see adficiō)

affīnitās, affīnitātis, f. (AFFINITY) *relationship by marriage*

afflictō, -āre, -āvī, -ātum *shatter, damage, wreck*

affligō See adfligō

affore = adfore

agellus, -i, m. (ager) *small field, little farm*

ager, agrī, m. *field, territory; pl., lands, country* 1

agger, aggeris, m. (ad + gerō) *rampart, material for a rampart, earth*

aggredior, -ī, aggressus sum (AGGRESSIVE) *approach, attack; attempt, undertake, begin*

aggregō, -āre, -āvī, -ātum (AGGREGATE) *collect; join*

agmen, agminis, n. *throng, flock; army [on the march* or *in marching order], line, procession*; agmen claudere, *to bring up the rear*; novissimum agmen, *the rear guard, the rear*; prīmum agmen, *the vanguard, the van* 8

agnus, -ī, m. *[male] lamb*

agō, -ere, ēgī, actum *drive, set in motion, do, act; pay attention to; perform, accomplish, conduct, guide, incite, discuss; spend, pass; devote; deal attend to, mind, observe, bring up sheds; age*, agite w. another imperative *come on, go on*; se agere *live, spend time*; cum + abl. agere *treat*; animam agere *give up the ghost*; rem agere *carry on one's business*; grātiās agere (w. dat. of ref.) *thank* 1

agricola, -ae, m. *farmer* I

āiō, ___, ___, ___(defective verb; forms are: āiō, āis, āit, āiunt, āiēbam, āiēbās, āiēbat, āiēbāmus, āiēbātis, āiēbant, āiās, āiat, āiant, āiēns) *say yes; affirm, assert, state* 2

āla, -ae, f. *wing; ala (a side alcove in an atrium); squadron (of cavalry)*

alacritās, alacritātis, f. *eagerness, ardor, alacrity*

alcēs, alcis, f. *moose, elk*

ālea, -ae, f. *die (one of a set of dice); game of dice*

ālēs, alitis *winged*; as noun, m. or f., *bird*

aliās (adv.) *at another time* I

alibi (adv.) *elsewhere* I

alicubi (indef. adv.) *somewhere, anywhere* I

alicunde (indef. adv.) *from somewhere, from anywhere* I

aliēnigena, -ae, m. (aliēnus + gignō) *foreigner; mongrel*

aliēnō, -āre (aliēnus) *alienate, estrange, render devoid*

aliēnus, -a, -um *of another, another's, someone else's; foreign, strange, alien*; aes aliēnum, *debt*; as noun, aliēnus, -ī, m., *foreigner, stranger* I

aliō (adv.) *to another place, elsewhere* I

aliquamdiū (adv.) *for some time, for a little while*

aliquandō (indef. adv.) *at some time, sometimes, at any time, once, at last* I

aliquantum, -i, n. *a little, considerable; something*

aliquantus, -a, -um (indef. adj.) *some little, of some size* I

aliquī, aliqua, aliquod (pron. adj.) *some; any, some other* I

aliquis, aliquid (indef. pron.) *someone, something, anyone, anything* I

aliquō (indef. adv.) *[to] somewhere, [to] anywhere* I

aliquot (indecl. indef. adj.) *several, some number of* I

aliquotiēns (indef. adv.) *several times* I

aliter (adv.) *otherwise, else, differently; in any other way*. aliter ac, *otherwise than* I

aliunde (adv.) *from another place* I

alius, alia, aliud (pron. decl.) *another, other, differ-*

ent; **alius . . . alius,** *one . . . another,* (pl.) *some . . . others* I

alō, -ere, aluī, alitum *feed, nourish, support, rear, keep, raise* I

altāria, -ium, n.pl. *altar*

altē, adv. *high, on high; far* I

alter, altera, alterum (pron. decl.) *the other, one [of two];* **alter . . . alter,** *the one . . . the other* I

altercātiō, altercātiōnis, f. (alter, ALTERCATION) *dispute, wrangling, debate; cross-examination*

altilis, -e (alō) *fattened, fat;* as noun, f. *a fattened bird*

altitūdō, altitūdinis, f. *height, altitude; depth* I

altus, -a, -um *high, lofty, tall, deep;* as noun, **altum, -ī,** n. *the deep, the sea* I

alveus, -ī, m. *hollow; [ship's] hold; [bath]tub; [river-]bed*

ambactus, ī, m. *retainer, dependent vassal*

ambāgēs, -is, f. *circuit; a long story, details; riddle, mystery*

ambō, -ae, -ō *both* I

ambulō, -āre, āvī, -ātum *walk* I

amentum, -ī, n. *thong, strap*

amiciō, -īre, amixī, amictum *clothe*

amīcitia, -ae, f. *friendship* I

amictus, -ūs, m. *cloak, outer garments*

amīcus, -a, -um *friendly, amicable* I

amīcus, -ī, m. *friend, ally* I

amita, -ae, f. *[paternal] aunt*

āmittō, -ere, āmīsī, āmissum *let go away, lose, send away* I

amnis, amnis, m. (i-stem) *river* I

amō, -āre, -āvī, -ātum *love, like;* **amābō** *please, if you please* I

amor, amōris, m. *love, affection* I

āmoveō, -ēre, -mōvī, -mōtum (moveō) *remove, move away*

amplector, -ī, amplexus sum *embrace; surround; include; encircle*

amplificō, -āre, -āvī, -ātum (amplus, AMPLIFY) *enlarge, magnify*

amplitūdō, amplitūdinis, f. (amplus, AMPLITUDE) *greatness, extent; breadth, size; importance*

amplus, -a, -um *great, ample, large; important, distinguished* 19

an (conj.) *or* (in disjunctive questions) I

anceps, ancipitis (ambō + caput) *two-headed; twofold; on two fronts*

ancora, -ae, f. *anchor;* **in ancorīs,** *at anchor*

anguis, anguis, m. or f. (i-stem) *snake* I

angustiae, -ārum, f. *narrow pass, strait; mountain pass; scarcity; distress, difficulties; narrowness*

angustus, -a, -um *narrow, close, steep;* as noun, **angustum, -ī,** n. *crisis*

anhēlitus, -ūs, m. *panting, breath*

anima, -ae, f. *breath, life, soul* I

animadvertō, -ere, animadvertī, animadversum (animus + ad + vertō, ANIMADVERSION) *notice, observe; turn the mind to; punish*

animal, animālis, n. (i-stem) (anima) *animal, living being*

animus, -ī, m. *soul, life; mind, courage, spirit; purpose; feelings;* **esse in animō,** *to intend;* (pl.) *morale* I

annōn (conj. + adv. in disjunc. questions) *or not* I

annus, -ī, m. *year* I

annuus, -a, -um (annus) *annual, yearly, year-long*

anser, anseris, m. (MERGANSER) *goose, gander*

ante (prep. w. acc.) *before, in front of, facing, ahead of* I

ante (adv.) *before, earlier, previously, in front* I

anteā (adv.) (ante) *before, hitherto, previously*

antecēdō, -ere, antecessī, antecessum (ante + cēdō, ANTECEDENT) *go before, precede, surpass,* with dat.

antecursor, antecursōris, m. (ante + currō) *scout, forerunner;* pl., *vanguard*

anteferō, -ferre, antetulī, antelātum (ante + ferō) *place before, prefer*

antepōnō, -ere, anteposuī, antepositum (ante + pōnō) *put before*

antīquitus, adv. (antīquus) *in former times, anciently*

antīquus, -a, -um *ancient; old-fashioned; former, previous* 17

anulus, ī m. (ANULAR) *finger-ring*

anus, -ūs, f. (ANILE) *old woman*

aperiō, -īre, aperuī, apertum *open, uncover; disclose, reveal;* **apertus, -a, -um** (aperiō, APERTURE) *open, uncovered; exposed; clear, manifest*

apīscor, -ī, aptus sum *attain, grasp;* **aptus, -a, -um** *fastened; prepared; fit, suitable; neat*

apparātus, -ūs, m. (parō) *preparation, equipment; splendor, pomp, display*

appareō, -ēre, -uī, -itum *appear, be apparent*

appellō, -āre, -āvī, -ātum (APPELLATION) *address; appeal to; name, call*

appellō, -ere, appulī, appulsum *push to, drive to, direct to* 1

appendō, -ere, appendī, appēnsum (pendō, APPEND) *weigh out, pay out* (to someone)

applicō, -āre, -āvī, -ātum *apply to;* **sē applicāre,** *to lean against*

apportō, -āre, -āvī, -ātum (ad + portō) *bring*

approbō, -āre, -āvī, -ātum *approve, assent to; prove*

appropinquō, -āre, -āvī, -ātum (ad + prope) *approach, come near*

aptō, -āre, -āvī, -ātum *fit, adapt; equip; adjust; prepare*

aptus, -a, -um see apīscor

apud (prep. w. acc.) *at, among, near, close to; at the house of; in the presence of; in the works of* I

aqua, -ae, f. *water; water supply, aqueduct* I

aquila, -ae, f. (AQUILINE) *eagle*

āra, -ae, f. *altar* I

arātrum, -ī, n. *plough*

arbitrium, -ī, n. *decision, judgment, choice; authority*

arbitror, -ārī, -ātus sum (ARBITRATION) *think, consider, believe*

arbor, arboris, f. *tree* 19

arboreus, -a, -um (arbor, ARBOREAL) *of a tree; branching*

arca, -ae, f. box, chest

accessō, -ere, accessīvī, accessītum *summon, send for, fetch, invite*

ardeō, -ēre, ārsī, ārsum *burn, be on fire;* **ardēns, -entis,** *burning, glowing* I

arduus, -a, -um *steep, high, tall; arduous*

argentum, -ī, n. *silver, money*

arguō, -ere, arguī, argūtum (argue) *declare, accuse*

āridus, -a, -um *dry, arid;* as noun, **āridum, -ī,** n. *dry land*

ariēs, arietis, m. (ARIES) *ram; battering ram*

arma, -ōrum, n. (no sing.) *arms, armor, weapons; implements* I

armāmenta, -ōrum, n. (arma, ARMAMENT) *rigging, equipment*

armātūra, -ae, f. (arma, ARMATURE) *equipment, armor;* **levis armātūrae peditēs,** *light infantry*

armātus, -a, -um (arma) *armed, equipped;* as noun, *armed man*

armō, -āre, -āvī, -ātum (arma) *arm, equip*

arō, -āre, -āvī, -ātum (ARABLE) *plow*

arripiō, -ere, arripuī, arreptum (rapiō) *snatch up, appropriate, seize with violence*

ars, artis, f. *art, skill, craft; knowledge, science* I

articulus, -ī, m. (ARTICULATION) *joint*

artificium, -ī, n. (ars + faciō, ARTIFICE) *art, trade; trick*

arvum, -ī, n. *field*

arx, arcis, f. (i-stem) *citadel, stronghold, castle; height* I

ascendō, -ere, ascendī, ascēnsum (ASCEND) *mount, climb, go up; embark*

ascēnsus, -ūs, m. *ascent; approach*

asper, aspera, asperum *rough, harsh, rugged, severe*

aspergō, -ere, aspersī, aspersum (-spargo, ASPERSION) *spatter, stain*

aspiciō, -ere, aspexī, aspectum (also **adspiciō**) *look at, behold, see; regard; catch sight of* I

assiduus, -a, -um (ad + sedeō) *constant, steady; assiduous* 20

assistō, -ere, adstitī, ——, (ASSIST) *stand near; appear before*

assuēsco, -ere, assuēvī, assuētum *become accustomed*

at (conj.) *but, yet, but yet* I

āter, -tra, -trum *black, dark*

atque or **ac** (conj.) *and, and even, and also; than; as;* **simul atque,** *as soon as;* **aliter atque,** *otherwise than* I

ātrium, -ī, n. *atrium* (chief reception room in a Roman house)

atrōcitās, atrōcitātis, f. (ATROCITY) *harshness, cruelty, severity*

atrōx, atrōcis *harsh, cruel, severe, atrocious*

attendō, -ere, attendī, attentum (ATTENTIVE) *exert, turn*

attexō, -ere, attexuī, attextum *add, join on; weave*

attineō, -ēre, -uī, attentum *touch on, concern*

attingō, -ere, attigī, attactum (tangō) *touch upon, touch; reach; border on*

attollō, -ere, ——, —— (tollō) *raise up, lift*

attonitus, -a, -um *astonished; thunderstruck*

attribuō, -ere, attribuī, attribūtum (ATTRIBUTE) *assign, allot*

auctor, auctōris, m. *originator, founder, author; authority* I

auctōritās, auctōritātis, f. (auctor) *authority, approval, power, influence; prestige*

audācia, -ae, f. (audāx) *boldness, rashness, daring, audacity*

audax, audācis *bold, rash, foolhardy, daring* 16

audeō, -ēre, ausus sum *dare* I

audiō, -īre, -īvī, -ītum *hear, listen to* I

auferō, auferre, abstulī, ablātum (ab + ferō) *carry off, steal, bear away* I

augeō, -ēre, auxī, auctum *increase, enlarge, enrich, strengthen* 4

auguror, -ārī, -ātus *prophesy, predict*

augustus, -a, -um (AUGUST) *consecrated, holy; majestic, dignified*

aula, -ae, f. *pot, jar*

aura, -ae, f. *air, breeze, open air*

aureus, -a, -um *golden, of gold* I

aurīga, -ae, m. *[racing] charioteer, driver*

auris, auris, f. (i-stem) *ear* 14

aurōra, -ae, f. (AURORA) *dawn*

aurum, -ī, n. *gold* I

auscultō, -āre, -āvī, -ātum *hear, listen to*

auspicium, -ī, n. (avis + -spicio) *auspice (religious interpretation of the behavior of birds); pl. auspices*

auspicor, -ārī, -ātus sum (avis + -spicio) *take the auspices* (see **auspicium**)

aut (conj.) *or; aut . . . aut, either . . . or* I

autem (postpositive conj.) *but, however, on the other hand, moreover* I

auxilior, -ārī, -ātus sum (auxilium) *help, aid*

auxilium, auxilī, n. *help, aid; pl. auxiliaries, troops*

avēna, -ae, f. *reed, straw; shepherd's pipe*

āversor, -ārī, -ātus sum (versō) *turn away, turn away from* (intrans.)

āversus, -a, -um (vertō, AVERSE) *turned away; behind, in the rear*

āvertō, -ere, āvertī, āversum (vertō) *turn away, turn aside, avert; alienate* (trans.)

avidus, -a, -um *eager, desirous; avid*

avis, avis, f. (i-stem) *bird; sign, omen* I

avītus, -a, -um *of a grandfather*

avūnculus, -ī, m. (AVUNCULAR) *uncle*

avus, -ī, m. *grandfather*

B

baculum, -ī, n. *staff, walking stick*

ballista or **bālista, -ae,** f. (BALLISTIC) *an engine for hurling*

balteus, -i, m. *belt*

barba, -ae, f. (BARBER) *beard*

barbarus, -a, -um *foreign; barbarous, uncivilized*

basilica, -ae, f. *basilica (a large hall in a Forum, used for public and private business)*

beātus, -a, -um (BEATITUDE) *blessed, happy*

bellicōsus, -a, -um (bellum, BELLICOSE) *warlike, fierce*

bellō, -āre, -āvī, -ātum (bellum) *wage war, fight*

bellum, bellī, n. *war* I

belua, -ae, f. *large animal, monster*

bene (adv.) *well, successfully* I

beneficium, -ī, n. (bene + facio, BENEFICIARY) *kindness, good deed, benefit*

benevolentia, -ae, f. (bene + volō) *good will, benevolence*

bibō, -ere, bibī *drink; imbibe* (trans. or intrans.) 10

biduum, -ī, n. (bis + diēs) *two days*

biennium, -ī, n. (bis + annus) *two years*

bīnī, -ae, -a *two by two, two at a time* I

bipertītō, adv. (bis + pārs, BIPARTITE) *in two divisions*

bis (adv.) *twice* I

blandior, -īrī, -ītus sum (blandus, BLANDISHMENT) *flatter; coax, wheedle*

blanditia, -ae, f. (blandus) *caressing; blandishment; pl., endearments*

blandus, -a, -um *flattering; alluring, charming; bland* 14

bonitās, bonitātis, f. (bonus, BOUNTY) *goodness, excellence; fertility*

bonus, -a, -um *good, advantageous; friendly; as noun,* **bonum, -ī,** n. *profit, advantage; pl., goods, possessions* I

bōs, bōvis (dat. and abl. pl. **bōbus** or **būbus**), m. or f. (BOVINE) *ox, cow, bull*

brācchium, -ī, n. *arm, forearm*

brevis, -e *short, brief* 4

brevitās, brevitātis, f. (brevis) *shortness, brevity*

bustum, -i, n. *tomb, mound*

buxus, -i, f. *boxwood*

C

C 100 I

cadaver, -eris, n. *corpse, cadaver*

cadō, -ere, cecidī, cāsum *fall, die; be slain* 3

caecus, -a, -um *blind; dark; invisible* I

caedēs, caedis, f. *slaughter, murder, killing* I

caedō, -ere, cecīdī, caesum *fell, cut down; cut, cut to pieces, kill* 3 caelebs, caelebis, m. *a widower*

caelestis, -e (caelum, CELESTIAL) *heavenly; as noun,* pl., *the Gods*

caelum, -ī, n. *sky, heavens* I

caerimōnia, -ae, f. *holiness, sacredness; [holy] awe; [sacred] ceremony*

caeruleus, -a, -um *sky blue, dark blue*

caespes, -itis, m. *sod, turf*

calamitās, calamitātis, f. *disaster, calamity, loss, damage, harm, defeat*

calcō, -āre, -āvī, -ātum *tread upon*

calīgō, -inis, f. *mist, darkness*

callidus, -a, -um *crafty, sly, shrewd*

cālō, cālōnis, m. *camp servant*

calor, calōris, m. (CALORIE) *heat; passion*

campus, -ī, m. *plain, meadow, level field.*

canis, canis, m. or f. (not an i-stem) (CANINE) *dog, bitch*

canō, -ere, cecinī, cantum *sing, tell; prophesy, foretell* 3

cantus, -ūs, m. (canō, CHANT) *singing, song, music*

cānus, -a, -um *old, venerable; white, hoary*

caper, caprī, m. (CAPRICORN) *goat*

capessō, -ere, -īvī, -ītum (capiō) *seize, take*

capiō, -ere, cēpī, captum *take, seize, capture; reach; captivate, please; receive;* cōnsilium capere *to form a plan* I

captīvus, -a, -um *captive.*

captō, -āre, -āvī, -ātum (capio) *seize, capture, try to catch*

caput, capitis, n. *head; person, soul, life; mouth [of a river];* capitis poena, *capital punishment*

carcer, carceris m. (INCARCERATE) *prison, jail; [race track] starting gate*

cardō, -inis, m. (CARDINAL) *hinge; crisis*

careō, -ēre, -uī, *lack, be without, do without* (w. abl. of sep.) I

carīna, -ae, f. (CAREEN) *keel, ship*

cāritās, -tātis, f. (carus, CHARITY) *love*

carmen, carminis, n. *song, poem; charm; prayer, incantation* I

carō, carnis, f. *meat, flesh*

carpentum, -ī, n. *[light two-wheeled] carriage*

carpō, -ere, carpsī, carptum *pluck; pursue; enjoy; cleave*

carrus, -ī, m. *[light freight] cart, wagon*

cārus, -a, -um *dear, expensive; precious* I

casa, -ae, f. *hut, cabin*

caseus, -i, m. (CASEIN) *cheese*

cassis, -idis, f. *a helmet of metal*

cassus, -a, -um *hollow, empty, devoid of*

castellum, -ī, n. (castra, CASTLE) *redoubt, fortress, stronghold, citadel*

castīgō, -āre, -āvī, -ātum (CASTIGATE) *reprove; punish*

castra, castrōrum, n. (pl. only) *camp, encampment;* castra pōnere, *pitch camp;* castra mōvēre, *break camp* I

cāsus, -ūs, m. *fall, accident, calamity; emergency, misfortune; fate, event, chance* I

catapulta, -ae, f. *catapult, (an engine which shot large arrows)*

catēnō, -āre, -āvī, -ātum (CONCATENATION) *chain together*

causa, -ae, f. *cause, reason; excuse, pretext;[legal] case;* causam cognōscō *hear a case;* abl. causā (w. preceding genitive) *for the sake of* I

causificor, -ārī, -ātus (causa + faciō) *pretend*

cautus, -a, -um *careful, cautious* 16

caveō, -ēre, cāvī, cautum *beware, take precautions against* 16

cēdō, -ere, cessī, cessum *move, yield, withdraw, go back, go away* (w. dat. of ref.) I

celer, celeris, celere *quick, swift, speedy* I

celeritās, -ātis, f. (celer, CELERITY) *speed, swiftness*

cēlō, -āre, -āvī, -ātum *conceal, hide*

celsus, -a, -um *high, lofty*

cēnō, -āre, -āvī, -ātum *dine*

cēnseō, -ēre, -uī, cēnsum *estimate, think; hold a census; give an opinion; decree, vote, determine* 9

cēnsus, -ūs, m. (censeō) *census, enumeration*

centēsimus, -a, -um *hundredth* I

centum (indecl.) *a hundred* I

centuria, -ae, f. (centum) *a century, a company of 60 to 100 men in a legion*

centūriō, centūriōnis, m. (centum) *centurion (a non-commissioned officer)*

cēra, -ae, f. *wax*

cernō, -ere, crēvī, crētum or certum *perceive, determine* I

certāmen, certāminis, n. (certō) *contest, struggle, rivalry*

certō, -āre, -āvī, -ātum *contend, struggle [in rivalry], vie* 8

certus, -a, -um *sure, certain, definite, specified, fixed;*

certiōrem facere, *inform;* certior fierī, *be informed;* certē, *at least, certainly* I

cervīx, cervīcis, f. *[nape of] the neck*

cervus, -ī, m. *stag*

cessō, -āre, -āvī, -ātum *cease; loiter; rest, pause, delay, hesitate* I

cēterum, adv. *for the rest, otherwise, but*

cēterus, -a, -um *other, the other;* pl. *the rest, the others* I

cibāria, -ōrum, n. *provisions*

cibus, -ī, m. *food*

cieō, -ēre, cīvī, citum *arouse; summon* 17

cingō, -ere, cīnxī, cīnctum *gird; surround, encircle* 7

cinis, cineris, m. *ashes* 14

circā (prep. w. acc.) *around, about, at the side of*

circā (adv.) *about, round about, approximately* I

circiter, adv. *about;* prep. with acc. *around, about*

circuitus, -ūs, m. (circum + eō) *circuit; roundabout way; circumference*

circum (prep. w. acc.) *around* I

circum (adv.) *around, round about, on all sides* I

circumarō, -āre, -āvī, -ātum *plow around*

circumcīdō, -ere, circumcīdī, circumcīsum (circum + caedō) *cut around, cut out*

circumclūdō, -ere, circumclūsī, circumclūsum (circum + claudō) *encircle*

circumdō, circumdāre, circumdedī, circumdatum (circum + dō) *put around, surround; border; envelop*

circumdūcō, -ere, circumdūxī, circumductum (circum + dūcō) *lead around*

circumferō, circumferre, circumtulī, circumlātum (circum + ferō, CIRCUMFERENCE) *bear around, carry around*

circumfundō, -ere, circumfūdī, circumfūsum (circum + fundō) *pour around; surround, hem in*

circummittō, -ere, circummīsī, circummissum (circum + mittō) *send around*

circumsistō, -ere, circumstitī, or circumstetī, ___ *surround, beset*

circumspectō, -āre, -āvī, -ātum (circum + spectō) *look around at*

circumspiciō, -ere, -spexī, -spectum (aspicio, CIRCUM-SPECTION) *look around, look over*

circumstō, -āre, circumstetī, circumstātum (circum + stō, CIRCUMSTANCE) *stand round, surround; beseige*

circumveniō, -īre, circumvēnī, circumventum (circum + veniō, CIRCUMVENT) *come around, go around, surround; deceive*

cis, prep. with acc. *on this side of*

citerior, -ius *on this side, hither; nearer, next*

citharoedus, -i, m. *singer (to the accompaniment of the cithara)*

citus, -a, -um (-cieō) *quick, speedy;* citō, *quickly*

cītō, -āre, -āvī, -ātum (cieō, CITE) *summon, urge on*

cītrā (prep. w. acc.) *on this side of*

cīvicus, -a, -um (cīvis) *relating to a citizen, civic, civil*

cīvīlis, -e (cīvis) *civic, of a citizen, of the citizens; courteous, polite, civil*

cīvis, cīvis, m. or f. (i-stem) *citizen, fellow citizen, townsman*

cīvitās, cīvitātis, f. *citizenship; citizenry, city, state* 2 (i-stem)

clādēs, -is, f. *destruction, disaster, defeat*

clam (prep. w. acc.) *without the knowledge of*

clam (adv.) *secretly, in private*

clāmitō, -āre, -āvī, -ātum *keep shouting, shout frequently*

clāmō, -āre, -āvī, -ātum *shout, cry; proclaim* I

clāmor, clāmōris, m. *clamor, shout, din, shouting, cry* 2

clangor, clangōris, m. *noise, clang, blare*

clārus, -a, -um *clear; bright; loud; famous* I

classicum, -ī, n. *[trumpet] call to advance*

classis, classis, f. (i-stem) *class; fleet; division of the people* 12

claudō, -ere, clausī, clausum *shut, close; beseige;* agmen claudere, *bring up the rear* I

clāvus, -ī, m. *nail, spike; a purple stripe [on the tunic]*

clēmentia, -ae, f. *mildness, mercy, clemency*

cliēns, clientis, m. *protegé, dependent [of a patrōnus]; client*

clientēla, -ae, f. *dependency*

clipeus, -ī, m. *[round metal] shield*

clīvus, ī, m. (DECLIVITY) *slope, ascent, sloping street*

cloāca, -ae, f. *sewer*

coacervō, -āre, -āvī, -ātum *heap, pile up*

coctilis, -e *burned, of burned bricks*

cocus, -i, m. (See coquus)

coëmō, -ere, coëmī, coëmptum (emō) *buy up*

coëō, coīre, coiī, or coīvī, coitum (eō) *come together, unite*

coepī, coepisse, coeptum (defect., perf. system only) *began* 1

coerceō, -ēre, uī, -itum (COERCE) *check, curb, control, confine, restrain*

cōgitātiō, cōgitātiōnis, f. *thought, plan, meditation, thinking*

cognātiō, cognātiōnis, f. *blood relations; kinsmen*

cognitiō, cognitiōnis, f. *understanding knowledge* (nāscor)

cognōmen, cognōminis, n. (nōmen) *cognomen* (a third or fourth name)

cognōscō, -ere, cognōvī, cognitum *come to know, find out, learn* (perf.) *know, recognize;* **causam cognōscō** *hear a case* 1

cōgō, -ere, coēgī, coactum *collect* (w. acc.); *compel* (w. inf. phrase) 1

cohors, cohortis, f. (i-stem) *cohort;* [general's] *bodyguard* 6

cohortātiō, -iōnis, f. *encouraging, exhortation*

cohortor, -ārī, -ātus *encourage, exhort, address*

collābor, -ī, collāpsus sum (lābor) *fall down, sink down, collapse*

collaudō, -āre, -āvī, -ātum (laudō) *praise highly*

collēga, -ae, m. *colleague*

collicō, -āre, -avī, -ātum *bind together*

colligō, -ere, collēgī, collēctum (-legō) *collect, assemble; obtain;* **sē colligere,** *rally, recover themselves* 1

collis, collis, m. (i-stem) *hill*

collocō, -āre, -āvī, -ātum (locus) *put, place, set, station; arrange*

colloquium, -ī, n. (loquor) *conversation, conference, colloquy*

colloquor, -ī, -locūtus (loquor) *talk with; hold a conference*

collum, -ī, n. (COLLAR) *neck*

colō, -ere, coluī, cultum *till, cultivate; live, dwell in, inhabit; worship, honor* 1

colōnus, -ī, m. (colō) *farmer, settler, colonist*

color, -ōris, m. *color, complexion*

coluber, -brī, m. *snake*

coma, -ae, f. *hair* [of the head]; *foliage* [of a tree] 4

combūrō, -ere, combussī, combustum (ūrō, COMBUSTION) *burn up, consume*

comes, comitis, m. or f. *companion, comrade, associate* 3

cominus (adv.) (see **comminus**)

comitās, comitātis, f. (comes, COMITY) *courtesy, civility, friendliness*

comitia, -ōrum, n. pl. (com + eō) *assembly* [of the Roman people]; *elections*

comitor, -ārī, -ātus sum (comes) *accompany, attend*

commeātus, -ūs, m. *free passage; leave* [of absence], *furlough; supplies; trip, voyage*

commemorō, -āre, -āvī, -ātum (memorō, COMMEMORATE) *mention, relate*

commendātiō, commendātiōnis, f. (mandō, COMMENDATION) *appeal*

commendō, -āre, -āvī, -ātum (mandō, COMMENDATION) *commend; introduce, present*

commeō, -āre, -āvi, -atum *go and come; pass to and fro*

commereor, -ērī, commeritus sum *commit be guilty of*

commīlitō, -ōnis, m. *comrade, fellow soldier*

comminīscor, -ī commentus sum *invent, think of*

comminus, odn. (com + manus) *hand to hand*

commissātiō, commissātiōnis, f. *drinking bout, drinking-party*

committō, -ere, commīsī, commissum *combine; entrust, commit; begin;* **proelium committere** *to join battle, fight* 1

commodō, -āre, -āvī, -ātum (ACCOMMODATE) (trans.) *lend, furnish;* (intrans.) *be obliging*

commodus, -a, -um (COMMODIOUS) *fitting, easy, suitable, convenient; favorable;* as noun, **commodum, -ī,** n. *convenience, advantage, profit*

commōveō, -ēre, commōvī, commōtum (moveo, COMMOTION) *move violently, move deeply, disturb, upset, excite; begin; influence*

communicō, -āre, -āvī, -ātum *share, communicate*

commūniō, -īre, -īvī, -ītum *strongly fortify, entrench*

commūnis, -e *common, general, shared, public* 15

commūtātiō, commūtātiōnis, f. (mūtō, COMMUTATION) *change*

commūtō, -āre, -āvī, -ātum (mūtō) *change, exchange, interchange; commute*

comparō, -āre, -āvī, -ātum (parō) *prepare, get together; furnish; get; buy, secure; compare*

compellō, -āre, -āvī, -ātum *address, accuse*

compellō, -ere, compulī, compulsum (pellō) *collect; confine; compel; drive together*

comperiō, -īre, comperī, compertum (cf. aperiō) *find out* [for certain]; *learn, discover; find guilty*

compēscō, -ere, compēscuī, ___ *restrain, check; quench* competītor, competītoris, m. (petō) *competitor, rival*

complector, -ī, complexus sum *embrace* 16

compleō, -ēre, complēvī, complētum *fill up, complete* 7

complexus, -ūs, m. (complector) *embrace*

complūrēs, complūra (plūrēs) *several, rather many; quite a few, a great many*

compōnō, -ere, composuī, compositum *put together, collect, arrange, quiet, compose; settle, conclude* I

comportō, -āre, -āvī, -ātum (portō) *carry, bring in, convey; collect*

comprecor, -ārī, -ātus *implore*

comprehendō, -ere, comprehendī, comprehēnsum *catch, seize, arrest, apprehend; comprehend*

cōnātus, -ūs, m. *attempt*

concēdō, -ere, concessī, concessum (intrans.) *retire, withdraw; (trans.) give up, submit; allow, concede, give in; permit* 16

concentus, -ūs, m. (canō) *singing [in a group]; serenade*

concidō, ere, -idī, -casum *fall*

concīdō, -ere, concīdī, concīsum (caedō, CONCISE) *cut, kill, destroy*

conciliō, -āre, -āvī, -ātum *reconcile, conciliate, win over; win, gain, procure*

concilium, -ī, n. *assembly, council;* concilium plēbis habēre *hold a meeting of the Comitia Tributa;* concilium populī habēre *hold a meeting of the Comitia Centuriata*

concitō, -āre, -āvī, -ātum (cieo) *stir up, rouse up, incite, excite; instigate*

conclāmō, -āre, -āvī, -ātum (clāmō) *shout together, cry aloud*

conculcō, -āre, -āvī, -ātum *tread, trample*

concupīscō, -ere, concupīvī, concupītum (cupiō, CONCUPISCENCE) *greatly desire*

concurrō, -ere, concurrī, concursum (currō, CONCUR) *run together, meet; fight; assemble*

concursō, -āre, ___, ___(currō) *rush to and fro, run about*

concursus, -ūs, m. (currō) *a running together, collision, meeting; concourse*

condemnō, -āre, -āvī, -ātum *condemn, sentence*

condiciō, condiciōnis, f. (con + dīcō) *condition, situation; terms*

condō, -ere, condidī, conditum *put together, collect, bury, conceal; found [a city]* I

condūcō, -ere, cōndūxi, conductum (dūcō, CONDUCE, CONDUCT) *bring together, collect*

cōnferō, cōnferre, contulī, collātus *bring together, collect;* (reflex.) *betake oneself, proceed, go;* (w. dat.) *compare* I

cōnfertus, -a, -um *crowded, dense, compact*

cōnfestim, adv. *at once, speedily*

cōnficiō, -ere, cōnfēcī, cōnfectum *do thoroughly, perform, finish, accomplish; compose; wear out, use up, weaken, kill* I

cōnfīdō, -ere, confīsus sum (fidēs, CONFIDE) *trust; rely, have confidence in, be confident*

cōnfirmō, -āre, -āvī, -ātum *confirm, assert, declare; encourage, strengthen; establish* I; cōnfirmātus, -a, -um *confident, encouraged*

cōnfiteor, -ērī, confessus sum *admit, confess*

cōnflagrō, -āre, -āvī, -ātum *be on fire, burn*

cōnflīgō, -ere, flīxī, flīctum (CONFLICT) *strike together, contend, fight*

cōnfluō, -ere, cōnflūxī, ___cf. (flūmen) *flow together, assemble*

cōnfodiō, -ere, confōdī, confossum (FOSSIL) *dig thoroughly; stab; assassinate*

cōnfugiō, -ere, confūgī, ___(fugiō) *flee, take refuge*

cōnfundō, -ere, confūdī, confūsum (fundō) *pour together; confuse, trouble, disturb*

congerō, -ere congessī, congestum (gerō, CONGEST) *bring together, heap, collect, construct*

congredior, -ī, congressus *meet, come together*

congregō, -āre, -āvī, -ātum *collect, assemble, congregate*

congressus, -ūs, m. (CONGRESS) *meeting, engagement*

coniciō, -ere, coniēcī, coniectum *throw together, hurl, drive, strike;* conicere in fugam *put to flight*

coniectūra, -ae, f. (coniciō) *guess, conjecture, inference*

coniectus, -ūs, m. (coniciō) *a throwing together; a hurling*

coniūnctim, adv. (iungō) *jointly, in common*

coniungō, -ere, coniūnxī, coniūnctum (iungō) *join, unite*

coniūnx (or coniux), coniugis, m. or f. *spouse, wife, husband* I

coniūrātiō, coniūrātiōnis, f. (iūrō) *sworn union, conspiracy, plot*

coniūrātus, -a, -um (iūrō) *conspiring;* n., *conspirator*

coniūrō, -āre, -āvī, -ātum (iūrō) *swear together, conspire* cōnor, -ārī, -ātus (conative) *try, attempt, undertake*

conquestus, -ūs, m. (queror) *[loud] complaint*

conquīrō, -ere, conquīsīvī, conquīsītum (quaerō) *seek out, hunt up; bring together, collect*

cōnsalūtō, -āre, -āvī, -ātum (salūs) *join in greeting, join in saluting*

cōnsanguineus, -a, -um (sanguis, CONSAGUINEITY) *of the same blood; related; n., kinsman, blood relation*

cōnscendō, -ere, cōnscendī, cōnscēnsum *mount, ascend; embark, go on board*

cōnscius, -a, -um (sciō) *conscious, aware*

cōnscrībō, -ere, cōnscrīpsī, cōnscrīptum (scrībo, CONSCRIPT) *write; enroll*

consecrō, -āre, -āvī, -ātum (sacer) *consecrate, devote [to a god]; dedicate; curse;* cōnsecrātus, -a, -um *consecrated, holy, sacred*

cōnsēnsiō, -ōnis, f. (sentiō) *agreement, unity, feeling*

cōnsēnsus, -ūs, m. (sentiō, CONSENSUS) *agreement, unanimity; consent*

cōnsentiō, -īre, cōnsēnsī, cōnsēnsum (sentio, CONSENT) *agree, resolve unanimously, conspire, harmonize, think together*

cōnsequor, -ī, cōnsecūtūs sum *follow [as a consequence], follow closely; overtake, catch up with; get, obtain* 2

cōnserō, -ere, cōñseruī, consertum *connect; join*

cōnservō, -āre, -āvī, -ātum (servo, CONSERVE) *preserve, save, spare; keep, observe*

cōnsīdō, -ere, cōnsēdī, cōnsessum (sēdēs) *sit down, settle, rest, encamp*

cōnsilium, -ī, n. *plan; advice, counsel; judgment, consent* I

cōnsimilis, -e (similis) *like, very similar*

cōnsistō, -ere, cōnstitī, cōnstitum *halt, stop; take a stand; find footing; stay, remain; settle; consist*

cōnsōlor, -ārī, -ātus *console, comfort*

cōnspectus, -ūs, m. *sight, view*

cōnspiciō, -ere, conspēxi, conspectum *observe, see;* pass. *be conspicuous*

cōnspicor, -ārī, -ātus *catch sight of, see*

cōnspīrō, -āre, -āvī, -ātum (spīrō) *sound together, unite, conspire*

cōnstīpō, -āre, -āvī, -ātum (CONSTIPATION) *crowd together*

cōnstituō, -ere, cōnstituī, cōnstitūtum *establish; decide, determine; put, place; draw up, arrange; construct; constitute* I

cōnstitūtiō, cōnstitūtiōnis, f. (cōnstituō, CONSTITUTION) *decision; settlement*

cōnstō, -āre, constitī, *consist; stand firm; depend on; impersonal,* cōnstat *it is established, it is well known, it is certain;* cōnstāns, cōnstantis, *constant* 11

cōnsuēscō, -ere, cōnsuēvī, cōnsuētum *accustom; become accustomed*

cōnsuētūdō, cōnsuētūdinis, f. *custom, habit; practice; intimacy*

cōnsul, cōnsulis, m. *consul*

cōnsulāris, -e *consular, of a Consul;* (noun) *ex-Consul*

cōnsulātus, -ūs, m. *consulship*

cōnsulō, -ere, cōnsuluī, cōnsultum (w. acc.) *consult;* (w. dat.) *take counsel for, consult the interests of, have regard for, look out for* I cōnsultum, -ī, n. (consulo) *deliberation, decree, decision* consultō, *purposely, on purpose; advisedly*

cōnsūmō, -ere, cōnsumpsī, cōnsumptum (sūmō) *consume, devour; burn up, destroy; spend*

contabulō, -āre, -āvī, -ātum *board over; build*

contagiō, cōntagiōnis, f. (tangō) *contact; contagion*

contegō, -ere, contēxī, contēctum (tegō) *cover; conceal*

contemnō, -ere, contēmpsī, contemptum *despise, feel contempt for, belittle, scorn, disdain* 2

contemptiō, cōntemptiōnis, f. (contemnō) *contempt*

contendō, -ere, contendī, contentum *strive, struggle, contend; hasten; march*

contentiō, contentiōnis, f. *effort; contention, strife; controversy*

contentus, -a, -um *satisfied, content*

conterminus, -a, -um *close by, near*

conterreō, -ēre, -uī, -itum *frighten thoroughly*

contexō, -ere, contexuī, contextum (CONTEXT) *weave, join, construct*

contiguus, -a, -um (contingō) *side by side, touching, contiguous*

contineō, -ēre, -uī, contentum *hold together, restrain, bound; shut in; hold back; embrace; bound;* sē continēre, *to remain;* continēns, continentis *bordering, adjacent, continuous; with* terra *understood, the mainland, continent* I

contingō, -ere, contigī, contactum *touch; concern;* contingit *it happens, it befalls* (w. acc. of the person) 10

continuus, -a, -um (contineō) *successive, continuous;* **continuō,** *immediately, forthwith*

contiō, contiōnis, f. *public meeting, assembly*

contollō, -ere, _____, _____(tollō) with **gradum,** *go to meet*

contrā (prep. w. acc.) *against, facing, contrary to, off; in reply to* I

contrā (adv.) *on the contrary; on the other hand; in return* I

contrahō, -ere, contrāxī, contrāctum (trahō) *bring together, assemble, collect; make smaller, contract*

contrārius, -a, -um (contrā) *facing, opposite; opposed; contrary*

contrōversia, -ae, f. (contrā + vertō) *controversy, dispute*

contubernaalis, -is m. (i-stem) *tent-mate*

contubernium, -ī, n. *a tent [for 10 men and an officer]; [military] apprenticeship*

contumēlia, -ae, f. (CONTUMELY) *insult, outrage*

cōnūbium, -ī, n. nūbō, (CONNUBIAL) *legal marriage; right of intermarriage*

conveniō, -īre, convēnī, conventum *come together, meet, assemble, convene; agree;* **convenit** *it is agreed, it is right* I

conventus, -ūs, m. (conveniō, CONVENT) *assembly, meeting;* **conventūs agere,** *to hold court*

convertō, -ere, convertī, conversus (verto, CONVERT) *turn round; direct the attention of; change;* **conversa sīgna īnferre,** *face about and advance*

convīva, -ae, m. (con + vīvō) *dinner guest, party guest*

convīvō, ere, -īxī, -victus, *to dine together*

convocō, -āre, -āvī, -ātum *call together, assemble, convoke; summon* I

coorior, -īrī, coortus sum (orior) *arise, appear, break out*

cōpia, -ae, f. *supply; plenty; opportunity* I; (pl.) *forces, troops; resources, wealth* 9

cōpiōsus, -a, -um (cōpia, COPIOUS) *well supplied, wealthy, rich*

coqua, -ae, f. or **coquus, -ī,** m. or **cocus, ī,** m. *cook*

cor, cordis, n. *heart* I

coram (prep. w. abl.) *in the presence of*

coram, adv. *face to face; in person*

cornū, -ūs, n. *horn; wing [of an army]* I

corōna, -ae, f. (CORONATION) *garland, wreath; crown;* **sub corōnā vēndere,** *to sell as slaves*

corpus, corporis, n. *body* I

corrumpō, -ere, corrūpī, corruptum (con + rumpō) *destroy, ruin; corrupt, bribe*

cortex, corticis, m. & f. *cork, piece of cork*

corvus, -ī, m. *blackbird, raven, crow*

coss. = cōnsulibus

cotīdiānus, -a, -um (quot + diēs, QUOTIDIAN) *daily; ordinary, usual*

cotīdiē (adv.) (quot + diēs, QUOTIDIAN) *daily, every day*

crās (adv.) *tomorrow* I

crāstinus, -a, -um *tomorrow's, belonging to tomorrow*

crātēs, -is, f. *wattle, wickerwork; bundle of brush*

crēber, crēbra, crēbrum *thick, crowded, close; repeated, frequent;* **crēbrō,** *frequently*

crēdō, -ere, crēdidī, crēditum (w. acc.) *trust, believe; think* (w. dat.) *entrust* I

cremō, -āre, -āvī, -ātum *burn, burn up, cremate*

creō, -āre, -āvī, -ātum *create, make, beget; elect, appoint* 7

crēscō, -ere, crēvī, crētum *grow, increase* 5

creta, -ae, f. *chalk, white earth*

crīmen, crīminis, n. *charge, accusation; crime, offense* 7

crīminātiō, crīminātiōnis, f. (crīmen) *accusation, charge; calumny*

croceus, -a, -um *of saffron; saffron colored, yellow*

cruciātus, -ūs, m. (EXCRUCIATING) *torture, suffering*

crūdēlis, -e *cruel*

crūdēlitās, crūdēlitātis, f. *cruelty*

cruentātus, -a, -um *blood stained*

cruentus, -a, -um *bloody, gory*

cruor, cruōris, m. *blood, gore*

crūs, crūris, n. *leg*

crux, crucis, f. (CRUCIFY) *cross, gallows*

cubiculārius, -ī, m. *chamber slave*

cubiculum, -ī, n. *bedroom*

cubīle, cubīlis, n. *bed, couch*

culpa, -ae, f. *blame, guilt, fault* 9

culter, cultrī, m. *knife*

cultūra, -ae, f. (colō, CULTURE) *cultivation*

cultus, -ūs, m. *care, cultivation; civilization, culture, refinement, adornment, dress; education; reverence* 15

cum (prep. w. abl.) *with* I

cum (adv. conj.) *when* I; *since; although* **cum . . .**

(**cum** *continued*)

tum, *as . . . so especially, not only . . . but also;*
cum primum, *as soon as* 18

cumulātus, -a, -um (ACCUMULATE) *heaped up*

cunctātiō, cunctātiōnis, f. *delay, hesitation*

cunctor, -ārī, -ātus sum *hesitate, linger, be slow*

cūnctus, -a, -um *altogether; all, the whole, entire*
12

cunīculus, -ī, m. *rabbit; tunnel*

cupiditās, cupiditātis, f. (cupiō) *eagerness, desire,
greed, lust; cupidity* I

cupīdō, cupīdinis, f. *longing, desire, eagerness* I

cupidus, -a, -um (cupiō, CUPIDITY) *desirous, eager
for* (w. obj. gen.)

cupiō, -ere, cupīvī, cupītum *want, long for, desire*
I

cūr (interrogative adv.) *why?* I

cūra, -ae, f. *care, carefulness, anxiety, trouble* I

cūrō, -āre, -āvī, -ātum *provide for, take care of,
watch over, manage* 19

currō, -ere, cucurrī, cursum *run* I

currus, -ūs, m. (currō) *chariot, car*

cursus, -ūs, m. *a running, course* I; **cursus honōrum**
political career (holding the magistracies in order
from lowest to highest) 18

curūlis, -e *curule* (of a higher magistrate)

curvāmen, -inis, n. *curve, bending*

custōdia, -ae, f. (custōs, CUSTODY) *guard, protection,
guardianship, keeping*

custōdiō, -īre, -īvī, -ītum (custōs) *guard, watch, keep*

custōs, custōdis, m. or f. *guard, watchman* 5

D

D 500 I

damnō, -āre, -āvī, -ātum *condemn, damn; sentence*

damnōsus, -a, -um *harmful*

dē (prep. w. abl.) *from, down from; about, con-
cerning; just after, during* I

dea, -ae, f. *goddess* I

dēbeō, -ēre, -uī, -itum *owe; ought, must* I

dēbilis, -e (dē + habeō, DEBILITATE) *weak, feeble*

dēcēdō, -ere, dēcessī, dēcessum (cedō, DECEASE) *go
away, depart; die*

decem (indecl.) *ten* I

dēcernō, -ere, dēcrēvī, dēcrētum (cernō) *decide;
decree; contend;* resolve; **dēcrētum, -ī,** n. *decree,
decision*

dēcertō, -āre, -āvī, -ātum (certō) *fight, fight a decisive
battle*

decet, -ēre, -uit, _____*it becomes, it is becoming*

decimus, -a, -um *tenth* I

dēcipiō, -ere, dēcēpī, dēceptum (capiō, DECEPTION)
cheat, deceive; catch

dēclīnō, -āre, -āvī, -ātum (decline) *bend aside, turn
away; close; lower; avoid, shun*

dēclīvis, -e *sloping, descending; as noun,* **dēclīvia,
-ium,** n. *slopes, declivities*

decor, decōris, m. (DECORATE) *beauty*

decōrus, -a, -um (DECOROUS) *beautiful, fitting; decorated*

dēcrētum, -ī, n. (cernō) *decree, decision*

decumānus, -a, -um (decem) *decuman, of a tenth
part; rear*

decuria, -ae, f. (decem) *decuria,* [cavalry] *squad* [of
ten men]

decuriō, decuriōnis, m. (decem) *decurion* (officer in
charge of a decuria)

dēcurrō, -ere, dēcurrī, dēcursum (currō) *run down;
hasten*

decus, decoris, n. *ornament, honor, glory, dignity;*
(pl.) *honorable exploits* I

dedecus, dedecoris, n. (decus) *dishonor, disgrace*

dēdicō, -āre, -āvī, -ātum *consecrate, dedicate*

dēditīcius, -a, -um (dē + dō) *surrendered;* n.,
prisoner of war, captive

dēditiō, dēditiōnis, f. (dē + dō) *surrender*

dēdō, -ere, dēdidī, dēditum (dē + dō) *give up,
surrender, devote*

dēdūcō, -ere, dēdūxī, dēductum *lead down, escort,
lead away; launch; induce* I

dēfendō, -ere, dēfendī, dēfēnsum *defend, guard;
ward off, repel* 4

dēfēnsiō, dēfēnsiōnis, f. (dēfendō) *defense*

dēfēnsor, dēfēnsōris, m. (dēfendō) *defender, protec-
tor*

dēferō, dēferre, dētulī, dēlātum (ferō, DEFER) *bring
down, take down; remove; bestow on; offer;
submit; register* [a name]; *cast ashore*

dēficiō, -ere, dēfēcī, dēfectum *fail, run out, fall short,
be deficient; revolt; rebel* I

dēfigō, -ere, dēfīxī, dēfīxum *drive in*

dēfleō, -ēre, dēflēvī, dēflētum (flēo) *weep for*

dēformō, -āre, -āvī, -ātum (fōrma) *uglify, deform; disgrace, dishonor*

dēfraudō, -āre, -āvī, -ātum *cheat, defraud, deceive*

dēfugiō, -ere, dēfūgī, ___ (fugiō) *flee; avoid*

dēfungor, -ī, dēfūnctus sum (fungor, DEFUNCT) (w. abl.) *finish, complete;* (w. vītā understood) *die*

dēgredior, -ī, dēgressus sum (PROGRESS, REGRESS) *go down, walk down*

dēiciō, -ere, dēiēcī, dēiectum (iaciō, DEJECTED) *throw down, lay down; dislodge, rout; drive; kill, destroy; disappoint*

dēiectus, -ūs, m. (iaciō) *slope, declivity*

deinceps (adv.) *one after another, successively; continuously*

deinde (adv.) *next, then; henceforth, hereafter, thereafter* I

dēlectus, -ūs, m. (deligō) *draft, conscription*

dēleō, -ēre, dēlēvī, dēlētum *wipe out, destroy, eradicate, erase, blot out; delete*

dēlīberō, -āre, -āvī, -ātum *weigh, consider, deliberate*

dēlictum, -ī, n. *offense*

dēligō, -āre, -āvī, -ātum (LIGAMENT, LIGATURE) *bind, tie, fasten*

dēligō, -ere, dēlēgī, dēlēctum *select, pick out, chose;* dēlēctus, -a, -um *picked, chosen;* (noun, pl.), *picked men, advisory staff* I

dēlīrō, -āre, -āvī, -ātum (DELIRIUM) *to be crazy, to rave*

dēlitēscō, -ere, delituī, ___ *hide, lie in wait*

dēlūdō, -ere, delūsī, dēlūsum (lūdō, DELUDE) *mock*

dēmetō, -ere, demessuī, demessum *reap, cut; gather*

dēmigrō, -āre, -āvī, -ātum *migrate, depart, withdraw*

dēminuō, -ere, dēminuī, dēminūtum (minus) *lessen, diminish, weaken*

dēmittō, -ere, dēmīsī, dēmissum (mittō) *let go down, lower, let fall, give up;* dēmissus, -a, -um *dropped; downcast, low*

dēmō, -ere, dēmpsī, dēmptum *take down; cut off; take away, subtract* I

dēmōnstrō, -āre, -āvī, -ātum *point out, demonstrate, show; explain* I

dēmum (adv.) *at length, at last;* tum dēmum *only then, then indeed*

dēnegō, -āre, -āvī, -ātum (negō) *refuse, reject [a request]*

dēnique (adv.) *finally, at last, in short* I

dēns, dentis, m. (DENTAL) *tooth, fang, tusk*

dēnsūs, -a, -um *dense, thick, close together* 20

dēnūdō, -āre, -āvī, -ātum *denude, strip; plunder*

dēnūntiō, -āre, -āvī, -ātum (nuntiō, DENOUNCE) *announce, declare; threaten; urge; admonish; order*

dēpellō, -ere, dēpulī, dēpulsum (pellō) *drive out, expel; remove*

dēpōnō, -ere, dēposuī, dēpositum (pōnō, DEPONENT) *put down, lay aside, give up; resign*

dēpopulor, -ārī, -ātus (dē + populus, DEPOPULATE) *lay waste, ravage; pass., be devastated*

dēportō, -āre, -āvī, -ātum (porto, DEPORT) *carry off; obtain*

dēprecātor, dēprecatōris, m. *intercessor*

dēprecor, -ārī, -ātus sum (DEPRECATE) *beg off; intercede; pray [on someone's behalf]*

dēprehendō, -ere, dēprehēndī, dēprehēnsum (PREHENSILE) *seize, catch; surprise*

dērēctus, -a, -um (rēgō) *straight, perpendicular*

dērīdeō, -ēre, dērīsī, dērīsum (rideō) *mock, deride, laugh at*

dēscendō, -ere, dēscendī, dēscēnsum *come down, go down, descend; dismount*

dēserō, -ere, dēseruī, dēsertum *leave, abandon, desert;* dēsertus, -a, -um *deserted, solitary, lonely* 4

dēsīderium, -ī, n. *longing, desire*

dēsidia, -ae, f. (dē + sedeō) *indolence, idleness*

dēsiliō, -īre, dēsiluī, dēsultum *leap down, dismount*

desinō, -ere, dēsiī, dēsitum *stop, cease* I

dēsistō, -ere, dēstitī, dēstitum (desist) *leave off, cease, stop; give up*

dēspērō, -āre, -āvī, -ātum (dē + spērō) *despair of, give up hope; give up*

dēspondeō, -ēre, dēspondī, dēspōnsum *promise in marriage*

dēstinō, -āre, -āvī, -ātum (DESTINATION) *select [for an office]; bind, fasten; settle; devote*

dēstituō, -ere, dēstituī, dēstitūtum (dē + stō, DESTITUTE) *desert, leave*

dēstringō, -ere, dēstrīnxī, destrictum *strip off, bare, uncover; draw [a sword]*

dēsum, dēesse, dēfuī, dēfutūrus *be away, be missing, be lacking, be wanting; fail, desert* I

dēsuper, adv. (dē + super) *from above*

dēterreō, -ēre, -uī, -itum *frighten off; deter, prevent*

detrāhō, -ere, detrāxī, detrāctum *drag down; remove; humiliate, slander* 2 dētrīmentum, -ī, n. (dē + terō) *loss, damage, defeat; detriment*

dētrūdō, -ere, dētrūsī, dētrūsum (INTRUDE, PROTRUDE,) *push away, push down, dislodge, drive out*

dēturbō, -āre, -āvī, -ātum (turba) *dislodge, cast down; drive off*

deus, -ī, m. *god* I

dēvehō, -ere, dēvexī, dēvectum (vehō) *carry away, remove; convey*

dēveniō, -īre, dēvēnī, dēventum (veniō) *come to, reach*

devinciō, -īre, devinxī, devinctum (vinciō) *put under obligation*

dēvorō, -āre, -āvī, -ātum *gulp down, devour*

dēvōtiō, dēvōtiōnis, f. (dē + vōveō) *curse*

dēvoveō, -ēre, dēvōvī, dēvōtum (dē + vōveō) *consecrate; devote [to death], vow the death of, curse*

dexter, dextera, dexterum (or dextra, dextrum) *on the right; handy, dexterous, skillful* I

dextimus, -a, -um (superl. of dexter) I

dicō, -āre, -āvī, -ātum *dedicate, devote*

dīcō, -ere, dīxī, dictum *say, talk; tell, call, name; set, appoint; plead* I

diēs, diēī, m. & f. *day;* multō diē, *late in the day;* in diēs, *every day, from day to day* I

differō, differre, distulī, dīlātum (ferō, DILATORY) *put off, postpone; differ; spread, scatter*

difficilis, -e *difficult, hard* I

difficultās, difficultātis, f. (difficilis) *difficulty; distress*

diffīdō, -ere, diffīsus sum (fidēs, DIFFIDENT) *distrust; despair*

diffundō, -ere, diffūdī, diffūsum (fundō) *pour out, spread out, diffuse*

digitus, -ī, m. *finger; toe; digit*

dīgnitās, dīgnitātis, f. *worth; dignity, reputation, honor; rank* 13

dīgnus, -a, -um *worthy,* (with abl.) I

dīgredior, -ī, dīgressus *come away, depart; digress*

dīiūdicō, -āre, -āvī, -ātum (iūdex) *decide, adjudicate*

dīligentia, -ae, f. *care, diligence; industry*

dīligō, -ere, dīlēxī, dīlēctum *love, value, esteem, feel affection for;* dīligēns, dīligentis *careful, diligent; industrious* I

dīmētior, -īrī, dimēnsus (DIMENSION) *measure; (of work) lay out*

dīmicātiō, -ōnis, f. *fight, struggle, contest*

dīmicō, -āre, -āvī, -atum *fight*

dīmidius, -a, -um (DEMI-) *half;* dīmidia pārs *one-half*

dīmittō, -ere, dīmīsī, dīmissus (mittō) *send away, send abroad, dismiss; let go, release; lose; leave*

dīripiō, -ere, dīripuī, dīreptum (rapiō) *tear apart, plunder, ransack*

discēdō, -ere, discessī, discessum *go away, depart, withdraw; give up;* ab armīs discēdere, *lay down arms* I

discernō -ere, discrēvī, discrētum (cernō) *see, discern; distinguish*

discessus, -ūs, m. (discēdō) *departure*

disciplīna, -ae, f. (discō) *instruction, teaching, learning, training, discipline*

discipulus, -ī, m. (discō, DISCIPLE) *pupil, student*

discō, -ere, didicī _____*learn* 9

discordia, -ae, f. (cor) *disagreement, discord*

discors, discordis (cor, DISCORD) *warring, disagreeing*

discrīmen, discrīminis, n. (cernō, DISCRIMINATE) *distinction; crisis*

discrīminō, -āre, -āvī, -ātum *separate, discriminate, discern*

discurrō, -ere, discurrī, discursum (currō, DISCURSIVE) *run about, run in different directions*

disertus, -a, -um *eloquent*

disiciō, -ere, disiēcī, disiectum (iaciō) *scatter; rout; drive apart*

disiungō, -ere, -iunxī, -iūnctum *separate*

dispār, disparis (PĀR) *unequal, disparate*

dispergō, -ere, dispersī, dispersum (spargō) *scatter, disperse*

dispertiō, -īre, _____, _____(pars) *divide*

dispōnō, -ere, disposuī, dispositum (pōnō) *place here and there; dispose; arrange; station, post*

disputātiō, dīsputātiōnis, f. (putō) *discussion, debate, dispute*

disputō, -āre, -āvī, -ātum (putō) *argue, dispute*

dissēnsiō, dīssēnsiōnis, f. (sentiō) *disagreement, dissension*

dissimilis, -e *unlike, dissimilar* I

dissimilitūdō, dissimilitūdinis, f. (dissimilis) *difference*

dissipō, -āre, -āvī, -ātum *scatter, disperse, dissipate*

dissolvō, -ere, dissolvī, dissolūtum (solvō, DISSOLVE) *loosen, break up, destroy;* dissolūtus, -a, -um *dissolute*

dissonus, -a, -um (sonō) *discordant, dissonant; disagreeing*

dissuādeō, -ēre, dissuāsī, dissuāsum (persuādeō, DIS-SUADE) *advise against, oppose [by argument]*

distineō, -ēre, -uī, distentum (teneō) *keep apart, separate*

distribuō, -ere, distribuī, distribūtum *distribute, divide, assign*

diū adv. *for a long time;* **quam diū,** *as long as* I

diūtinus, -a, -um (diū) *long lasting, long*

diūturnus, -a, -um (diū) *long lasting*

dīvellō, -ere, dīvellī, dīvolsum *tear away, tear to pieces*

dīvertō, -ere, dīvertī, dīversum *turn away, turn in a different direction; separate* **dīversus, -a, -um** *hostile; opposed; different, diverse; separate, apart* 18

dīves, dīvitis *rich, wealthy;* 11

dīvidō, -ere, dīvīsī, dīvīsum *divide, separate, share, distribute* 12

dīvīnitus (adv.) (dīvus) *by divine influence, by divine inspiration*

dīvīnus, -a, -um (divus) *divine, of the gods, godlike; prophetic*

dīvitiae, -ārum, f. *wealth, riches* 15

dīvus, -a, -um *divine; (of an emperor) deified* 11

dō, dare, dedī, datum *give, give up, surrender; grant;* **poenās dare,** *suffer punishment;* **negōtium dare,** *to direct;* **sē in fugam dare,** *take to flight* 19

doceō, -ēre, -uī, doctum *teach, inform, show, point out* I

doleō, -ēre, -uī, -itum *suffer pain, suffer, grieve; be moved; cause pain* (w. dat.); *lament* (w. acc.); *be sorry* (w. inf. phrase) I

dōlium, -ī, n. *[large earthenware] jar, vat*

dolor, dolōris, m. *pain, grief, sorrow* I

domesticus, -a, -um (domus) *domestic, household, native, civil, of the house*

dominātiō, dominātiōnis, f. (dominus) *domination, mastery; empire; tyranny*

dominus, -ī, m. *lord, master [of a household, of a political unit]* I

domō, -āre, domuī, domitum *tame, subdue, conquer, master*

domus, -ūs, f. *home* I

dōnec, conj. *as long as, until, while* 18

dōnō -āre, -āvī, -ātum *present; bestow, grant, give* 18

donum, -ī, n. *gift* 17

dormiō, -īre, -īvī, -ītum (DORMITORY) *sleep*

dōs, dōtis, f. *dowry, dower*

druidēs, -um, m. pl. *druids, Gallic priests*

dracō, dracōnis, m. *dragon, large serpent*

dubitātiō, dubitātiōnis, f. (dubitō) *doubt, hesitation*

dubitō, -āre, -āvī, -ātum *doubt, hesitate* I

dubius, -a, -um *doubtful, hesitating, at a loss;* **nōn dubium est** *there is no doubt* 20

ducentēsimus, -a, -um *two hundredth* I

ducentī, -ae, -a *two hundred* I

dūcō, -ere, dūxī, ductum *lead, guide* I; *think, consider; prolong, put off; of a trench, make, dig;* **in mātrimōnium dūcere,** *marry;* **spīritum dūcere,** *draw breath*

dulcis, -e *sweet, pleasant;* n. pl. **dulcia,** *sweets* 13

dum (adv. conj.) *while, as long as, until, provided that* 18

dum modo (or **dummodo**), conj. *provided, if only*

duo, duae, duo *two* I

duodecim (indecl.) *twelve* I

duodecimus, -a, -um *twelfth* I

duodēvīcēsimus, -a, -um *eighteenth* I

duodēvīgintī (indecl.) *eighteen* I

duplex, duplicis *double, twofold; two-faced* I

duplicō, -āre, -āvī, -ātum (duplex) *double; duplicate*

dūritia, -ae, f. *hardness; hardship*

dūrō, -āre, -āvī, -ātum *harden; endure, last*

dūrus, -a, -um (DOUR) *hard; harsh, rough; cruel; durable*

dux, ducis, m. *leader, guide* I

E

ē, ex (prep. w. abl.) *from, out of* I

eā, adv. *there, on that side; in that way*

ēbrius, -a, -um (INEBRIATE) *drunk*

ebur, eboris, n. *ivory; sheath of a sword, scabbard*

ecce (interjection) *here! see! see here!* **ecce nōs** *here we are*

ecquid, inter. adv. *at all?, any at all?*

edepol, interj. *by Pollux!*

ēdīcō, -ere, ēdīxī, ēdictum (dīcō, EDICT) *proclaim, appoint; publish; order, decree, ordain*

ēdiscō, -ere, ēdidicī, ___ (disco) *learn by heart; commit to memory*

ēdō, -ere, ēdidī, ēditum (ē + dō) *give out, put forth, publish; edit; inflict;* **mūnera ēdere** *sponsor gladiatorial games;* **lūdōs ēdere** *produce plays;* **ēditus, -a, -um** *high, elevated* edō, ēsse, ēdī, ēsum *eat* 16

ēdoceō, -ēre, -uī, ēdocitum *instruct, inform, apprise*

ēducō, -āre, -āvī, -ātum (edō) *bring up, rear, educate*

ēdūcō, -ere, ēdūxī, ēductum *lead out, raise up, draw up; rear* I

effēminō, -āre, -āvī, -ātum (fēmina) *weaken, enervate, make effeminate*

efferō, efferre, extulī, ēlātum (ferō) *bring out, bring forth, raise up; carry out; publish; praise, elate*

efficiō, -ere, effēcī, effectum *produce, accomplish, effect; bring about; build, make* I

effodiō, -ere, effōdī, effossum (FOSSIL) *dig out, excavate*

effugiō, -ere, effūgī, effugitum (fugiō) *flee, escape, elude*

effundō, -ere, effūdī, effūsum (ex + fundō, EFFUSIVE) *pour out, lavish, squander; effūsus, -a, um extravagant, immoderate*

egeō, -ēre, -uī, ___ *need, lack, want* (w. abl. of separation)

ego, meī (pers. & refl. pron.) I

ēgredior, -ī, ēgressus sum (EGRESS) *go out, walk out, leave; disembark*

ēgregius, -a, -um (EGREGIOUS) *outstanding, eminent, excellent*

ēheu, interj. *alas!*

ei, interj. *Ah, woe!*

ēiaculor, -ārī, -ātus sum *shoot forth, spout forth*

ēiciō, -ere, ēiēcī, ēiectum *throw out, cast out; drive out, expel; sē ēicere rush out* I

ēiulō, -āre, ___, ___ *wail, bewail, lament*

elephantus, -ī, m. *elephant*

ēliciō, -ere, ēlicuī, ēlicitum (ELICIT) *draw out, entice*

ēloquor, -ī, ēlocūtus (loquor, ELOCUTION) *speak out*

ēmicō, -āre, ēmicuī, ēmicātum *leap out, spring forth*

ēmineō, -ēre, -uī, ___ (eminent) *stand out; be prominent*

ēminus, adv *from a distance* (ē + manus)

ēmittō, -ere, ēmisī, ēmissum (mittō) *let go out, send out, emit; set free*

ēmō, -ere, ēmī, ēmptum *buy; acquire, obtain* I

ēn interj. *lo!, behold!, see!*

enim (postpositive conj.) *for* I

ēnsis, ēnsis, m. *sword*

ēnūntiō, -āre, -āvī, -ātum (nūntiō, ENUNCIATE) *speak out, report; reveal*

eō (adv.) *[to] here, [to] there, to this place, to that place* I

eō, īre, iī (īvī), itum *go, move, march, advance* I

eōdem (adv.) *to the (this, that) same place* I

epistula, -ae, f. *letter, epistle*

epulae, -ārum, f. *feast, banquet*

epulor, -ārī, -ātus sum *feast*

eques, equitis, m. *horseman; (as title) Knight; (pl.) cavalry* 8

equester, equestris, equestre (equus, EQUESTRIAN) *of horsemen; of knights; of horses; on horseback*

equidem, adv. (quidem) *truly, indeed; for my part*

equitātus, -ūs, m. (eques) *cavalry*

equus, -ī, m. *horse* I

ērādīcō, -āre, -āvī, -ātum *root out, eradicate*

ergā, prep. with acc. *towards*

ergō (adv.) *therefore, consequently, then* I

ērigō, -ere, ērēxī, ērēctum (regō) *raise up; encourage; ērēctus, -a, -um high, erect*

ēripiō, -ere, ēripuī, ēreptum *snatch away, tear out, remove, rescue; sē ēripere, escape* 3

errō, -āre, -āvī, -ātum *wander, stray, go wrong, be wrong* I

error, errōris, m. (errō) *a wandering, uncertainty; error, blunder; deception*

ērudiō, -īre, -īvī, -ītum (ERUDITE) *educate, teach*

ēruptiō, ēruptiōnis, f. (rumpō, ERUPTION) *sortie, rush*

erus, -ī, m. *master, owner*

essedārius, -ī, m. *charioteer*

essedum, -ī, n. *[heavy traveling or light fighting] chariot*

estō, fut. imperative 3rd sing. of sum, *shall be, so be it*

et (conj.) *and* I; et . . . et *both . . . and* I

et (adv.) *also, even* I

etiam (adv.) *even, yet, still, also* I nōn sōlum . . . sed etiam, *not only . . . but also*

etsī (adv.) *even if, although* I

ēvādō, -ere, ēvāsī, ēvāsum *go out, come out, evade, escape*

ēvellō, -ere, ēvellī, ēvulsum *pull out*

ēveniō, -īre, ēvēnī, ēventum *come out; ēvenit it happens, it turns out* (w. dat. of the person) 10

ēventus, -ūs, m. (ēveniō) *outcome, result; event; chance, fate, accident*

ēvertō, -ere, ēvertī, ēversum (vertō) *overturn; destroy, ruin*

ēvocō, -āre, -āvī, -ātum (vocō) *call out, call forth, summon, evoke; ēvocātus, -ī, m. veteran volunteer* ēvolō, -āre, -āvī, -ātum (volō) *fly out, fly up, leap out*

ex see ē, ex

exanimō, -āre, -āvī, -ātum (ex + anima) *deprive of breath, stun, shock; kill; weaken; pass. be exhausted, be out of breath*

exaudiō, -īre, -īvī, -ītum (audiō) *hear clearly; hear from afar*

excēdō, -ere, excessī, excessum (cēdō) *go out, depart; withdraw, leave; surpass, exceed*

excellēns, excellentis *distinguished, excellent, outstanding, superior*

excellō, -ere, —, excelsum *be eminent; excel;* excelsus, -a, -um *high, lofty*

excieō, -ēre, excīvī, excitum (cieō, EXCITE) *call forth; alarm*

excipiō, -ere, excēpī, exceptum *take, take out, except; catch* I

excitō, -āre, -āvī, -ātum (cieō) *call forth, rouse up; stir up, excite*

exclāmō, -āre, -āvī, -ātum (clāmō) *shout out, cry aloud, call out, exclaim*

exclūdō, -ere, exclūsī, exclūsum *shut out, exclude; hinder, prevent* I

excōgitō, -āre, -āvī, -ātum (EXCOGITATE) *think up, devise, invent*

excruciō, -āre, -āvī, -ātum (EXCRUCIATING) *torture*

excūsō, -āre, -āvī, -ātum (-ex + causa) *excuse, make excuses for*

exemplum, -ī, n. *copy, example; precedent* 9

exeō, -īre, exiī, exitum (-eō, EXIT) *go out, go forth; leave; perish*

exerceō, -ēre, -uī, -itum *tire out, weary; practise, manage; exercise*

exercitātiō, ēxercitātiōnis, f. *exercise, training, discipline*

exercitātus, -a, -um *exercised, trained, disciplined*

exercitus, -ūs, m. *army* I

exhauriō, -īre, exhausī, exhaustum *drain, exhaust, empty; impoverish*

exhorrēscō, -ere, exhorruī, — (HORRIBLE) *shudder*

exigō, -ere, exēgī, exactum (ex + agō, EXIGENT, EXACTION) *drive out, expel; complete; demand, require*

exiguitās, exiguitātis, f. cf. (EXIGUOUS) *smallness, paucity; shortness*

exiguus, -a, -um (EXIGUOUS) *small, thin, slender, scanty, mean, short, brief*

exiliō or exsiliō, -īre, exiluī or exsiluī —(RESILIENT) *spring forth, leap up*

eximius, -a, -um (eximō) *select, excellent, exceptional*

eximō, -ere, exēmī, exēmptum *take out, exempt* (w. abl. of separation) I

exīstimātiō, -iōnis, f. *judgment, opinion*

exīstimō, -āre, -āvī, -ātum *think, suppose, consider; estimate* I

exitium, -ī, n. (exeō) *destruction, ruin* (often used as dat. of purp. in double dat.)

exitus, -ūs, m. (exeō) *exit; end, mouth (of a river); outcome; departure; death*

exoptō, -āre, -āvī, -ātum (optō) *desire, long for*

exordior, -īrī, exorsus sum (ordō) *begin*

exorior, -īrī, exortus sum (orior) *come forth, rise up; appear; begin*

exornō, -āre, -āvī, -ātum (ornō) *[thoroughly] ornament, adorn, equip*

expallēscō, -ere, expalluī (PALLID) *turn pale*

expediō, -īre, -īvī, -ītum (-ex + pēs, EXPEDITE) *disengage, disentangle; explain; set free; despatch; be expedient; provide; find, procure, obtain;* expedītus, -a, -um *unencumbered; without baggage; light armed;* (n., m.) *light-armed soldier*

expellō, -ere, expulī, expulsum *push out, drive out, expel, banish* 1

experior, -īrī, expertus sum *try, prove, test; experience* 15

expiō, -āre, -āvī, -ātum (pius) *expiate, atone for*

expleō, -ēre, explēvī, explētum *fill out; complete* 7

explōrātor, explōrātōris, m. *explorer, spy, scout*

explōrō, -āre, -āvī, -ātum *investigate, explore, reconnoitre, test, gain*

expōnō, -ere, exposuī, expositum *put out, exhibit; expose, relate, explain; disembark* I

exprōmō, -ere, exprōmpsī, exprōmptum (prōmō) *show forth, utter*

expugnātiō, expugnātiōnis, f. (pugnō) *storming; taking by storm*

expugnō, -āre, -āvī, -ātum (pugnō) *take by storm; compel to surrender*

exquīrō, -ere, exquīsīvī, exquīsītum (quaerō, EXQUISITE) *seek out, search for, hunt up; inquire into*

exsanguis, -e (sanguis) *bloodless, pale; frightened*

exsecrātiō, exsecrātiōnis, f. (ex + sacer) *curse*

exsequor, -ī, exsecutus sum (sequor) *follow up, maintain, enforce* exserō, -ere, exseruī, exsertum (INSERT) *thrust out, put out*

exsilium -ī, n. *banishment, exile*

exsistō, -ere, exstitī, ___*stand out, project; arise; exist; be*

exspectātiō, -ōnis, f. (exspectō) *expectation*

exspectō, -āre, -āvī, -ātum *look for, wait for, await; expect* I

exstinguō, -ere, exstīnxī, exstīnctum *put out, extinguish; kill, destroy*

exstruō, -ere, exstrūxī, exstrūctum *pile up, build up, construct*

exter or exterus, -a, -um (ex) *outward, outer*

externus, -a, -um (ex) *outward, external, foreign*

extrā (adv. & prep. w. acc) (ex) *outside of, beyond, without*

extrahō, -ere, extrāxī, extrāctum (traho, EXTRACT) *draw out, bring out; prolong*

extrēmus, -a, -um *end of, outermost* n., **extrēmī, -ōrum** m. *the rear* I

exuō, -ere, exuī, exūtum *pull off, undress, take off, strip*

exūrō, -ere, exussī, exūstum (ūrō) *burn up*

F

faba, -ae, f. *[broad] bean*

fabricō, -āre, -āvī, -ātum (FABRICATION) *form, make, build*

fābula, fābulae, f. *story, fable* I

faciēs, -ēī, f. *shape, appearance; face* I

facilis, -e *easy; slight, little* I

facinus, facinoris, n. (faciō) *deed, action; crime, misdeed*

faciō, -ere, fēcī, factum *make, do; cause, bring about; obtain, accomplish; cause;* **certiōrem facere,** *to inform;* **iter facere,** *to march;* **vim facere,** *to use violence;* **imperāta facere,** *to obey commands;* **factum, -ī,** n. *deed, action, achievement* I

factiō, factiōnis, f. (faciō) *party, faction; chariot-racing team*

facultās, facultātis, f. (facilis) *ability; ease, facility; opportunity, faculty; chance; supply;* pl., *resources*

fāgus, -ī, f. *beech tree*

fallō, -ere, fefellī, falsum *deceive, cheat; fail, disappoint; escape the notice of;* **falsus, -a, -um** *false, feigned*

falx, falcis, f. (FALCHION) *sickle; hook [for tearing down walls]*

fāma, -ae, f. *report, rumor; fame, reputation* I

famēs, -is, f. *hunger, famine, want*

familia, -ae, f. *body of slaves; household; family;* **mātrēs familiae,** *matrons* I

familiāris, -e (familia) *of the family; familiar, intimate;* **rēs familiāris,** *private property;* n., m. or f., *friend*

fās (defective: nom. + acc. sing. only), n. *divine law, that which is permitted by the gods;* **fās est** *it is right, it is permitted, it is lawful* 16

fascina, -ae. f. *bundle of sticks*

fascis, -is, m. *bundle of sticks,* pl., *the fasces,* symbol of authority

fāstī, -ōrum, m. *calendar;* **fāstī diēs,** *court days*

fātālis, -e (fātum) *fated; fatal; deadly*

fāteor, -ērī, fassus sum *confess, admit*

fātum, -ī, n. *fate* I

fautor, fautōris, m. (faveō) *favorer, promoter, supporter, applauder*

faveō, -ere, fāvī, fautum (w. dat.) *favor;* **favēte linguīs** *keep silent* I

favor, favōris, m. (faveō) *favor, support, backing, goodwill*

fax, facis, f. *torch, firebrand* 14

fēcundus, -a, -um (FECUND) *fertile*

fēlix, fēlīcis (FELICITY) *fertile, lucky, successful, happy* I

fēmina, -ae, f. *woman, female* I

fenestra, -ae, f. (FENESTRATION) *window*

ferax, -ācis (ferō) *fruitful, fertile*

ferē (adv.) *almost, nearly, about; generally, usually;* **nōn ferē** *hardly* 2

ferō, ferre, tulī, lātum *bear, bring, take; relate, say, report, receive; suffer; withstand;* **lēgem ferō** *pass a law* I

ferrāmentum, -ī, n. (ferrum) *iron tool*

ferrum, -ī, n. *iron, steel; sword, dagger;* **ferrō et igne** *with fire and sword* 6

fertilitās, -ātis, f. (ferō) *fertility*

ferus, -a, -um *wild, savage;* (as n., m. or f.) *wild beast* I

fervefaciō, -ere, -fēcī, -factum *make hot; heat*

ferveō, -ēre, ferbuī, ___ (FERVENT) *be hot, boil;* **fervēns, ferventis** *red-hot*

fessus, -a, -um *weary, tired, worn out, exhausted* 20

fētus, -ūs, m. (FETUS) *offspring, young*

fidēlis, -e (fidēs, FIDELITY) *faithful*

fidēs, -eī, f. *faith, trust, belief; trustworthiness; pledge; safe-conduct; credit; protection* I

fīdus, -a, -um (fidēs, FIDO) *faithful, trusty, reliable, confident*

figō, -ere, fīxī, fīxum *fix, fasten; drive in*

figūra, -ae, f. *figure, form, shape*

fīlia, -ae, f. *daughter* I

fīlius, fīlī, m. *son* I

findō, -ere, fidī, fissum (FISSION) *split, cleave*

fingō, -ere, fīnxī, fictum *form, shape, mold; imagine, invent* I

fīniō, -īre, -īvī, -ītum (fīnis) *bound, limit; end, finish; define*

fīnis, fīnis, m. or f. *boundary, limit, border; end;* pl., *territory* 2

fīnitimus, -a, -um *adjacent, neighboring.* n., m. pl. *neighbors* I

fīō, fīerī, factus *become, happen; be made, be done;* **fit** *it happens, it is done* (w. abl. of specification of the person); **certior fīerī** *to be informed* 10

firmitās, -tātis, f. *strength*

firmiter, adv. *firmly, strongly*

firmus, -a, -um *strong, firm; steadfast, powerful*

fissus, -a, -um see **findō**

fistula, -ae, f. (FISTULA) *shepherd's pipe; water pipe*

flamma, -ae, f. *flame, blaze* I

flatus, -ūs, m. *a blowing*

flāvus, -a, -um *blond, yellow, golden*

flectō, -ere, flexī, flexum *bend, turn; influence* 1

fleō, -ere, flēvī, flētus *weep, cry, weep for*

flētus, -ūs, m. (fleō) *weeping*

flōreō, -ēre, -uī, —— (flōs) *bloom, flower; flourish, be prosperous*

flōs, flōris, m. *flower, blossom* 10

fluctus, -ūs, m. *wave, flood* 12

flūmen, flūminis, n. *river, stream* I

fluō, -ere, flūxī, flūxum (FLUID, FLUX) *flow*

foculus, -ī, m. *brazier*

fodiō, -ere, fōdī, fossum (FOSSIL) *dig; dig out*

foedus, -a, -um *foul, filthy, horrible, detestable, ugly* I

foedus, foederis, n. (FEDERATION) *league; treaty, agreement, contract*

follis, follis, m. *a leather money bag, a bag*

fōns, fontis, m. *spring, source; fountain* 17

forāmen, -inis, n. (foris) *hole, fissure*

forās (acc. of limit of motion) *[to] out, [to] outdoors* 17

fore future active infinitive of **sum**

forēnsis, -e (Forum, FORENSIC) *legal*

forīs (locative) *outdoors, out-of-doors, out, outside, not at home* 17

foris, -is, f. (i-stem) *door* 17

forma, -ae, f. *form, figure, shape, appearance; beauty* I

formīdō, formīdinis, f. (FORMIDABLE) *fear, dread, terror; scarecrow, bugbear*

formōsus, -a, -um (forma) *beautiful*

fors (defective; abl. **forte**), f. *chance, accident, luck* I

forsitan (= **fors sit an**) (adv.) *by chance; perhaps* (w. subjunctive) 11

fortis, -e *brave* I

fortitūdō, fortitūdinis, f. (fortis) *strength, courage, bravery; fortitude*

fortūna, ae, f. *fortune, chance; lot, rank* I

fortūnātus, -a, -um (fortūna) *lucky, fortunate; wealthy*

forum, -ī, n. *market place; forum*

fossa, -ae, f. (FOSSE) *ditch, trench*

fovea, -ae, f. *pit, pitfall*

fragor, fragōris, m. (frangō) *crashing sound, noise, crash*

frangō, -ere, frēgī, frāctum *break [to pieces]; dishearten; subdue* 13

frāter, frātris, m. *brother* I

fraudō, -āre, -āvī, -ātum *cheat, defraud, deceive*

fraus, fraudis, f. *deceit, deception, fraud*

fremitus, -ūs, m. *roar, noise; shouting*

fremō, -ere, fremuī, fremitum *murmur, growl, grumble*

frēnō, -āre, -āvī, -ātum *restrain*

frequēns, frequentis *crowded, frequented, well-attended; frequent*

fretum, -ī, n. *sea; strait, sound, channel* 12

frīgus, frīgoris, n. (FRIGID) *cold*

frōns, frondis, f. (FROND) *foliage*

frōns, frontis, f. *forehead, brow, front*

frūctus, -ūs, m. (fruor) *fruit, enjoyment; profit, income; result*

frūgēs, -um, f. (fruor, FRUGAL) *crops, fruits, produce*

frūmentārius, -a, -um (frūmentum) *grain-producing;* **rēs frūmentāria,** *grain supply* frūmentor, -ārī, -ātus (frūmentum) *get grain, forage*

frūmentum, -ī, n. *grain; pl. crops* I

fruor, -ī, frūctus sum (w. abl. of means) *enjoy* I

frūstrā (adv.) *in vain* 18

frūx, frūgis, f. *fruit;* frūgī dat. of purpose *honest*

fuga, -ae, f. *flight, a running away, escape, exile;* in fugam dare *put to flight* I

fugiō, -ere, fūgī, fugitum *flee, escape;* fugiēns, *a fugitive* I

fugitīvus, -a, -um (fugiō) *fugitive, runaway, fleeting*

fugō, -āre, -āvī, -ātum (fuga) *put to flight, rout*

fulmen, fulminis, n. *flash, lightning, thunderbolt* 11

fūmus, -ī, m. *smoke, fume*

fūnāle, fūnālis, n. (i-stem) *torch [of rope dipped in wax]*

funda, -ae, f. *sling*

funditor, -ōris, m. *slinger*

fundō, -ere, fūdī, fūsum *pour; melt; spread; throw down; rout:* fūsus, -a, -um *spread out, broad, flowing* 6

fungor, -ī, fūnctus sum (w. abl. of means) *perform; be engaged in* I

fūnis, -is, m. *funeral; death* 15

fūr, fūris, m. (FURTIVE) *robber*

furor, furōris, m. *rage, fury; madness; furor* 16

furtum, -ī, n. (FURTIVE) *theft*

fūsilis, -e (fundō) *molded*

G

galea, -ae, f. *helmet*

garriō, īre, -īvī, -ītum *chatter, praise*

gaudeō, -ēre, gāvīsus sum (semidep.) *be glad, rejoice* I

gaudium, -ī, n. *joy, gladness* I

gelidus, -a, -um (cf. CONGEAL) *ice cold, icy*

geminus, -a, -um (GEMINI) *twin*

gemitus, -ūs, m. *groan*

genae, -ārum, f. *cheeks*

genius, -ī, m. *guardian spirit; genius*

gēns, gentis, f. (i-stem) *family, clan, gens; tribe, people, nation* I

gentīlicius, -a, -um (gēns) *belonging to a particular family*

gentīlis, -e (gēns, GENTILE) *of a family;* nōmen gentīle *family name*

genū, -ūs, n. (GENUFLECT) *knee*

genus, generis, n. *race, birth; offspring; kind, class, rank; mode, method; sort, style* I

gerō, -ere, gessī, gestum *bear; carry on; wear; wage; accomplish; rēs gestae deeds, accomplishments;* sē gerere *act, behave* 7

gestiō, -īre, -iī or -īvī, -ītum *be eager*

gignō, -ere, genuī, genitum *beget; give birth to; pass. be born* 15

gladiātōrius, -a, -um *gladiatorial, of gladiators, of a gladiator;* mūnera gladiātōria *gladiatorial games*

gladius, -ī, m. *[Roman short] sword*

glāns, glandis, f. (GLAND) *acorn; bullet [thrown from a sling]*

glōria, -ae, f. *glory, fame* I

glōriōsus, -a, -um (glōria) *glorious, famous; honorable*

gracilis, -e *thin, slim, scrawny* I

gradus, -ūs, m. (GRADE) *step; position*

grandis, -e *large, great; grand*

grassor, -ārī, -ātus sum *proceed*

grātia, -ae, f. *favor, grace, gratitude, influence, pleasantness; (pl.) thanks* I; grātiā, with gen., *for the sake of;* grātiās agō (w. dat. of ref.) *thank* I; grātiam referre or habēre *show or feel gratitude*

grātus, -a, -um *pleasing, welcome; thankful, grateful*

gravis, -e *heavy, serious, important;* graviter, adv. *heavily; severly, bitterly;* graviter ferre *be annoyed* I

gravitās, gravitātis, f. (gravis) *heaviness, weight; importance, gravity; dignity*

gravō, -āre, -āvī, -ātum (gravis, AGGRAVATE) *weigh down, make heavy*

grex, gregis, m. (CONGREGATE, SEGREGATE) *flock, herd*

gula, -ae, f. (GULLET) *throat*

guttur, -uris, n. (GUTTERAL) *throat, mouth*

H

habeō, -ēre, -uī, -itum *have, hold, keep; consider, think, reckon; wear* I; ōrātiōnem habēre *deliver a speech;* cēnsum habēre *to take a census*

habilis, -e (habeō) *handy, ready*

habitō, -āre, -āvī, -ātum *live, dwell* I

habitus, -ūs, m. (habeō, HABIT) *holding, condition, appearance; dress, attire* haereō, -ēre, haesī, haesum (ADHERE, ADHESIVE) *stick, cling; hesitate*

harpagātus, -a, -um *hooked*

harundō, harundinis, f. *reed, arrow*

hasta, -ae, f. *spear*

hastātus, -a, -um *armed with a spear;* n. pl. m. substantive *the hastati, spear-men (first line of a Roman army in order of battle)*

haud (adv.) *not at all, by no means* I

hauriō, -īre, hausī, haustum *drink, drain, empty; exhaust; devour*

haustus, -ūs, m. *drink; draught*

heia (excl.) *how now!*

herba, -ae, f. *grass* I

hercle *by Hercules, by golly*

hērēditās, hērēditātis, f. (HEREDITY) *inheritance*

herī (adv.) *yesterday* I

heu (interj.) *alas!*

hīberna, -ōrum, n. (HIBERNATE) *winter camp; winter quarters*

hic, haec, hoc *this, the following; he, she, it [near me]; the latter* I

hīc (adv.) *here, in this place [near me]* I

hiemō, -āre, -āvī, -ātum *spend the winter; winter*

hiems, hiemis, f. *winter*

hinc (adv.) *from here, from this place [near me]; hence; hinc ... hinc ... from one side ... from another side ...* I

historicus, -ī, m. *historian*

hodiē (adv.) *today* I

homō, hominis, m. or f. *human being, person, (plural) people* I

honestās, honestātis, f. (honestus) *honor, honesty, integrity, honorableness*

honestus, -a, -um *honorable, upright; honest* 10

honor or honōs, -ōris, m. *an honor; public office;* in honōrem (w. gen.) *to honor, in honor [of]* I; cursus honōrum *political career (holding the magistracies in order, from the lowest to the highest)* 18

honōrificus, -a, -um (honor + facio, HONORIFIC) *honoring, causing honor, with honor*

hōra, -ae, f. *hour (a twelfth part of the day, from sunrise to sunset)* I

horribilis, -e *awful, horrible*

hortātus, -ūs, m. *encouragement, urging*

hortor, -ārī, -ātus *encourage, exhort; urge on*

hospes, hospitis, m. or f. *stranger; guest-friend, [house]guest, host* I

hostīlis, -e (hostis) *of the enemy, hostile*

hostis, hostis, m. (i-stem) *[public] enemy, foe;* pl. *the enemy* I

hūc (adv.) *(to) here, to this place [near me]* I

humānitās, -ātis, f. (humānus) *humanity; refinement, culture*

humānus, -a, -um *human; humane; civilized; refined* 2

humilis, -e *low, humble, insignificant* I

humus, -ī, f. *ground, earth, soil* I

I

I 1 I

iaceō, -ēre, -uī, -itum *lie, be situated; lie dead* I

iaciō, -ere, iēcī, iactum *throw, hurl* I

iactō, -āre, -āvī, -ātum (iterative of iaciō) *throw about, jerk about; talk repeatedly about; boast of* 6

iactūra, -ae, f. (iaciō) *loss, expense*

iactus, -ūs, m. (iaciō) *throwing, hurling, cast*

iaculum, -ī, n. (iaciō) *javelin*

iam (adv.) *now, already;* nōn iam *no longer;* nunc iam *right now* I; iam prīdem *long ago*

ianua, -ae, f. *[outer] door [of a house]*

ibi (adv.) *here, there, in this place, in that place* I

ibidem (adv.) *in the (this, that) same place* I

iciō, -ere, īcī, ictum (ICTUS) *strike, hit;* foedus icere *to make a treaty*

ictus, -ūs, m. (ICTUS) *blow, stroke*

īdem, eadem, idem *same* I

identidem (adv.) (īdem) *repeatedly; again and again*

ideō (adv.) *for that reason; therefore*

idōneus, -a, -um *suitable, fit, convenient* I

iecur, iecoris, n. *liver*

igitur (adv. and postpositive conj.) *therefore* I

ignārus, -a, -um *ignorant*

ignāvia, -ae, f. *laziness, worthlessness; cowardice*

ignāvus, -a, -um *slothful, lazy, cowardly*

igneus, -a, -um (ignis, IGNEOUS) *fiery, hot*

ignis, ignis, m. (i-stem) *fire* I

ignōrō, -āre, -āvī, -ātum (in + ⟨g⟩nōscō) *not know, be ignorant; ignore*

ignōscō, -ere, ignōvī, ignōtum (w. dative) (in + ⟨g⟩nōscō) *overlook, forgive, pardon*

ignōtus, -a, -um *unknown, strange; unacquainted with* 17

īlia, -ium, n. pl. *guts, side*

īlicō (adv.) *on the spot; immediately*

illāc (adv.) (ille) *that way*

ille, illa, illud *that; he, she, it* (not near the speaker or the person spoken to); *the former; the following;* (after its noun) *the famous, the well-known* I

illīc (adv.) *there, in that place* I

illigō, -āre, -āvī, -ātum (cf. LIGAMENT, LIGATURE) *bind, fasten*

illinc (adv.) *from there, from that place* I

illō (adv.) (ille) *there, thither, to that place*

illūc (adv.) *[to] there, to that place*

illūstris, -e *bright; illustrious*

imāgō, imāginis, f. *image, likeness, portrait, statue* I

imber, imbris, m. (i-stem) *rainstorm, shower* I

imitor, -ārī, -ātus sum *imitate, copy*

immānis, -e *huge, monstrous*

immemor, immemoris (memor) *unmindful, forgetful, unconscious, heedless*

immēnsus, -a, -um *immeasurable, immense* 6

immineō, -ēre, -uī, -itum *overhang; threaten; be imminent*

immītis, -e *cruel, rough, harsh*

immittō, -ere, -mīsī, -missum (mittō) *send in; hurl in; let go onto*

immō (particle expressing disagreement with what has been said or implied) *Oh, no! [no] indeed; nay; by no means*

immoderātus, -a, -um (modus, IMMODERATE) *unrestrained*

immodestia, -ae, f. (modus, IMMODESTY) *lack of discipline*

immolō, -āre, -āvī, -ātum *sacrifice; sprinkle [with sacred meal]; immolate*

immortālis, -e (mortālis) *deathless, immortal*

immūnis, -e *free from taxes, exempt; immune*

immūnitās, -ātis, f. *immunity, freedom from taxes*

impatiēns, -entis (patior) *impatient, intolerant*

impavidus, -a, -um *fearless, undaunted*

impedīmentum, -ī, n. *hindrance, impediment;* pl. *heavy baggage* I

impediō, -īre, īvī, -ītum *hinder, impede, obstruct;* impedītus, -a, -um *hindered, encumbered; difficult (of places); inaccessible* 20

impellō, -ere, impulī, impulsum *push on, set in motion, push forward, strike upon; persuade* I

impendeō, -ēre, ——, —— (pendō, IMPEND) *threaten, overhang*

imperātor, -ōris, m. (imperō) *commander, general; emperor*

imperfectus, -a, -um (in + per + faciō, IMPERFECT) *unfinished, incomplete*

imperītia, -ae, f. (cf. experior) *inexperience; clumsiness*

imperītus, -a, -um (cf. experior) *unskilled, inexperienced;* with gen.

imperium, -ī, n. (imperō) *power, authority; command, right to command; rule; the state, empire*

imperō, -āre, -āvī, -ātum *order, command; rule; demand* (w. acc. of thing, dat. of person), *give an order, give orders;* imperātum, -ī, n. *command, order* 7

impetrō, -āre, -āvī, -ātum *obtain [by asking]; accomplish [by trying]*

impetus, -ūs, m. (petō) *onrush, attack, charge; impetus, fury* 9

impiger, impigra, impigrum *not lazy, active, energetic*

impius, -a, -um (pius, IMPIOUS) *undutiful, godless, unpatriotic, disloyal*

impleō, -ēre, implēvī, implētum *fill up, complete* 7

implōrō, -āre, -āvī, -ātum *call upon with tears, beseech, implore*

impōnō, -ere, imposuī, impositum (w. acc. & dat.) *put in, put on; impose; mount;* (w. dat.) *deceive* I

importō, -āre, -āvī, -ātum (portō) *bring in; import*

imprecātiō, imprecātiōnis, f. (IMPRECATION) *curse*

imprecor, -ārī, -ātus sum (IMPRECATION) *utter as a curse; call down by prayer*

improbus, -a, -um *bad, wicked, depraved, shameless* 3

imprōmptus, -a, -um (in + prōmō, IMPROMPTU) *not ready; not quick*

imprōvīsus, -a, -um (in + prō + videō) *unforeseen, unexpected;* dē imprōvīsō, *unexpectedly, suddenly*

imprūdēns, -entis, f. (in + prō + videō) *unforeseeing, improvident; imprudent; off one's guard*

imprūdentia, -ae, f. (in + prō + videō) *imprudence; ignorance*

impulsor, -ōris, m. (impellō) *instigator*

impūne, adv. *unpunished, without punishment*

impūnitās, impūnitātis, f. (poena) *impunity, exemption [from punishment]*

īmus, -a, -um *bottom of* (also used as superl. of inferus, *lowest*) I

in (prep. w. acc. or abl.) *into, onto, upon, against,*

for (w. acc.); *in, on; among, within; in relation to; in the case of* (w. abl.) I

inamoenus, -a, -um (AMENITY) *cheerless*

inānis, -e (INANE) *empty, useless*

incautus, -a, -um (caveō) *incautious, heedless*

incēdō, -ere, incessī, incessum (cēdō) *come on, go on, advance*

incendium, -ī, n. (INCENDIARY) *fire, burning*

incendō, -ere, incendī, incēnsum *set on fire, burn; rouse, excite; incense*

incertus, -a, -um (certus, cernō) *uncertain; unsure*

incidō, -ere, incidī, ___ (cado, INCIDENT) *fall into, fall upon, happen to, occur, meet*

incīdō, -ere, incīdī, incīsum (caedo, INCISION) *cut into; cut short*

incipiō, -ere, incēpī, inceptum *begin, undertake* I

incitō, -āre, -āvī, -ātum (cieō) *urge on, incite; rouse, spur on*

inclemēns, inclementis (INCLEMENT) *unmerciful, harsh*

inclementer (adv.) *harshly, severely*

inclūdō, -ere, inclūsī, inclūsum *shut in, imprison, include* I

incognitus, -a, -um (in + cognōscō, INCOGNITO) *unknown*

incola, -ae, m. or f. (colō) *native, inhabitant*

incolō, -ere, incoluī, incultum (colō) (trans.) *inhabit;* (intrans.) *live, dwell*

incolumis, -e *unharmed*

incommodē (adv.) *disastrously, unfortunately*

incommodum, -ī, n. *disadvantage, inconvenience; defeat; disaster*

incrēdibilis, -e (crēdō) *incredible; extraordinary*

increpitō, -āre, -āvī, -ātum *reproach, chide*

increpō, -āre, increpuī, increpitum *shout out insultingly; reproach, rebuke*

incubō, -āre, incubuī, incubitum *lie upon, rest on*

incurrō, -ere, incurrī, incursum (currō) *run against, run into; attack; happen upon; incur*

incursiō, incursiōnis, f. (currō) *raid, incursion*

incursus, -ūs, m. (curro) *assault, attack*

incūsō, -āre, -āvī, -ātum (in + causa) *accuse, blame*

incutiō, -ere, incussī, incussum (cf. CONCUSSION) *strike upon, beat against*

inde (adv.) *from here, from there, from that place; thereupon* I

indicium, -ī, n. (indicō) *disclosure; sign, evidence; proof, indication*

indicō, -āre, -āvī, -ātum *point out, show, indicate; inform against* 10

indīcō, -ere, indīxī, indictum *proclaim, announce, appoint, declare*

indidem (adv.) *from the (this, that) same place* I

indīgnātiō, indīgnātiōnis, f. (dīgnus) *indignation; disdain*

indīgnitās, indīgnitātis, f. (dīgnus) *unworthiness, baseness, indignity*

indīgnor, -ārī, -ātus sum (dīgnus) *resent, be indignant, be indignant at*

indīgnus, -a, -um (dīgnus) *undeserved; unworthy, base, shameful, unbecoming*

indō, -ere, indidī, inditum (dō) *put on, give to*

indolēs, -is, f. *natural quality, genius, capacity*

indūcō, -ere, indūxī, inductum (dūcō, INDUCE) *bring in, lead in; lead on, influence*

induō, -ere, induī, indūtum (INDUE) *put on, clothe, cover; sē induere* *impale oneself*

industriē (adv.) *vigorously, industriously*

indūtiae, -ārum, f. *truce, armistice*

ineō, -īre, iniī, (inīvī), initum (eō, INITIAL) *begin, go into, enter; undertake; adopt, initā aestāte at the beginning of summer*

inermis, -e (in + arma) *unarmed, defenceless*

infāmō, -āre, -āvī, -ātum *disgrace, discredit*

īnfācundus, -a, -um *not eloquent, poor at speaking*

īnfāmia, -ae, f. (in + fāma) *disgrace, dishonor; infamy*

īnfandus, -a, -um *not to be spoken of, unspeakable, monstrous*

īnfectus, -a, -um (in + faciō) *unfinished*

īnfēlīx, īnfēlīcis (fēlīx, INFELICITY) *unfortunate, unhappy*

īnfēnsus, -a, -um *hostile, unfriendly, threatening*

īnferō, īnferre, intulī, illātum *bring in, import, carry onward;* (w. dat.) *bring upon, inflict; obtain; bellum īnferre* (with dat.) *to make war on;* **signa īnferre** *to advance* I

īnferus, -a, -um *below, underneath; īnferī, -ōrum, m. the gods below, the gods of the Lower World; inferior, -ius lower, inferior* I

īnfestus, -a, -um *hostile; dangerous; leveled*

īnficiō, -ere, īnfēcī, īnfectum (faciō, INFECT) *stain, dye, anoint*

īnfimus, -a, -um (superl. of īnferus) *lowest, at the bottom* I

īnfirmus, -a, -um *weak, infirm*

īnflectō, -ere, īnflexī, īnflexum (flectō) *bend*

īnfluō, -ere, īnflūxī, īnflūxum (INFLUX) *flow into, flow* īnfrā (adv., and prep. with acc.) *below*

ingemō, -ere, ingemuī, ingemitum *groan [over something], sigh deeply*

ingeniōsus, -a, -um (ingenium, INGENIOUS) *clever, talented, ingenious*

ingenium, -ī, n. *nature, character; talent, genius, ability* 13

ingēns, ingentis *huge, vast; mighty; remarkable* I

ingrātus, -a, -um (grātus, INGRATE) *unwelcome, unpleasant; ungrateful*

ingredior, -ī, ingressus sum (INGRESS) *enter, walk in, advance; undertake*

inhiō, -āre, -āvī, -ātum (HIATUS) *gape; covet, desire*

inhūmānus, -a, -um *inhuman*

iniciō, -ere, iniēcī, iniectum (iaciō) *throw in, strike in, inject; inspire*

inimīcitia, -ae, f. *enmity, unfriendliness*

inimīcus, -a, -um *unfriendly, hostile; as noun, m. personal enemy* I

inīquitās, inīquitātis, f. (in + aequus) *unfairness, injustice, inequity; iniquity*

inīquus, -a, -um (in + aequus, INIQUITY) *uneven, sloping; unfavorable; unequal; unfair, unjust*

initium, -ī, n. (in + eō, INITIAL) *beginning*

iniūria, -ae, f. (in + iūs) *wrong, injustice; injury*

iniussus, -ūs (abl. only) *without command*

iniūstus, -a, -um (in + iūstus) *unjust*

inliciō, -ere, inlexī, inlectum (ELICIT) *attract, entice, seduce*

inligō, -āre, -āvī, -ātum (LIGAMENT, LIGATURE) *bind, tie, fasten*

inlocābilis, -e (locus) *unable to be placed*

innītor, -ī, innīxus sum (w. abl. of means) *lean upon, rest on, bear down on*

innocēns, -centis (in + noceō) *blameless, innocent*

innoxius, -a, -um (cf. NOXIOUS) *harmless, unharmed*

inopia, -ae, f. *lack, need* I

inopīnāns, -antis (cf. OPINE) *unaware, off guard; unexpected*

inopīnātus, -a, -um (cf. OPINE) *unexpected, surprising*

īnops, inopis (opēs) *weak, poor, helpless; lacking*

inquam (defective verb: forms are inquam, inquis, inquit, inquiunt) *say, said* I

inquilīnus, -ī, m. *fellow lodger, traveler*

inquīsītor, inquīsītōris, m. (quaerō, INQUISITOR) *investigator; detective*

inrideō, -ēre, inrīsī, inrīsum (rideō) *laugh at, ridicule*

inrīsus, -ūs, m. (rideō) *laughter, mockery, derision*

inrītō, -āre, -āvī, -ātum See irrītō

inritus, -a, -um *void, invalid; ineffectual, vain, useless*

inrumpō See irrumpō

inruō, -ere, inruī, ___ *rush in, rush upon, attack*

īnsāniō, -īre, -īvī, -ītum *go insane; be insane*

īnsciēns, īnscientis (sciō) *not knowing*

īnsequor, -ī, īnsecūtus sum (sequor, ENSUE) *follow up, pursue*

īnserviō, -īre, -īvī, -ītum (serviō) *devote oneself to (with dat.)*

īnsideō, -ēre, īnsēdī, īnsessum (sedeō) *sit on*

īnsidiae, -ārum, f. (sedeō, INSIDIOUS) *ambush, trap; plot, stratagem*

īnsignis, -e *distinguished, remarkable;* (as noun) īnsigne, -is, n. *mark, emblem, badge, ensign, honor* 4

īnsiliō, -īre, īnsiluī, ___ *leap on*

īnsinuō, -āre, -āvī, -ātum (sinus) *push in, insinuate, wind in, twist in*

īnsistō, -ere, -stitī, ___ (INSIST) *stand upon, stand; press on; pursue*

īnsolēns, īnsolentis (soleō) *extravagant; arrogant, insolent*

īnsolitus, -a, -um (soleō) *unaccustomed*

īnspiciō, -ere, īnspexī, īnspectum (cf. aspiciō) *look into, inspect*

īnstar, n. (indecl.) *the equal*

īnstituō, -ere, -uī, -ūtum *build; construct; arrange, draw up; begin; establish, institute; teach;* īnstitūtum, -ī, n. *plan, arrangement; institution* I

īnstō, -āre, īnstitī, ___ *stand in, stand on; follow closely, press forward; be at hand, approach;* īnstāns, īnstantis *eager, urgent* I

īnstrūmentum, -ī, n. *tool; equipment; instrument*

īnstruō, -ere, īnstrūxī, īnstrūctum (INSTRUCT, CONSTRUCT) *set up, build; equip; draw up [troops]*

īnsuēfactus, -a, -um *well-trained*

īnsula, -ae, f. *island*

īnsum, inesse, īnfuī, īnfutūrus (sum) *be in*

intāctus, -a, -um (in + tangō) *untouched, intact, safe*

integer, integra, integrum *whole, untouched, unharmed, sound; innocent* 16; *as noun, m. pl. fresh troops*

intellegentia, -ae, f. (inter + legō) *intelligence*

intellego, -ere, intellēxī, intellēctum (inter + legō) *understand, realize, ascertain*

intemperāns, intemperantis *extravagant, immoderate, intemperate*

intendō, -ere, intendī, intentum *stretch out, aim; pay attention;* **intentus, -a, -um** *intent, attentive, eager*

inter (prep. w. acc.) *between, among; during within* I; **inter nōs, vōs, sē** *each other, one another*

intercēdō, -ere, intercessī, intercessum (inter + cēdō) *intercede, go between; intervene; take place; (of a tribune) impose a veto*

intercessiō, intercessiōnis, f. (inter + cedo) *intercession; [tribune's] veto*

intercipiō, -ere, intercēpī, interceptum (inter + capiō) *intercept; steal, cut off*

interclūdō, -ere, -clūsī, -clūsum (inter + claudō) *cut off; blockade; hinder, block up*

interdīcō, -ere, -dīxī, -dictum (inter + dīcō) *forbid, interdict, prohibit*

interdiū (adv.) (inter + diēs) *in the daytime*

interdum (adv.) *sometimes*

intereā (adv.) (intertea) *meanwhile*

intereō, interīre, interiī, interitum (inter + eō) *perish, die*

interficiō, -ere, interfēcī, interfectum *destroy, kill* I

intericiō, -ere, interiēcī, interiectum (inter + iaciō, INTERJECT) *put between; interpose;* **interiectus, -a, -um** *lying between*

interim (adv.) *in the meantime, meanwhile*

interimō, -ere, interēmī, interēmptum (inter + emō) *take away; kill, destroy*

interior, interiōris (comp.) *inner, interior (of), middle;* as noun, m. pl. *those within*

interitus, -ūs, m. (inter + eō) *death, destruction*

intermittō, -ere, intermīsī, intermissum (inter + mittō, INTERMITTENT) *send between; elapse; interrupt, discontinue [for a time]*

interneciō, interneciōnis, f. *slaughter*

interpōnō, -ere, interposuī, interpositum (inter + pōnō) *interpose, put between; present; elapse, allow to elapse*

interpretor, -ārī, -ātus *explain, interpret*

interrogō, -āre, -āvī, -ātum (inter + rogō) *ask, question, interrogate*

interrumpō, -ere, interrūpī, interruptum (inter + rumpō) *break in the middle; interrupt, break off*

interscindō, -ere, interscīdī, interscissum *cut down; cut through*

intersum, interesse, interfuī, interfutūrus (inter +

sum) *be between; be different; be involved in;* (impersonal w. gen.) **interest** *it is the concern*

intervallum, -ī, n. *interval, space, distance*

interveniō, -īre, intervēnī, interventum (inter + veniō) *come between, intervene, interrupt*

intimus, -a, -um *intimate*

intestīnus, -a, -um (INTESTINE) *internal*

intolerandus, -a, -um *unbearable, intolerable*

intrā (adv. & prep. with acc.) *within, inside; during*

intrō (adv.) *within, inside, inward, turned toward the inside*

intrō, -āre, -āvī, -ātum *enter*

intrōdūcō, -ere, intrōdūxī, intrōductum (dūcō) *bring in, take inside*

introeō, -īre, -īvī, ___ (eō) *enter, go into*

introitus, -ūs, m. (eo, INTROIT) *entrance*

intrōmittō, -ere, intrōmīsī, intrōmissus (mittō) *allow to enter, cause to enter*

intrōrsus (adv.) (intrōversus, vertō) *within, inside*

intrōrumpō, -ere, intrōrūpī, intrōruptum (rumpō) *break in*

intueor, -ērī, intuitus sum *look on; regard*

intus (adv.) *within, on the inside*

inūsitātus, -a, -um (in + ūsus) *unusual, strange, unfamiliar*

inūtilis, -e (in + ūtor) *useless*

invādō, -ere, invāsī, invāsum *advance, rush upon, attack; go in; invade*

inveniō, -īre, invēnī, inventum *come upon, find; meet with; invent; learn, discover, find out*

inventor, -ōris, m. (inveniō) *inventor*

investigō, -āre, -āvī, -ātum *discover, investigate*

inveterāscō, -ere, inveterāvī, ___ (vetus) *grow old, become established*

invicem *see* **vicis**

invictus, -a, -um (in + vincō) *unconquered, unbeaten*

invideō, -ēre, invīdī, invīsum (w. dat.) *envy;* **invīsus, -a, -um** *hated, unpopular* I

invidia, -ae, f. (invideō, INVIDIOUS) *envy; hatred, unpopularity*

invidus, -a, -um (invideō) *hateful, envious*

inviolātus, -a, -um (inviolate) *undamaged, unharmed*

invītō, -āre, -āvī, -ātum *invite; allure, attract*

invītus, -a, -um *unwilling*

invocō, -āre, -āvī, -ātum (vocō) *call upon, invoke*

iocus, -ī, m. *joke, jest*

ipse, ipsa, ipsum (intens. pron.) *myself, ourselves, yourself, yourselves, himself, herself, itself, themselves* I

īra, -ae, f. *wrath, anger, rage* I

īrāscor, -ī, īrātus sum *become angry;* **īrātus, -a, -um** *angered, enraged; irate* 19

irrītō, -āre, -āvī, -ātum (irritate) *anger, provoke, annoy, irritate; stimulate*

irritus or inritus, -a, -um *ineffective, useless, in vain*

irrumpō, -ere, irrūpī, irruptum (rumpō, IRRUPTION) *burst in, break into, rush in*

irruō See inruō

is, ea, id (adj.) *this, that;* (pron.) *he, she, it (the one[s] being spoken of)* **eō magis** *all the more* I

iste, ista, istud *that; he, she, it [near you]* I

istīc (adv.) *there, in that place [near you]* I

istinc (adv.) *from there, from that place [near you]* I

istūc (adv.) *[to] there, to that place [near you]* I

ita (adv. modifying verbs) *so, thus, in such a manner;* (modifying adjectives and adverbs) *so, to such a degree; (it is so)* = *yes* I

itaque (conjunction) *and so, therefore* I

item (adv.) (ITEM) *also; farther; just so, in like manner, likewise*

iter, itineris, n. *way, route, road; journey, march;* **magnum iter,** *forced march* I

iterātiō, iterātiōnis, f. (iterum, REITERATION) *repetition*

iterum (adv.) *again, a second time* I

itidem, adv. *in like manner, in the same way*

iubeō, -ēre, iussī, iussum *bid, order* (with acc. and infin.) I

iucundus, -a, -um *agreeable, pleasant, nice* 13

iūdex, iūdicis, n. *juryman, juror, judge* 15

iūdicium, -ī, n. (iūdex, JUDICIAL) *trial, judgement, decision; court; trial*

iūdicō, -āre, -āvī, -ātum (iūdex, ADJUDICATE) *judge, decide; think, infer; proclaim, declare*

iūgerum, -ī, n. (3d decl. in pl.: **iūgera, iūgerum**) *jugerum (a plot of land 240 by 120 feet)*

iugulō, -āre, -āvī, -ātum (JUGULATE) *cut the throat of*

iugum, -ī, n. *yoke; [mountain] ridge, summit, chain* 17

iūmentum, -ī, n. (iungō) *draft animal; beast of burden*

iungō, -ere, iūnxī, iūnctum *join, unite, connect; yoke* 11

iūnior (comp. of iuvenis) I

iūrō, -āre, -āvī, -ātum *swear* I; **iūs iūrandum** *oath* 14

iūs, iūris, n. *juice, broth, soup, sauce*

iūs, iūris, n. *right, law* I; **iūs iūrandum** *oath* 14

iussus, -ūs, m. (iubeō, JUSSIVE) *command, bidding*

iūstitia, -ae, f. (iūstus) *justice*

iūstus, -a, -um *just, right, fair; suitable, proper* 12

iuvenis, iuvenis (not an i-stem; no neuter) *young; as noun, young man* I

iuventūs, iuventūtis, f. (iūvenis) *youth (the time between the ages of 20 and 40); (collective) young men*

iuvō, -āre, iūvī, iūtum *help, assist; delight, please, gratify* I

iūxtā (adv. and prep. with acc.) (JUXTAPOSITION) *near, close to*

L

L *50* I

lābor, -ī, lāpsus sum *glide, slip, fall* 7

labor, labōris, m. *labor, toil, effort, hardship* I

labōriōsus, -a, -um *hardworking* (adv. *laboriously*)

labōrō, -āre, -āvī, -ātum *toil; suffer; be in difficulties; strive, struggle; be afflicted; be hard pressed* I

labrum, -ī, n. *lip; rim, edge*

lac, lactis, n. (LACTIC) *milk*

lacertus, -ī, m. *arm, upper arm*

lacessō, -ere, lacessīvī, lacessītum *provoke, harass, challenge; attack*

lacrima, -ae, f. *tear, teardrop* 13

lacrimō, -āre, -āvī, -ātum (lacrima, LACRIMATORY) *cry, weep [at]*

lacrimōsus, -a, -um (lacrima) *tearful, causing tears*

lacus, -ūs, m. *lake, pond, pool*

laetificō, -āre, -āvī, -ātum (laetus + facio) *delight, cheer, gladden*

laetitia, -ae, f. (laetus) *joy, gladness*

laetus, -a, -um *joyful, glad* I

laevus, -a, -um (LAEVOSE) *left, on the left hand; unpropitious*

lagōna, -ae, f. *flask, bottle*

lāmentum, -ī, n. *lament, lamentation*

laniō, -āre, -āvī, -ātum *tear, mangle, mutilate*

lanius, -i, m. *butcher*

lapis, lapidis, m. *rock, stone* 11

lapideus, -a, -um (lapis) *of stone*

laqueus, -i, m. *noose*

largē (adv.) (LARGE) *exceedingly*

largitiō, largitiōnis, f. (LARGESSE) *liberality, generosity; bribery*

lassitūdō, -inis, f. *weariness, exhaustion; lassitude*

latebra, -ae, f. *concealment; hiding-place; retreat*

lateō, -ēre, -uī, ___ (LATENT) *lie hidden; escape notice*

latericius, -a, -um *of brick*

lātitūdō, lātitūdinis, f. *width, breadth* I

latrō, lātrōnis, m. *bandit, robber*

latrōcinium, -ī, n. *brigandage, robbery*

lātus, -a, -um *wide, broad* I

latus, lateris, n. *side, flank* 14

laudātiō, laudātiōnis, f. (laudō) *eulogy*

laudō, -āre, -āvī, -ātum *praise, extol, laud* I

laurea, -ae, f. *laurel tree; laurel crown; wreath*

laus, laudis, f. *praise, fame, glory* I

lavō, -āre, -āvī, lautum or lōtum *wash, bathe, lave;* lautus, -a, -um *neat, elegant, splendid, luxurious, honorable*

laxō, -āre, -āvī, -ātum (RELAX) *loosen, extend*

lea, -ae, f. *lioness*

leaena, -ae, f. *lioness*

lectus, -ī, m. *couch, bed*

lēgātiō, lēgātiōnis, f. (lēgātus) *embassy, legation, delegation*

lēgātus, -ī, m. *ambassador, legate, envoy; lieutenant general; lieutenant, officer* I

legiō, legiōnis, f. *legion; (a division of the army containing 3000–6000 soldiers)* 19

legiōnārius, -a, -um (legiō) *legionary, of a legion*

legō, -ere, lēgī, lēctum *read; pick, collect, gather; appoint* I

lēnis, -e (LENIENT) *smooth; soft, mild, gentle*

lēnitās, lēnitātis, f. *smoothness; gentleness; lenience*

leō, leōnis, m. (LEONINE) *lion*

lepidē (adv.) *pleasantly*

lētum, -ī, n. (LETHAL) *death*

levis, -e *light, slight; fickle* 11

levitās, -ātis, f. (levis) *levity; lightness*

levō, -āre, -āvī, -ātum (levis, ELEVATE) *lift, raise*

lēx, lēgis, f. *law, rule* I; lēgem ferre *pass a law*

libellus, -ī, m. *little book*

libēns, libentis *willing; glad, with pleasure*

libenter (adv.) *gladly, willingly*

līber, lībera, līberum *free* I

līberālis, -e *generous, liberal*

līberāliter (adv.) (līber) *graciously, courteously; liberally*

līberī, līberōrum, m. *children* I

līberō, -āre, -āvī, -ātum *free, set free* I

lībertās, lībertātis, f. (līber) *liberty, freedom*

lībra, -ae, f. (LB.) *pound*

lībrō, -āre, -āvī, -ātum (EQUILIBRIUM) *balance, swing; hurl*

licentia, -ae, f. (licet) *freedom, license*

licet, -ēre, licuit, licitum *it is allowed; it is permitted* (w. dat. and inf.) 15

lignātiō, lignātiōnis, f. *getting wood*

lignum, -i, n. (LIGNEOUS) *log; pl. wood*

ligō, -āre, -āvī, -ātum (LIGAMENT, LIGATURE) *bind, unite*

līmen, līminis, n. *threshold* 14

līmes, -itis, m. *path, track; limit*

lineāmentum, -ī, n. *features, lineaments*

lingua, -ae, f. *tongue, language* I; favēte linguīs *keep silent*

linter, lintris, f. *boat, skiff*

līnum, -ī, n. *flax, linen thread*

liquidus, -a, -um *liquid; clear*

littera, -ae, f. *letter [of the alphabet]; (pl.) document, letter; literature* 2

lītus, lītoris, n. *seashore, coast* I

locō, -āre, -āvī, -ātum (locus, LOCATE) *place; put; arrange*

locus, -ī, m. *place; pl.* loca, -ōrum, n. *region, locality* I

locuplēs, -ētis *rich*

locuplētō, -āre, -āvī, -ātum *enrich*

longinquus, -a, -um *remote, distant; lasting*

longitūdō, longitūdinis, f. *length* I

longus, -a, -um *long; lasting; remote;* longē (adv.) *far, by far; far away* I; nāvis longa *warship*

loquor, -ī, locūtus sum *speak, talk; say, tell* 3

lōrīca, -ae, f. *coat of mail; breastwork, fortification*

lubet = libet

lūctus, -ūs, m. *grief, mourning*

lūcus, -ī, m. *grove, sacred grove*

lūdō, -ere, lūsī, lūsum *play, sport; (trans.) tease; deceive* 19

lūdus, -ī, m. *game, sport; school; pl. religious festival;* ludī circēnsēs *chariot races;* lūdī scaenicī *theatrical productions*

lūgeō, -ēre, lūxī, lūctum *grieve, mourn, bewail; deplore*

lūmen, lūminis, n. *light; eye; glory, ornament* 12

lūna, -ae, f. (LUNATE) *moon*

lūstrum, -ī, n. *lustrum* (an expiatory sacrifice offered every five years by the Censors; a five-year period)

lūsus, -ūs, m. (lūdō) *game, sport, play*

lūx, lūcis, f. *light, daylight;* **prima lūx** *dawn; at daybreak*

lūxuria, -ae, f. *luxury*

lūxuriōsus, -a, -um (LUXURIOUS) *self-indulgent*

M

macer, macra, macrum *thin, lean*

māchinātiō, māchinātiōnis, f. *contrivance, device; machinery; machination*

macte (voc. of **mactus,** *honored, worshipped, magnified*) *well done!*

madefactus, -a, -um *wet, soaked, stained*

madeō, -ēre, -uī, ___ *be wet, be dripping*

madēscō, -ere, maduī, ___ *become wet*

madidus, -a, -um *wet, moist; dripping*

maestitia, -ae, f. (maestus) *sadness*

maestitūdō, maestitūdinis, f. (maestus) *sadness*

maestus, -a, -um *sad, sorrowful, gloomy* 18

magis (adv.) *more, rather; more greatly* I

magister, magistrī, m. *master [of a school, of a ship, etc.]* I; **magister equitum** *Master of the Horse*

magistrātus, -ūs, m. (magister) *magistracy; magistrate*

magnitūdō, -inis, f. *size, magnitude; greatness* I

magnopere (adv.) (magnō opere) *greatly, very much, exceedingly*

magnus, -a, -um *great, large; loud; noble;* **magna pars** *the majority* I; **magnō opere** (magnopere) (adv.) *greatly, very much*

maiestās, maiestātis, f. (maior) *grandeur, dignity, majesty;* **patria maiestās** *paternal authority*

maior, -ius (comp. of **magnus**) *greater* I; as noun, m. pl. *ancestors, forefathers;* **maiōrēs nātū** *the elders, the older men*

male (adv.) *badly, ill* I

maledīcēns, -entis (male + dīcō) *abusive, critical*

maleficium, -ī, n. (male + facio, MALEFICENT) *wrongdoing, harm*

malitia, -ae, f. (malus) *ill will, malice*

malitiōsē, adv. (malus, MALICIOUS) *treacherously*

mālō, mālle, māluī, ___ *wish more, wish rather, prefer* 16

mālus, -ī, m. *mast*

malus, -a, -um *bad, evil, wicked* I

mandō, -āre, -āvī, -ātum *entrust; give instructions, instruct; command;* **mandātum, -ī,** n. *order, command; mandate* 7

māne, ___, n. (defective: sing., nom. **māne,** acc. **māne,** & abl. **māne,** only) *early morning;* **multō māne** *very early in the morning*

maneō, -ēre, mānsī, mānsum *stay, remain, last; continue* I

manipulus, -ī, m. (manus) *maniple* (military unit of two centuries)

mānsuēfaciō, -ere, mānsuēfēcī, mānsuēfactum *tame*

mānsuētūdō, mānsuētūdinis, f. *tameness, gentleness*

manūmittō, -ere, manumīsī, manumissum (manus + mittō, MANUMIT) *release, set free*

manus, -ūs, f. *hand; band [of men]* I; *power [of a father over his daughter or a husband over his wife], jurisdiction*

mare, maris, n. (i-stem) *sea* I

margō, -inis, m. *margin, edge; bank*

maritimus, -a, -um (mare) *of the sea, near the sea; maritime, coastal*

marītus, -a, -um *of marriage, nuptial*

marītus, -ī, m. *husband* I

marmoreus, -a, -um *of marble*

mās, maris, m. (MASCULINE) *male*

matara, -ae, f. *javelin, spear*

māter, mātris, f. *mother* I; **mātrēs familiae** *matrons*

māteria, -ae, f. *matter, material; timber, wood*

mātrimōnium, -ī, n. (mater) *marriage;* **in mātrimōniam dūcere** *to marry*

mātrōna, -ae, f. (māter) *matron, married woman*

mātūrō, -āre, -āvī, -ātum *hasten*

mātūrus, -a, -um (mature) *early; ripe, developed; timely*

maximus, -a, -um (superl. of **magnus**); **maximē** (adv.) *very greatly; especially; most* I

medicus, -ī, m. (MEDICAL) *doctor, physician*

mediocris, -e (medius) *moderate; ordinary, common; mediocre*

medium, ī, m. *middle, center* I

medius, -a, -um *middle of, middle; moderate;* **in mediō colle** *halfway up the hill;*

(medius continued)

media nox midnight; **medium, ī,** n. *middle, center* I

mel, mellis, n. (MELLIFLUOUS) *honey*

melior, melius (comp. of **bonus**) I

membrum, -ī, n. *part [of the body], organ, limb* 1

memimī, meminisse, __ (w. obj. gen.) *remember* I

memor, memoris *mindful, remembering* I

memorābilis, -e (memorō) *memorable; worth mentioning*

memoria, -ae, f. *memory* I; **memoriā tenēre** *remember*

memorō, -āre, -āvī, -ātum *call to mind, mention, recount, remember* 11

mēns, mentis, f. *mind, intellect; feeling, opinion*

mēnsis, -is, m. (i-stem) *month*

mēnsūra, -ae, f. (COMMENSURATE) *measure*

mentiō, mentiōnis, f. *mention*

mentior, -īrī, -ītus *lie, pretend*

mercātor, mercātōris, m. *trader, merchant*

mercātūra, -ae, f. *trade*

mercennārius, -a, -um *hired, paid, mercenary*

mercēs, mercēdis, f. *pay, wages; bribe*

mereō, -ēre, -uī, -itum + mereor, -ērī, -itus sum *earn, deserve, merit* 13; (w. **stipendium** understood) *serve in the army;* **meritum, -ī,** n. *merit, service; value* 13

mergō, -ere, mersī, mersum (IMMERSE, SUBMERGE) *dip, plunge; sink; overwhelm*

merus, -a, -um *pure, mere;* **merum, -ī,** n. *straight wine, wine not mixed with water* 18

merx, mercis, f. (MERCANTILE) *merchandise*

mēta, -ae, f. *turning-post [in a circus]; goal*

mētior, -īrī, mēnsus (METE, DIMENSION) *measure, distribute*

metō, -ere, messuī, messum *reap, mow, harvest*

metuō, -ere, metuī, metūtum *fear, dread;* (intrans.) *be afraid, feel dread* 8

metus, -ūs, m. *fear, dread* I

meus, -a, -um *my, mine* I

mi see **ego**

micāns, micantis *flashing*

mīgrō, -āre, -āvī, -ātum (migrate) *move [one's place of residence]; depart, remove*

mīles, mīlitis, m. *soldier* I

mīlia, mīlium, n. (pl. only) *thousands;* **mīlia passuum** *miles* I

mīliārium, -ī, n. (mīlia) *milestone*

mīlitāris, -e (mīles) *military, of a soldier, of soldiers;* **rēs mīlitāris** *the art of war*

mīlitia, -ae, f. (mīles) *military service;* (locative) **mīlitiae** *on military service*

mīlle (indecl. adj.) *a thousand, one thousand* I; **mīlle passūs, mīlle passuum,** m. *mile* (= 1.48 km.)

mīllēsimus, -a, -um *thousandth* I

mīlliārium See **mīliārium**

mināciter (adv.) *threateningly*

minae, -ārum, f. (MENACE) *threats*

minimus, -a, -um (superl. of **parvus**); **minimē** (adv.) *least, by no means; not at all* I

minister, ministrī, m. *waiter, attendant, servant* 1

ministerium, -ī, n. (minister, MINISTRY) *service, employment, duty*

minitābundus, -a, -um *threatening, menacing*

minitor, -ārī, -ātus sum *threaten repeatedly, go on threatening*

minor, -ārī, -ātus sum (MENACE) *threaten* (w. dat.)

minor, minus (comp. of **parvus**) I

minuō, -ere, -uī, -ūtum (minus, MINUTE) *diminish, lesson; settle*

mīrābilis, -e (mīror, ADMIRABLE) *amazing, wonderful, marvelous*

mīrāculum, -ī, n. (mīror) *a wonder, miracle*

mīror, -ārī, mīrātus sum *wonder, be amazed; wonder at, admire* 9

mīrus, -a, -um *amazing, wonderful, strange, remarkable* I

misceō, -ēre, -uī, mixtum *mix* I

miser, misera, miserum *poor, wretched, unhappy;* **miserē** (adv.) *wretchedly, pitiably; desperately* I

miserābilis, -e (miser) *wretched, miserable*

miseret, -ēre, -uit, __ *it causes pity (compassion, distress)* 17

miseria, -ae, f. (miser) *misery*

misericordia, -ae, f. (miser + cor) *pity; mercy, compassion*

miseror, -ārī, -ātus sum (miser) *pity*

mittō, -ere, mīsī, missum *let go, send, release; dismiss; throw, hurl; push, dispatch* I

mōbilis, -e (mōveō, MOBILE) *movable*

mōbilitās, mōbilitātis, f. (mōveō) *mobility; speed*

moderor, -ārī, -ātus (modus, MODERATE) *check, slow down, control*

modius, -ī, m. *modius* (a dry measure approx. = 1 peck)

modo (adv.) *only, just; just now;* modo . . . modo
at one moment . . . at another I; nōn modo . . .
sed etiam *not only . . . but also*

modus, -ī, m. *measure, limit; degree; manner, way;*
quō modō, quōmodō, quem ad modum, quemadmodum *how* I

moenia, moenium, n. *fortifications, walls* I

mōlēs, mōlis, f. (i-stem) *mass, bulk, heap; difficulty*
14

molestus, -a, -um (moles) *irksome, troublesome*

molior, -īrī, -ītus sum *set in motion; build; under-*
take; strive for, struggle, work on

molliō, -īre, -īvī, -ītum (mollis, EMOLLIENT) *soften;*
civilize

mollis, -e *soft, tender, gentle, smooth* 11

mōmentum, -ī, n. (mōveō) *movement, influence;*
moment; motive, [influencing] cause

moneō, -ēre, -uī, -itum *warn, advise; admonish;*
foretell I

monimentum See monumentum

monitus, -ūs, m. (moneō) *warning; advice*

mōns, montis, m. (i-stem) *hill, mountain* I

mōnstrum, -ī, n. (moneō) *portent; monster*

monumentum, -ī, n. (moneō) *memorial, monument,*
reminder

mora, -ae, f. *delay* 3

morbus, -ī, m. (MORBID) *disease, sickness*

morior, morī, moritūrus *die* 3

moror, -ārī, morātus sum *delay* I

mors, mortis, f. (i-stem) *death* I

morsus, -ūs, m. (MORSEL, REMORSE) *bite; jaws; teeth*

mortālis, -e *mortal* 5

mortuus, -a, -um *dead* 3

mōrus, -ī, *mulberry tree*

mōrum, -ī, n. *mulberry*

mōs, mōris, m. *habit, custom; (pl.) customs, morals;*
character 4

mōtus, -ūs, m. (mōveō) *motion, movement; uprising,*
revolt; terrae mōtus *earthquake*

mōveō, -ēre, mōvī, mōtum *move; stir up; remove;*
influence I; castra movēre *break camp*

mox (adv.) *soon* I

mucrō, mucrōnis, m. *sword, swordpoint*

muliēbris, -e *of a woman, womanly, feminine,*
woman's

mulier, mulieris, f. (the i is a consonant) *woman,*
wife

multa, -ae, f. (MULCT) *fine*

multitūdō, multitūdinis, f. *large number, number,*
multitude, crowd I

multō, -āre, -āvī, -ātum (MULCT) *fine, penalize;*
deprive

multus, -a, -um *much; (pl.) many* I; multō diē *late*
in the day

mundus, -ī, m. *world, universe, cosmos* 10

mūnīmentum, -i, n. (moenia) *fortification, defense,*
barrier

mūniō, -īre, -īvī, -ītum (moenia) *fortify, build [a*
fortification]

mūnitiō, mūnitiōnis, f. (moenia) *fortification, de-*
fenses

mūnus, mūneris, n. *service, duty; favor; funeral;*
gift I; (pl.) mūnera [gladiātōria] *gladiatorial*
show

mūrālis, -e *of a wall; mural*

murmur, -uris, m. *murmur, whisper*

mūrus, -ī, m. (INTRAMURAL) *wall*

mūsculus, -ī, m. (MUSCLE, MUSSEL) *a little mouse; in*
war *a shed, mantelet*

mutilus, -a, -um *broken, mutilated*

mūtō, -āre, -āvī, -ātum *change* I

mūtuor, -ārī, -ātus sum *borrow*

mūtus, -a, -um *dumb, silent, mute*

mystērium, -ī, n. *mystery rite, secret worship*

N

nam (conj.) *for* I

namque (conj.) *for, and in fact; for indeed* 20

nancīscor, -ī, nactus or nanctus sum *obtain, get;*
find, meet with

narrō, -āre, -āvī, -ātum *tell, narrate, recount*

nāscor, -ī, nātus sum *be born; arise; begin;* nātus,
-a, -um *born, arisen; [so many years] old;* as
noun, nāta, -ae, f. *daughter,* nātus, -ī, m. *son* I

nātālis, -e (nāscor) *natal, of birth*

nātiō, -ōnis, f. (nāscor) *nation, people; birth; race*

natō, -āre, -āvī, -ātum (NATATION) *swim, float*

nātūra, -ae, f. *birth, nature; character* I

nātūrālis, -e (nātūra) *natural*

nātus, -ūs, m. (nāscor) *birth;* minor nātū *younger;*
maior nātū *older*

naufragium, -ī, n. (nāvis + frangō) *shipwreck*

nauta, -ae, m. *sailor* I

nauticus, -a, -um (nauta) *nautical, naval*

nāvālis, -e (nāvis) *naval, nautical, of a ship, of ships*

nāvigātiō, -ōnis, f. (nāvigō) *sailing, navigation; trip*

nāvigium, -ī, n. (nāvigō) *sailing, navigation; a sailing-vessel, ship*

nāvigō, -āre, -āvī, -ātum *sail, navigate* I

nāvis, nāvis, f. (i-stem) *ship;* nāvis longa *warship* I; nāvis onerāria *transport ship, merchant ship*

nāvō, -āre, -āvī, -ātum *do with zeal;* operam nāvāre *do one's best*

nē (adv.) *not* 6 & 7; nē . . . quidem *not even* I; (conj.) *that . . . not, lest;* nē quis *that no one;* nē quid *that nothing*

-ne (interrog. enclitic particle) [?] I; -ne . . . an or -ne . . . -ne *whether . . . or* 11

nec See neque

nec . . . nec . . . See neque . . . neque . . .

necessārius, -a, -um (necesse) *necessary, urgent; household;* (as adv.)necessāriō *necessarily;* (as n.) necessārius, -ī, m. *close friend or relative*

necesse (defective adj., nom. & acc. neut. sing.) *necessary* 9

necessitās, necessitātis, f. (necesse) *necessity; inevitability; need*

necessitūdō, necessitūdinis, f. (necesse) *close connection; intimate friendship*

necne (conj. + adv.) *or not* (in disjunc. indirect questions) 11

necō, -āre, -āvī, -ātum *kill*

necopīnāns, necopīnantis *not expecting, unaware*

nefās, n. [defective: nom. & acc. s. only] (nē + fās) *sacrilege*

neglegenter, adv. (nec + legō, NEGLIGENT) *carelessly*

negligō or neglegō, -ere, neglēxī, neglēctum (nec + lego, NEGLIGENT) *neglect, overlook*

negō, -āre, -āvī, -ātum (w. acc.) *deny, refuse;* (w. indirect statement) *say . . . not* I

negōtium, -ī, n. (nec + ōtium, NEGOTIATE) *trouble; business, task*

nēmō, nēminis, m. *no one, nobody* I

nempe (conj.) *truly, certainly, of course*

nemus, nemoris, n. *grove* 20

nepōs, nepōtis, m. or f. *grandson, granddaughter* I

nēquāquam (adv.) (nē + quisquam) *in no way, by no means*

neque (conj.) *nor, and . . . not . . .* I

neque . . . neque . . . *neither . . . nor . . .* I

nequeō, nequīre, nequīvī, nequītum *be unable, be not up to*

nēquīquam (adv.) (nē + quisquam) *in vain*

nervus, -ī, m. *sinew muscle,* nerve; pl. *power, strings*

nēsciō, -īre, -īvī, ___ *not know, be ignorant* I; nēsciō quis *some one*

neu See nēve

neuter, neutra, neutrum (pron. decl.) *neither* I

nēve or neu (conj.) *and not, nor; and that . . . not*

nex, necis, f. (INTERNECINE) *death; murder*

nīdus, -ī, m. (NIDIFICATION) *nest*

niger, nigra, nigum *black* 14

nihil, nihilī (no dat.), nihil, nihilō (no pl.), n. *nothing; not at all; by no means* I

nihilō *in no way;* nihilō minus *none the less*

nihildum, nihilīdum, n. (nihil + dum) *nothing yet, nothing as yet*

nīl *a contraction of* nihil

nimis (adv.) *too much, greatly*

nimius, -a, um *too great, too much, excessive;* (as n.) nimium, -ī, n. *too much* 17

nisi (adv. conj.) *if . . . not, unless, except* I

niteō, -ēre, -uī, ___ *shine, glitter* 20

nītor, nītī, nīsus or nīxus sum *lean on* (w. abl. of means), *support oneself; struggle*

niveus, -a, -um *snow-white, snowy*

nō, -āre, -āvī, -ātum *swim*

nōbilis, -e *well-known, noted, renowned; noble, of high rank* I

nōbilitās, nōbilitātis, f. (nōbilis) *nobility; rank; nobles*

noceō, -ēre, -uī, -itum (w. dat.) *harm* I

noctū (adv.) (nox, NOCTURNAL) *by night, at night*

nocturnus, -a, -um (nox) *by night, nocturnal*

nōdus, -ī, m. (NODE) *knot*

nōlō, nōlle, nōluī, ___ *not wish, be unwilling* 16

nōmen, nōminis, n. *name, title; fame; account* I; nōmen gentīle *family name*

nōminātim (adv.) (nōmen) *by name*

nōminō, -āre, -āvī, -ātum (nōmen, NOMINATE) *name, call*

nōn (adverb) *not, no* I; nōn nūllī, -ae, -a *some, several* I; nōn numquam (adv.) *sometimes* I

nōnāgēsimus, -a, -um *ninetieth* I

nōnāgintā (indecl.) *ninety* I

nōndum (adv.) (nōn + dum) *not yet*

nōngentēsimus, -a, -um *nine hundredth* I

nōngentī, -ae, -a *nine hundred* I

nōnne (inter. adv.) *not? expects the answer 'Yes'* I

nōnus, -a, -um *ninth* I

nōs, nostrum (nostrī) (pers. & refl. pron.) *we* I

nōscō, -ere, nōvī, nōtum *come to know, find out, learn;* (perf.) *know* I

noster, nostra, nostrum *our, ours;* as noun, m. pl. *our men* I

nōtitia, -ae, f. (nōtus) *notice; acquaintance*

notō, -āre, -āvī, -atum (nōtus, NOTATION) *mark; express by signs; observe, notice*

nōtus, -a, -um *famous, well-known, familiar* I

novem (indecl.) *nine* I

novus, -a, -um *new, strange, novel* I; **novissimum agmen** *the rear;* **novissimī** *those at the rear*

nox, noctis, f. (i-stem) *night;* **prīmā nocte** *early in the night;* **multā nocte** *late at night* I

noxia, -ae, f. (noceō, NOXIOUS) *crime, fault*

nūbēs, nūbis, f. *cloud*

nūbō, -ere, nūpsī, nūptum (w. dat.) *be married;* **nūpta, -ae, f.** *bride* 16

nūdō, -āre, -āvī, -ātum (DENUDE) *lay bare, strip; leave unprotected*

nūdus, -a, -um *naked, bare, nude; unprotected*

nugae, -ārum, f. pl. *jokes, jest, trifles*

nūllus, -a, -um (pron. decl.) *no, not any, none*

num (interrogative particle expecting the answer *no*) I; **num quis** *anyone? any?* I; (introducing a yes-or-no indir. question) *whether, if* 11

nūmen, nūminis, n. *divine will, divine spirit, divinity* I

numerō, -āre, -āvī, -atum (numerus) *number, count; pay out; enumerate*

numerus, -ī, m. *number, quantity; group; position, rank* I

numquam (adv.) *never* I

nunc (adv.) *now, at this time;* **nunc iam** *right now* I

nūntiō, -āre, -āvī, -ātum *announce, report* I

nūntius, -a, -um *serving as a messenger*

nūntius, nūntī, m. *message, news; messenger* I

nūper (adv.) *recently, lately*

nūptiae, -ārum, f. (nūbō) *nuptials, wedding*

nūptiālis, -e (nūbō) *nuptial, of a wedding, wedding*

nusquam (adv.) *nowhere*

nūtrīx, nūtrīcis, f. (NUTRITION) *nurse, wet-nurse, nursemaid*

nūtus, -ūs, m. *nod; command;* **ad nūtum** *instantly*

O

ob (prep. w. acc.) *because of, on account of* I

obaerātus, -a, -um (ob + aes) *in debt;* noun, m. *debtor*

obdūcō, -ere, obdūxī, obductum (dūcō) *build, dig, close*

obeō, obīre, obiī, (obīvī), obitum *go to, go to meet, take part in* (trans.); *fall; die* (intrans.) I

obiciō, -ere, obiēcī, obiectum (iaciō) *throw before, cast; object; oppose, upbraid;* **obiectus, -a, -um** *opposite*

oblīvīscor, -ī, oblītus sum (w. obj. gen.) *forget* I

oboediō, -īre, -īvī, -ītum (w. dat.) (ob + audiō) *listen to, heed, obey; be subject; be obedient*

oborior, -īrī, obortus sum (orior) *arise, appear*

obscūrus, -a, -um *dark, in the dark; obscure*

obsecrō, -āre, -āvī, -ātum (ob + sacer, OBSECRATION) *beseech, implore*

obserō, -āre, -āvī, -ātum *bolt, bar, lock*

observō, -āre, -āvī, -ātum (servō) *watch, observe; heed*

obsēs, obsidis, m. or f. (ob + sedeō) *hostage; pledge, security*

obsessiō, -ōnis, f. (ob + sedeō) *blockade, siege*

obsideō, -ēre, obsēdī, obsessum (ob + sedeō) *besiege, blockade*

obsidiō, obsidiōnis, f. (ob + sedeō) *blockade, siege*

obsistō, -ere, obstitī, obstitum *oppose, resist*

obsolēscō, -ere, obsolēvī, obsolētum (ob + soleō, OBSOLETE) *wear out; lose value*

obsōnium, -ī, n. *food, provisions, shopping*

obsōnō, -āre, -āvī, -ātum *buy food, go shopping*

obstinātus, -a, -um *stubborn, obstinate, resolute*

obstipēscō, -ere, obstipuī, ___ *be amazed*

obstō, -āre, obstitī, obstātum (ob + stō, OBSTACLE) *stand in the way of; oppose, hinder* (with dat.)

obstringō, -ere, obstrīnxī, obstrictum *bind, bind by an oath*

obstruō, -ere, obstrūxī, obstrūctum (OBSTRUCT) *block up, barricade*

obstupefaciō, -ere, obstupefēcī, obstupēfactum *strike with amazement, astound*

obsum, obesse, obfuī, ___ (ob + sum) *hinder*

obtemperō, -āre, -āvī, -ātum *obey;* with dat.

obtestor, -ārī, -ātus sum *call to witness; implore*

obtineō, -ēre, -uī, obtentum (ob + teneō) (trans.) *hold on to; obtain;* (intrans.) *be successful, prevail*

obtingō, -ere, -tigī, ___ (ob + tangō) *befall, occur*

obtrectātor, obtrectātōris, m. (ob + trahō) *critic, disparager*

obtruncō, -āre, -āvī, -ātum *assassinate; kill; cut down*

obvertō, -ere, -tī, -tum *to turn toward, turn against*

obveniō, -īre, obvēnī, obventum (ob + veniō) *come in the way of; fall to the lot of*

obviam (adv.) (ob + via, OBVIOUS) *in the way; against, to meet*

occāsiō, occāsiōnis, f. (ob + cadō) *opportunity, occasion*

occāsus, -ūs, m. (ob + cadō) *setting;* **sōlis occāsus** *sunset; west*

occidentālis, -e (ob + cadō, OCCIDENTAL) *western*

occidō, -ere, occidī, occāsum *fall down; perish; set* **occidēns, occidentis** *setting; west* 3

occīdō, -ere, occīdī, occīsum *cut down, kill, slay* 3

occulō, -ere, occuluī, occultum (OCCULT) *hide*

occultō, -āre, -āvī, -ātum *hide, conceal, secrete*

occupātiō, occupātiōnis, f. (occupō) *occupation, employment*

occupō, -āre, -āvī, -ātum *seize, capture; occupy; attack* I

occurrō, -ere, occurrī, occursum (ob + currō) (w. dat.) *run to meet, go to meet; fall in with, happen upon; occur; resist, oppose*

ocrea, -ae, f. *a greave, legging*

octāvus, -a, -um *eighth* I

octingentēsimus, -a, -um *eight hundredth* I

octingentī, -ae, -a *eight hundred* I

octō (indecl.) *eight* I

octōgēsimus, -a, -um *eightieth* I

octōgintā (indecl.) *eighty* I

oculus, -ī, m. *eye* I

ōdī, ōdisse, ōsūrus (defective) (ODIOUS) *hate*

odium, -ī, n. (ODIOUS) *hatred, odium*

odōrātus, -a, -um *perfumed, fragrant*

offendō, -ere offendī, offēnsum *offend, be offensive*

offerō, offerre, obtulī, oblātus (ob + ferō, OBLATION) *offer, present; bestow*

officium, -ī, n. *duty, service; office* 2

oleō, -ēre, -uī, ___ (REDOLENT) *smell*

ōlim (adv.) *formerly; once, at one time, at some time* I

ōmen, ōminis, n. (audiō, OMINOUS) *sign, omen*

omittō, -ere, omīsī, omissum (ob + mittō) *lay aside; omit; let go; disregard*

omnīnō (adv.) (omnis) *altogether;* (after neg.) *at all;* (with numerals) *in all*

omnis, omne *all, every;* as noun, pl., m. *all men;* n. *all things* I

onager, onagrī, m. *wild ass, mechanical sling*

onerārius, -a, -um *for carrying freight;* **nāvis onerāria** *transport ship, merchant ship*

onus, oneris, n. *burden, load; cargo*

onustus, -a, -um *laden*

opācus, -a, -um *dark, shaded; opaque*

opera, -ae, f. *aid, assistance; service, effort; trouble; work, task; attention, time [spent on something];* **operae pretium** *worth the effort;* **operam dare** *pay attention, spend time*

operiō, -īre, -uī, -ertum *hide*

opifex, opificis, m. (opus + faciō) *workman*

opīniō, opīniōnis, f. *belief, idea, opinion; expectation; reputation*

opīnor, -ārī -ātus sum *opine, believe, think, suppose*

oportet, -ēre, -uit, ___ (impers.) *it is necessary, it is proper; ought, must;* with acc. and infin. 17

opperior, -īrī, oppertus sum *wait*

oppidānus, -ī, m. *townsman*

oppidō (adv.) *very much*

oppidum, -i, n. *town* I

oppōnō, -ere, opposuī, oppositum (ob + pōnō) *place against, place in opposition*

opportūnus, -a, -um *favorable; advantageous; opportune*

opprimō, -ere, oppressī, oppressum (ob + premō) *press against; overwhelm, crush; catch unawares; fall upon; oppress*

oppugnātiō, -ōnis, f. (ob + pugnō) *assault, siege, attack; storming*

oppugnō, -āre, -āvī, -ātum (ob + pugno) *attack [a fortified position]; assault; storm, beseige*

ops, opis, f. *help, power;* (pl.) **opēs, opum,** f. *might, power, influence, resources, assistance, wealth* 2

optimās, optimātis, m. (optimus) *aristocrat; Optimate* (member of the conservative party)

optimus, -a, -um superl. of **bonus** I

optō, -āre, -āvī, -ātum *choose, wish for; wish, desire* I

opus, operis, n. *work, task;* pl. *works, fortifications*

(opus *continued*)

I; **magnō opere** (**magnopere**) (adv.) *greatly, very much;* **tantō opere** (**tantopere**) (adv.) *so much, so greatly;* **opus est** *there is need*

ōra, -ae, f. *shore, coast*

ōrātiō, ōrātiōnis, f. (ORATION) *speech; eloquence;* ōrātiōnem habēre *deliver a speech*

ōrātor, ōrātōris, m. (ORATOR) *speaker, spokesman*

orbis, orbis, m. (ORBIT) *circle, ring, disk;* orbis terrārum *the circle of lands [around the Mediterranean] = the inhabited world*

ordinō, -āre, -āvī, -ātum (ordo, ORDAIN) *set in order, settle, arrange*

ordior, -īrī, orsus sum (ordo) *begin;* rem ordīrī *open a case [at law]*

ordō, ordinis, m. *order; row, series; rank, class; bank (of oars)* 8

orior, -īrī, ortus sum (oritūrus) *rise, arise; spring from; be descended;* oriēns, -entis, m. (*participle with* sol *understood*) *rising, the rising sun; the orient, the east* 7

ornātus, -ūs, m. (ornō) *dress, equipment; decoration, embellishment, arms*

ornō, -āre, -āvī, -ātum *decorate, adorn; honor; furnish, equip* 7

ōrō, -āre, -āvī, -ātum (ōs, ORATION) *beg, beseech; speak; plead*

ōs, ōris, n. *mouth, face* I

os, ossis, n. *bone* 14

ōsculor, -ārī, -ātus sum (ōs) *kiss*

ōsculum, -ī, n. *kiss; mouth, lip* 19

ōstendō, -ere, ōstendī, ōstentum *show, point out;* ōstentum, -ī, n. *prodigy, portent* I

ōstentātiō, ōstentātiōnis, f. *ostentation*

ostentō, -āre, -āvī, -ātum (ōstendō, OSTENTATION) *display, exhibit*

ostium, -ī, n. (ōs) *entrance, door; river-mouth*

ōtiōsus, -a, -um (ōtium, OTIOSE) *quiet, at leisure*

ōtium, -ī, n. *leisure, idleness, peace, rest, quiet* 14

P

pābulum, -ī, n. *fodder, forage*

pacīscor, -ī, pactus sum *make a bargain, compact, or agreement;* pactus, -a, -um *agreed upon, appointed;* pactum, -ī, n. *agreement; manner*

pācō, -āre, -āvī, -ātum (pāx) *pacify, subdue*

pactiō, -ōnis, f. *bargain, agreement*

paene (adv.) *almost* I

paenitet, -ēre, -uit, ___ *it causes repentance, (regret, displeasure), it repents, it grieves* (impers.) 17

pāgus, -ī, m. *district, canton*

pāla, -ae, f. *spade*

palam (adv.) *openly, publicly*

pallidus, -a, -um *pale, pallid*

pallor, pallōris, m. *paleness, pallor*

palma, -ae, f. *palm of the hand; hand; palm tree, palm branch*

pālus, -ī, m. *stake*

palūs, palūdis, f. *swamp, marsh*

pandō, -ere, pandī, passum (EXPAND) *spread out;* passīs manibus *with hands outstretched*

pānis, pānis, m. (i-stem) (PANTRY) *bread, loaf, piece of bread*

pār, paris *equal; even (of a number);* as m. noun *peer;* as n. noun *pair* I; pariter (adv.) *equally; together*

parcō, -ere, pepercī, pārsum (w. dat.) *spare* I

parcus, -a, -um (parcō) *sparing, frugal; scanty*

parēns, parentis, m. or f. *parent* I

pāreō, -ēre, -uī, -itum (w. dat.) *obey, submit to* I

pariēs, -etis, m. (PARIETAL) *wall, house wall*

pariō, -ere, peperī, partum *give birth to; bring forth; obtain* 16

parma, -ae, f. *[small round] shield*

parō, -āre, -āvī, -ātum *prepare, make ready; equip*

pārs, partis, f. (i-stem) *part, share; portion; region; party, faction; role;* magna pārs *the majority;* in omnīs partīs *in all directions;* ūnā ex parte *on one side* I

parsimōnia, -ae, f. (parcō, PARSIMONY) *thrift, frugality*

partim (adv.) (pārs) *in part; partly*

parum, n. (*only in nom. and acc. sing.*) *little, too little; not enough* I

parumper, adv. (parum + per) *for a short time*

parvulus, -a, -um (parvus) *very little, very small, tiny, very young; unimportant*

parvus, -a, -um *little, small* I

pāscō, -ere, pāvī, pāstum (PASTURE) *feed, feed on; graze*

passim (adv.) *here and there; everywhere*

passus, passūs, m. *pace (as unit of measure = 1.48 m., 4.85 ft.)* mille passūs *mile* I pāstor, pāstōris, m. (PASTOR) *shepherd, herdsman*

pateō, -ēre, uī, ___ *be open, lie open; extend, be accessible* 5

pater, patris, m. *father* I; patrēs cōnscrīptī *senators*

patientia, -ae, f. (patior) *endurance, patience*

patior, -ī, passum sum *suffer, endure, experience; allow, permit;* patiēns, patientis *patient, enduring*

patria, -ae, f. *fatherland, native land* I

patrius, -a, -um (pater) *of a father, native, ancestral*

paucitās, -ātis, f. (paucī) *scarcity; paucity*

paucus, -a, -um *little;* pl *few, a few* I

paulatim (adv.) (paulum) *little by little; gradually*

paulisper (adv.) (paulim + per) *for a short time*

paulum, n. (defective noun, abl. paulō) *a little* 8

pauper, pauperis, *poor, needy*

pauperiēs, -ēi, f. *poverty*

paupertās, -ātis, f. *poverty, need*

paveō, -ēre, pāvī, ___ *tremble, fear*

pavor, pavōris, m. *fear, panic*

pāx, pācis, f. *peace; peace treaty* 4

peccō, -āre, -āvī, -ātum (IMPECCABLE) *go wrong, do wrong, sin*

pectus, pectoris, n. *breast, heart* I

pecūnia, -ae, f. *money, property* I

pecus, pecoris, n. *cattle, herd, flock* 17

pedes, peditis, m. (pēs) *footsoldier, infantryman;* pl. *infantry*

pedester, pedestris, pedestre (pēs) *on foot, pedestrian*

peditātus, -ūs, m. (pēs) *infantry*

peior, peius (comp. of malus) *worse* I

pelagus, -ī, n. (ARCHIPELAGO) *sea*

pellis, -is, f. *skin, hide; pelt*

pellō, -ere, pepulī, pulsum *strike, push, drive away; defeat, rout* 1

pendeō, -ēre, pependī, ___ (pendō, PENDANT) *hang* (intransitive)

pendō, -ere, pependī, pēnsum *hang* (transitive); *weigh; pay* 6

penetrō, -āre, -āvī, -ātum *enter, penetrate*

penitus (adv.) *in (into) the inmost part, deeply*

penna, -ae, f. (PENNANT) *feather, wing*

per (prep. w. acc.) *through; across, among; during; by; by means of; by reason of* I

peragō, -ere, perēgī, perāctum (per + agō) *carry out, finish; agitate*

perbene (adv.) (per + bene) *very well*

percellō, -ere, perculī, perculsum *beat, strike, push [up of down]*

percieō, -ēre, percīvī, percitum (per + cieō) *stir up, arouse, excite*

percipiō, -ere, -cēpī, -ceptum (per + capio, perception) *secure, gain; perceive, feel*

percontor, -ārī, -ātus sum *inquire*

percurrō, -ere, percucurrī or percurrī, percursum (per + currō) *run through*

percutiō, -ere, percussī, percussum (PERCUSSION) *beat, strike; pierce*

perdiscō, -ere, didicī, ___ (per + discō) *learn thoroughly*

perdō, -ere, perdidī, perditum *destroy; waste; lose; ruin* 12

perdūcō, -ere, perdūxī, perductum (per + dūcō) *lead through, lead all the way; conduct; construct*

peregrē (adv.) (per + ager) *to or from abroad*

peregrīnus, -a, -um (per + ager, PILGRIM) *foreign*

pereō, perīre, periī (perīvī), peritum *perish, be*

perequitō, -āre, -āvī, -ātum (per + equus) *ride through; ride around*

perfacilis, -e (per + facilis) *very easy*

perferō, perferre, pertulī, perlātum (per + fero) *carry through; report; endure, suffer*

perficiō, -ere, perfēcī, perfectum (per + facio) *complete, do thoroughly, finish*

perfidia, -ae, f. (per + fidēs) *faithlessness, treachery, perfidy*

perfidiōsus, -a, -um (per + fidēs, PERFIDIOUS) *treacherous*

perfringō, -ere, perfrēgī, perfrāctum (per + frangō) *break through*

perfuga, -ae, m. (per + fuga) *deserter*

perfugiō, -ere, perfūgī, perfugitum (per + fugiō) *flee, desert; flee for refuge*

pergō, -ere, perrēxī, perrēctum (per + regō) *proceed, go on*

perīculōsus, -a, -um (perīculum) *dangerous, perilous*

perīculum, -i, n. *danger, peril; trial; risk* I

perimō, -ere, perēmī, perēmptum (per + emō, PEREMPTORY) *kill, destroy*

perītus, -a, -um (w. obj. gen.) *skilled, skillful; experienced*

perlegō, -ere, perlēgī, perlēctum (per + legō) *read through*

permaneō, -ēre, -mānsī, -mānsum (per + maneō, PERMANENT) *remain*

permātūrēscō, -ere, permātūruī, ___ *ripen thoroughly*

permittō, -ere, permīsī, permissum *let pass; entrust; permit, allow* 8

permoveō, -ēre, permōvī, permōtum (per + moveō) *move deeply, alarm; influence*

permulceō, -ēre, permulsī, permulsum *stroke*

permultus, -a, -um (per + multus) *very much;* (pl.) *very many*

pernegō, -āre, -āvī, -ātum (per + negō) *deny altogether*

perōdī, perōdisse, perōsum (perf. only) *hate*

perpaucī, -ae, -a (per + paucī) *very few; as noun,* m. *very few*

perpetuō (adv.) *continually*

perpetuus, -a, -um *continuous, continual, uninterrupted, lasting, perpetual*

perrumpō, -ere, perrūpī, perruptum (per + rumpō) *break through*

perscrībō, -ere, perscrīpsī, perscrīptum (per + scrībō) *write fully; report*

persequor, -ī, persecūtus sum *follow constantly, pursue, persecute; overtake; attack; accomplish* 2

persolvō, -ere, persōlvī, persōlutum (per + solvō) *pay*

perspiciō, -ere, perspexī, perspectum (cf. aspiciō, PERSPECTIVE) *perceive, see; observe*

perspicuē (adv.) *clearly, evidently*

persuādeō, -ēre, persuāsī, persuāsum (w. dat.) *persuade* 7

pertendō, -ere, pertendī, pertēnsum *continue*

perterreō, -ēre, -uī, -itum *frighten thoroughly; terrify*

pertinācia, -ae, f. (per + teneō) *perseverance; obstinacy; pertinacity*

pertināx, pertinācis (per + teneō, PERTINACIOUS) *persevering, stubborn, tenacious, obstinate*

pertineō, -ēre, -uī, ___ (per + teneō) *pertain, concern; extend; reach*

perturbātiō, perturbātiōnis, f. (per + turba, PERTURBATION) *disturbance; commotion*

perturbō, -āre, -āvī, -ātum (per + turba, PERTURB) *disturb, confuse*

perveniō, -īre, pervēnī, perventum *come all the way, arrive; attain* 1

pēs, pedis, m. *foot* (as measure, 11.65 inches) I; **pedem referre** *to retreat* I

pessimus, -a, -um (superl. of malus)

pestilentia, -ae, f. *pestilence, epidemic; plague, fever*

petītiō, petītiōnis, f. (petō) *attack; request, petition, candidacy*

petō, -ere, petīvī, petītum *aim at, seek; attack; ask; demand; secure* I

phalanx, phalangis, f. *phalanx; class formation*

pestilēns, -tis *pestilential*

pietās, pietātis, f. (pius) *dutifulness [towards gods, parents, or country]; devotion; piety*

piget, -ēre, -uit, ___ *it causes disgust (annoyance, regret, shame); it pains, it grieves* 17

pīla, ae, f. (PILASTER) *pillar*

pīlum, -ī, n. *javelin, pike*

pīlus, -ī, m. *maniple [in the army];* **prīmī pīlī centūriō** *first centurion of the first maniple* (first centurion of the legion in rank;) **prīmum pīlum dūcere** *hold the rank of first centurion*

pinguis, -e *fat, rich, fertile; dull, stupid*

pinna, -ae, f. (PINNACLE) *feather; battlement*

pīrāta, -ae, m. *pirate*

piscīna, -ae, f. *swimming-pool*

piscis, -is, m. (i-stem) (PISCES) *fish*

pius, -a, -um *loyal, dutiful [to gods, country, or relatives]* I

pix, picis, f. *pitch*

placeō, -ēre, -uī, -itum (w. dat.) *please* I

placidus, -a, -um *placid* 19

plācō, -āre, -āvī, -ātum *appease; placate*

plāga, -ae, f. *blow, stroke; tract, region*

plangor, plangōris, m. *outcry, shriek*

plānus, -a, -um *flat, level; plain, clear*

plēbēius, -a, -um (plēbs) *plebeian*

plēbs, plēbis, and plēbēs, -eī, or -is, f. *the multitude, the common people, plebeians* I

plēnus, -a, -um *full* (w. abl. of means or gen. of the whole) I

plērusque, plēraque, plērumque *the larger part of, the majority of;* **plerumque** (internal acc.) *generally, for the most part* 17

plorō, -āre, -āvī, -ātum (DEPLORE) *lament, weep*

plūma, -ae, f. *feather; plume*

plumbum, -ī, n. (PLUMB, PLUMBER) *lead*

plūrēs, plūra comp. of multī I

plūrimus, -a, -um superl. of multus I

plūs, plūris, n. (no dat. sing., no plural) *a larger amount, more* I

pluteus, -ī, m. *a shed [as a cover for besiegers]; a parapet*

pōculum, -ī, n. *[drinking-]cup*

poena, -ae, f. *punishment, penalty* 6; **poenam sūmere dē** or **ex** *punish;* **poenam dare** *be punished* poēta, -ae, m. *poet* I

pol (interj.) *by Pollux; truly; really*

pollex, pollicis, m. *thumb;* pollice versō *with up-turned thumb* (signalling the killing of a gladiator)

polliceor, -ērī, pollicitus sum *promise*

pollicitātiō, pollicitātiōnis, f. *promise*

pōmum, -ī, n. (POMEGRANATE) *apple, fruit*

pondō, n. (defective noun, abl. only) (POUND) *in weight* (with some form of lībra, *pound*)

pondus, ponderis, n. *weight* 6

pōnō, -ere, posuī, positum *put, place, lay down* I; castra pōnere *pitch camp*

pōns, pontis, m. (PONTOON) *bridge*

ponticulus, -ī, m. *small bridge*

pontificātus, -ūs, m. *pontificate, pontiffship*

pontus, -ī, n. *[the deep] sea* 12

populātiō, -iōnis, f. *ravaging, plundering*

populor, -ārī, -ātus *lay waste, devastate*

populus, -ī, m. *a nation, a people; populace* I

porrigō, -ere, porrēxī, porrēctum (prō + rego) *stretch out, extend*

porta, -ae, f. *gate, entrance; door* 17

porticus, -ūs, m. *portico, colonnade*

portō, -āre, -āvī, -ātum *carry, bring, bear* I

portus, -ūs, m. *harbor, port*

poscō, -ere, poposcī, ___ *ask, demand, require, beg*

possessiō, possessiōnis, f. (potis + sedeō) *possession*

possideō, -ere, possēdī, possessum (potis + sedeō) *possess, hold, occupy*

possidō, -ere, -sēdī, -sessum (potis + sedēs) *occupy, seize*

possum, posse, potuī, ___ *can, be able* I

post (prep. w. acc.) *after, behind, in back of;* (adv.) *afterward, after, later, behind* I

posteā (adv.) (post + is) *afterwards*

posteāquam (conj.) (post + is + quam) *after*

posterus, -a, -um *subsequent, following, next;* in posterum *for the future;* (as noun) posterī, -ōrum, m. *posterity, descendants;* posterior, -ius *later* I

posthāc (adv.) (post + hic) *hereafter, after this, in future*

postquam (adv. conj.) *after* I

postrēmus, -a, -um (superl. of posterus) *last;* ad postrēmum *finally;* postrēmō (abl. of time when) *at the last, last of all* I

postrīdiē (adv.) (posterus + diēs) *on the next day;* postrīdiē eius diēī *on the following day*

postulō, -āre, -āvī, -ātum (POSTULATE) *demand, ask; require; accuse, impeach*

postumus, -a, -um superl. of posterus I

potēns, potentis *powerful* 14

potentia, -ae, f. (potēns, POTENCY) *power, influence*

potestās, potestātis, f. (potēns) *power, strength; ability, chance, opportunity*

potiō, -ōnis, f. *drink, drinking*

potior, -īrī, potītus sum (w. obj. gen. or abl. of means) *gain, get possession of, obtain, acquire* I

potior, -ius *preferable:* (adv.) potius *rather, more preferably* I

potissimus, -a, -um *most important* I

prae (prep. w. abl.) *before, in front of, ahead of; in comparison with* I

praebeō, -ēre, -uī, -itum *offer, furnish, provide; show, exhibit* I

praecēdō, -ere, praecessī, praecessum (prae + cēdō) *go before, precede; surpass, excel*

praeceps, praecipitis (prae + caput) *headlong, hasty; inclined, steep; precipitous*

praecipiō, -ere, praecēpī, praeceptum *receive in advance; instruct, teach, order, anticipate;* praeceptum, -ī, n. *teaching, precept; order, command* I, I

praecipitō, -āre, -āvī, -ātum (prae + caput) PRECIPITATE) *throw headlong, cast down*

praecipuus, -a, -um (prae + capiō) *especial, special, particular*

praecō, praecōnis, m. *herald, town crier*

praeda, -ae, f. *(predatory) prey, booty*

praedicō, -āre, -āvī, -ātum *announce publicly, make publicly known*

praedīcō, -ere, praedīxī, praedictum (prae + dīcō) *say beforehand, predict; warn*

praedictiō, praedictiōnis, f. (prae + dīcō) *prediction, prophecy*

praedō, praedōnis, m. *bandit, robber, pirate*

praedor, -ārī, -ātus sum *pillage, plunder*

praefectus, -ī, m. (prae + faciō) *commander; prefect*

praeferō, praeferre, praetulī, praelātum (prae + ferō, PRELATE) *carry before, display; prefer;* praelātus, -a, -um *outstanding*

praeficiō, -ere, praefēcī, praefectum (prae + faciō, PREFECT) *put in charge of; place in command*

praemittō, -ere, praemīsī, praemissum (prae + mittō) *send ahead*

praemium, -ī, n. *reward, premium* 14

praenōmen, praenōminis, n. (prae + nōmen) *prae-nomen (first name)*

praeoptō, -āre, -āvī, -ātum (prae + optō) *prefer*

praerumpō, -ere, praerūpī, praeruptum (prae + rumpō) *break off in front;* **praeruptus, -a, -um** *steep, precipitous, overhanging*

praescrībō, -ere, praescrīpsī, praescrīptum (prae + scrībō) *direct; prescribe*

praesegmen, praesegminis, n. *paring*

praesēns See **praesum**

praesentia, -ae, f. (prae + sum) *present time; presence*

praesertim (adv.) *especially*

praesidium, -ī, n. (prae + sedeō) *protection, guard, defense; garrison*

praestō, -āre, praestitī, praestitum (w. dat.) *stand before, excel, be superior;* (w. acc.) *show; furnish, offer, present;* **praestat** *it is better;* **praestāns, praestantis,** *excellent, outstanding* I

praesum, praeesse, praefuī, praefutūrus *be at the head of, be in charge of;* (pres. part.) **praesēns, praesentis** *present, at hand, in person, immediate; propitious;* **in praesentia** *for the present*

praeter (prep. w. acc.) (PRETERNATURAL) *beyond, more than; except, besides*

praetereā (adv.) *further, besides that, in addition* 18

praetereō, praeterīre, praeteriī (praeterīvī), praeteritum *go by, pass by; neglect, disregard; surpass*

praetermittō, -ere, -mīsī, -missum (mittō) *pass over, overlook; let go*

praeterquam (adv.) *except, besides*

praetextus, -a, -um *bordered;* **toga praetexta** *purple-bordered toga*

praetor, praetōris, m. *praetor; judge; leader, commander*

praetūra, -ae, f. *praetorship*

praeūstus, -a, -um (prae + ūrō) *burnt at the end; hardened by burning*

praevaleō, -ēre, -uī, -itum (prae + valeō) *have more power, be stronger, prevail*

precēs, precum, f. (pl.) *prayers, entreaties*

precor, -ārī, -ātus sum (IMPRECATION) *pray, beseech, beg, entreat*

prehendō, -ere, prehendī, prehēnsum (PREHENSILE) *seize, grasp, catch, arrest*

premō, -ere, pressī, pressum *press, crush, follow closely; overwhelm* 11

prēndō, -ere, prēndī, prēnsum See **prehendō**

pretium, -ī, n. (PRECIOUS) *price, value; reward;* **operae pretium** *worth the effort*

prex, precis, f. *prayer, entreaty; curse, imprecation*

prīdem see **iam**

prīdiē (adv.) (prae + diēs) *the day before*

prīmīpīlus, -ī, m. *first centurion* (See **pīlus**)

primor, primōris (prīmus) *leading, foremost, high-ranking*

prīmus, -a, -um *first; earliest; foremost* I; (internal acc.) **prīmum** *first, for the first time;* (abl. of time when) **prīmō,** *first, at first;* **cum prīmum** *as soon as;* **quam prīmum** *as soon as possible;* **prīma lūx** *dawn;* (as noun) **prīmī, prīmōrum,** m. *chiefs, nobles;* **in prīmīs** *especially*

prīnceps, prīncipis, m. *chief, chieftain, leading man, prince, emperor* I

prīncipātus, -ūs, m. (prīnceps) *principate, emperorship, supremacy; chief command*

principium, -ī, n. (princeps) *beginning*

prior, prius *former, earlier, first;* as noun, m. pl. *those in advance;* **prius** (adv.) *before, earlier; first, rather* I

prīstinus, -a, -um *former, previous, early; old-time, original; pristine*

priusquam (conj.) *before, until; sooner than* I

prīvātus, -a, -um *private, personal;* **rēs prīvāta** *private property;* **prīvātus, -ī,** m. *private citizen*

prō (prep. w. abl.) *before, in front of; for (on behalf of, in exchange for, in proportion to)* I

probō, -āre, -āvī, -ātum *approve, recommend; try, test*

prōcēdō, -ere, prōcessī, prōcessum (prō + cēdō, PROCESSION) *go forth, go forward, advance*

procella, -ae, f. *storm, gust, squall, tempest, tumult*

procer, -eris, m. (usually plural) *chiefs*

prōclāmō, -āre, -āvī, -ātum (prō + clāmō) *shout out, cry out, burst out with, proclaim*

procul (adv.) *at a distance, far off* I

prōcumbō, -ere, prōcubuī, prōcubitum (cf. RECUMBENT) *sink down, lie down, lean forward*

prōcūrō, -āre, -āvī, -ātum (prō + cūrō, PROCURE) *take care of, attend to*

prōcurrō, -ere, prōcucurrī or prōcurrī, prōcursum (prō + currō) *run forward, advance*

prodeō, -īre, prodīvī or prodiī, proditum (prō + eō) *go forth, appear; advance*

prōdigium, -ī, n. (prō + agō) *prodigy, portent, omen; monster; wonder*

prōditor, prōditōris, m. (prōdō) *betrayer, traitor*

prōdō, -ere, prōdidī, prōditum *put forth, reveal, betray, hand down;* **memoriae prōdere** *relate, record* I

prōdūcō, -ere, prōdūxī, prōductum (prō + dūcō) *lead forth; prolong, extend; produce*

proelior, -ārī, -ātus sum (proelium) *fight*

proelium, -ī, n. *battle* I

profectiō, profectiōnis, f. (prō + faciō) *departure*

profectō (adv.) (prō + faciō) *surely, certainly; for a fact, in fact, actually*

prōferō, prōferre, prōtulī, prōlātum (prō + ferō) *bring forth, put forth; mention*

prōficiō, -ere, prōfēcī, prōfectum (prō + faciō) *make, accomplish, effect*

proficīscor, -ī, fectus sum (prō + faciō) *set out, start; proceed*

profiteor, -ērī, professus sum *declare; profess*

prōflīgō, -āre, -āvī, -ātum *overthrow, rout*

profugiō, -ere, profūgī, —(prō + fugiō) *flee, escape; take refuge*

prōfundō, -ere, prōfūdī, prōfūsum (prō + fundō, PROFUSE) *pour forth; rush; spend, lavish, squander*

prognātus, ī, n. (prō + nāscor) *descendant*

prōgredior, -ī, prōgressus sum *move forward, advance, progress*

prohibeō, -ēre, -uī, -itum *hold off, keep away; prevent, prohibit* I

prōiciō, -ere, -iēcī, -iectum (prō + iaciō, PROJECT) *throw forward, throw down*

proinde (adv.) (prō + inde) *hence, then*

prōlābor, -ī, prōlāpsus sum (prō + lābor, PROLAPSE) *slide forward, slip; fall, fall down, fail*

prōlēs, prōlis, f. *offspring, descendant* 1

prōloquor, -ī, prōlocūtus sum (prō + loquor) *speak out*

prōmittō, -ere, prōmīsī, prōmissum *send forth; promise;* **prōmissus, -a, -um** *flowing, hanging down* I

prōmō, -ere, prōmpsī, prōmptum *bring forth, bring out* I

prōmoveō, -ēre, prōmōvī, prōmōtum (prō + moveō, PROMOTION) *move forward*

prōnūntiō, -āre, -āvī, -ātum (prō + nūntiō, PRO-NOUNCE) *announce, declare*

prōnus, -a, -um (prō) *leaning forward; prone*

prope (prep. w. acc.) *near* I

prope (adv.) *nearby; nearly, almost* I

prōpellō, -ere, prōpulī, prōpulsum (prō + pellō) *drive forward; drive away, defeat*

propemodum (adv.) *nearly, almost*

properō, -āre, -āvī, -ātum (intrans.) *hasten, make haste;* (trans.) *hasten, accelerate* I

properus, -a, -um *quick, hasty, hurried;* **properē** (adv.) *speedily*

propinquitās, -ātis, f. (prope) *nearness, vicinity; propinquity; relationship*

propinquus, -a, -um (prope) *near, close, neighboring.* As noun, m. *relative* I

propior, -ius *nearer* I

propitius, -a, -um *propitious, favorable*

prōpōnō, -ere, prōposuī, prōpositum (prō + pōnō) *set forth, put forward; propose;* **prōpositum, -ī,** n. *plan; purpose; proposition*

proprius, -a, -um (PROPRIETOR) *[one's] own, characteristic*

propter (prep. w. acc.) *near; because of, on account of* I

proptereā (adv.) (propter + is) *therefore, for this reason;* **proptereā quod** *because of the fact that*

prōpugnō, -āre, -āvī, -ātum (prō + pugnō) *fight (on the defensive); take the offensive*

prōpulsō, -āre, -āvī, -ātum (prō + pellō) *drive off; drive back; repel*

prōrogō, -āre, -āvī, -ātum (prō + rogō, PROROGUE) *propose an extension of*

prōsequor, -ī, prōsecūtus sum (prō + sequor) *follow after, pursue*

prōsiliō, -īre, prōsiluī, —*leap forth, leap forward*

prōspectus, -ūs, m. (prospect) *view, sight*

prōsperus, -a, -um *fortunate, favorable, prosperous, successful*

prōspiciō, -ere, prōspexī, prōspectum (aspiciō, PROSPECT) *look forward, provide*

prōsum, prōdesse, prōfuī, prōfutūrus *be useful, be advantageous, be profitable* I

prōtegō, -ere, prōtēxī, prōtēctum (prō + tegō) *cover, protect*

prōtinus (adv.) *immediately, at once*

prōtrahō, -ere, prōtrāxī, prōtrāctum (prō + trahō) *draw forth; prolong, protract; defer*

prōturbō, -āre, -āvī, -ātum (prō + turba) *drive away; repulse*

prōvehō, -ere, prōvēxī, prōvectum (prō + vehō) *carry;* pass. *be carried, ride, sail*

prōverbium, -ī, n. (prō + verbum) *proverb*

prōvideō, -ēre, prōvīdī, prōvīsum (prō + videō) (with acc.) *foresee;* (with dat.) *provide for*

prōvincia, -ae, f. *province* I

prōvocō, -āre, -āvī, -ātum (prō + vocō) *call forth, challenge; provoke*

prōvolō, -āre, -āvī, -ātum (prō + volō) *fly forward; dash forth*

proximus, -a, -um *nearest, next, last* I

prūdēns, prūdentis (prō + videō) *prudent, foresighted, provident*

prūdentia, -ae, f. (prō + videō) *foresight; wisdom, prudence*

pruinōsus, -a, -um *frosty*

pūblicō, -āre, -āvī, -ātum (pūblicus) *make public; publish; confiscate*

pūblicus, -a, -um *public, belonging to the people* (populus) I

pudet, -ēre, -uit, ___ *it causes shame* 17

pudicitia, -ae, f. (pudet) *modesty; chastity*

pudīcus, -a, -um (pudet) *modest, virtuous*

pudor, pudōris, m. *shame, modesty, decency; [a woman's] honor* 3

puella, -ae, f. *girl* I

puer, puerī, m. *boy; child; slave boy; ā puerō from boyhood* I

puerīlis, -e (puer, PUERILE) *youthful, boyish; childish, silly*

pugna, -ae, f. *fight* 8

pugnō, -āre, -āvī, -ātum *fight* I; **pugnātum est** *the battle raged*

pugnus, -ī, m. *fist*

pulcher, pulchra, pulchrum *beautiful, handsome, fine, noble* I

pullus, -a, -um *dark-colored;* **vestis pulla** *mourning-garment*

pullus, -ī, m. (PULLET) *chicken*

pulsō, -āre, -āvī, -ātum (pellō) *beat; pulsate*

pulvis, pulveris, m. (PULVERIZE) *dust*

pūmex, pūmicis, m. *pumice stone*

puppis, -is, f. (POOP) *stern, ship*

pūrgō, -āre, -āvī, -ātum (PURGE) *make clean, excuse*

purpureus, -a, -um *purple, dark red*

putō, -āre, -āvī, -ātum *think, consider, believe* I

Q

quā (adv.) *where, by which way*

quadra, -ae, f. *square table*

quadrāgēsimus, -a, -um *fortieth* I

quadrāgintā (indecl.) *forty* I

quadrilībris, -e *that weighs four pounds*

quadringentēsimus, -a, -um *four hundredth* I

quadringentī, -ae, -a *four hundred* I

quadruplex, quadruplicis *fourfold* I

quaerō, -ere, quaesīvī, quaesītum *seek, search for, ask for* 1

quaesō, -ere, quaesīvī, quaesītum *seek, search for, ask for;* **quaesō** = *please; pray tell*

quaestiō, quaestiōnis, f. (quaerō) *questioning, inquiry; investigation*

quaestor, quaestōris, m. *quaestor; state-treasurer; quartermaster general*

quaestus, -ūs, m. *gain, profit*

quālis, -e *of such a kind* (rel.); *of what kind?* (interr.) I

quāliscumque, quālecumque (indef. rel. adj.) *of whatever kind* I

quam (adv. conj. modifying adjectives and adverbs) *as;* (interr. adv.) *how?* (w. comp.) *than;* (w. superl.) *as . . . as possible;* **tam . . . quam,** *as . . . as;* **quam diū** *as long as, how long;* **quam prīmum** *as soon as possible* I

quamobrem (inter.) *why, for which reason* I

quamquam (indef. adv.) *however* I

quamquam (adv. conj.) *although*

quandō (inter. adv.) *when? at what time?* (indef. adv.) *at any time;* (rel. adv.) *when, since* I

quandōcumque (indef. adv.) *whenever* I

quantus, -a, -um *of which size* (rel.); *how big? how large? how much?* (interr.) I; **quantō opere** *how much, how greatly;* **quantum** (internal acc.) *so much as; how much; how far*

quantuscumque, quantacumque, quantumcumque (indef. rel. adj.) *of whatever size; however big, however large, however much* I

quārē (interr. and rel. adv.) *wherefore, for which reason;* **why?** (in indirect questions) 11

quārtus, -a, -um *fourth* I

quāsi (adv.) *as if, just as if; as it were, sort of* 9

quater (adv.) *four times* I

quaternī, -ae, -a *four by four, four at a time* I

quatiō, -ere, ___ **quassum** *shake*

quattuor (indecl.) *four* I

quattuordecim (indecl.) *fourteen* I

-que (enclitic conjunction) *and* I

quemadmodum (adv.) (**quem ad modum**) *as* (rel.); *how?* (interr.) I

queō, quīre, quīvī, quītum *be able*

queror, -ī, questus sum *complain [of], lament*

quī, quae, quod (rel. & interr. pron.) *who, which, that; which?* (rel. & interr. adj.) *which; which?* (indef. adj.) *some; any* I

quia (adv. conj.) *because* I

quīcumque, quaecumque, quodcumque (indef. rel. adj.) *whichever* I

quīdam, quiddam (indef. pron.) *someone, something; a certain person, a certain thing* I

quīdam, quaedam, quoddam (indef. adj.) *some; a certain* I

quidem (postpositive adv.) *in fact; to be sure, at any rate;* **nē . . . quidem** *not even* I

quiēs, quiētis, f. (quiesco, QUIET) *rest, repose, sleep*

quiēscō, -ere, quiēvī, quiētum *rest, be quiet* 7

quiētus, -a, -um *quiet, calm, peaceful, at rest* 7

quīn (relative pronoun + adverb) *who . . . not; by which . . . not; from; that not, but that; that; why not? why don't you? why?* 20

quīndecim (indel.) *fifteen* I

quīngentēsimus, -a, -um *five hundredth* I

quīngentī, -ae, -a *five hundred* I

quīnī, -ae, -a *five by five, five at a time* I

quīnquāgēsimus, -a, -um *fiftieth* I

quīnquāgintā (indecl.) *fifty* I

quīnque (indecl.) *five* I

quīnquennium, -ī, n. (quīnque + annus) *a five-year period*

quīnquerēmis, quīnquerēmis, f. (i-stem) (quīnque + rēmus) *quinquereme (a ship with five banks of oars)*

quīnquiēns or **quīnquiēs** (adv.) *five times* I

quīnquiplex, quinquiplicis *fivefold* I

quīntus, -a, -um *fifth;* **quīntum** (internal acc.) *for the fifth time* I

quīque, quaeque, quodque (universal adjective) *each, every* I

quippe (adv.) *surely, indeed*

quis, quid (interr. pron.) *who?, what?* (indef. pron.) *someone, something; anyone, anything* I **sī quis**

quisnam, quidnam (inter. pron.) *who, pray? what, pray?*

quispiam, quaepiam, quidpiam or **quodpiam** (indef. pron.) *anyone, anything; as adj. any*

quisquam, quidquam (indef. pron.) *anyone, anything* I

quisque, quidque (universal pron.) *each one* I

quisquis, quidquid (indef. rel. pron.) *whoever, whatever* I

quīvīs, quaevīs, quidvīs (indef. pron.) (quī + vis) *anyone [you wish]; (adj.) any [you wish]*

quō (interrogative adverb) *where [to]?, whither?* (relative adverb) *to which place, to which, whither* (indef. adverb and conj.) *to any place; to some place* I

quoad (conj.) (quō + ad) *as long as, until*

quōcumque (indef. rel. adv.) *[to] wherever* I

quod (conj.) *because, in that; that;* (adv.) *with respect to which* I

quod sī (conj.) *but if* 13

quōminus (relative pronoun + adverb) *by which the less* 20

quōmodo (adv.) (quō modō) *as (rel.); how? in what way? (interr.)* I

quondam (adv.) *once; sometime* 18

quoniam (adv. conj.) *since, whereas, because* I

quōquam (indef. adv.) *[to] anywhere* I

quoque (adv.) *too, also* I

quōquō (indef. rel. adv.) *[to] wherever* I

quot (indecl.) *of which number (rel.); how many? (interr.)* I

quotannīs (adv.) (quot annīs) *every year, yearly*

quotcumque (indecl. indef. rel. adj.) *however many*

quotiēns or **quotiēs** (adv.) *as often (rel.); how often? (interr.)* I

quōtienscumque (indef. rel. adv.) *however often, as often as* I

quotquot (indecl. indef. rel. adj.) *however many* I

R

radius, -ī, m. (RADIUS) *ray; rod, staff*

rādīx, rādīcis, f. (RADICAL, RADISH) *root, root vegetable; base*

rāmus, -ī, m. (RAMIFICATION) *branch, bough, twig*

rapidus, -a, -um *seizing, tearing, violent; rapid, swift* 19

rapīna, -ae, f. (rapiō, RAPINE) *robbery, plunder, booty; rape*

rapiō, -ere, rapuī, raptum *snatch, seize, carry off; pillage* 3

raptim, adv. (rapio) *hurriedly*

ratiō, ratiōnis, f. *account; reasoning, reason; plan, method, system* 7

ratis, -is, f. (i-stem) *raft; vessel* 20

ratus, -a, -um *valid*

rebelliō, rebelliōnis, f. (bellum) *rebellion*

recēdō, -ere, recessī, recessum (cēdō) *recede, withdraw; retreat*

recēns, recentis *fresh; recent; late*

receptus, -ūs, m. (recipiō) *retreat*

recessus, -ūs, m. (cēdō) *retreat; recess*

recidō, -ere, recidī, ___ (cadō) *fall back*

recipiō, -ere, recēpī, receptum *take back, accept, receive;* sē recipere *retreat, recover* I

recitō, -āre, -āvī, -ātum *read aloud, recite*

reclīnō, -āre, -āvī, -ātum *bend back;* sē reclīnāre *lean back, recline*

recondō, -ere, recondidī, reconditum (condō, RECONDITE) *hide, conceal; put away*

rēctor, -ōris, m. *leader, ruler, master*

recuperō, -āre, -āvī, -ātum *recover, regain* (transitive); *recuperate*

recūsō, -āre, -āvī, -ātum (causa) *object, take exception; refuse, be unwilling* 20

reddō, -ere, reddidī, redditum *give back, restore; pay back; hand over; render, make* 1

redeō, redīre, rediī (redīvī), reditum *go back, come back, return* I

redigō, -ere, redēgī, redactum (agō) *drive back, bring back; render; reduce*

redimō, -ere, redēmī, redēmptum (emō, REDEMPTION) *buy back, redeem, ransom; buy off*

redintegrō, -āre, āvī, -ātum (integer) *renew; revive*

reditiō, reditiōnis, f. (eō) *returning; going back*

reditus, -ūs, m. (eō) *return*

redūcō, -ere, redūxī, reductum (dūcō) *lead back, bring back; restore; reduce*

referō, referre, rettulī, relātum *bring back, return; pay back; refer, relate; report back;* pedem referre *go back, return, give ground;* gratiam alicui referre *show gratitude to someone;* sē referre *go back* I

reficiō, -ere, refēcī, refectum (faciō) *rebuild, repair, restore*

refugiō, -ere, refūgī, refugitum (fugiō) *flee back, escape, avoid, take refuge*

refugus, -a, -um (fugiō) *fleeing, receding*

rēgālis, -e (rēx) *regal, royal*

rēgīna, rēgīnae, f. *queen* I

rēgiō, rēgiōnis, f. (rēgō) *region, country, district; direction*

rēgius, -a, -um (rēx) *royal, of a king;* [domus] regia *palace*

rēgnum, -ī, n. *kingdom, throne, kingship; power, dominion* I

rēgō, -ere, rēxī, rēctum *rule, direct, guide;* rēctus, -a, -um *right, proper; straight; honest* I

regredior, -ī, regressus sum (REGRESS) *go back; step back; retreat*

reiciō, -ere, reiēcī, reiectum (iaciō) *throw back; drive back; repulse; refuse, reject*

relābor, -lābī, relāpsus sum (lābor, RELAPSE) *fall back, vanish*

relanguēscō, -ere, relanguī, ___ (LANGUISH) *become faint, become weak; sink down*

relēgō, -āre, -āvī, -ātum *banish, remove; relegate* (relegation differs from exile in that a relegated person is confined to a particular place)

religiō, religiōnis, f. *scrupulousness, religious feeling, superstition*

relinquō, -ere, relīquī, relictum *leave behind, leave, abandon* I

reliquus, -a, -um *rest of, remaining. As noun, m. pl. the rest* I

remaneō, -ēre, remānsī, remānsum (maneō) *remain*

rēmigium, -ī, n. (rēmus + agō) *oarage, rowing*

remigrō, -āre, -āvī, -ātum (MIGRATE) *move back, go back*

reminīscor, -ī *remember, recollect*

remittō, -ere, -mīsī, -missum (mittō) *send back, remit; throw back, relax, diminish;* remissus, -a, -um *relaxed; remiss; mild*

remoror, -ārī, -ātus sum (moror) *delay*

remōveō, -ēre, remōvī, remōtum (mōveō) *move back, remove; move away;* remōtus, -a, -um *far off, remote*

rēmus, -ī, m. *oar* 12

renīdēns, renīdentis *shining, gleaming*

renūntiō, -āre, -āvī, -ātum (nūntiō) *report back, announce*

reor, rērī, ratus (RATIONAL) *think, believe; reckon*

repellō, -ere, reppulī, repulsum (pellō) *push back, repel, repulse*

repēns, repentis *sudden, unexpected*

repentē (adv.) *suddenly, unexpectedly*

repentīnus, -a, -um *sudden, unexpected*

reperiō, -īre, repperī, repertum *find, learn; discover* I

repetō, -ere, repetīvī, repetītum *demand back again, seek to recover; renew, begin again;* rēs repetundae *[case of] extortion* 18

repōnō, -ere, reposuī, repositum (pōnō, REPOSITORY) *put back, restore, renew*

reportō, -āre, -āvī, -ātum (portō) *carry back; report*

reposcō, -ere, ___, ___ *demand back, ask for again*

reprehendō, -ere, reprehendī, reprehēnsum *seize, catch; reprove, blame; reprehend*

repudiō, -āre, -āvī, -ātum (pudet, REPUDIATE) *refuse, reject; divorce; scorn*

repudium, ī n. *repudiation, separation, divorce*

repugnō, -āre, -āvī, -ātum (pugno, REPUGNANT) *fight back, oppose; resist*

reputō, -āre, -āvī, -ātum (putō, REPUTATION) *reckon; think over, consider, ponder*

requiēs, requiētis, f. (no dat.; acc. **requiem**) (quiēs, REQUIEM) *rest, repose*

requiēscō, -ere, requiēvī, requiētum (quiēscō) *rest*

requīrō, -ere, requīsīvī, requīsītus (quaerō) *to seek again, ask; require, miss*

rēs, -eī, f. *thing, object; affair, fact, circumstances, situation, reality; property; benefit; lawsuit; business, art, science;* **omnibus rēbus** *in all respects;* **rēs novae** *a revolution;* **rēs pūblica** *state, republic;* **rē vērā** *indeed, in fact* I; **rēs gestae** *deeds, accomplishments* 7; **rēs repetundae** *[case of] extortion* 18; **rēs frūmentāria** *grain supply;* **rēs mīlitāris** *military science*

resacrō, -āre, -āvī, -ātum (sacer) *free from a curse, reconsecrate*

rescindō, -ere, rescidī, rescissum *cut off, cut down, destroy; annul; rescind*

rescīscō, -ere, rescīvī, rescītum (sciō) *learn, find out*

resistō, -ere, restitī, ___ (w. dat.) *stop, stand; withstand, resist*

respectō, -āre, -āvī, -ātum (spectō) *look eagerly back, look about for*

respiciō, -ere, respexī, respectum *look back at; (of a god) look with favor upon; consider; respect* I

respondeō, -ēre, respondī, respōnsum *respond*

restituō, -ere, restituī, restitūtum (cf. cōnstituō, RESTITUTION) *replace, rebuild, restore; revive*

restō, -āre, restitī, ___ *remain behind, be left, be left over; (impersonal)* **restat** *it remains* 10

resupīnus, -a, -um (SUPINE) *lying on one's back*

retexō, -ere, retexuī, retextum *reverse, cancel*

retineō, -ēre, retinuī, retentum *hold back, retain; restrain; maintain* I

retrahō, -ere, retrāxī, retrāctum (trahō, RETRACT) *draw back, withdraw*

retrō (adv.) (RETROACTIVE, RETROGRESS) *backwards*

reus, -ī, m. *person accused*

revellō, -ere, revellī, revulsum (REVULSION) *pull back, tear away*

revertō, -ere, revertī, reversum (vertō) *turn back; (passive) return; revert*

revocō, -āre, -āvī, -ātum (vocō, REVOKE) *recall, call back; take back*

revolvō, -ere, revolvī, revolūtum (REVOLVE) *throw back, roll back*

rēx, rēgis, m. *king* I

rictus, -ūs, m. (RICTUS) *jaws; open mouth*

rīdeō, -ēre, rīsī, rīsum *laugh, smile; laugh at, deride* 18

rīma, -ae, f. *crack, chink; cleft*

rīpa, -ae, f. *river-bank* 5

rītus, -ūs, m. *rite; ceremony*

rīvālis, -is, m. *a neighbor, competitor, rival*

rīvus, -ī, m. *brook, stream*

rōbur or **rōbor, -ōris,** n. (ROBUST) *oak; strength*

rōdō, -ere, rōsī, rōsum (RODENT) *gnaw, peck*

rogitō, -āre, -āvī, -ātum (rogō) *keep asking, ask repeatedly*

rogō, -āre, -āvī, -ātum *ask, ask for; question* I

rogus, -ī, m. *funeral pyre*

Rōmānitās, -tātis, f. *Romanness*

rōstrum, -ī, n. (ROSTRA) *[ship's or bird's] beak*

rota, -ae, f. (ROTATE) *wheel*

rubus, -ī, m. *bramble, brier*

ruīna, -ae, f. *collapse, downfall; (pl.) ruins*

rūmor, rumōris, m. *muttering, grumbling; rumor, report*

rumpō, -ere, rūpī, ruptum *burst, break; destroy* 8

rūpēs, -is, f. *cliff, rock*

rūrsus or **rūrsum** (adv.) (reversus) *again; on the contrary* I

rūs, rūris, n. *country, countryside; country place* I

rūsticus, -a, -um *of the country, of farming, rural* I

S

sacer, sacra, sacrum *sacred; consecrated; accursed;* **sacrum, -ī,** n. *sacrifice; sacred vessel; pl. religious rites* I

sacerdōs, sacerdōtis, m. or f. *priest, priestess* 15

sacerdōtium, -ī, n. (sacerdōs) *priesthood*

sacrificium, -ī, n. (sacer + faciō) *sacrifice*

sacrificō, -āre, -āvī, -ātum (sacer + faciō) *offer sacrifice, consecrate, dedicate*

sacrilegium, -ī, n. *violation of sacred property, sacrilege*

saeculum, -ī, n. *age, generation, century* 1

saepe (adv.) *often* 1

saepēs, saepis, f. (i-stem) *hedge*

saepiō, -īre, saepsī, saeptum *hedge in, enclose, protect*

saevus, -a, -um *ferocious, cruel, fierce, savage, raging, harsh* 13

sagācitās, sagācitātis, f. (SAGACITY) *shrewdness*

sagitta, -ae, f. (SAGITTARIUS) *arrow*

sagittārius, -ī, m. (SAGITTARIUS) *bowman*

sagulum, -ī, n. *[travelling] cloak*

sagum, -ī, n. *[soldier's] cloak*

salīnum, -i, n. (SALINE) *salt-cellar*

saltem (adv.) *at least, even*

saltus, -ūs, m. *passage* [through a forest or over a mountain]

salūbris, -e (salūs, SALUBRIOUS) *healthful; healthy*

salūs, salūtis, f. *health, welfare, safety, salvation* 1

salūtō, -āre, -āvī, -ātum (salūs) *greet, salute*

salvus, -a, -um (salus, SALVATION) *safe, sound, well*

sambuca, ae, f. *bridge* [used in siegework]

sanciō, -īre, sanxī, sanctum *make sacred* [by a religious act]; *make irrevocable, confirm; sanction;* **sanctus, -a, -um** *sacred, holy, sanctified, inviolable; ordained* 9

sanctitās, sanctitātis, f. (sanciō) *sanctity, inviolabity, holiness*

sanguis, sanguinis, m. *blood, bloodshed*

sānitās, -ātis, f. *sanity, reason*

sānus, -a, -um *sound, healthy, sane, sober*

sānē (adv.) *certainly, of course*

sapiēns, sapientis (SAPIENT) *wise, discreet;* (as noun) m. *wise man, sage, philosopher*

sapiō, -ere, sapiī, ___ (INSIPID) *have taste, be sensible, be wise, understand*

sarcinae, -ārum, f. *baggage, pack*

sat (see satis)

satelles, satellitis, m. or f. (SATELLITE) *attendant; courtier*

satīn? = satisne?

satis, n. (only in nom. & acc. sing.) *a sufficient amount, a sufficient number, enough* 1

satisfaciō, -ere, satisfēcī, satisfactum (satis + faciō) *satisfy*

satisfactiō, satisfactiōnis, f. (satis + faciō) *satisfaction*

satrapēs, satrapis, m. *satrap* (Persian governor)

saucius, -a, -um *wounded; ill, sick*

saxum, -ī, n. *rock, stone* 5

scālae, -ārum, f. (scale, escalate) *ladder*

scapha, -ae, f. *skiff; light boat*

scelerātus, -a, -um (scelus) *wicked, criminal*

scelestus, -a, -um (scelus) *wicked, criminal, infamous*

scelus, sceleris, n. *wickedness, crime* 4

scientia, -ae, f. (sciō) *knowledge, science*

scīlicet (adv.) (sciō + licet) *one may know, certainly; of course*

scindō, -ere, scidī, scissum (RESCIND) *tear, split, divide*

scintillō, -āre, -āvī, -ātum (SCINTILLATE) *sparkle, glitter*

sciō, -īre, -īvī, -ītum *know, understand; perceive;* **sciēns, scientis** *knowing, understanding; skilled, expert* 6

scīpiō, scīpiōnis, m. *staff, wand*

scīscitor, -ārī, -ātus sum (sciō) *inquire*

scītum, -ī, n. (sciō, PLEBISCITE) *decree*

scorpiō, scorpiōnis, m. *scorpion; small catapult*

scrība, -ae, m. (scrībō) *scribe, secretary, clerk*

scrībō, -ere, scrīpsī, scrīptum *write* 136

scūtum, -ī, n. *[large] shield*

sēcēdō, -ere, sēcessī sēcessum (cedo) *withdraw, retire; revolt*

secundum (prep. with acc.) *along, next to, following*

secundus, -a, -um *following; favorable; second* 1

secūris, secūris, f. (i-stem; acc. **secūrim,** abl. **secūrī**) *axe; authority*

sēcūrus, -a, -um *carefree; secure* 20

sed (conjunction) *but; yet* 1

sēdecim (indecl.) *sixteen* 1

sedeō, -ēre, sēdī, sessum *sit, settle; encamp* 1

sēdēs, sēdis, f. *seat, chair; habitation, settlement* (pl.) *residence* 1

sēditiō, sēditiōnis, f. (dō) *dissension, sedition, insurrection, revolt, mutiny*

sēdō, -āre, -āvī, -ātum (sedēs, SEDATIVE) *calm, settle, assuage, put an end to* sēdūcō, -ere, sēdūxī, sēductum (dūcō) *lead apart, lead to another place; seduce*

sēdulō (adv.) (sedeō) *carefully*

segnis, -e *slow, lazy, tardy, sluggish*

sella, -ae, f. (sedeō) *seat, stool, bench, chair; sedan chair*

semel (adv.) *once* I

sēmentis, sēmentis, f. (i-stem) *a sowing*

sēmet see suī

semper (adv.) *always, continually, still*

senātor, -ōris, m. (senex) *senator*

senātōrius, -a, -um (senex) *of a senator; senatorial*

senātus, -ūs, m. (senex) *senate*

senectūs, senectūtis, f. (senex) *old age*

senēscō, -ēre, senuī, ___ (senex, SENESCENT) *grow old, become weak*

senex, senis (masc. only) *old; (as noun) old man* I

senīlis, -e (senex) *senile, aged*

senior (comp. of senex) I

sēnsus, -ūs, m. (sentiō) *feeling, sense*

sententia, -ae, f. (sentiō) *opinion, vote; in sententiam discēdō go over to an[other's] opinion, vote [with someone]*

sentiō, -īre, sēnsī, sēnsum *feel, think, realize; see, understand* I

sentis, -is, m. *thorn, brier*

sēparātim (adv.) (parō) *separately, apart*

sepeliō, -īre, -īvī, sepultum (SEPULCHER) *entomb, bury*

septem (indecl.) *seven* I

septendecim (indecl.) *seventeen* I

septentriō, septentriōnis, m. (septem) *north; [the seven stars forming the Big Dipper]*

septimus, -a, -um *seventh* I

septingentēsimus, -a, -um *seven hundredth* I

septingentī, -ae, -a *seven hundred* I

septuāgēsimus, -a, -um *seventieth* I

septuāgintā (indecl.) *seventy* I

sepulcrum, -ī, n. (SEPULCHER) *grave, tomb*

sequor, -ī, secūtus sum *follow, pursue; conform to* 2

sērius (adv.) *later, too late*

serius, -a, -um *serious*

sermō, sermōnis, m. *speech, talk, conversation* 1

serō, -ere, sēvī, satum (SATURN) *sow, plant*

serpēns, serpentis, m. or f. *serpent, snake*

sērus, -a, -um *late, too late*

serva, -ae, f. (servus) *slave-woman*

servīlis, -e (servus) *of a slave, slavish, servile*

serviō, -īre, -īvī, -ītum (w. dat.) *serve; be a slave* I

servitia, ōrum n. pl. *servants, slaves*

servitūs, -ūtis, f. (serviō) *slavery, servitude*

servō, -āre, -āvī, -ātum *keep, save, guard, watch, preserve* I

servus, -ī, m. *slave, servant* I

sescentēsimus, -a, -um *six hundredth* I

sescentī, -ae, -a *six hundred* I

sestertius, -ī, m. *sesterce (a silver coin, 1/100 of an aureus)*

seu See sīve.

seu . . . seu . . . See sīve . . . sīve . . .

sevēritās, sevēritātis, f. *severity, sterness, austerity*

sevērus, -a, -um *serious, severe, stern, grave*

sex (indecl.) *six* I

sexāgēsimus, -a, -um *sixtieth* I

sexāgintā (indecl.) *sixty* I

sextus, -a, -um *sixth* I

sī (adv. conj.) *if* I; quod sī, *but if* 13; sī quis *if anyone*, sī quid *if anything*

sīc *so, thus, in such a manner; (it is so) = yes* I

siccitās, siccitātis, f. *dryness*

siccō, -āre, -āvī, -ātum (DESICCATED) *dry, drain; exhaust*

siccus, -a, -um *dry; (as noun) siccum, -ī, n. dry land*

sīcut *just as, just as if* I

sīdus, sīderis, n. (SIDEREAL) *star, constellation, heavenly body*

signifer, signiferī, m. (signum + ferō) *standard-bearer*

significō, -āre, -āvī, -ātum (signum + faciō, SIGNIFICANT) *signify, indicate, show*

signō, -āre, -āvī, -ātum (signum) *mark, stamp; affix a seal (i.e. sign); designate*

signum, -ī, n. *sign, signal; [military] standard* I; *image, statue, seal*

silēns, silentis *silent, still*

silentium, -ī, n. *silence*

silva, -ae, f. *a wood, forest* I

silvestris, -e, (silva) *wooded*

similis, -e *like, similar* I

simplex, simplicis *single, simple* I

simpulum, -ī, n. *a small ladle for use in sacrifices*

simul (adv.) *at the same time; simul ac, simul atque (adv. conj.) as soon as* I

simulācrum, -ī, n. (similis) *likeness; portrait, image, statue*

simulātiō, -ōnis, f. (similis, SIMULATION) *pretense, deceit*

simulō, -āre, -āvī, -ātum (similis) *simulate, feign, pretend*

simultās, simultātis, f. (similis) *enmity, rivalry; hatred*

sīn (adv. and coord. conj.) *but if;* **sīn autem** *but if, on the other hand* I

sine (prep. w. abl.) *without* I

singillātim (adv.) (singulī) *one by one, singly*

singulāris, -e (singulī) *one by one, single; singular; remarkable*

singulī, -ae, -a *one by one, one at a time, separate* I

sinister, sinistra, sinistrum *on the left, lefthand, improper, adverse; inauspicious;* **sinistra, -ae,** f. *left hand* I

sinistrōrsus (adv.) (sinister + vertō) *to the left*

sinō, -ere, sīvī, situm *allow, permit* (w. infin. phrase)

sinus, -ūs, m. *bend, fold; bay, gulf; bosom [of a toga]* 8

sistō, -ere, stitī, statum (EXIST, CONSIST, RESIST) *stop, check; cause to stand; set up*

sitiō, īre, -īvī ___ *to thirst, be thirsty*

sitis, -is, f. *thirst*

situs, -a, -um (SITE) *placed*

situs, -ūs, m. *situation, site*

sīve (adv. and coord. conj.) *or if* I **sīve . . . sīve . . .** *whether . . . or . . . , if . . . or if . . .* I

sōbrius, -a, -um *sober*

socer, socerī, m. *father-in-law*

societās, societātis, f. (socius, SOCIETY) *companionship; partnership, company; alliance*

socius, socī, m. *ally, comrade* I

sodālis, -is, m. (i-stem) *friend*

sōl, sōlis, m. *sun* I

sōlātium, -ī, n. *consolation, comfort*

soleō, -ēre, solitus sum *be accustomed, do usually* I

sōlitūdō, sōlitūdinis, f. (sōlus) *solitude, loneliness, wilderness*

sollemnis, -e *festive; solemn, sacred; customary; annual; appointed*

sollicitō, -āre, -āvī, -ātum *disturb, stir; agitate, incite; solicit, tempt*

solum, -i, n. *ground, soil*

sōlus, -a, -um (pron. decl.) *alone, sole;* (as internal acc.) **sōlum** *only, alone;* **nōn sōlum . . . sed etiam** *not only . . . but also* I

solvō, -ere, solvī, solūtum *loosen, untie, undo, release; pay; break up;* (intrans.) *set sail* 7

somnium, -ī, n. (somnus) *dream*

somnus, -ī, m. *sleep* I

sonitus, -ūs, m. (sonō) *noise, din*

sonō, -āre, sonuī, sonitum *[make a] sound* 13

sordidātus, -a, -um *dressed in dirty clothing = in mourning*

soror, sorōris, f. *sister* I

sors, sortis, f. (i-stem) *lot, fate; oracular response* 8

spargō, -ere, spārsī, spársum *scatter, sprinkle, strew* 18

spatior, -ārī, -ātus (spatium, EXPATIATE) *take a walk, promenade*

spatium, -ī, n. *space, distance; length of time, period* 4

speciēs, -ēī f. *sight, appearance, show, splendor; kind* I

specimen, speciminis, n. *token, sample, specimen, pattern*

spectō, -āre, -āvī, -ātum *look at, watch, regard, see* I

speculātor, -ōris, m. *spy, scout*

speculātōrius, -a, -um *spying, scouting*

specus, -ūs, m. *cave, hole, chasm*

spēlunca, -ae, f. (SPELUNKER) *cave, cavern*

spērō, -āre, -āvī, -ātum *hope, hope for, expect* I

spēs, -ēī, f. *hope, expectation* I

spīritus, -ūs, m. *breath; life; spirit, soul; courage* **spīritum dūcō** *draw breath* 15

spīrō, -āre, -āvī, -ātum *breathe* 16

splendidus, -a, -um *splendid, glittering*

splendor, splendōris m. *splendor*

spoliō, -āre, -āvī, -ātum *rob, strip, despoil, plunder*

spolium, -ī, n. *spoil (the skin stripped from an animal, arms and clothing taken from a slain enemy)*

spondeō, -ēre, spopondī spōnsum (SPONSOR) *pledge oneself; betroth; promise;* **spōnsa, -ae,** f. *bride;* **spōnsus, -ī,** m. *bridegroom*

sponte (abl. only), f. *free will; with* **suā,** *voluntarily; of one's own accord, spontaneously*

spūmāns, spūmantis *foaming*

stabilitās, stabilitātis, f. (stō) *stability, steadiness*

statēra, -ae, f. *a steelyard, balance; a goldsmith's scales*

statim (adv.) *immediately, at once* I

statiō, statiōnis, f. (stō) *standing; station; [military] post, watch*

statua, -ae, f. (stō) *statue, image*

statuō, -ere, statuī, statūtum (stō, STATUTE) *set, place, set up, make stand, build; decide, think*

statūra, -ae, f. (stō) *stature, height [of a person]*

status, -ūs, m. (stō) *standing, status, position, state; status*

sternō, -ere, strāvī, strātum *spread out, smooth; pave; lay low, throw down* 5; **strātum, -ī,** n. *couch*

stīpendium, -ī, n. (STIPEND) *tax; [soldier's] pay;* **stīpendium facere** or **merērī** *serve in the army*

stirps, stirpis, f. *stock; source; male descendants*

stīva, -ae, f. *plough handle*

stō, stāre, stetī, stātum *stand, be fixed, remain* I

stolidus, -a, -um (STOLID) *foolish, dull, stupid*

strāmentum, -i, n. (sternō) *thatch*

strēnuus, -a, -um *active, vigorous, strenuous*

strepitus, -ūs, m. *din, noise, crash, uproar*

strīdeō, -ēre, strīdī, ___ (STRIDENT) *creak, roar, howl*

strīdulus, -a, -um *whizzing, hissing*

stringō, -ere, strīnxī, strīctum (STRICT) *draw tight; draw; graze; strip off*

struō, -ere, strūxī, strūctum (STRUCTURE) *pile up; contrive, arrange, build, construct*

studeō, -ēre, -uī ___, *be eager, strive after*

studiōsus, -a, -um (studium) *eager, studious*

studium, -ī, n. *eagerness, zeal, enthusiasm; study, hobby*

stultitia, -ae, f. *folly, stupidity*

stultus, -a, um (STULTIFY) *stupid, foolish*

suādeō, -ēre, suāsī, suāsum *recommend, speak in favor of, persuade, advise*

sub (prep. w. acc.) *to under, up to, to the foot of, close to, until;* (w. abl.) *under, at the foot of, beneath, during* I

subalāris, -e *placed under the arms*

subdūcō, -ere, subdūxī, subductum (sub + dūcō) *lead up, carry off, transfer; haul*

subeō, subīre, subiī (subīvī), subitum *go under, go up to, come up; approach, enter; undergo, submit to* I

subiciō, -ere, subiēcī, subiectum (sub + iaciō) *throw under, place under; make subject; expose;* **subiectus, -a, um** *lying near, adjacent*

subigō, -ere, subēgī, subactum (sub + agō) *drive under, subdue, conquer; compel*

subitō (adv.) (sub + eō) *suddenly*

subitus, -a, -um (sub + eō) *sudden, unexpected*

sublevō, -āre, -āvī, -ātum (sub + levis) *lift, lighten; support, assist*

sublicius, -a, -um *resting on piles*

sublustris, -e *somewhat light (e.g. starlit)*

submōveō, -ēre, submōvī, submōtum (sub + mōveō) *remove gradually; move away from beneath; get rid of*

subripiō See surripiō

subruō, -ere, subruī, subrūtum *undermine*

subsequor, -ī, subsecūtus sum (sub + sequor, SUBSEQUENT) *follow close upon, follow after*

subsidium, -ī, n. (sub + sedeō, SUBSIDY) *help, relief; reinforcement*

subsistō, -ere, substitī, ___ *stand still, halt; remain*

substituō, -ere, substituī, substitūtum (cf. constituō) *put under; put in the place of; substitute*

subsum, subesse, subfuī, ___ (sub + sum) *be near, be at hand*

subter (prep. with acc.) *beneath;* (with abl.) *underneath*

subveniō, -īre, subvēnī, subventum (sub + veniō, SUBVENTION) *come to help, assist; rescue*

succēdō, -ere, successī, successum (sub + cēdō) *go under; succeed to, come after, to be successful*

succendō, -ere, succendī, succēnsum *set on fire*

successor, successōris, m. (sub + cēdō) *successor*

succīdō, -ere, succīdī, succīsum (sub + caedō) *cut down*

succingō, -ere, succīnxī, succīnctum (SUCCINCT) *gird up [for action] (by pulling the tunic up through the girdle)*

succurrō, -ere, succurrī, succursum (sub + currō, SUCCOR) *run to the aid of, help*

sudis, sudis, f. (i-stem) *stake, log*

sufferō, -ferre, sustulī, sublātum (sub + ferō) *bear, endure, suffer*

suffīgō, -ere, suffīxī, suffīxum (SUFFIX) *nail up; fasten underneath; affix*

suffrāgium, -ī, n. *vote, suffrage*

suffrāgor, -ārī, -ātus *vote for support*

suī (no nom.) (refl. pron.) *himself, herself, itself, themselves* I

sum, esse, fuī, futūrus *be, exist* I

sumministrō, -āre, -āvī, -ātum (sub + minister) *supply, provide, furnish*

summittō, -ere, summīsī, summissum (sub + mittō) *furnish, supply; send*

summoveō, -ēre, summōvī, summōtum (sub + moveō) *force back, dislodge*

summus, -a, -um *top of* (also used as superl. of superus, *highest*) I as noun n. *top; summit, end;* summa, -ae, f. (rēs understood) *total, whole, sum; supremacy, control;* summa imperī *the chief command*

sūmō, -ere, sūmpsī, sūmptum *take, assume; put on* [clothing] 3; poenam sūmere dē or ex, *punish* 6; supplicium sūmere *to inflict punishment*

sūmptuārius, -a, -um (sūmō) *relating to expense, sumptuary*

sūmptuōsus, -a, -um (sūmō) *expensive, costly; sumptuous*

suppeditō, -āre, -āvī, -ātum *supply*

super (prep. w. acc.) *over, above, upon;* (prep. w. abl.) *over, upon, in addition to* I

superbia, -ae, f. (superbus) *haughtiness, pride, arrogance*

superbus, -a, -um *haughty, proud, overbearing, arrogant* I

superō, -āre, -āvī, -ātum (superus, INSUPERABLE) *surpass, overcome, defeat; be left over* I

superstes, superstitis (super + stō) *surviving*

supersum, superesse, superfuī, superfutūrus *be over and above; be left, be left over, survive* 19

superincidō, -ere, ___ ___ (super + in + cadō) *fall upon*

superus, -a, -um *above, upper, higher;* superior, -ius *higher; former; superior;* superī, -ōrum, m. *the gods above, the heavenly gods* I

suppetō, -ere, suppetīvī, suppetītum *be at hand; hold out*

suppleō, -ēre, supplēvī, supplētum (cf. compleō) *fill, supply*

supplex, supplicis *suppliant, kneeling, begging*

supplicātiō, supplicātiōnis, f. *thanksgiving; supplication*

supplicium, -ī, n. *punishment; torture; death penalty*

supplicō, -āre, -āvī, -ātum *pray, supplicate*

suprā (adv.) *above, before, formerly;* (prep. w. acc.) *above, over, beyond, more than* 19

suprēmus, -a, -um (superl. of superus) I

surgō, -ere, surrēxī, surrēctum *stand up, rise, lift; grow* 19

surripiō, -ere, surripuī, surreptum (sub + rapiō) *snatch away, steal, take away, filch*

suscipiō, -ere, suscēpī, susceptum (sub + capiō, SUSCEPTIBLE) *undertake, begin; suffer*

suspendō, -ere, suspendī, suspēnsum *hang up; suspend; keep in suspense* 6

suspiciō, -ere, suspexī, suspectum (cf. aspiciō) *look up to; admire; suspect;* suspectus, -a, -um *suspected, mistrusted*

suspiciō, suspiciōnis, f. *mistrust, suspicion*

suspicor, -ārī, -ātus sum *suspect, mistrust*

suspīritus, -ūs, m. (sub + spīritus) *sigh, deep breath*

sustentō, -āre, -āvī, -ātum *endure, hold out*

sustineō, -ēre, -uī, sustentum *hold up, support; sustain; restrain, hold in check, withstand* I

suus, -a, -um (refl. poss. adj.) *his* [own], *her* [own], *its* [own], *their* [own]; (as noun) m. pl. *his men, his friends;* n. pl. *his property;* sē suaque *themselves and their possessions* I

T

taberna, -ae, f. (TAVERN) *booth; shop; tent*

tabernāculum, -ī, n. (TABERNACLE) *small booth, hut; small tent, private tent*

tābēs, tābis, f. (i-stem) *melting, wasting away, pestilence*

tābēscō, -ere, -uī, ___ *melt; waste away*

tabula, -ae, f. *writing tablet; record; document.* pīcta tabula *painted tablet, painting*

taceō, ēre, -uī, -itum *be silent* (intrans.); *be silent about* (trans.); tacitus, -a, -um *silent, tacit* 11

taeda, -ae, f. *pine torch; marriage*

taedet, -ēre, -uit, ___ *it causes loathing* (disgust, weariness) 17

taedium, -i, n. (taedet) *weariness; tedium*

taenia, -ae, f. *headband*

tālāris, -e *of the heel;* n. pl. tālāria, *winged sandals of Mercury*

talentum, -ī, n. *talent* (a Greek weight = 100 Roman lbs., or a Greek sum of money = 120 denarii, equal to about $1200 in gold)

tālis, -e *such, of such a kind* I; tālis . . . quālis *such . . . as* tālus, -ī, m. *knucklebone* (used for games); *heel*

tam (adv. modifying adjectives and adverbs) *so, to such a degree* I

tamen (adv.) *nevertheless, however, but, yet, still*

tametsī (conj.) (tamen + etsī) *although, though*

tamquam (demonst. and rel. adv.) *just as; as if* I

tandem (adv.) *at length, at last;* (in questions) *pray tell?* 13

tangō, -ere, tetigī, tāctum *touch* 8

tantopere (tantō opere) (adv.) *so much, so greatly*

tantulus, -a, -um (tantus) *so very small, so trifling*

tantundem (adv.) (tantus) *just as much*

tantus, -a, -um *so great, so large* I; tantō opere (tantopere) (adv.) *so much, so greatly;* tantus . . . quantus *as great as;* tantī (gen. of indef. value) est *it is worth while;* tantum (internal acc.) *so much, only, merely*

tarditās, -tātis, f. *lateness, slowness*

tardō, -āre, -āvī, -ātum *check, retard; hinder*

tardus, -a, -um (TARDY) *slow, late; lame*

taurus, -ī, m. (TAURUS) *bull*

tegimentum, -ī, n. (tegō) *covering*

tegō, -ere, tēxī, tēctum *cover, protect, roof, shelter; conceal, hide; defend;* tēctum, -ī, n. *roof, covering; building, house* 5

tellūs, tellūris, f. *earth, land; the [planet] earth* 10

tēlum, -ī, n. *weapon, spear, dart; javelin* I

temerārius, -a, -um *rash, reckless to no purpose*

temerē (adv.) *rashly, blindly*

temeritās, temeritātis, f. *rashness, irresponsibility; temerity*

tēmō, tēmōnis, m. *pole, of a chariot*

temperō, -āre, -āvī, -ātum (TEMPER) *control oneself; restrain*

tempestās, tempestātis, f. (tempus, TEMPEST) *weather; storm*

templum, -ī, n. *[sacred] precinct, sanctuary, temple, shrine* 6

temptō, -āre, -āvī, -ātum *test; try, attempt; bribe* I

tempus, temporis, n. *time, season; necessity; occasion* I

tendō, -ere, tetendī, tentum (tēnsum) *stretch, extend; tend;* (intrans. w. ad or in) *head for*

tenebrae, -ārum, f. *darkness, gloom, obscurity* 17

teneō, -ēre, -uī, tentum *hold, grasp, maintain, keep, retain; occupy* I

tener, tenera, tenerum *tender, delicate, young* 17

tenuis, -e (TENUOUS) *thin, feeble, weak*

tepeō, -ēre, ___, ___ (TEPID) *be warm*

ter (adv.) *thrice, three times* I

tergum, -ī, n. *back;* ā tergō *in back* 4

ternī, -ae, -a *three each, three at a time*

terō, -ere, trīvī, trītum *rub; wear out; tread* 20

terra, terrae, f. *earth, land, ground, country* I; terrae mōtus *earthquake;* orbis terrārum *the circle of lands [around the Mediterranean] = the inhabited world*

terreō, -ēre, -uī, -itum *frighten, alarm, terrify*

terrestris, -e (terra, TERRESTRIAL) *on land*

terror, terrōris, m. *terror, panic, alarm, fear*

tertius, -a, -um *third* I; (internal acc.) tertium *a third time*

testimōnium, -ī, n. *witness, proof, testimony*

testis, testis, m. or f. (i-stem) *witness*

testor, -ārī, -ātus sum *bear witness, testify; call to witness*

testūdō, testūdinis, f. *tortoise; testudo* (movable shed)

tetulī, for tulī, from ferō

thōrāx, -ācis, m. (THORAX) *breastplate, cuirass*

tībīcina, -ae, f. *female flute player*

tībīcen, tībīcinis, m. (canō) *flute player*

tigillum, -ī, m. *small beam; cottage*

tigris, tigridis, m. or f. *tiger, tigress*

timeō, -ēre, -uī, ___ *fear, be afraid* I

timidus, -a, -um (timeō) *timid, fearful, cowardly*

timor, timōris, m. *fear, dread* I

tingō or tinguō, -ere, tīnxī, tīnctum (TINCTURE, TINT) *dye, wet, moisten*

toga, -ae, f. *toga* (male Roman citizen's official outer garment); toga praetexta *purple-bordered toga;* toga virīlis *[unbordered] toga of manhood;* toga candida *[unbordered] toga of political candidates;* toga exigua *single toga*

togātus, -a, -um *wearing a toga* (civilian dress)

tolerō, -āre, -āvī, -ātum *bear, endure, tolerate*

tollō, -ere, sustulī, sublātum *lift up, raise, remove, steal; extol* I

tōnsor, -ōris, m. (TONSORIAL) *barber*

tormentum, -ī, n. *windlass; rack [for torture]; artillery piece*

torquis, torquis, m. or f. *torque* (a twisted necklace worn by the Gauls)

torreō, -ēre, torruī, tōstum (TORRID, TOAST) *roast, burn, parch; bake* (of water: *boil, rush, stream*)

tot (indecl. adj.) *so many*

totidem (indecl.) *just as many*

totiēns (adv.) *so often* I

tōtus, -a, -um (pron. decl.) *all, whole, entire, total* I

trāctō, -āre, -āvī, -ātum (trahō) *draw, haul, pull; handle, manage, treat*

trādō, -ere, trādidī, trāditum *hand over, deliver; hand down; relate, teach* I

trādūcō, -ere, trādūxī, trāductum (trāns + dūcō, TRADUCE) *lead across, transfer*

trāgula, -ae, f. *dart, javelin*

trahō, -ere, trāxī, trāctum *drag, draw* 2

trāiciō, -ere, trāiēcī, trāiectum *throw across, lead across; transfix, pierce* I

trāiectus, -ūs, m. (traiciō, TRAJECTORY) *crossing, passage*

trāmes, trāmitis, m. *path*

trānō, -āre, -āvī, -ātum *swim across*

trāns (prep. w. acc.) *across, over; beyond* I

trānseō, trānsīre, trānsiī (trānsīvī), trānsitum *go over, go across, cross* (transitive) I

trānsferō, trānsferre, trānstulī, trānslātum (trāns + ferō) *carry across, transfer, translate*

trānsfigō, -ere, trānsfīxī, trānsfīxum *transfix, pierce through*

trānsfuga, -ae, m. (trāns + fuga) *deserter*

trānsfugiō, -ere, trānsfūgī, trānsfugitum (trāns + fugiō) *desert [to the enemy]*

trānsgredior, -ī, trānsgressus sum (TRANSGRESSION) *cross, go over*

trānsigō, -ere, trānsēgī, trānsāctum (trāns + agō) *drive through, stab; transact, finish, perform; pass, spend*

trānsitus, -ūs, m. (trānseō, TRANSIT) *crossing, passage*

trānsportō, -āre, -āvī, -ātum (trāns + portō) *carry across, transport*

trānsversus, -a, -um (trāns + vertō, TRANSVERSE) *crosswise, oblique*

trecentēsimus, -a, -um *three hundredth* 122

trecentī, -ae, -a *three hundred* I

tredecim (indecl.) *thirteen* I

tremebundus, -a, -um *trembling*

tremō, -ere, -uī, ___ (tremor) *tremble, shake, shudder*

tremulus, -a, -um (tremulous) *trembling*

trepidātiō, trepidātiōnis, f. *fear, alarm, trepidation*

trepidō, -āre, -āvī, -ātum (TREPIDATION) *be agitated, be afraid, tremble, waver*

trepidus, -a, -um (INTREPID) *alarmed; alarming*

trēs, tria *three* I

triārius, -ī, m. *third rank soldier*

tribūnal, tribūnālis, n. (i-stem) *tribunal (a raised platform for magistrates)*

tribūnātus, -ūs, m. *tribunate, tribuneship*

tribūnicius, -a, -um *tribunician, of a tribune, of a tribune's rank;* as a masc. noun *ex-tribune*

tribus, tribūs, m. *tribe*

tribūnus, -ī, m. *tribune;* **tribūnus plēbis** *tribune of the people;* **tribūnus mīlitum** *tribune of the soldiers*

tribuō, -ere, tribuī, tribūtum *allot, assign; ascribe; attribute*

tribūtum, -ī, n. *tribute, tax*

trīcēsimus, -a, -um *thirtieth* I

trīciēns or **trīciēs** (adv.) *thirty times*

trīduum, -ī, n. (trēs + diēs) *three days*

triennium, -ī, n. (trēs + annus, TRIENNIAL) *three years*

trīgintā (indecl.) *thirty* I

trīnī, -ae, -a *three by three, three at a time, triple, threefold* I

triplex, triplicis *triple, threefold* I

trirēmis, trirēmis, f. (i-stem) (trēs + rēmus) *trireme (a ship with three banks of oars)*

trīstis, trīste *mournful, sad, sorrowful, grim, gloomy* I

triumphālis, -e (trumphus) *triumphal; having won a triumph*

triumphus, -ī, m. *triumph (a solemn procession awarded by the Senate to some victorious generals)* 11

trux, trucis (TRUCULENT) *wild, savage, fierce*

tū, tuī (pers. & refl. pron.) *you* (sing.) I

tuba, -ae, f. (TUBE) *[straight] war-trumpet*

tueor, -ērī, tūtus sum (TUTOR) *guard, protect; watch over, gaze upon*

tugurium, -ī, n. *[peasant's] cottage*

tulī, see ferō

tum or **tunc** (adv.) *then, at that time* I; **tum dēmum** *only then, then indeed;* **cum . . . tum** *not only . . . but also, as . . . so especially*

tumultuōsus, -a, -um *disquieted, tumultuous, confused, thick*

tumultus, -ūs, m. *uproar, confusion, tumult*

tumulus, -ī, m. *mound, hillock, tomb*

tunc See **tum**

turba, -ae, f. *crowd, throng; distrubance* I

turbō, -āre, -āvī, -ātum (turba, TURBID) *disturb, throw into disorder, alarm, confuse*

turma, -ae, f. *[cavalry] troop*

turmātim (adv.) *in bands, in troops*

turpis, -e *ugly, disgraceful, base; shameful* 16

turpitūdō, turpitūdinis, f. (turpis) *baseness, disgrace; turpitude* turris, -is, (i-stem) (acc. sing. **turrim**, abl. **turrī**), f. *tower*

tussiō, -īre, -īvī, -ītum *cough*

tussis, tussis (i-stem: acc. sing. **tussim**, abl. **tussī**), f. *cough (or any disease with this symptom)*

tūtus, -a, -um *safe, protected* 6

tuus, -a, -um *your, yours (one person's)* I

tyrannis, tyrannidis, f. *tyranny, absolute rule*

tyrannus, -ī, m. *monarch; despot, tyrant*

U

ūber, ūberis *fertile, rich, abundant*

ubi (interrogative adverb) *where [at]? when?* (relative adverb) *where, when* I

ubicumque (indef. rel. adv.) *wherever* I

ubique (adv.) *anywhere, everywhere* I

ubiubi (indef. rel. adv.) *wherever* I

ulcīscor, -i, ultus sum (trans.) *avenge; punish;* (intrans.) *take vengeance*

ūllus, -a, -um (pron. decl.) *any* I

ulterior, -ius *farther, beyond* I

ultimus, -a, -um *farthest, last* I

ultor, ultōris, m. *avenger*

ultrā (adv. and prep. w. acc.) (ULTRAVIOLET) *beyond, more than, besides*

ultrō (adv.) *spontaneously, of one's own accord; without provocation*

ululātus, -ūs, m. (ULULATION) *howling, shrieking, wailing, yelling*

umbō, umbōnis, m. *[the central] boss [of a shield]*

umbra, -ae, f. *shade, shadow, ghost* I

umerus, -ī, m. (HUMERUS) *upper arm, shoulder*

umquam (adv.) *ever* I

uncus, -a, -um *hooked, curved*

unda, -ae, f. (UNDULATE) *wave*

unde (interrogative adverb) *where from?* (rel. adv.) *from which place, from which* I

ūndecim (indecl.) *eleven* I

ūndecimus, -a, -um *eleventh* I

undecumque (indef. rel. adv.) *from wherever* I

undeunde (indef. rel. adv.) *from wherever* I

ūndēvīcēsimus, -a, -um *nineteenth* I

ūndēvīgintī (indecl.) *nineteen* I

undique (adv.) *from all sides, on all sides* I

unguis, -is, m. *nail, claw, talon*

ūnicus, -a, -um (ūnus) *only, sole, unparalleled, unique*

ūniversus, -a, -um (ūnus + vertō) *entire, whole, universal*

ūnus, -a, -um *one, sole, single, only;* ūnā (modifying viā understood) *at the same time, together, along* I

urbānus, -a, -um (urbs) *urban; urbane; citified; witty, humorous, roguish*

urbs, urbis, f. (i-stem) *city* I

urgeō, -ēre, ursī, ___ *press hard; urge*

urna, -ae, f. *urn, jar*

ūrō, -ere, ūssī, ūstum *burn (transitive)* 20

ūrus, -ī, m. *wild ox*

usquam (adv.) *anywhere*

ūsque (adv.) *all the way, continuously, constantly; as far as, up to* 18

ūsus, -ūs, m. *usefulness, advantage; habit, practice*

ut or utī (rel. adv.) *in order that; that, so that; as, when;* (interr. adv.) *how?* **ut prīmum** *as soon as*

utcumque (indef. rel. adv.) *however, somehow*

uter, utra, utrum (pron. decl.) *which [of two]?* I

ūter, ūtris, m. *bag, bag of hide, leathern bottle*

uterque, utraque, utrumque (pron. decl.) *each [of two]* I

ūtilis, -e (ūtor, INUTILE) *useful; advantageous*

ūtilitās, ūtilitātis, f. (ūtor, UTILITY) *usefulness, advantage*

utinam (particle introducing wishes impossible of fulfillment) *if only, would that, Oh! that* 6

ūtor, -ī, ūsus sum (w. abl. of means) *use, employ, make use of; enjoy* I

utrimque (adv.) (uterque) *from both sides, on both sides*

utrum (interrog. particle introducing a disjunctive question) *whether* I; **utrum ... necne** *whether ... or not*

ūva, -ae, f. *grape*

uxor, uxōris, f. *wife* I

V

V 5 I

vacātiō, vacātiōnis, f. (VACATION) *exemption*

vacō, -āre, -āvī, -ātum *be empty; be vacant; be idle*

vacuus, -a, -um *empty, vacant, unoccupied; free* 5

vadum, -ī, n. *ford, shoal; channel*

vae (interj.) *alas! woe!*

vādō, -ere, ___, ___ (INVADE) *advance, go*

vāgīna, -ae, f. *sheath, scabbard*

vagor, -ārī, -ātus sum (vagus) *ramble, rove*

vagus, -a, -um *wandering, roving* 5

valeō, -ēre, -uī, -itum *be strong, be well; prevail; be worth;* (imperative) valē, valēte *farewell, goodby*

valētūdō, valētūdinis, f. (valeō, VALETUDINARIAN) *health; ill-health, weakness*

validus, -a, -um (valeō, VALID, INVALID) *strong, powerful*

vallēs, vallis f. *valley*

vallum, -ī, n. *fortification [of a Roman camp], wall, rampart*

vānus, -a, -um *empty; vain, idle, groundless; ostentatious; fickle*

varietās, varietātis, f. (varius) *variety, difference; mottled appearance*

varius, -a, -um *various, varying, varied, different, diverse* I

vās, vāsis, n. (vase) *vessel, pot, jar;* (pl.) *personal baggage*

vastō, -āre, āvī, -ātum *lay waste, devastate, ravage*

vāstus, -a, -um *empty, desolate, devastated; vast, enormous, frightful*

vātēs, vātis, m. or f. (not an i-stem) *soothsayer, seer, prophet; bard* 7

-ve (enclitic conj.) *or, or possibly* I

vectīgal, vectīgālis, n. *tax, tribute, revenue*

vehō, -ere, vexī, vectum *transport, bear, carry;* (passive) *travel, ride, sail* 13

vel (conj.) *or, or even, or in fact, or if you please*

vel . . . vel . . . *either . . . or . . .* I

vēlāmen, vēlāminis, n. *veil, covering*

vēles, vēlitis, m. *a light-armed soldier;* pl. m. *skirmishers*

vēlō, -āre, -āvī, -ātum *veil, cover*

vēlōcitās, vēlōcitātis, f. *speed, swiftness; velocity*

velut or velutī (adv.) *as, just as, just as if, as for example* 16

vēna, -ae, f. *vein*

vēnātiō, vēnātiōnis, f. (VENISON) *the hunt, hunting; a wild-animal show*

vēnātor, vēnātōris, m. *hunter*

vēndō, -ere, vēndidī, vēnditum *sell* I

venēnum, -ī, n. *poison, venom, drug*

venerius, -a, -um (Venus, VENEREAL) *of love*

veneror, -ārī, -ātus sum *venerate, respect*

venia, -ae, f. (VENIAL) *favor, indulgence; permission; forgiveness*

veniō, -īre, vēnī, ventum *come* I

vēnor, -ārī, -ātus sum *hunt*

venter, ventris, m. (VENTRAL) *belly; stomach; abdomen; womb*

ventitō, -āre, -āvī, -ātum (veniō) *keep coming*

ventus, -ī, m. *wind* I

verber, verberis, n. (REVERBERATION) *lash, whip; flogging*

verberō, -āre, -āvī, -ātum (REVERBERATION) *beat, whip, flog*

verbum, verbī, n. *word* I

vereor, -ērī, veritus sum *stand in awe of, revere; fear, dread; respect* I

vergō, -ere, ___, ___ (verge) *incline, lie, slope*

versō, -āre, -āvī, -ātum *keep turning; shift, change; occupy,* (pass.) *be employed; move about; live, dwell; be* I

versus (adv. and prep. w. acc.) (vertō, VS., VERSUS) *toward, in the direction of*

versus, -ūs, m. *a turning; a verse [of poetry]; a line [of prose]* I

vertex, verticis, m. *whirlpool, whirlwind; top [of the head]* 20

vertō, -ere, versī, versum *turn, direct, change* I

vērus, -a, -um *true, real;* (as noun) vērum, -ī, n. *truth;* (abl. as adv.) vērō *truly, in truth, indeed, really* I

verūtum, -ī, n. *dart*

vēscor, -ī, ___ (w. abl. of means) *feed upon* I

vesper, vesperī and vesperis, m. (VESPERS) *evening;* (locative) vesperī *in the evening*

vester, vestra, vestrum *your, yours (more than one person's)* I

vestibulum, -ī, n. *entrance-court, vestibule, antechamber*

vestīmentum, -ī n. *garment, clothing*

vestīgium, -ī, n. (VESTIGE) *foot-sole, footstep, footprint, trace;* ē vestīgiō *on the spot, immediately*

vestiō, -īre, -īvī, -ītum (vestis) *clothe, dress*

vestis, vestis, f. (i-stem) *garment, clothing;* (pl.) *clothes* I; vestis pulla *mourning garment*

vestītus, -ūs, m. (vestis) *clothing*

veterānus, -a, -um (vetus) *old, veteran*

veterrimus, -a, -um (superl. of vetus) I

vetō, -āre, -uī, -itum (veto) *forbid*

vetus, veteris (not an i-stem) *old, former, ancient*

vetustior, -ius (comp. of vetustus, *old*) I

vexātiō, vexātiōnis, f. (VEXATION) *harassment, persecution, ill-treatment*

vēxillum, -ī n. *flag, banner*

vexō, -āre, -āvī, -ātum *abuse, vex, molest*

via, -ae, f. *way, road, street; journey* I

vīcēnī, -ae, -a *twenty each*

vīcēsimus, -a, -um *twentieth* I

vīcīnia, -ae, f. (vīcīnus) *neighborhood; proximity*

vīcinitas, -tātis f. *neighborhood, vicinity*

vīcīnus, -a, -um *near, neighboring; (as noun) m. or f. neighbor* I

___, vicis, f. (no nom. sing. or gen. plur.) *interchange, alternation; in vicēs, per vicēs alternately, in turn, by turns; vice, vicem, ad vicem, in vicem (invicem) in place [of], instead [of]* 20

victima, -ae, f. *victim; animal for sacrifice*

victor, victōris, m. *conqueror, winner (in apposition = victorious, triumphant)* 9

victōria, -ae, f. *victory* 4

victus, -ūs, m. (vīvō) *living, food, victuals; way of life*

vīcus, -ī, m. (VICINITY) *street, row of houses; village, hamlet*

videō, -ēre, vīdī, vīsum *see, perceive; observe, understand; (passive) seem, seem best* I

vigeō, -ēre, -uī ___, *thrive, be vigorous, be strong*

vigilia, -ae, f. (VIGILANT) *wakefulness; watchfulness; a watch (¼ of the night, a measure of time)*

vīgintī (indecl.) *twenty* I

vigor, -ōris, m. *liveliness, vigor*

vīlis, -e (VILE) *cheap, of small price*

vīlla, -ae, f. *farmhouse, villa* I

villōsus, -a, -um *shaggy*

villula, -ae, f. *small farmhouse*

vīmen, vīminis, n. *twig, shoot*

vinciō, -īre, vinxī, vinctum *tie, bind; restrain* I

vincō, -ere, vīcī, victum *conquer, defeat; surpass, exceed* I

vinculum, -ī, n. *bond, fetter, chains; pl. imprisonment* 7

vindicō, -āre, -āvī, -ātum (VINDICATE) *lay claim to; set free; avenge, take vengeance on*

vīnea, -ae, f. (vīnum) *vineyard, wickershed used in seigework*

vīnolentus, -a, -um (vīnum) *hard-drinking*

vīnum, -ī, n. *wine* 18

violō, -āre, -āvī, -ātum (vis) *violate, profane*

vīpera, -ae, f. (vīvus + pariō) *viper, serpent*

vir, virī, m. *man; husband; hero* I

vīrēs, -ium, f. *strength (see vis)* I

virga, -ae, f. *twig; whip; rod; wand*

virgō, virginis, f. *maiden, girl* I

vīrīlis, -e (vir, VIRILE) *manly, of a man, of manhood; toga vīrīlis [unbordered] toga of manhood*

viritim (adv.) (vir) *man by man; individually*

virtūs, virtūtis, f. *manliness, virtue, worth, courage*

vīs, vīs, f. (i-stem) *force, violence; (plural)* vīrēs, vīrium, *strength* 115

viscus, -eris, n. (VISCERAL) *entrails, vitals*

vīsō, -ere, vīsī, vīsum (video) *go to see, visit, look at*

vīsus, -ūs, m. (video) *look, sight, appearance; vision*

vīta, -ae, f. *life* I

vitiō, -āre, -āvī, -ātum (vitium) *make faulty, spoil, damage; vitiate*

vitium, -ī, n. *fault, defect, vice* 17

vītō, -āre, -āvī, -ātum *shun, avoid*

vīvō, -ere, vīxī, victum *live, dwell; be alive* I

vīvus, -a, -um *alive, living* I

vix (adv.) *scarcely, barely, with difficulty* I

vocō, -āre, -āvī, -ātum *call, summon, invoke* I

volātus, -ūs, m. (volō) *flight*

volō, -āre, -āvī, -ātum *fly, move swiftly, speed, rush, hover over* I

volō, velle, voluī, ___, *wish, want, be willing; mean* 16

volucer, volucris, volucre (volō) *winged, flying; (as noun) m. bird*

voluntās, voluntātis, f. (volō) *will, wish, desire; good will; favor, consent*

voluptās, voluptātis, f. (VOLUPTUARY) *pleasure, delight, enjoyment* 1

volvō, -ere, volvī, volūtum *roll, revolve*

vorāgō, vorāginis, f. *pit, chasm, abyss; whirlpool*

vōs, vestrum (vestrī) (pers. & ref. pron.) *you (pl.)*

voveō, -ēre, vōvī, vōtum *vow, dedicate, consecrate;* vōtum, -ī, n. *vow, prayer* 12

vōx, vōcis, f. *voice; utterance, sound* I

vulgus, -ī, n. *common people, the public, the mob;* vulgō (abl. as Adv.) *publicly, commonly, generally, usually* 13

vulnerō, -āre, -āvī, -ātum (vulnus, VULNERABLE) *wound, injure, harm, pain*

vulnus, vulneris, n. *wound* 10

vultus, -ūs, m. *face, countenance, expression* 5

X

X *10* I

ENGLISH–LATIN VOCABULARY

A

about: *circum, circā, dē;* ____ to, see Lesson 1; be silent ____, *taceō;* talk repeatedly ____, throw ____, *iactō*

above: *super, suprā;* be over and ____, *supersum*

absent: *absēns*

accomplishments: *rēs gestae*

account: *ratiō*

accusation: *crīmen*

act: *agō, agitō;* in the ____ of, see Lesson 1

add: *addō;* be ____ ed *accēdō, addor*

addition: in ____, *praetereā*

admire: *mīror*

adorn: *ornō*

adornment: *cultus*

advise: *moneō*

affirm: *āiō*

after: *post, postquam*

again: *iterum, rūrsus;* begin ____, demand back ____, *repetō*

against: *contrā, in;* guard ____, *caveō;* inform ____, *indicō*

age: *aetās, aevum, saeculum*

agreeable: *iucundus*

aim at: *petō*

all: *cunctus, omnis;* ____ the way, *usque;* in ____ respects, *omnibus rēbus*

alluring: *blandus*

ally: *socius*

almost: *ferē, paene*

along: *per*

also: *et, etiam, quoque;* not only . . . but ____, *cum . . . tum, nōn sōlum . . . sed etiam*

alternately: *vicēs, per vicēs*

although: *cum, etsī, quamquam*

always: *semper*

amaze: be ____ ed, *mīror*

ample: *amplus*

ancient: *antīquus*

and: *ac, atque, et, -que;* ____ not, *neque, nēve;* be over ____ above, *supersum*

angry: *īrātus;* become ____, *īrāscor*

annoy: see Lesson 17

anything: *aliquid, quidquam, quid*

appraise: *cēnseō*

arise: *orior*

army: *agmen, exercitus*

arouse: *cieō*

arrogant: *superbus*

as: *ut, velut;* ____ if, ____ it were, *quāsi;* ____ long ____, *dōnec, dum;* ____ . . . so especially, *cum . . . tum;* ____ soon ____, *cum prīmum, simul ac, simul atque;* ____ often ____, *quotiēns . . . totiēns, quotiēnscumque;* just ____, just ____ if, *velut;* so ____ to, see Lesson 6

ashamed: see Lesson 17

ashes: *cinis*

ask: *petō, quaerō, rogō;* ____ for, *rogō*

assert: *āiō*

at: ____ last, *dēnique, postrēmō, tandem;* ____ length, *tandem;* ____ that time, *tum, tunc;* aim ____, *petō;* laugh ____, *rideō;* wonder ____, *mīror*

attack: *impetus, petō*

attendant: *minister*

attention: pay ____, see Lesson 1 Vocabulary Notes

audience: the ____, *audientēs*

away: turn ____, *dīvertō*

B

back: *rūrsus, tergum;* come ____, *redeō;* demand ____ again, *repetō;* give ____, *reddō*

bad: *improbus, malus*

badges: *īnsīgnia*

bank: river- ____, *rīpa*

bard: *vātēs*

barely: *aegrē, nōn ferē, vīx*

bay: *sinus*

be: *sum;* ____ amazed, *mīror;* ____ born, *nāscor;* be far, *absum;* ____ frightened, *timeō;* ____ in favor

of, *faveō;* ____ left, ____ left over, *restō, supersum;*
____ married, *nūbō;* ____ missing, *dēficiō;* ____
open, *pateō;* ____ over and above, *supersum;* ____
quiet, *quiēscō;* ____ silent, ____silent about, *taceō;*
____ unwilling, *nōlō;* ____ visible, *pateō:*
____ willing, *volō;* ____ worried, *vereor;* ____
wrong, *errō*

bear: *ferō, gerō, gignō, pariō*

become: *fīo;* ____ angry, *īrāscor*

befall: *accidō contingō*

before: *ante, apud, prae, prō*

begin: *incipiō;* began, *coepī;* ____ again, *repetō*

beget: *gignō*

behind: remain ____, *restō*

believe: *crēdō*

belittle: *contemnō*

below: *īnferus;* those ____, *īnferī*

bend: *flectō, sinus*

besides that: *praetereā*

beware of: *caveō*

big: so ____, *tantus*

birth: give ____ to, *gignō, pariō*

black: *niger*

blame: *culpa*

blind: *caecus*

boast of: *iactō*

bodyguard: *cohors*

bond: *vinculum*

bone: *os*

bosom: *sinus*

boundary: *finīs*

boy: *puer*

brass: *aes*

break: *frangō, rumpō;* ____ up, *solvō*

breath: *anima, spiritus*

breathe: *spīrō*

bride: *nūpta*

bronze: *aes*

building: *tectum*

burn: *ardeō, ūrō*

burst: *rumpō*

business: see Lesson 1 Vocabulary Notes

but: *at, autem, sed;* see also Lesson 20 ____ if,
quodsī, sīn; not only . . . ____ also, *cum . . . tum,*
nōn sōlum . . . sed etiam

by: *ā abs;* abl. of means; see also Lesson 2; ____ no
means, *haud;* ____ turns, *vicēs, per vicēs;* ____
which not, *quīn;* ____ which the less, *quōminus*

C

can: *possum*

care: *cūra;* ____ for, take ____ of, *cūrō*

carefree: *sēcūrus*

careful: *cautus*

carry: *portō;* ____ on, *gerō*

catch up with: *cōnsequor*

cautious: *cautus*

cavalry: *equitēs*

census: hold a ____ of, *cēnseō*

certain: *certus, quīdam;* it is ____, *cōnstat*

character: *ingenium, mōrēs*

citizenry: *cīvitās*

citizenship: *cīvitās*

city: *cīvitās, urbs*

class: *classis, ordō*

close: ____ together, *dēnsus;* it is very ____, *nōn
multum abest, parum abest*

cohort: *cohors*

coin: gold ____, *aureus*

collect: *cōgō, colligō*

come: *veniō;* ____ back, *redeō:* ____ on (w. imperative), see Lesson 1 Vocab. Notes; ____ out, *ēveniō*

command: *imperō, mandō*

common: *commūnis*

companion: *comes*

compel: *cōgō*

complain, complain of: *queror*

concern: *contingō*

conquered: the ____, *victī*

conqueror: *victor*

consider: *habeō*

consist: *cōnstō*

constant: *assiduus;* follow ____ly, *persequor*

consult: *cōnsulō:* ____ the interests of, *cōnsulō*

contempt: feel ____ for: *contemnō*

contend: *contendō*

continuously: *usque*

conversation: *sermō*

copper: *aes*

countenance: *vultus*

courage: *animī, spiritus, virtūs*

cover: *tegō*

create: *creō*

cross: *trānseō*

crime: *scelus*

cruel: *saevus*
cry: *clāmor*
dress: *cultus*
custom: *mōs*
cut: *caedō;* ____ **down,** *caedō, occīdō*

D

damned: **the** ____, *īnferī*
dare: *audeō*
daring: *audāx*
darkness: *tenebrae*
daughter: *fīlia, nāta*
day: *diēs*
dead: *mortuus*
debt: *aes aliēnum*
deceive: *fallō, impōnō, lūdō*
decency: *pudor*
deeds: *rēs gestae*
defect: *vitium*
defend: *dēfendō*
deified: *dīvus*
delay: *mora, moror*
delicate: *tener*
demand: ____ **back again,** *repetō*
dense: *dēnsus*
deny: *negō*
depart: *abeō, discēdō*
depraved: *improbus*
desert: *dēficiō, dēserō*
deserve: *mereor*
despise: *contemnō*
destine: ____d **to,** see Lesson 1
destroy: *perdō*
devote: see Lesson 1 Vocabulary Notes
die: *morior*
different: *dīversus;* **turn in** ____ **directions,** *dīvertō*
difficult: *difficilis*
difficulty: *mōlēs;* **with** ____, *aegrē*
direct to: *appellō*
direction: *pārs;* **turn in different** ____s, *dīvertō*
discuss: see Lesson 1 Vocabulary Notes
disgraceful: *turpis*
disgust: see Lesson 17
distance: *spatium*
distinguished: *īnsīgnis*

divide: *dīvidō*
divine: *dīvus;* ____ **law,** *fās*
do: *agō, agitō, faciō;* ____ **not,** see Lesson 16; **be** ____ **ne,** *fīō;* **why** ____**n't you?,** *quīn*
document: *litterae*
door: *foris*
doubt: *dubitō;* **there is no** ____, *nōn dubium est*
doubtful: *dubius*
down: **cut** ____, *caedō, occīdō;* **drag** ____, *dētrahō;* **fall** ____, *accidō, occidō;* **throw** ____, *fundō, sternō*
drag: *trahō;* **drag away,** *abstrahō;* **drag down,** *dētrahō*
draw: *trahō*
dread: *metuō, metus*
drink: *bibō*
drive: *agō, agitō;* **drive to,** *appellō*
duty: *officium*

E

ear: *auris*
earn: *mereor*
earth, **the** ____: *tellus;*
easy: *facilis*
eat: *edō*
education: *cultus*
effect: *efficiō*
either . . . or: *aut . . . aut, vel . . . vel*
elect: *creō*
embrace: *complector*
empire: *imperium*
empty: *vaccus*
end: *fīnis*
enemy: *hostis, inimīcus*
entire: *cunctus, tōtus*
entrust: *mandō*
equip: *ornō*
escape: *fugiō;* ____ **the notice of,** *fallō*
especially: *in prīmīs;* **as . . . so** ____, *cum . . . tum*
eternal: *aeternus*
even: *et, etiam, vel;* ____ **if,** *etsi;* **or** ____, *vel*
every: *omnis, quīque;* ____ **time,** *quotiēns . . . totiēns, quotiēnscumque*
everything: *omnia*
evil: *malus*
example: *exemplum*

excessive: *nimius*
experience: *experior*
express an opinion: *cēnseō*
excel: *praestō, superō*
exchange: in ____ for, *prō*
expel: *expellō*
expression: *vultus*
extend: *pateō*
extent: to such an ____, *ita, tam*
eye: *oculus, lūmen*

F

fall: *cadō, lābor:* ____ down, *accidō, occidō;* fall to, *accidō*
false: *falsus*
far: *longē;* be far, *absum*
fast: *celer*
fate: *casus, fātum, sors*
father: *pater*
fatherland: *patria*
fault: *culpa, vitium*
favor, be in favor of, *faveō*
fear: *metus, metuō, timor, timeō, vereor*
feed: *alō;* ____ on, ____ upon, *vēscor*
feel contempt for: *contemnō*
fell: *caedō*
ferocious: *saevus*
fickle: *levis*
fight: *pugna, pugnō*
fill up: *compleō, expleō, impleō*
finally: *dēnique, postrēmō*
find: *inveniō, reperiō*
finger: *digitus*
firm: stand ____, *cōnstō*
fit: see Lesson 19; ____ ting, *idōneus;* it is ____ ting, *oportet*
flank: *latus*
flattering: *blandus*
fleet: *classis*
flock: *agmen, pecus*
flower: *flōs*
fold: *sinus*
foliage: *coma*
follow: *consequor, sequor;* follow constantly, *persequor*

foolhardy: *audāx*
for: *enim, nam, prō;* ____ indeed, *namque;* ____ the most part, *plerumque;* ____ the purpose, ____ the sake, *causā grātiā;* ask ____, *rogō;* care ____, *curō;* feel contempt ____, *contemnō;* in exchange ____, *prō;* look ____, *quaerō*
forest: *silva*
found: *condō*
fountain: *fōns*
friend: *amīcus*
frightened: be ____, *timeō*
from: *ā, ab, dē, ē, ex;* see also Lession 20
full: *plēnus*
funeral: *funus*

G

generally: *ferē*
gentle: *mollis*
get: *cōnsequor*
ghost: see Lesson 1 Vocabulary Notes
gird: *cingō*
girl: *puella, virgō*
give: *dō;* ____ back, *reddō;* ____ birth to, *gignō pariō;* ____ in, *concēdō;* ____ up, *concēdō,* & see also Lesson 1 Vocabulary Notes
glide: *lābor*
glitter: *niteō*
go: *eō;* ____ ing to, see Lesson 1; ____ on (w. imperative): see Lesson 1 Vocabulary Notes
god: *deus*
go: ____ ing to, see Lesson 2; ____ wrong, *errō*
gold coin: *aureus*
golden: *aureus*
good: *bonus;* ____s, *bona;* it seems best, *vidētur*
grain: *frūmentum*
great: *magnus* (comp. *maior,* superl. *maximus*); so ____, *tantus;* too ____, *nimius*
grieve: *doleō;* see also Lesson 17
grove: *nemus*
grow: *crēscō, surgō*
guard: *custōs, servō;* ____ against, *caveō*
guest: *hospes*
guilt: *culpa*
gulf: *sinus*

H

hair: *coma*

hang: *pendō;* ____ up, *suspendō*

happen: *accidō, contingō, ēveniō, fīo*

happy: *fēlīx*

hardly: *aegrē, nōn ferē, vīx*

harm: *noceō*

hasten: *properō*

haughty: *superbus*

have: ____ to, see Lesson 2

he: *hic, ille, is, iste*

head: *caput*

healthful: *salūtī*

heap: *mōlēs*

help: *auxilium, iuvō;* see also Lesson 20

helpful: *auxiliō*

heart: *cor*

herd: *pecus*

here: *hīc*

high: ____ er, *superior;* ____ est, *suprēmus*

hinder: *impediō*

hold a census of: *cēnseō*

holy: *sanctus*

honor: *decus, honor;* a woman's ____, *pudor*

honorable: *honestus*

hope: *spērō, spēs*

horn: *cornū*

horse: *equus*

horseman: *eques*

hostile: *dīversus, inimīcus*

hour: *hōra*

house: *aedēs*

how: *quemadmodum, quōmodo, ut*

human: *hūmānus*

humane: *hūmānus*

humble: *humilis*

humiliate: *dētrahō*

husband: *coniunx, marītus*

I

I: *ego*

if: *num, sī;* see also Lesson 3; ____ not; *nisī* ____

only, see Lesson 6; as ____, *quasī;* but ____, *quodsī, sīn;* even ____, *etsī;* just as ____, *velut;* or ____, *seu, sīve*

ill: *aeger*

imagine: *fingō*

immense: *immēnsus*

important: *amplus;* more ____, *potius;* most ____, *potissimus*

in: *in;* ____ addition, *praetereā;* ____ all respects, *omnibus rēbus;* ____ back, *ā tergō;* ____ exchange for, *prō;* ____ order that, ____ order to, see Lesson 6; in place, *vice, vicem, invicem, in vicem;* ____ such a way, *ita, sīc;* in turn, *vicēs, per vicēs;* ____ vain, *frūstrā;* be ____ favor of, *faveō;* give ____, *concēdō; keep* ____ suspense, *suspendō;* turn ____ different directions, *dīvertō*

increase: *augeō*

indeed: *quidem, rē vērā, vērō;* for ____, *namque*

indicate: *indicō*

influence: *addūcō*

inform against: *indicō*

innocent: *integer*

insignia: *īnsīgnia*

instead: *vice, vicem, invicem, in vicem*

instruct: *mandō, praecipiō*

intend: ____ing to see Lesson 1

interest: consult the ____s of, *cōnsulō*

invent: *fingō*

inviolable: *sanctus*

iron: *ferrum*

irrevocable: make ____, *sanciō*

it: *hoc, id, illud, istud;* ____ is certain, *cōnstat;* ____ is fitting; *oportet;* ____ is lawful, *fās est;* ____ is necessary, *oportet;* ____ is permitted, *fās est, licet;* ____ is right, *fās est;* ____ is very close, *nōn multum abest, parum abest;* ____ is well-known, *cōnstat;* ____ seems best, *vidētur;* as ____ were, *quasī*

J

join: *iungō*

judge: *iūdex*

juryman: *iūdex*

just: *iūstus, modo;* ____ as, ____ as if, *velut*

K

keep in suspense: *suspendō*
kill: *interficiō, occīdō*
kind: *genus;* of such a ____, *tālis*
king: *rēx*
kingdom: *rēgnum*
kiss: *osculum*
know: *cognōvī, nōvī, sciō;* not ____, *nesciō*

L

lament: *queror*
land: *tellus, terra*
large: *amplus, magnus;* the ____r part of, *plērusque*
last: *suprēmus, ultimus;* at ____, *dēnique, postrēmō, tandem*
laugh, laugh at: *rideō*
law: *iūs, lēx;* divine ____, *fās*
lawful: it is ____, *fās est*
lay low: *sternō*
lead to: *addūcō*
leader: *dux*
learn: *dīscō*
learned: the ____, *doctī*
leave: *abeō, discēdō, relinquō*
left: *sinister;* ____ hand, *sinistra;* be ____, be ____ over, *restō, supersum;* on the ____, *ā sinistrā*
legion: *legiō*
leisure: *otium*
length: *longitūdō;* at ____, *tandem*
less: *minor;* by which the ____, *quōminus*
let: *patior, permittō;* see also Lesson 5
letter: *littera, litterae*
life: *anima, spiritus, vīta*
light: *levis, lūmen*
like: *amō, similis;* should ____, would ____, see Lesson 16
limb: *membrum*
literature: *litterae*
little: *parvus;* a ____, *paulum;* too ____, *parum*
loath: see Lesson 17
long: *diū, longus:* as ____ as, *dōnec, dum*

look: ____ at, *aspiciō, spectō;* ____ for, *quaerō*
loosen: *solvō*
lose: *perdō*
lot: *sors*
lover: *amāns*
low: ____ est, *īnfimus;* lay ____, *sternō*

M

madness: *furor*
majority: *magna pārs;* the ____ of, *plērīque*
make: *faciō;* ____ a sound, *sonō;* ____ irrevocable, ____ sacred, *sanciō;* be made, *fīō*
man: *homo, vir;* or use adjective in masculine; young ____, *iuvenis*
many: *multī;* so ____, *tot;* so ____ times, *totiēns*
married: be ____, *nūbō*
mass: *mōlēs*
matter: *rēs*
may: see Lesson 7
meet: *conveniō*
melt: *fundō*
mention: *memorō*
mere: *merus*
merit: *meritum*
might: see Lesson 7
mind: *animus, mēns;* see also Lesson 1 Vocabulary Notes
missing: be ____, *dēficiō*
mix: *misceō;* wine not ____ed with water, *merum*
mob: *vulgus*
modesty: *pudor*
mold: *fingō*
money: *pecūnia*
morals: *mōrēs*
more: *magis, plūres, plūs;* wish ____, *mālō*
mortal: *mortālis*
most: *potissimum;* for the ____ part, *plērumque*
motion: set in ____, put in ____, *agō, agitō*
much: *multus;* so ____, *tantus;* too ____, *nimius* (see also **most**)
must: see Lessons 2 & 17
my: *meus*

N

nearly: *fere, prope*
necessary: *necesse;* it is ____, *necesse est, oportet*
neglect: *praetereo*
neither: *neuter*
never: *ne umquam, numquam*
nevertheless: *tamen*
new: *novus*
night: *nox*
no: *ne quid, ne ullus, nullus;* ____ one, *ne quis, nemo;* by ____ means, *haud;* there is ____ doubt, *non dubium est*
nor: *neque, neve*
not: *ne, non;* ____ know, *nescio;* only . . . but also, *cum . . . tum, non solum . . . sed etiam;* ____ wish, *nolo;* and ____, *neque, neve;* by which not, *quin;* do, ____, see Lesson 16; if ____, *nisi;* or ____, *annon necne;* surely not?, *num;* who ____, why ____, *quin;* wine ____ mixed with water, *merum;* wish ____, *nolo*
nothing: *ne quid, nihil*
notice: escape the ____ of, *fallo*
nourish: *alo*
number: *numerus;* large ____, *multitudo*

O

oar: *remus*
oath: *ius iurandum*
obey: *pareo*
obscurity: *tenebrae*
observe: see Lesson 1 Vocabulary Notes
obtain: *consequor, pario*
of: ____ such a kind, *talis;* be in favor ____, *faveo;* beware ____, *caveo;* boast ____, *iacto;* complain ____, *queror;* consult the interests ____, *consulo;* escape the notice ____; hold a census ____, *censeo;* out ____ the question, see Lesson 20; sort ____, *quasi;* take care ____, *curo:* that ____ yours, *iste;* the large part ____, *plerusque;* the majority ____, *plerique*
offspring: *proles*
often: as ____ as: *quotiens . . . totiens, quotienscumque;* very often, *saepissime*

oh, to . . .!: see Lesson 6
old: *antiquus, senex, vetus*
old-fashioned: *antiquus*
on: ____ the left, *a sinistra;* ____ the right, *a dextra;* carry ____, *gero;* push ____, *impello;* put ____, *impono, sumo*
once: *olim, quondam, semel*
only: *solum, tantum;* if ____, see Lesson 6; not ____ . . . but also, *cum . . . tum, non solum . . . sed etiam*
onrush: *impetus*
open: be ____, *pateo*
opinion: express an ____, *censeo*
or: *an, aut, seu, sive, -ve, vel;* ____ even, *vel;* ____ if, *seu, sive;* ____ not, *annon, necne*
order: *impero, iubeo, mando, ordo;* in ____ that, in ____ to, see Lesson 6
organ: *membrum*
other: *alius*
ought: *debeo;* see also Lesson 2
our: *noster*
ourselves: *nos*
out: *foras, foris;* ____ of the question, see Lesson 20; come ____, *evenio;* push ____, *expello;* snatch ____, *eripio;* spread ____, *sterno;* turn ____, *evenio;* wear ____, *tero*
outdoors: *foras, foris*
outside: *foras, foris*
over: be ____ and above, *supersum;* be left ____, *resto, supersum*
own: her ____, his ____, its ____, their ____, *suus;* my ____, *meus;* our ____, *noster;* your ____, *tuus, vester*

P

painfully: *aegre*
parent: *parens*
part: *membrum, pars;* for the most ____, *plerumque;* the larger ____ of, *plerusque*
pave: *sterno*
pay: *pendo, solvo;* ____ attention: see Lesson 1 Vocabulary Notes
peace: *otium, pax*
peaceful: *quietus*

people: *hominēs;* or use masculine of adjective
perceive: *cernō*
perform: *fungor*
perhaps: *forsitan, haud sciō an*
period: *spatium*
permit: *patior, permittō;* it is ____ted, *fās est, licet*
persecute: *persequor*
persuade: *persuādeō*
pity: see Lesson 17
place: *locus, pōnō;* in ____, *vice, vicem, invicem, in vicem*
placid: *placidus*
play: *canō, lūdō, sonō;* see also Lesson 1 Vocabulary Notes
pleasure: *voluptās*
poem: *carmen*
point: to that ____, *adeō, eō*
posterity: *posterī*
pour: *fundō*
powerful: *potēns*
pray tell: *tandem*
precinct: *templum*
prefer: *mālō*
present: *dōnō*
press: *premō*
prevent: *prōhibeō;* see also Lesson 20
previous: *antīquus, prior*
priest, priestess; *sacerdōs*
prophesy: *canō*
protect: *tegō*
provided that: *dum*
punish: *poenam sūmō dē (ex);* be ____ed, *poenam dō*
punishment: *poena*
pure: *merus*
purpose: for the ____, *causā, gratiā*
pursue: *persequor*
push: *pellō;* ____ on, *impellō;* ____ out, *expellō;* ____ to, *appellō*
put on: *impōnō, sūmō*

Q

question: out of the ____, see Lesson 20
quick: *citus*
quiet: *quiētus;* be ____, *quiēscō*

R

raft: *ratis*
rank: *dīgnitās, ordō*
rapid: *rapidus*
rash: *audāx*
rather: *magis, potius,* or use comparative; wish ____, *mālō;* would ____, see Lesson 16
read: *legō*
rear: *alō*
reason, reasoning: *ratiō*
recover: seek to ____, *repetō*
refuse: *recūsō*
regret: see Lesson 17
rejoice: *gaudeō*
release: *solvō*
remain: *maneō;* ____ behind, *restō*
remarkable; *īnsīgnis*
remember: *meminī, memoriā teneō*
remove: *dētrahō*
render: *reddō*
renew: *repetō*
repeatedly: talk about ____, *iactō*
repent see Lesson 17
rescue: *ēripiō*
resist: *restō*
resources: *opēs*
respect: in all ____s, *omnibus rēbus*
rest: *quiēscō;* the ____ of, *cēterī, reliquus*
restrain: *contineō*
retire: *concēdō*
reverence: *cultus*
reward: *praemium*
riches: *divitiae*
ridge: *iugum*
right: *dexter, iūs, iūstus;* it is ____, *fās est*
rise: *orior, surgō*
river: *amnis;* ____ -bank, *rīpa*
rock: *saxum*
roof: *tegō*
rout: *fundō, pellō*
route: *iter*
roving: *vagus*
row: *ordō*
rub: *terō*

S

sacred: *sacer, sanctus;* make ___, *sanciō*
sad: *maestus*
safe: *tūtus*
sail: *nāvigō, sinus;* set ___, *solvō*
sake: for the ___, *causā, grātiā*
same: *īdem*
sanction: *sanciō*
sanctuary: *templum*
say: *dīcō;* ___ no, *negō;* ___ yes, *āiō*
scarcely: *aegrē, nōn ferē, vīx*
scatter: *spargō*
sea: *frētum, mare, pontus*
search for: *quaerō*
secure: *sēcūrus*
see: *videō;* ___ to it, *faciō*
seek: *petō, quaerō;* ___ to recover, *repetō*
seem: *videor;* it ___s best, *vidētur*
seek: *petō, quaerō*
seize: *rapiō:* seizing, *rapidus*
servant: *minister*
serve: *serviō*
set sail: *solvō*
shame: *pudor*
shameless: *improbus*
share: *dīvidō;* ___ ed, *commūnis*
she: *ea, haec, illa, ista*
shine: *niteō*
short: *brevis*
should: see Lessons 2, 5, 7, 13, & 17; ___ like,
shout: *clāmor*
sick: *aeger*
side: *latus*
silent: be ___ about: *taceō*
since: *cum, quoniam;* see also Lesson 3
sing: *canō*
sink: *cadō*
slander: *dētrahō*
slip: *lābor*
small: *parvus*
smooth: *sternō*
snatch: *rapiō;* snatch out, *ēripiō*
so: *adeō, eō, ita, sīc, tam;* ___ as to, see Lesson 6;
___ big, ___ great, *tantus;* ___ many, *tot;*
___ many times, *totiēns;* ___ much, *tantus;*
___ that, see Lesson 6; as ... ___ especially:
cum ... tum

soft: *mollis*
soldier: *mīles*
someone: *aliquis, quīdam, quis, quisquam*
sometime: *ōlim, quondam*
son: *fīlius, nātus*
soon: *mox;* as ___ as, *cum prīmum, simul ac, simul atque*
soothsayer: *vātēs*
sorrowful: *maestus*
sorry: see Lesson 17
sort of: *quāsī*
sound: *integer, sonō;* make a ___: *sonō*
source: *fōns*
space: *spatium*
speak: *loquor*
speedy: *citus*
spend: see Lesson 1 Vocabulary Notes
spirit: *animus, spiritus*
spread: *fundō;* ___ out, *pateō*
spring: *fōns*
sprinkle: *spargō*
stand: *stō;* ___ firm, *cōnstō;* ___ up, *surgō*
state: *cīvitās, rēs publica, āiō*
statue: *imāgō, sīgnum*
stay: *maneō*
steady: *assiduus*
steal: *auferō*
steel: *ferrum*
steersman: *magister*
still: *tamen*
stone: *lapis*
strait, straits; *frētum*
strike: *pellō;* ___ upon, *impellō*
struggle: *contendō*
style: *cultus*
such: *tālis;* in ___ a way, *ita, sīc;* of ___ a kind, *tālis;* to ___ an extent, *ita, tam*
suffer: *patior*
suitable: *idōneus*
summon: *cieō*
sun: *sōl*
support: *alō*
supreme: *suprēmus*
survive: *supersum*
suspend: *suspendō*
suspense: keep in ___, *suspendō*
sweet: *dulcis*
sympathize: *miseret*

T

take: *sumō;* ____ care of, *cūrō*
talent: *ingenium*
talk: *sermō;* ____ repeatedly about, *iactō*
teacher: *magister*
tear: *lacrima*
tease: *lūdō*
tell: *dīcō, narrō;* pray ____, *tandem*
tender; *tener*
test; *experior*
thank: see Lesson 1 Vocabulary Notes
that: *ille, iste, is;* see also Lessons 8 & 20; ____ of
   yours, *iste;* at ____ time, *tum, tunc;* besides ____,
   praetreā; in order ____, so ____, see Lesson 6; to
   ____ point, *adeō eō;* would ____, see Lesson 6;
   provided ____, *dum*
there: *eō, ibi, illīc, illūc, istīc, istūc;* ____ is no doubt,
   see Lesson 20
thin: *gracilis* (superlative *gracillimus*)
thing: *rēs;* or adjective in neuter
this: *hic, is*
three: *tres*
threshold: *līmen*
throng: *agmen*
throw: *iaciō;* ____ about, *iactō;* ____ down, *fundō,*
   sternō
thunderbolt: *fulmen*
time: *tempus;* at that ____, *tum, tunc;* every ____,
   quotiēns ... totiēns, quotiēnscumque; so many
   ____s, *totiēns;* spend ____, see Lesson 1 Vocabu-
   lary Notes
tired: *fessus;* see also Lesson 17
to: *ad:* see also Lessons 6 & 7; ____ such an extent,
   ita tam; ____ that point, *adeō, eō;* direct ____,
   drive ____, *appellō;* fall ____, *accidō;* give birth
   ____, *gignō, pariō;* going ____, have ____, see
   Lesson 2; in order ____, see Lesson 6; lead ____,
   addūcō; oh, ____ ... !, see Lesson 6; push ____,
   appellō; see ____ it, *faciō;* seek ____ recover,
   repetō; so as ____, see Lesson 6
toe: *digitus*
together: close ____, *dēnsus*
tokens: *īnsīgnia*
too: *nimium,* or use comparative; ____ great, ____
   much, *nimius*
top: *vertex*
torch: *fax*

touch: *contingō, tangō*
tradition: *mōs maiōrum*
transport: *vehō*
travel: *vehor*
treat: see Lesson 1 Vocabulary Notes
tree: *arbor*
triumph: *triumphus*
trivial: *levis*
turn: *vertō;* ____ away, ____ in a different direction,
   dīvertō; ____ out, *ēveniō;* in ____, by ____, *vicēs,*
   per vicēs

U

ugly: *foedus, turpis*
unharmed: *integer*
unite: *iungō*
universe: *mundus*
unknown: *ignōtus*
unless: *nisī*
unlike: *dissimilis* (superl. *dissimillimus*)
unmeasurable: *immēnsus*
untie: *solvō*
until: *dōnec, dum*
unwilling *nōlēns;* be ____ *nōlō*
up: break ____, *solvō;* catch ____ with, *consequor;*
   fill ____, *compleō, expleō, impleō;* give ____,
   concēdō; hang ____, *suspendō;* stand ____, *surgō*
upon: strike ____, *impellō*
use: *ūsus, ūtor;* ____d to, use imperfect
useful: *ūsuī;* be ____, *prōdō*
usually: *fere*

V

vain: in ____, *frūstrā*
verse: *versus*
very: use superlative; ____ often: *saepissimē;* it is
   ____ close, *nōn multum abest, parum abest*
vessel; *ratis*
vice: *vitium*
victor, victorious: *victor*
victory: *victōria*
vie: *contendō*

violent: *rapidus*
visible: be ____, *pateō*
vote: *cēnseō*
vow: *vōtum, vōveō*

W

waiter: *minister*
walk: *ambulō*
wandering: *vagus*
want: *cupiō, volō*
war: *bellum*
warn: *moneō*
waste: *perdō*
watchman: *custōs*
water: *aqua;* wine not mixed with ____, *merum*
wave: *fluctus*
way: *via;* all the ____, *usque;* in such a ____, *ita, sīc*
wealth: *dīvitiae*
wealthy: *dīves*
wear: *gerō;* ____ out, *terō*
weary: see Lesson 17
weep, weep for: *fleō*
weigh: *suspendō*
weight: *pondus*
well: *bene;* ____ -worn, *terō;* it is ____ -known, *cōnstat*
what: *id quod, quid*
when: *cum, quandō, ubi;* see also Lesson 3
whether: *an, num, seu, sīve, utrum*
which: *quī, uter;* see also Lesson 3; by ____ not, *quīn;* by ____ the less, *quōminus*
while: *dum;* see also Lesson 1
whirlpool: *vertex*
whirlwind: *vertex*
who *quī, quis, uter;* see also Lesson 3; ____ not, *quīn*

whole: *interger;* the ____, *cunctus, tōtus*
why: *cūr, quārē, quīn;* ____ don't you, why not, *quīn*
wickedness: *scelus*
willing: *volēns;* be ____, *volō*
wine: *vīnum;* ____ not mixed with water, *merum*
wish: *optō, volō;* ____ more, *mālō;* ____ not, *nōlō;* ____ rather, *mālō;* I ____, see also Lesson 6; not ____ *nōlō*
with: *cum;* see also Lesson 3; ____ difficulty, *aegrē;* catch up ____, *cōnsequor;* wine not mixed ____ water *merum*
withdraw: *concēdō*
without: *sine*
woman: *fēmina*
wonder, wonder at: *mīror*
worried: be ____, *vereor*
worse: *peior*
worst: *pessimus*
worth: use genitive of indefinite measure; see also Lesson 19
would: see Lessons 7 & 13; ____ like, ____ rather, see Lesson 16; ____ that, see Lesson 6
wound: *vulnus*
wrong: be ____, go, *errō*

Y

yes: say ____, *āiō*
yet: *tamen*
yoke: *iugum*
young: ____ er, *iūnior, minor nātū;* young man, *iuvenis*
you: *tū, vōs;* why don't you, *quīn*
your, yours; *tuus, vester;* that of ____s, *iste*
yourself: *tuī, tibi, tē*

GRAMMATICAL INDEX